FILM COSTUME

An Annotated Bibliography

SUSAN PEREZ PRICHARD

The Scarecrow Press, Inc.
Metuchen, N.J., & London
1981

Library of Congress Cataloging in Publication Data

Prichard, Susan Perez, 1953-
  Film costume, an annotated bibliography.

  Includes index.
  1. Costume--Bibliography. I. Title.
Z5691.P75 [PN1995.9.C56]   016.79143'026 81-5274
ISBN 0-8108-1437-4   AACR2

This book is dedicated to my mother,
Virginia Perez Prichard, and to
the memory of my father,
Robert E. Prichard

CONTENTS

Foreword (Anthony Slide)   vii

Introduction   ix

The Bibliography   1

Index   483

FOREWORD

At the outset I should state that my personal involvement in the area of costume design is limited; limited, in fact, to coordinating two motion-picture costume-design exhibits at the Academy of Motion Picture Arts and Sciences in 1977 and 1978. In the preparation of those exhibits, which included original costumes from motion pictures back to the mid-thirties, I came to know a number of costume designers-- in particular Sheila O'Brien, President of the Costume Designers Guild, and Bill Theiss, whose credits include the television series Star Trek and Bound for Glory (could anything be more disparate?)-- and to learn something of the manner of their work, their accomplishments, and their contribution to the sum total of a film.

In recent years the history of motion-picture costume design has begun to receive long-overdue recognition both through exhibits and several books on the subject. As a film historian, I have used those books and also started to wonder what else, if anything, might have been written on the subject in the past. Now Susan Prichard has produced another book on costume design, and I daresay it will be used far more by me and other film historians than any other volume on this subject. What Prichard has done is compile an annotated bibliography to almost 4,000 books and periodical articles on costume design in the film industry, telling us all precisely what has been written in the past 70 years in this field. Costume design is a glamorous occupation to most people outside of the industry, and the recent costume-design books have been equally glamorous with their pretty pictures and glossy texts. Susan Prichard's book is not glamorous, because it is a basic, working textbook. It is a serious, scholarly, carefully considered work, and as such comes far closer to the reality of costume design in motion pictures. Costume design is not New York socialites gazing over champagne glasses at beautiful dresses at the Metropolitan Museum, but rather scores of hard-working women individually sewing sequins on gowns. The other books dealing with costume design have been for the dilettantes; this volume is for the working student or scholar.

It is a revelation for me to glimpse just how much has been

documented on this subject, and to find it so meticulously indexed and annotated. A number of times of late I have picked up a so-called bibliography to find it littered with inaccurate data and descriptions of the contents of articles that bear no resemblance to the articles when actually checked by the researcher. One need find no such irritation with Prichard's book. She has read every item listed in this bibliography--not only read it but summarized it carefully and yet in a highly personal and often amusing manner. Here is a bibliographer who loves her work, and how much it shows in the finished product and how much we film historians, students, and scholars owe her a debt of gratitude!

Bibliographies seldom make good reading in their own right, but here is one that does. The enthusiasm of its compiler shines through on every page. Of course, one expects to find dozens of references to Edith Head, but how pleasing to come across references to people whom one knows, who are the unsung heroines of costuming, such as Irene D. Caine, credited with the wardrobe for "The Children's Hour," "Two for the Seesaw," and others. How interesting it is to find references to Chaplin discussing his costumes or to Colleen Moore announcing that the 30 gowns she will wear in "Irene" will be made by her personal modiste. From the entries relating to MGM's best-known costume designer, Adrian, we learn probably more about the man than we would from most entries in available reference works. I see, in the Ladies' Home Journal in 1933, that he was crediting Garbo with influencing fashion more than any other actress and that a 1935 trip to Mexico had influenced his own designs. As well as discovering how much has been written on costume design, this bibliography indicates how little has been devoted to certain individual designers. Harold Grieve, a prominent and still-living art director and costume designer of films in the twenties, has no references.

When Susan Prichard asked me to write a foreword to her bibliography, she told me that her ultimate objective was to write an accurate but readable reference book. She has most certainly succeeded. It is my privilege to recommend this definitive bibliography on costume design not only as a source book in its own right but, one hopes, as a model for future bibliographies on such much-needed topics as art direction, makeup, cinematography, and publicity.

Anthony Slide
Studio City, California

INTRODUCTION

Millions of people in audiences all over the world have been dazzled by the work of the film-costume designer, captured "forever" on celluloid. Twentieth-century fashion, manipulated by skillful designers who tailored it to the camera's eye, was influenced by the motion picture as by no other medium.

Because the techniques of theatrical and retail fashion design were often inappropriate for motion-picture needs, film-costume designers originated solutions to problems posed by the camera and by the industry itself as they evolved. The literature documents how greatly film costume affected, and was affected by, for example, changing silhouettes and hemlines, and the transition to pants in the 1920s through the 1970s. Technological innovations in fashion, such as mass-produced clothes, synthetic fabrics, and the zipper, also greatly influenced film--and in turn received much support through the designers' endorsement. The film-costume designers also adapted well to such innovations as sound and color films.

The Designers

Some designers have excelled with costumes for both the theatre and film: Karinska, Cecil Beaton, and Irene Sharaff are notable examples. Many succeeded in both film and retail fashions: Adrian, Travis Banton, Bonnie Cashin, Oleg Cassini, Howard Greer, Irene, Jean Louis, Omar Kiam, Bernard Newman, and Edward Stevenson are some of them. Others have made their mark with period costumes, like Walter Plunkett, who was also one of only three designers to specialize in costumes for men (the other two were Gile Steele and Valles). One person, Sheila O'Brien, worked her way up from the wardrobe department to become a designer and founder of the Costume Designers Guild.

Whatever their area of expertise, the film-costume designers helped elevate the field to the art it is, together with the many others on the wardrobe team: costumes, jewelers, furriers, shoemakers, armorers, beaders, embroiderers, agers, and so on.

In addition to surveying the designers' education and training, work methods, and specific films, the literature chronicles their famous partnerships. To name a few: in the teens, George Hopkins designed for Theda Bara; in the 1920s, Charles Le Maire for the Talmadge sisters and Howard Greer for Pola Negri; in the 1920s and '30s, Adrian for Greta Garbo, as well as for Joan Crawford and Norma Shearer; in the 1930s, Travis Banton for Marlene Dietrich, Carole Lombard, and Mae West and Orry-Kelly for Bette Davis; in the 1940s, Edith Head for Barbara Stanwyck and Dorothy Lamour and Jean Louis for Rita Hayworth; in the 1950s, Edith Head for Grace Kelly.

Though contemporary films are hardly as numerous or as challenging in terms of costuming as those made in the great decades of the '20s, '30s, and '40s, excellent designers continue in the tradition. Bob Mackie's talent ranks him alongside the greatest, Adrian and Travis Banton. Like predecessors Cecil Beaton and Tony Walton, Polly Platt excels in both costume and set design. Two designers whose careers span almost 50 and 60 years, respectively, continue at their craft: Yvonne Wood and Edith Head.

The field has not been limited to designers trained in costume and fashion. Directors who have received costume-design credit include Claude Autant-Lara, Lou Burns, Michael Cacoyannis, Louis J. Gasnier, Mitchell Leisen, Erich von Stroheim, and Orson Welles. Directors Joseph Henaberry and Clarence Brown researched costumes for their films, and both Mervyn Le Roy and writer Ayn Rand worked in wardrobe departments at the start of their careers.

The demands of the job have brought about their casualties. Adrian died in 1959 at the age of 56 from a heart attack. Irene committed suicide in 1962 at the age of 54. Travis Banton lost his job as Paramount's chief designer due to alcoholism.

The Literature

From the first motion picture in 1895 until the early 1920s little was written on film costume, until it became apparent that film would be a significant medium for establishing and spreading twentieth-century fashion. Film-fan magazines enthusiastically covered the subject until World War II and the "death of glamour," as some magazines called it. In the teens and 1920s the magazines featured the "how-to" approach toward film costuming, often behind-the-scenes with the wardrobe mistress or designer. The subject was popular enough by the 1930s to be featured in monthly articles in most of the fan magazines. With the austerity of the war in the 1940s the magazines switched slowly to reporting on the lifestyles and gossip of the stars off the screen. In the latter half of the 1960s the studios and press seemed to remember what great publicity the costumes of a film could be, but the trend was short-lived.

The "Romantic and Glamorous Hollywood Design" exhibit in 1974 at the Metropolitan Museum of Art's Costume Institute created a new wave of interest in and literature about costumes in the movies for years to come. Other exhibits and permanent collections of film costumes in such museums as the Smithsonian Institution, the National Film Archives, and the Los Angeles County Museum of Art speak well of the craftsmanship and significance of film costume as art.

The Metropolitan Museum exhibit paved the way for the publication of three books in 1976 (as well as provided the inspiration for this bibliography). Costume Design in the Movies (Leese) is an excellent, liberally illustrated book with brief biographies of and credits for about 150 designers, with a title index giving some 6,000 credits. The book is indispensable. In addition, Hollywood Costume --Glamour! Glitter! Romance! (McConathy with Vreeland) and Hollywood Costume Design (Chierichetti), and the recent In a Glamorous Fashion (La Vine), are all excellent for their readability and illustrations of the work of the major designers in the studio system.

Film-costume designers who have written autobiographies include Cecil Beaton, Erté, Howard Greer, Edith Head, Bob Mackie, Helen Rose, and Irene Sharaff. Fashion designers who have written briefly of their films in their autobiographies include Christian Dior, Lady Lucile Duff Gordon, Mary Quant, and Schiaparelli.

It is safe to say that the fashion-industry press has generally ignored the subject of costumes in the movies. For three centuries Paris has dominated American fashion sense, and the scarcity of literature in such magazines as Vogue and Harper's Bazaar suggests that the fashion press chose to follow likewise, rather than recognize Hollywood as a style center.

How to Use This Book

I have included literally any literature relevant to film costume in this bibliography, even the most trivial. I have excluded articles that dealt solely with the personal wardrobe of an actor or actress, as well as the hundreds of articles in which the costumes discussed were not specifically identified as having been worn in a film.

Arrangement is alphabetical by author. A full index at the end of the volume provides access by subject.

Articles consisting essentially of costume stills or original sketches appear here because they are indispensable to costume research, often providing important credits. For the silent era they document costumes for many films that no longer exist. Most studios dispose of their stills, which are often sold in a handful of memorabilia shops and then become impossible to locate altogether. Although libraries, among them those of the Academy of Motion Picture Arts and Sciences, University of Southern California, University of California at Los Angeles, and Stanford University, maintain archives, it is often impossible to reconstruct the costumes of a film by searching these collections.

The credits gathered from the American Film Institute Catalog are not intended to substitute for those found in either Costume Design in the Movies (Leese) or Hollywood Costume Design (Chierichetti), though the AFIC often supplements credits found in the two books. Because this bibliography is not just about film-costume designers, many costumers and other wardrobe-department workers have also been included.

With each person's credits I have used the same wording as the credit found in the catalog. I have interpreted its use of "cost." to mean costumes; it is impossible to determine which credits should have read "costumer" instead, as the abbreviation was used for "costume, costumer, costumes."

Persons whose credits read either "wardrobe" or "cost." were included in this bibliography if they worked independently on at least one film without a costume or wardrobe "designer." I have listed up to ten films for each person, in chronological order, or else I have noted the number of credits for which he or she received costume/wardrobe credit. The credits are intended to give an overall view of a person's work in the decades covered by the catalog: 1921-30 and 1961-70. Therefore, a film's entire wardrobe credits should be reviewed in the catalogs themselves if one is in doubt about the designer of a certain film, since (1) not every person and credit in the catalogs was included in this bibliography, and (2) the credits in the annotations have not been cross-referenced, although they have been indexed.

The studios and unions should examine the industry-wide practice of using numerous and confusing credits. For example, there are credits for "clothes," "costumer," "costumes," "costumes created by," "fashions," and "gowns," any of which can imply designer, besides the obvious titles of costume designer, dress designer, fashion designer, and wardrobe designer.

Unions fortunately exist to protect workers from the unreasonable working conditions that still plague the crews of nonunion independent films. To some extent the favorable working conditions exist at the cost of creative freedom. For example, a member of the Motion Picture Costumers union cannot design a costume without some form of warning or penalty, if caught. Similarly, a member of the Costume Designers Guild cannot perform duties a member of the Costumers union would. Clearly, if a person wants to design and sew costumes, the choice is not to join a union and pursue the whole range of costuming for nonunion films.

Also, the Costume Designers Guild will not let its members receive credit for both costume and set design (i. e. , production design). For that reason, credits for Polly Platt were inadvertently omitted from this bibliography because she received "production design" credit in lieu of costume design, as were credits for Veniero Colasanti and John Moore for their costumes of "The Fall of the Roman Empire."

My research was generally limited to libraries within California and to what I could obtain through interlibrary loan. A supplement may be forthcoming in several years to keep up with newly published books, articles, and biographical reference books, and to complete runs of early film-fan magazines.

I welcome correspondence, which readers should send in care of Scarecrow Press.

1 "Abar-Baranovskaya, Mayya. " <u>American Film Institute Catalog,</u>
1961-70, p. 2.
Mayya Abar-Baranovskaya is credited with the costumes of "The
Red and the White. "

2 Abbott, John. "What It Costs to Be a Well-Dressed Sheik. "
<u>Motion Picture Classic,</u> 24 (1): 43, September 1926.
Rudolph Valentino models four costumes from "Son of the Sheik. "
Included is a lengthy list of the costumes and jewelry he pur-
chased for the film, which came to a total of $11, 260.

3 Abrams, Michael. "Edith Head" [Letters]. <u>Films in Review,</u>
23 (2): 116, February 1972.
Biographical information on Edith Head, with credits listed; sent
in a letter from a fan.

4 "Accessories of Fashion. " <u>Screen News,</u> 3 (8): 18, February 23,
1924.
John Francis Dillon, director with First National, was interviewed;
he gives final approval on all costumes worn in his films. The
secret to being well dressed lies in selecting correct accessories.

5 "Accordion Plaits!" <u>Silver Screen,</u> 5 (11): 48, September 1935.
A trend in film costumes is to have accordion plaiting, especially
with gold lamé fabric, as shown in costumes worn by Lyda Roberti in "The Big Broadcast of 1936"; closeups of Greta Garbo;
and Jean Muir in "Orchids to You. "

6 "Actress Designs Own Gowns for Screen Appearances. " <u>Screen
News,</u> 3 (36): 10, September 6, 1924.
Marguerite de la Motte designs and sews all of her film costumes. When she is very busy she will cut out the garments and
let a dressmaker complete them.

7 "Actress Prefers Costume Pictures. " <u>MGM Studio News,</u> 3 (6):
n. p. , December 16, 1935.
Elizabeth Allen prefers costume pictures since she has learned
more about the history of costume through them and can better
appreciate modern clothing. She predicted that the sleeves and
full skirts of "David Copperfield" would influence fashion, as
would the fabrics and jewelry worn by herself and others in "A
Tale of Two Cities. "

1

8   "Adair, Maudine."   American Film Institute Catalog, 1961-70,
        p. 4.
    Maudine Adair is credited with the wardrobe of "One Way Wa-
    hine."

9   "Adams, Dell."   American Film Institute Catalog, 1961-70, p. 4.
    Dell Adams is credited with the wardrobe of "Invasion of the
    Star Creatures."

10 Adams, J. A.   "Modes a la Hollywood" [Letters].   Photoplay,
        46 (5): 13, April 1934.
    Sir Charles Higham, in a speech in London, discussed the influ-
    ence of Hollywood film costume on British fashion.   Included is
    an extract of the speech, in which films were praised for help-
    ing women to make themselves more attractive.

11 Adams, Phobe-Lou.   Review of Hollywood Costume, by Dale
        McConathy with Diana Vreeland.   Atlantic Monthly, 239
        (1): 93-4, January 1977.
    In this brief book review it is noted that there is more "guff
    than gusset," along with an abundance of old publicity stills.

12 "Adamson, Betty."   American Film Institute Catalog, 1961-70,
        p. 5.
    Betty Adamson is credited with the wardrobe of "Nine Hours to
    Rama," "The Curse of the Mummy's Tomb," and "A Dandy in
    Aspic"; she was the wardrobe mistress of "The Roman Spring
    of Mrs. Stone," "Waltz of the Toreadors," and "Duffy" and the
    wardrobe supervisor of "The 7th Dawn," "Woman of Straw,"
    "Brotherly Love," and "Goodbye Gemini."

13 "Adhere to Your Type Religiously if You Would Be Smartly
        Gowned."   Screen News, 4 (47): 12, November 28, 1925.
    Constance Bennett bought trunks of clothes especially made for
    her in New York, which MGM is having duplicated for her to
    wear in "Sally, Irene, and Mary."   She models one of the pieces.

14 Adrian.   "Clothes," in Behind the Screen: How Films Are Made,
        edited by Stephen Watts.   London: Barker, 1938, p. 53-7.
    Adrian discusses how he designs for a film, and notes that Greta
    Garbo insists on costumes with belts and that Joan Crawford pre-
    fers the color blue and formal gowns.

15 _____.   "Costumes for the Screen," in Movie Merry-Go-
        Round, by John Paddy Carstairs.   London: Newnes, 1937,
        p. 80-7.
    Adrian discusses how he designs for a film, with mention of con-
    struction procedures, closeups, and the importance of dramatic
    value in costume.

16 _____.   "Do American Women Want American Clothes?"
        Harper's Bazaar, 2656: 36-41, 135-6, February 1934.
    Adrian states that films have popularized American fashion more

than any other medium could have; that he cannot copy Parisian couture because of the time it takes for a film to be produced, and that he would not want to; that dramatic and exaggerated costumes are important for symbolism; and that sound films brought in realistic costuming. He discusses designing for Greta Garbo in "Queen Christina, " Jean Harlow in "The Blonde Bombshell, " Diana Wynyard in "Rasputin, " and Kay Francis in an unnamed film, and his feelings about the popularity of the famous gown worn by Joan Crawford in "Letty Lynton. " Costumes from "Riptide" are modeled by Norma Shearer, from "Going Hollywood, " by Marion Davies and a model wears a gown worn by Jean Harlow in "The Blonde Bombshell. " Dorothea Wieck models a gown from "Miss Fane's Baby Is Stolen, " by Travis Banton.

17 _____. "Garbo as Camille. " Vogue, 88 (10): 70-1, November 15, 1936.
Adrian briefly discusses researching and designing costumes worn by Greta Garbo and Lenore Ulric in "Camille, " noting that it was especially difficult to locate sources regarding costumes worn by the demi-monde. Includes four sketches of costumes worn by Greta Garbo.

18 _____. "The Garbo Girl Sways the Mode. " Screenland, 18 (3): 26-7, 90, 101, January 1929.
Adrian discusses designing for Greta Garbo, with mention of a costume she wears in "A Woman of Affairs. "

19 _____. "Garbo Goes 'Different!' " Movie Classic, 8 (5): 34-5, 75, July 1935.
Adrian discusses the extent to which Great Garbo's costumes in "Anna Karenina" will influence fashion; with one sketch of Garbo. He was not sure if the very feminine costumes would be popular since women are used to more practical clothing.

20 _____. "How Adrian Dresses a Star. " Hollywood, 17 (27): 16-7, August 15, 1928.
Adrian discusses the designing and constructing of a butterfly-like gown worn by Aileen Pringle in "A Single Man, " which she models. The gown took eight women two weeks to make. Discussion also of other costumes worn by Pringle in the film.

21 _____. "How the 'Deb' Should Dress. " Screenland, 18 (5): 44-5, 105, March 1929.
Adrian discusses designing for Anita Page. Includes four sketches of costumes she wears in "Modern Maidens"; she models two additional costumes from the film.

22 _____. " 'Romeo and Juliet' Costumes. " "Romeo and Juliet"; A Motion Picture Edition, by William Shakespeare. New York: Random House, 1936, p. 259-63.
Adrian discusses researching and designing the costumes for "Romeo and Juliet, " with references to the paintings from which some of the costumes were adapted. All of Norma Shearer's

costumes were only slightly modified from paintings from the 14th
and 15th centuries.

23 _____. "Setting Styles Through the Stars." Ladies' Home
         Journal, 50 (2): 10-11, 40, February 1933.
Adrian discusses film-costume design and designing for many
actresses. He notes that Greta Garbo has influenced fashion more
than any other actress; she models a costume from "Romance,"
with the popular Empress Eugenie hat. Every gown should have
a prevailing note, as with the ruffles of the "Letty Lynton" gown
worn by Joan Crawford, which she models.

24 _____. "What the Woman of the World Should Wear." Screen-
         land, 19 (1): 54-5, 107-8, May 1929.
Adrian discusses designing for Aileen Pringle, as in "The Dream
of Love."

25 "Adrian." American Film Institute Catalog, 1921-30, p. 940-1.
67 credits are listed for designer Adrian.

26 "Adrian." Celebrity Register. 1st ed., 1959, p. 7-8.

27 "Adrian." [A leaflet prepared by] Cheltenham Township Senior
         High School, Wyncote, Pennsylvania. Circa 1978.
Joseph S. Simms and his students have done an extensive and
praiseworthy job of searching out and preserving sketches, paintings, film costumes, and retail fashions by Adrian. Includes a
discussion of how the collection has grown since 1969, the type
of research done, and brief mention of where many exhibitions
have taken place. Numerous stills show some of the collection,
without film titles; photos indicate that the collection includes costumes worn by Katharine Hepburn in "The Philadelphia Story,"
Greta Garbo in "Two-Faced Woman," and Gladys George in "Marie
Antoinette."

28 "Adrian." Dictionary of Film Makers, by Georges Sadoul.
         Berkeley: University of California Press, 1972, p. 2.

29 "Adrian." International Encyclopedia of Film. New York:
         Crown, 1972. p. 59.
Credits Adrian as having received his first screen credit in 1928,
for "Love."

30 "Adrian." Motion Picture Almanac. 1943-4, p. 2.
After starting his own business in 1942 Adrian designed the cos-
tumes for "They Got Me Covered," "Flight for Freedom," "Hit
Parade of 1943," and "Shadow of a Doubt" (he designed only for
Teresa Wright in the latter).

31 "Adrian." World of Fashion. 1976, p. 311-2.
Adrian, in part through the influence of his film costumes, was
a major factor in "establishing Hollywood as the glamour capital
of the world from the 1930's to the 1950's."

32 "Adrian, Gilbert." <u>American Film Institute Catalog, 1921-30</u>,
        p. 941.
    Gilbert Adrian (he soon dropped his first name) is credited with
    the gowns for "Cobra."

33 "Adrian, Gilbert." <u>Current Biography</u>. 1941, p. 11-2.
    Lengthy biographical information on Adrian. Brief mention of his
    trend-setting hats for Greta Garbo in "As You Desire Me" and
    Hedy Lamarr in "I Take This Woman."

34 "Adrian, Gilbert." <u>Fairchild's Who's Who in Fashion</u>. 1975,
        p. 4.
    Adrian was the most expensive couturier in Hollywood and proba-
    bly the most trend-setting of any American designer. Notes er-
    roneously that he designed all of Greta Garbo's film costumes.

35 "Adrian, Gilbert" (Milestones). <u>Time</u>, 74 (12): 100, September
        21, 1959.
    Brief obituary of Adrian, who designed sequined slacks for Greta
    Garbo (in "Mata Hari").

36 "Adrian--American Artist and Designer," by the Humanities
        Committee (of Cheltenham High School, Wyncote, Pennsyl-
        vania). (Housed at the Academy of Motion Picture Arts
        and Sciences.) Circa 1976, 22p.
    A biography of Adrian prepared by the History of the American
    Cinema students at Cheltenham High School. Few of Adrian's
    original costumes and sketches exist, since they were torn up
    both by Adrian, after a film's production, and allegedly by Irene,
    due to jealousy, when she succeeded him as MGM's chief designer.
    Adrian's encounters with other film designers included his being
    "discovered" by Natacha Rambova; inspired by Erté; and, before
    either of them were film designers, almost ruined by Charles Le
    Maire, since Le Maire rejected some of Adrian's sketches be-
    cause he designed "only to suit yourself, and no one else."

37 "Adrian Answers 20 Questions on Garbo." <u>Photoplay</u>, 48 (4):
        36-7, 76, September 1935.
    Adrian discusses his friendship with Greta Garbo and notes that
    her favorite film costumes thus far are those she wore in "Anna
    Karenina" (with illustrations). She prefers unconventional hair-
    styles, so he designs hats to suit them, and although they do not
    suit the current mode, they usually become fashionable.

38 "Adrian Buys 'Glass Fabric.'" <u>MGM Studio News</u>, 3 (13): n. p.,
        May 12, 1936.
    Adrian will return in June from a trip to New York, where he is
    buying some of the "glass fabric" that has created a sensation in
    recent Paris collections.

39 "Adrian Collects Odd 'Antoinette' Styles." <u>MGM Studio News</u>,
        4 (11): n. p., July 26, 1937.
    While in Europe researching the costumes for "Marie Antoinette"

Adrian also collected over 50 complete peasant costumes--the
purpose of which is not noted.

40   "Adrian Creations." MGM Studio News, 5 (11): n.p., November
        5, 1938.
     One gown worn by Joan Crawford in "The Shining Hour" consists
     of a gingham vestee top and an organza skirt, worn over a hooped
     petticoat; by Adrian.

41   "Adrian Deplores Fashion Rivalry." New York Times, October
        18, 1941, p.12.
     Adrian thinks that East and West Coast manufacturers should think
     more of "American" design and quit competing with each other.
     He has ended his film designing career and hopes to dress practi-
     cal women in practical clothes.

42   "Adrian, Designer, Is Dead on Coast." New York Times, Sep-
        tember 14, 1959, p.29.
     Adrian died at the age of 56 from a stroke.   Includes biographical
     information.

43   "Adrian Designs for Norma Shearer." Vogue, 91 (9): 83, May
        1, 1938.
     Includes three sketches by Adrian of two costumes worn by Norma
     Shearer and one by Alma Kruger, the actress who portrayed her
     mother in "Marie Antoinette." Of the 1,200 costumes made for
     the film Shearer will wear 34 gowns.

44   "Adrian Has Novel Idea for Crawford." MGM Studio News,
        4 (3): n.p., February 27, 1937.
     Adrian's novel idea for Joan Crawford's costumes in "Mannequin"
     is completely practical gowns that she could also wear in her
     private life.

45   "Adrian: Painter and Designer." Look, 15 (24): 93-6, 98-9,
        November 20, 1951.
     Brief biographical information on Adrian, with mention of his re-
     turning to film-costume design.

46   "Adrian Suits Constance Bennett." Screenland, 49 (11): 52-3,
        September 1945.
     Constance Bennett models six costumes from "Paris--Underground,"
     by Adrian, comprising her total wardrobe for the film.

47   "Adrian Tours to Study Americana." MGM Studio News, 2 (11):
        n.p., August 8, 1935.
     Adrian noted that his trips, as to Mexico, had influenced his
     costumes, and that fashion was also being influenced by national
     costumes, as with his Russian costumes for Greta Garbo in "Anna
     Karenina."

48   "Adrian Uses Sketches from School Books for 'Wizard of Oz'
        Costumes." MGM Studio News, 6 (22): n.p., August 14, 1939.

Some of Adrian's costumes for "The Wizard of Oz" were based
on childhood sketches he had made in his old textbooks; it was
his favorite book. He sent to his home in Naugatuck, Connecticut,
for his textbooks, in which he had sketched the Munchkins and
others.

49 "Adrian Using Own Schoolboy Art in Designs for 'Oz.'" MGM
       Studio News, 5 (5): n.p., May 31, 1938.
    Identical to the previous article.

50 "Adrian's Career as Studio Designer Background for Today's
       Success." The Californian, 9 (4): 30, May 1950.
    Adrian was Cecil B. De Mille's costume designer for three years
    and then was with MGM for about 12 years, when he left to con-
    tinue his trend-setting as a fashion designer. General information,
    with stills of his most famous partners, Greta Garbo, Norma
    Shearer, and Joan Crawford.

51 "Advance New Models for Next Season's Wear." Screen News,
       4 (9): 15, February 28, 1925.
    Paulette Duval models two fur coats from "Cheaper to Marry."

52 "The Affairs of Susan." Motion Picture, 69 (4): 58, May 1945.
    Joan Fontaine plays four separate personalities in "The Affairs
    of Susan," each with a complete wardrobe--for a total of 28
    costumes.

53 Affron, Charles. Star Acting: Gish, Garbo, [and] Davis. New
       York: Dutton, 1977.
    Numerous references to the significance of costume to the plots
    of films starring Lillian Gish, Greta Garbo, and Bette Davis.
    Indexed.

54 Agel, Jerome, ed. The Making of Kubrick's "2001." New York:
       New American Library, 1970.
    Many designers submitted sketches of futuristic costumes for
    "2001: A Space Odyssey" to director Stanley Kubrick, who se-
    lected Hardy Amies. Kubrick selected the costumes and fabrics
    to be nondistracting, to anticipate clothing changes 35 years into
    the future, for instance, the absence of buttons, and the wearing
    of padded hats for the stewardesses to cushion collisions. He
    also consulted NASA experts before selecting the spacesuits. A
    computer printout suggested that the ape costumes would take nine
    years to construct, though it eventually took three months. In-
    cludes costume descriptions for extraterrestrial beings that were
    eliminated from the film.

55 Ager, Cecelia. "Mae West Reveals the Foundation of the 1900
       Mode." Vogue, 82 (5): 67, 86, September 1, 1933.
    Mae West feels that the fashions of the late 1800s, like those she wore
    in "She Done Him Wrong," will influence evening clothes, though they
    would be impractical for daytime wear. Discussion of the corset she
    wore in the film, which she models; made by Madame Binner.

56 "Aghayan, Ray." American Film Institute Catalog, 1961-70, p. 6.
Ray Aghayan was the wardrobe designer of "Gaily, Gaily"; the
costume designer of "The Art of Love," "Do Not Disturb," "Our
Man Flint," "Caprice," and "Doctor Dolittle" and for Doris Day
in "The Glass Bottom Boat"; and is credited with the costumes of
"Father Goose" and "In Like Flint."

57 "Aghayan, Ray." Fairchild's Who's Who in Fashion. 1975, p. 5.
Biographical information on Ray Aghayan, whose film-costume
credits include "Hannie Caulder," "Lady Sings the Blues," and
"Funny Lady."

58 "Aghayan, Ray/Bob Mackie." World of Fashion. 1976, p. 207-8.
The two designers formed their own business, Ray Aghayan/Bob
Mackie; through which they design for ready-to-wear, the theater,
television, and films. Bob Mackie had previously designed for
films as Jean Louis's assistant.

59 Agnes, Frances (pseudonym of Frances May Schering). "Cos-
        tumes," in Motion Picture Acting. New York: Reliance
        Newspaper Syndicate, 1913, p. 76-7.
Basic references to film costume: for example, actors supplying
their modern wardrobes and the studios providing their period
costumes, and avoidance of white costumes due to their poor
photogenic quality. Recommends that actors and actresses be
prepared for working in interior scenes if the studio stage is not
available, or if the weather is wrong for outdoor filming (much of
early film production took place outdoors without a stage, or on
stages that were not enclosed within a building; hence the use of
the phrase "interior scenes").

60 "Aileen Pringle Sets New Style in Wedding Dress." Screen News,
        3 (31): 26, August 2, 1924.
Description of a wedding gown of gold cloth worn by Aileen Pringle
in "His Hour."

61 "Aileen Pringle Wears the Most Expensive Gown Ever Made at the
        Metro-Goldwyn-Mayer Studios...." Photoplay, 34 (5): 70,
        October 1928.
Aileen Pringle models a gown that took eight women 15 days to
make, sewing each bead and sequin by hand, in "A Single Man"
--"which is why he stayed single."

62 "Alan, Geoffrey." American Film Institute Catalog, 1961-70,
        p. 7.
Geoffrey Alan is credited with the wardrobe of "Lad: A Dog" and
"Dead Ringer," the costumes of "Spencer's Mountain," and the
men's wardrobe of "Assault on a Queen."

63 "Albee Kin Will Do Designs Here." Hollywood Vagabond, 1 (9):
        7, June 7, 1927.
Eve Gardner will be a freelance film-costume designer. She has
studied in Europe and has already established herself as a well-

known fashion designer.

64   Albert, Dora. "How to Dress Smartly on Nothing at All."
        Movie Mirror, 3 (4): 56-7, 86, February 1933.
     Kay Francis discusses her fashion image. She notes that most
     women should not copy film costumes but consult the leading fash-
     ion magazines, since too often film costumes are not realistic,
     or are appropriate only for the scenes in which they appear, as
     with costumes she wears in "One Way Passage" and "Trouble in
     Paradise"; she models a gown from the former.

65   Albert, Katherine. "Hollywood Leads Paris in Fashions!"
        Photoplay, 36 (6): 56-7, 138, November 1929.
     Howard Greer has reluctantly admitted that many Parisian fashions
     were started one or two years before in Hollywood. He feels
     that too many film costumes are tight-fitting and in poor taste
     since they exploit the audience's interest in sex (though the camera
     does photograph such curved lines better). He also discusses
     changing hemlines in Hollywood and Paris, as with the longer
     skirts worn by Corinne Griffith in "Lilies of the Field," one of
     which she models.

66   _____. "What the Stars Do With Their Old Clothes." Screen
        Guide, 1 (7): 12-3, 48, November 1936.
     Shirley Temple's film costumes are given anonymously to charity
     when she no longer needs them. Gary Cooper wears many of his
     old suits in his films; actors are required to have many suits,
     as they provide their own film wardrobes.

67   "Albray, Maurice." American Film Institute Catalog, 1961-70,
        p. 8.
     Maurice Albray was the costume designer for "La bonne soupe,"
     "The Champagne Murders," and "La femme infidèle" and is
     credited with the costumes of "Landru" and "Les biches."

68   Albright, Diane. " 'Grease' Brings a 1950s Boom to U.S.
        Fashion." National Enquirer, 53 (4): 17, September 5,
        1978.
     Such films as "Grease" and "Annie Hall" have been profitable for
     stores selling vintage clothing, for example, Macy's and I. Mag-
     nin, and for Screenland, a New York wholesaler that sells used
     clothing to many department stores. The boom started with
     "Annie Hall," but 'Grease" has especially influenced fashion
     through a return to 1950s styles.

69   "Aldredge, Theoni V." American Film Institute Catalog, 1961-
        70, p. 9.
     Theoni V. Aldredge is credited with the costumes of "You're a
     Big Boy Now," "Uptight," "Last Summer," "I Never Sang for My
     Father," and "Promise at Dawn" and with the clothes for Lee
     Remick and Eileen Heckart in "No Way to Treat a Lady."

70   "Aldredge, Theoni V." Biographical Encyclopaedia and Who's

Who in the American Theatre.   1966, p. 238.
Biographical information on designer Theoni V. Aldredge, with
theatrical-costume design credits, and a credit for the film "Girl
of the Night."

71   "Aldredge, Theoni V."   Who's Who in the Theatre.   16th ed.,
          1977, p. 342-3.

72   "Aldredge, Theoni V."   Who's Who of American Women.   8th
          ed., 1974-5, p. 10.

73   "Aldrich, Georganne."   American Film Institute Catalog, 1961-70,
          p. 9.
     Georganne Aldrich is credited with the costumes of "Come Spy
     with Me."

74   "Alec B. Francis Is Assembling a Wardrobe...."   Screen News,
          4 (39): 6, October 3, 1925, col. 3.
     Alec B. Francis has gathered a wardrobe of hand-me-downs for
     the lead role in "The Fighting Parson."

75   "Aleksandrova, Ye."   American Film Institute Catalog, 1961-70,
          p. 9.
     Ye. Aleksandrova is credited with the costumes of "The Day the
     War Ended" and "A Home for Tanya."

76   "Alexander, Angela."   American Film Institute Catalog, 1961-70,
          p. 9.
     Angela Alexander is credited with the wardrobe of "The Manchurian
     Candidate," "Sergeants 3," "Seven Days in May," and "What Ever
     Happened to Baby Jane?"; the costumes of "Winter A-Go-Go"; and
     the ladies'/women's costumes in "Fitzwilly" and "Gaily, Gaily."

77   "Alford, Vi."   American Film Institute Catalog, 1961-70, p. 10.
     Vi Alford is credited with the wardrobe of "The Liberation of L.
     B. Jones" and the women's wardrobe of "The Collector."

78   "Aline Bernstein, Designer, Dead."   New York Times, Sep-
          tember 8, 1955, p. 31.
     Theatrical-costume designer Aline Bernstein died at age 74 after
     a long illness.   Does not include references to her brief film-
     costume designing period.

79   "All-Gold Gown."   Screen News, 2 (49): 30, December 8, 1923.
     Discussion of a period costume of pure gold cloth worn by Betty
     Francisco in "Maytime."

80   "Almine."   American Film Institute Catalog, 1961-70, p. 13.
     Almine is credited with the costumes of "Nights of Shame."

81   "Alpert, Jerry."   American Film Institute Catalog, 1961-70, p. 13.
     Jerry Alpert is credited with the wardrobe of "The Comedy of
     Terrors," "Love with the Proper Stranger," "Soldier in the Rain,"

"Young Billy Young, " and "Suppose They Gave a War and Nobody Came"; the costumes of "The Green Berets" and "2000 Years Later"; and the men's costumes of "Billie. "

82 "Altieri, Ezio. " American Film Institute Catalog, 1961-70, p. 13.
Ezio Altieri is credited with the costumes of "The Tiger and the Pussycat" and "The Pizza Triangle. "

83 "Altman, I. " American Film Institute Catalog, 1961-70, p. 13.
I. Altman is credited with the costumes of "Don Quixote" (1961).

84 American Fashion: The Life and Lines of Adrian, Mainbocher,
        McCardell, Norell, and Trigère. Edited by Sarah Tomer-
        lin Lee for the Fashion Institute of Technology. New York:
        Quadrangle/New York Times, 1975.
Robert Riley writes on Adrian, Dale McConathy on Mainbocher, Sally Kirkland on McCardell, Bernadine Morris on Norell, and Eleni Sakes Epstein on Trigère.

85 The American Film Institute Catalog of Motion Pictures Pro-
        duced in the United States. Edited by Kenneth W. Munden.
        New York: Bowker, 1971.
Elsewhere in this bibliography this source is abbreviated as American Film Institute Catalog, with the year of the volumes, either 1921-30 or 1961-70, and the page number. There are two volumes for each of the catalogs. The American Film Institute has planned on covering films from 1893 on but is reportedly hav- ing financial difficulties with the enormous task. One volume con- sists of synopses of about 6,000 films, and the companion volume lists persons and companies alphabetically so that one may find all credits listed under their name. With only one exception ("Here We Go 'Round the Mulberry Bush"), all credits listed in this bibliography were gathered from the credit indexes.

86 "Amies, (Edwin) Hardy. " International Who's Who. 41st ed. ,
        1977-8, p. 36.

87 "Amies, (Edwin) Hardy. " Who's Who in the World. 3rd ed. ,
        1976-7, p. 19.

88 "Amies, Hardy. " American Film Institute Catalog, 1961-70, p.
        16.
Hardy Amies is credited with Tony Randall's costumes in "The Alphabet Murders, " Albert Finney's clothes in "Two for the Road, " the wardrobe of "2001: A Space Odyssey, " and the costumes for Joan Greenwood in "The Playgirl and the War Minister. "

89 "Amies, Hardy. " Celebrity Register. 3rd ed. , 1973, p. 11.

90 "And Now Something New--a Movie 'Undie' Parade. " Photoplay,
        38 (3): 36-7, August 1930.
Joan Crawford models lingerie from "Our Blushing Brides. "

91 "And Now Tomorrow." <u>Motion Picture</u>, 68 (5): 52, December
        1944.
    Edith Head was challenged in designing for Loretta Young and
    Susan Hayward in "And Now Tomorrow" since the costumes had
    to resemble those of the 1930s and yet not appear comical or out-
    dated by 1940s standards.

92 "Anderson, John A." <u>American Film Institute Catalog, 1961-70</u>,
        p. 17.
    11 wardrobe-related credits are listed for John A. Anderson.

93 Anderson, Lindsay. <u>Making a Film</u>. London: Allen & Unwin,
        1952.
    In this diary kept during the production of "Secret People" the
    costume references are: Anthony Mendleson was the costume
    designer, Ernest Farrer was the wardrobe master, Lily Payne
    was the wardrobe mistress, Ben Foster was the wardrobe as-
    sistant. Mendleson reused a chausable for a person who played
    a priest, which had first been worn by Alec Guinness in "Kind
    Hearts and Coronets" (which Mendleson also costume designed);
    he improvised fascist uniforms for extras; hired extras to fit
    into some ethnic costumes; and hired several Chinese men to
    wear their own clothes. Notes also the psychological influence
    of the costumes upon those extras who played dukes and duchesses.

94 Anderson, Milo. "Styles That Last." <u>Silver Screen</u>, 17 (2):
        56-7, 88-9, January 1947.
    Milo Anderson, a designer with Warner Brothers for 15 years,
    discusses costumes worn by Ida Lupino, Andrea King, and Martha
    Vickers in "The Man I Love" and by Geraldine Fitzgerald in "No-
    body Lives Forever." Includes two sketches of costumes worn by
    Lupino in "The Man I Love"; she models two costumes copied
    from the sketches, though in different colors from the film cos-
    tumes.

95 Anderson, Nancy. "Photoplay on Location." <u>Photoplay</u>, 84 (2):
        60-2, 102, 104, 106, August 1973.
    For "Mame" Lucille Ball will wear her own moonstone and dia-
    mond jewelry, with the rest being supplied by the wardrobe de-
    partment. She was padded for four inches around her body with
    bird seed. Theadora Van Runkle designed about 700 "pieces" for
    the film, at a cost of about $300,000 alone for Miss Ball. In-
    cludes costume and accessory descriptions.

96 "Anderson, Sara." <u>American Film Institute Catalog, 1961-70</u>,
        p. 18.
    Sara Anderson is credited with the wardrobe of "The Name of
    the Game Is Kill" and was the wardrobe mistress of "Psych-
    Out."

97 "Andre." <u>American Film Institute Catalog, 1961-70</u>, p. 18.
    Andre is credited with the costumes of "Mundo Depravados."

98 "André-Ani." American Film Institute Catalog, 1921-30, p. 947.
    43 credits are listed for designer André-Ani.

99 "André-Ani, Clement." American Film Institute Catalog, 1921-30,
        p. 947.
    André-Ani Clement (before he dropped the "Clement") is credited
    with the wardrobe of "His Secretary" and "Soul Mates."

100 "Andre Leon Talley Talks with the World's Leading Designers
        About the International Influence of Hollywood." Hollywood
        Reporter 49th Annual [1979], p. 41-4, 46-8, 57-62.
    The author, an associate fashion editor and correspondent for
    Women's Wear Daily, has interviewed 11 fashion designers as to
    whether or not films have influenced them. He notes that Adrian
    received credit for Joan Crawford's wearing her personal ward-
    robe in "Humoresque." Oscar de la Renta briefly discusses de-
    signing 45 pieces for Marsha Mason in "Chapter II," his first
    film. Hubert de Givenchy discusses briefly his films with Audrey
    Hepburn, his favorite being "Funny Face," and designing for
    Elizabeth Taylor in "The V. I. P. s." Norma Kamali has been in-
    spired in her collections by Gene Tierney, especially in "Laura,"
    and Mary McFadden by Irene Papas in "Iphigenia." McFadden,
    de la Renta, and Bill Blass each admitted to being inspired by
    various films of (Luchino) Visconti.

101 "Andrzejewski, Jean Marie." American Film Institute Catalog,
        1961-70, p. 19.
    Jean Marie Andrzejewski is credited with the wardrobe of "Brew-
    ster McCloud."

102 "Anemoyannis, George." American Film Institute Catalog, 1961-
        70, p. 19.
    George Anemoyannis is credited with the costumes of "Antigone."

103 Anesely [Anesley], Alice. "Alice in Screenland." Screenland,
        9 (4): 72-3, 95, July 1924.
    Discussion of a bathing suit worn by Annette Kellerman in "Venus
    of the South Seas." The knitted one-piece suit that bore her name
    [the "Kellerman"] has been adopted by even the most proper peo-
    ple, but the "police regulations are sometimes annoying"; as a
    result Miss Kellerman will wear a "two-in-one" bathing suit with
    a short skirt.

104 Anesley, Alice. "Alice in Screenland." Screenland, 9 (2): 72-
        3, May 1924.
    Discussion of costumes worn by Claire Windsor and Mae Busch
    in "Nellie, the Beautiful Cloak Model"; with sketches.

105 "Angel, Jack." American Film Institute Catalog, 1961-70, p. 19.
    Jack Angel is credited with the costumes of "The Young Savages"
    and "One Man's Way," and the wardrobe of "Mr. Sardonicus,"
    "Sail a Crooked Ship," "Zotz!," and "13 Frightened Girls."

106 Anger, Kenneth. <u>Hollywood Babylon.</u> San Francisco: Straight
          Arrow, 1975.
     Virginia Rappe was placed under contract by William Fox when
     she won an award as "Best Dressed Girl in Pictures," though
     she died soon after in the scandal that ruined the career of Fatty
     Arbuckle.   Includes a yearly itemization of Gloria Swanson's cloth-
     ing expenditures (for instance, $9,000 for stockings and $50,000
     for shoes) in the 1920s.   Erich von Stroheim was removed as the
     director from "Merry-Go-Round" because of his extravagant spend-
     ing--he ordered silk underpants for the film's Guardsmen, em-
     broidered with the Imperial Guard monogram.   Discussion of
     Marlene Dietrich's "ambisextrous" appeal in men's clothing; she
     appeared "dressed as a man" in each of her films with director
     Josef von Sternberg.   This book is not for the squeamish and in-
     cludes what many film biographers prefer to ignore.

107 "Annamode." <u>American Film Institute Catalog, 1961-70,</u> p. 20.
     Annamode was the costume designer of "Marriage Italian Style"
     and is credited with the costumes of "Casanova '70" and the ward-
     robe of "The Young, the Evil and the Savage."

108 "Annenkov, Georges." <u>American Film Institute Catalog, 1961-70,</u>
          p. 20.
     Georges Annenkov was the costume designer of "Modigliani of
     Montparnasse."

109 "Another Reason." <u>It</u>, 2(9): 22, May 1, 1920.
     Discussion of the influence of film costume on fashion, noting that
     stores must change their inventory more often with the latest
     styles being shown so quickly in the films.   Before the motion
     picture stores could wait several years to sell their clothing goods,
     but now must advertise more to keep their stock moving.

110 "Ansell, Gail." <u>American Film Institute Catalog, 1961-70,</u> p. 20.
     Gail Ansell was the costume designer of "My Lover, My Son" and
     the wardrobe designer of "Change of Mind."

111 Ansen, David.   "Stunt Man." <u>Newsweek</u>, 92 (8): 67, August
          21, 1978.
     In a review of "Hopper" it is noted that Burt Reynolds does not
     want to tamper with a successful formula--in many of his recent
     films he has been wearing the same blue and white checkered
     shirt with tight jeans.

112 "Anthony Adverse Fashion Contest." <u>Modern Screen</u>, 13 (4):
          20-1, September 1936.
     Includes three sketches of costumes worn by Olivia de Havilland
     and one worn by Anita Louise in "Anthony Adverse," by Orry-Kelly;
     copies are marketed by Studio Styles, Inc.   The contest requires
     that one discuss "How Screen Clothes Have Helped Me to Dress
     Smartly."

113   " 'Anthony Adverse' Fashion Contest. "   Modern Screen, 13 (5):
        74-5, 98, October 1936.
      Olivia de Havilland and Anita Louise model copies of their cos-
      tumes from "Anthony Adverse"; both copies and originals were
      designed by Orry-Kelly and marketed by Studio Styles.   The prizes
      include the costume copies and shoes copied from the film.

114   " 'Antoinette' Costume Proves Heavy Burden for Cecilia Parker. "
        MGM Studio News, 5 (2): n.p. , March 23, 1938.
      Brief mention of the inconvenience for Cecilia Parker in dressing
      as Marie Antoinette in a ball sequence of "Judge Hardy's Children. "
      The director, wanting an especially feminine gown for Miss Parker,
      selected the period costume.

115   "Antonelli, A. "   American Film Institute Catalog, 1961-70, p.21.
      A. Antonelli is credited with the costumes of "The Slave. "

116   "Antonelli, Franco. "   American Film Institute Catalog, 1961-70,
        p.21.
      Franco Antonelli is credited with the wardrobe of "Doctor Faustus"
      and "Midas Run" and the costumes of "A Long Ride from Hell. "

117   "Appel, Wendy. "   American Film Institute Catalog, 1961-70, p.
        21.
      Wendy Appel is credited with the costumes of "Pound. "

118   Arbasino, Alberto.   "The Fantastic Tosi. "   Vogue, 156 (4): 385-
        6, 420, September 1, 1970.
      Discussion of the fashion influence of Piero Tosi's costumes for
      "The Damned, " with biographical information on the designer, who
      briefly discusses designing for "The Damned, " "Fellini Satyricon, "
      "Death in Venice, " "Metello, " "La Viaccia, " and others.

119   "Arbuthnot, Molly. "   American Film Institute Catalog, 1961-70,
        p.22.
      19 wardrobe-related credits are listed for Molly Arbuthnot.

120   Archerd, Armand.   "Photoplay Visits a Movie Set. "   Photoplay,
        52 (4): 73-7, October 1957.
      Dorothy Jeakins, the costume designer of "Desire Under the Elms, "
      authenticated her costumes for Anthony Perkins by checking with
      the New-York Historical Society.   Sophia Loren's costumes of
      1850 were a compromise--no petticoat, but worn with a waist-
      cincher.

121   Ardmore, Jane.   The Self-Enchanted.   Mae Murray: Image of
        an Era.   New York: McGraw-Hill, 1959.
      Costumes were very important for Mae Murray's characterizations
      and allure, ranging from the wearing of cheap silk hosiery in
      "The Merry Widow" and 13-inch platform shoes in "Fashion Row"
      to spending hours in the wardrobe department experimenting with
      costumes for "At First Sight. "   When a studio head argued with
      her over a wedding dress for the latter film she quit and left for

another studio. For "On with the Dance," the director left the
selection of costumes up to her because of her diligence in selecting them; while researching in New York's Russian slums she was
given an authentic shawl for the film. Nor did expense bother her:
a fringed costume beaded with mirrors for "The French Doll"
cost $1,500; a hand-embroidered Russian dress with headdress
for "Fashion Row" cost $2,700; and a peacock costume made of
flesh-colored wool tights covered with sequins for "Peacock Parade" required that 30 women resew the sequins each night since
they melted in the hot lights. For "The Gilded Lily" she rejected
advice that the lily costume for a color prologue would not show
up in its gold and white colors--it did and she unwound from the
lily costume to a jeweled G-string. The book is a touching portrait of the actress--she helped Rudolph Valentino and John Gilbert
in their careers, was a top box-office draw of the 1920s, and was
blackballed and left bankrupt in the 1930s. It is disturbing that
the book ends with her sleeping on a park bench in the 1930s--
she lived several decades longer.

122   "Argüello, Luis." American Film Institute Catalog, 1961-70, p.
      23.
      Luis Argüello is credited with the costumes of "The Young Rebel."

123   "Arithmetic à la Gloria." Picture Play, 11 (2): 32, October
      1919.
      Gloria Swanson models four gowns from "Male and Female," "but
      all these smart frocks are zeros unless the wearer has Gloria's
      beauty."

124   "Armand, Edward." American Film Institute Catalog, 1961-70,
      p. 24.
      Edward Armand is credited with the wardrobe of "Journey to
      Shiloh," and was the costume supervisor of "Bullet for a Badman"
      and "Gunfight at Comanche Creek."

125   "Armand, Jean-Marie." American Film Institute Catalog, 1961-
      70, p. 24.
      Jean-Marie Armand is credited with the robes of "The Young Girls
      of Rochefort."

126   "Armstrong, Tony." American Film Institute Catalog, 1961-70,
      p. 24.
      Tony Armstrong is credited with the costumes of "The Jokers,"
      and with Gabriella Licudi's wardrobe in "You Must Be Joking!"

127   "Armstrong Boutique, Tony." American Film Institute Catalog,
      1961-70, p. 24.
      The Tony Armstrong Boutique was the costume designer of "No
      Blade of Grass."

128   Arnold, Alan. Valentino. New York: Library Publishers, 1954.
      Jetta Goudal had designed such bizarre costumes for "The [A]
      Sainted Devil" that they "would have ruined scenes and were in

any case impossible to make" (other sources attribute the designs
to Natacha Rambova, though Norman Norell also designed for the
film); two couturiers refused to make some of the especially difficult costumes.   The author praises Natacha Rambova, Rudolph
Valentino's second wife, for stepping in--as the production delays
were costly--and for replacing Goudal with Dagmar Godowsky.
Notes also that Natacha Rambova and Rudolph Valentino spent
$40,000 of studio money for costumes and props for "The Scarlet
Power," the title of which was changed to "The Hooded Falcon,"
which was never completed; with brief mention of Nita Naldi's
fittings in Paris of the costumes Rambova had designed for her
in "The Hooded Falcon."

129   Arons, Rana. "Hollywood Costume Parade." Photoplay, 87
        (2): 62-4, 91, March 1975
Concerns the premiere of the "Romantic and Glamorous Hollywood
Design" exhibit, with photos of seven of the gowns in the exhibit,
ranging from Irene Castle in "Patria," 1917, to Barbra Streisand
in "Funny Lady," 1977. The accessories, such as the collars,
headdresses, and capes for the costumed mannequins were made
by Julia Feathers.

130   "Arrico, Charles." American Film Institute Catalog, 1961-70,
        p.25.
Charles Arrico is credited with the wardrobe of "Dondi" and "The
Fortune Cookie," and was the wardrobe supervisor of "Young
Americans."

131   "The Arrival of Pola Negri from Europe...." Grauman's Mag.,
        6 (10): 3, March 11, 1923.
Pola Negri's first American film, "Bella Donna," will also be the
first film in which she has worn contemporary costumes.   She
wore costumes from the French Revolutionary period in "Passion,"
Spanish costumes in "Carmen," and Arabian costumes in "One
Arabian Night."

132   L'Art du Costume dans le Film. La Revue du Cinema, 19-20:
        1-113, Autumn 1949.
This was a single issue of La Revue du Cinema, featuring one
article each by Jacques Manuel, director and designer Claude
Autant-Lara, Lotte H. Eisner, and Jean George Auriol and Mario
Verdone. Includes excellent illustrations of American, British,
French, German, and Italian films.

133   "Artists in Evening Dress Get Black Gold Shower." Screen
        News, 2 (17): 20, April 28, 1923.
The entire cast of "The Meanest Man in the World" was required
to attend a shower from an oil pump while in formal evening
clothes.   Doubles could not be used because of many closeups.

134   Arvad, Inga. "You See It in the Movies." Collier's, 116 (14):
        22-3, October 6, 1945.
Walter Plunkett prefers designing for period films so that he need

not worry about the costumes being outdated by the time the film
is released, and so that he can claim a costume is authentic and
avoid pleas to modernize it.   Shown are costumes worn by, but
not modeled by, Katharine Hepburn and Joan Fontaine in "Quality
Street, " Deanna Durbin in "Can't Help Singing, " Vivien Leigh in
"Gone with the Wind, " and lingerie from "Duel in the Sun" (worn
by Jennifer Jones).   Also modeled are retail copies of the costumes, and a hat worn by Hepburn in "Mary of Scotland. "

135   "As a Rule the Ordinary Man Is Content with Three Suits.... "
        Screen News, 1 (28): 14, September 2, 1922, col. 1.
Lewis Stone wears 11 suits in "The Dangerous Age, " varying from
golf clothes to formal evening wear.

136   "As Fresh as the First Crocus--Fashions Worn by Deanna Dur-
        bin. " Silver Screen, 11 (5): 54-7, March 1941.
Deanna Durbin models eight costumes from "Nice Girl. "

137   "As Week After Week Passes into Film History. " Screen News,
        3 (13): 10, April 5, 1924.
Viola Dana will wear a bathing suit for the second time in a film,
in "The Beauty Prize. "   Helene Chadwick is busy sewing a wardrobe now that she is a freelance actress; since the studio had
previously provided her film costumes, she will now need her
own wardrobe.

138   "Asbestos B. V. D. 's. " Senator Newsette, 3 (33): 4, August 13,
        1927.
Wallace Beery and Raymond Hatton wore asbestos underpants for
"Fireman, Save My Child" since the script required that their
pants be set afire; designed and tailored by the Paramount wardrobe department.

139   "Ashman, Gene. " American Film Institute Catalog, 1961-70,
        p. 27.
Gene Ashman is credited with the costumes of "Head" and "The
Model Shop, " and the wardrobe of "Getting Straight, " "The Liber-
ation of L. B. Jones, " and "Watermelon Man. "

140   Astaire, Fred. Steps in Time. New York: Harper, 1959.
Fred Astaire's leading ladies usually rehearsed in slacks, so that
dance routines often had to be changed if the costume restricted
movement or injured Mr. Astaire.   He describes an incident with
Ginger Rogers and a feathered gown in "Top Hat, " the feathers
of which kept flying off when she moved, causing a blizzard on
the stage, and which they found did not photograph.   In "Follow
the Fleet" Rogers wore a heavily beaded gown that kept hitting
Astaire in the face through 20 filmings of the dance; they learned
that the first slap from the costume was not noticeable, as first
filmed.   Such costumes also wrapped around Astaire's legs while
dancing.   He was also careful to have his partners, including
Rita Hayworth, wear heels that kept him several inches taller.
In a wartime bond sale his old tap shoes sold for $100,000, and

his laces for $16,000.

141 Aster, Janet. "Silent Clothes for the Talkies." <u>Photoplay,</u>
        36 (2): 86, July 1929.
     Charles Le Maire discusses how film costumes have changed with
     the talkies. Photogenic fabrics, such as taffetas, metallic fabrics,
     and those with beads and bead fringe, have been replaced by vel-
     vet, lace, chiffons, and trims of bows, flowers, and silk fringe,
     to reduce the noise. Loose jewelry, such as pearls and bangles,
     will be replaced by fitted and engraved or jewel-studded bracelets
     or bands, and tight necklaces.

142 "At Last a Role for Which He Has the 'Wardrobe'...."
        <u>Screen News</u>, 1 (22): 27, July 22, 1922, col. 3.
     Fenwick Oliver's next role will be that of a British officer in
     "Pink Gods," for which he will wear the uniform he wore during
     most of the war.

143 "At Last--Buster Keaton Without His Pancake Hat." <u>Screen</u>
        <u>News,</u> 2 (29): 13, July 21, 1923.
     Discussion of a suit and hat worn by Buster Keaton in a comedy
     set in 1820, "Our Hospitality", designed by Walter Israel.

144 "At Last Jane Novak, Outdoor Girl of Screen, Is to Wear
        Evening Gown." <u>Screen News,</u> 1 (31): 27, September 23,
        1922.
     Jane Novak, famous for her western and outdoor roles, has worn
     only two evening gowns in her four-year-long film career. She
     is now the head of her film company, and will wear evening gowns
     in two of her four forthcoming films--also outdoor stories.

145 "At the Head of the Crowd." <u>Los Angeles Times,</u> September
        23, 1975, sec. 4, p.8.
     Edith Head presented a fashion show to the Textile Association of
     Los Angeles, consisting of old film costumes and a new gown for
     Jill Clayburgh in "Gable and Lombard."

146 "Athena." <u>American Film Institute Catalog, 1961-70</u>, p.28.
     Athena is credited with the costumes of "Voice of the Hurricane."

147 "Attired in Blue and Purple Trailing Robes...." <u>Screen News,</u>
        1 (20): 31, July 1, 1922, col. 1.
     250 persons were costumed in blue and purple robes to give an
     astral appearance for their roles as ghosts in "Borderland."

148 Atwell, Lee. "Women in the Industry; Designer Edith Head."
        <u>Hollywood Reporter,</u> 242 (5): 5, June 28, 1976.
     Edith Head was responsible for 15,000 male costumes in "The
     Man Who Would Be King."

149 "An Audrey Hepburn Fantasy." <u>Vogue,</u> 142 (10): 126-33,
        December 1963.
     Audrey Hepburn models many hats and costumes worn by others
     in the Covent Garden and Ascot sequences of "My Fair Lady."
     Includes comments and color and black-and white photos by the de-

signer, Cecil Beaton.

150   "Autant-Lara, Claude." International Encyclopedia of Film.
        New York: Crown, 1972, p. 86, passim.
      The emphasis is upon Claude Autant-Lara's directorial career,
      with brief mention of his having been a designer (does not specify
      sets or costumes) in the 1920s.

151   "Autre, Tanine." American Film Institute Catalog, 1961-70,
        p. 31.
      Tanine Autre was the costume designer of "Lost Command" and
      "The Brain"; nine other costume/wardrobe credits are listed.

152   "Autumn Artistry." Photoplay, 36 (5): 93, October 1949.
      Edward Stevenson briefly discusses the appropriateness of one of
      his suits for Lucille Ball in "Interference" to current fashions.

153   Aydellote, Winifred. "The Miseries of Nudism." Photoplay,
        46 (4): 26-7, 119-20, September 1934.
      Maureen O'Sullivan discusses the inconveniences created by the
      brief costume she wore in "Tarzan." She frequently caught colds
      and could not stay warm enough during the long shooting production
      schedules. She did not mind the costume itself, though some fans
      wrote in to say that they thought it was immodest and unattractive.

154   "Azevedo, Tereza." American Film Institute Catalog, 1961-70,
        p. 32.
      Tereza Azevedo is credited with the wardrobe of "Tarzan and the
      Jungle Boy."

155-7 No entries.

158 Babcock, Muriel. "Hollywood--Is One Year Ahead." <u>Silver</u>
     <u>Screen</u>, 3 (5): 30-1, 60, March 1933.
Adrian discusses designing the costumes for "Rasputin" noting that
the hats worn by Ethel Barrymore will influence fashion and that
the sable coat worn by Greta Garbo in "Mata Hari" is still a best-
seller in department stores. Adrian has been especially inspired
by the men's costumes of the 14th century in designing for Garbo.
Joan Crawford models three costumes from "Today We Live."

159 "Baburina, N." <u>American Film Institute Catalog, 1961-70</u>, p.
     33.
N. Baburina is credited with the costumes of "When the Trees
Were Tall."

160 "Baer, Virginia." <u>American Film Institute Catalog, 1921-30</u>,
     p.958.
Virginia Baer is credited with wardrobe of "Doughboys" and "Remote Control."

161 Bahrenburg, Bruce. <u>The Creation of Dino De Laurentiis'</u>
     <u>"King Kong."</u> New York: Pocket Books, 1976.
Jessica Lange, the female lead in "King Kong," was sewn into
her costume for the sacrificial sequence, by costumer Fern Weber.
Besides a reference to the natives' costumes being adapted from
native costumes in Borneo, there are few other references to the
costumes or designers. Moss Mabry was the costume designer,
and Anthea Sylbert was credited with the gowns and native costumes. Of the two wardrobe persons, Arny Lupin and Fern
Weber, biographical information of Weber is included. For location work on "The Ten Commandments" (1954), Weber notes
that Cecil B. De Mille sent a plane to India to get some tiger
skins since he did not like the skins the studio already had. Also,
lengthy references to the costumes worn by the star in the title
role, King Kong, portrayed by both a 40-foot mechanical marvel
and a man in a monkey suit, with specific references to the costumes worn by both.

162 _____. Filming "The Great Gatsby." New York: Berkley,
                1974.
When problems occurred with casting Ali McGraw for the woman's
lead in "The Great Gatsby," the press believed the coverstory--
costume problems. The major costume problem was that of a
low budget of a quarter-million dollars. Designer Theoni Aldredge
discusses designing for Robert Redford, Mia Farrow (casted instead of McGraw), Lois Chiles, Bruce Dern, Karen Black, and
Sam Waterston. 80 percent of the costumes not worn by the principals were rented from costume companies, and the remaining consisted of either original flapper costumes or were made by Barbara Matera and by Aldredge's assistants, Marilyn Putnam, George
Newman, Erica Eames, and Ray Beck. $895,000 worth of
jewelry, 58 pieces, was supplied by Cartier's; the extras wore
costume jewelry. Hats were often worn several times by changing
the trim. 2,500 pairs of shoes were bought, but, along with the
costumes, many were damaged due to weather problems, requiring
that more be bought or remade. Seamed, silk stockings were
worn by the women. The male extras wore rented or specially
made tuxedos, and the lead men wore clothing bought from Ralph
Lauren, sold under the Polo label.

163 Bainbridge, John. Garbo. Garden City, N.Y.: Doubleday, 1955.
Adrian said that he left MGM because they tried to make Greta
Garbo into a sweater girl and the all-American type in "Two-
Faced Woman." "When the glamour ends for Garbo, it also ends
for me. She has created a type. If you destroy that illusion,
you destroy her. When Garbo walked out of the studio, glamour
went with her, and so did I." The National Legion of Decency
condemned the film, in part, because of the suggestive costumes.

164 Bair, Frederick H. "A Guide to the Study of 'Maid of Salem'; Cos-
                tumes." Photoplay Studies, 3 (1): 12, January 1937.
Many of the principals in "Maid of Salem" required at least six
costumes each due to scenes that were especially hard on the
costumes. At least 40 persons required a minimum of four costumes with complete accessories as duplicates. Costumes were
also made for 2,000 extras.

165 "Baiza, Libertad de." American Film Institute Catalog, 1961-
                70, p.35.
Libertad de Baiza is credited with the costumes of "Violated Love."

166 "Bake, Hartmut." American Film Institute Catalog, 1961-70,
                p.35
Hartmut Bake was the costume designer of "Girl from Hong Kong."

167 Baker, Bob. "Cecil Beaton." Film Dope, 3: 14, August 1973.
"There's a monograph to be written about clothes in the movies.
Nobody'd read it but it might look nice in the shop window." In
such a book the author states that Cecil Beaton would merit a
paragraph since he designs for himself, rather than for the character.

168 "Baker, Hylan." American Film Institute Catalog, 1961-70,
                p.35.
Hylan Baker is credited with the wardrobe of "The Shuttered Room."

169 "Baker, Ivy." <u>American Film Institute Catalog, 1961-70</u>, p. 35.
Ivy Baker was the costume designer of "The Green Helmet"; the wardrobe mistress of "Pussycat Alley" and "One Million Years B.C." (1967); the costume/wardrobe supervisor of "Man in the Middle," "Invasion Quartet," "Lisa," "In the Cool of the Day," "Great Catherine," "Anne of the Thousand Days," and "Scrooge"; and is credited with the wardrobe of "Inspector Clouseau."

170 "Balchus, Frank." <u>American Film Institute Catalog, 1961-70</u>, p. 36.
Frank Balchus is credited with the costumes of "The Bridge at Remagen" and "The Undefeated."

171 "Balenciaga." <u>American Film Institute Catalog, 1961-70</u>, p. 36.
Balenciaga is credited with the gowns of "The Empty Star."

172 "Balestra." <u>American Film Institute Catalog, 1961-70</u>, p. 36.
Balestra is credited with the gowns for "Dark Purpose" and for Carroll Baker in "The Sweet Body of Deborah."

173 "Balkan, Adele." <u>American Film Institute Catalog, 1961-70</u>, p. 36.
Adele Balkan was the men's-costume designer of "John Goldfarb, Please Come Home!" and is credited with the wardrobe of "Star!"

174 "Ballard, Lucinda." <u>Biographical Encyclopaedia and Who's Who of the American Theatre</u>. 1966, p. 269-70.
Biographical information of Lucinda Ballard, who was the costume designer of "Portrait of Jenny" and "A Streetcar Named Desire."

175 "Ballard, Lucinda. (Mrs. Howard Dietz)." <u>Who's Who in America.</u> 37th ed., 1972-3, p. 143.

176 "Ballard, Lucinda." <u>Who's Who in the World.</u> 3rd ed., 1976-7, p. 47.

177 "Ballard, Lucinda." <u>Who's Who of American Women.</u> 8th ed., 1974-5, p. 43.

178 "Ballerino, Louella," in <u>Fashion Is Our Business</u>, by Beryl Williams [Epstein]. Philadelphia: Lippincott, 1945, p. 156-70.
Before becoming a successful fashion designer Louella Ballerino studied with André Ani of MGM, though the book does not say if she was employed by the studio. She has designed for (unnamed) films, though not full-time.

179 "Balmain, Pierre." <u>American Film Institute Catalog, 1961-70</u>, p. 37.
14 credits are listed for designer Pierre Balmain.

180 "Balmain, Pierre." <u>Celebrity Register.</u> 3rd ed., 1973, p. 29.

181 "Balmain, Pierre." Fairchild's Who's Who in Fashion. 1975,
       p. 17.

182 "Balmain, Pierre." Who's Who in the World. 3rd ed., 1976-
       7, p. 47.

183 "Balmain, Pierre." Who's Who. 130th ed., 1978-9, p. 117.

184 "Balmain, Pierre Alexandre." International Who's Who. 41st
       ed., 1977-8, p. 93.

185 Banks, Edgar J. "Archaeology and Motion Pictures." Art and
       Archaeology, 15 (1): 2-13, January 1923.
     The author, a specialist in oriental archaeology, discusses his
     association with Sacred Films, Inc., and its purpose in filming
     only biblical films. He discusses the costuming of Sarah, Abra-
     ham, and others in a film ("Abraham") based on the Bible. (This
     writer has found no record of the film company or its proposed
     films.)

186 _____, Ph. D. "How Did Sarah Dress Her Hair?" Photo-
       Dramatist, 3 (10): 23-4, March 1922.
     Dr. Banks, archaeologist and research director for Sacred Films,
     Inc., discusses the costuming of Sarah in a film based on the life
     of Abraham.

187 "Banks, Seth." American Film Institute Catalog, 1961-70, p.
       38.
     13 wardrobe-related credits are listed for Seth Banks.

188 Banton, Travis. "Amusing Fashions from 'Auntie Mame.'"
       Theatre Arts, 41 (2): 70-1, 86, February 1957.
     Travis Banton briefly discusses the differences in designing for
     the theater and films, how he became a costume designer, and
     his costumes for Rosalind Russell in the stage version of "Auntie
     Mame."

189 _____. "Fashion Forecast for Autumn." Photoplay, 48 (1):
       53, 84, September 1935.
     Includes sketches of two costumes worn by Marlene Dietrich in
     "The Pearl Necklace" ("Desire"), by Travis Banton.

190 _____. "Fashions for the Stars." Motion Picture Studio
       Insider, 1 (1): 26-7, May 1935.
     Travis Banton discusses fashion trends for the coming season
     and predicts that his costumes for Marlene Dietrich in "Caprice
     Espagnole" ("The Devil Is a Woman") will influence fashion.
     Dietrich models one costume from the film; with sketches of two
     additional costumes.

191 _____. "Paris + Hollywood = What Smart Women Will Wear
       This Fall." Screenland, 21 (5): 34, 117, September 1930.
     Travis Banton discusses film-costume design and notes that Holly-

wood has not influenced Parisian fashion and never will.   Includes
a sketch of a costume worn by Jeanette MacDonald in "Monte Carlo."

192 _____.   "Personality Wardrobes."   <u>Silver Screen</u>, 16 (12):
          58-9, 92-3, October 1946.
Travis Banton discusses his costumes for Susan Hayward in
"Smash-Up" ("Smash-Up, the Story of a Woman"), Zorina and
Lucille Ball in "Lover Come Back," Maria Montez in "Pirates of
Monterey," and Geraldine Fitzgerald in "Uncle Harry."   Hayward
models one, and Ball two costumes from these films.

193 _____.   "The Winter-Summer Wardrobe."   <u>Silver Screen</u>,
          19 (1): 46-7, 66-7, November 1948.
Travis Banton discusses designing Rosalind Russell's costumes in
"The Velvet Touch," six of which she models.

194 "Banton, Travis."   <u>American Film Institute Catalog, 1921-30</u>,
          p. 961.
Travis Banton is credited with the wardrobe of "Doomsday,"
"The Fifty-Fifty Girl," "His Tiger Lady," "The Wild Party," and
"The Vagabond King" (1930).

195 "Banton, Travis."   <u>Fairchild's Who's Who in Fashion</u>.   1975,
          p. 17.
Travis Banton began designing for Paramount in the 1920s, but
moved to Twentieth Century-Fox when his contract expired in
1938; he later worked less frequently for Universal.   He designed
for the retail industry in the 1950s and is best known for the
"Paramount Look" of understated costumes, often with a bias
cut.

196 "Banton, Travis."   <u>Motion Picture Almanac.</u>   1930, p. 122.

197 "Banton, Travis."   <u>Who's Who in California; a Biographical
          Reference Work of Notable Living Men and Women of
          California</u>.   Los Angeles: Who's Who Publications,
          1942-3, p. 45-6.
Travis Banton designed for Madame Francis [sic] from 1919 to
1924, was with Paramount from 1924 to 1937 (1938), and was the
costume director of Twentieth Century-Fox at this time.

198 "Banton, Travis."   <u>World of Fashion.</u>   1976, p. 313-4.
Notes that some of Travis Banton's film costumes were adapted
for wholesale collections.

199 "Banucha, Jan."   <u>American Film Institute Catalog, 1961-70</u>,
          p. 38.
Jan Banucha is credited with the costumes of "Lotna."

200 "Barbara Coming West with Own Personal Modiste."   <u>Screen
          News</u>, 2 (40): 2, October 6, 1923.
Barbara La Marr hired Madame Doria, of an exclusive dress
shop in Rome, to design all of her future film costumes, beginning with "Thy Name Is Woman."

201 "Barbara La Marr Selects the Latest Jewelry." Screen News, 3 (17): 19, April 26, 1924.
Discussion of jewelry worn by Barbara La Marr in "The White Moth." Includes sketches and one photo.

202 "Barbara La Marr Wears Charming Gowns in 'Quincy Adams Sawyer.'" Screen News, 1 (23): 3, July 29, 1922.
Discussion of several gowns worn by Barbara La Marr in "Quincy Adams Sawyer."

203 "Barbier, George." American Film Institute Catalog, 1921-30, p. 961.
George Barbier is credited with the costumes of "Monsieur Beaucaire" (1924).

204 "Bardon, Henry." American Film Institute Catalog, 1961-70, p. 39.
Henry Bardon is credited with Clive Revill's costumes in "Fathom."

205 "Bardon, Henry." Who's Who in the Theatre. 16th ed., 1977, p. 384.

206 Baremore, R.W. "The Modern Cloth of Gold." Picture-Play, 8 (5): 19-24, July 1918.
Notes that the costumes for Lina Cavalieri in "Gismonda" cost over $5,000--one example of standard costs in making a film.

207 "Barnes, Gloria." American Film Institute Catalog, 1961-70, p. 40.
Gloria Barnes is credited with the wardrobe of "The Last Shot You Hear."

208 "Barrett, Alan." American Film Institute Catalog, 1961-70, p. 41.
Alan Barrett was the costume designer of "Far from the Madding Crowd" and "Lock Up Your Daughters" and is credited with the costumes of "Start the Revolution Without Me."

209 Barrett, E.E. "Clothes That Count." Picturegoer, 16 (94): 24-5, October 1928.
Costumes are often vital to the success of an actor or actress, as with Betty Balfour and Charles Ray, whose careers were ruined when they forsook their shabby costumes for more elegant roles. Mary Pickford's future career is uncertain since she started playing in well dressed roles. Irene Rich was unsuccessful in "The Lost Lady," presumably because she was not as well dressed as the public expected her to be. Adolphe Menjou and Lew Cody are most popular in well-dressed roles, as Douglas Fairbanks is in period costumes. Janet Gaynor and Mabel Poulton should avoid fashion-plate roles.

210 "Barrie, Scott." Fairchild's Who's Who in Fashion. 1975, p. 18.
Biographical information on Scott Barrie, who designed the costumes for "Blood."

211 Barry, Eleanor. "You'll Be in Hollywood Yet." Harper's
        Bazaar, 2668: 39-43, 65, 116, February 1935.
     The text does not mention film costumes, but costumes from
     "Gilded Lily" are modeled by Claudette Colbert, wearing jewelry
     designed for her role by Trabert and Hoeffer; from "Folies
     Bergères de Paris" ("Folies Bergère"), by Princess Natalie Paley,
     designed by Omar Kiam and reproduced for Saks Fifth Avenue;
     from "Caprice Espagnole" ("The Devil Is a Woman"), by Marlene
     Dietrich, designed by Travis Banton, (with closeups of her head-
     dress); and worn by Joan Crawford (in "Chained"), but not modeled
     by her, by Adrian.

212 Barthes, Roland. Erté (Romain de Tirtoff). Testo di Roland
        Barthes. Seguito dai Ricordi di Erté. Parma: Franco
        Maria Ricci, 1970.
     The Italian edition of the following book.

213 _____. Erté (Romain de Tirtoff). Text by Roland Barthes.
        With an Extract from Erté's Memoirs. Translated by
        William Weaver. Parma: Franco Maria Ricci, 1972.
        (The Sign of Man Series.)
     Roland Barthes notes that both Erté and Hollywood were an im-
     portant part of 1925, "one of the most strongly individual dates
     in the history of style." Excerpts from Erté's autobiography
     (see Erté, Things I Remember) include his experiences as a de-
     signer in Hollywood; he had three contracts with MGM in 1925.

214 "Barthet, Jean." American Film Institute Catalog, 1961-70,
        p. 43.
     Jean Barthet is credited with the hats of "The Young Girls of
     Rochefort."

215 "Barto, Pat." American Film Institute Catalog, 1961-70, p.
        43.
     Pat Barto was the costume designer of "Gidget Goes to Rome"
     and "Diamond Head" and is credited with the wardrobe of "Mr.
     Sardonicus" and "Batman," and the costumes for (for Janet Leigh)
     "Bye Bye Birdie" and "The Man from the Diners' Club," and the
     costume coordination of "The Big Bounce."

216 "Bartolini Salimbeni, Giancarlo." American Film Institute
        Catalog, 1961-70, p. 43.
     Giancarlo Bartolini Salimbeni is credited with the wardrobe of
     "The Mystery of Thug Island" and the costumes of "The Pharaoh's
     Woman," "Queen of the Pirates," "Constantine and the Cross,"
     "Cleopatra's Daughter," "Sodom and Gomorrah," "Queen of the
     Nile," "Tiger of the Seven Seas," "Invasion 1700," "Sandokan the
     Great," and "The Lion of St. Mark."

217 "Basket Weaver Makes Hat for Clark Gable." MGM Studio
        News, 5 (13): n. p., January 14, 1939.
     The straw hat worn by Clark Gable in "Idiot's Delight" was hand-
     woven by Edward Johnston, who wove a new brim onto an old hat
     of Gable's.

218   Baskette, Kirtley.   "The Amazing Inside Story of How They
               Made 'Snow White.'"   Photoplay, 52 (4): 22-3, 68, 70,
               April 1938.
For the animated film of "Snow White and the Seven Dwarfs"
paints were developed to simulate satin and velvet for the Queen's
costumes, linen for Snow White, and homespun for the Dwarfs.

219   "Bathsheba."   American Film Institute Catalog, 1961-70, p.45.
Bathsheba is credited with the costumes of "Hallelujah the Hills"
and "The Double-Barrelled Detective Story."

220   Batterberry, Michael and Ariane.   Mirror Mirror: A Social
               History of Fashion.   New York: Holt, Rinehart and Win-
               ston, 1977.
Clara Bow helped popularize exposed legs and short skirts worn
by the flappers, when she wore stockings rolled to her knees.
Cecil B. De Mille was the first person to arrange for studio designers, since actresses had previously purchased all of their
costumes.   Samuel Goldwyn hired Gabrielle Chanel in the mid-
1930s (1931) to help his actresses with their costumes--though
it was not successful.   The Legion of Decency made Mae West
their first target of censorship; includes a photo of West in a
sheer costume from "Night After Night."   Circa the late 1920s
"Hollywood did not set the style" because a film was often cir-
culated three years after production, although it did influence
fashion through the photogenic sequined and satin fabrics worn by
the actresses.   Youth of the 1960s copied films of the 1920s to
the 1940s rather than the films of their own decade.   Includes
many costume photos, as with Gregory Peck in "The Man in the
Gray Flannel Suit," which lent the name to the stereotypical image
of businessmen.

221   "Baudot, Colette."   American Film Institute Catalog, 1961-70,
               p.46.
Colette Baudot is credited with the wardrobe of "Secret World,"
and was the wardrobe mistress of "End of Desire."

222   "Bayance, Rita."   American Film Institute Catalog, 1961-70,
               p.47.
Rita Bayance is credited with the costumes of "Benjamin."

223   "Baykova, L."   American Film Institute Catalog, 1961-70,
               p.47.
L. Baykova is credited with the costumes of "A Kiev Comedy."

224   "Bayless, Luster."   American Film Institute Catalog, 1961-70,
               p.47.
Luster Bayless is credited with the costumes of "Rio Lobo" and
"The Undefeated," the wardrobe of "Chisum," and the men's
wardrobe/costumes of "Advance to the Rear" and "Norwood."

225   "Be Not Too Serious--Wrinkles Are Result."   Screen News,
               1 (40): 20, November 25, 1922.

Dorothy Gish has been studying the characteristics and clothing
of girls in the sailors' district in London, to authenticate her role
in "Fury."

226 "Bear, Jack." American Film Institute Catalog, 1961-70, p.47.
      Jack Bear was the costume designer of "The President's Analyst,"
      "The Odd Couple," and "Darling Lili" and is credited with the
      costumes of "What Did You Do in the War, Daddy?," "Gunn,"
      "Waterhole #3," and "The Party"; the wardrobe of "Hitler" and
      "Kisses for My President"; and the men's wardrobe of "Inside
      Daisy Clover."

227 Beard, Charles R. "Why Get It Wrong?" Sight and Sound,
          2 (8): 124-5, Winter 1934.
      The author, a costume and armor historian, discusses the cos-
      tuming of "Henry VIII," the most successful film in Britain in
      1933. Frequently referring to the original period, he has found
      an abundance of inaccuracies in the men's costumes.

228 Beaton, Cecil. Cecil Beaton: Memoirs of the 40's. New York:
          McGraw-Hill, 1972.
      Cecil Beaton designed the costumes for "An Ideal Husband" and
      "Anna Karenina" at the same time, while having problems with the
      weather, fabric scarcities due to the war, and a wardrobe-union
      revolt. Technicolor adviser Natalie Kalmus, and her assistant,
      Joan Bridge, were apparently annoying with their suggestions con-
      cerning costume colors. The costumes for the leading actresses
      in "Anna Karenina" were made by Madame Paulette. Beaton de-
      cided to make the costumes more authentically Russian than those
      Greta Garbo had worn in the 1935 version. Garbo had avoided
      wardrobe tests of her film costumes since she felt that looking at
      a costume was sufficient to tell how it would photograph. Includes
      sketches and stills of costumes worn by Paulette Goddard and
      Diana Wynyard in "An Ideal Husband" and by Vivien Leigh in
      "Anna Karenina."

229 _____. Cecil Beaton's "Fair Lady." New York: Holt, Rine-
          hart and Winston, 1964.
      As the only book of its kind, this is the single most comprehen-
      sive record of a film's costuming and designing. Cecil Beaton's
      diary chronicles a year spent on the sets and costumes of "My
      Fair Lady"; he was in charge of the total look of the film. Joe
      Hiatt was in charge of wardrobe, Anne Laune was the production
      forelady of wardrobe, Leah Barnes was the milliner, and Geoff
      Allan was in charge of aging the costumes. The book is not
      liberally illustrated, but it does include stills of Audrey Hepburn,
      Rex Harrison, Gladys Cooper, Wilfred Hyde-White, Stanley Hollo-
      way, and Bina Rothschild.

230 _____. The Glass of Fashion. Garden City, N.Y.: Double-
          day, 1954.
      Cecil Beaton notes that Greta Garbo, through her film costumes
      and makeup, had, in the 1930s, the most influence of any person

over the appearance of a generation. Her early film costumes
were in questionable taste, but her later costumes suited her
personality to the extent that she did not care for wardrobe tests.

231 _____. The Happy Years, Diaries: 1944-8. London: Weiden-
            feld and Nicolson, 1972.
The English edition of Cecil Beaton: Memoirs of the 40's.

232 _____. "Hollywood Goes Refined." Vogue, 77 (12): 34-5,
            98, June 15, 1931.
Cecil Beaton criticizes the pretentiousness and bad taste of the
lifestyles and film costumes of Hollywood in the silent era. He
praises the talents of Adrian, as with his photogenic and exaggerated film costumes, and the hiring of Mlle. Chanel by Samuel
Goldwyn. Also praised is the "exotic" Joan Crawford, who, two
years before, wore "vulgar costumes" in Hollywood, which "was
formerly considered a wilderness of vulgarians."

233 _____. " ' ... in Making Gigi.' " Vogue, 131 (10): 88-90,
            151, June 1958.
Cecil Beaton discusses the research and filming of his costumes
for "Gigi"; with stills of stars Leslie Caron, Louis Jourdan, and
Maurice Chevalier.

234 _____. "My Fair Lady." Ladies' Home Journal, 81 (1):
            56-65, January/February 1964.
Includes excerpts from a diary kept by Cecil Beaton during the
production of "My Fair Lady" (see Cecil Beaton's "Fair Lady"),
with references to the research, fittings, fabrics, and aging of
the costumes. Includes numerous sketches and stills of costumes
and hats, modeled by Audrey Hepburn and others.

235 _____. The Restless Years, Diaries: 1955-63. London:
            Weidenfeld and Nicolson, 1976.
Cecil Beaton discusses costume designing for "Gigi," including
the research and color selection of costumes and working with
costumer Madame Karinska. He would have liked to design the
costumes for Marilyn Monroe in "The Prince and the Showgirl,"
when asked by Sir Laurence Olivier, but refused because of a
personal feud with Olivier. He also discusses briefly designing
for Audrey Hepburn in "My Fair Lady" and notes that "thirty-five
years ago I could think of nothing more wonderful than going to
Hollywood to work on designing a great film. But Hollywood has
changed and so have I."

236 _____. The Strenuous Years, Diaries: 1948-55. London:
            Weidenfeld and Nicolson, 1973.
Irene Castle, hired as the clothes adviser for "The Story of Vernon
and Irene Castle," drove her car filled with photograph albums
to Hollywood, only to have the original records of her clothing
ignored.

237 "Beaton, Cecil." American Film Institute Catalog, 1961-70,
            p. 47.

Cecil Beaton was the costume designer of "My Fair Lady" and of the period costumes of "On a Clear Day You Can See Forever," which he also created.

238   "Beaton, Cecil." Biographical Encyclopaedia and Who's Who of the American Theatre. 1966, p. 280.

239   "Beaton, Cecil." Celebrity Register. 2nd ed., 1963, p. 42.

240   "Beaton, Cecil." Fairchild's Who's Who in Fashion. 1975, p. 20.

241   "Beaton, Cecil (Walter Hardy)." Current Biography. 1944, p. 34-7.

242   "Beaton, Cecil (Walter Hardy)." Current Biography. 1962, p. 31-4.

243   "Beaton, Cecil (Walter Hardy)." Who's Who in the World. 3rd ed., 1976-7, p. 62.

244 "Beaton, Sir Cecil." Who's Who in the Theatre. 16th ed., 1977, p. 398.

245   "Beaton, Sir Cecil Walter Hardy." International Who's Who. 41st ed., 1977-8, p. 120.
Includes a unique costume-design credit for Cecil Beaton not listed in any other source, for "Black Vanities."

246 "Beaton, Sir Cecil Walter Hardy." Who's Who. 130th ed., 1978-9, p. 163.

247 "Beaton, Sir Cecil Walter Hardy." World of Fashion. 1976, p. 101-2.
Biographical information on Cecil Beaton, whose costumes for "My Fair Lady" influenced fashion in the early 1960s through colors, silhouette, and mood.

248   "The 'Beau Brummell' of Mansfield and Barrymore--a Study in Stage and Screen Contrasts--by an Old-Timer." Screen News, 3 (16): 22, 31, April 19, 1924.
In "Beau Brummell" John Barrymore wears costumes based on authentic color plates that he selected; he models one costume.

249   "Beauty and the Boot." Picture Play, 31 (6): 54-5, February 1930.
Eight actresses model costumes with boots, including Billie Dove from "The Painted Angel."

250   "Beauty Blitz." Screenland, 49 (4): 29, February 1945.
Rita Hayworth and Janet Blair each model one costume from "Tonight and Every Night"; in color.

251 Beck, Marilyn. "Designer Sees Stars at Their Worst." San
Francisco Examiner, September 21, 1976, p.20.
Bill Thomas, who started designing in Hollywood over 30 years
ago, discusses the many stars he has designed for and candidly
offers suggestions for some. He favors realism in costumes that
reinforce the character, rather than start fashion trends. He won
an Academy Award for "Spartacus."

252 "Beck, Ron." American Film Institute Catalog, 1961-70, p.48.
12 costume-related credits are listed for Ron Beck.

253 Beckwith, C.J., R.A. "Interior Decoration." Cinema Arts
(Preview Issue), 1 (1): 43, 88, September 1937.
Notes the similarities of film costume and furniture and set design in their influence on the audience. Generally, the interior
design of films has not been as publicized as film costume, though
the budgets and amount of detail given to each are similar.

254 "Beer, Vivian." American Film Institute Catalog, 1921-30,
p.968.
Vivian Beer is credited with the wardrobe of "Way for a Sailor."

255 "Beery Shoes Shod Like Mules' Hoofs." MGM Studio News,
7 (7): n.p., April 23, 1940.
Metal plates were attached to the soles of Wallace Beery's shoes,
which he had worn in many previous films, for "20 Mule Team"
since borax crystals during filming could quickly slice through
leather.

256 "Beetson, Frank, Jr." American Film Institute Catalog, 1961-
70, p.50.
Frank Beetson, Jr., is credited with the costumes of "The Glory
Guys" and "Nevada Smith," the men's costumes of "Hatari!," and
the costume supervision of "McLintock!"

257 "Beetson, Frank, Sr." American Film Institute Catalog, 1961-
70, p.50.
Frank Beetson, Sr., is credited with the wardrobe of "The Deadly
Companions" and "Donovan's Reef" and the costume supervision
of "Cheyenne Autumn."

258 Beetson, Frederick W. "Now." Los Angeles Times Annual
Pre-View, April 18, 1928, sec. 1, p.7-8.
Discussion of problems in the film industry caused by such large
forces of labor, as with the 10,000 registered extras and 25,000
casual extras. Only 5 percent of the extras make a living wage,
and they usually have a wardrobe valued at $1,000. Those items
that the dress extra must have are listed.

259 "Begins 'Fashion Row.'" Screen News, 2 (38): 2, September
22, 1923.
Mae Murray will wear about 100 costumes in "Fashion Row."

260   "Behind the Scenes at Hollywood's Famed Costume Houses. "
          Motion Picture Costumers, 1960, n. p.
      The two main costume houses in Hollywood are Western Costume
      Company, the world's largest, and Berman's & Sons, which is
      associated with Berman's in London.   Western Costume Company
      also employs more members of the Costumer's Local 705 than
      any other organization.

261   Behlmer, Rudy, ed.   Memo from David O. Selznick.   New
          York: Viking, 1972.
      David O. Selznick was well known for his voluminous memos.
      He felt that the producer's function with costuming was to approve
      the sketches and emphasize the dramatic points needed for the
      costumes, conferring with the designer.   Concerning "Gone with
      the Wind, " his complaints with designer Walter Plunkett and ward-
      robe chief Edward P. Lambert were that the costumes looked
      too new; the costume colors of the opening Twelve Oaks sequence
      were not bright enough to contrast with the dull-colored worn
      during the war sequences; and the colors of costumes worn in the
      bazaar sequence were too bright, but needed to be somewhat
      bright to contrast with Vivien Leigh's widow costume.   He also
      felt that Clark Gable's costumes looked awful and were poorly
      fitted; he was angry that someone had told Gable not to use his
      usual tailor, Eddie Schmidt, since Gable usually looked reason-
      ably well dressed, had always liked Schmidt, and occasion-
      ally had even assisted him in the sketching.   Since the film had
      influenced fashion "at least fifty percent" with snoods and corsets,
      for example, he thought this should be publicized, but limited to
      women's and fan magazines.   He also felt that the success of
      "The Garden of Allah, " "Becky Sharp, " "La Cucaracha, " "Vogues
      of 1938, " and "Goldwyn Follies" had been due in part to the color
      photography of the costumes.

262   "Behold the Tailored Bathing Suit. "   Screen News, 3 (10): 17,
          March 8, 1924.
      Discussion of current trends in bathing suits, with mention of
      bathing suits worn in "Lilies of the Field. "   (The illustration dis-
      cussed was not shown until the following issue.)

263   "Behold the Tailored Bathing Suit. "   Screen News, 3 (11): 31,
          March 15, 1924.
      An unidentified woman models a bathing suit from "Lilies of the
      Field. "   (See previous entry.)

264   "Bei, Leo. "   American Film Institute Catalog, 1961-70, p. 50.
      Leo Bei is credited with the costumes of "Almost Angels, " "For-
      ever My Love, " "The Good Soldier Schweik, " "Miracle of the
      White Stallions, " and "Emil and the Detectives" and the wardrobe
      of "The Secret Ways. "

265   "Belew, Bill. "   American Film Institute Catalog, 1961-70, p. 50.
      Bill Belew was the wardrobe designer of "Elvis--That's the Way It Is. "

266 Bell, Caroline. "What Do We Have Here? Everything!" Picture
        Play, 25 (6): 83-5, 105, February 1927.
Western Costume Company was founded 12 years earlier with an
investment of $500, and has since amassed a stock of over one
million costumes. The over 200 employees, including cobblers
and armorers, can make anything that is not already owned; and
research is done in a company library. Ten films recently costumed are listed, e.g., Douglas Fairbanks models a costume from
"Robin Hood." Cinema Mercantile Corporation, essentially a
property rental company, was founded six years earlier by Harry
Arnold. The costume department houses 9,000 garments, with
seamstresses employed who can design and construct modern clothing on one-day notice.

267 Bell, Lisle. "Cornbelt Silk." Review of Designing Male, by
        Howard Greer. New York Herald Tribune Book Review, 28
        (18): 13, December 16, 1951.
Discussion of Howard Greer's "cornbelt point of view," his book
Designing Male, and his mother, Minnie, who once had Greta
Garbo mash potatoes for dinner.

268 "Belle Bennett Signs to Play in Revival of 'East Lynne.'"
        Screen News, 4 (16): 11, April 18, 1925.
Belle Bennett has one week to gather a wardrobe of period clothes
for "East Lynne."

269 " 'The Belle' of the Nineties." Movieland, 3 (2): 48-9, 75,
        March 1945.
Don Loper discusses designing for Gypsy Rose Lee and Dinah
Shore in "Belle of the Yukon," with mention of how the costumes
might influence fashion. The costumes were authentic and inspired
by painters Boldini, John Sargeant, and Gainsborough. The 33
actresses wore custom-made corsets, averaging $150 to $300
each. Includes eight costume sketches.

270 "Belloni, Nanda." American Film Institute Catalog, 1961-70,
        p. 51
Nanda Belloni is credited with the costumes of "Night Affair."

271 Ben-Allah [Ben-Allah Newman]. Rudolph Valentino: His Ro-
        mantic Life and Death. Hollywood: Ben-Allah Co., 1926.
Uninformative book about Rudolph Valentino, with comments about
his wife, Natacha Rambova, being overdomineering in his film
productions.

272 Bender, Marilyn. "Cassini Faces New Frontier in Fashion with
        Few Regrets for Past Designs." New York Times, March
        15, 1961, p. 35.
Includes biographical information on Oleg Cassini and a discussion
of his fashion-design career, noting that he designed 36 films for
Paramount and Twentieth Century-Fox, beginning in 1940.

273 _____. The Beautiful People. New York: Coward-McCann,
        1967.
Film-costume references: Michael Caine's costumes for the title
role in "Alfie" were an "instrument of social protest"; Norman
Norell began his designing career as a film-costume designer;
Pierre Cardin received acclaim and his start as a designer after
creating the costumes of "The Beauty and the Beast," based on the
sketches of Christian Bérard; and Douglas Hayward, a London
men's tailor, noted for his costumes in "Casino Royale" and
"Modesty Blaise," flew to Hollywood to make four suits for Tony
Curtis in "Don't Make Waves." Film costume influenced fashion
considerably in the 1930s, but in the 1960s "Hollywood was a
wasteland." Discussion of the influence, or doubtful influence,
of costumes worn in "Dr. Zhivago" and "Viva Maria," e.g., the
bomb bag worn in the latter. Foreign films listed as having influenced fashion are "Morgan," "The Knack," "Darling," "Blow-
Up," "Last Year at Marienbad," and "Jules et Jim."

274 Bendick, Jeanne. "Casting, Costuming, and Make-Up," in
        Making the Movies. New York: Whittlesey House,
        McGraw-Hill, 1945, p. 57-65.
Includes a discussion of the differences in being a dress extra as
opposed to an extra: a dress extra must have a large wardrobe to
be ready for a variety of films. Written for young persons and
very basic concerning film costume.

275 Benesh, Carolyn L. E. Reflections of Edith Head; an Exhibition
        of Costumes and Sketches. Los Angeles: California
        Museum of Science and Industry, 1976.
Edith Head was interviewed for an exhibition of her film costumes,
organized by Stuart Iverson. Much of the text also comes from
The Dress Doctor, and other sources, as found in the bibliography.
Discussion of costumes worn in "The Golden Bed," "Artists and
Models Abroad," and by Lupe Velez in "The Wolf Song," Mae
West in "She Done Him Wrong," Charles Laughton in "Sign of the
Cross" and "White Woman," "Shirley Temple in "Little Miss Marker,"
Claudette Colbert in "Zaza," Barbara Stanwyck in "The Lady Eve,"
Ginger Rogers in "Lady in the Dark," Olivia de Havilland in "The
Heiress," and others. Includes 47 sketches and stills from the
above and other films.

276 "Benson, John Brock." American Film Institute Catalog, 1961-
        70, p. 53.
John Brock Benson is credited with the costumes of "Bacchanale"
and "The Corporate Queen."

277 Bentley, Byron. "Vertès' Paris Is Broadway's Plum." Theatre
        Arts, 39 (7): 30-1, 92-3, July 1955.
Marcel Vertès prefers painting to film and theatrical costume and
set design. He considered the seven months spent on the costumes
and sets for "Moulin Rouge" too long an absence from painting,
but sold about 75 of the sketches in exhibits in New York and Lon-

don. He won two Academy Awards for the color costumes and
sets of "Moulin Rouge."

278 "Beranková, Anna." American Film Institute Catalog, 1961-70,
         p. 54.
Anna Beranková is credited with the costumes of "Daisies."

279 Berges, Marshall. "Home Q & A: Dorothy Jeakins." Los
         Angeles Times, October 31, 1976, Home sec., p. 32-4.
A biography of designer Dorothy Jeakins, touching for the insight
about her early years. She worked for the advertising department
of a department store before being hired for her first film, "Joan
of Arc," for which she received an Academy Award. She discusses designing for "Fat City," working with decreasing budgets,
and how she designs for a film.

280 "Berman, David." American Film Institute Catalog, 1961-70,
         p. 56.
David Berman is credited with the costumes of "Jack the Giant
Killer."

281 "Berman, Wally." American Film Institute Catalog, 1961-70,
         p. 56.
Wally Berman is credited with the costumes of "Tarzan and Jane
Regained Sort Of."

282 "Berman's." American Film Institute Catalog, 1961-70, p. 56.
Berman's is credited with the wardrobe of "Guess What Happened
to Count Dracula."

283 "Berman's of London." American Film Institute Catalog, 1961-
         70, p. 56.
Berman's of London is credited with the wardrobe of "30 Is a
Dangerous Age, Cynthia" and the costumes for Ursula Andress
and Joanna Pettet in "Casino Royale."

284 "Bernard Newman Is Dead at 63; Designer for Bergdorf Good-
         man." New York Times, December 1, 1966, p. 47.
Bernard Newman died at age 63 from an undisclosed cause. The
information concerns his skill as a fashion designer, briefly noting
that he was a designer with Warner Brothers in 1934 (actually
RKO--he did not work for Warner Brothers until 1946-7).

285 "Berne, Israel." American Film Institute Catalog, 1961-70,
         p. 56.
Israel Berne is credited with the wardrobe of "13 West Street,"
"Diamond Head," "Under the Yum Yum Tree," and the men's
costumes of "Taras Bulba."

286 Bernique, Jean. "Costumes: The Art of Dressing for the
         Movies," in Motion Picture Acting for Professionals and
         Amateurs: A Technical Treatise on Make-up, Costumes
         and Expression. Chicago: Producers Service Co., 1916,

p. 181-90.
Sensible advice for selecting appropriate modern clothing for actresses and actors, including lengthy lists, particularly for the
men, of specific clothes recommended for a variety of scenes;
also information on such accessories as shoes, purses, gloves,
and jewelry.

287 "Berselli, Adriana." American Film Institute Catalog, 1961-70,
        p. 57.
Adriana Berselli was the costume designer of "Better a Widow"
and is credited with the costumes of "Damon and Pythias,"
"Prisoner of the Iron Mask," "The Bobo," and "Pussycat, Pussycat, I Love You."

288 "Best=Dressed" [sic]. American Magazine, 131 (2): 74,
        February 1941.
Rita Hayworth was voted "the best-dressed girl in the movies"
the previous year by Hollywood designers.

289 "Best Dressed Woman of the Month." Motion Picture, 70 (2):
        91, September 1945.
In "Christmas in Connecticut" Barbara Stanwyck will wear cos-
tumes designed by Edith Head and Milo Anderson. (Head designed
Stanwyck's costumes, and Anderson the others.)

290 "Best Dressed Woman of the Month." Motion Picture, 73 (2):
        117, March 1947.
Loretta Young models a suit from "The Perfect Marriage," by
Edith Head; she bought it for her personal wardrobe.

291 "Best Dressed Woman of the Month." Motion Picture, 73 (6):
        67, July 1947.
Shirley Temple models a dress from "The Bachelor and the Bobby-
Soxer."

292 "Best, Marjorie." American Film Institute Catalog, 1961-70,
        p. 58.
Marjorie Best was the costume designer of "The Comancheros,"
"Tender Is the Night," and "Spencer's Mountain" and the assistant
costume designer of "The Greatest Story Ever Told" and is credited
with the costumes of "State Fair" (1962).

293 "Betrue, Gloria." American Film Institute Catalog, 1961-70,
        p. 58.
Gloria Betrue is credited with the wardrobe of "Wild Wheels."

294 "Bette Davis." Movies, 6 (1): 49, July 1942.
Bette Davis wore glasses and 25 pounds of cotton padding to
achieve a dowdy appearance in "Now Voyager."

295 "Betty Compson Wears Coat Made from Lion's Skin." Screen
        News, 3 (35): 8, August 30, 1924.
Betty Compson wears a cape with collar made of lion skin in "The

Female. " The wardrobe department made it from two lion-skin rugs.

296 Beymer, William Gilmore. "Costuming All Creation. " Woman's
           Home Companion, 55 (1): 18-9, 162, 164, February 1928.
The author discusses his tour with Mr. Lambert (probably Edward P.)
of a building (never identified; it was Western Costume Company)
that houses thousands of costumes. Described are many of the
floors, such as the library, and many of the costumes housed in
the collection, e.g., those worn in "The Queen of Sheba" and
"The Birth of a Nation. " Costumes discussed at greater length
include those worn in "Beau Geste" (1926), "Across the Pacific, "
"Captain Sazarac, " "The Wedding March, " "The Golden Journey, "
and worn by Elaine Hammerstein in "Rupert of Hentzau. "

297 "Bibas. " American Film Institute Catalog, 1961-70, p. 59.
Bibas is credited with Carol White's wardrobe in "I'll Never Forget What's 'Is Name. "

298 Biery, Ruth. "Clothes Habits of Hollywood. " Photoplay, 39
           (6): 72-3, 120-4, May 1931.
Discussion of the personal clothing preferences of many actors
and actresses. Alice White refused to wear the longer hemlines
in "The Widow from Chicago"; the producer and designer (not
identified) could not talk her out of it, so she wore her costumes
at knee-length.

299 _____. "What Her Every Fan Should Know. " Motion Pic-
           ture, 38 (6): 32-3, 94, January 1930.
Leatrice Joy has final approval over her film costumes, which
the studio provides, and are made of the best fabrics so that they
can be made over for extras. She would not care to keep the
costumes since they reflect the different characters she plays and
are often inappropriate for her off-screen life, as with the indiscreet costumes she wore in "A Most Immoral Lady. "

300 "Big Uniform Factory Put in Operation for Romantic Play. "
           Screen News, 1 (40): 11, November 25, 1922.
An entire plant has been working on court and military costumes
for a fictitious kingdom in "If I Were Queen. "

301 "Biggest Sewing Job on Record. " Screen News, 4 (26): 15,
           July 4, 1925.
40 seamstresses worked several months on tapestries and on costumes for 1,500 extras and the cast in "The Wanderer. " Half of
the 44,000 square yards of fabric was used for the costumes and
the other half for drapes and other coverings.

302 "Biki of Milano. " American Film Institute Catalog, 1961-70,
           p. 60.
Biki of Milano was the special wardrobe designer for Maureen
O'Hara in "The Battle of the Villa Fiorita. "

303   "Bilabel, Barbara." American Film Institute Catalog, 1961-70,
         p. 60.
Barbara Bilabel was the costume designer of "The Castle."

304   "Bill Hart Has a Wonderful Wardrobe." Screen News, 4 (36):
         4, September 12, 1925.
Lists many items from William S. Hart's film wardrobe, all
authentic, and many historical, western costumes.

305 The Biographical Encyclopaedia and Who's Who of the American
         Theatre. Edited by Walter Rigdon.   New York: James
         H. Heineman, 1966.
This biographical dictionary includes biographies of many theatrical-
costume designers who also design for films.   Because of the large
numbers of entries from this dictionary, the bibliographical ci-
tation has been shortened to include only the book's title and date.
To date, it has not been revised.

306   Bird, Adelia. " ... A Star and Her Designer Talk Clothes."
         Modern Screen, 14 (1): 64-6, 86-8, December 1936.
Lengthy discussion of costumes worn by Ruth Chatterton in "Dodsworth," by Omar Kiam.   Chatterton models seven costumes; with
two of the original sketches.

307   _____.   "And the Bride Wore...." Modern Screen, 13 (2):
         64-6, 80-1, July 1936.
Discussion of wedding gowns, including one each worn by Irene
Dunne in "Showboat" and by Shirley Deane in "The First Baby,"
which Deane models.

308   _____.   "Don't Try to Be a Clotheshorse." Modern Screen,
         13 (6): 64-6, 83-5, November 1936.
Travis Banton does not plan on allowing the current historical-
costume trend to influence his modern costume designs.

309   _____.   "Dresses You Could Really Wear." Modern Screen,
         10 (3): 56-8, 80, February 1935.
Discussion of the trend toward more practical film costumes, as
with costumes by Orry-Kelly, copies of which are marketed throughout the country.   Ruby Keeler models one costume from "Flirtation
Walk."

310   _____.   "Hollywood Fads in the Making." Modern Screen,
         11 (6): 48-50, 71-2, November 1935.
Discussion of costumes worn by Joan Crawford in "I Live My
Life," by Adrian; Dolores Del Rio in "I Live for Love," by Orry-
Kelly; and Ginger Rogers in "In Person" and Lily Pons in "Love
Song," both by Bernard Newman.   Crawford models one costume
and one headdress, and Del Rio four costumes and one headdress,
from the above films.

311   _____.   "Hollywood Sets the Tempo for Your Spring Shopping."

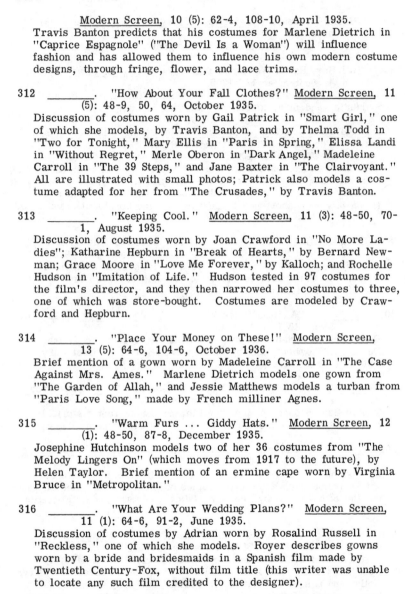

Modern Screen, 10 (5): 62-4, 108-10, April 1935.
Travis Banton predicts that his costumes for Marlene Dietrich in
"Caprice Espagnole" ("The Devil Is a Woman") will influence
fashion and has allowed them to influence his own modern costume
designs, through fringe, flower, and lace trims.

312 _____. "How About Your Fall Clothes?" Modern Screen, 11
        (5): 48-9, 50, 64, October 1935.
Discussion of costumes worn by Gail Patrick in "Smart Girl," one
of which she models, by Travis Banton, and by Thelma Todd in
"Two for Tonight," Mary Ellis in "Paris in Spring," Elissa Landi
in "Without Regret," Merle Oberon in "Dark Angel," Madeleine
Carroll in "The 39 Steps," and Jane Baxter in "The Clairvoyant."
All are illustrated with small photos; Patrick also models a cos-
tume adapted for her from "The Crusades," by Travis Banton.

313 _____. "Keeping Cool." Modern Screen, 11 (3): 48-50, 70-
        1, August 1935.
Discussion of costumes worn by Joan Crawford in "No More Ladies"; Katharine Hepburn in "Break of Hearts," by Bernard Newman; Grace Moore in "Love Me Forever," by Kalloch; and Rochelle
Hudson in "Imitation of Life." Hudson tested in 97 costumes for
the film's director, and they then narrowed her costumes to three,
one of which was store-bought. Costumes are modeled by Crawford and Hepburn.

314 _____. "Place Your Money on These!" Modern Screen,
        13 (5): 64-6, 104-6, October 1936.
Brief mention of a gown worn by Madeleine Carroll in "The Case
Against Mrs. Ames." Marlene Dietrich models one gown from
"The Garden of Allah," and Jessie Matthews models a turban from
"Paris Love Song," made by French milliner Agnes.

315 _____. "Warm Furs ... Giddy Hats." Modern Screen, 12
        (1): 48-50, 87-8, December 1935.
Josephine Hutchinson models two of her 36 costumes from "The
Melody Lingers On" (which moves from 1917 to the future), by
Helen Taylor. Brief mention of an ermine cape worn by Virginia
Bruce in "Metropolitan."

316 _____. "What Are Your Wedding Plans?" Modern Screen,
        11 (1): 64-6, 91-2, June 1935.
Discussion of costumes by Adrian worn by Rosalind Russell in
"Reckless," one of which she models. Royer describes gowns
worn by a bride and bridesmaids in a Spanish film made by
Twentieth Century-Fox, without film title (this writer was unable
to locate any such film credited to the designer).

317 _____. "What They Like to Wear." Modern Screen, 12 (4):
        56-7, 86-8, March 1936.
Jane Froman models one costume by Orry-Kelly from "Stars over
Broadway," which she bought for her personal wardrobe. Director
John Stahl had gowns sent over from Hattie Carnegie's salon so

that he, Anita Louise, and Irene Dunne could select their costumes for "The Magnificent Obsession."

318 Bird, Adelia E. "Allure, Romance, Charm, Youth." Modern
          Movies, 1 (7): 40-3, January 1938.
One costume by Gwen Wakeling is each modeled by Marlene Dietrich from "Desire" and Loretta Young from "Second Honeymoon."

319 _____. " 'First Lady' in Cinema Smartness." Modern
          Movies, 1 (6): 44-5, December 1937.
Kay Francis models four costumes by Orry-Kelly from "First Lady."

320 _____. "There's a DRESS-UP Feeling to Fashions."
          Modern Movies, 1 (5): 44-5, November 1937.
Gail Patrick models five costumes by Edith Head from "Artists and Models."

321 Bird, Adelia F. [sic]. "Technicolor Costumes." Modern
          Movies, 1 (4): 42-5, October 1937.
Joan Bennett models seven costumes from "Vogues of 1938."

322 Birdwell, Russell. "Career Insurance." Jones' Magazine, 4
          (1): 26-8, 48-50, February 1939.
Seven formerly famous and wealthy actors and actresses including Jean Acker Valentino (the first wife of Rudolph Valentino), Rosemary Theby, Alice Lake, Elinor Fair, and director Henry Otto, were all working as extras when they sent a petition to Sacramento to have a law enacted to require that studios deduct 10 percent of the stars' earnings to be kept by the state treasurer for their future, so that at least others would be protected from becoming bankrupt when their careers waned. Nearly all of them broke, they were earning $7.50 a day as extras, or $16.50 if they were dress extras and provided their own clothes. Theby never saved her money since she spent it all on the costumes she supplied for her films.

323 "Black for Formal Occasions." Screen News, 5 (2): 6,
          January 16, 1926.
Betty Jewel models a gown by Paul Poiret from "The Necessary Evil."

324 Blackford, Marion. "Miss Temple's Best Bib and Tucker."
          Screen Play, 20 (137): 33, 54-5, August 1936.
Shirley Temple insists upon immaculate and matching costumes. She is allowed to keep all of her film costumes, though she prefers simple garments when home, where she has several hundred dresses. Her designer, William Lambert, discusses designing for her.

325 "Blaine, Madame." American Film Institute Catalog, 1921-30,
          p. 978.

Madame Blaine is credited with the costumes of "Potash and Perlmutter."

326   "Blake, Yvonne." American Film Institute Catalog, 1961-70,
          p. 64.
Yvonne Blake was the costume designer of "Judith," "Assignment
K, " "Charlie Bubbles," "Duffy," and "The Best House in London";
the associate costume designer of "Fahrenheit 451"; and is credited
with the costumes for "The Idol," "The Spy with a Cold Nose,"
and Susannah York's in "Brotherly Love."

327   Blakeslee, Fred Gilbert.   "Costume Research." Motion Picture
          Classic, 17 (5): 18-9, 81, 84, July 1923.
Historical films seldom have authentic costumes despite their
advertising claims.   The author suggests a central bureau be
established so that experts in various areas of film production
can be listed in a central file.   Lengthy analysis of costumes
worn in "When Knighthood Was in Flower," with references to
Marion Davies, Lynn Harding, and many others, and in "Robin
Hood," with references to Douglas Fairbanks and other actors
in the film.

328   Blakesley, Richard.   "One Designing Male Makes Good." Re-
          view of Designing Male, by Howard Greer.   Chicago
          Tribune, December 16, 1951, sec. 4, p. 13.

329   Blayney, Laura.   "Do Movies Influence the Paris Designers?"
          Movie Classic, 8 (4): 34-5, 58, June 1935.
The author attends the Paris collections four times per year and
interviewed leading couturiers for their opinions on film costume's
fashion influence.   Previous films that had influenced fashion in-
clude "The Private Life of Henry VIII," "Catherine the Great,"
"She Done Him Wrong," and "Little Women." Captain Molyneux,
Jeanne Lanvin, Jean Charles Worth, Lucien Lelong, Marcel
Rochas, and Jean Patou all admitted to being influenced by the
movies and/or the way in which the actresses wear their clothes.
Katharine Hepburn models a gown by Bernard Newman from
"Break of Hearts." Lili Damita models six costumes by Marcel
Rochas from an unidentified film.

330   _____.   "Paris Answers Hollywood!" Motion Picture, 46
          (5): 44-5, 74, 76, December 1933.
Gabrielle Chanel discusses the photography of film costumes,
noting that films excel in promoting seductive styles, and states
that film costumes are continually adapted from Parisian couture,
as with the famous "Letty Lynton" gown.   Elsa Schiaparelli is
impressed by the film designers but does not feel they can replace
Paris because of the limited nature of film costume.   Other
Parisian designers, Captain Molyneux, Madame Paray, Jean Patou,
and Jacques Worth agree, denying any competition with Hollywood
and noting also that films are a good medium for spreading Parisian fashions.

331   "Bliss, Bert." American Film Institute Catalog, 1961-70,
          p. 65.
Bert Bliss was the costume designer of "SINderella and the Golden
Bra" and "Divorce Las Vegas Style."

332   "'Blood and Sand' Faithful Reproduction of the Story." Screen
          News, 1 (18): 27, June 17, 1922.
John Robertson, a Paramount director, purchased three toreador
suits for Rudolph Valentino, and some Spanish mantillas for the
women in "Blood and Sand." The suits required three months of
handwork on the silver embroidery for each, made by Spanish
experts.

333   "Blue Collars Due to Film Influence Says La Rocque." Screen
          News, 3 (26): 28, June 28, 1924.
Actor Rod La Rocque attributes the fad for men's shirts in blue
and other colors to the movies, since white is seldom used for
shirts or props due to excessive reflection of light. Yellow is
also frequently used.

334   "The 'Bluebird' of Leningrad." San Francisco Chronicle,
          March 11, 1975, p. 17.
Edith Head discusses designing for Maya Plitsetskaya and Elizabeth Taylor, who wore seven costumes in "The Bluebird," and
some of her experiences on location in Russia. Includes one
sketch each of costumes worn by Cecily Tyson, Elizabeth Taylor,
and Ava Gardner.

335   Blyth, Ann. "'Or Would You Rather Be a Fish?'" Modern
          Screen, 37 (1): 64-5, 110, June 1948.
Ann Blyth discusses wearing an approximately 45-pound mermaid
tail in "Mr. Peabody and the Mermaid," made by Bud Westmore.
Brief mention of how the tail was made.

336   "Boehm, Werner." American Film Institute Catalog, 1961-70,
          p. 67.
Werner Boehm is credited with the costumes of "A Glass of Water."

337   "Bohan, Marc." American Film Institute Catalog, 1961-70,
          p. 67.
Marc Bohan is credited with Elizabeth Taylor's wardrobe in
"Secret Ceremony" and was the costume designer for "The Lady
in the Car with Glasses and a Gun." (Christian Dior was credited
with the dresses for Samantha Eggar and Stéphane Audran in this
film, though Bohan had been designing for the House of Dior since
a year after Dior's death.)

338   "Bohan, Marc." Celebrity Register. 3rd ed., 1973, p. 53.

339   "Bohan, Marc." Current Biography. 1965, p. 41-3.
Biographical information on Marc Bohan, chief designer of the
House of Dior. Helps clear the confusion of the organization of

the House of Dior after Christian Dior's death in 1957, when
Yves St. Laurent was chosen to carry on in the designer's place,
though he eventually left due to differences between himself and
Bohan.   Notes that he occasionally designs for films.

340   "Bohan, Marc."   Who's Who in France.   6th ed. , 1963-4,
             p. 475.

341   "Bolongaro, Massimo."   American Film Institute Catalog, 1961-
             70, p. 68.
Massimo Bolongaro is credited with the costumes of "Samson and
the Seven Miracles of the World. "

342   "Bond, Janice."   American Film Institute Catalog, 1961-70,
             p. 69.
Janice Bond was the costume designer of "Kenner. "

343   "Bonnay, Yvette."   American Film Institute Catalog, 1961-70,
             p. 69.
Yvette Bonnay is credited with the costumes of "Time Bomb. "

344   Booker, Janice L.   "Costumes by Adrian--The Story of an
             Era."   Leader Suburbanite (Philadelphia), June 22, 1972,
             p. 5.
Teachers Joseph Simms and Tom Stretton, and the high school
students of Cheltenham High in Wyncote, Pennsylvania, have
amassed considerable material on or by Adrian, including sketches,
paintings, and film and nonfilm fashions, and two suits worn by
Claudette Colbert in "Without Reservations. "   Discussion of their
research methods, and biographical information on Adrian.

345   "Booth, May."   American Film Institute Catalog, 1961-70, p. 70.
May Booth is credited with the wardrobe of "Clambake" and
"Change of Habit" and the women's costumes of "Palm Springs
Weekend. "

346   "Borque, Ralph."   American Film Institute Catalog, 1961-70,
             p. 71.
Ralph Borque is credited with the costumes of "The Texican. "

347   "Bos, Jerry."   American Film Institute Catalog, 1961-70, p. 71.
Jerry Bos is credited with the wardrobe of "Flight That Disappeared" and "The Scarface Mob. "

348   "Boss, Reeder."   American Film Institute Catalog, 1961-70,
             p. 72.
Reeder Boss is credited with the wardrobe of "Hero's Island. "

349   "Botti, Sartoria Sorelle."   American Film Institute Catalog,
             1961-70, p. 72.
Sartoria Sorelle Botti is credited with Cyd Charisse's dresses in
"Five Golden Hours. "

350 "Bourman, Einar." American Film Institute Catalog, 1961-70,
        p. 73
     Einar Bourman is credited with the wardrobe of "Gun Fight,"
     "When the Clock Strikes," "You Have to Run Fast," and "Saintly
     Sinners" and "Boy, Did I Get a Wrong Number!" and the costumes
     of "Gun Street," "Secret of Deep Harbor," "Deadly Duo," "Inci-
     dent in an Alley," "Shock Corridor," and "The Naked Kiss."

351 Bowers, Ronald. "Romantic and Glamorous Hollywood Designs."
        Films in Review, 26 (6): 379-80, June-July 1975.
     Discussion of the film costume exhibit at the Metropolitan Museum
     of Art. Designers who recreated lost costumes included Bill
     Blass, Giorgio de Sant'Angelo, and Jean Louis, who recreated
     the original gown worn by Rita Hayworth in "Gilda." The exhibit
     included a coat by Travis Banton worn by Theda Bara in "Fedora"
     in 1920.

352 "Box, Brian." American Film Institute Catalog, 1961-70, p. 74.
     Brian Box was the costume designer of "The Vampire Lovers."

353 "Boxer, John." American Film Institute Catalog, 1961-70, p. 74.
     John Boxer is credited with the wardrobe of "Requiem for a
     Heavyweight."

354 "Boyce, Eddie." American Film Institute Catalog, 1961-70,
        p. 74.
     Eddie Boyce is credited with the wardrobe of "Laughter in the
     Dark" and was the wardrobe supervisor for "The Long Day's
     Dying," "Before Winter Comes," and "The Executioner."

355 Bradbury, Ray. "When Hollywood Stars Were Costume-Made."
        Review of Hollywood Costume: Glamour! Glitter! Romance!,
        by Dale McConathy with Diana Vreeland. Los Angeles
        Times, November 28, 1976, Books sec., p. 6.
     "True, these costumes are mere molehills. But what molehills!"

356 Brady, James. Superchic. Boston: Little, Brown, 1974.
     James Brady, former publisher of Women's Wear Daily and
     Harper's Bazaar, notes that Parisian fashion designers flocked to
     see "Les Annees Follies," a collection of old newsreels. Conse-
     quently, the next season's collections featured clothes influenced
     by the 1920s.

357 "Brady, John." American Film Institute Catalog, 1961-70, p. 76.
     John Brady is credited with the wardrobe of "Billion Dollar
     Brain" and was the wardrobe master of "Dr. No," "Tarzan's
     Three Challenges," and "On Her Majesty's Secret Service."

358 "Brandi, Rose." American Film Institute Catalog, 1961-70,
        p. 77.
     Rose Brandi is credited with the wardrobe of "Brainstorm," the
     women's wardrobe of "There Was a Crooked Man...." and the
     ladies' costumes of "Inside Daisy Clover."

359 "Brandley, Majo." American Film Institute Catalog, 1961-70, p. 77.
Majo Brandley is credited with the wardrobe of "Temptation" (1962).

360 "Brandt, John, cost." American Film Institute Catalog, 1961-70, p. 77.
John Brandt is credited with the costumes of "Wild Gypsies."

361 "Brawd, Rose." American Film Institute Catalog, 1961-70, p. 78.
Rose Brawd is credited with the wardrobe of "The Incredible Mr. Limpet."

362 "Brdečka, Jiří." American Film Institute Catalog, 1961-70, p. 78.
Jiří Brdečka is credited with the costumes of "Lemonade Joe."

363 "Breath-Taking Hedy Lamarr...." Modern Screen, 20 (5): 100, April 1940.
Hedy Lamarr models a gown by Adrian from "I Take This Woman."

364 "Breed, Jackie." American Film Institute Catalog, 1961-70, p. 79.
Jackie Breed was the costume designer of "Isadora"; the wardrobe mistress of "Wonderful to Be Young!," "Summer Holiday," and "Prehistoric Women"; the wardrobe supervisor of "The Yellow Rolls-Royce," "Blow-Up," and "The Long Duel"; and is credited with the wardrobe of "The Hands of Orlac."

365 Breitinger. "Modas: Columbia Presenta a Rosalind Russell en 'El que juega con fuego.'" Cinelandia, 18 (3): 44-5, March 1944.
Rosalind Russell models six costumes by Travis Banton from "El que juega con fuego" ("Roughly Speaking"). The costumes are discussed, along with a fashion title Russell had recently received. One gown shows an oriental influence from a recent visit by Mme. Chiang Kai-shek. Spanish text.

366 _____. "Orry-Kelly." Cinelandia, 18 (1): 42-3, 46, January 1944.
Orry-Kelly is ranked with Travis Banton, Adrian, and Omar Kiam as the four most famous designers of Hollywood, all having done for Hollywood what designers Patou and Schiaparelli have done for Paris. Orry-Kelly is the only one of the four designers who remains in film, though he also hopes to open a salon, in South America. Orry-Kelly feels that costumes worn in films eight years earlier would have looked ridiculous if worn off-screen, and that film costume has greatly influenced American fashion, particularly after the Paris occupation. Having served in the army during WWII, he felt disillusioned about the field of film costume, which seemed almost ridiculous in comparison to the gravity of war. One costume each is modeled by Bette Davis from "Mr. Skeffington," Alexis Smith from "La ninfa constante" ("The Constant Nymph"), and Ann Sheridan from "Luna sobre la

cosecha" ("Shine on Harvest Moon") and "Gracias a tu buena
estrella" ("Thank Your Lucky Stars").   Also includes two sketches
of costumes worn by Sheridan from "La Cantena de Hollywood"
(the title obviously translates into "Hollywood Canteen," though
she did not appear in this).   Spanish text.

367   "Brenner, Albert."   American Film Institute Catalog, 1961-70,
         p. 79.
Albert Brenner was the costume designer of "Monte Walsh."

368   Bresler, Riva T.   Review of The Dress Doctor, by Edith Head
         and Jane Ardmore.   Library Journal, 84 (2): 187,
         January 15, 1959.
Less-than-flattering review of The Dress Doctor.

369   Breting.   "Edith Head: Directora de Modas en Paramount."
         Cinelandia, 17 (11): 44-5, November 1943.
A biography of Edith Head, who has traveled to Arizona and
Mexico for inspiration in her costume designs.   She has also had
some fabrics specially made in Mexico for her creations (films?).
Spanish text.

370   _____.   "El Puente de San Luis Rey."   Cinelandia, 17 (12):
         6-7, December 1943.
Reynaldo Luza was the technical adviser and costume and set
designer of "El Puente de San Luis Rey" ("The Bridge of San
Luis Rey"), one of few films having a South American setting--
Peru; and the designer's first film assignment.   Biographical information includes his having worked as a fashion illustrator for
Harper's Bazaar and as a designer who has traveled throughout
the world.   Includes three of his sketches for star Lynn Bari,
with four sketches of adapted costumes and three photos of one
costume from sketch to fitting.   Spanish text.

371   _____.   "Irene."   Cinelandia, 17 (10): 44-6, October 1943.
A biography of Irene, who discusses the coming of color films
and what it will mean to costume designing, and the influence of
the war on film costuming--e.g., requirements to use the least
fabric possible.   She notes that it would be absurd to try and
keep up with fashion under the circumstances.   Spanish text.

372   "Brichetto, Bice."   American Film Institute Catalog, 1961-70,
         p. 80.
Bice Brichetto was the costume designer of "Disorder," the
assistant costume designer of "The Leopard," and is credited
with the costumes of "Sandra."

373   "Bride on a Budget."   Silver Screen, 11 (6): 54-7, April 1941.
Ann Rutherford models a wedding gown and eight costumes by
Dolly Tree from "Keeping Company."

374   "Bridge, Joan."   American Film Institute Catalog, 1961-70,
         p. 80.

Joan Bridge was the costume designer of "Behold a Pale Horse" and "The Liquidator," the color costume designer of "A Man for All Seasons" and "The Prime of Miss Jean Brodie," and is credited with the costumes of "The Amorous Adventures of Moll Flanders," "Arrivederci, Baby!," "Chitty Chitty Bang Bang," and "Half a Sixpence."

375 "Briggs, John." American Film Institute Catalog, 1961-70, p. 81.
John Briggs was the costume designer of "Isadora"; the wardrobe master of "Greyfriars Bobby," "The Roman Spring of Mrs. Stone," "In Search of the Castaways"; "The Three Lives of Thomasina," and is credited with the wardrobe of "The Curse of the Mummy's Tomb," "Promise Her Anything," "Attack on the Iron Coast," and "Submarine X-1."

376 "Brighten Up Your Evenings." Motion Picture, 68 (5): 60-1, December 1944.
Claims that Hollywood is still a greater source of fashion trends, with its many designers, even though Paris has been liberated.

377 "Brighton, Billy." American Film Institute Catalog, 1921-30, p. 988.
Billy Brighton was the wardrobe technical director for "Seven Days Leave."

378 "The British Show Us Some Neat Styles (With a Little Help from Paris)." Screen Book, 17 (120): 44, March 1935.
British films are beginning to influence world fashions. The costumes modeled are not identified as film costumes.

379 "Brooks, Donald." American Film Institute Catalog, 1961-70, p. 83.
Donald Brooks was the costume designer of "The Cardinal" and is credited with the costumes of "Star!," Julie Andrews's costumes in "Darling Lili," and Elizabeth Ashley's clothes in "The Third Day."

380 "Brooks, Donald." Biographical Encyclopaedia and Who's Who of the American Theatre. 1966, p. 321.

381 "Brooks, Donald." Celebrity Register. 2nd ed., 1963, p. 76.

382 "Brooks, Donald." Fairchild's Who's Who in Fashion. 1975, p. 39.

383 "Brooks, Donald (Marc)." Current Biography. 1972, p. 47-9.
Donald Brooks's success with theatrical-costume designing led to his designing the costumes for Romy Schneider and Carol Lynley in "The Cardinal," spanning 1917 to 1948, for which he received an Academy Award nomination. He commuted from his New York headquarters to Hollywood and London for one and a half years while designing 130 costumes for Julie Andrews in "Star!" and

about 3,500 for the cast. He influenced fashion when he included some copies of Andrews's costumes in his collection. He was nominated for an Academy Award, also, for Andrews's costumes in "Darling Lili."

384 "Brooks, Jane." American Film Institute Catalog, 1961-70,
        p. 83.
Jane Brooks was the costume designer of "Tuck Me In."

385 Brown, Betty. "The Latest Fashions on Parade." Picture
        Play, 24 (6): 62-3, 111, August 1926.
The author attended the commencement exercises at the Paramount School and discusses the costumes designed by Gilbert Clark, the costume-department dean. Includes one sketch of a costume worn by Mary Brian in "Beau Geste" (1926).

386 "Brown, Louis." American Film Institute Catalog, 1961-70,
        p. 85.
Louis Brown was the costume designer of "Husbands" and "I Walk the Line."

387 "Brown, Morris." American Film Institute Catalog, 1961-70,
        p. 85.
Morris Brown is credited with the wardrobe of "How to Save a Marriage--and Ruin Your Life," "The Manchurian Candidate," "Boy, Did I Get a Wrong Number!," and "Murderers' Row."

388 Brownlow, Kevin. The Parade's Gone By. New York: Knopf,
        1969.
A massive account of the silent-film era, with the following references, too numerous to discuss: Joseph Henaberry's research for the costumes of "Intolerance" and "The Mother and the Law"; Clarence Brown's assembling the costumes for Olga Petrova in "Law of the Land" and "Exile"; Sophie Wachner's hosiery for Lois Moran in "Stella Dallas" (1925); the Pathécolor process of hand-tinting their fashion films, as with "Figleaves"; Gloria Swanson wearing her first bathing suit in "The Pullman Bride"; Dorothy Gish's research for her film costumes at the library; inauthentic period costumes, as with Adrian's for Rudolph Valentino in "The Eagle"; Mitchell Leisen's costumes for "Robin Hood," with simulated chain-mail; Charlie Chaplin having first worn his tramp costume in "Mabel's Strange Predicament" (see McCabe, John), and eating his boots made of licorice, in "The Gold Rush"; Harry Langdon's clothing style, developed in his vaudeville days; Buster Keaton's receiving costume-design credit in "The Playhouse"; Harold Lloyd's popularity in relation to his glasses; Geraldine Farrar's 80-pound armor made of "aluminum silver" for "Joan the Woman"; and disasters associated with costumes: the train of a gown worn by Leatrice Joy was removed so that she could run from tigers, if necessary, in "Manslaughter"; stuntman Dick Grace doubled for an unnamed actress, since the script called for her dress being set ablaze; and star Martha Mansfield died when her period costume caught fire during the filming of "The Warrens

of Virginia" (1923).   Also, brief mention of her 36 costumes for
"The Queen of Sheba, " and of wardrobe person Margaret Whistler;
of the importance of costume to the performances of Lois Wilson,
and Marlene Dietrich.

389   Bruce, "Spider. "   " 'Coney Island' " (Production).   Modern
           Screen, 26 (3): 44-5, 103, February 1943.
Betty Grable had to wear green, a color she hates, in her biggest
dance number in "Coney Island" because the only silk tights available had already been dyed.   A wardrobe person was required to
follow her around to protect the tights.   Production was scheduled
in half-hour intervals, since Grable wore a corset that cinched
her waist to 18", causing great discomfort.   Since only 350 extras
were available, they were required to change costumes often to
appear as a larger crowd.   War restriction prohibited the making
of elaborate costumes, so auctions and clearances were searched
out--though the old hats and costumes were authentic.

390   Brunell, Kay.   "An American in Paris Features a Star in
           Jersey. "   Motion Picture, 82 (6): 43, January 1952.
Leslie Caron models a dress designed by Orry-Kelly, from "An
American in Paris, " a copy of which can be ordered from the
magazine.

391   _____.   "Campus or Career. "   Motion Picture, 84 (1): 52-3,
           August 1952.
Virginia Mayo models two costumes by Travilla, and two retail
copies, from "She's Working Her Way Through College. "

392   _____.   "Designed for Lounging. "   Motion Picture, 81 (6):
           52-3, July 1951.
Loretta Young models two costumes by Travilla from "Half Angel. "

393   _____.   "Fall Trends in Fashion. "   Motion Picture, 82 (2):
           50-1, September 1951.
Arlene Dahl models two costumes by Helen Rose, and a hat by
Rex, from "No Questions Asked. "

394   _____.   "Fashion Selections from Paramount's 'Dear Wife. ' "
           Silver Screen, 20 (3): 54-5, January 1950.
Joan Caulfield models two costumes from "Dear Wife. "

395   _____.   "Good Mixers. "   Motion Picture, 82 (5): 46-7,
           December 1951.
One suit each is modeled by Gloria De Haven from "Friendly Island, " by Travilla, and Shelly Winters from "The Raging Tide, "
by Bill Thomas.

396   _____.   " 'Ivanhoe' Inspired Fashions. "   Motion Picture,
           84 (3): 56-7, October 1952.
Seven photos of retail garments show alleged influence of the
medieval costumes of "Ivanhoe. "

397 _____. "Paramount Presents 'Dear Wife' Fashion Selections."
        Screenland, 54 (3): 54-5, January 1950.
Joan Caulfield models a suit from "Dear Wife." Virtually identical in text and photos to the entry entitled "Fashion Selections
from Paramount's "Dear Wife," also by Brunell.

398 _____. "Picture Yourself Dressed Like a Star." Motion
        Picture, 82 (1): 46-7, August 1951.
One costume each is modeled by Constance Bennett from "As
Young as You Feel," by Charles Le Maire, and Jeanne Crain
from "Take Care of My Little Girl."

399 _____. "Starred for Spring." Motion Picture, 83(2): 55,
        March 1952.
Betsy Drake models a costume by Leah Rhodes from "Room for
One More."

400 _____. "Swing into Spring." Motion Picture, 83 (3): 52-3,
        April 1952.
Virginia Gibson models a costume by Leah Rhodes from "About
Face."

401 _____. "Two for the Show." Motion Picture, 83 (1): 46-7,
        February 1952.
Janet Leigh models a costume by Michael Woulfe from "Two
Tickets to Broadway."

402 Brunner, John. "Lisa Gastoni Talks Fashions." Preview.
        London: Andrew Dakers, 1959, p. 15-7.
Lisa Gastoni discusses her fashion philosophy and the significance
of a mink coat to her performance in "Intent to Kill."

403 "Bruno, Richard." American Film Institute Catalog, 1961-70,
        p. 86.
15 costume-related credits are listed for Richard Bruno.

404 "Bryce, Hope." American Film Institute Catalog, 1961-70,
        p. 87.
Hope Bryce was the costume coordinator for "Advise and Consent,"
"The Cardinal," "Bunny Lake Is Missing," "In Harm's Way,"
"Hurry Sundown," "Skidoo," and "Tell Me That You Love Me,
Junie Moon."

405 Brynn, Celia. "Ladies' Day." Picture Play, 14 (4): 73-7,
        98-9, June 1921.
Claire [Clare] West began taking care of gowns for Cecil B.
De Mille's films and eventually became chief designer. Some of
her film costumes have been exhibited at the Metropolitian Museum
of Art. Sophie Wachner, head of the Goldwyn wardrobe department, costumes both men and women and supervises a large staff
of cutters and fitters. Natacha Rambova, set and costume designer for Nazimova, will work on "Camille" and "Aphrodite."
Ethel Chaffin, of the Lasky studios, prefers draping her designs

to pattern making. Betty Brown has worked as a freelance art
director and as a set and costume designer.

406 _____. "The Story of a Designing Man." Picture Play,
          11 (2): 59-61, October 1919.
George Hopkins, of Fox Studio, writes Theda Bara's scenarios
and designs her costumes; he had previously designed for Ziegfeld's Follies and designed Emily Stevens' costumes for "The
Unchastened Woman." He first worked with Bara and Fox on her
14 costumes for "Madame duBarry," one of which she models.
He has also written and designed for her in "The She-Devil" and
"A Woman There Was," as discussed. Sketches and stills are
included, without identification.

407 "'Bubbles' That Did Not Float in the Air." Screen News,
          1 (2): 30, March 4, 1922.
A small fiasco occurred on the set of "A Blind Bargain," when
actresses in suits of metal jumped into a pool of bluing, taking
in more liquid than had been anticipated.

408 Buck, Genevieve. "She's Dressed the Stars." Chicago Trib-
          une, July 20, 1975, sec. 5, p.3.
Edith Head states that too many contemporary fashions look like
costumes, rather than sensible fashions. She hopes the elegant
costumes in "Gable and Lombard" will not set fashion trends
since fashion need not look to the past for inspiration.

409 "Budz, Frank R." American Film Institute Catalog, 1961-70,
          p. 88.
Frank R. Budz is credited with the costumes of "War Party."

410 "Bulgarelli, Enzo." American Film Institute Catalog, 1961-70,
          p. 89.
Enzo Bulgarelli is credited with the military uniforms of "Frau-
lein Doktor" and the costumes of "The Mongols," "Death Rides a
Horse," and "The Five Man Army."

411 "Bull Montana All Dressed Up." Screen News, 2 (32): 2,
          August 11, 1923.
A San Francisco tailor has made two trick suits for Bull Montana,
for his role as a criminal in "Held to Answer."

412 "Bürger, Hildegard." American Film Institute Catalog, 1961-
          70, p.90.
Hildegard Bürger is credited with the costumes of "Seven Consenting Adults."

413 Burke, Howard. "But Is It Art? 'Yes,' Declares Film De-
          signer." Los Angeles Examiner, June 19, 1960, sec.
          5, p. 11.
Edith Head discusses why she believes films and film costumes
are art.

414 Burke, Marcella. "Fashion Mandates from a Famous French
         Expert. " Hollywood, 20 (8): 46-7, 63, September 1931.
     Gabrielle Chanel has been hired by Samuel Goldwyn in the hope
     that her film costumes will be as popular as her couture designs.
     Chanel noted that she was intrigued and proud to be a film de-
     signer, and that she would not try to convert the actresses to her
     style.

415 "Burlison, Heather. " American Film Institute Catalog, 1961-
         70, p. 90.
     Heather Burlison is credited with the wardrobe of "Color Me
     Dead. "

416 "Burns, Paul. " American Film Institute Catalog, 1921-30, p.
         997.
     Paul Burns was the master of wardrobe and/or costumes for "The
     Three Musketeers" (1921), "The Thief of Bagdad" (1924), "The
     Gaucho, " and "The Iron Mask" (1929) and is credited with the
     wardrobe of "Don Q, Son of Zorro. "

417 Burroughs, Annette. "Erté Speaks His Mind. " Photoplay, 29
         (3): 32-3, February 1926.
     Erté, who found film actresses no more attractive or inspiring
     than other women, discusses designing for Renee Adoree in "The
     Big Parade" and Lillian Gish in "La Bohème. " Both women,
     among other factors, were enough for him to quit gladly and re-
     turn to Paris.

418 "Burrows, Rosemary. " American Film Institute Catalog, 1961-
         70, p. 91.
     25 wardrobe-related credits are listed for Rosemary Burrows.

419 "Burza, Norman. " American Film Institute Catalog, 1961-70,
         p. 92.
     Norman Burza is credited with the costumes of "Support Your Lo-
     cal Sheriff!" and "The Strawberry Statement" and the wardrobe
     of "Get Yourself a College Girl, " "Sunday in New York, " "Your
     Cheatin' Heart, " and "The Traveling Executioner. "

420 Bush, W. Stephen. "Nudity on the Screen. " Moving Picture
         World, 27 (1): 49-50, January 1, 1916.
     Discussion of the occurrence of nudity and near-nudity in history,
     noting that the screen has remained remarkably free of it during
     its brief history. The author recommends that those associated
     with the screen adhere to societal standards and traditions, with
     modest covering of the figure.

421 "Busy Mr. Adrian!" MGM Studio News, 3 (7): n.p., December
         26, 1935.
     Adrian has been creating evening and dancing gowns for Joan Crawford
     in "Elegance" (apparently never made), the costumes of which will be
     harmonized with the mood suggested by each dance and the music.

422   "Butler, Forrest T." American Film Institute Catalog, 1961-
          70, p. 92.
      Forrest T. Butler is credited with the wardrobe of "Days of Wine
      and Roses," "Hitler," "Married Too Young," "El Dorado," "Good
      Times," "If He Hollers, Let Him Go!," and "The Out-of-Towners."

423   "Buyers Vote Adrian Top U. S. Designer." MGM Studio News,
          7 (6): n.p., April 16, 1940.
      1,000 U. S. buyers voted for their favorite designers in an un-
      specified poll. Adrian received third place, but was first among
      American designers. The list, in order, included Schiaparelli,
      Hattie Carnegie, Adrian, Chanel, Lelong, Elizabeth Hawes, Travis
      Banton, Howard Greer, and Valentina (all of whom were associated
      with film costume in one way or another).

424   "Buzina, N." American Film Institute Catalog, 1961-70, p. 93.
      N. Buzina was the uniform designer of "War and Peace" (1968).

425   "Bykhovskaya, M." American Film Institute Catalog, 1961-70,
          p. 93.
      M. Bykhovskaya is credited with the costumes of "Apartment in
      Moscow."

426   "Byrne, Kiki." American Film Institute Catalog, 1961-70, p.
          93.
      Kiki Byrne was the costume designer of "Stop the World--I Want
      to Get Off" and "Perfect Friday," and the wardrobe designer and
      consultant of "Fathom."

427   "Byrne, Kiki." Fairchild's Who's Who in Fashion. 1975, p. 42.

428   The Bystander. "Over the Teacups." Picture Play, 16 (4):
          66-7, 88, June 1922.
      Mabel Ballin will wear 14 modern costumes in her new film, the
      title of which is not given, with husband Hugo Ballin (they made
      many films together; might possibly be "Married People"). Brief
      descriptions of several of the costumes.

429   _____. Picture Play, 18 (1): 56-8, 92, March 1923.
      Edith Roberts will wear many costumes in "Backbone," designed
      by Adrian, who has just come over from Paris to design for
      the Music Box Revue. (The earliest reference to Adrian design-
      ing for a film.)

430   _____. Picture Play, 26 (1): 48-51, 109, March 1927.
      Lilyan Tashman returned from Paris with a wardrobe for "Don't Tell
      the Wife," which she will have copied for the film rather than
      wear the originals. Marion Davies's costumes for "Tillie the
      Toiler" will be considerably exaggerated for comic effect.

431 "Cabrera, Vicente." American Film Institute Catalog, 1961-
70, p. 94.
Vicente Cabrera is credited with the wardrobe of "Beach Red"
and "The Losers."

432 "Cacoyannis, Michael." American Film Institute Catalog, 1961-
70, p. 94.
Michael Cacoyannis was the costume designer of "The Day the
Fish Came Out."

433 "Caffin, Yvonne." American Film Institute Catalog, 1961-70,
p. 95.
15 credits are listed for designer Yvonne Caffin.

434 Cahn, William. Harold Lloyd's World of Comedy. New York:
Duell, Sloan and Pearce, 1964.
Mack Sennett replaced his films featuring cops and comedians
with bathing-girls on a hunch that the scanty costumes would make
for greater publicity. Harold Lloyd consequently left the Sennett
studios, and, realizing the need for a costume he could be identified with, he came up with the "glass character," featuring himself in ordinary attire with horn-rimmed glasses, with the glass
removed to prevent glare. A lengthy discussion follows concerning his glasses, which he wore for all on-screen roles, but never
off-screen, whether for roles as a girl or athlete.

435 "Caine, Irene." American Film Institute Catalog, 1961-70,
p. 95.
Irene Caine is credited with the wardrobe of "The Children's
Hour," "Kid Galahad," "Two for the Seesaw," and "Kiss Me,
Stupid."

436 "Calder, Bob." American Film Institute Catalog, 1961-70,
p. 95.
Bob Calder is credited with the wardrobe of "2,000 Weeks."

437 "Calder, Magg." American Film Institute Catalog, 1961-70,
p. 95.
Magg Calder is credited with the wardrobe of "2,000 Weeks."

438   Calhoun, Dorothy.   "Hollywood Starts a Big Clean-Up."   Movie
            Classic, 6 (1): 44-5, 68-9, March 1934.
      Discussion of the censorship taking place concerning publicity
      stills with actresses scantily clad, as with chorus girls in "Flying
      Down to Rio," "Wonder Bar," and "Fashions of 1934."   Actresses
      may be photographed in bathing suits but not lingerie, and may
      still wear, within reason, whatever they want to on the screen.
      Includes a list of "must-nots" from the Hays Office.

439   _____.   "Off with the New Clothes, and On with the Old!"
            Motion Picture, 45 (5): 54-5, 92-3, June 1933.
      Discussion of the popularity of period films and costumes, with
      examples of costumes worn by Mary Pickford in "Secrets," Edna
      May Oliver and Ann Harding in "The Conquerors," Irene Dunne
      in "The Secret of Madame Blanche," Diana Wynyard in "Caval-
      cade," Ethel Barrymore in "Rasputin and the Empress," and Mae
      West in "She Done Him Wrong," with brief mention of many others.
      The period costumes have influenced fashion designers, and may
      change the currently popular mannish fashions to more feminine
      ones; though Marlene Dietrich, as with a diamonded, white, silk
      tuxedo in "Blonde Venus," is wearing pants in order to influence
      women to avoid frequently changing women's fashions.   (See also
      entries by Dorothy Donnell.)

440   _____.   "The Inside Story of Garbo's Great Success!"
            Motion Picture, 43 (5): 28-9, 80-1, June 1932.
      Discussion of the evolution of Greta Garbo's appearance since her
      arrival in the U.S. in 1925; designer Adrian is credited with much
      of the change.   MGM receives many requests for patterns of her
      costumes.   Illustrations include a sketch and closeup still of a
      gown worn by Garbo in "Inspiration."

441   Calthrop, Dion Clayton.   "Modes and Movies."   Picturegoer,
            17 (104): 8-9, August 1929.
      Discussion of the overly ornate and unrealistic costuming of many
      character types, as with vamps and English gentlemen; the author
      recommends that research play a greater role in costuming.

442   "Candid Parade."   Screen Guide, 13 (4): 35-7, April 1948.
      Marguerite Chapman models five western costumes, including one
      from "Relentless."

443   Cannell, Kathleen.   "Designing Dresses for the Stars."   Re-
            view of The Dress Doctor by Edith Head and Jane Kesner
            Ardmore.   Christian Science Monitor, April 2, 1959, p.
            7.
      Positive review of The Dress Doctor, by the "veritable Emily
      Post of fashion," Edith Head.

444   Cantor, Hermine.   "Shape of Suits to Come."   Motion Picture,
            85 (1): 56-7, February 1953.
      An original suit and a copy are modeled by Virginia Mayo from
      "She's Back on Broadway," and by Peggy Lee from "The Jazz

Singer" (both films by Howard Shoup).

445 _____. "Shipshape Fashions from Hollywood." Motion
        Picture, 86 (6): 48-9, January 1954.
Jane Powell models two original dresses by Moss Mabry, and retail copies from "Three Sailors and a Girl."

446 "Cantrell, Rebecca." American Film Institute Catalog, 1961-70,
        p. 99.
Rebecca Cantrell is credited with the wardrobe of "Johnny Tiger."

447 "Capel, Fred." American Film Institute Catalog, 1961-70,
        p. 99.
Fred Capel is credited with the costumes of "Jules and Jim."

448 "Capucci, Roberto." American Film Institute Catalog, 1961-
        70, p. 100.
Roberto Capucci is credited with Silvana Mangano's clothes in
"Teorema."

449 Carco, Francis. Vertès. New York: Atheneum, 1946.
A biography of Marcel Vertès, without mention of his film-
costume designing.

450 "Cardi, Gloria." American Film Institute Catalog, 1961-70,
        p. 101.
Gloria Cardi is credited with the costumes of "Sesso."

451 "Cardin, Pierre." American Film Institute Catalog, 1961-70,
        p. 101-2.
Pierre Cardin is credited with the Paris originals for "A New
Kind of Love" and "The V. I. P. s"; Jeanne Moreau's costumes in
"Eva," "The Yellow Rolls-Royce," and "The Immortal Story";
Laurence Harvey's and Mia Farrow's costumes in "A Dandy in
Aspic"; the costumes/wardrobe of "Mata Hari, Agent H-21" and
"You Only Love Once"; and the racing leather designs of "Little
Fauss and Big Halsy."

452 "Cardin, Pierre." Celebrity Register. 3rd ed., 1973, p. 90.

453 "Cardin, Pierre." Current Biography. 1965, p. 69-71.
When working at the Paris salon of Pacquin, Pierre Cardin agreed
to make the costumes for "Beauty and the Beast," sketched by
Christian Bérard.

454 "Cardin, Pierre." International Who's Who. 41st ed., 1977-
        8, p. 272.

455 "Cardin, Pierre." Who's Who in America. 40th ed., 1978-9,
        p. 526.

456 "Cardin, Pierre." Who's Who in France. 6th ed., 1963-4, p. 620.

457 "Cardin, Pierre." Who's Who in the World. 2nd ed., 1974-5,
       p. 177.

458 "Cardinale, Frank." American Film Institute Catalog, 1961-
       70, p. 101.
     Frank Cardinale is credited with the costumes of "Yours, Mine,
     and Ours."

459 Carlile, Tom. "Sartorial Menace." Motion Picture, 71 (5):
       128, 130-1, June 1946.
     Discussion of the fashion style of Clifton Webb, which is briefly
     compared with Adolphe Menjou's; they are competitors for Holly-
     wood's "best dressed" title.

460 Carlisle, Helen. "Confessions of the Stars' Modiste." Motion
       Picture, 27 (6): 43-5, July 1924.
     Ethel Chaffin, the costume designer for Famous Players for over
     five years, discusses the styles of many of the actresses she has
     designed for, as well as film-costume design. She has found it
     easier to have the costumes made in studio workrooms, rather
     than sent out; the collection of costumes number over 3,000.
     The costumes are eventually altered and used again. One sketch
     of Agnes Ayres in "Bluff."

461 Carnegie, Hattie. "Even a Queen's Fads Aren't Fashion."
       Pictorial Review, 39 (12): 21, 63-4, September 1938.
     Discussion of the cumbersome period costumes worn by Norma
     Shearer in "Marie Antoinette," e.g., steel-hoop underskirts and
     clothes so wide that doors in rooms and carriages had to be ex-
     panded. One gown took many seamstresses over three months to
     complete; it was worn with a petticoat made with 60 yards of
     organdy, which took three weeks to complete. Hattie Carnegie
     had previously designed clothes for her collection based on cos-
     tumes worn by Shearer in "Romeo and Juliet," and discusses how
     some of the costumes of "Marie Antoinette" would influence her
     next collection.

462 "Carnegie, Hattie," in Fashion is Our Business, by Beryl
       Williams [Epstein]. Philadelphia: Lippincott, 1945,
       p. 53-68.
     Includes references to the previous entry, written by Hattie
     Carnegie, concerning the folly of some historical costumes, as
     worn by Norma Shearer in "Marie Antoinette"; eight women helped
     Miss Shearer put on one 80-pound ball gown.

463 "Carpio, Roberto." American Film Institute Catalog, 1961-70,
       p. 103.
     Roberto Carpio is credited with the costumes of "Dr. Coppelius."

464 Carpozi, George Jr. Cher. New York: Berkley, 1975.
     Sonny and Cher Bono's film, "Good Times," bombed, but they
     earned some extra money by marketing copies of their film cos-
     tumes. Available nationally in stores before the film's release,

the collection included bell-bottom pants and matching cotton-knit
tops designed by Cher and made by Gordon & Marx of California.
Two fake-fur vests, worn by Sonny Bono, were marketed by Lou
Nierenberg of New York.   (Leah Rhodes was credited as the film's
costume designer.)

465   Carr, Larry.   Four Fabulous Faces; the Evolution and Meta-
            morphosis of Garbo, Swanson, Crawford [and] Dietrich.
            New Rochelle, N.Y.: Arlington House, 1970.
An extensive, essentially photographic study of those four women
who have influenced fashion and cosmetics the most, and endured
the longest, of twentieth-century actresses.   Greta Garbo influenced fashion, and continues to, through the pillbox hat, the
Empress Eugenie hat from "Romance," slouch hats, berets, trench
coats, and high collars.   She designed one of her most memorable
hats, resembling a funnel, for "Ninotchka."   Concerning Gloria
Swanson, designer Captain Edward Molyneux stated in 1929 that
she was the best-dressed woman in both films and the world.
Includes stills of Swanson in hats from "A Society Scandal," "Fine
Manners," and "What a Widow."   Joan Crawford's many fashion
influences included square shoulders, huge puffed sleeves, wide-
lapelled coats, and large hats.   Marlene Dietrich, with her "ambi-
sextrous" appeal, appeared alluring in ultrafeminine gowns and in
men's-styled clothes, as with the cowboy costumes she wore in
"Rancho Notorious."   Travis Banton dressed her in satins, feathers,
chiffon, and sequins, and in "Shanghai Express" he collaborated
with director Josef Von Sternberg.   Also states that Dietrich was
Banton's "favorite of all stars."

466   Carrick, Edward (pseudonym of Edward Anthony Craig).   Art
            and Design in the British Film: A Pictorial Directory of
            British Art Directors and Their Work.   London: Dennis
            Dobson, 1948.
The production designer of a film is responsible for the "visual
composition" of a film and often works with the costume designer
in achieving this.   As an art director for the Crown and Army
Film Units during World War II in England the author felt that a
casualty of the realism cult was "Caesar and Cleopatra," made
by the unit with costume designer Oliver Messel.   See entries for
art director/costume designers Roger Furse, Hein Heckroth, and
Oliver Messel.

467   _____.   Designing for Films.   London and New York:
            Studio Publications, 1949.
A second edition of the following book; including sketches by the
author of shoes and collars used as research material for "Lorna
Doone," found in both editions.

468   _____.   Designing for Moving Pictures.   London: Studio
            Publications, 1941.
Notes that the costume department should work with the art director, who should also assist in the costume designing.   Includes
four of the 36 sheets of costumes and props that the author sub-

mitted to help in the preliminary scripting of "Lorna Doone"; he
also designed about 60 of the costumes.

469   Carringer, Robert, and Barry Sabath.   Ernst Lubitsch; a Guide
        to References and Resources.   Boston: Hall, 1978.
Includes rare costume-design credits for German films made from
1918 to 1923: Ali Hubert was the costume designer for "Carmen,"
"Madame Dubarry" (released in the United States as "Passion"),
"Sumurun" ("One Arabian Night"), and "Anne Boleyn" (Deception,"
1920); Kurt Richter, for "Die Puppe" ("The Doll"); and Ernst
Stern, for "Die Bergkatze" ("The Mountain Cat" or "The Wild
Cat"), with co-costume credit for Emil Hassler.   "Das Weib Des
Pharao" ("The Loves of Pharaoh") was designed by Stern, Hubert,
and Ernö Metzer.

470   _____.   Review of Hollywood: Legende und Wirklichkeit, by
             Ali Hubert, in Ernst Lubitsch; a Guide to References and
             Resources.   Boston: Hall, 1978.
According to this review, Ali Hubert, the usual costume designer
of Ernst Lubitsch's films, has here written of his experiences in
Hollywood, as with his costumes for "The Patriot" and "The Student Prince" (released as "The Student Prince in Old Heidelberg").

471   Carroll, Jane.   "Design for Livelihood."   Movie Classic, 9
             (3): 30-1, 62, 77, November 1935.
Ethel Traphagen, who manages her own school of costume design,
discusses career opportunities in the field.   Film costume has
taught American women how to dress better, popularized American
fashion despite competition with Paris, and helped the industry by
employing American designers.   Bernard Newman, who graduated
from her school, earns $100,000 per year; film-costume designers
are the highest paid American designers.

472   Carroll, Roger.   "Pick Your Movie Job."   Motion Picture, 63
             (5): 24-7, June 1942.
Includes career-opportunity information for aspiring film-costume
designers, e.g., expected working conditions, qualifications required, and recommended preparation.   Natalie Visart, at age
22, became a designer for Cecil B. De Mille by preparing hundreds of sketches for "Cleopatra" (1934) before she met him, and
by having influential connections.

473   "Carroll and Co."   American Film Institute Catalog, 1961-70,
             p.104.
Carroll and Co. is credited with Frank Sinatra's wardrobe in
"Marriage on the Rocks."

474   "Carroll, Vana."   American Film Institute Catalog, 1961-70,
             p.105.
Vana Carroll is credited with the wardrobe of "The Black Klansman" and the costumes of "A Man Called Dagger."

475   "Carroll, Veda."   American Film Institute Catalog, 1961-70, p.
        105.

Veda Carroll is credited with the wardrobe of "Apache Uprising."

476   Carstairs, Burks.   "Scrap Book."   Harper's Bazaar, 2669:
         92-3, March 1935.
Merle Oberon models a black taffeta cape from "The Scarlet
Pimpernel," which is being widely copied in London.

477   "Carteney, Marilù."   American Film Institute Catalog, 1961-70,
         p. 105.
Marilù Carteney is credited with the costumes of "Bandits of
Orgosolo," "Salvatore Giuliano," "A Bullet for the General," and
"Mafia"; the wardrobe of "Once Upon a Time in the West"; and
the wardrobe coordination of "Burn!"

478   Carter, Ernestine.   20th Century Fashion: A Scrapbook--1900
         to Today.   London: Eyre Methuen, 1975.
A pictorial record of twentieth-century fashion.   Illustrations of
(from the 1920's) Joan Crawford in a costume from "Our Dancing
Daughters" and Josephine Baker in "Les Femmes des Folies
Bergère."   Of the 1930s, it is noted that Hollywood became a
leading influence in fashion, especially with Adrian: Photos of
Joan Crawford in "Letty Lynton" and Crawford, Norma Shearer,
and Rosalind Russell in "The Women."   From the 1940s illustrations include Rita Hayworth in a costume from "Gilda," by
Jean Louis (captioned "Adrian's bare midriff").   Films again began to influence fashion in the 1960s, as with "Jules et Jim,"
"Bonnie and Clyde," and "Dr. Zhivago"; western films popularized
jeans.   Film costumes from the 1920s-1940s were also revived
in the 1970s.

479   Carter, Randolph.   The World of Flo Ziegfeld.   New York:
         Praeger, 1974.
Includes many references to designer Lucile Duff Gordon and Flo
Ziegfeld as having worked famously together; both Ziegfeld and
"Lucile, Ltd.," Lady Duff Gordon's fashion line, were bankrupted
as a result of the Depression.   Brief mention of Charles Le Maire,
Adrian, Erté, and Howard Greer as designers for the Greenwich
Village Follies, before they designed for films.   Brief mention
also of designer Gretl Urban; William Randolph Hearst loved
Marion Davies to wear lavish and period costumes.

480   Cartnal, Alan.   "Compleat, As Is Her Costume."   Los Angeles
         Times, February 24, 1976, sec. 4, p. 1, 5.
The California Museum of Science and Industry held a 12-week
retrospective of the career of Edith Head, who has been a designer for over 50 years, worked on about 1,500 films, and designed over 250,000 costumes.   Most of the costumes and sketches
on display are from Head's own collection.   David Chierichetti,
author of Hollywood Costume Design, has called her "the ultimate
collaborator" and "the greatest realist of costume."

481   "Casa d'Arte-Firenze."   American Film Institute Catalog, 1961-
         70, p. 106.
Casa d'Arte-Firenze is credited with the wardrobe of "The Agony

and the Ecstasy" and the costumes of "The Mystery of Thug Island" and "Chronicle of Anna Magdalena Bach."

482 "Casey, Gertrude." American Film Institute Catalog, 1961-70, p. 107.
15 costume credits are listed for Gertrude Casey, most in conjunction with a costume designer.

483 Cashin, Bonnie. "Cool and Charming Cotton." Silver Screen, 17 (9): 66-7, 90-2, July 1947.
Bonnie Cashin discusses designing June Haver's costumes for "Scudda Hoo, Scudda Hay," seven of which Haver models.

484 _____. "Double Duty Clothes." Silver Screen, 19 (7): 46-7, 67-8, May 1949.
Shirley Temple models one costume from "Mr. Belvedere Goes to College," and seven others that may or may not be from the film; designed by Bonnie Cashin.

485 _____. "Notes from a Designer's Diary." Screenland, 49 (8): 36-7, 62-4, June 1945.
Bonnie Cashin discusses designing for Dorothy McGuire, Joan Blondell, and Peggy Ann Garner in "A Tree Grows in Brooklyn"; Joan Leslie in "Where Do We Go from Here?"; and Jeanne Craine in "Home in Indiana." Includes ten stills of models in hats from "Billy Rose's Diamond Horseshoe," and Gene Tierney models a gown from "Laura."

486 "Cashin, Bonnie." Current Biography. 1970, p. 69-71.
Bonnie Cashin became a costume designer with Twentieth Century-Fox after having designed for the Roxy Theatre, a manufacturer, and the military. She designed for over 60 Fox films from 1943-1949.

487 "Cashin, Bonnie." Fairchild's Who's Who in Fashion. 1975, p. 50.

488 "Cashin, Bonnie." Who's Who in America. 39th ed., 1976-7, p. 529.

489 "Cashin, Bonnie." Who's Who in the World. 2nd ed., 1974-5, p. 183.

490 "Cashin, Bonnie." Who's Who of American Women. 8th ed., 1974-5, p. 153.

491 "Cashin, Bonnie." World of Fashion. 1976, p. 215.

492 "Cassini, Oleg." American Film Institute Catalog, 1961-70, p. 108.
Oleg Cassini is credited with Elsa Martinelli's clothes in "Rampage," and the dresses and costumes of "The Ambushers."

493 "Cassini, Oleg." Celebrity Register. 1st ed., 1959, p. 137.

494 "Cassini, Oleg." Fairchild's Who's Who in Fashion. 1975,
     p. 51.
Oleg Cassini began film-costume designing in "1929" (actually
1940) with Paramount and later became a designer for Twentieth
Century-Fox in 1942.

495 "Cassini, Oleg." World of Fashion. 1976, p. 215-6.

496 "Cassini, Oleg (Loiewski)." Current Biography. 1961, p. 96-8.
Lengthy biography of Oleg Cassini, who designed for 36 films
before losing interest and returning to fashion designing.

497 "Cassini, Oleg (Loiewski)." Who's Who in the World, 3rd
     ed., 1976-7, p. 149.
Oleg Cassini was a designer for Paramount from 1940-1941, for
Twentieth Century-Fox from 1941-1942, and was head of the wardrobe
department at Eagle-Lion Studios from 1946-1947.

498 "Cassini, Oleg (Lolewski)" [sic]. Who's Who in America.
     39th ed., 1976-7, p. 531.

499 "Castillo." American Film Institute Catalog, 1961-70, p. 108.
Castillo is credited with Ingrid Bergman's wardrobe in "The
Yellow Rolls-Royce."

500 Castle, Irene, as told to Bob and Wanda Duncan. Castles
     in the Air. Garden City, N.Y.: Doubleday, 1958.
Throughout her dancing career Irene Castle had a devoted fashion
following, and she appeared in a number of films. She writes
briefly but engagingly of her association with designer Lady Duff
Gordon. She was hired as a technical adviser for "The Story of
Vernon and Irene Castle," a film based on her life with her husband, Vernon, who died young and tragically. Although she had
driven out to Hollywood with all of their old costumes, and
Yvonne Wood had been hired to sketch them, Ginger Rogers,
portraying Irene Castle, rejected everything. Rogers refused to
wear ankle-length dresses and insisted on shoulder pads in everything, including a 1910 bathing suit. Fred Astaire had all of his
costumes designed exactly like Vernon Castle's originals and was
the only one to come and view all of the costumes she had brought.
She was one of many such technical advisers who were kept on the
payroll but who were hindered from assisting with such matters
as authentic costuming.

501 "Catalina." American Film Institute Catalog, 1961-70, p. 109.
Catalina is credited with the sportswear and swimwear of "Ride
the Wild Surf."

502 Catalogue [of] the Estate of Rudolph Valentino. To Be Sold at
     Public Auction Commencing December 10, 1926.

S. George Ullman, Administrator. A. H. Weil, Auctioneer.
Los Angeles, [1926].
A catalogue of the impressive and valuable possessions of Rudolph
Valentino, including antique arms and armor, and a book collection,
of which it is noted, "It is doubtful if there is another collection
of books on costumes in this country so extensive and complete
as this one." There was no doubt as to his love of costumes, as
seen in the lists of costumes, shoes, gloves, stockings, belts,
and hats worn in "Blood and Sand," "Monsieur Beaucaire," "Son
of the Sheik," "The Four Horsemen" ("The Four Horsemen of the
Apocalypse"), and many costumes never worn in the canceled production of "The Hooded Falcon."

503 "Catherine (cost.)." American Film Institute Catalog, 1961-70,
        p. 109.
Catherine was the costume designer of "Peek-a-boo."

504 Catlin, Elizabeth. "Acting Isn't the Only Movie Career."
        Movie Classic, 8 (5): 32-3, 70, July 1935.
The studio research department gathers photos of costumes for
designers to help them in researching and designing a film's costumes. Seamstresses and wardrobe women are paid about $32.50
per week.

505 "Caudrelier, Lily." American Film Institute Catalog, 1961-70,
        p. 109.
Lily Caudrelier is credited with the wardrobe of "Love at Night"
and "Pleasure and Vices," and was the wardrobe mistress of
"Woman of Sin."

506 "Cavanagh, John." American Film Institute Catalog, 1961-70,
        p. 109.
John Cavanagh was the women's-costume designer of "The Secret
of My Success."

507 " 'The Caviar Collection' by Schrader in Celanese Fibers."
        Vogue, 147 (5): 29-35, March 1, 1966.
The 12 women's fashions modeled are supposed to be inspired by
"Dr. Zhivago," but only two include direct references to the film,
the details being limited to frog fastenings; marketed by Abe and
Mort Schrader.

508 "Cecchi, Dario." American Film Institute Catalog, 1961-70,
        p. 110.
Dario Cecchi is credited with the costumes of "The Best of Enemies."

509 "Cecil B. De Mille Is at Work...." Grauman's Magazine, 4
        (18): 6, May 8, 1921.
This small advertisement stated that Clare West had elaborately
costumed "The Lady and the Laurels" (the title was changed to
"Fool's Paradise," and no designer received credit).

510   "Ceraceni." American Film Institute Catalog, 1961-70, p. 111.
      Ceraceni is credited with the wardrobe of "Better a Widow."

511   Chaffin, Ethel. "Paramount Designer Awaits Results of Color
            Photography." Screen News, 3 (24): 5, June 21, 1924.
      Discussion of Ethel Chaffin's costumes for Billie Dove and
      Kathlyn Williams in "Wanderers of the Wasteland," her first color
      film.

512   "Chaffin, Ethel P." American Film Institute Catalog, 1921-30,
            p. 1010.
      Ethel P. Chaffin is credited with the costumes of "Confessions of
      a Queen" and the wardrobe of "The Big Parade," "The Circle,"
      and "The Sporting Venus."

513   "Chalif, S. L." American Film Institute Catalog, 1921-30, p.
            1010.
      S. L. Chalif was the assistant wardrobe master of "The Iron Mask."

514   Chambers, Florence Allen. "Screen Fashions." Cinema Art,
            3 (7): 39-42, January 1924.
      One costume each is modeled by Mae Marsh from "Paddy-the-
      Next-Best-Thing," Winifred Bryson from "Pleasure Mad," and
      Jeanne Balzac and Carmel Myers from "Slaves of Desire."

515   Champlin, Charles. "Edith Head Cuts Success Pattern." Los
            Angeles Times, August 12, 1966, sec. 4, p. 6.
      Biographical information of Edith Head, who discusses film-
      costume designing. Some of her costumes for Carroll Baker in
      "Harlow" were criticized for being transparent, but were found
      "amusing" when they were copied by Paris couturiers.

516   "Chanel." American Film Institute Catalog, 1961-70, p. 113.
      Chanel is credited with Delphine Seyrig's gowns in "Last Year at
      Marienbad."

517   "Chanel, Gabrielle (Bonheur)." Current Biography. 1954, p.
            169-71.

518   "Chanel, Gabrielle (Bonheur). Current Biography (Necrology).
            1971, p. 461.

519   Chaplin, Charles. My Autobiography. New York: Simon and
            Schuster, 1964.
      Charles Chaplin discusses how he needed a comedy outfit for a
      film and came up with a tight derby and coat, and large pants
      and shoes. The costume transformed him into the Tramp, and
      as a result of the borrowed clothes he thought up many gags:
      "As the clothes had imbued me with the character, I then and
      there decided I would keep to this costume, whatever happened."

520   "Chapman, Ceil." American Film Institute Catalog, 1961-70,
            p. 113.

Ceil Chapman was the wardrobe designer for Marie McDonald in "Promises! Promises!"

521 _____. Who's Who of American Women. 8th ed., 1974-5, p.159.

522 "Characters and Clothes." New York Times, June 8, 1924, sec. 7, p.2.
Frank Lloyd, the director of "Sea Hawk," asked for quality, but not ornate, costumes, and spent $85,000. He discusses the importance of film costume and the need for realism in costuming.

523 "Charge It to Sex!" Screenland, 7 (4): 28-30, July 1923.
The author, an unnamed shop model, discusses the film and non-film clothing purchases and habits of many actresses, some also unnamed; mostly refers to their temperament and whether or not they are well dressed on the screen.

524 "'Charity' is 1100th Film for Designer Edith Head." Hollywood Reporter, 199 (12): 1, January 15, 1968.
Edith Head has designed 58 costumes for Shirley MacLaine, Chita Rivera, Paula Kelly, and 20 models and dancers in "Sweet Charity."

525 "Charles Puffy, Three Hundred Pound Comedian...." Screen News, 4 (38): 8, September 26, 1925, col. 2.
Charles Puffy's head is so large that the wardrobe department of Universal had to search all the local hat shops until an ancient but standard derby was found, for an upcoming comedy.

526 Chase, Donald. "The Costume Designer," in Filmmaking: The Collaborative Art. Boston: Little, Brown, 1975, p.193-211, 308.
Edith Head and Thea Van Runkle each discuss designing authentic costumes for period films, researching and designing for a film, and working with actors/actresses and other members of the production crew. Head refers to costumes for Joan Bennett, for Grace Kelly in "To Catch a Thief," for Olivia de Havilland in "The Heiress," for Paul Newman in "Hud," and for Bette Davis in "All About Eve." Van Runkle refers to Faye Dunaway and Estelle Parsons in "Bonnie and Clyde," Dunaway in "The Thomas Crown Affair," Lucille Ball in "Mame," Raquel Welch in "Myra Breckenridge," as well as costumes for "The Reivers" and "The Arrangement." Polly Platt discusses collaboration between the designer and the costumer; she has been a costumer on several films that were designed by Van Runkle. Includes illustrations of many of the abovementioned films and partial credits for the designers on p.308.

527 Chase, Edna Woolman, and Ilka Chase. Always in Vogue. Garden City, N.Y.: Doubleday, 1954.
Edna Woolman Chase rose from an envelope addresser in 1895 to editor-in-chief of Vogue by the time she semiretired in 1952. In 1929 Paris dictated that hemlines, currently above-the-knee, be

lengthened, which made the actresses in unreleased films appear
comical when the films were finally released, with the no-longer-
fashionable actresses revealing their knees.

528 Cheatham, Maude. "Costuming the Silent Drama." Motion
        Picture Classic, 10 (5): 24-6, 73, 84, January 1923.
Discussion of the researching of costumes for Theodore Roberts
and the women in "The Old Homestead" and Mitchell Leisen's
costumes for Douglas Fairbanks in "Robin Hood." John S. Robertson bought Rudolph Valentino's costumes and ragged clothes for
"Blood and Sand" while in Seville, Spain. Rudolph Bylek researched the costumes for "Burning Sands." Discussion also of
the jobs of Ethel Chaffin, designer, and Roy Diem, men's-costume
designer, both with Famous Players-Lasky. Costumes modeled
include Kathleen O'Connor in "The Old Homestead," Bert Lytell
in "To Have and to Hold," Enid Bennett in "Robin Hood," and
extras in "Manslaughter" and "Burning Sands."

529 _____. "Kitty Gordon's Fashion Parade." Motion Picture,
        17 (2): 40-1, March 1919.
Kitty Gordon has designed all of her film costumes.

530 _____. "Of Interest to Women." Grauman's Magazine, 5
        (5): 20, February 5, 1922.
Motion pictures have taken over the theater as a means of promoting the most recent fashions, so that poor costumes could ruin
a film--though theatrical actors have passed unnoticed for decades
with frequent costume inaccuracies. Many film actresses realize
the influence of their costumes upon the audience and themselves;
they often consider the psychology of clothing in their costume
selections, for instance, Leatrice Joy in "Saturday Night."

531 _____. "Of Interest to Women." Grauman's Magazine, 6 (1):
        6, 20, January 7, 1923.
The revival of the costume drama means that the costumes form
a subbackground, which the costume designer must develop through
subtle impressions, as with Bert Lytell and Betty Compson's costumes of 1620 in "To Have and to Hold," rather than overshadow
the story or actors.

532 _____. "Of Interest to Women." Grauman's Magazine, 6
        (9): 8, March 4, 1923.
Douglas Fairbanks evolved his costumes for "Robin Hood" through
long fittings until he felt more like the character. Many weeks
were spent researching the costumes for authenticity, and testing
colors, lines, and fabrics.

533 "Chepurko, A." American Film Institute Catalog, 1961-70, p. 116.
A. Chepurko is credited with the costumes of "Age of Youth."

534 "Chiari, Maurizio." American Film Institute Catalog, 1961-
        70, p. 116.
Maurizio Chiari is credited with the costumes of "The Magnificent
Cuckold," The Devil in Love," and "Treasure of San Gennaro."

535 Chic, Mlle. "Mlle. Chic's Hollywood Fashion Tips. " Motion
          Picture, 52 (5): 17, December 1936.
Film-costume accessories that have influenced fashion include the
gloves worn in "Love on the Run" and the shawls from "Camille. "

536 _____. Motion Picture, 52 (6): 73, 87, January 1937.
Greta Garbo wears a set of earrings, necklace, and cameo ring
with gold filigree settings, cut in camellia shape in "Camille. "

537 _____. Motion Picture, 53 (2): 23, March 1937.
A gown by Travis Banton worn by Carole Lombard in her new
film, "Swing High Swing Low," is described; it has only silver
zippers with her monogram for decoration.

538 _____. Motion Picture, 56 (4): 17, November 1938.
Bette Davis had one of her costumes from "The Sisters," set in
1904, copied for her personal wardrobe. For "The Lady and the
Cowboy" Merle Oberon needed a costume that the story required
already be onboard a boat; this was resolved by her wearing a
shirt and necktie borrowed from co-star Gary Cooper, the shirt
reaching her knees.

539 _____. Motion Picture, 56 (5): 78, December 1938.
Bette Davis has had some of her costumes from "The Sisters"
copied for her personal wardrobe; one "dust ruffle" is described.

540 _____. Motion Picture, 58 (5): 25, June 1939.
A dress designed by Lola Lane is described; Howard Shoup wants
to copy it for Lane's next film.

541 _____. Motion Picture, 59 (6): 61, July 1940.
Description of one gown worn by Anna Neagle in "Irene. "

542 _____. Motion Picture, 60 (5): 69, December 1940.
Jeanette MacDonald wore pink in her first color film, and purple
and cerise in the Technicolor film "Bitter Sweet"--colors generally
considered taboo for redheads.

543 _____. Motion Picture, 61 (4): 57, May 1941.
Constance Moore liked the U.S. Air Force uniforms she wore in
"I Wanted Wings" and has had them adapted for her personal
wardrobe.

544 "A Chic Costume. " Screen News, 4 (38): 14, September 26,
          1925.
Eleanor Boardman models a costume from "Proud Flesh. "

545 Chierichetti, David. "David Chierichetti Reviews the Oscar-
          Winning Designers. " Hollywood Reporter 49th Annual,
          [1979], p. 63-4.
Film-costume historian David Chierichetti reviews many films
Academy Awarded since the beginning of the Best Costume Design
category, first awarded formally on March 24, 1949. He also

discusses criteria by which a film's costumes should be judged,
e.g., disguising an actress' figure flaws or predicting trends in
contemporary costume design. Films were judged in two separate
categories, color and black-and-white, from 1948 to 1957, and
then from 1959 to 1967; no films in black-and-white were nominated in 1958, so the two categories were reinstated until 1967,
when black-and white films were no longer being made. If the
award had begun a decade earlier, competition would have been
stiff between the two costume designers generally considered the
best, Adrian and Travis Banton.

546 _____. "Edith Head, a Lively Legend in Design." Fabric
        News, 10 (1): 21-4, August 1979.
Edith Head usually shows film costumes along with clothes made
from her Vogue Pattern designs when traveling on the road--her
way of referencing her contemporary designs to her past ones.
She discusses, often with mention of how they compare with her
patterns, costumes she designed for Ginger Rogers in "The Major
and the Minor," "Lady in the Dark," "Tender Comrade," and
"Forever Female"; for Grace Kelly in "To Catch a Thief"; and
others. Head notes that Rogers wore two mink dresses, designed
in part with director Mitchell Leisen, in "Lady in the Dark"; a
heavily jeweled top with a mink skirt in the restaurant sequence;
and then a heavily sequined leotard more exaggerated than the top
first worn, also worn with the mink skirt.

547 _____. "Edward Stevenson." Film Fan Monthly, 95: 20-3,
        May 1969.
Lengthy account of the career of Edward Stevenson, film and television designer. In 1924 he began working for André-Ani as a
sketch artist and moved with him to MGM in the same capacity
in 1925. Their contracts were not renewed, and Stevenson moved
to Fox, again as a sketch artist but with more opportunities to
design; his contract was not renewed--it was given to Orry-Kelly.
After a brief time at Hal Roach studios he left in 1932 to start
his own business designing for studios without wardrobe departments, but longed to return to studio film work. He was hired
as Bernard Newman's sketch artist at RKO for "Roberta"; Newman designed solely by draping but the studio system requiring
a number of approvals before a costume is made necessitated a
sketch artist. Newman returned to Bergdorf Goodman's, and
Stevenson stayed at RKO for 13 years designing most of the "A"
films; his assistant, Renie, designed most of the "B" films. Orson Welles once had him study Marion Davies's wardrobe from
the 1920s for Dorothy Comingore in "Citizen Kane." He left RKO,
designed for Fox and later Universal, and in 1954 began designing
for Lucille Ball's television shows until his death in 1968 of a
heart attack. Illustrations include wardrobe tests of one costume
each worn by Susan Hayward in "David and Bathsheba," Thelma
Todd in "Kismet," and Linda Darnell in "Two Flags West."

548 _____. "Fashion Designers View the Reel Versus the Real."
        San Jose Mercury, February 16, 1979, sec. C, p.1-2.

Edith Head is anything but impressed by the fad for 1940s and
1950s film costumes in recent Paris collections. Renee Connely's
costumes for "Kitty Foyle," designed over 30 years ago, are also
making a comeback in Paris. Briefly discussed are Donald Brook's
costumes for "The Bell Jar," Burton Miller's for "Airport 79:
The Concorde," and Joe Tompkins's for "Coal Miner's Daughter."

549 _____. Hollywood Costume Design. New York: Harmony,
      1976.
To date, the definitive book on film costume. The book is divided
by chapters on the major studios. The designers are studied chronologically, with reference to their most significant films, the actresses they worked with, and the political climate of the various
studios. By looking at film-costume history chronologically through
the different studios, one also gets a "corporate" picture of filmmaking and costuming; for example, MGM proudly lavished money
on costumes but had difficulty retaining a designer until Adrian
arrived in 1925. Paramount's situation was unique in that Edith
Head began as an assistant to Howard Greer and Travis Banton
in 1923, became chief designer in 1938, and dominated the studio's
costumes until 1967, when the studio changed hands and she left
for Universal. Based mainly on interviews by the author, the
book is enjoyable and informative, well illustrated, and well researched. The author often mentions, alongside the stills, how
the costumes were designed to correct an actress' figure flaws,
or enhance her assets. A filmography of numerous designers is
similar to, but not as comprehensive as, Costume Design in the
Movies (#1734); many films and designer credits are unique to each
book, so that they sould be used together.

550 _____. Hollywood Director: The Career of Mitchell Leisen.
      New York: Curtis, 1973.
Typical of Chierichetti's works, this is an excellent biography
and filmography of director and costume and set designer Mitchell
Leisen. The book abounds with references to his costume de-
signs (most of which he never received credit for); he usually
designed costumes for each of his films, even when directing.
There are references to or illustrations of his costumes for
"Male and Female"; Douglas Fairbanks in "Robin Hood" and "The
Thief of Bagdad" (1924); Mary Pickford in "Rosita" and "Dorothy
Vernon of Haddon Hall" (he was her adviser for "The Taming of
the Shrew" [1929]); "The Godless Girl"; Claudette Colbert in "The
Sign of the Cross," "Cleopatra" (1934), "Tonight Is Ours," and
"Midnight" (the latter with gowns by Irene and Colbert); "Murder
at the Vanities"; for Fred MacMurray in "Hands Across the
Table"; Mary Parker in "Artists and Models Abroad"; Constance
Moore in "Take a Letter, Darling"; Paulette Goddard and John
Lund in "Bride of Vengeance"; Steve Forrest in "Bedevilled"
(with gowns for Anne Baxter by Jean Desses and Helen Rose).
Mention is also made of working with Travis Banton; Ralph Jester
and Natalie Visart on "Cleopatra" (1934); Adrian on "The Volga
Boatman"; Edith Head for Olivia de Havilland in "Hold Back the
Dawn"; and of costumes by Edith Head, Raoul Pène du Bois,

Valentina, Babs Wilomez, Mme. Karinska, and his own costumes
--for Ginger Rogers and Ray Milland in "Lady in the Dark."
Leisen also inspired a costume that Edith Head designed for
Ginger Rogers in "Lady": a red sequined, mink-lined gown. Ayn
Rand began her writing career while an RKO wardrobe department
employee. War restrictions by the government placed a $5,000
ceiling on new costumes and sets per film.

551 _____. "How They Dress the Hollywood Heroes." Los
          Angeles Times, Fashion 80, April 4, 1980, p.2, 7.
Discussion of the history of men's wear in television, with the
following references to film: Ralph Bellamy wore his own clothes
in "The Awful Truth," Ray Milland his own in most of his films
except "Lady in the Dark," and Fredric March in "Susan and
God." Though all were dressed well, the studio paid little attention to their costumes, unlike current treatment of actors in
television. Walter Plunkett designed Fred Astaire's costumes
for "The Story of Vernon and Irene Castle," but Astaire wore
his own clothes in "Flying Down to Rio" and "The Gay Divorcee."

552 _____. "How to Dress Buck Rogers--and Other Sci-Fi
          Tales." Los Angeles Times, Fashion 79, October 26,
          1979, p.9-10.
A number of television-costume designers have been interviewed
concerning their most recent science-fiction assignments, including frequent film designers Jean-Pierre Dorleac and Yvonne Wood.
Science-fiction film costumes have been understated in comparison
to those of television, as with the subdued colors used by John
Mollo for the costumes of "Star Wars." Producer Gordon Carroll
discusses Mollo's costumes for "Alien," with brief mention of
Sigourney Weaver and Harry Dean Stanton. Robert Fletcher discusses his costumes for "Star Trek--The Motion Picture," with
brief mention of Persis Khambatta. Bill Thomas discusses color
symbolism of his costumes for "Logan's Run," and his costumes
for Robert Forster, Joseph Bottoms, and Yvette Mimieux in "The
Black Hole." Joe Tompkins discusses his costumes for the space
women in "Cheech and Chong Go Hollyweed"; illustrations include
two of his sketches for the women. This is the only source in
this bibliography that deals at length with science-fiction film
costumes.

553 _____. "Movies Inspire Designs for Living." Hollywood
          Reporter's 48th Annual, [1978], p.119-22.
Discussion of the impact of film makeup, settings, and ideas on
American lifestyles. The influence of film costume on American
fashion is mentioned in quotes from Gloria Vanderbilt on jeans
and on "Annie Hall," which brought about renewed film-fashion
influence; from Andy Warhol, on John Travolta in "Saturday Night
Fever"; and from Erté, on freedom and happiness in Hollywood
(he mentions that Lillian Gish would wear only silks due to allegedly delicate skin).

554 _____. "Sheila O'Brien." Film Fan Monthly, 148: 19-24,

October 1973.
Sheila O'Brien rose from dress extra to founder of the Designer's
Guild in 1953. She has been the only seamstress to move up to
the ranks of designer.   After an uneventful career as an actress
she worked as a seamstress for Frank Richardson in Paramount's
wardrobe department, where Edith Head and she became good
friends.   She soon left to become a wardrobe girl at MGM, where
Adrian was the chief designer; she felt that "the extras there were
better dressed than some of the stars at Paramount. " She later
worked as general assistant for Adrian's successor, Irene, but
left and began costume designing for Joan Crawford over a ten-
year period, her only non-Crawford assignment being the construction of Bette Davis's costumes for "Winter Meeting, " designed by Bill Travilla.   An unnamed New York designer made
two complete wardrobes for Crawford in "Humoresque, " but she
wore instead one suit Adrian had designed for her personal wardrobe and had O'Brien design the rest.   Many of their other films
together are discussed.

555 _____.   "Sitcom Chic: TV's Influence on the Way We Wear. "
        Los Angeles Times, Fashion 78, December 15, 1978,
        p. 10, 11, 14.
Film designers Elois Jenssen and Edward Stevenson both designed
for the "I Love Lucy" television show; Jenssen from 1953 to 1954,
Stevenson from 1955 until his death in 1968.   Lucille Ball wore
shifts and muumuus from Sears in "Yours, Mine and Ours, " and
during the film's wedding sequence with Henry Fonda wore the
suit that she had worn when she married Gary Morton.

556 _____.   "Star Style: Hollywood's Legendary Fashion Firsts. "
        Los Angeles Times, Fashion 78, October 27, 1978, p. 6.
Discussion of designers and their most innovative costumes, in-
cluding Adrian's ruffled sleeves and padded shoulders for Joan
Crawford in "Letty Lynton" and "Today We Live, " respectively.
A strapless gown he designed for Jean Harlow in "Personal
Property" was before its time, and the Hays office had the scene
refilmed.   The strapless gown was popular from the 1940s until
the 1960s for evening wear, especially as a result of Rita Hayworth's "Put the Blame on Mame" gown from "Gilda, " by Jean
Louis; she had worn one by Travis Banton two years earlier in
"Cover Girl, " but it did not catch on.   Renie's "Kitty Foyle"
dress for Ginger Rogers, in navy wool with white cuff and collars,
became a staple for working women and continues to be popular;
she was inspired in part by a dress she had designed for herself
as a student and by a dress worn by Joan Crawford in "Grand
Hotel, " by Adrian.   Edith Head's many innovative costumes include those worn by Barbara Stanwyck in "The Lady Eve, " Audrey
Hepburn in "Sabrina, " Doris Day in "The Man Who Knew Too
Much, " and Elizabeth Taylor in "A Place in the Sun. "   Her
sarongs for Dorothy Lamour, first worn in "The Jungle Princess"
(see "Daring, But Decent!, " below), influenced fashions during
World War II through tropical prints (disguising poorly made fabrics)
and sarong draping, a method useful for low-quality rayons.

557 "Chikovani, Mikhail." American Film Institute Catalog, 1961-
        70, p. 117.
     Mikhail Chikovani is credited with the costumes of "War and
     Peace" (1968).

558 "Chodorowicz, Katarzyna." American Film Institute Catalog,
        1961-70, p. 117.
     Katarzyna Chodorowicz was the costume designer of "Ashes and
     Diamonds."

559 "Chojkowska, Wieslawa." American Film Institute Catalog,
        1961-70, p. 118.
     Wieslawa Chojkowska is credited with the costumes of "The
     Passenger."

560 "Christine." American Film Institute Catalog, 1961-70, p. 118.
     Christine is credited with the costumes of "Take Her By Surprise."

561 Christy, George. "The Good Life." Hollywood Reporter, 237
        (16): 10, July 17, 1975.
     Edith Head discusses the golden age of fashion, as revived in
     "Gable and Lombard," and discusses briefly some of the people
     she has designed for, including Carole Lombard in "True Con-
     fession" (Travis Banton received credit for designing for Lombard
     in "True Confession").

562 Churchill, Lillian. "Modes à la Movies." New York Times
        Magazine, January 7, 1940, p. 8-9, 18.
     Discussion of the influence of costumes worn in "Cimarron,"
     "Snow White," and "Little Women"; those worn by Norma Shearer
     in "Romeo and Juliet" and "The Barretts of Wimpole Street," by
     Greta Garbo in "Inspiration" and "The Painted Veil," and by Hedy
     Lamarr in "I Take This Woman" (all by Adrian), and by Vivien
     Leigh in "Gone with the Wind," with costumes by Walter Plunkett
     and hats by John Frederics. Also discussed are average costs
     for period and contemporary film costumes; the costumes of "Gone
     with the Wind" cost about $98,154. Most of these films are
     illustrated with photos of the original costumes and retail copies.
     Churchill considers how much Paris and Hollywood influence each
     other, and whether or not Hollywood is a major style center.

563 "Cicoletti, Piero." American Film Institute Catalog, 1961-70,
        p. 119.
     Piero Cicoletti is credited with the costumes of "Bora Bora" and
     was the costume assistant of "The Hawks and the Sparrows."

564 " 'Cinderella.' " Photoplay, 19 (4): 36-7, March 1921.
     Agnes Ayres, Kathlyn Williams, Forrest Stanley, Julia Faye,
     and an extra each model one costume from the Cinderella Ball
     sequence of "Forbidden Fruit," with two additional sketches.
     Clare West is credited with "making the gorgeous gowns for this
     one episode." (The sequence was designed by Natacha Rambova
     and Mitchell Leisen, according to Costume Design in the Movies,

with West having designed the rest of the film.)

565 "The Cinema and Paris Fashions." Unifrance, 16: 20-1, March
     1952.
     Martine Carol will wear lingerie created by the house of Jacques
     Griffe, in "Gibier de Potence." Discussion of the publicity chiefs
     of six couture houses, who promote their fashions through film
     and other media. English text provided.

566 "Cinema Arts Presents Authentic Costumes of Mysterious
              Tibet...." Cinema Arts, 1 (2): 47-50, July 1937.
     18 color sketches of costumes worn in "Lost Horizon," though few
     persons are identified; sketched by Dan Grossbeck.

567 "Cinema Fashions." Fortune, 15 (1): 38, 44, January 1937.
     Ben Waldman's first attempt to market copies of film costumes--
     of a wedding gown designed by I. Frank & Sons for "The King of
     Jazz"--was not a success, but it led him to start the Modern
     Merchandising Bureau. The Bureau cooperates with all studios
     (except for Warner Brothers, which markets its own) by selecting
     stills of films in production and contacting manufacturers to copy
     the costumes so that they can be advertised when the film is re-
     leased. The studios first took 1 percent of the gross, but have
     since stopped because of the publicity value. The Bureau makes
     a 5 percent commission from its 400 stores and the 1,400 stores
     that occasionally sell the copies; it made the most money from
     copies of 15 gowns worn in "Roberta."

568 "A City with a Fence Around It." MGM Presents "Marie
              Antoinette"; a Souvenir Program. 1938, p. 23.
     The MGM wardrobe department contains enough costumes to clothe
     2,300 persons; with 8,000 women's costumes and 1,500 men's
     costumes.

569 "A City with a Fence Around It." MGM Studio News, 4 (8): n.p.,
              May 2, 1937.

570 "Claire Adams in Bathing Suit." Close Up, 10 (4): 13, Sep-
              tember 5, 1923.
     Claire Adams wore her first bathing suit, a one-piece, in "Satan's
     Secret."

571 "Claire Wears Asbestos Suit in Fire Scene." Screen News,
              2 (46): 8, November 17, 1923.
     Claire Windsor wore an asbestos suit as she ran through flames
     in "Nellie, the Beautiful Cloak Model."

572 "Claire Windsor--Blond Beauty...." Screen News, 1 (14): 12,
              May 22, 1922.
     Claire Windsor models four costumes, with closeups of a hat and
     pair of shoes, from "One Clear Call."

573 "Claire Windsor--Blond Beauty...." Screen News, 1 (44): 24,
              December 23, 1922.

574 "Clairval, Laurence." <u>American Film Institute Catalog, 1961-</u>
        <u>70</u>, p. 122.
     Laurence Clairval is credited with the costumes of "The Married
     Woman" and was a dresser for "The Young Girls of Rochefort."

575 "Clara Kimball Young Favors American Style of Clothes."
        <u>Screen News</u>, 1 (27): 21, August 26, 1922.
     Clara Kimball Young, as an Italian prima donna, needed costumes
     that looked foreign-made for "Enter Madame." She remembered
     some Italian fashions she had seen on a previous trip and arranged
     the elaborate and numerous costumes with her modiste, several
     of which are described.

576 "Clark, Buddy." <u>American Film Institute Catalog, 1961-70</u>,
        p. 122.
     Buddy Clark is credited with the costumes of "The Patsy" and
     "Young Fury" and the wardrobe of "Escape from Zahrain," "Wives
     and Lovers," "The Disorderly Orderly," and "Red Line 7000."

577 Clark, Edith. "Designing Clothes for Movie Folk," in <u>Oppor-</u>
        <u>tunities in the Motion Picture Industry</u>. Los Angeles:
        Photoplay Research Society, 1922, p. 79-82.
     Edith Clark, the costume designer for Christie Film Co., dis-
     cusses the attitudes and abilities aspiring costume designers should
     have.

578 "Clark, Gilbert." <u>American Film Institute Catalog, 1921-30</u>,
        p. 1016.
     25 credits are listed for designer Gilbert Clark.

579 "Clark, Ossie." <u>American Film Institute Catalog, 1961-70</u>,
        p. 123.
     Ossie Clark is credited with Goldie Hawn's wardrobe in "There's
     a Girl in My Soup."

580 "Clarke, Vanessa." <u>American Film Institute Catalog, 1961-70</u>,
        p. 123.
     Vanessa Clarke is credited with the costumes of "Privilege" and
     "The War Game."

581 "Classic Stresses Practical Dresses--That Are Easy to Make."
        <u>Movie Classic</u>, 9 (5): 49, January 1936.
     Claire Trevor models an ensemble from "Navy Wife," which has
     been sketched and was available as a pattern.

582 "Classic's Fashion Parade." <u>Movie Classic</u>, 8 (5): 43, July
        1935.
     Dixie Lee models a gown by Rene Hubert from "Redheads on
     Parade."

583 "Classic's Fashion Parade." <u>Movie Classic</u>, 9 (4): 43, De-
        cember 1935.
     Margaret Lindsay models one gown by Orry-Kelly from "Personal
     Maid's Secret."

584 "Classic's Fashion Parade." Movie Classic, 9 (6): 51, 54-7,
       February 1936.
     Wendy Barrie models one costume from "Millions in the Air" and
     Mona Barrie three from "King of Burlesque," both by Gwen Wakel-
     ing, credited as the only high-ranking woman costume designer.
     Helen Vinson models one costume from "King of the Damned,"
     by Elsa Schiaparelli, and Marlene Dietrich one hat from "Desire."

585 "Claudette, Your New Screen Clothes Are Grand!" Photoplay,
       41 (4): 52-3, March 1932.
     Claudette Colbert models four costumes and one hat from "The
     Wiser Sex."

586 "Claudette's Fashion Favorites." Screenland, 51 (4): 56-7,
       February 1947.
     Claudette Colbert models five costumes by Irene from "The Secret
     Heart."

587 "Clavé, Antoni." American Film Institute Catalog, 1961-70,
       p. 124.
     Antoni Clavé is credited with the costumes of "Black Tights."

588 "Cleavage & the Code." Time, 48 (6): 98, August 5, 1946.
     Joseph Breen has been in London explaining the voluntary censor-
     ship system of American filmmakers to the British, who must
     refilm parts of "Wicked Lady" because of the low-cut period cos-
     tumes worn by Margaret Lockwood and Patricia Roc and "Pink
     String and Sealing Wax," also in part because Googie Withers
     wears low-cut gowns.

589 "Clive of London." American Film Institute Catalog, 1961-70,
       p. 125.
     Clive of London is credited with the wardrobe of "Maroc 7."

590 "A Cloak Literally 'Worth Its Weight in Gold'...." Screen
       News, 2 (12): 30, March 24, 1923, col. 1.
     Katherine MacDonald wears a peach velvet cloak with gold brocade
     lining in "Refuge."

591 "Closer-Ups." It, 3 (36): 26, January 22, 1921.
     Priscilla Dean's costumes in "False Colors" cost $8,000.

592 "Closeup of Karinska." Vogue, 87 (10): 44-5, 138-9, May 15,
       1936.
     A biography of Mme. Karinska, stage- and film-costume designer
     and seamstress, with emphasis on her life in Russia.

593 "Clothes and Alimony." It, 2 (3): 23, February 1, 1920.
     The wife of actor Frank Lorimer Mayo asked for one-half of her
     husband's $300-per-week salary, but was denied, during divorce
     proceedings. Mr. Mayo protested, since each of his films re-
     quire three to four suits, costing about $110 each.

594 "Clothes Filler in Discard." Screen News, 1 (14): 25, May
       27, 1922.
Actors and actresses known for their clothes-horse roles are
slowly being edged out of films by the audiences' desire for more
realistic characters.

595 "Clothes for All Kinds of People--Wardrobe Department," in
       Masters and Masterpieces of the Screen, compiled by
       C.W. Taylor. New York: P.F. Collier & Son, 1927,
       p.105.
One still of a portion of First National's large wardrobe department, with many racks of period costumes.

596 "Clothes for Skylarking." Photoplay with Movie Mirror, 19
       (4): 59-63, September 1941.
Claudette Colbert models five costumes by Irene from "Skylark."

597 "The Clothes Line." Picturegoer, 11 (66): 16-7, 63, June 1926.
Some of the film costumes sold at a recent auction are noted,
with reference to the actresses who wore them, how much they
originally cost, and what they were sold for. Unfortunately, no
film titles are given.

598 "Clothes Only Help to Portray a Role, Says Gloria Swanson."
       Screen News, 3 (30): 21, July 26, 1924.
Gloria Swanson feels that film costumes should reinforce a role,
rather than just make one more attractive; in "Manhandled" she
begins with no concern for clothes, and wears more beautiful
clothes as the character changes.

599 "A Clothes Story." Close Up, 9 (1): 10, January 20, 1923.
In "Her Fatal Millions" Viola Dana wears a black derby hat and
a man-tailored suit made in an inexpensive tailor's shop, with
a stiff shirt and huge shoes, collar, black trousers, and swallow-
tailed coat.

600 "Clothes 'Torn to Order.' " Senator Newsette, 2 (39): 4, Sep-
       tember 25, 1926.
Harry Langdon's worn-out film costumes often require as much
work to make as new clothes, as with an unusual coat (not described) and extra-long pants worn in "The Strong Man."

601 Cocteau, Jean. "Beauty and the Beast": Diary of a Film.
       Translated by Ronald Duncan. New York: Dover, 1972
       [1947].
Jean Cocteau kept this diary, in spite of many health problems,
during the production of "Beauty and the Beast" ("La Belle et la
Bête"). Christian Bérard designed the costumes, which were
made at couturier Pacquin's establishment. Cocteau especially
enjoyed the costumes because they did not look like they were
made for a costume ball. References to the aging of the costumes;
the importance of Bérard's costumes in reinforcing the charac-

ters; jewelry, limited to that worn by Beauty when she was dressed
as the princess; some costumes being made from anything available; and costumes created by Marcel Escoffier, in charge of
wardrobe, and by Cocteau, for the statue of Diana and extras.

602 "Coffin, Gene." American Film Institute Catalog, 1961-70,
          p. 126.
Gene Coffin was the costume designer of "The Happening"; the
wardrobe designer of "Goodbye, Columbus"; and is credited with
Shelley Winters's costumes in "Lolita," George C. Scott's ward-
robe in "The Yellow Rolls-Royce," and the costumes of "Act One,"
"The Producers," and "Don't Drink the Water."

603 Cohen, Ronny H. "Couture Goes to the Movies." Art in
          America, 63 (4): 26-7, July/August 1975.
Discussion of the "Romantic and Glamorous Hollywood Design"
exhibit, with mention of different aspects of costume as viewed
from behind the camera; and the significance and symbolism of
costume, as with the role of motion. The exhibit had over 100
costumes, with only one worn by a man, tails worn by Fred
Astaire. The author also notes that "there exists little in the
way of Hollywood shoe iconography," since most film costumes
are seen in full-view only briefly.

604 "Cohen, Shura." American Film Institute Catalog, 1961-70,
          p. 127.
Shura Cohen is credited with the wardrobe of "If ... " and
"Husbands" and was the wardrobe supervisor of "Joanna" and
"Women in Love."

605 Cohn, Art, ed. Michael Todd's "Around the World in 80 Days."
          New York: Random House, 1957.
The costumes made and rented for "Around the World in 80 Days"
were the most used in any film yet made, a total of 74,685 costumes, 34,685 of which were needed on location for shooting
around the world; 36,092 pieces of jewelry were also required.
Includes biographical information on the costume designer, Miles
White.

606 Cohn, Lawrence. "Fashions," in Movietone Presents the
          Twentieth Century. New York: St. Martin's, 1976, n. p.
The latest fashions were presented in the Movietone newsreels
beginning in 1919, with Vyvyan Donner as the fashion editor.
Over 75 photos are presented in the 40-page chapter, including
fashions inspired by sheik Rudolph Valentino.

607 "Colasanti, Veniero." American Film Institute Catalog, 1961-
          70, p. 127.
Veniero Colasanti was the costume designer of "El Cid" and "55
Days at Peking" and is credited with the costumes of "Carthage
in Flames."

608 Colbert, Claudette. "Wear Something Simple!" Movie Life,

1 (2): 54-5, 60, December 1937.
Claudette Colbert especially liked her costumes for "I Met Him
in Paris," in which she played a fashion designer, but her costumes were not as elaborate as those, also designed by Travis
Banton, for her next film, "Bluebeard's Eighth Wife"; she feels
that Banton is the world's best designer. Many actresses welcome
roles that require simple wardrobes so that their talent will not
be competing with the costumes for the audience's attention.

609 Colby, Anita. "The New Look." Photoplay, 31 (6): 74-5, 86,
        November 1947.
Edith Head designed a new-personality wardrobe for Betty Hutton
in "Dream Girl," which Hutton bought for her personal use.

610 "Cole, Elizabeth, makeup." American Film Institute Catalog,
        1961-70, p. 127.
Elizabeth Cole is credited with the costumes of "Peer Gynt."
(The "makeup" after Cole's name is used to distinguish her from
another woman with the same name; it is in error since she had
nothing to do with the film's makeup.)

611 "Cole, Grover." American Film Institute Catalog, 1961-70,
        p. 127.
Cole Grover is credited with the costumes of "Mission Mars."

612 "Colleen Moore to Become Fashion Plate in 'Irene.'" Screen
        News, 4 (40): 5, October 10, 1925.
Colleen Moore will wear 30 gowns in "Irene," made by her
personal modiste.

613 Colling, Bill. "Do Clothes Mean More Than Beauty?" Picture
        Play, 27 (1): 28-9, 116, September 1927.
Director Herbert Brenon discusses the importance of clothing and
personality to an actress's success. Generally the women in the
audience make the success of an actress, and clothing is very
important to them.   One costume each is modeled by Pola Negri
from "Hotel Imperial," Betty Bronson from "Peter Pan," and
Gloria Swanson from "The Humming Bird."

614 "Collins, Chris." American Film Institute Catalog, 1961-70,
        p. 129.
Chris Collins is credited with the costumes of "The Gladiators."

615 Colman, Hila. "Costume Designer," in Making Movies: From
        Student Films to Features. New York: World, 1969,
        p. 84-6.
Virtually nothing is said about the costume designer, but the
wardrobe man, unnamed, for "Alice's Restaurant" found it harder
to costume than "The Cardinal," since no costumes were supplied
and he had to make sure the extras wore the same clothes each
day. (George Newman was credited with the wardrobe of both
films.)

616   Colman, Wes.   "Fads: Hollywood Ideas That Spread over the
            World."   Silver Screen, 2 (12): 44, October 1932.
      Discussion of fashion fads started by actors and actresses, in-
      cluding the sleeves worn by Joan Crawford in "Letty Lynton" and
      hats worn by Greta Garbo in "As You Desire Me" and "Romance."

617   Colonnelli, Elaine.   "Dress Designer Misses Fantasy."   Times-
            Picayune (New Orleans), November 11, 1973, sec. 2,
            p. 17.
      Edith Head misses the old days when glamour and fantasy were
      the main ingredients in the movies.   Anything could come true,
      the movies seemed to say, if you wore the correct clothes.
      (However, she was the main crusader for more realistic cos-
      tumes.)

618   "Color Photography Will Not Alter Good Taste in Dressing of
            Stars Says Sylvia."   Screen News, 3 (20): 29, May 17,
            1924.
      Color photography will allow for greater variety in dress selection,
      since the actresses won't have to worry that each color worn will
      still look like a variation of gray.   Sylvia Breamer matches all
      of her costumes and accessories in spite of the black-and-white
      results.

619   "Color Sequence Will Feature Next Picture."   Screen News, 4
            (41): 6, October 17, 1925.
      "Stage Struck" will include a color dream sequence with servants
      dressed in gold and crimson, and court ladies and men colorfully
      dressed.

620   "Colors Can Give You Charm of Variety Says Norma Talmadge."
            Screen News, 3 (22): 20, May 31, 1924.
      In "The Song of Love" Norma Talmadge wore the vivid Oriental
      colors one would expect of a brunette and in "Secrets" wore the
      pastel colors one associates with a blonde, though Talmadge is a
      brunette.   She models a costume from "Secrets."

621   "Colt, Alvin."   American Film Institute Catalog, 1961-70, p.
            129.
      Alvin Colt is credited with the costumes of "Stiletto."

622   "Colt, Alvin."   Biographical Encyclopaedia and Who's Who of
            the American Theatre.   1966, p. 365-6.
      Biographical information on costume designer Alvin Colt, whose
      film credits include "Top Banana" and "Li'l Abner."

623   "Colt, Alvin."   Who's Who in the Theatre.   16th ed., 1977,
            p. 502.

624   "Coltellacci, Giulio."   American Film Institute Catalog, 1961-70,
            p. 129-30.
      Giulio Coltellacci was the costume designer of "Casanova '70,"
      "The 10th Victim," and "More Than a Miracle," and is credited

with the costumes of "A Quiet Place in the Country."

625 "Colvig, Helen." <u>American Film Institute Catalog, 1961-70,</u>
          p. 130.
     21 credits are listed for designer Helen Colvig.

626 "Comeau, Barbara." <u>American Film Institute Catalog, 1961-70,</u>
          p. 131.
     Barbara Comeau is credited with the costumes of "Atlas."

627 "Comfort, with Glamor." <u>Movie Classic,</u> 10 (1): 48, March
          1936.
     Marlene Dietrich models a costume from "Desire."

628 "Completely Suited!" <u>Movie Classic,</u> 8 (4): 50, June 1935.
     Claire Trevor models a suit by Rene Hubert from "Spring Tonic."

629 "Compliments of Peggy Hamilton, 'Lucile of the West,' Triangle
          Designer." <u>Moving Picture World,</u> 37 (3): 446, July 20,
          1918.
     An advertisement of the kind frequently placed to advertise one-
     self and to give thanks to others in the film industry.

630 "Compton, Sharon." <u>American Film Institute Catalog, 1961-70,</u>
          p. 132.
     Sharon Compton is credited with the wardrobe of "The Secret
     Invasion" and "Beach Ball" and was the costume supervisor of
     "Queen of Blood."

631 "Confidential Agent." <u>Motion Picture,</u> 70 (5): 49, December
          1945.
     Charles Boyer appeared to wear only one suit in "Confidential
     Agent," but he required four suits with 38 shirts, and wore two
     raincoats and three hats because of the stress on the clothing
     from the many action scenes.

632 Conlon, Lillian. "My Lady Favorite's Wardrobe De Luxe."
          <u>Motion Picture Classic,</u> 3 (1): 53, September 1916.
     Notes that actresses no longer have to wear studio costumes lent
     them by the wardrobe mistress, since too often the audiences
     recognize them as having been worn by someone else; that no
     cost is spared by the studio; and that Paris and New York have
     supplied films with the latest fashions.

633 "Connelly, Glenn." <u>American Film Institute Catalog, 1961-70,</u>
          p. 132.
     Glenn Connelly was the costume designer for Doris Day in "Where
     Were You When the Lights Went Out?" and "With Six You Get
     Eggroll."

634 "Connely, Renee." <u>American Film Institute Catalog, 1961-70,</u>
          p. 132.
     Renee Connely was the dress designer of "Angel, Angel, Down
     We Go."

635   "Connolly, Sybil." _American Film Institute Catalog, 1961-70_,
          p. 132.
Sybil Connolly is credited with Hayley Mills's wardrobe and the
nuns' habits in "The Trouble with Angels."

636   "Consider 'Claudia' and Her Clothes." _Screenland_, 47 (4): 52-
          3, August 1943.
Dorothy McGuire models three dresses from "Claudia."

637   "Constance Talmadge at Work on 'East Is West.'" _Screen
          News_, 1 (17): 8, June 10, 1922.
Constance Talmadge and Charles Le Maire went shopping around
New York for fashion accessories for "East Is West," while he
took a break from designing for the Ziegfeld Follies. He sketched
the color plates from which Talmadge's costumes were made;
they featured fabric of heavily embroidered silks and brocades
from China.

638   "Constance to Wear Wig with Pigtail." _Screen News_, 1 (20):
          21, July 1, 1922.
Information identical to that found in the previous article.

639   "Constance to Wear Wig with Pigtail." _Screen News_, 1 (29):
          29, September 9, 1922.

640   "Constructing the Crude, Odd-Looking Fur Costume...."
          Screen News, 2 (14): 24, April 7, 1923, col. 3.
The cavemen and cavewomen costumes worn in "Adam's Rib"
appeared natural and photographed well as a result of the many
skins used, 12 of which are listed.

641   "A Continued Interest in Novel Sleeves...." _Screen News_, 1
          (32): 26, September 30, 1922, col. 2.
In "Money, Money, Money" Katherine MacDonald wears a pleated
gown of yellow chiffon, gold lace, and black trim with immense
sleeves.

642   Cook, Joan. "Fade-In on Donald Brooks, Backstage Star."
          New York Times, May 22, 1967, p. 49.
Donald Brooks discusses designing for his third film, "Star!"
He immersed himself in the various decades of the film for the
approximately 100 costumes worn by Julie Andrews in the starring
role, and up to 3,000 costumes for the entire cast. Includes
two of his sketches, and Andrews models one costume.

643   Cook, Ted. "Ted Cook's Hollywood Fashion Cook-Coos." _New
          Movie_, 7 (5): 43, 100-1, May 1933.
Brief mention of Adrian, erroneously noted as a Londoner, and
the fashion influence of his costumes for Norma Shearer, including a tight gown she wore in "Strange Interlude"; Joan Crawford's
large sleeves and broad shoulders in "Letty Lynton"; and a hat
worn by Greta Garbo in "Romance." Notes also Marlene Dietrich's

fad for wearing pants, about which Adrian said, "Miss Dietrich
has gone to extremes.... They are unbecoming to most women.
Dietrich just happens to look chic in men's clothes."

644   Cooke, David C. Behind the Scenes in Motion Pictures. New
            York: Dodd, Mead, 1960.
Brief mention of the studio wardrobe department and how a film
is costumed.

645   Cooper, Miriam, with Bonnie Herndon. Dark Lady of the
            Silents: My Life in Early Hollywood. Indianapolis and
            New York: Bobbs-Merrill, 1973.
Miriam Cooper writes engagingly of her film career, from 1911
to 1923, with D. W. Griffith and his company of players. As in
"The Tide of Battle," her early roles often required that she be
disguised as a boy. Mae Marsh received her big break with
Griffith when he gave her the lead in "Man's Genesis," after Mary
Pickford turned down the role because she refused to wear a grass
skirt and reveal her legs. Cooper and the other actresses in
"The Birth of a Nation" selected their costumes, with the help of
wardrobe mistress Mrs. Harris, from Civil War-era magazines.
Cooper wore the complete costume, including pantalettes and hoop
skirt, in 100-degree heat and over. For most of her films she
simply told Western Uniform Company (Western Costume Company)
what the role required, though they would usually send dresses
that were too nice for the simple-girl roles she had, and she
would instead go to secondhand stores for the clothes. She did
not like the girl she played in "Intolerance," and dressed for the
role accordingly. She spent more than she could afford on her
costumes for "The Oath" because that was the sort of role it was.
Her costumes for "Kindred of the Dust" consisted of calico and
homespun fabrics.

646   "Cooperation of New York and Hollywood to Preserve Our Style
            Leadership Urged." New York Times, April 23, 1945,
            p. 16.
Makeup expert Perc Westmore proposed that a mediation board
be established with Hollywood and New York representatives so
that the fashion industry could coordinate hair, hat, and dress
fashions in order to help sell the American fashion image and
industry abroad. Otherwise women would only be confused if the
industries in New York and Hollywood did not coordinate periodicals and predictions.

647   "Corinne Griffith in the Role of Madame Zattiany...." Screen
            News, 2 (51): 8, December 22, 1923, cols. 1-2.
Corinne Griffith models a costume from "Black Oxen."

648   "Corinne Griffith Is Busy with Her Modiste...." Screen News,
            3 (20): 29, May 17, 1924, col. 2.
Corinne Griffith is planning her wardrobe for "Single Wives" with
a dressmaker.

649   "The Corn Is Green." Motion Picture, 69 (5): 52, June 1945.
      Bette Davis wore 30 pounds of padding, and period costumes, in
      "The Corn Is Green," for a "fortyish" appearance.

650   "Cornejo, Humberto." American Film Institute Catalog, 1961-
          70, p. 138.
      Humberto Cornejo is credited with the costumes of "Lazarillo" and
      the wardrobe of "A Few Bullets More."

651   "Cornelius, Marjory." American Film Institute Catalog, 1961-
          70, p. 138.
      Marjory Cornelius was the costume designer of "On Her Majesty's
      Secret Service."

652   "Cornwell, O'Kane." American Film Institute Catalog, 1921-
          30, p. 1031.
      O'Kane Cornwell was the costume designer of "Scaramouche."

653   "Corso, Marjorie." American Film Institute Catalog, 1961-70,
          p. 138.
      23 credits are listed for designer Marjorie Corso.

654   Corson, Grace. "Announcing Grace Corson, Fashion Authority."
          Photoplay, 26 (3): 66-7, 99, August 1924.
      Grace Corson has sketched one costume each worn by Carmel
      Myers in "Broadway After Dark" and Leatrice Joy in "Triumph."
      She discusses the frequent poor taste in the selection of film cos-
      tumes, as with the above two costumes, though she notes film
      costumes are the greatest influencer of fashion in America.

655   _____. "As Others See Us." Motion Picture, 32 (5): 35,
          103, 106, December 1926.
      Discussion of some costumes worn by Florence Vidor in "The
      Popular Sin."

656   _____. "As Others See Us." Motion Picture, 33 (1): 33-5,
          February 1927.
      Includes sketches of six costumes worn by Gloria Swanson in
      "Sunya."

657   _____. "The Extravagance of Screen Fashions." Photoplay,
          26 (5): 41-3, 123, October 1924.
      Discussion of the extravagant and often bizarre costumes worn in
      Cecil B. De Mille's films, especially as worn by Gloria Swanson,
      who is known more as a "clothes horse" than as an actress.   In-
      cludes sketches of three costumes that are examples of bad taste;
      for instance, those worn by Lillian Knight and Vera Reynolds in
      "Feet of Clay"; one sketch of a costume worn by Julia Faye from
      the same film displays good taste.   Other costumes in good taste
      are sketched, as worn by Claire Windsor in "Born Rich," Norma
      Shearer in "Broken Barriers," and Gloria Swanson in "Manhandled."

658   _____. "In the Studios and on Fifth Avenue." Photoplay,
          27 (2): 75-6, January 1925.

Includes one sketch each of costumes worn by Diana Kane, Francesca Billings (refers to her also as Frances; her correct name
was Florence), and Bebe Daniels in "Miss Bluebeard."

659 _____. "Miss Corson Selects Best Screen Clothes of the
          Month." Photoplay, 26 (4): 56-7, September 1924.
Includes three sketches of Aileen Pringle in costumes from "True
as Steel" and one of Alma Rubens and two of Constance Bennett
in costumes from "Cytherea."

660 _____. "New Costumes from New Pictures." Photoplay, 27
          (3): 49-51, February 1925.
Discussion, and two sketches each of costumes worn by Norma
Shearer in "The Snob" and Jetta Goudal in "Salome of the Tene-
ments" and one sketch each of costumes worn by May Allison in
"The Interpreter's House," Madge Evans in "Classmates," Marie
Prevost in "Lover of Camille," Pauline Frederick in "Married
Flirts," and Betty Compson in "Locked Doors."

661 _____. "Paris Is in Short Skirts Again." Photoplay, 27
          (4): 53, 94, March 1925.
Anna Nilsson feels that her film costumes are awful in comparison
to her personal wardrobe because studio persons insist on adding
trim for fear that the comparatively plain clothes will not photograph well. Includes sketches of two costumes worn by Nilsson
in "One Way Street."

662 _____. "Screen Inspired Readymades." Photoplay, 27 (6):
          49-53, May 1925.
Includes one sketch each of costumes worn by Doris Kenyon in
"I Want My Man," Dorothy Mackaill in "Chickie," and Adalyn
Mayer in "The Dressmaker from Paris"; two sketches of Constance Bennett in "My Son"; and three of Lillian Rich in "A Kiss
in the Dark." Includes prices and information for purchasing
copies of the costumes through the magazine.

663 "Corteny, Marilu." American Film Institute Catalog, 1961-70,
          p. 139.
Marilu Corteny is credited with the costumes of "God Forgives--
I Don't."

664 "Cortés, Antonio." American Film Institute Catalog, 1961-70,
          p. 139.
Antonio Cortés was the costume designer of "The Viscount."

665 "Costanzi, Elio." American Film Institute Catalog, 1961-70,
          p. 139.
Elio Costanzi is credited with the costumes of "Two Women" and
"Love, the Italian Way."

666 "Co-Starring Barbara Stanwyck and Edith Head." Screenland,
          50 (7): 54-5, May 1946.
Barbara Stanwyck models seven costumes by Edith Head, three

seen as closeups, from "The Strange Love of Martha Ivers."

667 "Coste, Christiane." American Film Institute Catalog, 1961-
           70, p.139.
     Christiane Coste is credited with the costumes of "The Rise of
     Louis XIV."

668 "Costich, Thomas." American Film Institute Catalog, 1961-
           70, p.140.
     Thomas Costich is credited with the costumes of "Bloody Mama,"
     the wardrobe of "Blindfold," and was the wardrobe master of
     "Up in the Cellar."

669 "Costly Wardrobe." Screen News, 4 (40): 2, October 10, 1925.
     Corinne Griffith and her personal modiste designed her gowns for
     "Caesar's Wife," valued at $50,000, some of which are described.
     Since she can only wear her costumes in one film, she sells
     them to a costume company, which rents them to other actresses.

670 "Costume and Make-Up." What's Happening in Hollywood, 28:
           6p., April 5, 1943.
     Discussion of how Edith Head is economizing on fabric for film
     costumes as a result of the government's restriction; her cos-
     tumes for Ginger Rogers in "Lady in the Dark," and other films;
     and costumes worn by Joan Fontaine in "Jane Eyre," by Bette
     Davis and Miriam Hopkins in "Old Acquaintance," by Olivia de
     Havilland in "Devotion" (by Milo Anderson), by Ann Harding in
     "Mission to Moscow," and by Irene Dunne in "A Guy Named Joe."
     Greer Garson's costumes in "Madame Curie" were exact replicas of
     clothes found in portraits of the era.

671 "Costume ... Award ... Winners." The Costumer, June 1950,
           n.p.
     Leah Rhodes had been Orry-Kelly's assistant for many years
     when she was given her "big opportunity" with the costumes for
     "Saratoga Trunk." Marjorie Best joined Warner Brothers in
     1942, and has since designed the men's costumes for their im-
     portant films. Gile Steele designed the men's costumes for
     "Samson and Delilah" and "The Heiress," for which he received
     an Academy Award.

672 "Costume Ball Marks Start of Production of 'Christine of the
           Hungry Heart.'" Screen News, 3 (34): 6, August 23,
           1924.
     Great care was required for costuming hundreds in the ball
     sequence of "Christine of the Hungry Heart." Each person wore
     costumes individually designed for him or her, except for Ian
     Keith, who wore a costume lent him by John Barrymore, who
     had previously worn it in "Beau Brummell."

673 "Costume Design." What's Happening in Hollywood, 2 (30):
           n.p., April 14, 1945.
     Discussion of costumes designed by Irene and worn by Greer

Garson in "The Valley of Decision," Lucille Bremer in "Yolanda
and the Thief," Hedy Lamarr in "Her Highness and the Bellboy,"
Kathryn Grayson in "Anchors Aweigh," and waitresses in "The
Harvey Girls." Discussion also of MGM's wardrobe department,
with mention of Alice Whitehouse and her duties as a wardrobe
mistress. The writer recommends that an Academy Award be
established for best costume design--it was started with films
made in 1948.

674 "Costume Design." What's Happening in Hollywood, 4 (21):
        n.p., February 9, 1947.
Discussion of the influence of film costume on fashion; of Travis
Banton's research and designing for "Time Out of Mind"; and of
costumes by Edith Head worn by Loretta Young in "The Farmer's
Daughter," Ann Todd and Valli in "The Paradine Case," and Claudette Colbert in "The Egg and I." Brief mention of many other
films.

675 "Costume Design for Pictures." What's Happening in Hollywood,
        3 (17): n.p., January 12, 1946.
Discussion of costumes worn by Linda Darnell and Irene Dunne in
"Anna and the King of Siam" and Jennifer Jones in "Cluny Brown,"
both by Bonnie Cashin; Merle Oberon in "A Night in Paradise,"
by Travis Banton; Maureen O'Hara in "The Strange Adventures of
Sinbad," by Edward Stevenson; Marjorie Reynolds and Joan Caulfield in "Monsieur Beaucaire"; Loretta Young in "The Perfect
Marriage" and Ingrid Bergman in "The Bells of St. Mary's," both
by Edith Head; and costumes worn in "City of Flowers," by Rene
Hubert. Brief mention of many other films. Notes that the three
types of film costume are modern, character, and period.

676 "Costume Director Tells of Clothing Characters." New York
        Times, January 10, 1926, sec. 7, p. 5.
H. M. K. Smith discusses how he designs for a film and supervises
costumes that are purchased for contemporary films. Gloria
Swanson, also with Paramount, has her costumes designed by
Rene Hubert, whom she brought over from Paris; he supervised
the construction of her costumes for "Tamed" in New York. Brief
mention of jewelry she and others wear in their films, authentic
and costume. Brief mention also of her costumes for an unnamed
film, bought by Smith and a shopgirl on New York's 14th Street.
Thomas Meighan had his costumes for "Irish Luck" made in London and his policeman's uniform for the film made by a New York
tailor.

677 "Costumer of the Year--Alex Velcoff." The Costumer, June
        1950, p. 16.
Alex Velcoff's invention of an infrared evaluator has saved many
hours of work for costumers, since one can now see exactly how
a fabric will photograph on infrared film now being used for color
movies--thus eliminating the need for expensive wardrobe tests.

678 "The Costumers Link the Present and the Past with a Cavalcade

of Outstanding Costumes. Part One: Contemporary. "
Motion Picture Costumer, 1962, n. p.
Includes stills of costumes worn by Jesse Pearson and Janet Leigh
in "Bye Bye Birdie" and Yvette Mimieux in "Diamond Head," both
by Pat Barto; Jane Fonda in a costume she designed for "A Period
of Adjustment"; Hope Lange in "Pocketful of Miracles," by Edith
Head; Mimieux and Russ Tamblyn in "The Wonderful World of the
Brothers Grimm," by Mary Wills; Leslie Caron in "The Man Who
Understood Women," by Charles Le Maire; and Natalie Wood and
Barbara Watson in "Gypsy" and Glynis Johns in "The Chapman
Report," both by Orry-Kelly. Not all costumes modeled by the
actresses.

679   "The Costumers Link the Present and the Past with a Cavalcade
         of Outstanding Costumes. Part Two: The Past." Motion
         Picture Costumer, 1962, n. p.
Stills of costumes worn by Robert Morley and Norma Shearer in
"Marie Antoinette" and Jeanette MacDonald in "Maytime," by
Adrian; Judy Garland in "Meet Me in St. Louis" and Yul Brynner
and Deborah Kerr in "The King and I, " by Irene Sharaff; Ginger
Rogers in "Lady in the Dark" and Mae West in "She Done Him
Wrong," by Edith Head; Maureen O'Hara in "At Sword's Point, "
by Edward Stevenson; Katharine Hepburn in "A Woman Rebels, "
by Walter Plunkett (the last two not modeled by the actresses);
Anne Baxter in "All About Eve," by Charles Le Maire; Jill St.
John in "The Lucky Mr. Pennypacker," by Mary Wills; Virginia
Mayo in "The Silver Chalice," by Rolfe Gerard; Errol Flynn in
"Don Juan" ("The Adventures of Don Juan"), by Travilla and Leah
Rhodes; and Bette Davis in "Elizabeth and Essex" ("The Private
Lives of Elizabeth and Essex"), by Orry-Kelly.

680   "The Costumes for 'First a Girl' Cost Thousands of Pounds. "
         Film Pictorial, 9 (211): 3, March 7, 1936.
A Lux soap ad with a "testimony" by a Gaumont-British wardrobe
mistress (not named) and including photos of costumes from "First
a Girl. "

681   "Costumes from Spain." Screen News, 1 (6): 25, April 1, 1922.
John S. Robertson shipped three toreador costumes from Spain for
Rudolph Valentino to wear in "Blood and Sand." The suits, in
blue, brown, and crimson (this information conflicts with other
articles, which say purple instead of crimson), with matching
pants and silk waist and sash, are all worn with a black cap with
a black topknot, according to the Spanish custom. Two pink capes
with silver embroidery may be interchanged with each suit, one
cape lined with green and the other with crimson silk.

682   "Costumes Gorgeous Creations. " Screen News, 4 (30): 7,
         August 1, 1925.
Claire Windsor wears over 26 costumes in "Souls for Sables. "

683   "The Costumes [of 'Earthquake']. " American Cinematographer,
         55 (11): 1325, November 1974.

Burton Miller, the costume designer, with Edith Head, of "Earthquake," discusses some of the problems that occurred in costuming over 1,000 persons. The major problem was that each person needed about five changes of each costume to reflect the
deterioration of their costumes that occurred during and after the
earthquake. The principal cast needed at least six changes each,
as with a beige suit worn by Ava Gardner. Sheila Mason was the
wardrobe supervisor.

684   "Coulter, Lucia." American Film Institute Catalog, 1921-30,
           p.1033.
       22 costume-related credits are listed for Lucia Coulter.

685   "Courcelles, Christiane." American Film Institute Catalog,
           1961-70, p.140.
       Christiane Courcelles is credited with the costumes of "Judex."

686   Courtlandt, Roberta. "My Lady's Wardrobe." Motion Picture
           Classic, 3 (4): 15-7, December 1916.
       Many actresses and their film costumes are shown, unfortunately
       without film titles. Dorothy Kelly wears a gown designed by
       Vitagraph's Mrs. Jane Lewis; Juanita Hansen models a gown from
       "The Secret of the Submarine."

687   Cowley, Susan Cheever. "The Travolta Hustle." Newsweek,
           91 (22): 97, May 29, 1978.
       The fad for wearing copies of John Travolta's white suit in
       "Saturday Night Fever" is replacing the jean uniform for many
       men. The suit is worn with a black shirt and gold chain, as
       shown in photos of John Travolta and others in retail copies.

688   "Cox, Brian." American Film Institute Catalog, 1961-70, p.
           141.
       Brian Cox is credited with the costumes of "Hammerhead" and
       "The Man Who Had Power over Women."

689   "Cox, David." American Film Institute Catalog, 1921-30, p.
           1034.
       47 costume-related credits are listed for David Cox.

690   "Cox, James David." Motion Picture Almanac. 1930, p.122.
       Brief biographical information on designer David Cox, with credits
       listed for "The Man Who Laughs" and "Our Dancing Daughters."

691   Coyle, Richard. "Auction Day in Hollywood." Motion Picture,
           33 (2): 46-7, 93, 101, March 1927.
       Discussion of the annual auction of the Paramount wardrobe depart-
       ment, where $100,000 worth of costumes had just been sold.
       Lists prices of many of the costumes, as with a dress worn by
       Mary Brian in "The Little French Girl." The other costumes
       discussed, with one still each, include those worn by Florence
       Vidor in "You Never Know Women," Bebe Daniels in "Stranded"
       and "The Campus Flirt," Betty Bronson and Arlette Marchal in

"The Cat's Pajamas," and Pola Negri in "Good and Naughty."

692   Craig, Carol.   "A New Robin Hood--in Color!"   Motion Picture,
            54 (6): 42-3, 60, January 1938.
      Milo Anderson, the designer of "The Adventures of Robin Hood,"
      discusses the creation of chain-mesh armor for the film.   After
      it had been made for the knights and soldiers it was too noisy for
      the microphones; instead, a mesh of woven string and metal paint
      was made which photographed the same as the chain-mesh.

693   _____.   "This Is Hepburn."   Movie Classic, 9 (6): 40-1,
            84-5, February 1936.
      Katharine Hepburn once visited Muriel King's salon and liked her
      sketches enough to send 100 to director George Cukor to consider
      for her role in "Sylvia Scarlett."   The director wired King to
      come to Hollywood, which was unusual since there were so many
      designers in Hollywood.   King discusses at length designing for
      Hepburn and the film.   Includes biographical information on the
      designer and a photo collage of Hepburn in costumes from the
      film, though generally in closeups.

694   "Craig, Marla."   American Film Institute Catalog, 1961-70,
            p. 142.
      Marla Craig is credited with the costumes of "The Phantom
      Planet."

695   "Cramer, Claire."   American Film Institute Catalog, 1961-70,
            p. 142.
      Claire Cramer is credited with the wardrobe of "Teenage Million-
      aire" and "Brushfire!"

696   Crawford, Joan.   My Way of Life.   New York: Simon and
            Schuster, 1971.
      Joan Crawford wore no bra or girdle for a sensual look for her
      role as a prostitute in "Grand Hotel."   For Adrian and Crawford,
      her films were a showcase of his designs--simple costumes for
      dramatic scenes and vice versa.   Also, she wore dark colors
      and little jewelry for dramatic scenes.   They both made fashion
      history when Adrian decided to make her broad shoulders even
      broader with shoulder pads.   Director Michael Curtiz did not like
      that look when she tried out for "Mildred Pierce," and ripped her
      housedress from Sears from "neck to hemline" only to find that
      she had no shoulder pads on.

697   _____, with Jane Kesner Ardmore.   A Portrait of Joan:
            The Autobiography of Joan Crawford.   Garden City, N.Y.:
            Doubleday, 1962.
      F. Scott Fitzgerald called Joan Crawford "the best example of the
      flapper, ... gowned to the apex of sophistication...."   Adrian
      designed all of her film costumes for 14 years, giving her the
      tailored look and, for a change, "simpler" styles for "Sadie Mc-
      Kee."   After wearing a $40,000 wardrobe in "The Women" Craw-
      ford wore three dresses valued under $40 in "Strange Cargo,"

including one that was aged each day and soaked in mud and dried,
which she then had to wear.   After more clothes-horse roles she
eventually starred in "Mildred Pierce."   The studio-designed
housedresses looked too good for director Michael Curtiz, so
Crawford bought a $2.98 dress from Sears, which Mr. Curtiz
tore up during her wardrobe tests (the story here varies from
that in the above entry).   They became good friends later, and
she gave him a gift of Adrian's shoulder pads.

698 Crawford, M. D. C.   The Ways of Fashion.   New York: Fair-
        child, 1948.
Includes brief biographical information of Lady Duff Gordon, known
also as Lucile; Adrian; Travis Banton, who was working for Hattie
Carnegie at that time; Irene; and Omar Kiam.   Chanel made the
mistake of accepting an offer to design film costumes; Jeanne
Lanvin and Captain Molyneux, who were also asked, did not.
Brief mention of fashion trends started by some of the above de-
signers, and Royer and Gwen Wakeling.

699 "Crawford Models Advance Fashions for Coming Year."   MGM
        Studio Picture News, 5 (1): n.p., January 7, 1938.
Adrian has designed 28 gowns for Joan Crawford in "Mannequin,"
which reflect European influence from a recent trip.   One Russian
peasant costume was translated into a gown of gold cloth with sable
trim.

700 "Crawford, One Star Style Show, in New 'Ice Follies of 1939.'"
        MGM Studio News, 6 (15): n.p., February 25, 1939.
Adrian has designed elaborate costumes with furs of every kind
for Joan Crawford in "Ice Follies of 1939," including one costume
with a wrap skirt of white fox and a tight bodice of silver metallic
cloth and large fur sleeves.

701 "Creation by Adrian."   Motion Picture Studio Insider, Intro-
        ductory number: 18, February 1935.
Joan Crawford models two gowns by Adrian, from "Chained."

702 Crisler, B. R.   "The Stylists Declare for Peace."   New York
        Times, May 7, 1938, sec. 10, p. 5.
The author finds it ludicrous that film designers should be so
worried about the impending European war because their fashions
might be out of date when the films were released.   Royer discussed how trivial this all might seem, but was quite concerned,
for example, that his costumes for Sonja Henie and others in
"Second Fiddle" would be out of date, though he had designed
them conservatively in case the war did break out.

703 Croce, Arlene.   The Fred Astaire and Ginger Rogers Book.
        New York: Galahad, 1972.
The film "Roberta" featured a fashion show that, the author notes,
had ugly costumes.   Irene Castle was employed as a technical adviser for "The Story of Vernon and Irene Castle," though she was
given little chance to help with the costumes despite the fact that

she and her husband had been great trend setters in the fashions
of their times.   Some of Ginger Rogers's costumes were patterned
after those of Mrs. Castle.

704   Cruikshank.   " 'I'm No Trilby' says Marlene Dietrich." Motion
            Picture, 46 (5): 24-5, 68, June 1935.
Marlene Dietrich noted that she liked Hollywood fashions, especially
to wear in Hollywood, and that the fashions had influenced European designers, particularly in sportswear.   She still wore trousers for comfort, but not as evening clothes, since it had been
a fad.

705   Cruikshank, Herbert.   "Forecasting About--Views and Previews
            of Impending Events." Motion Picture, 36 (3): 66, 112,
            119, October 1928.
Paper costumes will soon be used for some films, as in chorus
scenes, to reduce soaring costume and production costs.   Time
and money can be saved, and interesting effects can be achieved,
by painting the costumes to harmonize with the sets.

706   Crump, Irving.   "Wardrobe and Make-Up," in Our Movie
            Makers.   New York: Dodd, Mead, 1940, p. 124-7.
Discussion of the typical wardrobe department: the duties of the
workers; the storage of modern and period film costumes; and
its role in the costuming of a film.   The services of costume
companies are often required for especially large casts, so that
a wardrobe truck often must go on location and have a sufficient
supply and selection of costumes to anticipate needs.

707   "Cummings, Patrick." American Film Institute Catalog, 1961-
            70, p. 147.
Patrick Cummings is credited with the costumes of "Promises!
Promises!," "Convict Stage," and "Fort Courageous"; the ward-
robe of "Woman Hunt"; the men's wardrobe of "Seven Women from
Hell"; and the wardrobe supervision of "Nightmare in the Sun."

708   "Cummins, Jackie." American Film Institute Catalog, 1961-
            70, p. 147.
13 wardrobe-related credits are listed for Jackie Cummins.

709   " 'Curly Top' Sets the Fashion for Little Girls." Photoplay,
            48 (5): 5, October 1935.
Shirley Temple models three dresses by Rene Hubert from "Curly
Top."

710   Curran, Doris.   "Hollywood Welcomes Erté: Missionary of
            Beauty." Motion Picture Classic, 29 (6): 28-30, July
            1925.
General biographical information on Erté, who discusses film-
costume design briefly.

711   Curry, George.   "Locations, Sets and Costumes," in Copper-
            field '70.   New York: Ballantine, 1970, p. 33-47.

Includes brief references to the costumes of "David Copperfield," designed by Anthony Mendleson, and worn by Pamela Franklin, Edith Evans, Susan Hampshire, Robin Phillips, Corin Redgrave, Sir Michael Redgrave, Ron Moody, Sir Laurence Olivier, and Richard Attenborough. Brief mention also of the costumes being based on the original Phiz drawings; color selection; and that Berman's was the costumer. Susan Hampshire models a costume, shown with the original sketch, from the film.

712 "Curtis, Mary Ann." American Film Institute Catalog, 1961-
     70, p. 148.
Mary Ann Curtis is credited with the costumes of "Nashville Rebel."

713 Cuskelly, Richard, and Dale Kern. "Dressing Up the Movies."
     Los Angeles Herald-Examiner, February 17, 1974, sec.
     F, p. 1, 7.
Includes sketches or stills of costumes worn by Bette Davis in "All About Eve," by Edith Head; Diana Ross in "Lady Sings the Blues," by Bob Mackie; Karen Black in "The Day of the Locust," by Ann Roth; Barbra Streisand and others in "The Way We Were," by Moss Mabry (Dorothy Jeakins also designed the film); Jack Nicholson in "Chinatown," by Anthea Sylbert; and Liv Ullmann "Forty Carats," by Jean Louis. The above designers, and Ron Talsky, discuss how they design for a film, their preference for modern or period costumes, their favorite actors and actresses, and the extent to which film costumes influence fashion.

714   Daché, Lilly. "Stargazing," in <u>Talking Through My Hats.</u>
        Edited by Dorothy Roe Lewis. New York: Coward
        McCann, 1946, p. 154-71.
Travis Banton often sent his costume sketches to Lilly Daché so
that she could design the hats, as for Carole Lombard.   No
mention of specific films.   Daché's hats for Marlene Dietrich's
films included her famous and widely copied hats for "Desire"--
Daché sent about 50 hats to Hollywood for Dietrich to select.
She also made many unique hats for Carmen Miranda, including
the hats and jewelry for one film (unnamed).

715   _____. "Talking Through My Hats."   <u>Woman's Home Com-</u>
        <u>panion,</u> 73 (4): 18+, April 1946.
A very long article consisting of excerpts from Lilly Daché's
autobiography (see the previous entry), with mention of her having
designed hats worn by Marlene Dietrich in many of her films and
jewelry and hats worn by Carmen Miranda in an unnamed film.
Illustrations include closeups of Paulette Goddard in a hat from
"Kitty," and Marlene Dietrich (from "Desire").

716   "Daché, Lilly."   <u>Current Biography</u>.   1941, p. 198-9.

717   "Dache, Lilly." <u>Who's Who in America</u>.   37th ed., 1972-3, p. 719.

718   "Dache, Lilly."   <u>Who's Who of American Women</u>.   8th ed.,
        1974-5, p. 214.

719   Dade, Helen.   "What Becomes of the Clothes the Stars Wear
        on the Screen."   <u>Motion Picture,</u> 45 (1): 49, 84, 89,
        February 1933.
The 6 million dollars' worth of costumes worn in films each year
are either remade for, or reworn by, extras, sold to someone
who distributes them to secondhand shops, sold at the studios on
"bargain days," are renovated and sold as new, or are bought by
costume companies or by the actresses who wore them.   Marion
Davies and Mary Pickford once started a store but could not obtain enough film costumes to keep it supplied.   Includes photos
of the same costume passed on by Lili Damita in "The Woman
Between" to Jeanne Helbling in "Une Femme Libre" and an extra
in "Traveling Husbands."

720 "Dahlke, Edith." _American Film Institute Catalog, 1961-70_,
         p. 150.
     Edith Dahlke is credited with the wardrobe of "U-47 Lt. Com-
     mander Prien."

721 "Dahlman, Rynol." _American Film Institute Catalog, 1961-70_,
         p. 150.
     Rynol Dahlman is credited with the wardrobe of "A Yank in Viet-
     Nam."

722 Dale, Edgar. "Costuming," in _How to Appreciate Motion Pic-
         tures._ New York: Macmillan, 1933, p. 46-50.
     H. M. K. Smith discusses generally the costuming of a film and
     notes that while the costumes are diligently researched for authen-
     ticity and good taste, the average woman should not imitate the
     actresses because they often wear the wrong clothes, usually
     their own selections. He was for many years the Famous Players-
     Lasky costume director.

723 "Dalton, Phyllis." _American Film Institute Catalog, 1961-70_,
         p. 151.
     Phyllis Dalton was the costume designer of "Lawrence of Arabia,"
     "Doctor Zhivago," "Lord Jim," and "Oliver!"; the wardrobe de-
     signer of "Fury at Smuggler's Bay"; and is credited with the cos-
     tumes of "Becket."

724 "Damiani, Luciano." _American Film Institute Catalog, 1961-
         70_, p. 151.
     Luciano Damiani is credited with the costumes of "Cavalleria
     Rusticana."

725 "Danduryan, A." _American Film Institute Catalog, 1961-70_,
         p. 152.
     A. Danduryan is credited with the costumes of "Chelkash" and
     "Bolshoi Ballet 67."

726 "Danielle." _American Film Institute Catalog, 1961-70_, p. 152.
     Danielle is credited with the costumes of "Come One, Come All!"

727 D'Arcy, Rita Jean. "Fashionable Debutante--or Well-Dressed
         Working Girl?" _Motion Picture,_ 48 (6): 56-7, 89, January
         1933.
     Discussion of many costumes worn by Adrienne Ames in "Gigol-
     lette," six of which she models.

728 _____. "'Know Clothes, and You'll Know Success'--Peggy
         Fears." _Motion Picture,_ 48 (5): 54-6, 77, 79, Decem-
         ber 1934.
     Peggy Fears, a successful writer and producer of plays, a Zieg-
     feld girl, and an owner of a Hollywood dress shop, has been given
     a contract at Fox Studios as an actress, costume designer, writer,
     producer, and director. She attributes her success to her fashion
     sense and feels that Norma Shearer's success, and that of other

actresses, is also due in large part to their costumes. Rene
Hubert has designed the costumes for her first film, "Lottery
Lover."

729 d'Arcy, Susan. "A Head of Fashion." Films Illustrated,
     4 (39): 30-1, September 1974.
In Hollywood's heyday Edith Head designed for about 50 films per
year, but now designs for about five per year. Includes two
sketches of Robert Redford in "The Great Waldo Pepper."

730 Dare, Janet. "The $25-a-Week Girl Can Dress Well, Too!"
     Movie Classic, 8 (6): 50-1, 72, August 1935.
Orry-Kelly notes that American women have been allowed to keep
up with the latest fashions through film costumes; he discusses
wardrobe selection. A still shows Orry-Kelly and Ruby Keeler
in his office examining her latest film wardrobe.

731 "Darieux, Robert." American Film Institute Catalog, 1961-70,
     p. 154.
Robert Darieux is credited with the costumes of "Orgy of the
Dead."

732 "Daring, But Decent!" Screen Guide, 4 (9): 16-7, November
     1939.
Dorothy Lamour has often had her film costumes copied for her
personal wardrobe. She models original costumes, and adaptations,
from "Disputed Passage," by Travis Banton; she collaborates with
Banton on the adapted costumes. She wore her first sarong in
"The Hurricane" (designed by Omar Kiam; she wore a sarong
also in "The Jungle Princess," by Edith Head, the same year).

733 "The Dark Corner." Motion Picture, 71 (4): 54, May 1946.
Clifton Webb, heir to the best-dressed title, wears an extensive
number of his 125 suits in "The Dark Corner."

734 "Date-Raters in Summer Style." Photoplay with Movie Mirror,
     21 (2): 59-61, July 1942.
Patricia Morison models three costumes from "Mr. and Mrs.
Cugat," by Edith Head; with original sketches.

735 Daves, Jessica. Ready-Made Miracle: The American Story of
     Fashion for the Millions. New York: Putnam's, 1967.
Los Angeles began to be a fashion center through the fashions of
Adrian, whose famous "Letty Lynton" gown for Joan Crawford
was the "first recorded instance" of film costume's specific influence; the next event was Lana Turner's tight sweaters. Adrian,
Irene, and Howard Greer were the nucleus in establishing Los
Angeles as a ready-to-wear center. Turner's wearing of sweaters was a boon for the knitting industry, but was not yet widely
popular because of its association with the movies.

736 "Davidoff, Alexis." American Film Institute Catalog, 1961-70,
     p. 156.

Alexis Davidoff is credited with the costumes of "The Hoodlum Priest," the men's wardrobe of "A Distant Trumpet," and the wardrobe of "The Explosive Generation," "House of Women," "PT 109," and "Apache Rifles."

737   Davies, Dentner (pseudonym of David Sentner). "Jean's Influence on Styles," in Jean Harlow: Hollywood Comet. London: Constable, 1937, p. 90-8, passim.
Jean Harlow was referred to as "sexquisite" after her appearance in a gown that may have caused more conversation than any previously worn film costume--a tight, skimpy, slinky, satin gown worn in "Hell's Angels." (She also had one of her most memorable lines when she said, " ... excuse me ... while I slip into something more comfortable.") Her influence on fashion was in general ways--for instance, satin and beltless evening gowns-- rather than with specific styles copied faithfully. She was particularly fond of off-the-shoulder evening gowns; one worn in her last completed film, "The Man in Possession" (U.S. title: "Personal Property"), was pasted onto her body after she was first covered with glue, and was steamed off for removal. (Author David Chierichetti [see "Star Style"] notes that Adrian designed the boned-bodice, strapless gown but the Hays office required that MGM refilm the scene [for the U.S. version]). Also, her evening gowns often lacked shoulder straps; they were held up instead by whalebone in the bodice.

738   Davies, Marion. The Times We Had: Life with William Randolph Hearst. Edited by Pamela Pfau and Kenneth S. Marx. New York: Bobbs-Merrill, 1975.
The filming of "Little Old New York" was delayed when the studio burned down. Filming resumed at another studio, and Marion Davies's costumes were remade.

739   Davis, Bette. "Where Did You Get That Hat?" Screen Guilds' Magazine, 3 (2): 14, April 1936.
Bette Davis welcomes the trend toward more realistic films and hopes that it will include more realistic costumes. She wore "bizarre" costumes and headdresses during her first three years in films, but has since tried to dress more appropriately for her roles, as in "The Golden Arrow," designed by Orry-Kelly.

740   "Davis, Francesca." American Film Institute Catalog, 1961-70, p. 157.
Francesca Davis is credited with the costumes of "Coming Apart."

741   Davis, Lucy. "The Girl on the Cover." Photoplay, 7 (2): 35-7, January 1915.
Actress Winifred Kingston feels that films have influenced fashion more than fashion books or the theater, especially since women in small towns can copy the costumes.

742   "Dawson, Beatrice." American Film Institute Catalog, 1961-70, p. 159.

22 credits are listed for designer Beatrice Dawson. (See also "Dawson, Bumble.")

743 _____. Who's Who in the Theatre. 16th ed., 1977, p. 539-
          40.
Beatrice Dawson has designed for over 50 films. The credits
listed are "The Importance of Being Earnest," "The Assassination
Bureau," and "The Prince and the Showgirl."

744 "Dawson, Bumble." American Film Institute Catalog, 1961-70,
          p. 159.
Bumble Dawson was the costume designer of "The Roman Spring
of Mrs. Stone," and the costume supervisor of "Modesty Blaise."
(See also "Dawson, Beatrice.")

745 "Dawson, Gordon." American Film Institute Catalog, 1961-70,
          p. 159.
Gordon Dawson is credited with the wardrobe of "In Harm's Way,"
"Hour of the Gun," "The Way West," and "The Wild Bunch" and
the men's costumes of "Ride Beyond Vengeance."

746 "Dawson, Tom" American Film Institute Catalog, 1961-70,
          p. 159.
Tom Dawson is credited with the costumes of "Major Dundee"
and the wardrobe of "Shenandoah."

747 "Day, Richard." American Film Institute Catalog, 1921-30,
          p. 1048-9.
Richard Day is credited with the costumes of "Merry-Go-Round"
and "The Merry Widow" (1925).

748 Deaner, Frances. "The New Janet Gaynor--Designed by Adrian."
          Movie Mirror, 14 (2): 16-7, 59, January 1939.
Discussion of the transformation of Janet Gaynor and her appearance since her marriage to Adrian. They had previously worked
together in 1933, when Fox arranged to have Adrian design Gaynor's costumes for "Paddy, the Next Best Thing." (See Riley,
Robert. "Adrian.")

749 Deans, Marjorie. "The Costumes and Decor," in Meeting at
          the Sphinx. London: MacDonald, 1946, p. 108-10, passim.
George Bernard Shaw, author of the play and the screenwriter for
"Caesar and Cleopatra," also helped with costume advice. Includes
lengthy excerpts of correspondence between Shaw and producer
Gabriel Pascal concerning the costumes of Cecil Parker and
Claude Rains, and for Flora Robson, for whom he changed lines
to suit her appearance. Costume designer Oliver Messel did not
follow Shaw's pale color suggestions for Stewart Granger, choosing
instead bright colors. Bombs dropped during London air raids
hit the studio wardrobe workrooms, and since most of the workers
fled London, the 2000-plus costumes were finished by a handful
of persons. Due to fabric shortages Messel improvised the uniforms for 1,200 Egyptian troops, who were provided by the

Egyptian government for location shooting. Messel also selected
Indian saris, curtains, cotton bedspreads, and plain gauze fabric
that was specially handblocked, stenciled, and dyed by himself
and Scott-Slymon. Messel and Beatrice Dawson handmade the
authentic jewelry; Hugh Skillan made the special headdresses;
Matilda Etches carried out Messel's sketches, which are reproduced throughout this book; and Elinor Abbey, his assistant,
and Maggie (or Margaret) Furse helped with the wardrobe. Includes costume stills in color and black-and-white.

750   " 'Declassé' Shows New Gown Styles. " Senator Newsette, 1
         (16): 2, April 5, 1925.
Corinne Griffith's gowns in "Declassé" were designed for her by
New York designers Mme. Frances and Gilbert Clarke.

751   de Courtais, Georgine. Women's Headdress and Hairstyles in
         England from A. D. 600 to the Present Day. London:
         Batsford, 1972.
Mentions the popularity of hats from 1930 to 1939, including the
"Juliet" cap (from "Romeo and Juliet") and the "Robin Hood" hat
(from "The Adventures of Robin Hood").

752   Dee, Vincent. Taped Lecture. University of Southern Califor-
         nia Special Collections Library, no date.
Vincent Dee has been the head of Universal's wardrobe department
for men and women for over 15 years. He discusses how a film
is costumed; job opportunities; the advantage of working on a low-
budget film, as with "Psycho"; and notes that the art department
can override the wardrobe department since the expense of the
sets and the length of time and work involved in making the sets
are more important than what will be worn inside the sets. The
tape, which runs for over one hour, can be hard to listen to: the
lecture was disorganized and features a considerable amount of
profanity.

753   "Dee, Vincent. " American Film Institute Catalog, 1961-70,
         p. 161.
Vincent Dee is credited with the costumes of "Texas Across the
River" and the costume supervision of "Marnie, " "The Raiders, "
and "Dark Intruder. " (Dee was not solely responsible for the
wardrobe of the above films, but is included for reference to the
preceding entry.)

754   Deere, Dorothy. "The Most Envied Profession. " Movieland,
         2 (12): 36-9, 60-1, January 1945.
Discussion of the life and career of hosiery designer Willys DeMond,
with references to hosiery worn by Claudette Colbert in "It Happened
One Night" and "Zaza, " Ginger Rogers in "International" and
"Stage Door, " Deanna Durbin in "Mad About Music, " Alice Faye
in "Rose of Washington Square" and "Old Chicago, " Marlene
Dietrich in "The Flame of New Orleans, " Barbara Stanwyck in
"Queen of Burlesque, " Rita Hayworth in "You Never Looked
Lovelier" ("You Were Never Lovelier"), Carole Landis in
"One Million B. C. , " Joan Blondell in "Good Girls Go to

Paris, " and Jack Benny in "Charley's Aunt. "

755 "Defend Salome's Lack of Clothing. " Movie Picture World,
         38 (8): 1059, February 22, 1919.
Theda Bara and J. Gordon Edwards, the director of "Salome,"
discuss the appearances of Bara and the person (unnamed) who
played the part of John the Baptist--which have been widely
criticized in the press.   Bara denies that she tried to appear
seductive; she tried to deter the audience from wickedness, rather
than inspire them to it.   There is no mention of specific costumes.

756 "Deighton, Gordon. " American Film Institute Catalog, 1961-70,
         p. 162.
Gordon Deighton is credited with Michael York's costumes in
"The Guru. "

757 "Delamare, Rosine. " American Film Institute Catalog, 1961-
         70, p. 163.
Rosine Delamare was the costume designer of "The Wonders of
Aladdin"; the wardrobe designer of "Hello--Goodbye"; and is
credited with the costumes of "The Green Mare, " "Maxime, "
"The Most Wanted Man, " "The Story of the Count of Monte
Cristo, " "The Night of the Generals, " "The 25th Hour, " "The Mad-
woman of Chaillot, " and "Rider on the Rain. "

758 "De Luca of Rome. " American Film Institute Catalog, 1961-70,
         p. 165.
De Luca of Rome is credited with the special costumes for Jac-
queline Sassard in "Accident" and created the costumes for "Red
Desert. "

759 "De Marchis, Marcella. " American Film Institute Catalog,
         1961-70, p. 165.
Marcella De Marchis is credited with the wardrobe of "Navajo
Joe" and the costumes of "Teorema. "

760 "Demarez, Andrée. " American Film Institute Catalog, 1961-
         70, p. 165.
Andrée Demarez is credited with the costumes of "The Man with
Connections. "

761 "De Matteis, Maria. " American Film Institute Catalog, 1961-
         70, p. 165.
Maria De Matteis was the costume designer of "The Girl and the
General" and is credited with the costumes of "Neapolitan Ca-
rousel, " "Barabbas, " "The Reluctant Saint, " "Son of Samson, "
"The Story of Joseph and His Brethren, " "Son of the Red Cor-
sair, " "The Bible ... In the Beginning, " "Kiss the Girls and
Make Them Die, " and "Fraulein Doktor. "

762 De Mille, Cecil B.   The Autobiography of Cecil B. De Mille.
         Edited by Donald Hayne.   Englewood Cliffs, N. J. :
         Prentice-Hall, 1959.

Bessie McGaffey no longer had to visit libraries for the researching of films after Cecil B. De Mille advised her to buy whatever
books she needed, founding the first research department for a
studio, at Famous Players. "Joan the Woman" was made in 1916,
when period films were not generally considered box-office draws.
Geraldine Farrar, in the title role, wore silver-aluminum armor
rather than the heavier iron used for the men's armor, though it
was still burdensome. The film's costumes were publically exhibited, which was probably the first time this had been done.
Gloria Swanson's success was due in part to her film costumes,
designed by Alphareta (or Alphretta) Hoffman and later by Mitchell
Leisen, who designed the costumes for the Babylonian sequence
of "Male and Female." No one but De Mille was allowed to
speak to H.B. Warner when he was in his costume as Christ for
"The King of Kings." Clare West's lavish costumes for Julia
Faye in "Saturday Night" included a patent-leather bathing suit,
the top of which came off while she was swimming--the footage
was retained in the film, since the accident was not noticeable.
Faye helped design and sew some of Estelle Taylor's costumes
for "The Ten Commandments."

763 "deMille Emerald Gives Leatrice Joy a Scare." Screen News,
        1 (18): 10, 14, June 17, 1922.
For "Manslaughter," Cecil B. De Mille lent Leatrice Joy a
valuable emerald necklace, which Joy thought she had damaged;
the crack turned out to be a natural flaw.

764 "Demore, Don." American Film Institute Catalog, 1961-70,
        p. 166.
Don Demore was the costume designer of "Voyage to the End of
the Universe."

765 "Denial Is the Price Stars Pay for Fame." Screen News, 3
        (37): 2, September 13, 1924.
Colleen Moore spent one month off between films studying the
costumes and customs for the four periods of a woman's life
she will play in "So Big."

766 Denis, Paul. "Scenic, Costume and Lighting Designers," in
        Your Career in Show Business. New York: Dutton, 1948,
        p. 133-9.
Discussion of film-costume design by Aline Bernstein, Raoul Pène du
Bois, and Bonnie Cashin, who recommends that aspiring designers
start their careers apprenticing with a good couturier. Michael
Woulfe obtained a studio contract after establishing his reputation
in two years as a New York fashion designer. Brief mention of
many designers who travel frequently between New York and Hollywood as both fashion and film designers, including Travis Banton,
Don Loper, Max Ree, and others not specifically noted as film
designers.

767 "Dennis, Frances." American Film Institute Catalog, 1961-70,
        p. 167.

Frances Dennis is credited with the wardrobe of "The Red, White and Black."

768 "Dennis, Kathleen." American Film Institute Catalog, 1961-70, p. 167.
Kathleen Dennis is credited with the wardrobe of "Madison Avenue."

769 Denton, Frances. "'Ride, Swim and Dance.'" Photoplay, 19 (6): 55-6, 97, May 1921.
To obtain a job as an extra women should have a complete change of modern wardrobe for every occasion, and men should have a complete wardrobe of the latest fashions. Al Christie's rules for his film company include that one must have dancing and walking shoes with coordinated hats, and sport, street, afternoon, and evening dresses or suits.

770 "De Pinna." American Film Institute Catalog, 1961-70, p. 167.
De Pinna is credited with the clothes of "Light Fantastic."

771 "Derek, John." American Film Institute Catalog, 1961-70, p. 167.
John Derek was the costume designer of "A Boy ... A Girl."

772 "Desideri, Giorgio." American Film Institute Catalog, 1961-70, p. 168.
Giorgio Desideri is credited with the costumes of "The Wonders of Aladdin," "Gladiator of Rome, "The Golden Arrow" (1964), "Torpedo Bay," "Kill or Be Killed," and "Payment in Blood."

773 "Designer." American Magazine, 117 (2): 32, February 1934.
Adrian notes that there will be "keen competition as to who is going to create the popular, big-selling models" between Hollywood and Paris.

774 "Designer, Daisy." American Film Institute Catalog, 1961-70, p. 168.
Daisy Designer is credited with the costumes of "Space Thing."

775 "Designer Edith Head Signs Long-Term Universal Pact." Box Office, 90 (21): W-2, March 13, 1967.
Edith Head will leave Paramount for Universal, effective March 27, 1967. She had already been loaned out to Universal for the costumes worn by Sylva Koscina in "Meanwhile, Far from the Front" and Julie Andrews in "Torn Curtain."

776 "A Designer for Miss Average America." Photoplay, 33 (3): 89, August 1948.
Mary Grant briefly discusses designing for Diana Lynn in "Texas, Brooklyn and Heaven."

777 "The Designer's Dreams Come True." Motion Picture, 28 (7): 30-1, August 1924.
13 sketches and/or stills of costumes worn by Rudolph Valentino,

Bebe Daniels, Lowell Sherman, Lois Wilson, and Doris Kenyon in "Monsieur Beaucaire," by Barbier.

778 "Designs for Women by a Woman." Hollywood Pattern, 7 (1): 8-9, Spring 1938.
Includes sketches of costumes for Shirley Ross, Martha Raye, Dorothy Lamour, and Grace Bradley in "Big Broadcast of 1938," by Edith Head, who discusses designing for them. She notes that the "worst shock" of her film-designing career was seeing an extravagant film costume copied for a daytime dress.

779 "Dessès, Jean." Current Biography. 1956, p. 149-51.
As a child Jean Dessès studied Italian films with a fascination for the costumes. He designed the costumes for "Can-Can" and for Ludmila Tcherina in "Oh Rosalinda."

780 _____. Current Biography (Necrology). 1970, p. 461.

781 _____. Who's Who in America. 28th ed., 1954-5, p. 680.

782 _____. Who's Who in France. 1st ed., 1953-4, p. 271.

783 "Devaud, Ginette." American Film Institute Catalog, 1961-70, p. 169.
Ginette Devaud was the costume designer of "The 300 Spartans."

784 "Devine, Sophie." American Film Institute Catalog, 1961-70, p. 169.
Sophie Devine was the dress designer of "This Sporting Life"; the costume designer of "The Fearless Vampire Killers; or, Pardon Me but Your Teeth Are in My Neck"; and is credited with the costumes of "The Innocents" and the wardrobe of "Burn, Witch, Burn."

785 "Devore, Sy." American Film Institute Catalog, 1961-70, p. 170.
Sy Devore is credited with the wardrobe design for Dean Martin in "The Ambushers" and "The Wrecking Crew," Pat Boone in "The Yellow Canary," and Cameron Mitchell in "Nightmare in Wax"; the men's wardrobe of "The Nutty Professor" and "Three on a Couch"; and the haberdashery of "The Patsy."

786 Dew, Gwen. "Fashion Foreword." Movie Classic, 9 (1): 42, 79, September 1935.
The costumes worn in "The Crusades" are influencing fashion through square necklines, long and flowing lines, velvet fabric, and heavy antique belts. Bernard Newman's costumes for Ginger Rogers in "Top Hat" will also influence fashion.

787 _____. "Fashion Foreword." Movie Classic, 9 (5): 42, 70, January 1936.
Madge Evans models a costume from "Transatlantic Tunnel," designed for 50 years into the future.

788 "Dialogue on Film; Edith Head." American Film, 3 (7): 33-48,
     May 1978.
     Virtually nothing new is said here by or about Edith Head, except
     in regard to two new films, "The Big Fix" and "The Short Night."
     Still, this article is helpful since it includes, in one source, such
     topics as conditions today in costume design--for instance, time
     and budgets for a film; the difference of working with directors
     Alfred Hitchcock, George Roy Hill, Jeremy Paul Kagan, William
     Wyler, and Joseph Mankiewicz; color symbolism, selection, and
     photography; and the importance of Western Costume Company in
     supplying costumes.

789 "Dialogue on Film: George Cukor." American Film, 3 (4): 33-
     48, February 1978.
     The interviewer commented that Greta Garbo's costumes in
     "Camille" seemed to make a statement for each scene; director
     George Cukor approves and comments on the costumes' appropri-
     ateness to scenes in his films. (Asked if it was his idea for Garbo
     to use a handkerchief in the film, he commented, "No, but when
     you're dying of TB it's a handy thing to have.")

790 "Diamonds & The Stars." Picturegoer, 8 (48): 62, December
     1924.
     One costume each is modeled by Huguette Duflos from "Konigs-
     mark," Barbara La Marr from "The Eternal City," and Nita Naldi
     from "Lawful Larceny," with brief and inconsequential comments
     concerning their jewelry.

791 "Di Bari, Dina." American Film Institute Catalog, 1961-70,
     p. 171.
     Dina Di Bari is credited with the costumes of "Divorce--Italian
     Style."

792 Dickens, Homer. The Films of Marlene Dietrich. New York:
     Citadel, 1968.
     The author finds Irene's costumes for Marlene Dietrich in "Seven
     Sinners" wild and often in bad taste, including her jewelry. In
     her New York Herald Tribune column in 1962 fashion editor Eu-
     genia Sheppard described a classic suit worn by Dietrich in "De-
     sire" (she had just watched the film) but found the remaining cos-
     tumes in terrible taste by 1962 standards.

793 "Dickson, Muriel." American Film Institute Catalog, 1961-70,
     p. 172.
     Muriel Dickson is credited with the costumes of "Devils of Dark-
     ness" and was the wardrobe supervisor of "Only Two Can Play"
     and the wardrobe mistress of "Faces in the Dark," "The Ipcress
     File," and "Monique."

794 "Did Balzac Start These Ankle Bracelets?" Screen News, 2
     (30): 21, July 28, 1923.
     Discussion of an ankle bracelet worn by Carmel Myers in "The
     Magic Skin."

795 "Did You Ever Hear a Dream Gown Talking?   Listen to These!"
       Motion Picture, 47 (2): 44-5, March 1934.
     Veree Teasdale and Virginia Dabney model one gown each from
     "Fashions of 1934."

796 Dietrich, Marlene, as told to Howard Carter.   "I'd Rather Wear
       Rags!" Motion Picture, 67 (4): 48-9, 107, May 1944.
     A somewhat astonishing article, in which Marlene Dietrich claims
     that though her film costumes have been spectacular, they have
     always been inappropriate and often in poor taste.   She feels that
     being glamorous can hinder one's dramatic ability and the audience's
     acceptance of the performance; she would have preferred some
     shabbily dressed roles.

797 Dietrich, Noah, and Bob Thomas.   Howard, the Amazing Mr.
       Hughes.   Greenwich, Connecticut: Fawcett, 1972.
     As Howard Hughes took over RKO he began approving all costumes;
     he wrote a lengthy memo after viewing wardrobe tests of Jane
     Russell in "Macao" (actually Russell's costumes in "The Outlaw").
     The memo was sent to several RKO personnel, including the ward-
     robe woman, who was allowed only to read the memo several times
     so that it could be destroyed lest the subject seem indelicate or
     unkind.   One metallic dress worn by Russell was fine, though
     high-necked, but Hughes wanted the remainder of her dresses to
     be "as low as the law allows" and as tight as possible around her
     bosom "so that the customers can get a look at the part of Russell
     which they pay to see...." Hughes recommended at length the
     design and construction of a brassiere that would allow her breasts
     to be well supported and revealed, either through a "half-brassiere"
     or one made of very thin fabric.   (In both the biography of Hughes
     by Albert B. Gerber and in the television film "The Amazing
     Howard Hughes" [1977], based on Dietrich's book, the above infor-
     mation is attributed to Russell's costumes in "The Outlaw".)

798 "Dietrich on Display!" Photoplay, 54 (12): 56, December 1940.
     Marlene Dietrich models seven costumes from "Seven Sinners."

799 Dietz, Howard. Dancing in the Dark.   Words by Howard Dietz.
       An Autobiography.   New York: Quadrangle/New York
       Times, 1974.
     The few references to Howard Dietz's third wife, film and the-
     atrical costume designer Lucinda Ballard, are inconsequential.

800 "Diliberto, Carolyn." American Film Institute Catalog, 1961-
       70, p. 172.
     Carolyn Diliberto is credited with the wardrobe of "How to Make
     It."

801 Dillon, Franc.   "Shirley Temple, Saver of Lives." Modern
       Screen, 12 (1): 26-7, 78-9, December 1935.
     Three seamstresses are employed nearly year round for Shirley
     Temple's film costumes, designed by Rene Hubert; each dress
     averages $35-$45.   Miss Temple is allowed to keep them after

each film since the studio does not need a stock of them in her size. Discussion of some of her costumes for "Curly Top," four of which she models.

802 "Dimitrovová, Olga." American Film Institute Catalog, 1961-
       70, p. 173.
Olga Dimitrovová is credited with the wardrobe of "Closely Watched Trains" and the costumes of "Capricious Summer."

803 "Dimmitt, Joseph." American Film Institute Catalog, 1961-70,
       p. 173.
Joseph Dimmitt is credited with the costumes of "The Silent Call" and "Winter A-Go-Go" and the wardrobe of "20,000 Eyes," "Rider on a Dead Horse," "Raiders from Beneath the Sea," "Arizona Raiders," "Wild on the Beach," and "40 Guns to Apache Pass."

804 Dior, Christian. Christian Dior and I. Translated by Antonia
       Fraser. New York: Dutton, 1957.
Christian Dior notes that although he has designed for films and the theater, he never found it very pleasurable because of the need for improvisation at the cost of craftsmanship. He has the temperament of a fashion designer rather than a costume designer.

805 "Dior, Christian." American Film Institute Catalog, 1961-70,
       p. 173.
Christian Dior is credited with the Paris originals of "A New Kind of Love," the gowns of "The Cheaters" and for Ingrid Bergman in "Goodbye Again"; the wardrobe of "You Only Love Once" and for Sophia Loren in "Arabesque" and Elizabeth Taylor in "Secret Ceremony"; Olivia de Havilland's costumes in "Light in the Piazza"; the clothes for Gina Lollobrigida in "Woman of Straw" and Moira Lister in "The Double Man"; and the dresses for Sophia Loren in "Yesterday, Today and Tomorrow" and Samantha Eggar and Stéphane Audran in "The Lady in the Car with Glasses and a Gun." (See also "Bohan, Marc.")

806 "Dior, Christian." Current Biography. 1948, p. 147-8.

806a "The Dirt on 'Poseidon.'" Los Angeles Times, January 1, 1973,
       sec. 4, p. 12.
Paul Zastupnevich, the costume designer of "The Poseidon Adventure," had a problem with the modern wash-and-wear fabrics since they kept appearing clean and dry when photographed. Eric Shea's clothes were doused with mineral oil to make them look wet. A minimum of six copies were required for each garment to show the continual deterioration.

807 "Discuss Screen Fashions." New York Times, March 24,
       1933, p. 14.
After hearing Adelia Bird (fashion editor of Photoplay) and Ruth Katash (of the "Cinema Shop" at R. H. Macy and Company) promote Hollywood as a fashion center, and designer Elizabeth Hawes oppose its influence, the Fashion Group in New York voted that

Hollywood fashions are most influential in promoting specific styles and that Hollywood is not a fashion "creative center." Hawes said that no "fundamental style" had been promoted from Hollywood; Katash said that the fashions were "different at any cost," and Bird that the stores were eager for Hollywood fashions.

808 "Do Costume Pictures Influence Styles?" Motion Picture Studio Insider, 2 (1): 46, 62, January 1937.
Walter Plunkett discusses the extent to which his costumes for Katharine Hepburn in "Quality Street," "Mary of Scotland," "A Woman Rebels," and "Little Women" have influenced fashion. He believes that Paris and costume pictures have the most radical influence on fashion. Includes sketches and stills of Hepburn in costumes from "Quality Street."

809 "Do You Know--." Screen News, 2 (52): 17, December 29, 1923.
Norma Talmadge wore seven hoop skirts in "Secrets." Schenk studio designer Clare West has ordered Emily Fitzroy not to sit down for the sake of her bustles for a film set in 1888, not named ("Secrets," though she was in the 1865 sequence).

810 "Do You Pick Flaws in Movies?" Screen News, 3 (34): 18, August 23, 1924.
Errors are often caused in movies because scenes are not filmed in the same sequence as they will appear on the screen. For example, an actress may be filmed outside a house and yet not be filmed inside it for several weeks, yet her appearance must be alike in every detail.

811 "Dobrovolskaya, Ya." American Film Institute Catalog, 1961-70, p.175.
Ya. Dobrovolskaya is credited with the costumes of "Song of the Forest."

812 Dodson, Mary Kay. "Glamour by Candlelight." Silver Screen, 18 (8): 46-7, 68-9, June 1948.
Mary Kay Dodson discusses many of the costumes she designed for Audrey Totter in "The Saxon Charm." Totter models five of the costumes. With two original sketches.

813 _____. "Practical, Individual and Smart." Silver Screen, 17 (7): 52-3, 88-9, May 1947.
Mary Kay Dodson had contract offers from three studios as a costume designer before signing with Paramount. She discusses her costumes for Virginia Welles in "Ladies' Man"; Paulette Goddard, who models three costumes, and Arleen Whelan, who models two, one from "Suddenly It's Spring" and a bathing suit worn in "Catalina."

814 "Doelnitz, Marc." American Film Institute Catalog, 1961-70, p.175.
Marc Doelnitz was the wardrobe designer of "Vice and Virtue"

and is credited with the costumes of "Zazie" and "Circle of Love."

815 "Does Color Enhance Dramatic Realism?" Moving Picture
World, 29 (1): 84, July 1, 1916.
J. A. Berst, the Vice President and General Manager of Pathé,
had "A Matrimonial Martyr" specially color processed, in part
because of the summer dresses worn by Ruth Roland.

816 "Does Hollywood Create?" Vogue, 81 (3): 59-61, 76-7, February 1, 1933.
A thorough and competent discussion of whether Hollywood or
Paris has been influencing fashion the most. Analyses of costumes designed by Adrian, Howard Greer, and Hattie Carnegie,
who designs all of Constance Bennett's clothes; of costumes worn
by Katharine Hepburn, Norma Shearer, Lilyan Tashman, and Kay
Francis; and of Marlene Dietrich in "Morocco" and Greta Garbo
in "Mata Hari" and "Grand Hotel."

817 "Does Hollywood Set the Styles?" Motion Picture Studio Insider, 2 (2): 46, 56, April 1937.
Travis Banton feels that too often Hollywood receives credit for
styles it did not start, and deplores the fads caused by historical
costumes influencing modern fashion, though he did adapt some
costumes from "Souls at Sea." He discusses costumes worn in
"Champagne Waltz"; by Carole Lombard in "Swing High Swing
Low"; by Frances Dee, Gary Cooper, Virginia Weidler, Tully
Marshall, Frances Dee, Olympe Bradna, and Cecil Cunningham,
all in "Souls at Sea"; and the coming of Technicolor films.

818 "Donati, Danilo." American Film Institute Catalog, 1961-70,
p. 176-7.
Danilo Donati was the costume designer of "The Taming of the
Shrew" (1967) and "Romeo and Juliet" (1968), and is credited with
the wardrobe of "The Steppe" and the costumes of "The Gospel
According to St. Matthew," "El Greco," "Mandragola," "The
Hawks and the Sparrows," "On My Way to the Crusades, I Met
a Girl Who ...," "Fellini Satyricon," and "The Lady of Monza."

819 Donfeld. "Donfeld on Design." Show, 1 (7): 44-5, June 25,
1970.
Donfeld, who spent six months researching the costumes of "They
Shoot Horses, Don't They?," discusses the influence on fashion
of film costumes of the 1930s, and as worn in the period films
"The Damned" and "Bonnie and Clyde." Includes three stills of
Jane Fonda and one of Susannah York from "They Shoot Horses."

820 "Donfeld." American Film Institute Catalog, 1961-70, p. 177.
Donfeld was the costume designer of "The Cincinnati Kid," "The
Chase," "The April Fools," and "They Shoot Horses, Don't They?"
and is credited with the costumes of "Hombre," "Luv," and "The
Phynx" and the wardrobe of "Don't Make Waves" and for Jacqueline Bisset in "The Grasshopper" and Ingrid Bergman in "A Walk
in the Spring Rain."

821 Donnell, Dorothy. "Are You a Screen Shopper?" Motion
           Picture, 40 (2): 70-1, 114, 117, September 1930.
     Discussion of the influence of films on the purchases of the audi-
     ence. The fashion discussion is limited to short-reel fashion
     shows seen in "Fashion Features," conceived by Meredith Fulton
     and George Gibson. Film actresses model fashions that were not
     originated in Hollywood but that have considerable influence upon
     the audience.

822 _____. "Sex Appeal and the Clothes You Wear." Motion
           Picture, 47 (3): 28-31, 74, 76, April 1934.
     Discussion by Charles Le Maire, Orry-Kelly, Adrian, and Travis
     Banton concerning the trend in brief costumes and how it will
     influence fashion. Charles Le Maire is covering up the chorus
     girls in "George White's 1935 Scandals." Some of Orry-Kelly's
     film costumes and some of Adrian's costumes for Greta Garbo in
     "Queen Christina" are being adapted for retail sale by Studio
     Styles.

823 _____. "Will They Soon Be Dressing Like Mother Eve?"
           Motion Picture Classic, 26 (5): 16-7, 70, January 1928.
     Alice Day and Betty Bronson lost their film contracts because they
     would not wear skimpy costumes. Most actresses do, as dis-
     cussed, with brief mention of costumes worn by Lois Weber in
     "The Naked Truth," Leatrice Joy in "Madame Eve," Corinne
     Griffith in "The Garden of Eden," and Sue Carol in "Soft Cush-
     ions" and also worn in "The Private Life of Helen of Troy,"
     "The Volga Boatman," "The Triumph of Venus," and "Daughter
     of Neptune."

824 _____, Dorothy Calhoun. "Styles Are Dictated in Hollywood
           and Paris Designers Follow Them." Motion Picture,
           29 (2): 28-9, 110-1, 116-7, March 1925.
     Discussion of the influence of film costume on American and
     Parisian fashion. Ethel Chaffin discusses film-costume design,
     as with Paulette Duval's costumes in "Cheaper to Marry" (with
     one sketch of Duval). Howard Greer discusses designing for
     Betty Compson in "Locked Doors" (with one sketch) and for
     Dorothy Cummings in "The Female." Corinne Griffith purchased
     her wardrobe for "Declassé" on Fifth Avenue (see also "'Declassé'
     Shows New Gown Styles."). Clare West, credited as the first
     studio designer with "Intolerance," discusses a costume worn by
     Claire Windsor in "For Sale" and some of her 34 costumes for
     Mae Murray in "The Merry Widow." (The credits of this film are
     at best confusing. The American Film Institute Catalog credits
     Erich von Stroheim and Richard Day with the film's costumes.
     Murray's biographer, Jane Kesner Ardmore, and the authors of
     Hollywood Costume credit Adrian. In this article and in Holly-
     wood Costume Design, Clare West receives credit. Costume De-
     sign in the Movies does not include the film.)

825 _____. "The Sennett School for Girls." Motion Picture,
           30 (6): 36-8, 113, 115, January 1926.

Mack Sennett discusses the qualities needed to be a screen beauty, for instance the ability to wear clothing correctly. Costume tests are part of the decision-making process before an actress is hired.

826 _____. "What Do the Film Stars Do with All Their Old Clothes?" Motion Picture, 29 (3): 32-3, 116, April 1925. Most actors have about 25 suits to wear in their films; Rudolph Valentino has 40. Holmes Herbert spent $40,000 on his wardrobe in the previous year. Famous Players studios auctions off their film costumes. Pola Negri usually wears hers out, Louise Fazenda gives hers away, Betty Blythe wears them in her personal life, and other stars send them to fans. (See also items by Dorothy Calhoun.)

827 Donovan, Maria. "How to Get That Smooth Look...." Silver Screen, 19 (6): 46-7, 73, April 1949. Maria Donovan discusses designing the costumes for Ella Raines in "Impact," six of which Raines models.

828 "Dont [sic] All Speak at Once!" Motion Picture, 31 (5): 42, June 1926. Corinne Griffith appears in four costumes from "Mademoiselle Modiste."

829 "Don't Be Crewel." People Weekly, 6 (12): 98, September 20, 1976. Gossipy report of a feud begun between designers Edith Head and Burton Miller when they collaborated on the costumes for "Airport 1977." Head was to design for the actresses and Miller for the actors, but actress Lee Grant asked Miller to design her costumes, causing the problem.

830 "Doris of Mariposa." American Film Institute Catalog, 1961-70, p. 178. Doris of Mariposa is credited with the wardrobe of "Doctor, I'm Coming!"

831 "Doris Pawn." Screen News, 1 (14): 22, May 27, 1922. Doris Pawn models an evening gown from "One Clear Call."

832 "Dorothy Gish in 'The Bright Shawl.' " Screen News, 1 (43): 8, December 16, 1922. Dorothy Gish researches her roles before a film begins production, as with "The Bright Shawl." Her costumes are faithful copies from those of 1850, and she will wear a shawl that is almost two centuries old.

833 "Dorothy Lamour: Mrs. William Howard Always Carries a Sarong." Photoplay, 82 (1): 60-1, 106, 110, 113, July 1972. Dorothy Lamour would like to be remembered for more than her sarongs since she wore them in only eight of her 60 films. She was, however, proud to have one displayed in a Smithsonian Institution exhibit.

834 "Dorothy Mackaill Wears Some Gorgeous Creations...." Screen
        News, 4 (42): 9, October 24, 1925, col. 3.
     Dorothy Mackaill designed most of her costumes for "Joanna."

835 "Dorothy Mackaill's Idea of What a Well-Dressed Star Wears
        on the Screen." Motion Picture, 42 (5): 64-5, December
        1931.
     Dorothy Mackaill models four costumes from an unnamed film.

836 "Dorothy Malone." Movie Fan, 3 (2): 59, July-August-
        September 1948.
     Dorothy Malone models a western costume by Leah Rhodes from
     "Two Guys from Texas."

837 "Dorothy Phillips, Famous Screen Artiste...." Screen News,
        2 (6): 23, February 10, 1923, col. 1.
     Mme. Yvonne Le Croix, of Paris, has created a $2,500 skating
     costume for Dorothy Phillips to wear in "Slander the Woman,"
     made of broadcloth fabric with white astrakhan trim.

838 Dove, Billie. "Among My New Costumes." Hollywood, 18
        (13): 20, December 1929.
     Billie Dove models four costumes from "The Other Tomorrow"
     and discusses the hemline lengths of the costumes.

839 "Dragonwyck." Motion Picture, 71 (3): 50, April 1946.
     Gene Tierney was eventually able to discard the heavy, whaleboned
     corsets needed for authentic costumes of the mid-1800s when it
     was found that she could fit easily into her costumes for "Dragon-
     wyck."

840 "Drama for Autumn." Hollywood, 26 (11): 45, November 1937.
     One gown each is modeled by Pat Paterson from "52nd Street"
     and Betty Douglas from "Vogues of 1938."

841 "Drama in Design." Silver Screen, 11 (3): 52-5, January 1941.
     Carole Lombard models six costumes by Irene from "Mr. and
     Mrs. Smith."

842 "The Dream Wizards." Newsweek, 89 (22): 61, 63, May 30,
        1977.
     The "wookiee" costume of "Star Wars" was designed by makeup
     artist Stuart Freeborn. Director George Lucas decided not to
     film any scenes on the wookiee planet because of the enormous
     cost of 300 wookiee costumes.

843 " 'The Dreamers' at Work." Screen Romances, 13 (74): 26,
        July 1935.
     Stills of Verree Teasdale in a 145-pound mesh costume; James
     Cagney, whose costume is being repaired; and Joe E. Brown cos-
     tumed as Flute, all from "A Midsummer Night's Dream."

844 "Drecol." American Film Institute Catalog, 1921-30, p.1062.
     Drecol is credited with the gowns of "The Recoil."

845 "Dress and the Picture." Moving Picture World, 7 (2): 73-4,
         July 9, 1910.
     Moving pictures suffer from being considered a lower-class form
     of entertainment, though the theater remains popular. Theater
     fashions are often reported the following morning in the news-
     papers; such publicity should also help moving pictures become
     more popular since women will go to see the latest fashions and
     refined people will go to see other refined people dressed real-
     istically and dignified.

846 "Dress Like Claudette Colbert!" Silver Screen, 2 (12): 45,
         October 1932.
     Claudette Colbert models a costume from "The Phantom President,"
     a pattern of which can be ordered.

847 "Dress Rehearsal." Motion Picture, 59 (4): 40-1, May 1940.
     Zorina models eight costumes by Royer from "I Was an Adventuress."

848 "Dressed for Action." Screenland, 50 (1): 52-3, November
         1945.
     Esther Williams models six Spanish-influenced costumes from her
     new film, "Fiesta."

849 "Dressed Up and Ready to Invade London." Screen News, 2
         (32): 27, August 11, 1923.
     Matt Moore has spent "two tons sterling" on his clothes for
     "Strangers of the Night," which he ordered by cable through a
     Bond Street tailor.

850 "Dressed Women." It, 16 (4): 15, May 1, 1919.
     Universal Studios has hired Irene Duncan, formerly with Bon Ton
     of New York, to head the staff of 11 wardrobe persons; she has
     been given an unlimited budget.

851 "Dresses Worth $1,600 Were Stolen...." Screen News, 1 (34):
         14, October 14, 1922, col. 3.
     Priscilla Dean's costumes for "White Tiger" were stolen from
     her dressing room and are being duplicated as police try to find
     the originals.

852 "Dressing a Picture Serious Problem: Miss Anita Stewart Talks
         About Actress' Clothes." Screen News, 1 (4): 7, 18,
         March 18, 1922.
     Anita Stewart discusses problems she encountered in purchasing
     enough costumes in New York for "Playthings of Destiny" and
     "The Invisible Fear," in which she wore over 25 costumes.

853 "Dressing for the Movies." Photoplay, 7 (2): 117-20, January
         1915.
     The most important contribution an actress may make to her films
     is often the care and research she uses in selecting her costumes.
     By making a "dress plot" from the script, she must then either
     sew or order her costumes. The studio provides historical cos-

tumes. Clara Kimball Young, Barbara Tennant, Margarita Fischer, Adele Lane, and others discuss color selection and psychology in relation to their film-costume selections.

854   "Dressing for the Movies." Photoplay, 7 (3): 115-8, February
         1915.
      Six actresses model gowns from their current movies, including Frances M. Nelson from "Ambition" and Vivian Martin from "The Wishing Ring"; the others without titles.

855   "Dressing for the Movies." Photoplay, 7 (4): 111-3, March
         1915.
      Beverly Bayne considers herself one of the best-dressed actresses in the movies.

856   "The Dressing Room." It, 2 (3): 12, February 1, 1920.
      Discussion of many of the gowns worn by Louise Glaum in "Sex," which she designed and her modiste made.

857   "Dressing the Part." Movies, 5 (3): 38, September, 1941.
      Ten stills show Jack Benny being fitted into his period gown for "Charley's Aunt," designed by Travis Banton--from his whale-boned corset to his lace and ruffled petticoat.

858   "Dressing the Part." What's Happening in Hollywood, 12: n. p.,
         November 27, 1943.
      Discussion of many films currently being costumed, including Jennifer Jones in "Song of Bernadette," Joan Fontaine in "Jane Eyre," Merle Oberon in "The Lodger," and "Wilson," all by Rene Hubert. Actresses are no longer trendsetting, since the war has brought about a change in the type of roles they play, with less stress on glamour.

859   "Dressing the Stars." Christian Science Monitor, April 2,
         1959, p. 8.
      Excerpts included from Edith Head's The Dress Doctor, concerning Mary Martin and Betty Hutton in "The Stork Club."

860   "Dressing to Type." Motion Picture, 72 (2): 42-3, September
         1946.
      Lauren Bacall models a gown by Leah Rhodes from "The Big Sleep."

861   "Dressmaker, Painter, Architect, Suggested for Movie Con-
         ference." Screen News, 2 (17): 31, April 28, 1923.
      Adolph Zukor, President of Famous Players-Lasky, is gathering lecturers to attend an international conference on motion pictures. It has been suggested by Paul Iribe that three Frenchmen be in-cluded, including dressmaker (or couturier) Paul Poiret.

862   Drew, Janice. "Colorful Wools to Keep You Cozy." Silver
         Screen, 14 (12): 52-3, October 1944.
      Trudy Marshall models one costume from "Ladies in Washington."

863 "Drury, Joe." <u>American Film Institute Catalog, 1961-70</u>, p.
       181.
     Joe Drury is credited with the costumes of "The Scalphunters."

864 Dryden, Ernst. "Actresses Can Look Like People." <u>Screen</u>
       <u>Guilds' Magazine</u>, 3 (4): 11, 28, June 1936.
     In a previous article written by Bette Davis (see "Where Did You
     Get That Hat?"), she stated that actresses seldom look like real
     people. Designer Ernst Dryden agrees and attributes this to an
     inferiority complex on the part of the actresses, who overcom-
     pensate by wearing outlandish costumes. Some of the blame also
     falls on the directors, producers, and designers. He also dis-
     cusses the three main types of dress--modern, period, and fantasy,
     with brief mention of his fantasy costumes for "Lost Horizon."

865 "Dubois, Ilse." <u>American Film Institute Catalog, 1961-70</u>, p.
       182.
     Ilse Dubois is credited with the costumes of "Situation Hopeless--
     But Not Serious" and "Unwilling Agent."

866 "Du Bois, Raoul Pène." <u>Who's Who in the Theatre</u>. 16th ed.,
       1977, p.563.
     Raoul Pène du Bois was a film-costume designer from 1941 to
     1945, three credits of which are listed--"Louisiana Purchase,"
     "Lady in the Dark," and "Dixie."

867 Dudley, Fredda. "Donkeys for Diversion." <u>Hollywood</u>, 31 (4):
       56-7, April 1942.
     Biographical information on Edith Head, who had recently designed
     five hostess gowns and a pair of pajamas for Betty Field in "Mr.
     and Mrs. Cugat."

868 _____. "Dress Like a Movie Star!" <u>Screenland</u>, 52 (6):
       22-3, 81-2, April 1948.
     Betty Hutton models two costumes from "Dream Girl," with three
     additional sketches of costumes by Edith Head. Head is currently
     teaching costume design at UCLA. She discusses current fashions,
     which she feels should not be faddish--for example, the fad for the
     Empress Eugenie hat worn by Greta Garbo in "Romance."

869 Duer, Caroline. "Modes and Manners--in Current Films."
       <u>Stage</u>, 14 (3): 102-3, December 1936.
     The author discusses how Hollywood modernizes historical films,
     and does it so poorly, as with the costumes worn in "Mary of
     Scotland" and with costumes worn by domestic servants in many
     films.

870 Duff Gordon, Lady Lucile. <u>Discretions & Indiscretions</u>.
       London: Jarrolds; New York: Stokes, 1932.
     Reminiscences of Lady Lucy Christiana Duff Gordon, who went
     from designing and constructing her own clothes at home to es-
     tablishing "Maison Lucile" in London, Paris, New York, and
     Chicago. At one time she was designing for all of Ziegfeld's

productions and most of the film stars, though here she discusses briefly only designing for Mary Pickford and Betty Blythe in unnamed films. She will perhaps best be remembered for her striking and innovative changes in early-twentieth-century women's fashions. Some of her innovations include freeing women from steel or whalebone-reinforced high collars, which often scarred the neck, and from corsets in favor of brassieres. Both changes allowed women to appear more natural and to be more comfortable. Other innovations included beautiful and daring underclothes of chiffon and lace rather than of the customary linen and wool; split skirts that revealed women's legs; colored wigs; mannequin or dress parades (or "fashion shows") in which women actually moved, which led to the concept of the "show girl" in the Ziegfeld Follies; and the introduction of the word "chic" into the English language. One of the greatest mistakes she made was turning over the financial management of "Lucile" to a manufacturer so that she might tend to the creative aspects. The wealth and fashion empire that she had spent decades building was eventually lost and "Lucile" bankrupted. She then turned to writing fashion articles and her autobiography, which describes in detail her survival of the sinking of the <u>Titanic</u>.

871   Duggan, Louise. "Hot from Paris: Mlle. Chanel Tells Hollywood and You How to Dress." <u>Motion Picture Classic</u>, 33 (4): 29, June 1931.
Gabrielle Chanel has been hired by Samuel Goldwyn, with plans of establishing a branch of the House of Chanel at the United Artist studios, to be managed by her associate, Madame Magna. Chanel states that she had never costumed an actress before and never had time to visit the cinema. The author notes that, unlike Romain de Tirtoff Erté, "Chanel does not pull any artistic stuff about 'inspiration.'"

872   "Dunayeva, I." <u>American Film Institute Catalog, 1961-70</u>, p. 183.
I. Dunayeva is credited with the costumes of "House with An Attic."

873   Dunn, Theodora. "Screen Fashions." <u>Photo-Play World</u>, 2 (6): 41-3, February 1919.
An unnamed actress models pajamas from "Too Many Millions."

874   "Dunne--in the Romantic Mood." <u>Motion Picture</u>, 69 (1): 58, February 1945.
Irene Dunne models three costumes from "Together Again," by Jean Louis.

875   Dunne, John Gregory. <u>The Studio.</u> New York: Farrar, Straus and Giroux, 1969.
The author spent a year behind the scenes at Twentieth Century-Fox studios. Richard Zanuck, son of Darryl--the former studio chief, once lost a lot of money on a Gary Cooper comedy film, allegedly because Cooper's hat was too small. William Travilla

discusses making the custom-tailored work clothes for Tony Curtis
in "The Boston Strangler." Julie Andrews wore $200,000 worth
of jewelry from Cartier's in "Star!," some of which is described
here.   Also discussed are problems with a gown by Irene Sharaff
worn by Barbra Streisand in "Hello, Dolly!" and problems with
a bathing suit worn by Jacqueline Bisset in "The Sweet Ride."
An inaccuracy in "From the Terrace" was that the actors wore
white dinner jackets while portraying wealthy men in Southampton.
Rex Harrison wore two different costumes in one sequence in
"Dr. Dolittle," but it was left in since it was assumed that no
one would notice. The promotion of "Dr. Dolittle" included the
marketing of such items as hats, watches, sewing sets, and costumes.   How costumes fit into "below-the-line" expenditures is
discussed; and it is noted that Sid Mintz was Jack Oakie's wardrobe man.

876   "Dupont, Jacques." American Film Institute Catalog, 1961-70,
         p. 184.
Jacques Dupont was the costume designer of "Hotel Paradiso" and
is credited with the costumes of "The Lovers of Teruel."

877   "Duquette, Tony." Biographical Encyclopaedia and Who's Who
         of the American Theatre. 1966, p. 426.
Biographical information on Tony Duquette, whose film credits
include the costumes for the ballet sequence of "Yolanda and the
Thief," "Lovely to Look At" (the chorus costumes), "Kismet"
(1955), and the design and execution of costumes for "The Four
Horsemen of the Apocalypse" (1962; he did not receive credit for
this in the American Film Institute Catalog).

878   "During the Production of 'East Lynne'...." Screen News, 4
         (47): 12, November 28, 1925, col. 3.
The typical woman's costume worn in "East Lynne" was made of
28-32 yards of fabric, with a train of an additional six yards.

879   Durling, E. V. "Film Fact and Fable." Screen News, 1 (27):
         25, August 26, 1922.
The only work Rudolph Valentino wants his wife, Natacha Rambova, to do is to assist occasionally in designing his costumes.

880   "Duse, Anna." American Film Institute Catalog, 1961-70, p.
         185.
Anna Duse was the costume designer of "The Chairman" and
"Decline and Fall ... of a Bird Watcher" and is credited with the
costumes of "That Riviera Touch."

881   "Dushina, L." American Film Institute Catalog, 1961-70, p.
         185.
L. Dushina is credited with the costumes of "A Night Before
Christmas."

882 "Each of Crawford's Films Leaves Its Mark on Fashions."
MGM Studio News, 2 (13): n.p., September 24, 1935.
A survey was made of international fashions, and Adrian's costumes for Joan Crawford were found to be widely adopted; Adrian
attributes this to young American women who want to be like
Crawford. Fashion trends created by her films include extra-
wide lapels from "Today We Live," shorter skirts from "Chained,"
modernized hoop skirts from "Forsaking All Others," the necklines of "No More Ladies," and a polo coat of metallic fabric
and an envelope evening bag from "I Live My Life."

883 Easton, Carol. The Search for Sam Goldwyn: A Biography.
New York: Morrow, 1976.
For the Goldwyn Girls, Sam Goldwyn bought lavish costumes, for
example, $45 plain sandals, spending large sums as Florenz
Ziegfeld had done with his Ziegfeld Girls. Goldwyn hated the
bustle and liked Merle Oberon's shoulders, so he advanced the
period of "Wuthering Heights" forty years to 1841 (bustles were
in fact not worn in the early 1800s). He also spent thousands
on each of Virginia Mayo's costumes in "Up in Arms," designed
by Adrian. Edith Head once worked in the prop room washing
stockings when working for Cecil B. De Mille (undoubtedly at the
start of her career!). Omar Kiam, a member of the Gimbel
family (of the New York department store), was fired from the
Goldwyn studio when he got drunk at a Goldwyn party. William
Wyler had Irene Sharaff barred from the set of "Glory for Me"
(later titled "The Best Years of Our Lives") because she was
neither suited to nor willing to design simple clothes, as for
Teresa Wright. Sharaff was also barred from the lot and fired
by Goldwyn at this time. She was brought back for "The Secret
Life of Walter Mitty," though Goldwyn felt that some of Virginia
Mayo's costumes were improper. Mary Wills became Sharaff's
assistant in 1945 and became the chief designer when Sharaff left
in 1947; Wills left in 1952. Wills discusses at length working
with Sam Goldwyn and his mediator and wife, Frances; Edith
Head's and her own costumes for Teresa Wright in "Enchantment";
and, briefly, her costumes for June Havoc in "Our Very Own"
and Virginia Mayo in "Ball of Fire." Walter Brennan was so
thin during the filming of "Barbary Coast" that muscles were built
into his costumes.

884   "Easy Lies the Head That Wears a Pith Helmet." Screen News,
        3 (36): 12, September 6, 1924, col. 1.
      A pith helmet will be worn by both Milton Sills in "Pandora La
      Croix" and Frank Mayo in "If I Marry Again."

885   "Eckart, Jean." Biographical Encyclopaedia and Who's Who of
        the American Theatre. 1966, p.429.
      Biographical information on Jean Eckart, who designed the cos-
      tumes for "The Pajama Game."

886   "Eckart, Jean (née Jean Levy)." Who's Who in the Theatre.
        16th ed., 1977, p.574.
      Film-costume design credits listed for Jean Eckart include "Damn
      Yankees" and "The Night They Raided Minsky's" (the American
      Film Institute Catalog listed Anna Hill Johnstone as the costume
      designer and the Eckarts as the production designers for the
      latter film).

887   "Eckart, William J." Who's Who in the Theatre. 16th ed.,
        1977, p.574-5.
      William J. Eckart's film-costume design credits are the same as
      those for his wife, Jean--"The Pajama Game," "Damn Yankee,"
      and "The Night They Raided Minsky's." See previous entry.

888   "Eckart, William Joseph." Biographical Encyclopaedia and
        Who's Who of the American Theatre. 1966, p.429.

889   "Edith Head--Biography." Motion Picture News (Press De-
        partment, Universal Studios). Circa 1977, 4p.
      Edith Head--costume designer, coordinator of film-costume fashion
      shows, fashion editor, lecturer, and author--was a schoolteacher
      after completing B.A. and M.A. degrees in foreign languages.
      She has since designed for five studios and over 1,000 films.

890   Edith Head Collection #104: Costume Workbook for "Butch
        Cassidy and the Sundance Kid." (Housed in the University
        of Southern California Special Collections Library.)
        Circa 1969.
      Edith Head donated to the university library the workbook com-
      piled for the research and designing of the costumes of "Butch
      Cassidy and the Sundance Kid." Consists of the men's and
      women's costume plot, and the script with per-scene requirements.
      For Etta Place (Kathryn Ross) only, there are photos of the
      original sketches with fabric swatches attached.

891   "Edith Head Says...." Photoplay, 32 (3): 98, February 1948.
      A dress by Edith Head for Betty Hutton in "Dream Girl" has been
      sketched, with additional sketches of how it has been adapted for
      other actresses (no film titles given).

892   "Edith Roberts in ... 'The Dangerous Age'...." Screen News,
        1 (40): 27, November 25, 1922, col. 3.
      Edith Roberts models a gown from "The Dangerous Age," with

detailed description. (The following two entries show her modeling different gowns.)

893 "Edith Roberts in ... 'The Dangerous Age'...." Screen News,
        1 (41): 14, December 2, 1922, col. 1.

894 "Edith Roberts in ... 'The Dangerous Age'...." Screen News,
        1 (42): 7, December 9, 1922, cols. 1-3.

895 "Edith, Who Protects the Working Girl." Photoplay, 31 (5):
        88, 91, October 1947.
     Edith Head discusses designing costumes for Joan Caulfield in
     "Welcome Stranger" and "Dear Ruth" and for Lizabeth Scott in
     "Desert Fury."

896 The Editors of Photoplay. "For the Last Time We Say: Carroll,
        Put Your Clothes On--Your Talent Is More Than Skin Deep!"
        Photoplay, 68 (1): 56-7, 90-1, July 1965.
     The editors, with the support of many readers, think that Carroll
     Baker ought to dress more modestly in her films, as in "Baby
     Doll," when she wore a dress that she thinks probably cost 98
     cents. Baker felt that wearing a $900 black-beaded gown (in "The
     Big Country") was sexier than appearing nude.

897 "Edna Mayo's Latest Gown by Lucille [sic]." Motion Picture,
        11 (2): 48-9, December 1916.
     Edna Mayo models four gowns by Lucile from "The Strange Case
     of Mary Page."

898 Edwards, Anne. Vivien Leigh. New York: Simon and Schuster,
        1977.
     The opening scene of "Gone with the Wind" was reshot so that
     Vivien Leigh would appear virginal in a white ruffled gown, de-
     signed by Walter Plunkett. She originally had worn the green
     sprig muslin gown that she wore to the party in the next sequence.
     Leigh did not appreciate director Victor Fleming's request that
     she look bustier, which required that her bosom be taped
     for deeper cleavage. For "Caesar and Cleopatra" she wore thin
     gowns in the cold weather, which was meant to appear stifling
     hot, resulting in a serious illness. For "Anna Karenina" (1947) she
     and designer Cecil Beaton traveled to Paris for fabrics that Lon-
     don couturiers did not have. She then had to wear furs and heavy
     costumes in the stifling heat during filming. Lucinda Ballard, her
     costume designer for "A Streetcar Named Desire," flew to Eng-
     land, where they approved the sketches; they became lifelong
     friends, as Leigh did with designer Bumble Dawson (though they
     never worked together). Leigh's costumes for "The Roman
     Spring of Mrs. Stone" were designed by Pierre Balmain and fitted
     in Paris.

899 "Edwards, Bill." American Film Institute Catalog, 1961-70,
        p. 189.
     Bill Edwards is credited with the wardrobe of "The Clown and the
     Kid" and "The Cat."

900   "Edwards, Sally." American Film Institute Catalog, 1961-70,
             p. 189.
       Sally Edwards is credited with the wardrobe of "Harper."

901   "Egidi, Carlo." American Film Institute Catalog, 1961-70,
             p. 190.
       Carlo Egidi is credited as the costumer of "Seduced and Aban-
       doned," with his assistants being Angela Sammaciccia and Lilli
       Menichelli credited respectively for costumes and assistant cos-
       tumes.

901a   "The Egyptian Influence in Dress Makes Erté's Designs for the
             'Restless Sex' Most Interesting." Harper's Bazaar, 55
             (4): 66-7, April 1920.
       Presented are nine of Erté's sketches for costumes of deities
       as worn in the ball sequence of "Restless Sex," without identifi-
       cation of the persons for whom they were designed.

902   Ehren, France. "Jacob Had the Right Idea." Silver Screen,
             18 (7): 46-7, 71-2, May 1948.
       France Ehren was educated at a fashion academy in Europe and
       was a designer there before becoming the chief designer for
       Eagle Lion Studios. She has designed the costumes for "Raw
       Deal" and "The Noose Hangs High."

903   Eichelbaum, Stanley. "Back over the Yellow Brick Road."
             San Francisco Sunday Examiner Chronicle, December
             11, 1977, Scene/Arts, p. 12.
       A review of The Making of "The Wizard of Oz," by Aljean Har-
       metz, the daughter of a former MGM wardrobe assistant-chief;
       with references to the costumes of Margaret Hamilton, Bert Lahr
       in a suit of real lion skin, and Judy Garland.

904   _____. "It's a Bird, a Plane, a Pinball Game." San
             Francisco Sunday Examiner and Chronicle, December
             24, 1978, Scene, p. 6.
       The marketing blitz for "Superman--the Movie" is the biggest
       ever leveled at the movie public, surpassing the hypes for "King
       Kong" (1976), "Jaws," and "Star Wars." Garments marketed in-
       clude bathing suits, T-shirts, jackets, jeans, and shoes. $10
       million was spent on the promotion and merchandising, with over
       1,000 items being licensed in connection with the film.

905   "Elaborate Biblical Scenes to Be Made for 'So This Is Marriage.'"
             Screen News, 3 (36): 2, September 6, 1924.
       Sophie Wachner has designed especially colorful costumes for the
       biblical sequence of "So This Is Marriage"; the sequence will be
       filmed in color.

905a   "An Elaborate Fashion Play." Moving Picture World, 29 (5):
             794, July 29, 1916.
       "Beauty and the Beast" will feature gowns made solely by Maison
       Maurice, of New York's Fifth Avenue. The costumes for star

Mineta Timayo are worth over $2,000.

906   "Elaboration Hurting Realism in Movies Says Blanche Sweet."
           Screen News, 3 (24): 18, June 14, 1924.
       Too many movie sets and costumes are unrealistic and hurt the
       plot--for instance, actors who are seen in suits with never a
       wrinkle, or eating dinner in formal attire.

907   "Eleanor Boardman in 'The Strangers' Banquet'...." Screen
           News, 1 (30): 13, September 16, 1922, col. 3.
       Eleanor Boardman removed the shoulder straps from an evening
       gown she wears in "The Strangers' Banquet" since she found the
       straps annoying. The gown is held in place with milliners' paste,
       and the Goldwyn studios are copying the gown.

908   "Elfstrom, Katherine." American Film Institute Catalog, 1961-
           70, p.191.
       Katherine Elfstrom is credited with the costumes of "Peer Gynt."

909   "Elissa Langston." Jones' Magazine, 1 (5): 52-3, December
           1937.
       Elissa Langston has been a model, fashion designer, and assisted
       Ernst Dryden with the costume designing of "Lost Horizon" and
       "The Garden of Allah." As a fashion designer at Bullock's Wil-
       shire, she designed some of the costumes for "Vogues of 1938"
       and "Shall We Dance?," under the Irene label (costumes for which
       Irene received credit).

910   "Ellacott, Joan." American Film Institute Catalog, 1961-70,
           p.191.
       Joan Ellacott was the dress designer of "The League of Gentlemen"
       and "In the Doghouse"; the costume designer of "Circle of Decep-
       tion," "Watch Your Stern," "Carry on Regardless," "Carry on
       Cabby," and "A Stitch in Time"; and is credited with the costumes
       of "Beware of Children" and "The Swingin' Maiden."

911   "Elliot, Courtney." American Film Institute Catalog, 1961-70,
           p.192.
       Courtney Elliot was the dress designer of "The Double Man."

912   Elsworth, Elmer. "A Brief History of the Motion Picture
           Costumers." Motion Picture Costumers, 1966, n.p.
       Elmer Elsworth, one of the founders of the Associated Motion
       Picture Costumers, AFL Local 18067, discusses the secrecy
       necessary at the time the union was formed, and the subsequent
       growth of the union.

913   "Elmquist, Marion." American Film Institute Catalog, 1961-
           70, p.192.
       Marion Elmquist is credited with the wardrobe of "The Hostage."

914   Emerson, John, and Anita Loos. "How to Dress for a Picture,"
           in Breaking into the Movies. New York: McCann, 1921,
           p.22-5.

The authors discuss the need of extras for a large and constantly
replenished wardrobe, which can be a considerable strain on the
budget since the same clothes cannot be worn in another picture,
and each picture may have many different scenes. Basic wardrobe needs are listed for male and female extras.

915   "Enid Bennett Takes Firm Stand on Present Day Women's
            Fashions." Screen News, 2 (3): 27, January 20, 1923.
Discussion of many costumes worn by Enid Bennett in "Your
Friend and Mine."

916   Ennis, Bert. "Fame Came to Chaplin with Borrowed Clothes."
            Motion Picture Classic, 23 (5): 36-7, 76, July 1926.
When working for the Keystone Company, Charlie Chaplin was
once rushed for a scene and hurriedly borrowed Fatty Arbuckle's
huge pants, Ford Sterling's oversized comedy shoes, and a derby
and cane. Soon after the film's release many comedians were
imitating his attire, but without the same successful results.

917   Epstein, Eleni Sakes. "Trigère," in American Fashion. New
            York: Quadrangle/New York Times, 1975, p. 409-96.
After establishing himself as a costume designer in Hollywood
Travis Banton worked for Hattie Carnegie; his assistant was
Pauline Trigère, then at the start of her fashion designing career.

918   "Equini, Arrigo." American Film Institute Catalog, 1961-70,
            p. 195.
Arrigo Equini is credited with the costumes of "The Avenger."

919   "Erbele, Carl." American Film Institute Catalog, 1961-70,
            p. 195.
Carl Erbele is credited with the costumes of "Barquero."

920   "Erdmann, Ernst." American Film Institute Catalog, 1961-70,
            p. 195.
Ernst Erdmann is credited with the wardrobe of "U-47 Lt. Commander Prien."

921   Ergenbright, Eric L. "Mae West Answers Your Questions."
            Motion Picture, 46 (1): 54-5, 74-5, August 1933.
Mae West does not cover her body for the simple reason that she
is not ashamed of it, and she wore padded dresses in "She Done
Him Wrong" because of stage experience, rather than modesty.

922   "Ericksen, Leon." American Film Institute Catalog, 1961-70,
            p. 195.
Leon Ericksen designed the wings worn by Bud Cort in "Brewster
McCloud."

923   "Ernst, Lone." American Film Institute Catalog, 1961-70,
            p. 196.
Lone Ernst is credited with the costumes of "Danish Blue."

924 Erté. Erte Fashions. London: Academy Editions; New York:
        St. Martin's, 1972.
Includes autobiographical information by Erté, who designed his
MGM film costumes so that they would not be soon outdated and
could be shown for several years.

925 Erté. "Erté Writes His Own Biography." Harper's Bazaar,
        54 (3): 31, 102, March 1919.
Erté was born in Russia but found greater success in Paris. His
favorite occupation is designing theatrical costumes.

926 Erté. Things I Remember: An Autobiography. New York:
        Quadrangle/New York Times, 1975.
Erté was commissioned to design the costumes for Cecil B. De
Mille's "The Prodigal Son," but William Randolph Hearst learned
of it and signed him to a three-year contract; he was already
under contract to Hearst to design the Harper's Bazaar covers
and write fashion articles. He designed the costumes for Marion
Davies and others in the ball sequence of "Restless Sex," but
no others during the contract. He discusses at length, with frequent illustrations, his costumes for MGM (with which Hearst's
studio had merged) films starring Carmel Myers in "Ben-Hur,"
Aileen Pringle in "The Mystic" and "Dance Madness," Theodore
Kozloff (or Kosloff) in "Time the Comedian," "Paris," and for
Renée Adorée and Lillian Gish in "La Bohème," with his version
of the problems with the two actresses. Erté was provided with
his own wardrobe department, where Mme. Van Horn executed
his costumes.

927 Erte. New York: Rizzoli, 1978.
Erté notes in the Foreword that "I find it difficult to add to the
information contained in the many articles and books published
about my life and in my memoirs Things I Remember." Thomas
Walters mentions that Erté designed for MGM in 1925 and soon
found himself "at the centre of the 1920's."

928 "Erté." Fairchild's Who's Who in Fashion. 1975, p.79.
Erté simplified his name, Romain de Tirtoff, by using his initials,
R.T., pronounced "air-tay." He designed film costumes in 1925
but left after seven months due to creative and financial restrictions.

929 "Erte, Gown Artist, Here with Movie Costumes." New York
        American, February 26, 1925, p.8.
Erté, well known for his Harper's Bazaar covers, has arrived
on his first visit to the United States to design film costumes.

930 "Erte: Greatest Fashion Genius Now in Pictures." Photoplay,
        27 (6): 78, May 1925.
Erté has temporarily left his Paris and Monte Carlo establish-
ments for MGM since he believes motion pictures influence fashion
to the greatest extent in the world.

931 "Erté, the World's Foremost Fashion Genius Has Designed Breath-
        Taking Styles for Robert Z. Leonard's Production 'Paris'
        ...." Moving Picture World, 75 (1): 2, July 4, 1925.
     An ad that boasts of Erté's costumes for "Paris." (According to
     biographer Charles Spencer, "Paris" was a major factor in Erté's
     leaving Hollywood, because of its unrealistic portrait of a Parisian
     couturier, which Erté also discussed in articles at the time he
     left. (It is not known how many of his costumes were eventually
     used in the film. This ad was premature.)

932 "Escoffier, Marcel." American Film Institute Catalog, 1961-
        70, p. 196.
     Marcel Escoffier was the costume designer of "Lady L" and is
     credited with the costumes of "Blood and Roses," "Madame,"
     "La Bohème" (1965), "Time of Indifference, "Woman Times
     Seven," "Senso," "Mayerling," and "The Head of the Family."

933 "Esquimeaux Wearing Sport Clothes." Screen News, 4 (42): 7,
        October 24, 1925.
     Laska Winter could not find the 3-4 simple calico housedresses
     she needed for "Rocking Moon" in Hollywood, and then had more
     difficulty on location in Alaska, for the Indian-Russian girl she
     portrays.

934 "Estévez." American Film Institute Catalog, 1961-70, p. 197.
     Estévez was the costume designer of "Hurry Sundown."

935 "Ethel Chaffin, Head of the Wardrobe Department of the Lasky
        Studio...." Grauman's Magazine, 5 (50): 8, December
        31, 1922.
     Ethel Chaffin, who designs all of the Paramount costumes except
     for those worn in Cecil B. De Mille's films, has gone to New
     York to interview some of the greatest designers with the hope of
     hiring one as her assistant.

936 "Ethel Clayton." Screen News, 1 (29): 14, September 9, 1922.
     Ethel Clayton will wear colorful and imaginative costumes for her
     role in the imaginary "Three Cornered Kingdom," including a
     pearl headdress, and a regal train of embossed gold velvet with
     embroidered gold leaves and ermine trim.

937 "Eugene O'Brien Voices Trouble." Senator Newsette, 2 (33):
        2, 4, August 15, 1926.
     Eugene O'Brien is tired of well-dressed roles and hopes for cow-
     boy roles with cowboy costumes.

938 "Evans, Clive." American Film Institute Catalog, 1961-70,
        p. 197.
     Clive Evans is credited with the gowns of "Negatives."

939 "Evans, Felix." American Film Institute Catalog, 1961-70,
        p. 197.
     Felix Evans is credited with the wardrobe of "Murder She Said"

and is given additional wardrobe supervision credits.

940   "Evein, Bernard." American Film Institute Catalog, 1961-70,
          p. 198.
      Bernard Evein was the costume designer of "Cleo from 5 to 7"
      and is credited with the costumes of "Last Year at Marienbad."

941   "Even Coat Hangers Go Colossal for Hollywood Demand." MGM
          Studio News, 5 (6): n.p., August 15, 1938.
      The weight of Norma Shearer's 34 costumes in "Marie Antoinette"
      was enough to break hangers placed in the walls; 34 special eight-
      foot-across hangers were developed by the property department.

942   "Evening Elegance." Modern Movies, 1 (9): 36-7, March 1938.
      One costume each is modeled by Rita Johnson from "Manproof,"
      Peggy Corklin from "Having a Wonderful Time," Claire Trevor
      from "Big Town Girl," and Dolores Del Rio from "International
      Settlement."

943   "Everyone Who Is Interested in What Still Will Be Fashion-
          able...." Screen News, 2 (14): 31, April 7, 1923, col.
          3.
      New York dress shops were searched for gowns and models to
      model them in the fashion-show sequence of "The Glimpses of the
      Moon."

944   "Everything's on the Block." Life, 68 (19): 42-8, May 22, 1970.
      The biggest auction ever held was for the MGM collection of 45
      years of costumes and props. Numerous photographs include cos-
      tumes worn by Greer Garson in "Pride and Prejudice" and "Mrs.
      Parkington," Robert Taylor in "Camille" (1936), Norma Shearer
      in "Marie Antoinette," Jeanette MacDonald in "Girl of the Golden
      West," Katharine Hepburn in "Sea of Grass," and Greta Garbo in
      "Conquest." Clark Gable had three copies of a Burberry trench
      coat, which he wore in many movies, including "Homecoming"
      and "Comrade X," with a photo from the latter film.

945   "Evolution of a Dress." Movie Classic, 9 (2): 47, October
          1935.
      The steps of making a dress for Helen Mack are shown through
      fittings, by fitter Marie Ree, to its completion. The dress, de-
      signed by Walter Plunkett, may have been worn in "The Return
      of Peter Grimm"; text is not specific.

946   "The Evolution of a Dress." Picture Play, 26 (2): 26-7, April
          1927.
      Joe Rapf, the head of MGM's wardrobe department, and Andre-
      Ani, the chief designer, help Gertrude Olmstead in the selection
      and creation of a dress, as illustrated; without film title.

947   Ewing, Elizabeth. History of Twentieth Century Fashion.
          London: Batsford, 1974.
      In its influence on fashion, film was "universal as no previous

influence could have been." In Hollywood, Coco Chanel promoted
her boyish fashions. Mae West sent a plaster cast of her body
to Elsa Schiaparelli for costumes for "Sapphire Sal" ("Every Day's
a Holiday"); later Schiaparelli came from Paris to design in Hollywood. There Adrian "followed her lead" with shoulder pads and
influenced fashion worldwide through costumes for Joan Crawford
and Greta Garbo. British manufacturer Julian Lee marketed
thousands of clothes copied from those worn by Joan Crawford and
Ginger Rogers. British designer Charles Creed visited Hollywood,
where he designed film costumes, sometime before 1939 (he was
associated with films from the mid-1930s through the 1940s).
"Hollywood's last fling" was the cone-shaped bra popularized by
sweater girls like Jane Russell in "The French Line." Film costume's influence declined in the 1950s with the decline in movie
attendance.

948   "Experiment Perilous." Motion Picture, 68 (6): 66, January
            1945.
Hedy Lamarr wears 16 period costumes in "Experiment Perilous."

949   "Exploitation; Antoinette's Ring." MGM Studio News, 5 (6):
            n.p., August 15, 1938.
A ring worn by Norma Shearer in "Marie Antoinette" will be exactly copied and sold throughout the country, with the same in-
scription as found in Shearer's ring: "Everything Leads to Thee."

950   "Exploitation; Crown Jewels." MGM Studio News, 4 (16): n.p.,
            October 15, 1937.
Greta Garbo wore authentic jewelry originally from the court of
Napoleon in "Conquest," lent from a private collector.

951   No entry.

952 "Fabiani." American Film Institute Catalog, 1961-70, p. 199.
Fabiani is credited with Susan Hayward's costumes in "Stolen
Hours."

953 "Facts from Film." MGM Studio News, 4 (16): n.p., October
15, 1937.
Nathalie Bucknall, head of MGM's research department, helped
uncover thousands of costume facts for "Conquest."

954 "Facts That Make 'Antoinette' Most Fabulous Picture Screen
Ever Attempted." MGM Studio News, 5 (2): n.p., March
23, 1938.
"Marie Antoinette" required four years of research; with 1,250
costumes designed by Adrian for over 150 persons.

955 "Fageol, Christiane." American Film Institute Catalog, 1961-
70, p. 200.
Christiane Fageol is credited with the costumes of "My Life to
Live" and was the dresser for "The Young Girls of Rochefort."

956 Fairchild's Who's Who in Fashion. Compiled by Josephine
Ellis Watkins. New York: Fairchild, 1975.
This biographical dictionary of fashion designers is referred to
often in this bibliography. Some designers who have designed
for films infrequently have not been included here.)

957 "Fairlie, Jean." American Film Institute Catalog, 1961-70, p.
200.
20 wardrobe-related credits are listed for Jean Fairlie.

958 "Falk, Gabriella." American Film Institute Catalog, 1961-70,
p. 201.
Gabriella Falk was the dress designer of "In Search of Gregory"
and is credited with the costumes of "The Adding Machine" and
"Two Gentlemen Sharing" and the wardrobe coordination of "Don't
Raise the Bridge, Lower the River."

959 "Fall Figure Flattery." Photoplay, 36 (6): 92, November 1949.
Yvonne Wood designed a simple wardrobe with clean lines for
Marta Toren in "Illegal Entry."

960   "Fall--for These." Motion Picture, 56 (3): 38-41, October
         1938.
      Merle Oberon models six costumes and Ursula Jeans four from
      "Over the Moon," made by Maggy Rouff from sketches by Rene
      Hubert.

961   Farrar, John. "Movie Frills and Furbelows." Ladies' Home
         Journal, 51 (10): 41, October 1924.
      Film costumes are handled by the wardrobe, costume, and re-
      search departments; the latter also studies the author's script for
      inaccuracies and to anticipate any research needed. Discussed
      are the destination of costumes after a film's production has ended,
      and the need for simplicity in film costumes, as with the "stark
      simplicity" of Natacha Rambova's costumes for Nazimova in
      "Salome" (1922). The costumes of "Monsieur Beaucaire" (1924)
      cost $90,000.

962   "Farrar's Gowns Count Big in Her Play of 'Shadows.'" Moving
         Picture World, 39 (4): 480, January 25, 1919.
      Geraldine Farrar has a hard time outdoing her previous film cos-
      tumes for each Goldwyn film and never wears the same gown
      twice in public; they are donated to the Stage Women's War Re-
      lief. Some of the gowns worn by Farrar in "Shadows" are de-
      scribed; she models two of the gowns.

963   "Farrer, Ernie." American Film Institute Catalog, 1961-70,
         p. 203.
      11 wardrobe-related credits are listed for Ernie Farrer.

964   Farrington, Mrs. Frank. "In the Costume Room." Moving
         Picture World, 33 (3): 389-90, July 21, 1917.
      Mrs. Farrington, once a theatrical-costume designer, is the
      chief costume mistress for Thanhouser Film Corporation. She
      discusses costume design, noting that theatrical and film pro-
      ducers spend similar amounts of money for costumes, but the-
      atrical costumers are allowed more time.

965   "Fascination for 1943." Photoplay with Movie Mirror, 22 (3):
         59-61, February 1943.
      Carole Landis models three costumes by Adrian from "The Powers
      Girl."

966   "Fashion Arbiter Gerrard Settles Movie Argument." Screen
         News, 2 (39): 15, September 29, 1923.
      Charles Gerrard never feels properly dressed unless he is wear-
      ing wool suits made by Burk, the London tailor, and his hat is
      made by Strand. He was called upon to decide the proper collar
      that should be worn by a British character (unnamed) in "Her
      Temporary Husband."

967   "A (Fashion) Bouquet for Belinda." Preview, 1957, p. 132-5.
      Julie Harris discusses costume designing in general, and design-
      ing for Belinda Lee.

968 "Fashion Departs from Strict Rule of Simplicity Early in Morn-
        ing and Late at Night." Screen News, 3 (6): 19, Feb-
        ruary 9, 1924.
     Anna Q. Nilsson models two costumes from "Flowing Gold"; with
     a sketch of an additional costume.

969 "Fashion Flashes." Modern Movies, 2 (6): 81, December 1938.
     Description of a suit and turban by Adrian worn by Paulette God-
     dard in "Dramatic School."

970 "Fashion Flashes." Modern Movies, 3 (1): 77, July 1939.
     Edith Head has designed the costumes for Dorothy Lamour in
     "Disputed Passage," with oriental accents, such as embroidery,
     and mostly black-and-white colors with silk or linen fabrics, for
     her seven day-costumes.

971 "Fashion Flashes." Motion Picture, 55 (2): 39-41, March 1938.
     Joan Crawford models three costumes by Adrian from "Mannequin."

972 "Fashion Focus on Heather Sears." Preview, 1958, p.15-7.
     Heather Sears models two costumes by Julie Harris from "The
     Story of Esther Costello."

973 "Fashion Foibles." Screen News, 1 (31): 24, September 23,
        1922.
     Discussion of costumes worn by Marcia Manon in "The Masquer-
     ader," Dorothy Phillips in "Hurrican's [sic] Gal," Mary Thurman
     in "The Bond Boy," and Ruth Clifford in "The Dangerous Age."

974 "Fashion Forecast." Hollywood, 28 (3): 66, March 1939.
     Actor and "dummy" Charlie McCarthy models four costumes from
     "You Can't Cheat an Honest Man." Includes a photo of his ward-
     robe closet.

975 "Fashion Illustration and Costume Design." Design, 52 (9):
        16-7, June 1951.
     Biographical information on Edith Head and Bonnie Cashin, with
     references to their film-costume designing, and their advice to
     would-be costume designers. Includes a sketch and still of a
     completed costume by Edith Head worn by Hedy Lamarr in "Sam-
     son and Delilah."

976 "Fashion Influences." Hollywood Pattern, 7 (2): 12-3, Summer
        1938.
     One costume each is modeled by Alice Faye from "In Old Chicago,"
     Franciska Gaal from "The Buccaneer," Deanna Durbin from "Mad
     About Music," and Sonja Henie from "Happy Landing"; with brief
     mention of how the costumes have influenced fashion.

977 "Fashion Note." New York Times, September 14, 1947, sec.
        2, p. 5.
     Edith Head and Milo Anderson doubted that the American woman
     would want to pad her hips and/or hide her legs with the new

Parisian fashions (the New Look). It was suggested by the author that the designers' opinions were part of an alleged campaign by the studios to protect films that were still in production--it was feared the new fashions would date films that had not yet been released.

978 "Fashion Notes." Screen News, 1 (34): 14, October 14, 1922. Discussion of gowns worn by Mary Thurman in "The Bond Boy," Colleen Moore in "Slippy McGee," and Ruth Clifford in "The Dangerous Age."

979 "Fashion Pageant in 'Mlle. Modiste.'" Senator Newsette, 2 (20): 4, May 16, 1926.
In "Mlle. Modiste," a sequence entitled "The Storm" features numerous models dressed symbolically as elements of an April shower. Corinne Griffith appears after the storm modeling many gowns; with one description. Adrian, "noted Paris designer" (sic), is credited as the designer. (On the dustjacket of Costume Design in the Movies, but not in the book's credits, Mme. Frances is credited with this film.)

980 "Fashion Preview." Screen Book, 14 (4): 44, May 1935.
Ginger Rogers models five gowns by Bernard Newman from "Star of Midnight."

981 "Fashion Row." Picture Play, 46 (6): 30-1, August 1937.
Includes photos of Joan Bennett, Helen Vinson, Alma Kruger, and Warner Baxter in costumes from "Vogues of 1938."

982 "Fashion Says: You'll See the Latest on the Late Show." Photoplay, 79 (1): 62-4, January 1971.
Lynda Day models five outfits made from Simplicity patterns, presumably inspired by "Dead End," "Desire," "Morning Glory," "The Great Ziegfeld," and "Public Enemy"; with brief references to how the patterns compare with the costumes.

983 "Fashion Show in Pictures." Moving Picture World, 26 (2): 271, September 9, 1915.
A new World Film picture, unnamed, will feature a woman who selects gowns to recapture her fiancé from an Indian princess. Gowns from the film will be shown throughout the country in "Mrs. Whitney's Fashion Show," organized by Belle Armstrong Whitney and featuring gowns designed by Worth, Pacquin, Jenny, Georgette, and Cheruit.

984 "Fashion Story of a Woman." Screenland, 51 (5): 56-7, March 1947.
Susan Hayward models seven costumes by Travis Banton from "Smash Up--Story of a Woman."

985 "Fashion-Wise." What's Happening in Hollywood, 10: n.p., November 13, 1943.
The fashions of the "roaring twenties" were liberally adapted for

"Rhapsody in Blue" so that the audience would not find them
humorous.   Loretta Young in "When Ladies Fly" and Irene Dunne
in "A Guy Named Joe" will mainly wear uniforms.   Many of
Raoul Pène Du Bois's costumes for Ginger Rogers in "Lady in the
Dark" are discussed, as are costumes worn by Joan Fontaine and
Ralph Forbes in "Frenchman's Creek," which were researched by
Madame Hilda Grenier.   Brief mention of many other films in
production, and of the influence of past films on fashion.

986   "Fashion Yourself a Fall Wardrobe!" Movie Classic, 9 (2): 51,
         October 1935.
Genevieve Tobin models a costume from "Here's to Romance!,"
which has been sketched for this pattern offer.

987   "Fashionable Frocks in Films." Pictures and the Picturegoer,
         9 (89): 99, October 30, 1915.
The latest in film fashion is discussed, as can be seen in "Pathé's
Animated Gazette," with one still of a woman modeling a hat.
Violet Mersereau models a hat, also, from "The Wolf of Debt."

988   "Fashioned for Winter." Movies, 6 (5): 48-9, December 1942.
Ilka Chase models a dress by Orry-Kelly from "Now Voyager,"
and others that may or may not be from the film.

989   "Fashions." Feature Movie, 5 (2): 24-5, March 1916.
Fritzi Brunette models three of her 18 costumes from "Unto
Those Who Sin," and Kathlyn Williams models two from an un-
named film.

990   "Fashions." Picture Play, 48 (5): 39-43, July 1938.
Doris Nolan models two gown by Kalloch from "Holiday."

991   "Fashions." Picture Play, 49 (4): 57-61, December 1938.
Gail Patrick models two costumes from "King of Alcatraz"; and
three costumes by Edith Head each are modeled by Joan Bennett
from "Artists and Models Abroad" and Frances Mercer from "The
Mad Miss Manton."

992   "Fashions." Picture Play, 49 (5): 60-1, January 1939.
Jeanette MacDonald models three costumes by Adrian from "Sweethearts."

993   "Fashions." Silver Screen, 12 (5): 48-9, March 1942.
Loretta Young models four costumes by Irene from "Bedtime
Story."

994   "Fashions a la Ferguson." Photoplay, 16 (3): 84-5, August
         1919.
Elsie Ferguson models six gowns from "Avalanche."

995   "Fashion$ and Figure$." Modern Screen, 20 (3): 38, Febru-
         ary 1940.
Tyrone Power models some outfits from his wardrobe; with a list

of the average prices he pays.   He spends about $7,000 per year
since each film requires new clothes.

996   "Fashions and Films."   Unifrance, 4: 19-20, June 1950.
      Discussion of the need for authentic period-film costumes versus
      nonauthentic; contributions to film costume by the late Christian
      Bérard; and film costume's fashion influence.   Designers often
      design period-film costumes but have others sew them since they
      lack the resources, with the exception of Christian Dior and his
      costumes for "Lit à Colonnes," made before he was famous as a
      designer; brief mention of his costumes for Yvonne Printemps in
      "Valse de Paris."   Maggy Rouff completed Renée Saint Cyr's cos-
      tumes for "Fusillé à l'Aube," designed by Rosine Delamare, the
      designer for "Monsieur Sanfoin."   One costume each is modeled
      by Martine Carol from "Les Amants de Verone," Danielle Darrieux
      from "Occupe-Toi D'Amélie," and Sophie Desmarets from "Mon
      Ami Sanfoin."   English text provided.

997   "Fashions Anticipated for Screen Productions."   New York
            Times, June 14, 1925, sec. 8, p.2.
      Howard Greer discusses the challenge of predicting fashion trends
      so that a film and its costumes are not soon out of date; clothes
      are never store-bought for that reason.   Greer and Travis Banton
      take turns visiting Paris to keep up with the latest fashions, which
      is especially helpful to women in isolated areas who depend on
      films for such news.   Designers must also be in continual con-
      tact with fabric designers and manufacturers.

998   "Fashions for Men."   Hollywood, 26 (7): 30, 51, July 1937.
      Studio stylist Hugh Daniels discusses the fashion images of many
      actors.

999   "Fashions from the Films."   Picture Play, 1 (11): 27, June 19,
            1915.
      Notes that women watch films to learn of the latest fashions since
      the actresses and studios lavish money on the costumes.   Two
      unnamed actresses each model one gown from unnamed films.

1000 "Fashions from the Screen."   Cinema Arts, 1 (1): 70-3, June
            1937.
      One gown each is modeled by Miriam Hopkins from "Woman
      Chases Man" and Doris Weston from "The Singing Marine."

1001 "Fava, Otello."   American Film Institute Catalog, 1961-70,
            p.203.
      Otello Fava is credited with the costumes of "Bebo's Girl."

1002 "Favorites in a Movie Star's Wardrobe."   Movie Classic, 8
            (2): 50, April 1935.
      Ann Dvorak models three costumes by Orry-Kelly from "Sweet
      Music."

1003 "Favorites in Furs."   Silver Screen, 11 (12): 42-3, October
            1941.

Ann Sothern models two gowns and two furs, and Eleanor Powell one gown and one fur, from "Lady Be Good," all by Adrian.

1004   "Fax, Peg." American Film Institute Catalog, 1961-70, p. 204.
Peg Fax is credited with the costumes of "What!"

1005   "Fay, Addalyn." American Film Institute Catalog, 1961-70,
       p. 204.
Addalyn Fay is credited with the wardrobe of "The Sadist."

1006   "Fea, Anna Maria." American Film Institute Catalog, 1961-
       70, p. 204.
Anna Maria Fea is credited with the wardrobe of "Kelly's Heroes,"
"Reflections in a Golden Eye," and "Anzio" and was the wardrobe
mistress of "The 300 Spartans."

1007   "Fearless." "The Truth About Stars' Figures...." Photoplay
       with Movie Mirror, 19 (4): 28-9, 76-7, September 1941.
"Fearless" is frank concerning the many actresses and actors
who have figure problems, either too much or too little. Includes
references to costumes worn by Loretta Young in "Clive of India,"
Carmen Miranda and Alice Faye in "That Night in Rio," James
Stewart in "The Philadelphia Story," and Mae West, whose costumes were limited to dark colors in "Every Day's a Holiday,"
designed by Travis Banton (actually by Schiaparelli). The comments range from a discussion of Carmen Miranda's huge platform
shoes and turbans, to the attribution of the decline in popularity
of Mae West and Sylvia Sidney to their being overweight; to this
comment about Constance Bennett: " ... the interior of Connie's
screen costumes look like the storage department of a baby pillow
factory."

1008   "February Fashion Plate." Photoplay with Movie Mirror, 24
       (3): 57-9, February 1944.
Alexis Smith models a costume by Milo Anderson from "One More
Tomorrow."

1009   "Feld, Don." American Film Institute Catalog, 1961-70, p.
       204-5.
19 credits are listed for designer Don Feld.

1010   Feldkamp, Phyllis. "Joe Simms' Quest: Yesteryear's Dress."
       The Evening Bulletin (Philadelphia), October 5, 1977,
       p. 21-2.
Discussion of teacher Joe Simms's search for remaining film and
nonfilm fashions designed by Adrian. He has been a fan of Adrian,
and a collector, since he first saw Norma Shearer in "Marie
Antoinette."

1011   _____. "Movie Modes." Christian Science Monitor, March
       25, 1974, sec. F, p. 2.
As with her costumes for "Bonnie and Clyde," Theadora Van
Runkle's costumes for "Mame" are also influencing fashion. In-
cludes brief descriptions of some of the 35 costumes Lucille Ball

wore in the film, and notes some of the manufacturers that will
market adapted fashions and accessories, including a cloche, which
is modeled.

1012   "Feminine Note." Senator Newsette, 2 (4): 3, January 24,
           1926.
A number of fashion designers (not identified) lent their latest
fashions to D. W. Griffith for "That Royale Girl," for models in
the modiste-shop sequence.

1013   Fenin, George N., and William K. Everson. "The Western
           Costume," in The Western: From Silents to Cinerama.
           New York: Bonanza, 1962, p. 180-90.
Discussion of the history of costume in western films, especially
of the 1920s-40s; authenticity was seldom important, though symbolism always separated the hero from the villain. The most
authentic costumes were worn in Ince westerns of 1910-13; "The
Iron Horse"; "Shane"; and films starring William S. Hart. Inauthentic costumes discussed include those worn by John Wayne
in "Stagecoach" and in French westerns, as with "The Hanging
at Jefferson City." The styles of many actors are discussed,
including Tom Mix, Gene Autry, Roy Rogers, Buck Jones, William
Boyd, and Tim McCoy. Costumes worn by women and Indians
are discussed in one paragraph each; women's costumes have reflected current fashions rather than been authentic. "The Outlaw"
brought in sexy costumes for women in westerns.

1014   _____. "The Western Costume," in The Western: From
           Silents to the Seventies. New York: Grossman, 1973,
           p. 180-90.
Reprint of the 1962 edition.

1015   "Fennell, Elsa." American Film Institute Catalog, 1961-70,
           p. 206.
Elsa Fennell is credited with the wardrobe of "Journey to the
Far Side of the Sun" and the wardrobe supervision of "Lolita,"
"The War Lover," "The Victors," "The Hill," "The Blue Max,"
and "The Heroes of Telemark."

1016   "Féraud, Louis." American Film Institute Catalog, 1961-70,
           p. 206.
Louis Féraud is credited with Elga Andersen's dresses in "Coast
of Skeletons" and the gowns of "Vice and Virtue."

1017   Ferguson, Elsie. "Clothes and Good Taste." Photoplay,
           17 (4): 57-8, 119, March 1920.
Ferguson notes that Paris was the fashion center until the World
War, when New York designers were forced to originate and
popularize their own designs (both Hollywood and New York were
in a similar situation during World War II). The actresses are
usually dressed in the newest American or Parisian designs, with
no regard to cost.

1018   _____, as told to Carolyn Van Wyck. "My Ideals of Dress."
        Photoplay, 21 (4): 52-3, March 1922.
        Elsie Ferguson designs her own film costumes, which are then
        made in a fashion house; she discusses her fashion preferences.

1019   "Ferris, Gamp." American Film Institute Catalog, 1961-70,
        p. 207.
        Gamp Ferris is credited with Craig Douglas's wardrobe in "Ring-
        a-Ding Rhythm."

1020   "Ffolkes, David." American Film Institute Catalog, 1961-70,
        p. 207-8.
        Davis Ffolkes was the costume designer of "The Long Ships" and
        is credited with the costumes of "Heavens Above!"

1021   Field, Alice E. "Costuming Today's Pictures." Scholastic,
        42 (2): 22, February 8, 1943.
        Discussion of how a film is costumed and how the war is affect-
        ing film costume, with examples from costumes worn by Loretta
        Young in "China," Rosalind Russell in "Flight for Freedom,"
        Ingrid Bergman in "For Whom the Bell Tolls," Maureen O'Hara
        in "This Land Is Mine," and Ann Harding in "Mission to Moscow."

1022   Field, Alice Evans. "Costume Design," in Hollywood, U.S.A.:
        From Script to Screen. New York: Vantage, 1952, p.
        114-21.
        Discussion of film-costume design; MGM's costume department,
        housed in seven buildings; the careers of Adrian, Irene, Edith
        Head, and Rene Hubert; and, briefly, the history of film costume
        in relation to theatrical costume. Brief mention of the psycho-
        logical importance of costumes worn by Judith Anderson in "The
        Pursued," Katie Nolan and Joan Blondell in "A Tree Grows in
        Brooklyn," Bette Davis in "Mr. Skeffington," and Irene Dunne in
        "Together Again."

1023   Field, Gertrude Hamilton. "The Vogue of Norma Talmadge."
        Motion Picture, 15 (3): 71-3, 118, April 1918.
        The latest fashion news can be found in the moving pictures, rather
        than Vogue, according to Norma Talmadge, who discusses her
        color selections and the psychological significance of costumes
        worn in "The Moth," "Poppy," and "The Secret of the Storm
        Country."

1024   "15-Cent Hat Costs $42.65 for Picture." Senator Newsette,
        1 (6): 3, January 25, 1925.
        Earl Hudson, production supervisor for First National, made the
        wardrobe plot for Colleen Moore in "So Big," set in 1890, and
        found that clothing prices have risen considerably. Moore's cos-
        tumes were reproduced by studio dressmakers, bought secondhand,
        and some imported. The 1925 costs were about $42 for hats,
        $22 for corsets, $95 for men's suits, and $38 for children's
        suits, the last three being specially manufactured for the film.

1025 "The $1,500 Dress." Screenland, 21 (3): 16, July 1930.
Norma Shearer models a gown from "The Divorcée" that was made
with gold woven into the fabric. Includes two of Adrian's original
sketches.

1026 "5th Avenue Girl." Hollywood, 28 (10): 34, October 1939.
Ginger Rogers models four costumes from "5th Avenue Girl."

1027 "Figuring Proper Costume for Artist Puzzles 'Your Friend and
        Mine' Company." Screen News, 2 (1): 30, January 6,
        1923.
After Otto Lederer had selected a smock for his role as an artist
in "Your Friend and Mine" many artists were interviewed to find
out if this was the correct type; the results were inconclusive, so
he wore the one he had selected.

1028 "Fill, Dennis." American Film Institute Catalog, 1961-70,
        p. 209.
Dennis Fill is credited with the wardrobe of "For Singles Only."

1029 "Film Gossip of the Month." Modern Screen, 2 (1): 15, June
        1931.
Sam Goldwyn spent thousands of dollars duplicating Gabrielle
Chanel's Paris salon for her studio wardrobe department, as de-
scribed.

1030 "Film Styles by Adrian on Display." Hollywood Citizen-News,
        July 6, 1967, sec. B, p. 11.
22 film costumes by Adrian were shown at the Los Angeles County
Museum of Art, loaned by MGM. (No catalogue was prepared
for the exhibit.)

1031 "Films and Fashions." Times (London), August 24, 1933,
        p. 7.
Trevor Fenwick, of Messrs. Fenwick, Limited, discusses the
influence of American film costume on British fashion.

1032 "Filmy Frills." Screen News, 1 (29): 9, September 9, 1922.
Includes descriptions of costumes worn by Ruth Sinclair in "The
Masquerader" and costumes Norma Talmadge had adapted for her
personal use, from "The Eternal Flame."

1033 "Find Modern Girl Can't Squeeze into Wasp-Waist Corset."
        Screen News, 2 (41): 6, October 13, 1923.
The actresses in "The Spanish Dancer" had difficulty fitting into
the iron and canvas corsets required for their costumes of 1750,
due to their modern, corsetless figures. The costumes were
altered to make their waists look smaller, but were authentic reproductions copied from paintings of the period.

1034 "Fine Feathers." Motion Picture, 24 (7): 66, August 1922.
Gloria Swanson models three costumes from "The Gilded Cage."

1035   "Fine Feathers, Etc." Photoplay, 27 (5): 34-5, April 1925.
One costume each is modeled by Yola D'Arvil, Olive Borden,
Clara Morris, Dorothy Seastrom, Sally Rand, Jocelyn Lee, Christina Montt, Etta Lee, and Adalyn Mayer from "The Dressmaker
from Paris," by Travis Banton.

1036   "Fine Feathers Really Don't--!" Screen News, 1 (13): 30,
        May 10, 1922.
Caustic remarks about an extra in "Our Leading Citizen," who
wore vintage fashions of 1904, presumbly because she was from
the country; but was dressed right for the film.

1037   "Fini, Leonor." American Film Institute Catalog, 1961-70,
        p. 211.
Leonor Fini is credited with the costumes of "A Walk with Love
and Death."

1038   Firth, Rena. "Smart for Your Age." Photoplay, 40 (2): 67,
        August 1951.
Includes biographical information on designer Helen Rose.

1039   "Fischer, Lee." American Film Institute Catalog, 1961-70,
        p. 212.
Lee Fischer is credited with the wardrobe of "The Ribald Tales
of Robin Hood" and the costumes of "Trader Hornee."

1040   "Fitzer, Gwen." American Film Institute Catalog, 1961-70,
        p. 212.
Gwen Fitzer is credited with the costumes of "Flareup."

1041   "500 Pair of Felt Overshoes Help Sound in Picture." MGM
        Studio News, n. d., n. p. (Housed at the Academy of Motion
        Picture Arts and Sciences). 1938.
Several hundred dress extras wore felt shoes over their regular
shoes for a dance sequence in "The First Hundred Years," to reduce the shuffling noise; most required one pair per day.

1042   Flake, Kolma. "Irene." Movieland, 2 (11): 46-7, 86-8,
        December 1944.
Irene is solely responsible for every costume worn in an MGM
film, though she is essentially a supervisor of specialized assistants. Irene first designed for films when Constance Bennett
came to her for her "Topper" costumes. Except for "Kismet"
and "Yolanda and the Thief" her designing had been simplified
due to war scarcities and restrictions. Lana Turner models
five costumes by Irene from "Marriage Is a Private Affair."

1043   _____. "Man-Hunting Clothes." Movieland, 3 (1): 46-7,
        67-8, February 1945.
Lengthy biographical information on Yvonne Wood, who has worked
with film designers William Lambert, Bernard Newman, Edward
Stevenson, Muriel King, Royer, and Irene Saltern. Includes

several sketches of costumes for Carmen Miranda and the chorus
in "Something for the Boys" and for Lynn Bari in "Sweet and Lowdown. "

1044   Flamini, Roland.   Scarlett, Rhett, and a Cast of Thousands:
          The Filming of "Gone with the Wind."   New York:
          Macmillan, 1978.
Walter Plunkett signed a 15-week contract to design the costumes
of "Gone with the Wind," but when his contract expired David O.
Selznick, the film's producer, tried to induce Plunkett to stay on
without salary since other designers were eager to design the
film's costumes without pay; he stayed a total of 162 weeks; after
the 15 weeks he received only $400 per week of the $600 he had
previously received.   Selznick had also had Howard Greer, Adrian,
and Milo Anderson submit sketches.   Plunkett visited Margaret
Mitchell, the book's author, to obtain her permission to design
costumes in colors other than green, which the author had in-
advertantly mostly limited Scarlett to; and in Atlanta he obtained
fabric swatches from museums, which were then made up by a
Pennsylvania manufacturer in exchange for the right to market
fabrics bearing the film's name.   Another problem to be worked
out by Margaret Mitchell, and Susan Myrick, the liaison between
Selznick and Mitchell, was Selznick's insistence upon Vivien Leigh
wearing a bonnet in the bazaar sequence; neither Mitchell nor
Myrick could convince him to abandon this, though he was per-
suaded not to have a scene in which the ladies' gowns were to be
seen standing up against a wall, since the hoops and whalebone
construction of the bodices would have made this impossible.
Plunkett's staff included seamstresses for the dresses and uniforms, weavers with two old looms, a woman who constructed
the antebellum corsets, and an ironmonger to solder the hoops
worn under the dresses.   In addition to the previously mentioned
designers who hoped to work on "GWTW," Irene Mayer Selznick
tried to convince her husband that she could design the costumes.
Discussion also of Natalie Kalmus's work on the film, as selecting
colors and fabrics: "For many Hollywood producers, she was a
strong argument in favor of sticking to black-and-white film. "
Includes references to Vivien Leigh's breasts being taped for more
cleavage in one gown, a white gown being made for the first
scene since she appeared in the green sprig muslin dress too
often, and the aging of the calico dress that she wore through
about a third of the film, 27 copies of which were required.   The
women's wardrobe came to about $98,154; the total wardrobe
costs were $153,818.   While Howard Strickling was in charge of
MGM's publicity actors were not allowed to appear in fashion articles or to receive awards based on their appearance lest they
appear effeminate.   Emily Torchia, of the Strickling staff, developed the "Sweater Girl" image of Lana Turner by having her
pose without a blouse under her sweater.

1045   "Flemming, Charlotte."   American Film Institute Catalog,
          1961-70, p.213.
Charlotte Flemming is credited with the costumes of "Hippodrome"

and "The Girl and the Legend" and was the costume adviser of "Heldinnen."

1046 Fletcher, Adele Whitely. "Look Out, Paris! Here Comes
        Hollywood." Picture Play, 34 (1): 54-5, 114, March
        1931.
Discussion of many garments considered Paris originals but that
were really originated on the screen, including a costume worn
by Sharon Lynn in "Sunny Side Up," which she models, and costumes designed by Travis Banton and Adrian.

1047 _____. "Who Is Hollywood's Best Dressed Woman?"
        Photoplay with Movie Mirror, 22 (4): 32-4, 84-5, March
        1943.
Seven designers discuss Hollywood's best-dressed women. No
film-costume references, but mention of two new film designers,
Mrs. Leslie Morris of RKO, and Valentina, who is designing
Ginger Rogers's costumes in "Lady in the Dark" (Rogers's cos-
tumes in the film were the work of a handful of designers).

1048 "Fletcher, Robert." American Film Institute Catalog, 1961-
        70, p. 214.
Robert Fletcher is credited with Stella Stevens's costumes in
"The Ballad of Cable Hogue."

1049 "Fletcher, Robert." Biographical Encyclopaedia and Who's
        Who of the American Theatre. 1966, p. 455-6.

1050 "Fletcher, Robert." Who's Who in the Theatre. 16th ed.,
        1977, p. 614-5.

1051 "The Flick Chick." Newsweek, 70 (25): 113, December 18,
        1967.
A tongue-in-cheek letter from one woman to another describing
all of her recent clothing purchases, all inspired by film costumes, recent and classic. Retail fashions modeled include one
garment each "inspired" by "Camelot," "Dr. Zhivago," "Gone
with the Wind," and "Bonnie and Clyde."

1052 "Flicker Fashions." Cosmopolitan, 117 (3): 6, September
        1944.
Discussion of film costume's influence on fashion, with brief
mention of "Letty Lynton" and "For Whom the Bell Tolls."
Recommends that designers design film costumes that women can
afford to buy copies of. Rene Hubert's costumes for the two
wives of President Wilson and three daughters in "Wilson" have
influenced fashion through retail copies by Nettie Rosenstein,
as seen in one costume from the film and an adaptation.

1053 Floherty, John J. Moviemakers. New York: Doubleday,
        Doran, and the Junior Literary Guild, 1935.
General discussion of the importance of the wardrobe department
and how an actress is costumed; actors provide their own costumes.

1054   "'Flop' Hats Now Favored Instead of Sailors in Katherine's
                Wardrobe." Screen News, 1 (29): 29, September 9, 1922.
        Katherine MacDonald has temporarily discarded the sailor hat,
        which she popularized, for a number of innovative hats worn in
        "The Lonely Road," for her role as a hat designer.

1055   "Florence, Gay." American Film Institute Catalog, 1961-70,
                p. 214.
        Gay Florence is credited with the wardrobe of "The Mini-Affair."

1056   "Flowers Are in Vogue Again." Screen News, 3 (22): 9,
                May 31, 1924.
        In "Cytherea, Goddess of Love" Constance Bennett wears a gown
        of black satin with orchids on the shoulder, which she models.

1057   "Foale & Tuffin." American Film Institute Catalog, 1961-70,
                p. 215.
        Foale & Tuffin are credited with Audrey Hepburn's clothes in
        "Two for the Road."

1058   "Foale, Marion." American Film Institute Catalog, 1961-70,
                p. 215.
        Marion Foale is credited with Susannah York's costumes in "Ka-
        leidoscope."

1059   Foley, Edna. "Starting at the Bottom." Picture Play, 17 (2):
                87, October 1922.
        Actress Doris May does not wear the same pair of shoes in more
        than one film.   Includes 14 photos of her shoes.

1060   "Fonssagrives, Mia." American Film Institute Catalog, 1961-
                70, p. 215.
        Mia Fonssagrives was the costume designer for Richard Burton,
        Ewa Aulin, Florinda Bolkan, Marilù Tolo, and Nicoletta Machia-
        velli in "Candy"; the clothes designer for Paula Prentiss in
        "What's New Pussycat?"; and is credited with the costumes for
        Elizabeth Taylor in "The Only Game in Town" and Samantha Eggar
        in "The Walking Stick" (codesigned with Vicki Tiel).

1061   "Fontana (Roma), Sorelle." American Film Institute Catalog,
                1961-70, p. 215.
        Sorelle Fontana (of Roma) is credited with the costumes of "Le
        Amiche," and Ava Gardner's in "The Bible ... In the Beginning";
        Ursula Andress's clothes in "The 10th Victim"; the fashion-show
        clothes for Jessie Royce Landis; and the "special outfit" for Cindy
        Carol in "Gidget Goes to Rome."

1062   "Fonteray, Jacques." American Film Institute Catalog, 1961-
                70, p. 215.
        Jacques Fonteray was the costume designer of "Barbarella,"
        "Castle Keep," "The Devil by the Tail," and "Borsalino" and is
        credited with the costumes of "Rapture," "Marco the Magnificent,"
        "King of Hearts," "The Upper Hand," and "Spirits of the Dead."

1063 "For Evening Wear, Myrtle Stedman ... Prefers the Regal
        Dignity of Ermine." Screen News, 2 (7): 2, February
        17, 1923, cols. 1-3.
Myrtle Stedman models two fur coats and Helen Ferguson one from
"The Famous Mrs. Fair."

1064 "For the First Time in Her Long Screen Career...." Screen
        News, 4 (40): 9, October 10, 1925, col. 1.
Charlotte Mineau has spent very little on her slovenly costume
and wornout shoes for "Scraps," in contrast to costumes of a
previous film, which cost over $1,000. The calico robe and used
shoes cost her $1.98.

1065 "For the Sake of Art." Hollywood, 19 (2): 9, February 1930.
One costume each is modeled by Merna Kennedy from "Broadway,"
Evelyn Brent from "Underworld," Betty Boyd from "Lilies of the
Field," and Ethlyn Clair from "Show of Shows."

1066 "For Those Secret Scarlett O'Haras." New York Times,
        September 27, 1967, p. 36.
The revival of "Gone with the Wind" led several designers to in-
corporate romantic fabrics of silhouettes reminiscent of the movie
into their collection; the resemblance is doubtful.

1067 Forbes, Pamela Pratt. "The Men Behind the Gowns."
        Cinema Arts, 1 (1): 74-5, June 1937.
Brief biographies of designers Adrian, Edward Stevenson, John
Harkrider, Travis Banton, Orry-Kelly, Robert Kalloch, Gwen
Wakeling, and Walter Plunkett. One sketch is included of cos-
tumes for Joan Crawford in "The Last of Mrs. Cheyney," by
Adrian; Lily Pons in "That Girl from Paris," by Edward Steven-
son; Virginia Bruce in "When Love Is Young," by John Harkrider;
Claudette Colbert in "I Met Him in Paris," by Travis Banton;
Kay Francis in "Another Dawn," by Orry-Kelly; and Joan Perry
in "The Devil Is Driving," by Kalloch.

1068 "Forman, Ron." American Film Institute Catalog, 1961-70,
        p. 217.
Ron Forman was the costume designer of "The Affairs of Aphrodite."

1069 "Forquet." American Film Institute Catalog, 1961-70, p. 217.
Forquet is credited with Ira von Fürstenberg's costumes in "Matchless."

1070 Forsee, Aylsea. "Edith Head: Designer for the Stars," in
        Women Who Reached for Tomorrow. Philadelphia:
        Macrae Smith, 1960, p. 152-77.
This book was written for young persons; the biography of Edith
Head does not reveal much that could not be found in her auto-
biography. (See Head, Edith. The Dress Doctor.)

1071 "Fortini, Luciana." American Film Institute Catalog, 1961-

<u>70</u>, p.217.
Luciana Fortini is credited with the costumes of "A Minute to
Pray, a Second to Die" and "Ace High."

1072   "Fortune in Furs on Review in New Santell Fortune." <u>Senator</u>
           <u>Newsette</u>, 2 (46): 4, November 13, 1926.
Gilbert Clarke of Milgrim's in New York designed the gowns and
costumes of the fashion-show sequence in "Subway Sadie."

1073   " '44 Fashions." <u>Silver Screen</u>, 14 (3): 52-3, January 1944.
Six fashions that were adapted by Nettie Rosenstein from "Jane
Eyre" are modeled.   Includes closeups of Joan Fontaine and Or-
son Welles in costumes from the film.

1074   "Forum of Events; Lord & Taylor's Second Annual Series of
           Awards...." <u>Architectural Forum</u>, 71 (1): 18, July 1939.
Adrian received a $1,000 award from Lord & Taylor for his
ability as a costume designer.

1075   "Fouquet, Marie-Claude." <u>American Film Institute Catalog</u>,
           <u>1961-70</u>, p.218.
Marie-Claude Fouquet is credited with the costumes of "The
Young Girls of Rochefort."

1076   Fowler, H.E.   "A Guide to the Appreciation of the Historical
           Photoplay 'Victoria the Great.'" <u>Photoplay Studies</u>, 3
           (8): 8-9, Series of 1937.
Nine historical paintings are shown, with stills of Anna Neagle,
Anton Walbrook, and others, to prove the importance of research
to the costumes of "Victoria the Great."

1077   Fox, George.   <u>"Earthquake": The Story of a Movie</u>.   New
           York: New American Library, 1974.
Burton Miller, the costume designer of "Earthquake" (with Edith
Head), discusses the difficulty created by having thousands of
costumes reflect the action of the actors during and after the
disaster sequences; with brief mention of Ava Gardner.

1078   "Fox, Ree." <u>American Film Institute Catalog, 1961-70</u>, p.
           219.
Ree Fox is credited with the wardrobe of "Wanda (The Sadistic
Hypnotist)."

1079   Frances.   "Fashion Letter from Frances." <u>Movies</u>, 5 (4):
           43-5, 51, October 1941.
Discussion of costumes worn by Barbara Stanwyck in "You Belong
to Me," by Edith Head; Ann Sheridan in "The Man Who Came to
Dinner," by Orry-Kelly; Joan Perry in "Nine Lives Are Not
Enough," by Howard Shoup; Ilona Massey in "International House,"
by Edward Stevenson; Cobina Wright and Alice Faye in "Weekend
in Havana," by Gwen Wakeling; and Deanna Durbin in "Almost an
Angel," by Vera West.   Illustrations include costumes modeled by
Evelyn Keyes in "Here Comes Mr. Jordan," Ann Sothern in "Lady

Be Good," and by Stanwyck, Perry, and Faye, from the above
films.

1080   "Frances, Madame." American Film Institute Catalog, 1921-
            30, p.1100.
Madame Frances is credited with the costumes of "Potash and
Perlmutter."

1081   "Frances Made a Perfectly Simple Little Serge Frock...."
            Screen News, 2 (24): 20, June 16, 1923, col. 3.
Description of a suit worn by Hope Sutherland in "Potash and
Perlmutter"; it cost about $300 and was designed by Madame
Frances.

1082   "Francis X. Bushman." Motion Picture Costumer, 1957,
            n.p.
Francis X. Bushman traveled to Berlin so that costume and armor
specialists could create an authentic warrior's costume, at his
own expense, for the silent version of "Ben-Hur." He was honored by the Costumers for his regard for authentic costuming in
his films.

1083   "Francois Nazare Aga Is the Creator of the Startling Persian
            Costumes...." Screen News, 1 (24): 20, August 5, 1922,
            col. 3.
Francois Nazare Aga created the costumes for "Omar the Tentmaker."

1084   Frank, Stanley. "Style King of Ready-to-Wear." Saturday
            Evening Post, 235 (37): 76-7, 79-80, October 20, 1962.
Cary Grant chose two suits and an evening gown off-the-rack at
Norman Norell's showroom for Doris Day to wear in "That Touch
of Mink." An inexperienced Norman Levinson, who changed his
name to Norell, found employment as a costume designer for
movies with Gloria Swanson and Rudolph Valentino at the Astoria,
New York, Paramount studio because "designers were so scarce";
the job ended when the studio closed. It was Norell's first paid
job as a designer.

1085   Fraser, Grace Lovat. "Scenes from the Shows." Studio,
            119 (566): 176-9, May 1940.
The author found the costumes of "The Hunchback of Notre Dame,"
including Charles Laughton's, so correct that they were boring--
except for those worn in the Mystery Play sequence, as shown.
Discussion also of costumes worn in "The Wizard of Oz."

1086   _____. "Scenes from the Shows." Studio, 119 (567): 210-2,
            June 1940.
The costumes of "The Private Lives of Elizabeth and Essex,"
designed by Orry-Kelly, are historically accurate, with the exception of the farthingale worn by the women, which ruins the
otherwise correct silhouettes. The farthingales (hoops) worn are
from the wrong century.

1087 _____. "Scenes from the Shows." <u>Studio,</u> 121 (574): 20-1,
           January 1941.
The costumes of "Pride and Prejudice," by Adrian, were authentic
and not of excessive proportions, as too often occurs with historical costumes.   The correct texture, weight, and pattern in the
fabrics were used, along with authentic trimmings, caps, bows,
and other accessories.   Includes stills of Laurence Olivier, Greer
Garson, Ann Rutherford, and Edna May Oliver.

1088 _____. "Scenes from the Shows." <u>Studio,</u> 122 (569): 36-41,
           August 1941.
Discussion of Adrian's costumes for "Bittersweet," which Jeanette
MacDonald models, and Cecil Beaton's costumes for "Kipps," with
stills of Diana Wynyard, Michael Redgrave, and Phyllis Calvert.

1089 _____. "Scenes from the Shows." <u>Studio,</u> 122 (570): 78-81,
           September 1941.
Discussion of Rene Hubert's authentic costumes for "That Hamilton
Woman," with stills of stars Laurence Olivier and Vivien Leigh, and
inauthentic costumes worn by Marlene Dietrich in "The Flame of
New Orleans," a wedding dress from which Dietrich models.

1090 "Fratini, Gina." <u>American Film Institute Catalog, 1961-70,</u> p. 222.
Gina Fratini was the costume designer of "Stop the World--I Want
to Get Off."

1091 "Frazer, Henrietta." <u>American Film Institute Catalog, 1921-
           30,</u> p. 1102.
Henrietta Frazer is credited with the wardrobe of "Brotherly
Love," "Honeymoon," "Show People," "All at Sea," "Desert
Nights," "Hallelujah," "So This Is College," "The Bishop Murder
Case," and "Caught Short" and the costumes of "The Hollywood
Revue of 1929."

1092 "Freak Fashions of the Films." <u>Photoplay,</u> 26 (1): 31, June 1924.
Viora Daniel models a costume by Ethel Chaffin from "Triumph."
Other costumes by Chaffin, from unnamed films, are modeled.

1093 "Fredericks of Hollywood." <u>American Film Institute Catalog,
           1961-70,</u> p. 223.
Fredericks of Hollywood is credited with the bras worn in "What's
Up Front."

1094 French, William F.   "Hollywood Really Goes Colossal!"
           <u>Motion Picture,</u> 63 (6): 44-5, 82-3, July 1942.
Discussion of the plot and cast of "Tales of Manhattan" and the
various roles played by the star--a tailcoat that descends the
social ladder with each man who wears it.

1095 _____. "Working Girl!" <u>Screenland,</u> 30 (4): 29, 80-2,
           February 1935.
Jean Muir discusses her clothing likes and dislikes and her en-
thusiam over Orry-Kelly's 24 costumes for her in "Desirable."

1096 "Freshy Playclothes as Featured in 'Song of the Open Road.'"
      Modern Screen, 28 (6): 71, May 1944.
All the starlets in "The Song of the Open Road" wore playclothes
designed and made by the Goldman Company, sold under the label
of Freshy Playclothes. Peggy O'Neil models one of the outfits.

1097 Friedman, Arlene. "Theadora Van Runkle: Costume Designer,
      Painter, Writer." Cinema (Beverly Hills), 35: 34-5,
      1976.
Theadora Van Runkle briefly discusses designing the costumes for
"Mame" and for her first film, "Bonnie and Clyde"; with sketches
of Lucille Ball in "Mame," and "Bonnie and Clyde" and "Godfather
II." She had never designed anything before "Bonnie and Clyde"
and learned what she knows through sewing her own clothes.

1098 "Frigerio, Ezio." American Film Institute Catalog, 1961-70,
      p. 225.
Ezio Frigerio is credited with the costumes of "The Best of Enemies."

1099 "Frills O' the Films." Screen News, 2 (33): 14, August 18,
      1923.
Discussion of gowns worn by models in a fashion-show sequence
in "Potash and Perlmutter."

1100 "Frills O' the Films." Screen News, 2 (42): 20, October 20,
      1923.
Discussion of costumes worn by Colleen Moore and Myrtle Stedman in "Flaming Youth" and by Anna Q. Nilsson in "Ponjola,"
in which she proceeds from women's to men's clothes, and wears
a new moiré fabric.

1101 "Frocks and Frills." Picture Play, 27 (1): 77, September
      1927.
One costume each is modeled by Billie Dove from "The Stolen
Bride" and Kathryn Carver from "Service for Ladies."

1102 "Frocks, Brock." American Film Institute Catalog, 1961-70,
      p. 226.
Brock Frocks is credited with the costumes of "The Lusting
Hours."

1103 "From a Costume Designer's Sketch Book." Jones' Magazine,
      1 (1): 34-5, August 1937.
Helen Taylor has been the costume designer for most of Walter
Wanger's films, including "52nd Street"; includes six sketches of
costumes from the film, in color, without identification of characters.

1104 "From 'Fade-In' to 'Fade-Out'; Wardrobe," in The Blue Book
      of the Screen. Edited by Ruth Wing. Hollywood: The
      Blue Book of the Screen, 1923, p. 365.
The actress in a modern film outlines the script to determine the

number of costumes she will need, the wardrobe mistress designs
and makes them, and the director approves them.

1105   "From 'Slavey' to Social Leader." Screen News, 1 (14): 26,
            May 27, 1922.
Leatrice Joy models two costumes from "Her Man."

1106   Fuir, Charles.   "Costuming a Cinema Spectacle." Motion
            Picture, 14 (12): 47-50, January 1918.
Informative article on the research and costuming of principals
and extras in "The Woman God Forgot," with stills of Geraldine
Farrar, Theodore Kosloff, and the armor and headdresses.   Includes also a lengthy list of costumes required for the film.

1107   "Furness, John." American Film Institute Catalog, 1961-70,
            p. 228.
John Furness was the costume designer of "The Long Duel,"
"The Viking Queen," "Those Daring Young Men in Their Jaunty
Jalopies," and "The Kremlin Letter"; the wardrobe designer of
"The Valley of Gwangi"; and is credited with Ursula Andress's
wardrobe in "The Blue Max" and the other costumes (other than
Julie Harris's) for "Eye of the Devil."

1108   "Furs Worth Fortune Used in 'The Alaskan.'" Screen News,
            3 (36): 4, September 6, 1924.
Native Alaskan Indians created and loaned to the cast furs from
every local fur-bearing animal for "The Alaskan," to be worn in
native-life sequences.

1109   "Furse, Margaret." American Film Institute Catalog, 1961-
            70, p. 228.
14 credits are listed for designer Margaret Furse.

1110   Furse, Roger.   "Design and Costumes," in The Film "Ham-
            let": A Record of Its Production.   Edited by Brenda
            Cross.   London: Saturn, 1948, p. 36-42.
Roger Furse discusses his sets for "Hamlet," without mention of
the costumes; though included are eight of his sketches of the costumes, including some for star Laurence Olivier and others not
identified.   Furse's film credits include the costumes of "Odd
Man Out."

1111   _____.   "Middle Ages Through Modern Eyes." Films and
            Filming, 1 (8): 10-1, May 1955.
Discussion by Roger Furse of designing period film costumes that
will not appear distracting for the modern audience--for example,
modifying medieval shoes and hats for "Richard III"--and of cos-
tumes worn by Sir Laurence Olivier, with brief mention of others.
Includes a sketch of a costume worn by Sir Cedric Hardwicke.
Furse was helped with the costumes, and on the previous films
"Henry V" and "Hamlet," by art director Carmen Dillon.

1112   _____.   "A Wardrobe for Richard." Films and Filming,

1 (7): 8-9, April 1955.
Roger Furse discusses film-costume design and the need for
adapting period costumes for "Richard III," as with his previous
costumes for "Henry V" and "Hamlet." Discussion also of costumes worn by Mary Kerridge, Claire Bloom, and Pamela Brown.
Illustrations include one sketch each of costumes worn by Laurence
Olivier, Ralph Richardson, John Gielgud, and William Catesby.

1113   "Furse, Roger," in Art and Design in the British Film, by
           Edward Carrick.   London: Dobson, 1948, p. 61-3.
Roger Furse was temporarily released from the Navy to design
the costumes and armor of "Henry V," having already established
himself as an authority on Shakespearian productions in the theater;
he is also noted for his realistic costumes.

1114   "Furse, Roger."   Who's Who in the Theatre.   15th ed., 1972,
           p. 810-1.
Roger Furse was the costume designer of "Henry V," "Under
Capricorn," "The Angel with the Trumpet," "Ivanhoe," "Knights
of the Round Table," and "Helen of Troy." (The other films he
designed are listed, but with production instead of costume credits.)

1115 Gabree, John. "Clothes," in <u>Gangsters: From Little Caesar to the Godfather</u>. New York: Galahad, 1973, p.17.
Good clothes are essential to the successful gangster to reflect his success to others; brief mention of the principal characters in "The Public Enemy," "Little Caesar," and "Scarface."

1116 Gaddis, Pearl. "Dressing for the Movies." <u>Motion Picture Classic</u>, 2 (6): 56-8, August 1916.
Discussion of gowns worn by Dorothy Gish in "Susan Rocks the Boat" and Alice Joyce in "The Theft of the Crown Jewels," one of which she models. Mabel Trunnelle designs many of her film costumes.

1117 _____. "Maid in America." <u>Motion Picture Classic</u>, 4 (1): 36-8, March 1917.
Since the war has prohibited the importation of foreign fashions, women are turning to the movies for inspiration. Billie Burke models a costume from an unnamed film, designed by Lady Duff Gordon.

1118 Gaines, William P. "Hollywood Snubs Paris." <u>Photoplay</u>, 46 (5): 78-9, 107, April 1934.
Travis Banton has stopped traveling to Paris because Hollywood has become independent with its fashion designs and influences New York more than Paris; instead, he travels around the United States. His designs for Marlene Dietrich in "The Scarlet Empress" (the ruche collar, for example) will probably influence fashion. Dietrich models a costume from the film. The talkies were the greatest factor in establishing Hollywood as a style center, Banton feels.

1119 "Gainsford, Anne." <u>American Film Institute Catalog, 1961-70</u>, p.229.
Anne Gainsford is credited with the costumes of "Inadmissible Evidence."

1120 "Galanos." <u>American Film Institute Catalog, 1961-70</u>, p.230.
Galanos is credited with the costumes for Rosalind Russell in "Oh Dad, Poor Dad, Mama's Hung You in the Closet and I'm Feelin' So Sad."

1121 Galante, Pierre. <u>Mademoiselle Chanel</u>. Translated by Eileen
        Geist and Jessie Wood. Chicago: Regnery, 1973.
      The author quotes at length from the article written by Laura
      Mount, with incorrect bibliographical information, concerning
      Chanel's period as the designer for Goldwyn studios. Chanel felt
      it would be a way to advertise her styles, and it was assumed
      that she would revolutionize film costume, but after "compro-
      mising" somewhat, she left Hollywood. Erroneous reference to
      Chanel remodeling Greta Garbo so that "Greta would leave the
      screen at the peak of her glory."

1122 "Gaminerie, La." <u>American Film Institute Catalog, 1961-70</u>,
        p. 231.
      La Gaminerie is credited with the costumes of "A Matter of Days."

1123 "Ganevskaya, G." <u>American Film Institute Catalog, 1961-70</u>,
        p. 231.
      G. Ganevskaya is credited with the costumes of "Mumu" and
      "Resurrection."

1124 "García, Rosa." <u>American Film Institute Catalog, 1961-70</u>,
        p. 232.
      Rosa García is credited with the costumes of "Tristana."

1125 Gardner, Ava. "I Dress as I Please." <u>Movieland</u>, 7 (11):
        26-9, 70-1, December 1949.
      Ava Gardner has learned from designer Irene that she needs to
      wear simple, tailored clothes for the screen.

1126 "Gardner, Brenda." <u>American Film Institute Catalog, 1961-
        70</u>, p. 232.
      Brenda Gardner is credited with the wardrobe of "The Hand" and
      "Dutchman" and was the wardrobe mistress of "The Innocents,"
      "Fury at Smuggler's Bay," and "The Man Who Couldn't Walk."

1127 "Garlandiana." <u>Time</u>, 81 (16): 111-2, April 19, 1963.
      In this review of "I Could Go On Singing" Edith Head was credited
      with costuming Judy Garland (in a red chiffon gown) as though
      "somebody had tried to stuff eight great tomatoes into a little
      bitty gown." (See Edith Head's reply, "Tomato Surprise.")

1128 "The Garments Preferred by the Gold-Digger." <u>Motion Pic-
        ture</u>, 35 (1): 64-5, February 1928.
      Ruth Taylor models six costumes from "Gentlemen Prefer Blondes."

1129 "Garr, Phyllis." <u>American Film Institute Catalog, 1961-70</u>,
        p. 233.
      Phyllis Garr was the wardrobe designer of "Tell Me That You
      Love Me, Junie Moon" and is credited with the wardrobe of "The
      Graduate," "Hurry Sundown," "Skidoo," and "Pieces of Dreams."

1130 "Gaskin, Bill." <u>American Film Institute Catalog, 1961-70</u>,
        p. 234.

Bill Gaskin was the assistant costume designer of "Gypsy."

1131   "Gasparinetti, Alessandro (Maj.)." American Film Insti-
          tute Catalog, 1961-70, p.234.
Major Alessandro Gasparinetti was the military-uniform consultant
for "The Leopard."

1132   "Gay Performers." Photoplay with Movie Mirror, 22 (2):
          51-3, January 1943.
Ginger Rogers models three costumes from "Once Upon a Honeymoon"; with sketches.

1133   Gay, Valerie.   "Are You Up-to-Date About Helen Vinson?"
          Movie Classic, 9 (2): 39, 66-7, October 1935.
Though she is considered one of the screen's "best-dressed,"
Helen Vinson prefers to concentrate on her acting, rather than on
her costumes.   Because she wears many gowns in each film,
many fans think she owns them and deluge her with requests.
The average film wardrobe requires two full weeks of work, including examination of sketches and lengthy fittings.   The costumes
wear out quickly due to daily laundering and pressing, and because
they are worn for weeks; they are then passed on to the wardrobe
department for extras.   Vinson wonders if all of this had ever been
explained to the readers.

1134   "Gazing into Life's Mirror." Motion Picture, 18 (11): 54-5,
          December 1919.
One costume each is modeled by Peggy Davis, Vanda Hawley,
Bebe Daniels, Violet Hemming, and an unidentified extra from
"Everywoman."

1135   Geduld, Carolyn.   "The Production," in Filmguide to "2001:
          A Space Odyssey." Bloomington: Indiana University Press,
          1973, p.21-8.
The costumes of "2001: A Space Odyssey," designed by Hardy
Amies, were developed over one year.   They were meant to look
as though they would be worn 35 years in the future.

1136   Geduld, Harry M.   "The Production," in Filmguide to "Henry
          V." Bloomington: Indiana University Press, 1973, p.13-
          25.
The costume designers for "Henry V" were Margaret and Roger
Furse and Roger Ramsdell.   Real armor could not be used because of war restrictions and the shortage of metal.   Roger
Furse had imitation chain mail made by spraying metal paint
upon knitted twine, concealed in part by the banners, worn with
historically authenticated coats of arms.

1137   "Gee of London, Cecil." American Film Institute Catalog,
          1961-70, p.236.
Cecil Gee of London is credited with the CIA suit worn by Tom
Courtenay in "Otley."

1138   "Gellert, Trudy." American Film Institute Catalog, 1961-70,
       p. 236.
       Trudy Gellert is credited with the wardrobe of "For Singles Only."

1139   "Gentili, Carlo." American Film Institute Catalog, 1961-70,
       p. 237.
       Carlo Gentili is credited with the costumes of "A Pistol for
       Ringo."

1140   "Georgiadis, Nicholas." American Film Institute Catalog, 1961-
       70, p. 237.
       Nicholas Georgiadis is credited with the costumes of "Romeo and
       Juliet" (1966; the ballet version).

1141   "Geradino, Zoraida." American Film Institute Catalog, 1961-
       70, p. 237.
       Zoraida Geradino is credited with the wardrobe of "Terror in the
       Jungle."

1142   Gerber, Albert B. Bashful Billionaire: The Story of Howard
       Hughes. New York: Lyle Stuart, 1967.
       The costumes and sets of "Hell's Angels" cost $540,000. After
       "The Outlaw" censorship eventually relaxed, but before and during
       its time "a woman's possession of breasts could be hinted at, but
       never demonstrated." Howard Hughes, the film's director and
       producer, was unhappy with the photography of Jane Russell's
       bustline and eventually decided to design a new type of brassiere,
       the design and construction of which is not discussed.

1143   "Gerdago." American Film Institute Catalog, 1961-70, p. 238.
       Gerdago is credited with the costumes of "Forever My Love" and
       "The Fountain of Love."

1144   "Germès-Vergne, Jeannine." American Film Institute Catalog,
       1961-70, p. 238.
       Jeannine Germès-Vergne is credited with the costumes of "Leda"
       and "Time Bomb."

1145   "Gernreich, Rudi." American Film Institute Catalog, 1961-
       70, p. 238.
       Rudi Gernreich is credited with the Roman Discotheque wardrobe
       of "2000 Years Later" and was the costume designer of "Skidoo."

1146   "Gernreich, Rudi." Current Biography. 1968, p. 141-3.

1147   "Gernreich, Rudi." Who's Who in America. 37th ed., 1972-
       3, p. 1137.

1148   "Gernreich, Rudi." Who's Who in the West. 14th ed., 1974-
       5, p. 245.

1149   "Gernreich, Rudi." Who's Who in the World. 2nd ed., 1974-
       5, p. 371.

1150 "Gettinger, Muriel."   American Film Institute Catalog, 1961-
            70, p. 239.
      Muriel Gettinger was the costume designer of "The Incident."

1151 "Gherardi, Piero."   American Film Institute Catalog, 1961-70,
            p. 239.
      Piero Gherardi was the costume designer of "The Appointment"
      and is credited with the costumes of "La Dolce Vita," "8 1/2,"
      "The Hunchback of Rome," "Juliet of the Spirits," "La Fuga,"
      "Danger: Diabolik," "Three Nights of Love," and "Burn!"

1152 "Gherardi, Piero."   International Encyclopedia of Film.
            New York: Crown, 1972, p. 236, passim.
      Biographical information on Piero Gherardi (1909-1971), Italian
      set and costume designer.   Notes his famous collaborations with
      Federico Fellini.

1153 "Ghidini, Giuliana."   American Film Institute Catalog, 1961-
            70, p. 239.
      Giuliana Ghidini is credited with the costumes of "Sword of the
      Conqueror."

1154 Gibbon, Monk.   "The Protagonists--Powell, Pressburger and
            Heckroth," in "The Red Shoes" Ballet: A Critical Study.
            London: Saturn, 1948, p. 49-56.
      Hein Heckroth, the art director and costume designer of "The
      Red Shoes," created over 2000 sketches for the film.   Brief
      mention of the color schemes and his working with other members
      of the production crew.

1155 "Gibbs, Evelyn."   American Film Institute Catalog, 1961-70,
            p. 240.
      12 wardrobe-related credits are listed for Evelyn Gibbs.

1156 "Giboyau, Catherine."   American Film Institute Catalog, 1961-
            70, p. 240.
      Catherine Giboyau is credited with the costumes of "Checkerboard."

1157 "Gibson, Freda."   American Film Institute Catalog, 1961-70,
            p. 240.
      Freda Gibson is credited with the wardrobe of "Horror Hotel"
      and "Clue of the Twisted Candle" and was the wardrobe mistress
      of "Foxhole in Cairo."

1158 "Gibson, Mary."   American Film Institute Catalog, 1961-70,
            p. 240.
      Mary Gibson is credited with the wardrobe of "The Frozen Dead,"
      "It!," "The Anniversary," and "The Lost Continent" and was the
      wardrobe mistress of "Die! Die! My Darling!" and "The Nanny."

1159 "Gilbert, Bates."   American Film Institute Catalog, 1921-30,
            p. 1113.
      Bates Gilbert is credited with the fashions of "Lilies of the Field"
      (1924).

1160 "Gilbert, Hylda." American Film Institute Catalog, 1961-70,
         p. 241.
      Hylda Gilbert is credited with the costumes of "The 7th Dawn."

1161 "Gilda." Motion Picture, 71 (4): 4, May 1946.
      "Gilda" features Rita Hayworth in a $60,000 wardrobe

1162 "Gill, Betina." American Film Institute Catalog, 1961-70,
         p. 242.
      Betina Gill is credited with the wardrobe of "The Householder."

1163 "Gillett, Barbara." American Film Institute Catalog, 1961-
         70, p. 242.
      11 wardrobe-related credits are listed for Barbara Gillett.

1164 "Gimbel, Sophie." Celebrity Register. 1st ed., 1963, p. 239.

1165 _____ Haas." Who's Who of American Women. 8th ed.,
         1974-5, p. 341.

1166 "Gimbel, Sophie Haas." Who's Who of American Women, 8th ed.,
         p. 243.
      Paula Giokaris was the costume designer of "Wild, Wild Winter"
      and is credited with the costumes of "The Long Rope" and "Lord
      Love a Duck" the wardrobe of "The Purple Hills," "Teenage
      Millionaire," "The Broken Land," "A Rage to Live," and "The For-
      tune Cookie" and the women's wardrobe of "The Two Little Bears."

1167 "Giokaris, Vou Lee." American Film Institute Catalog, 1961-
         70, p. 243.
      Vou Lee Giokaris is credited with the costumes of "Promises!
      Promises!" and the wardrobe of "What Ever Happened to Baby
      Jane?" and "They Shoot Horses, Don't They?"

1168 "Giorgi, Marinella." American Film Institute Catalog, 1961-
         70, p. 243.
      Marinella Giorgi is credited with the wardrobe of "To Bed or
      Not to Bed."

1169 "Giorsi, Mario." American Film Institute Catalog, 1961-70,
         p. 243.
      Mario Giorsi was the costume designer of "Gold for the Caesars"
      and is credited with the wardrobe of "Gladiators Seven" and the
      costumes of "The Centurion," "The Huns," "Marco Polo," "The
      Slave," "Duel of Champions," "Hercules in the Haunted World,"
      "Nightmare Castle," and "The Secret Seven."

1170 "Girl in a Glass Skirt." Life, 22 (14): 142-4, April 7, 1947.
      Cathy Downs, a model, wears a gown designed by Bonnie Cashin
      for six chorus girls in "I Wonder Who's Kissing Her Now." As
      seen in four stills, the gown is made of 20 yards of a nylon fiber
      that resembles glass, has a wire hoop frame, cost $754, and took
      12 persons eight days to make.

1171   "The Girl in the Black Dress." Photoplay, 21 (3): 52, Febru-
          ary 1922.
        Actress Dorothy Hall attributes her start in films to a gown she
        was wearing when spotted by a casting director. She designs,
        cuts, and sews all of her clothes and does not plan on buying any
        of her clothes for her forthcoming comedies.

1172   "Girls, Here's Your Chance to Get Mae Murray's Gowns."
          Screen News, 3 (4): 11, January 26, 1924.
        Mae Murray, one of the screen's best-dressed actresses, sells
        her gowns when picture work is finished since the gowns would
        be too easily recognized if worn in another picture.

1173   "Girls of America Prettier Than French, States Paulette
          Duval." Screen News, 3 (29): 3, July 19, 1924.
        Rene Hubert, Parisian designer, recently worked with the cos-
        tuming of "Monsieur Beaucaire."

1174   Gish, Lillian. Dorothy and Lillian Gish. Edited by James
          E. Frasher. New York: Scribner's, 1973.
        Original stills include Lillian Gish in a gown worn in "Captain
        Macklin," made by Madame Frances; she wore her best gowns
        in her films, and, as with this gown, she and other actresses
        were not paid by the studio for providing their own. D.W.
        Griffith conceived the costumes for "Intolerance." Rudolph Valen-
        tino was so concerned with his appearance in "Out of Luck" that
        he held up the shooting schedule. Gish selected the costumes for
        sister Dorothy Gish in "Remodeling Her Husband" (1920) since
        "we had no designers then." She "dressed" two cousins for
        "Orphans of the Storm" in the style of Gainsborough and Greuze;
        the costumes were heavy enough to cause Dorothy to faint. Con-
        cerning her feud with Erté, she felt that worn-out silks rags
        would look and move better than the new calico fabrics he wanted
        for "La Bohème"; she wore only one of his costumes for the film,
        a small photo of which is included, and designed the rest with
        Mother Coulter. Renée Adorée did wear Erté's costumes, which
        Gish still considers unattractive. Many of their films are well
        illustrated, as with two gowns worn by Lillian in "Way Down
        East," from Henri Bendel's, and six vamp gowns worn in "Diane
        of the Follies." Dorothy Gish models a $25,000 Cuban shawl
        from "The Bright Shawl."

1175   _____, with Ann Pinchot. The Movies, Mr. Griffith, and
          Me. Englewood Cliffs, N.J.: Prentice-Hall, 1969.
        Lillian Gish discusses her costumes, and often the research re-
        quired, for "The Birth of a Nation" and "Intolerance," many of
        which were designed by D.W. Griffith; "Hearts of the World";
        "The Chink and the Child," by wardrobe mistress Mrs. Jones;
        "Way Down East," with one gown by Henri Bendel; and "The Two
        Orphans," designed with the help of Herman Tappé. She notes
        erroneously that Erté was brought over from Paris to design the
        costumes for "La Bohème," discusses their feud, which led her
        to redesign the costumes with Mother Coulter, and notes that she

could not talk Renée Adorée out of wearing Erté's costumes.
Genuine uniforms from the Civil War could not be worn by the
men of "The Birth of a Nation" because of the difference in body
sizes, so they were provided by the company that became Western
Costume Company. Mrs. Morgan Belmont wore gowns by Lucile
in "Way Down East."

1176   _____, as told to Carolyn Van Wyck. "Individuality in
          Dress." Photoplay, 22 (1): 56-7, June 1922.
Lillian Gish does not select her film costumes for their appearance
since she is usually limited to poor-girl roles, as in "Broken
Blossoms," "Way Down East," and "Orphans of the Storm."

1177   "Giusti, Silvano." American Film Institute Catalog, 1961-70,
          p. 244.
Silvano Giusti is credited with the costumes of "The Brute and the
Beast."

1178   "Givenchy." American Film Institute Catalog, 1961-70, p. 244.
Givenchy is credited with Elizabeth Taylor's wardrobe in "The
V. I. P. 's," and Audrey Hepburn's clothes/wardrobe in "Breakfast
at Tiffany's," "Charade," and "How to Steal a Million."

1179   "Givenchy, Hubert de." American Film Institute Catalog, 1961-
          70, p. 244.
Hubert de Givenchy is credited with Audrey Hepburn's wardrobe
in "Paris When It Sizzles."

1180   "Givenchy, Hubert (James Taffin) De." Current Biography.
          1955, p. 228-9.

1181   "Glamor Wardrobe for Rita." Pictorial Movieland: A Magazine
          Within a Magazine [insert in] Movieland, 5 (11): 46-7,
          December 1947.
Rita Hayworth models five costumes designed by Jean Louis from
"The Lady from Shanghai," with four of his original sketches.

1182   "Glamour Fashions for You." Picture Play, 49 (6): 57-61,
          February 1939.
Merle Oberon models one hat from "The Cowboy and the Lady";
Constance Bennett, two costumes by Irene from "Topper Takes a
Trip"; and Lucille Ball, three costumes by Renie from "Annabelle
Takes a Tour."

1183   "Glamour Glitter." Movies, 3 (9): 44-5, March 1940.
Barbara Stanwyck models one gown from "Remember the Night,"
and Mary Martin models a copy of one of her costumes, by Edith
Head, from "The Great Victor Herbert."

1184   "The Glass of Fashion." What's Happening in Hollywood, 3
          (32): n. p., April 28, 1945.
Brief mention of Bonnie Cashin's costumes for Joan Leslie in
"Where Do We Go from Here" and chorus girls in "Billy Rose's

Diamond Horseshoe," dressed as tropical fruits, seasonings, and desserts, by three unnamed designers.

1185   "Glazman, Linda." American Film Institute Catalog, 1961-70, p. 245.
Linda Glazman is credited with the costumes of "Latitude Zero."

1186   "Glenn, Charles." American Film Institute Catalog, 1961-70, p. 245.
Charles Glenn is credited with the wardrobe for Sammy Davis, Jr., in "Salt & Pepper."

1187   "Glinkova, G." American Film Institute Catalog, 1961-70, p. 246.
G. Glinkova is credited with the costumes of "Battle Beyond the Sun."

1188   Gloria. "Style Notes from the Gay Musical, Roberta." Screen Book, 14 (2): 48-9, March 1935.
The 150 costumes for "Roberta," designed by Bernard Newman, cost $50,000. Irene Dunne wears 15 costumes in the film; she and Ginger Rogers each model two costumes.

1189   "Gloria Swanson Completes Work in 'The Humming Bird.'"
Screen News, 3 (1): 9, January 5, 1924.
For the first time since she appeared in Sennett comedies, Gloria Swanson has worn boy's clothes in "The Humming Bird."

1190   "Gloria Swanson Explains Art of Wearing Clothes." Screen News, 2 (29): 10, July 21, 1923.
Gloria Swanson assisted in the designing of her costumes for "Bluebeard's Eighth Wife."

1191   "Gloria Swanson Re-Acts to the Clothes She Wears." Screen News, 1 (9): 12, April 21, 1922.
Gloria Swanson is transformed into almost any character if realistically costumed for the role. For "Beyond the Rocks" she wore two period costumes for historical sequences in the contemporary film.

1192   "Gloria Swanson Returns from Europe with Six Trunks of Paris Gowns." Screen News, 1 (19): 8, June 24, 1924.
Gloria Swanson bought six trunkfuls of gowns in Paris, most to be worn in "The Impossible Mrs. Bellew."

1193   "Gloria Swanson to Produce 'Mme. Gêne' in Paris." Screen News, 3 (31): 25, August 2, 1924.
The French government has made many historical costumes and military uniforms available for use in "Madame Sans-Gêne."

1194   "Gloria Swanson Wears Many Stunning Gowns in Modiste Shop Scene." Screen News, 3 (28): 19, July 12, 1924.
Gloria Swanson is transformed from a drab shopgirl to a chic

woman in "Manhandled." The modiste shop was designed with the help of Gilbert Clarke, who has his own modiste shop, and H. M. K. Smith, formerly with Lady Duff Gordon. Most of Swanson's gowns were designed by Gilbert Clarke.

1195 "Gloria's New Clothes and Coiffure." Photoplay, 36 (6): 32-3, November 1929.
Gloria Swanson models an ermine wrap from "The Trespasser," with costume jewelry; other costumes may not be from the film.

1196 "Gloria's Shoe-Out." People Weekly, 10 (1): 47, July 3, 1978.
Gloria Swanson cleaned out 37 years of clothing and 200 pairs of shoes from her closet. Some of the shoes were worn in her films; she planned on donating them to charity, probably to be auctioned off.

1197 "Glunt, Ruth." American Film Institute Catalog, 1961-70, p. 246.
Ruth Glunt is credited with the special costumes of "Wilbur and the Baby Factory."

1198 Glynn, Prudence. "The Performing Arts as Catalyst," in In Fashion: Dress in the Twentieth Century. New York: Oxford University Press, 1978, p. 67-83, passim.
Of the handful of books that deal with twentieth-century fashion this is one of the few to cover film costume more than superficially: " ... it is, naturally, the performed arts which most affect fashion." Writer Jacques Manuel has credited a costume by Louis Gasnier worn by Pearl White in an unnamed serial in 1916 as the "first specially created film costume." White appears in a photo in another costume created by Gasnier, from "Plunder," 1922-3; both of White's costumes were copied and became virtual uniforms for working women. Like Erté, two other protégés of Paul Poiret (actually, Erté only briefly worked for Poiret) entered film designing: Georges Lepape designed the costumes of "Phantasmes" and Paul Iribe the costumes of "Male and Female." Of those who could not adjust to the studio system "the most famous failure is Erte," and though he was a "supreme illustrator," his sketches did not translate well onto the human body. Notes also his feud with Lillian Gish. The wire-framed cantilevered bra, developed in 1946, helped bring international renown to Jane Russell in "The Outlaw." Brief mention of designers Norman Norell (incorrectly stated to have begun his designing in Hollywood --actually, the Paramount studio in Astoria, New York), Adrian (with mention of his "Letty Lynton" costumes for Joan Crawford), Howard Greer, Travis Banton, Walter Plunkett, Jean Louis, Helen Rose, Edith Head, and Irene Sharaff. The influence of film costume on fashion waned in the early 1960s when pop music replaced it as a fashion trendsetter. Includes also a comment by Mrs. D. W. Griffith, who once said that her husband turned down an actress but offered to pay her five dollars for her hat so that Mary Pickford could wear it in a film.

1199 Godowsky, Dagmar. First Person Plural: The Lives of Dag-
          mar Godowsky. New York: Viking, 1958.
The credits of "A Sainted Devil" will probably always remain a
puzzle. Dagmar Godowsky notes that she got the lead role in
"A Sainted Devil" after Natacha Rambova fired Jetta Goudal (other
sources say the studio fired her) from the film due to their argu-
ments over Goudal's wardrobe. Most sources say that Rambova
designed the bizarre costumes, but Godowsky says of her wardrobe
that "Norman Norell did mine and it was divine." (Adrian has
also been credited with the film, and it is anyone's guess as to
whether Rambova's wardrobe was replaced, or redesigned.)

1200 " 'Gold Diggers' at Work Again!" Screen Guide, 3 (2): 37-9,
          June 1938.
The Gold Diggers' costumes for the "South Sea Island" sequence in
"Gold Diggers in Paris" were made with one yard each of batik
fabric costing 20 cents per yard. The approximately 20 Gold
Diggers each wore out about five pairs of opera-length, specially
made stockings at $5 apiece and two pairs of shoes each.

1201 Gold, Zachary. " 'Standing Room Only'; Production." Modern
          Screen, 28 (4): 34-5, 112, March 1944.
Paulette Goddard will not wear stockings in "Standing Room Only,"
using leg makeup instead. (Undoubtedly due to war scarcities or
to boost morale of women who had no stockings.)

1202 Goldman, James. Robin and Marian. New York: Bantam,
          1976.
The costumes of "Robin and Marian" are hardly discussed, and
only partial credits are listed. One costume sketch each of Sean
Connery and Audrey Hepburn is included; a magnifying glass indicates the designer was Yvonne Blake. When some local resi-
dents persisted in watching the filming they were given costumes
and allowed to remain.

1203 Goldwyn, Samuel, as told to Eric L. Ergenbright. "Women
          Rule Hollywood." New Movie, 11 (2): 18-9, 53, March
          1935.
Women rule Hollywood by choosing which films their families will
see and because they comprise the majority of the audience. Film
costumes are also a major factor in bringing women into a theater,
and Gloria Swanson ensured her appeal and career by her lavish
costumes, as did Norma Shearer.

1204 "A Good Bet--'Wilson.'" Motion Picture, 68 (1): 50, August
          1944.
Geraldine Fitzgerald wears 47 costumes in "Wilson."

1205 " 'The Good Old Days,' and What the Motion Picture Costumers
          Did About Them." Motion Picture Costumers, 1956, n.p.
The Associated Motion Picture Costumers was formed in 1929 to
correct the poor work conditions endured by those associated with
film costuming. A history is given of the union, Costumers'

Local 705, which oversees some 60 job classifications. In the
early days the prop man was in charge of costumes unless it was
necessary to rent items from Western Costume Company. By the
mid 1920s, Famous Players-Lasky founded the first costuming
department.

1206   Gordon, James. "One Man Who Suits Women." American
            Magazine, 141 (3): 46-7, 101, March 1946.
Adrian's preference for clothing with broad shoulders first came
about when designing for Joan Crawford, to make her broad hips
look smaller. Claudette Colbert models a suit by Adrian from
"Without Reservations."

1207   "Gorgeous Gloria." Picturegoer, 1 (5): 22-3, May 1921.
Gloria Swanson briefly discusses her transformation by Triangle
designer Peggy Hamilton for her first big role.

1208   "Gorgeous Gowns Cause Stampede at Powers Studio." Screen
            News, 2 (28): 28, July 14, 1923.
Discussion of two gowns worn by Ruby Miller in "Alimony."

1209   "Gorgeous Gowns Enhance Pola's Beauty on Screen." Screen
            News, 5 (3): 2, January 23, 1926.
Discussion of jewelry and costumes worn by Pola Negri in "A
Woman of the World."

1210   "Görlich, Grete." American Film Institute Catalog, 1961-70,
            p.252.
Grete Görlich is credited with the costumes of "The Goose
Girl."

1211   Gostelow, Mary. "Romantic and Glamorous Hollywood Design
            --The Costume Institute, The Metropolitan Museum of
            Art, New York." Journal of the Costume Society, 9:
            58, 1975.
The oldest of the over 100 costumes displayed in the "Romantic
and Glamorous Hollywood Design" exhibit was worn by Lillian
Gish in "Way Down East." Brief mention of the psychological
importance of a gown worn by Joan Crawford in "The Gorgeous
Hussy" and of historical inaccuracies in costumes worn by Norma
Shearer, Gladys George, and an unnamed actress in "Marie
Antoinette," all by Adrian. Fabrics discussed include a wedding
gown by John Truscott worn by Vanessa Redgrave in "Camelot"
and gowns by Travis Banton worn by Marlene Dietrich in "Angel"
and by Bob Mackie worn by Barbra Streisand in "Funny Lady."

1212   Gottlieb, Carl. The "Jaws" Log. New York: Dell, 1975.
Obviously not a "costume" picture. The single reference to the
wardrobe of "Jaws" is that of the actors buying wetsuits and being
handsomely rewarded by the studio with rental fees. Robert
Ellsworth is credited with the men's wardrobe and Louise Clark
with the women's wardrobe.

1213 Gow, Gordon. "Them and Us." Films and Filming, 24 (1):
          12-6, October 1977.
      Shirley Russell, wife of director Ken Russell, discusses her cos-
      tumes for Twiggy, Georgina Hale, and extras in "The Boy Friend";
      Glenda Jackson and Oliver Reed in "Women in Love"; Oliver Reed
      and Ann-Margret in "Tommy"; Roger Daltry and Fiona Lewis in
      "Lisztomania"; Richard Chamberlain in "The Music Lovers"; Robert
      Powell in "Mahler"; Dorothy Tutin in "Savage Messiah"; Stanley
      Donen in "The Little Prince"; and her only film without husband
      Ken Russell, "Inserts." She discusses collaborating with director
      Russell, their training, and careers; the fire that burned the
      costumes of "Tommy"; and her collection of costumes, which are
      often rented out for other films. She also designed many furs for
      "Billion Dollar Brain," which were made in France by Chombert.
      Illustrations of Twiggy from "The Boy Friend," Oliver Reed in
      "The Devils," and many of the cast members of "Valentino,"
      particularly Rudolf Nureyev and Michelle Phillips.

1214 "The Gown Goes to Town." Collier's, 111 (20): 18-9, May 15,
          1943.
      Because of war scarcities and fabric restrictions, Rene Hubert
      reused fabric for many film costumes, as with a gown worn by
      Alice Faye in "Hello, Frisco, Hello," which was used for cos-
      tumes worn by Lynne Roberts in "School for Scandal," Vivian
      Blaine and Gerrie Noonan in "Coney Island," Doris Merrick in
      "I Escape from Hong Kong," Roseanne Murray in "War Corres-
      pondent," and Rhonda Fleming in "Sweet Rosie O'Grady"; one still
      of each.

1215 "Gown of Gems." MGM Studio News, 3 (16): n.p., August
          5, 1936.
      Adrian has commissioned a Los Angeles jeweler to create a gown
      made entirely of jewels, attached to fine gold mesh with crown
      settings, for Greta Garbo in "Camille." The jewels to be used
      are square-cut emeralds and French rose-cut diamonds, to be
      worn with a set of tiara, bracelets, and necklace. (She wore no
      such gown in the film.)

1216 "Gowns, and What Becomes of Them." Screen News, 1 (30):
          10, September 16, 1922.
      Colleen Moore donates her film costumes to her favorite charity
      after a film's completion, often ranging from 20 to 30 costumes.
      She also maintains a stock wardrobe, which includes various sports
      outfits.

1217 "Gowns Designed in the Perior [sic] of Sixteenth Century."
          Screen News, 1 (2): 11, March 4, 1922.
      Sophie Wachner has found that the costumes of "The Dust Flower,"
      circa 1500, can easily be adapted for modern wardrobes, as with
      the batwing sleeves.

1218 "Gowns Insured for £8,000!" Pictures and the Picturegoer,
          10 (122): 238, June 17, 1916.

Billie Burke's costumes for "Gloria's Romance" were insured for
£8,000, or $40,000, not to cover the original cost of the gowns
but in case anything should happen while the gowns were not worn
during breaks in filming of specific sequences.

1219 "Gowns Made for Stars." Motion Picture, 30 (6): 52, January
        1926.
Irene Rich and May McAvoy each model one gown by Sophie Wach-
ner, with an additional sketch of one costume for each, from
"Lady Windermere's Fan."

1220 "Grace Moore Steps Out." Vogue, 87 (10): 78-9, May 15,
        1936.
Presented are four sketches by Ernst Dryden of costumes worn
by Grace Moore in "The King Steps Out."

1221 Graham, Sheila. "Is Hollywood Carrying Sex Too Far?"
        Photoplay, 43 (2): 36-7, 84-5, February 1953.
Discussion of the trend toward lower moral standards in films,
and revealing costumes, as worn by Jane Wyman in "Just for
You," Corinne Calvet in "What Price Glory," Janet Leigh in
"Houdini," and June Allyson in "Remains to Be Seen."

1222 "Grani, Tina." American Film Institute Catalog, 1961-70,
        p. 255.
Tina Grani was the costume designer of "Black Sabbath" and is
credited with the costumes of "Erik the Conqueror" and "The War
of the Zombies" and the wardrobe of "Black Sunday."

1223 Grant, Hank. "Hollywood." San Francisco Chronicle, August
        4, 1978, p. 51.
Anita Ekberg is making a comeback in "Treasure of the Amazon
Women," wearing a scanty costume designed by Gucci's. Carmen
Miranda's trademark costume with a three-foot-high turban stacked
with fruit, will be worn by Maureen Reagan in a guest appearance
on "Love Boat."

1224 Grant, Jack. " 'The White Sister'--Seen Through Hollywood's
        Eyes." Motion Picture, 45 (4): 40-1, 76-7, 81, May
        1933.
Colonel Beuf, a former Italian officer, acted as a technical adviser for "The White Sisters." As an Italian soldier in a German
prison camp, Clark Gable wore the crown of his hat completely
indented to signify discharge (the hat could be worn five other
ways for different meanings). Also, fatalities were averted
because aviators who had crashed during filming of aerial scenes
had worn heavily padded snowsuits made of leather like those worn
by the real Italian aviators.

1225 "The Great Costume Cycle." Silver Screen, 5 (7): 36-41,
        May 1935.
17 stills show numerous actors and actresses appearing in period
films, with brief mention of the "wardrobe activity" created by

the trend.   Includes a photo of Lucia Coulter, age 68, a wardrobe
mistress with MGM for 15 years.

1226   "Great Fashion Exposition for Colleen Moore's 'Irene.'"
         Screen News, 4 (44): 9, November 7, 1925.
Cora MacGeachy, stage designer, has designed over 200 costumes
for "Irene." 60 women in the fashion sequence will model about
200 gowns and accessories, costing over $75,000.

1227   Greenberg, Abe.   "Abe Greenberg's Voice of Hollywood; Edith
         Head Goes to Universal." Hollywood Citizen-News, March
         6, 1967, p. 5.
Edith Head will leave Paramount for Universal, effective March
27, 1967.   She has been nominated for at least one Academy
Award each year for costume design since the award began.

1228   Greene, Alice Craig, and Margaret Bramwell Charles.   "Occupa-
         tion Please...." Movieland, 4 (4): 46-7, 78-82, May 1946.
Brief mention of many behind-the-scenes film occupations, including those who prepare character and costume plots, sketchers,
cutters, fitters, drapers, seamstresses, and agers.   One aged
and torn dress worn by Jennifer Jones in "Duel in the Sun" required weeks of work.   It was boiled, bleached, sandpapered,
soaked in oil, and made in duplicates at certain stages for five
different scenes.   A snag became a tear in one scene, and then
appeared mended in the following scene.

1229   "Greenwood, Jane."   American Film Institute Catalog, 1961-70,
         p. 259.
Jane Greenwood is credited with the wardrobe of "Hamlet" (1964).

1230   "Greenwood, Jane."   Who's Who in the Theatre.   16th ed.,
         1977, p. 675-6.

1231   Greer, Howard.   Designing Male.   New York: Putnam's, 1949.
   Howard Greer discusses, for most of the book, working with Lady
   Duff Gordon, with whom he was associated as a designer for her
   establishment, the House of Lucile, and as a companion.   Im-
   poverished in Paris, he worked briefly for Erté and Paul Poiret.
   At the House of Lucile he worked with future film designers
   Robert Kalloch and Gilbert Clarke.   Clarke suggested to Famous
   Players-Lasky that they hire Greer instead of himself to be Pola
   Negri's designer, for her second American film and on, at a
   salary of $200 per week.   Constance Bennett refused to wear
   studio-provided costumes and instead bought hers in New York.
   He also discusses designing lavish and excessive costumes for
   Negri, as in "The Spanish Dancer"; designing a wardrobe in
   "Hell's Angels" for Greta Nissen, who was replaced two years
   later by Jean Harlow, for whom he made another wardrobe; working with Travis Banton and Edith Head, who consecutively succeeded
   him; and crossing over to design retail fashions in his own salon
   when he tired of designing ostentatious costumes for black-and-
   white films.

1232 _____. "I've Dressed Them All." <u>Modern Screen,</u> 7 (1):
          44-5, 76-7, 95, December 1933.
The first of four parts, in which Howard Greer discusses many
actresses he has designed for in his establishment, including
Greta Garbo, noting that she prefers very simple clothes off
screen in contrast to her exotic film costumes.

1233 _____. "I've Dressed Them All." <u>Modern Screen,</u> 7 (2):
          62-3, 99-100, January 1934.
A tulle gown designed by Howard Greer and worn by Mary Pickford in "Coquette" was photographed while on a dressform so that
she could study it from various angles objectively.

1234 _____. "I've Dressed Them All." <u>Modern Screen,</u> 7 (3):
          44-6, 90-1, February 1934.
Howard Greer mentions designing dark and simple clothes for
Ann Harding in "The Animal Kingdom," at her own request, and
designing many costumes worn by Clara Bow in her early films,
and in "Call Her Savage." Illustrations include a still of each,
and of Irene Dunne being fitted for an unnamed film (the writer
could find no record of the film with Greer receiving credit).

1235 _____. "I've Dressed Them All!" [sic] <u>Modern Screen,</u>
          7 (4): 48-9, 96, March 1934.
Brief mention of the excessively elaborate film costumes worn by
many actresses, as compared with their personal wardrobes.

1236 "Greer, Howard." <u>Fairchild's Who's Who in Fashion.</u> 1975,
          p. 106.
Howard Greer designed costumes for Paramount for five years,
until 1926 (actually, he was at Paramount 1923-8), when he opened
his own establishment. His clothes were sophisticated, wearable,
and not extreme. He retired in 1962.

1237 "Greet, Dinah." <u>American Film Institute Catalog, 1961-70,</u>
          p. 259.
Dinah Greet was the costume designer of "Help!," "How I Won
the War," and "The Looking Glass War"; the assistant dress
designer of "Macbeth" (1963); the dress designer of "The Italian
Job"; the associate costume designer of "Those Magnificent Men in
Their Flying Machines; or How I Flew from London to Paris in
25 Hours and 11 Minutes"; and is credited with the wardrobe for
"Inspector Clouseau" and for Michèle Mercier in "You Can't Win
'Em All."

1238 Gregory, Nina Dorothy. "The 'Designing' Pauline Frederick."
          <u>Motion Picture Classic,</u> 5 (3): 26, November 1917.
Having amassed a stock of film costumes, many of which were
specially designed for her, Pauline Frederick lost them all in a
fire at Famous Players' studio; she later designed and sewed costumes for "Zaza," "Bella Donna," "Sappho," "The Eternal City,"
"Her Better Self," and others not mentioned.

1239   "Greta Garbo's Negligee." Screenland, 18 (2): 32, December
       1928.
       Greta Garbo models a negligee designed by Adrian from "A Woman
       of Affairs"; the negligee will be awarded as a contest prize.

1240   Griffith, Corinne, as told to Carolyn Van Wyck. "Make Your
       Clothes Expressive!" Photoplay, 22 (3): 54-5, 102,
       August 1922.
       Corinne Griffith discusses her fashion preferences, noting that
       she prefers to design her clothes and have a dressmaker make
       them.   She loves dressed-up roles so that she can wear startling
       costumes, which her fans expect.

1241   Griffith, Richard. Anatomy of a Motion Picture. New York:
       St. Martin's, 1959.
       Includes one wardrobe-test each of James Stewart, Lee Remick,
       Arthur O'Connell, Eve Arden, Kathryn Grant, Murray Hamilton,
       Don Ross, Howard McNear, Brooks West, Alex Campbell, and
       Ken Lynch from "Anatomy of a Murder." Lana Turner turned down
       the lead role since she could not have a glamorous wardrobe; director
       Otto Preminger insisted upon a realistic wardrobe.   Includes a
       still of costume coordinator Hope Bryce.

1242   Griswold, J.B. "How Do You Look?" American Magazine,
       145 (5): 28-9, 143-5, May 1948.
       Lengthy article with advice by Edith Head concerning improving
       one's appearance.   Her first New Look wardrobe was for Betty
       Hutton in "Dream Girl." The only inauthentic thing she ever de-
       signed, she states, was Dorothy Lamour's sarong, since the au-
       thentic one would have been censored.

1243   "Gross, Laurence." American Film Institute Catalog, 1961-
       70, p.262.
       Laurence Gross is credited with the costumes of "Slaves."

1244   "Gründel, Dorit." American Film Institute Catalog, 1961-70,
       p.263.
       Dorit Gründel is credited with the costumes of "Pinocchio."

1245   "Gryś, Lidia." American Film Institute Catalog, 1961-70,
       p.263.
       Lidia Gryś is credited with the costumes of "Lotna."

1246   "Guerin, Charles." American Film Institute Catalog, 1961-
       70, p.263.
       Charles Guerin is credited with the wardrobe of "The 7th Dawn,"
       "Psycho-Circus," "Don't Raise the Bridge, Lower the River,"
       and "The Virgin Soldiers" and was the wardrobe master/super-
       visor for "Immoral Charge," "There Was a Crooked Man," and
       "The Long Duel."

1247   Guiles, Fred Lawrence. Marion Davies: A Biography. New
       York: McGraw-Hill, 1972.

William Randolph Hearst was fond of seeing Marion Davies, his
companion, in male costumes, and particularly slacks, so that
such sequences were often written into her films. She wore male
costumes in "Little Old New York," "The Red Mill, " "When
Knighthood Was in Flower," "Beverly of Graustark," "Operator
13," "Blondie of the Follies," and "Marianne." There was a
rumor at the time that Hearst would buy any film property that
allowed her to wear male attire. Theatrical-set designer Joseph
Urban and daughter Gretl Urban, a costume designer, collaborated
on Hearst films for almost a decade. Urban lost his valuable
collection of costume and set designs when a fire destroyed the
studio in which "Little Old New York" was being made. All of
the costumes were destroyed, but they were remade and the film
completed.

1248 "Gunter, Daisy." American Film Institute Catalog, 1961-70,
       p. 265.
Daisy Gunter is credited with the wardrobe of "The Devil's Bedroom. "

1249 "Guyot, Jacqueline." American Film Institute Catalog, 1961-
       70, p. 266.
Jacqueline Guyot was the costume designer of "Lady L," created
the costumes of "The Milky Way," and is credited with the costumes of "Lafayette" and "Yo Yo."

1250 Gwynn, Edith. "Dress Parade." Photoplay, 30 (6): 52-3,
       92-3, May 1947.
A handbag manufacturer will be producing copies of Joan Fontaine's handbag from "Ivy," which producer Bill Menzies commissioned for her, featuring an ornamental secret compartment.

1251 _____. "Gay Gadabouts." Photoplay, 31 (5): 64-5, 100-1,
       October 1947.
Ann Blyth models a wool plaid dress from "Brute Force," which
she bought for her own wardrobe.

1252 _____. "Peacock Parade." Photoplay, 32 (2): 60-1, 77,
       January 1948.
Description of a gown designed by Edith Head and worn by Gail
Russell in "The Night Has a Thousand Eyes," which she models,
and bought for her own wardrobe.

1253 "H. M. K. Smith, Head of the Costume Department at Famous
        Players...." Screen News, 3 (31): 26, August 2, 1924,
        col. 2.
After visiting Paris H. M. K. Smith traveled to Algiers, where he
purchased materials and studied Arab dress and customs for
"Wages of Virtue."

1254 "Haack, Morton." American Film Institute Catalog, 1961-70,
        p. 266.
Morton Haack was the costume designer of "The Unsinkable Molly
Brown," "Walk, Don't Run," "Planet of the Apes," and "Beneath
the Planet of the Apes"; the wardrobe designer of "Buona Sera,
Mrs. Campbell"; and is credited with the gowns of "Come Sep-
tember" and the costumes of "Jumbo."

1255 Haber, Joyce. "Edith Head Dresses Down the Fashion Flit-
        ters." Los Angeles Times, April 1, 1973, Calendar, p.
        17.
A review of the career of Edith Head, who had just become the
first fashion editor of Holiday.

1256 "Hackett, Florence." American Film Institute Catalog, 1961-
        70, p. 267.
Florence Hackett is credited with the costumes of "Support Your
Local Sheriff!" and the wardrobe of "House of Women," "Get
Yourself a College Girl," "Looking for Love," "Sunday in New
York," "36 Hours," "The Legend of Lylah Clare," and "Zigzag."

1257 "Haddock, Lillias." American Film Institute Catalog, 1961-
        70, p. 267.
Lillias Haddock is credited with the wardrobe of "To the Shores
of Hell."

1258 Haedrich, Marcel. Coco Chanel: Her Life, Her Secrets.
        Translated by Charles Lam Markmann. Boston: Little,
        Brown, 1972.
Charlie Chaplin once told Coco Chanel that he had copied her
fashions for the actresses in "City Lights" and would do so again,
since her styles are timeless.

1259 "Haffenden, Elizabeth." American Film Institute Catalog, 1961-
          70, p.267.
      Elizabeth Haffenden was the color costume designer of "A Man for
      All Seasons" and "The Prime of Miss Jean Brodie"; the costume
      designer of "Kill or Cure," "Behold a Pale Horse," and "The
      Liquidator"; the dress designer of "I Thank a Fool"; and is credited
      with the costumes of "The Amorous Adventures of Moll Flanders,"
      "Arrivederci, Baby!," "Chitty Chitty Bang Bang," and "Half a
      Sixpence."

1260 "Hagen, Lilo." American Film Institute Catalog, 1961-70,
          p.268.
      Lilo Hagen was the costume designer of "Town Without Pity."

1261 "Hahn, Birgitta." American Film Institute Catalog, 1961-70,
          p.268.
      Birgitta Hahn is credited with the costumes of "Night Games"
      and the costumes/technical costume advice of "Loving Couples."

1262 "Hahn, Manon." American Film Institute Catalog, 1961-70,
          p.268.
      Manon Hahn is credited with the costumes of "Die Fastnachts-
      beichte," "The Judge and the Sinner," and "Maedchen in Uniform."

1263 Hall, Gladys. "Hollywood Has Designs on You." Photoplay,
          47 (2): 62-4, 105-6, February 1955.
      Charles Le Maire, Edith Head, Bill Thomas, and Helen Rose
      discuss actresses they have designed for. Rose designed approxi-
      mately 27 costumes for Elizabeth Taylor in "The Last Time I
      Saw Paris." All costumes designed by Rose are worn over a
      brassiere and cinch combined for a good foundation. Edith Head
      describes a cocktail-into-dinner dress worn by Grace Kelly in
      "Rear Window."

1264 _____. "I'm a Career Girl Says Norma Shearer." Motion
          Picture, 63 (3): 32-3, 61-3, April 1942.
      Includes several stills of Norma Shearer in costumes by Robert
      Kalloch from "We Were Dancing."

1265 _____. "It for the Itless." Motion Picture, 36 (3): 64-5,
          84-5, October 1928.
      Biographical information on Howard Greer and a discussion of his
      new establishment, "Howard Greer, Incorporated."

1266 _____. "Women Are What They Wear." Screenland, 52
          (8): 40-1, 56, June 1948.
      Cecil Beaton discusses designing for Paulette Goddard in "An
      Ideal Husband" and Vivien Leigh in "Anna Karenina" (1947); he
      designed about 140 costumes for the former. Includes stills of
      both actresses.

1267 Hall, Helen Forrist. "Cinema Fashions." Cinema Arts
          (Preview Issue), 1 (1): 27, September 1936.

Discussion of how film costumes and West Coast designers are influencing fashion in the United States and abroad; copies of costumes worn in "Mary of Scotland" and by Grace Moore in "The King Steps Out" and by Shirley Temple can be bought in stores. Even before the films were released Lucien Lelong was copying a dress from "Ramona," and Marcel Rochas was featuring "Anthony Adverse" costume copies in his collection. One costume each is modeled by Carole Lombard and Gail Patrick from "My Man Godfrey," Patrick's designed by Brymmer (or Brymer); Patrick also models a costume by Travis Banton from "Murder in Pictures," and Margaret Sullavan one from "Next Time We Live."

1268   _____. "Hollywood at Work: Fashions from the Past. Fashions for the Future. Fashions in the Making." Cinema Arts [Preview Issue], 1 (1): 28-9, September 1936.
Includes quotes by the following designers (as well as Orry-Kelly): Adrian notes that each film influences fashion for at least 500,000 women. (Erroneously credits Adrian as working for Paramount.) Sketches are included of an adapted costume by Vera West worn by Jean Arthur in "Diamond Jim" and costumes worn by Gladys Swarthout in "Rose of the Rancho," by Travis Banton; Joan Crawford in "Letty Lynton," by Adrian; Shirley Temple in "The Little Colonel," by William Lambert; Loretta Young in "Private Number," by Gwen Wakeling; Katharine Hepburn in "Mary of Scotland," by Walter Plunkett; Grace Moore in "The King Steps Out," by Ernst Dryden; and unidentified actresses in the finale of "The Great Ziegfeld," by John Harkrider, and in "Roberta," by Bernard Newman. Designers West, Lambert, and Plunkett adapted the above costumes for retail sale.

1269 "Hall, Leslie." American Film Institute Catalog, 1961-70, p. 270.
Leslie Hall is credited with the wardrobe of "Journey to Shiloh."

1270 "Hall, Peter." American Film Institute Catalog, 1961-70, p. 270.
Peter Hall was the costume designer of "Doctor Faustus."

1271 "Halston." American Film Institute Catalog, 1961-70, p. 271.
Halston is credited with the wardrobe of "Pieces of Dreams," and Kay Thompson's costumes in "Tell Me That You Love Me, Junie Moon."

1272 "Halston." Current Biography. 1972, p. 200-2.

1273 Hamilton, Sara. "Secrets of the Fitting Room." Photoplay, 46 (4): 34-5, 104, March 1934.
Improbable article concerning how many actresses get hysterical over their film costumes: Carole Lombard screams with excitement over Travis Banton's costumes; Miriam Hopkins always finds parts that need fixing; Norma Shearer likes everything in white,

Joan Crawford everything in blue, with weights in the hem to prevent sagging; Greta Garbo likes new and humorous styles, as with
the pillbox hat in "As You Desire Me." Travis Banton designed
a normal-waistline wardrobe for Lilyan Tashman in an unnamed
film when the long waistline was in fashion, but fashion was changing as the film was released, and she was in the height of fashion.
A not-so-funny job of the designer occurs when an actress has
been removed from a film and does not find out until she shows
up at the wardrobe department to find her costumes are being
made over for another actress. Brief mention of Marlene Dietrich's coque feathered turban in "Shanghai Express."

1274   "Hamilton-Kearse, Virginia." American Film Institute Catalog,
        1961-70, p. 271.
Virginia Hamilton-Kearse was the clothes designer of "Joanna."

1275   Hampton, Edgar Lloyd. "A 1,200 Mile Style Parade." Nation's
        Business, 25 (4): 78, 80, 82, 84, 86, 88, 90, April 1937.
Discussion of the differences between Hollywood and Paris fashion
industries; their respective fashion influence in America; film-
costume design; and some of the manufacturers that market film
costumes. Examples of the influence of film costume on fashion
include Clara Bow's high waist, which was eventually adopted
worldwide; the "sex dress," which is tight-fitting; the youthful
style for women; and two types of hats, the small hat and the
brimless hat, both designed because of the camera--the brimmed
hat casts a shadow over the face that the camera photographs.

1276   Hampton, Hope. "For Women Only." Screen News, 2 (47):
        2, November 24, 1923.
Hope Hampton discusses assembling a screen wardrobe and the
importance of having a director's approval so that costumes in
each scene are harmonized with each actor. While shopping for
"The Gold Diggers" she had a jeweler make a monocle of blue
glass so that she could see how the colors would be photographed
by the camera.

1277   "Hancock, Ruth." American Film Institute Catalog, 1961-70,
        p. 273.
Ruth Hancock is credited with the wardrobe of "Lad: A Dog,"
"Wall of Noise," and "Dead Ringer."

1278   "Handiwork of Expert Revealed." Screen News, 1 (11): 21,
        May 6, 1922.
Biblical and archaeological authority Dr. Edgar James Banks is
the costume adviser, among other things, for "Abraham," produced by Sacred Films, Inc.

1279   Hannay, Evelyn. "An Easy-to-Take Fashion Pill." Review
        of The Dress Doctor by Edith Head and Jane Kesner
        Ardmore. San Francisco Chronicle, This World, March
        22, 1959, p. 16.
The author finds The Dress Doctor an exciting blend of "a motion

picture gossip magazine and Vogue."

1280 _____. "To All Appearances--"Winnie' for Adrian."
    San Francisco Chronicle, February 25, 1945, p.21.
Adrian, "a movie dressmaker" for 17 years, created a gown with
a peasant bodice and long sleeves for Greta Garbo in "Ninotchka,"
which was copied and marketed for tens of thousands of women.
(Adrian worked for film studios from 1925 to 1942, but created
film costumes less frequently before and after his studio contracts.)

1281 "Hanoszek, Anna." American Film Institute Catalog, 1961-70,
    p.273.
Anna Hanoszek is credited with the costumes of "Seven Daring
Girls."

1282 "Harbeck, Celine." American Film Institute Catalog, 1961-70,
    p.274.
Celine Harbeck is credited with the costumes of "Crazy Quilt."

1283 Harbert, Ruth. "Assignment in Hollywood; Hollywood's Store-
    house." Good Housekeeping, 137 (4): 16-7, 323, October
    1953.
Western Costume Company, owned by six major studios, houses
countless costumes and accessories rented for films. Employed
are many dressmakers, milliners, shoemakers, and others, so that
any garment or accessory not already in the collection can be made
in hours. A history is given of the company; its collection includes
costumes worn in "Call Me Madam," "Gone with the Wind," "Joan
of Arc," and "Blood and Sand" (1922).

1284 _____. "Assignment in Hollywood; The Robe." Good
    Housekeeping, 137 (1): 16-7, 199-200, July 1953.
Dorothea Hulse, who has her own weaving studio, discusses the
research and making of a seamless robe for "The Robe," with
reference to selecting the yarn and chemical cleaning and treatment. Four robes were made by Hulse, who also wove the fabrics for "David and Bathsheba." Charles Le Maire designed the
film's costumes and collaborated with Hulse on the robe's research.

1285 "Harkrider, John." American Film Institute Catalog, 1921-
    30, p.1138.
John Harkrider was the costume designer of "Whoopee!"

1286 Harmetz, Aljean. "'Below the Line,'" in The Making of "The
    Wizard of Oz." New York: Knopf, 1977, p.205-42,
    passim.
This book is distinguished by its lengthy and rare information
concerning the costuming of "The Wizard of Oz," for which many
wardrobe persons were interviewed, from laundry workers to
beaders. Frank Morgan's coat, for his role as Professor Marvel,
was first owned by the author of the book, L. Frank Baum; this
was reported in only one article (see "Hot from Hollywood"). Extensive references to costumes worn by Judy Garland, Jack Haley,

Bert Lahr, Ray Bolger, and Billie Burke, all of whose costumes were based on the original illustrations by W.W. Denslow as found in the Baum book, or according to the text, if described; and mention of inaccuracy in publicity reports--a little less than 1,000 costumes were made, rather than the 3,210 reported; problems with costume colors and lighting for Technicolor, as with light bouncing off the Tin Man's costume; Adrian's never using a sketch artist (unlike many film designers, who are actually supervisors rather than designers). Includes a wardrobe breakdown of costumes worn in the Emerald City sequence, prepared by the author's mother, Rose Meltzer, who prepared wardrobe plots and estimated costs for most MGM films from 1937 to 1951. Natalie Kalmus received credit on every Technicolor picture as part of her divorce settlement from husband and Technicolor president Herbert Kalmus; she showed up several times for the film. Lengthy references to the construction of the ruby slippers, and to what happened to many of the film's costumes when MGM auctioned over 30,000 of its costumes. One might wish for more references to Adrian, the film's costume designer.

1287 "Harold Lloyd in the Philippines." Screen News, 1 (17): 25, June 10, 1922.
One Harold Lloyd fan wrote him to say that suits he wears in his films are widely copied by men in the Philippines, and tailors frequently view his films to copy the suits.

1288 "Harris, Grace." American Film Institute Catalog, 1961-70, p.277.
Grace Harris is credited with the wardrobe of "Girls! Girls! Girls!," "Donovan's Reef," "In Harm's Way," "Blindfold," and "The Out-of-Towners" and the ladies' costumes of "The Stalking Moon."

1289 Harris, Julie. "Costume Designing." Films and Filming, 4 (2): 17, November 1957.
Julie Harris discusses breaking down a script in designing for a film, keeping up with fashion trends, period versus modern costume designing, color versus black-and-white films, and other aspects of designing. Brief mention of her costumes for "House of Secrets" and the researching of "Miracle in Soho" and "Across the Bridge."

1290 "Harris, Julie." International Motion Picture Almanac. 1974, p.95.

1291 "Harris, Julie, cost." American Film Institute Catalog, 1961-70, p.277.
28 credits are listed for designer Julie Harris.

1292 "Harris, Margaret F." Who's Who in the Theatre. 16th ed., 1977, p.704.
See "Motley." Who's Who in the Theatre.

1293 "Harris, Margaret Frances." <u>Who's Who</u>. 125th ed., 1973,
        p. 1410.

1294 Harris, Warren G. <u>Gable and Lombard</u>. New York: Simon
        and Schuster, 1974.
      Discussion of Carole Lombard wearing film and personal clothes
      by Travis Banton, and then by Irene when Banton left Paramount.
      Husband Clark Gable was a "fashion plate, like Lombard," having
      started trends for turtleneck sweaters and unusual hats. Gable
      did not want to make "Parnell" because he detested wearing period
      costumes. Notes also that Jean Harlow did not wear lingerie,
      effective during the filming of sexier scenes, and that Marion
      Davies wore a Venetian wedding gown made of 185 yards of satin
      and lace in "Cain and Mabel."

1295 Harrison, Helen. "Adrian's Fashion Secrets." <u>Hollywood</u>,
        23 (9): 42-3, 55, September 1934.
      Adrian notes that Greta Garbo's costumes must be very original
      and express "old world repose and maturity." Research for
      "Queen Christina" indicated that the Queen had no interest in
      clothes, so he dressed Garbo to suit her screen image during
      formal court functions, and in pants, like the real queen, for
      other occasions. His costumes for Joan Crawford in "Letty
      Lynton" had huge sleeves to suggest action.

1296 _____. "Headline Fashions!" <u>Screenland</u>, 30 (4): 26-7,
        82-4, February 1935.
      Adrian designs simple clothes for Jean Harlow's films, but with
      exaggerated details, since her roles require "revealing, exotic,
      even bizarre clothes." Often a designer must design clothes that
      tell the audience in a short moment what much dialogue could not,
      as with Norma Shearer in "Riptide," accomplished with slit skirts
      and other novelties. Greta Garbo has placed all of her faith in
      Adrian and allows him the freedom to dress her accordingly; he
      dresses her to suit her mind. Joan Crawford's huge sleeves in
      "Letty Lynton" suggested the restlessness of the character by the
      constant vibration in the sleeves as she moved. He also discusses
      adapting film costumes to one's wardrobe. Shearer models a
      gown from "Riptide," Crawford one from "Forsaking All Others,"
      and Garbo one from "The Painted Veil."

1297 _____. "Hollywood's Own Fashion Revolt!" <u>Screenland</u>,
        30 (5): 32-3, 87-8, March 1935.
      Travis Banton discusses the need for more realistic film cos-
      tumes; designing for Claudette Colbert in "The Gilded Lily"; and
      hats worn by Marlene Dietrich. Dietrich's costumes in "Caprice
      Espagnole" ("The Devil Is a Woman") will influence fashion.

1298 _____. "Screen Style Secrets!" <u>Screenland</u>, 30 (6): 32-3,
        75-6, April 1935.
      Bernard Newman describes some of the 150 costumes he designed
      for "Roberta," which cost approximately $50,000; it is his first
      film assignment. Irene Dunne and Ginger Rogers each model two

costumes from the film.

1299 _____. "Sculpturing with Scissors!" <u>Screenland,</u> 30 (7):
        56-7, 74-5, May 1935.
Rene Hubert discusses some of the actresses he has designed for
--including Gloria Swanson, and Claire Trevor in an unnamed
film--and how he designs for a film, with references to fabric
and color selections.

1300 _____. "Streamlining the Stars." <u>Screenland,</u> 30 (3): 26-
        7, 90-1, January 1935.
Orry-Kelly discusses film-costume designing, with brief mention
of a gown worn by Kay Francis in "Mandalay."

1301 "Harrison, Vangie." <u>American Film Institute Catalog, 1961-</u>
        <u>70,</u> p.278.
Vangie Harrison was the costume designer of "The Magic Christian" and is credited with the costumes of "De Sade" and "There's
a Girl in My Soup."

1302 "Harry Langdon's Overcoat." <u>Screen News,</u> 2 (40): 9, 21,
        October 6, 1923.
Harry Langdon has eight triangular overcoats, which have been
his trademark in both vaudeville and his three films; they were
made by a Chicago tailor. The importance of the coat is discussed; it is as much a trademark to Langdon as glasses are to
Harold Lloyd, a bamboo cane to Charlie Chaplin, and the check-
ered cape to Lloyd Hamilton. Langdon models the coat.

1303 Hart, William S. <u>My Life East and West.</u> Boston and New
        York: Houghton Mifflin, 1929.
Wardrobe forelady Mrs. Harris told William S. Hart that a laced
shirt was probably not an authentic shirt for him to wear in "The
Cold Deck." She took out a costume-history book and inside was
a portrait of a cowboy in a laced shirt--Hart himself in a shirt
his sister had made for him to wear in "The Squaw Man."

1304 "Harte, Michael." <u>American Film Institute Catalog, 1961-70,</u>
        p.278.
Michael Harte is credited with the wardrobe of "Advise and Consent," "The Illustrated Man," and "Chisum."

1305 Hartley, Katharine. "Not the Best-Dressed--But the Most
        Important." <u>Movie Classic,</u> 8 (6): 38-9, 79, August
        1935.
Discussion of the strong influence upon fashion of the costumes
and hats, all designed by Travis Banton, worn by Marlene Dietrich in "Shanghai Express," "The Song of Songs," and "The Devil
Is a Woman." Designers Kiviette and Lucien Lelong admitted to
being influenced by Dietrich's costumes. Banton said that his
greatest claim to fame was being Dietrich's designer. The author
calls her "the most important fashion influence in the world today,"
a more important distinction than being considered the "best-dressed."

1306   Hartmann, Cyril Hughes.   "The Technical Expert in British
       Films."   Hollywood Quarterly, 4 (4): 332-7, Summer
       1950.
Discussion of common errors in historical films, noting that en-
suring accuracy of sets and costumes in a historical film is less
important than authenticating the speech, behavior, and sentiments
of the period.

1307   "Hartnell, Norman."   American Film Institute Catalog, 1961-
       70, p. 279.
Norman Hartnell is credited with Fidelma Murphy's wardrobe in
"Never Put It in Writing."

1308   "Harton, Wally."   American Film Institute Catalog, 1961-70,
       p. 279.
Wally Harton is credited with the wardrobe of "Operation Eichmann," "Convicts 4," and "The T. A. M. I. Show" and the men's
wardrobe of "Hell Is for Heroes."

1309   "Harvest of the Motion Picture Plants."   It, 3 (29): 12, De-
       cember 4, 1920.
May Allison entered the ocean fully clothed for a scene in "Are
Wives to Blame," ruining a $1,400 gown.

1310   _____.   It, 3 (32): 12, December 25, 1920.
Designer Ethel Chaffin has returned from abroad, where she studied the latest fashion trends.

1311   Harwell, Richard, ed.   Margaret Mitchell's "Gone with the
       Wind" Letters, 1936-1949.   New York: Macmillan, 1976.
After selling her film rights to "Gone with the Wind" author
Margaret Mitchell repeatedly told David O. Selznick that she would
not give any advice, including with costumes, but did recommend
Susan Myrick as a period adviser; she was hired and acted as a
liaison between them.   Myrick, in working with costume designer
Walter Plunkett, did have one scene changed, where the young
ladies took a nap and their dresses were supposed to stand on
their own--impossible, since the metal hoops in their petticoats
were collapsible.   Mitchell was horrified when she heard, and
eventually saw, that Vivien Leigh, as Scarlett O'Hara, was wearing a black bonnet and long veil in the bazaar sequence, both of
which she felt were in bad taste to wear at a party while other
women wore décolleté gowns.   She also felt mortified at the fashion for Scarlett O'Hara bonnets (before the film's release), and
expressed concern over a need for "copyright of literary property,"
mainly as to commercial tie-ins, her example being Scarlett O'Hara
panties.

1312   Harwood, Jim.   "Of All the Head Gowns Sewn, Only a Few
       Can Be Reaped."   Variety (Daily), February 20, 1976,
       p. 6.
Only about a dozen gowns could be found for the Edith Head exhibit at the California Museum of Science and Industry, since most

of the costumes had been remade or reused, until they wore out.
The exhibit included one costume each worn by Mae West in "She
Done Him Wrong," Elizabeth Taylor in "A Place in the Sun,"
Shirley MacLaine in "Sweet Charity," Zizi Jeanmaire in "Anything
Goes," and Dorothy Lamour in "Road to Morocco." Also shown
was a wedding gown for Barbara Stanwyck in "The Lady Eve,"
which could not be worn because it was white satin and did not
photograph well, and a costume originally worn by Carole Lombard, worn by an unnamed person in "Gable and Lombard."

1313 Haskell, Marilyn. From Reverence to Rape. New York:
         Holt, Rinehart and Winston, 1974.
The power of the film studios (and the actresses, through their
costumes) in the 1930s was such that they could change the trend
of fashion.

1314 Hastings, Baird. Christian Bérard: Painter, Decorator, De-
         signer. Boston: Institute of Contemporary Art, 1950.
"Directly or indirectly," Christian Bérard "exerted a decisive influence over the careers of many a fashion designer. Vertès
developed a style similar to Bérard's; Cecil Beaton has a manner
which in some ways recalls that of his lifelong friend...." Includes mention of Bérard's contribution, through his costume designs, to "La Belle et la Bête" ("Beauty and the Beast"); the costumes were made by Pacquin (Pierre Cardin made them while employed by the couturier). He had been working on Jean Cocteau's
"Orphée" at the time of his death. Includes sketches of his costumes for "La Belle et la Bête" and "La Machine Infernale."

1315 "Hats Chosen to Accompany Frocks." Screen News, 4 (6):
         14-5, February 7, 1925.
Discussion of three hats worn by Norma Talmadge in "The Only
Woman," which she models.

1316 "Have Toga, Will Travel! And Jeff Dickey Has, Turning
         Campuses into Animal Houses." People Weekly, 10 (18):
         116-7. October 30, 1978.
$60,000 was spent by Universal on a toga-promotion campaign for
"National Lampoon's Animal House." Literally tens of thousands
of university students have appeared on campuses be-togaed (and
wearing laurel wreaths) "in what resembled the world's largest
white sale."

1317 Hawes, Elizabeth. Fashion Is Spinach. New York: Random
         House, 1938.
Notes that Greta Garbo reportedly wears whatever her designer,
Adrian, designs for her, including sequined day dresses for "Mata
Hari." One of the best "stunts" pulled by the fashion industry was
a fad for Eugenie hats, as worn by Greta Garbo in "Romance,"
which ceased to be fashionable as soon as the industry used up its
surplus supply of feathers.

1318 _____. "Hollywood Fashion Is Spinach." Screenland, 37
         (6): 24-7, October 1938.

Elizabeth Hawes analyzes film costume in relation to her fashion philosophy, as found in her book Fashion Is Spinach. She blames the poor taste of much of film costume upon the public, the actresses, and the designers, all of whom should plead for more functional designs. Examples of "Spinach" shown are costumes worn by Bette Davis, Joan Crawford, Loretta Young, and Claudette Colbert, most of whom the author feels would not wear such clothes in their private lives. She also discusses women who copy film costumes and says of the designers and actresses, "Since they both get paid plenty of money, it is idle to waste too much sympathy on them, I suppose, although neither seems very happy about the clothing situation." The only film designer she has met is Adrian, who "has all my sympathy and no blame" since, as Adrian notes, some actresses have misconceptions of themselves and insist upon costumes that are not flattering. (See Orry-Kelly's reply, "Hollywood Fashion Defended.")

1319   "Hayes, David." American Film Institute Catalog, 1961-70,
          p. 282.
David Hayes is credited with the fashions of "Beyond the Valley of the Dolls."

1320   "Hayes, Sadie." American Film Institute Catalog, 1961-70,
          p. 282.
Sadie Hayes is credited with the costumes of "Chastity."

1321   "Haynes, Harry." American Film Institute Catalog, 1961-70,
          p. 282.
Harry Haynes was the costume designer of "The Brides of Fu Manchu" and "Baby Love"; wardrobe supervisor of "Portrait of a Sinner" and "Captain Sinbad"; and wardrobe master of "Double Bunk," "Ladies Who Do," "The Model Murder Case," "Saturday Night Out," and "The Devil's Own."

1322   "Hayward, Douglas." American Film Institute Catalog, 1961-
          70, p. 282.
Douglas Hayward is credited with the costumes for Terence Stamp in "Modesty Blaise," and Noel Coward in "Boom!," Stephen Boyd's clothes in "Assignment K," and Peter Lawford's wardrobe in "Salt & Pepper."

1323   "He Speaks for Fashion's 'Perverse Truth.'" New York Times,
          December 19, 1971, sec. 1, p. 62.
Cecil Beaton feels that Hollywood was "at its worst point from a sartorial point of view" in the 1940s and does not like the return to fashions of that period.

1324   Head, Edith. "Be Glad You're Small." Movieland, 4 (6): 58-
          9, 70-1, July 1946.
Edith Head discusses designing for short women, with one sketch each of costumes worn by Veronica Lake in "The Blue Dahlia," Virginia Welles in "To Each His Own," Olivia de Havilland in "The Well-Groomed Bride," and Olga San Juan in "Blue Skies."

1325 _____. "Change-About." Photoplay, 33 (5): 87, October
        1948.
Edith Head discusses some of her costumes for Gail Russell in
"The Night Has a Thousand Eyes."

1326 _____. "A Costume Problem: From Shop to Stage to
        Screen." Hollywood Quarterly, 2 (1): 44-8, October
        1946.
Edith Head shows through sketches how a typical suit was adapted
for numerous actresses by changing the color and accessories,
with one sketch each of Barbara Stanwyck in "Cry Wolf!," Veronica
Lake in "The Blue Dahlia," Joan Fontaine in "The Affairs of
Susan," Ingrid Bergman in "The Arch of Triumph," Dorothy La-
mour in "My Favorite Wife," and Loretta Young in "The Perfect
Marriage."

1327 _____. "Edith Head's Fashion Flashes." Screenland, 52
        (12): 44-5, 66, October 1948.
Edith Head discusses fashion trends, with brief mention of a
gown worn by Ilka Chase in "Miss Tatlock's Millions," which
Chase models.

1328 _____. "Edith Head's Fashion Flashes." Screenland, 53
        (1): 46-7, 57-8, November 1948.
Wanda Winter models six costumes by Edith Head from "Miss
Tatlock's Millions."

1329 _____. "Edith Head's Fashion Flashes." Screenland, 53
        (2): 46-7, 71-2, December 1948.
Barbara Stanwyck models a gown and blouse by Edith Head from
"Sorry, Wrong Number."

1330 _____. "Edith Head's Fashion Flashes." Screenland, 53
        (3): 46-7, 62-3, January 1949.
Biographical information on Edith Head, her typical duties as a
designer, and her reflections on how film costume has changed
since she first started. She briefly mentions that her wardrobes
for Lizabeth Scott in "Bitter Victory," Wanda Hendrix in "Miss
Tatlock's Millions," and Loretta Young in "The Accused" could
be worn by women in the professions in which the actresses are
portrayed in their films.

1331 _____. "Head on Fashion." Holiday, 53 (1): 24, 65-6,
        January/February 1973.
Edith Head discusses selecting clothing for traveling purposes,
with brief mention of Ava Gardner in "The Life and Times of
Judge Roy Bean" and Jane Fonda in "A Doll's House."

1332 _____. "Head on Fashion." Holiday, 56 (5): 20,
        September/October 1975.
Edith Head discusses traveling to location shooting in Russia for
"The Bluebird" and to Morocco for "The Man Who Would Be
King," where she set up a wardrobe factory.

1333 _____. "Head on Fashion." Holiday, 57 (2): 18, March
          1976.
Edith Head had a hard time locating authentic satins and jewelry
as worn in the 1930s for Jill Clayburgh in "Gable and Lombard."
She discusses how contemporary the period costumes are, and
some of the designers, and the actresses they designed for, who
have particularly influenced fashion.   She avoids the use of fur for
costumes unless it was bred for fashion purposes; fake fur photographs like the real thing.   Much of the jewelry worn was authentic, though some pieces were made for the film.   Zippers
were also not available then, so dresses were fastened with hooks
and eyes (zippers were in fact available but were not yet fashionable; Carole Lombard wore at least one gown with a zipper in
"Swing High Swing Low").

1334 _____. "Head on Fashion; Body by Head." Holiday, 54
          (1): 8, 10, July/August 1973.
Brief mention of fashion preferences of some of the actresses and
actors Edith Head has designed for: Cary Grant liked the color
scheme of his wardrobe planned around that of his leading lady,
and Mae West always wanted her dresses tighter.

1335 _____. "Head on Fashion; In Fitting Detail." Holiday, 55
          (5): 6, 16, September/October 1974.
Discussion of the basics of costume designing, how some film
actors and actresses have reacted to fitting sessions, and period
costuming versus modern-day.   Brief mention of costumes by
Edith Head worn by Karen Black, Charlton Heston, and others in
"Airport '75."

1336 _____. "Head on Fashion; Purple and Other Passions."
          Holiday, 56 (2): 12-3, March 1975.
Discussion of color preferences and dislikes of many actresses
and actors and the symbolism color plays in telling a story in
films; with brief mention of Katharine Hepburn in "Rooster Cogburn"; Paul Newman in "Winning," "Butch Cassidy and the Sundance Kid," and "The Sting"; Robert Redford; and "The Bluebird."

1337 _____. "Head on Fashion; The Imagists." Holiday, 55
          (6): 12, 15, November/December 1974.
Discussion of creating images and typecasting in Hollywood and
of how Edith Head reinforced such images through costume, including Dorothy Lamour's in "The Jungle Princess" and the "Road"
films.   Like Lamour, June Allyson was typecast by her image
and costumes and was not successful when she tried to break that
image in "The Shrike."

1338 _____. "Head on Fashion; Uncovering the Subject." Holiday,
          56 (1): 8, 12, January/February 1975.
Discussion of the trend toward brief costumes, including the bikini
worn by Hugh O'Brian in "Love Has Many Faces," by Edith Head,
who notes that it was the first of its kind.   Cary Grant refused to
wear brief bathing trunks in his films; another example of modesty--

Bing Crosby refused to wear women's clothes in "White Christmas. " Brief mention also of Marlon Brando in "One-Eyed Jacks"
and of censorship, as with the barely covered men in the jungle
pictures that starred Dorothy Lamour, who was comparatively
well covered.

1339   _____. "Honesty in Today's Film Fashions. " Show, 1 (10):
           14-5, August 6, 1970.
Edith Head states that contemporary film costumes no longer set
fashion trends because women tend to find their own style. Also,
today's films stress reality and are often hard-hitting, so that
costumes offer nothing new or innovative. References to Audrey
Hepburn in "Sabrina, " with one sketch; Kim Darby in "Red Sky
at Morning"; and Mae West in "Myra Breckenridge, " with one
sketch.

1340   _____. "Many Styles in New Film. " Hollywood Citizen-
           News, April 1, 1969, sec. A, p. 7.
Edith Head briefly mentions the types of clothing worn in "Sweet
Charity, " as with "classic" for John McMartin, "super chic" for
Ricardo Montalban, and "self-expression" for Sammy Davis, Jr.

1341   _____. "The Season for Party Pretties. " Silver Screen,
           18 (3): 50-1, 80-2, January 1948.
Discussion of gowns by Edith Head worn by Betty Hutton in "Dream
Girl" and by Gail Russell in "The Night Has a Thousand Eyes, "
two of which she models; Lizabeth Scott models a gown from "I
Walk Alone. "

1342   _____. Taped Lecture. University of Southern California,
           Special Collections Library. May 7, 1972. [About 35
           minutes.]
Edith Head discusses career opportunities as a film-costume designer; war restrictions of fabrics in World War II; film costume
in the silent era; and current conditions of costume in film, where
the emphasis is on social conditions. References to costumes
worn in "The Golden Bed" and worn by Lauren Bacall in "Applause, " Olivia de Havilland in "The Heiress, " Shirley MacLaine
in "What a Way to Go, " Bette Davis in "Pocketful of Miracles, "
and others; and film costumes she did not design, including those
in "Gaslight, " and Ali McGraw's in "Love Story. "

1343   _____. "Tomato Surprise. " [Letters to the Editor]. Time,
           81 (17): 16, April 26, 1963.
In a previous review of "I Could Go On Singing" (see "Garlandiana"),
it was said that Judy Garland looked "as though 8 large tomatoes
had been stuffed into a small dress. " Edith Head wrote a witty
reply to say that she had never seen the dress, though she had
designed Garland's costumes for the film.

1344   _____, and Jane Kesner Ardmore. The Dress Doctor.
           Boston: Little, Brown, 1959.
In her autobiography Edith Head says comparatively little about

herself in relation to the many films and actresses she has designed for. The book makes for pleasant reading, particularly
for those new to film costume, but much of it has been repeated
considerably in other sources. Illustrated with 24 black-and-white
stills.

1345   _____, and _____. "I Dress the World's Most Glamor-
              ous Women." Good Housekeeping, 148 (3): 64-7, 127-31,
              March 1959.
Excerpts from The Dress Doctor concerning costumes worn by
Marlene Dietrich in "Witness for the Prosecution," and Audrey
Hepburn in "Sabrina," with one still of each; Grace Kelly in "The
Country Wife," "Rear Window," and "To Catch a Thief"; Sophia
Loren in "Houseboat" and "One Black Orchid," with a photo from
"Heller"; Kim Novak in "Vertigo"; Rita Hayworth in "Separate
Tables"; and Eva Marie Saint in "That Certain Feeling."

1346   _____, as told to Bee Bangs. "Let's Be Glamourous!"
              Movie Show, 5 (10): 62-3, 95-7, June 1947.
Edith Head discusses designing for Lizabeth Scott in "Desert Fury"
and suggests how readers can adapt the costumes to their own
wardrobe. Scott models two costumes, with two sketches.

1347   _____, as told to Gladys Hall. "Dress Your Type."
              Screenland, 68 (11): 33-7, 78, 80, September 1944.
Edith Head discusses the fashion styles of many actresses she
has designed for so that the reader can find her type and dress
accordingly. The actresses discussed include Veronica Lake,
Paulette Goddard, Barbara Stanwyck, Betty Hutton, Ginger Rogers,
Loretta Young, and Dorothy Lamour.

1348   _____, as told to Gladys Hall. "Simple Chic for Small In-
              comes." Silver Screen, 16 (11): 46-7, 93-5, September
              1946.
Discussion of costumes worn by Loretta Young in "The Perfect
Marriage," five of which she models. Includes also a sketch of
one costume each worn by Veronica Lake in "The Blue Dahlia"
and Virginia Welles in "To Each His Own."

1349   _____, with Joe Hyams. How to Dress for Success. New
              York: Random House, 1967.
A book of Edith Head's philosophy on successful dressing, with
the following references to film costumes, and other very general
ones: visiting Macy's pet department with Natalie Wood to obtain
an authentic smock for her role in "Love with the Proper Stranger";
clothes copied after film costumes are usually less flamboyant,
with examples of the ruffled shirt from "Tom Jones," the hat from
"My Fair Lady," and the bias-cut gowns from "Harlow"; having a
bike in the fitting room for Julie Andrews to practice on with a
costume from "Torn Curtain"; Shirley MacLaine climbing the
social ladder with $500,000 worth of gowns and $3,000,000 worth
of jewels in "What a Way to Go"; reactions to color psychology,
and color preferences, of some actresses; and the importance of

lingerie in changing one's figure, as with Julie Andrews's silhouette in "Mary Poppins," "Torn Curtain," "Hawaii," and "Thoroughly
Modern Millie."

1350 "Head, Edith." <u>American Film Institute Catalog, 1961-70,</u>
         p. 283.
91 credits are listed for designer Edith Head.

1351 "Head, Edith." <u>Celebrity Register</u>. 3rd ed., 1973, p. 228.
Edith Head was born in 1907 (sources conflict) and grew up in
Mexico and on Indian reservations in the Southwest. She discusses
briefly her dislike of contemporary films and film fashions.

1352 "Head, Edith." <u>Current Biography</u>. 1945, p. 276-8.

1353 "Head, Edith." <u>Fairchild's Who's Who in Fashion</u>. 1975,
         p. 115.
Edith Head became the chief designer for Paramount in 1938 when
Travis Banton left. She has been nominated for an Academy Award
at least 30 times, has written two books, and articles for newspapers and magazines, and now designs for Universal Studios.

1354 "Head, Edith," in <u>Fashion Is Our Business</u>, by Beryl Williams
         [Epstein]. New York: Lippincott, 1945, p. 138-55.
Discussion of Edith Head's early life, her duties as a film de-
signer, and her costumes for Dorothy Lamour in "Road to Utopia,"
Claudette Colbert in "Zaza," and Louise Campbell in "Men with
Wings."

1355 "Head, Edith." <u>International Encyclopedia of Film</u>. New
         York: Crown, 1972, p. 260.

1356 "Head, Edith." <u>Who's Who in America</u>. 37th ed., 1972-3,
         p. 1379.

1357 "Head, Edith." <u>Who's Who of American Women</u>. 8th ed.,
         1974-5, p. 407.

1358 "Head, Edith." <u>World Who's Who of Women</u>. 2nd ed., 1974-
         5, p. 523.

1359 Heath, Lance. "Wells Fargo." <u>Jones' Magazine</u>, 1 (5): 51-3,
         86-7, December 1937.
For "Wells Fargo" "Hollywood's wardrobe facilities were taxed to
the limit, on several occasions every costume of the 1850s available being 'in work.'"

1360 "Heavy Costumes." <u>MGM Studio News</u>, 5 (6): n.p., August
         15, 1938.
The weight of Norma Shearer's 34 costumes in "Marie Antoinette"
came to 1,768 pounds, about 17 times her weight.

1361 "Heckroth, Hein." <u>American Film Institute Catalog, 1961-70,</u>
         p. 284.

Hein Heckroth was the costume designer of "Three Penny Opera."

1362   "Heckroth, Hein," in Art and Design in the British Film, by
          Edward Carrick.   London: Dobson, 1948, p. 64-6.
Hein Heckroth, German artist and theatrical and ballet designer,
designed the costumes of "Caesar and Cleopatra," "Black Narcissus," and "The Red Shoes."

1363   "Hegarty, Hazel."   American Film Institute Catalog, 1961-70,
          p. 284.
Hazel Hegarty is credited with the costumes of "Young Fury."

1364   "Heim."   American Film Institute Catalog, 1961-70, p. 284.
Heim is credited with the gowns of "The Cheaters."

1365   "Helen Chadwick in Universal Photoplay."   Screen News, 4
          (24): 3, June 13, 1925.
Helen Chadwick has been selecting her film costumes for "The
Still Alarm" from fashion magazines of 1908--though she will age
17 years in the film and also wear modern-day fashions.

1366   "Helen Chadwick Is More Popular in Beautiful Clothes...."
          Screen News, 4 (46): 7, November 21, 1925, col. 1.
Helen Chadwick receives more fan mail after films are released
in which she wears beautiful clothes.   In her next two films,
"The Still Alarm" and "The Golden Cocoon," she will proceed
from plain to beautiful clothes as the stories unfold.

1367   "Helen Chadwick to Become Costume Designer."   Screen News,
          3 (22): 21, May 31, 1924.
Helen Chadwick is no longer satisfied as an actress and is studying with a New York designer so that she can design her film
costumes.   She has previously worn some studio-designed costumes but will design her costumes for "Her Own Free Will."
Notes (erroneously) that she is the only actress who designs her
own costumes.

1368   "Helen Jerome Eddy Turns Back Pages of Fashion's Calender
          --Finds She Leads."   Screen News, 1 (34): 8, 13, Oc-
          tober 14, 1922.
While selecting her wardrobe for "When Love Comes" Helen
Jerome Eddy found that the fashions of a few years earlier, in
which the film is set, would be the fashions for the next year,
so that her costumes would be fashionable when the film was released.   For her role as a village girl in New England she selected longer and fuller costumes, avoiding the flapper look.

1369   "Helen Lynch, One of the Stars in ... 'The Dangerous
          Age'...."   Screen News, 1 (41): 30, December 2, 1922,
          col. 1.
Helen Lynch models a gown from "The Dangerous Age."

1370   "Helen Vinson in 'Vogues of 1938.'"   Vogue, 90 (1): 72,

July 1, 1937.
Helen Vinson models a gown (seen from the back) from "Vogues of 1938," of which Macy's will be selling copies.

1371 "Helfgott, Ann." American Film Institute Catalog, 1961-70,
            p. 285.
Ann Helfgott is credited with the women's wardrobe of "The Caretakers" and the costumes of "Flap."

1372 "Helm, Jacques." American Film Institute Catalog, 1961-70,
            p. 285.
Jacques Helm is credited with Marina Vlady's wardrobe in "Don't Tempt the Devil."

1373 Henderson, Jessie. "A Day with a Queen." Hollywood, 27
            (8): 32, 40-1, August 1938.
In "Marie Antoinette" Norma Shearer wore a wedding gown equal to her own weight, 110 pounds. Her wardrobe consists of 34 costumes, none weighing less than 52 pounds (she wore at least one nightgown, also). The steel hoop worn under the gowns was fastened to a type of foundation that allowed the weight to hang from her shoulders. Over this was worn three frilled petticoats (a departure from history, since ladies of the French court allegedly wore no lingerie).

1374 Hendrick, Kimmis. " 'Paris' Clothes by Helen Rose."
            Christian Science Monitor, August 13, 1965, p. 6.
Helen Rose has designed the "Parisian" costumes for "Made in Paris," which will include a fashion-show sequence of 36 purposely far-out and elegant costumes.

1375 "Henze, Jurgen." American Film Institute Catalog, 1961-70,
            p. 287.
Jurgen Henze was the costume designer of "The Mercenary."

1376 "Herberg, Claudia." American Film Institute Catalog, 1961-
            70, p. 287.
Claudia Herberg was the costume designer of "Fanny Hill: Memoirs of a Woman of Pleasure" and is credited with the costumes of "Faust."

1377 Herbert, H. "Passing the Censors Without Clothes." Motion
            Picture, 20 (9): 56, 108, October 1920.
The success with which Bob Gordon broke into the movies is attributed to his not having money for clothes, and consequently in acting in character parts that included studio-provided clothes.

1378 "Herbert, Jocelyn." American Film Institute Catalog, 1961-
            70, p. 287.
Jocelyn Herbert was the costume designer of "Ned Kelly" and is credited with the costumes for the National Theatre of Great Britain in "Othello."

1379   "Herbert, Jocelyn." _Who's Who in the Theatre._ 16th ed.,
         1977, p. 724-5.

1380   "Here, Girls, Are Screen Clothes That Will Start Something!"
         Photoplay, 40 (6): 38-41, November 1931.
       Joan Bennett, Ina Claire, and Madge Evans model costumes from
       "The Greeks Had a Word for Them," designed by Gabrielle Chanel,
       who also designed Gloria Swanson's costumes in "Tonight or Never."

1381   "Here They Are! Joan's Latest." _Modern Screen,_ 10 (4): 48-
         50, March 1935.
       Joan Crawford models three costumes by Adrian from "Forsaking
       All Others."

1382   "'Here We Go 'Round the Mulberry Bush.'" _American Film
         Institute Catalog, Feature Films, 1961-70,_ p. 473.
       The following designers, credited with "special fashion coopera-
       tion," were left out of the companion volume, the Credit Index,
       of the _American Film Institute Catalog_: Veronica Marsh, Graziella
       Fontana, Clare and Deborah, Ritva, and Moya.

1383   "Here's How Chanel of Paris Dresses Ina and Joan." _Motion
         Picture,_ 42 (6): 56-7, January 1932.
       Joan Bennett models one costume from "The Greeks Had a Word
       for Them," and Ina Claire, two, including a $40,000 chinchilla
       coat, and a hat influenced by the Empress Eugenie hat worn by
       Greta Garbo in "Romance," designed by Gabrielle Chanel.

1384   "Here's One Reason Why Men Do Not Get Movie Struck,"
         Screen News, 1 (21): 13, July 8, 1922.
       David Powell has the equivalent of a small shop of men's clothing,
       with at least 57 suits. He does not keep changing his suits in a
       film so that he will not call attention to them if worn in another
       film, or distract the audience by constantly changing them.

1385   Herrick, Hal. "He Decides Fashions for the Stars." _New
         Movie,_ 9 (3): 53, March 1934.
       Adrian's hats for Greta Garbo in "Romance" and "As You Desire
       Me" were instantly copied by "millions" of women, though the
       small, flat, pill-box hat she wore in "As You Desire Me" was
       first laughed at. Joan Crawford's puffed sleeves in "Letty Lynton"
       became the rage with women and clothing manufacturers.

1386   "Herrington, George." _American Film Institute Catalog, 1961-
         70,_ p. 288.
       George Herrington is credited with the wardrobe of "Surf Party."

1387   "Herschel." _Photoplay,_ 34 (5): 85, April 1949.
       Herschel briefly discusses his costumes for Susan Hayward in
       "Tulsa."

1388   Herwood, Marion. "Suit Yourself in Your First Job." _Silver
         Screen,_ 18 (10): 40-1, 70-1, August 1948.

Jane Wyman models six costumes designed by Marion Herwood from "No Minor Vices." Herwood, once an assistant to Irene, is chief designer for Enterprise Productions.

1389   Herzberg, Max J.   "A Preliminary Guide to the Study and
          Appreciation of the Screen Version of Shakespeare's
          'Romeo and Juliet,'" in "Romeo and Juliet": A Motion
          Picture Edition, by William Shakespeare.   New York:
          Random House, 1936, p. 269-90.
In "Facts About the Photoplay Production" it is noted that Adrian and Oliver Messell designed 1,250 costumes for "Romeo and Juliet" and sketched the most costumes for any film yet made. Several of the artworks used for research are noted, including a gown adapted for Norma Shearer from a Botticelli painting.

1390   _____.   "A Preliminary Study Guide to the Screen Version
          of Shakespeare's 'Romeo and Juliet'; Facts About the
          Photoplay Production."   Photoplay Studies, 2 (3): 16,
          March 1936.
See the previous entry.

1391   Heston, Charlton.   The Actor's Life, Journals 1956-76.   Edited
          by Hollis Alpert.   New York: Dutton, 1978.
Charlton Heston's diary, spanning 20 years, has necessarily brief entries.   References include: that a Mexican tailor made his suit for "A Touch of Evil"; briefly, his costumes for "The Buccaneer" and "Ben-Hur"; the civilian clothes in "The Pigeon That Took Rome" did not seem right; his clothes in "Diamond Head" first looked like costumes rather than clothes; his researching and sketching his uniform for "55 Days at Peking," which was eventually designed by studio designers; his simple wardrobe in "The Agony and the Ecstasy" was copied from portraits of Michelangelo; unhappiness with the pants, chain-mail, and new-looking costumes for "The War Lord"; his period costumes in "The Hawaiians" were modern in appearance; his armor for "Julius Caesar," made by Nathans, did not fit right; and he notes that Hildegard Neil wore Greek costumes in "Antony and Cleopatra" because Cleopatra was an Alexandrian Greek, not an Egyptian.   The sketches and the costumes, made in Florence, for "El Cid" were excellent, though fitting the 11 fifteenth-century costumes and armor was torturous; with discussion of his chain-mail for this and "The War Lord," which he authenticated in a London museum.   He flew to London for fittings of "The Three Musketeers" (1973) costumes, which fit badly; and he notes that the costume designer copied the wrong character found in engravings of the period and consequently designed two wrong costumes, one of which he wore.

1392   "Hi, Miss Winter!"   Photoplay with Movie Mirror, 20 (2): 45-
          9, January 1942.
Barbara Stanwyck models three costumes from "You Belong to Me," with the original sketches by Edith Head.

1393   "Hickson of Fifth Avenue."   American Film Institute Catalog,
          1921-30, p. 1151.

Hickson of Fifth Avenue designed the furs for "Ermine and Rhine-stones."

1394   Higham, Charles.   Marlene: The Life of Marlene Dietrich.
          New York: Norton, 1977.
       Includes references to Marlene Dietrich's bisexual appeal, demon-
       strated with a tuxedo she wore in "Blonde Venus"; how, with ex-
       tensive costume fittings with the "neurotic" Travis Banton, she
       endured costume tests with heavy costumes under hot lights for
       "The Scarlet Empress"; how she would tape her bosom for uplift
       rather than wear a brassiere; and how she was fired, and the film
       eventually canceled, when she glamorized her appearance for the
       nonglamorous lead role in "Hotel Imperial." Her costumes for
       "Stage Fright" were designed by Christian Dior, with mention of
       how Dietrich instructed the wardrobe department to care for them.

1395   "Hilborn, Thelma."   American Film Institute Catalog, 1961-70,
          p. 291.
       Thelma Hilborn is credited with the wardrobe of "The Sergeant
       Was a Lady."

1396   "Hildebrandt, Gudrun."   American Film Institute Catalog, 1961-
          70, p. 291.
       Gudrun Hildebrandt is credited with the costumes of "Die Fleder-
       maus."

1397   Hill, Gertrude.   "Hollywood Leads the Fashion Parade."
          Movie Classic, 8 (3): 40-1, 80-1, May 1935.
       Discussion of many costumes by Travis Banton worn by Mae West
       in "How Am I Doin'?" ('Goin' to Town"), one of which she models.
       Banton notes that her costumes are amusing because they make
       men nervous.   Brief mention of costumes by Omar Kiam worn by
       Ann Sothern in "Folies Bergère."

1398   _____.   "Looking Over the New Hollywood Fashions."
          Movie Classic, 8 (1): 38-9, 73, March 1935.
       Discussion of costumes worn by Joan Crawford in "Forsaking All
       Others," one of which she models, and by Ginger Rogers in
       "Roberta," which will feature a fashion show in which 105 cos-
       tumes, designed by Bernard Newman, will be modeled.

1399   Hill, Gladwin.   "Noted Film Gowns Face Retirement."   New
          York Times, November 29, 1960, p. 44.
       Edith Head is the caretaker of a collection of historically impor-
       tant film costumes that have been stored since they were worn
       out due to occasional showings.   The collection includes gowns
       worn by Jean Harlow in "Hell's Angels," Gloria Swanson in "Male
       and Female," Mae West in "She Done Him Wrong," and Clara
       Bow in "It."

1400   "Hime, Marvin."   American Film Institute Catalog, 1961-70,
          p. 292.
       Marvin Hime is credited with the jewelry worn by Julie Andrews

in "Darling Lili."

1401 "A Hint to Brides." Screen News, 3 (12): 28, March 22, 1924.
Lucille Ricksen models a gown from "The Galloping Fish."

1402 Hirsch, Virginia Antoinette. Edith Head, Film Costume Designer. University of Kansas, Ph. D. dissertation, 1973.
When this was written it was the only Ph. D. thesis related to
film costume, and is the only graduate work included in this
bibliography. Leaning considerably on Edith Head's autobiography,
The Dress Doctor, this has little new information on how a film
is costumed or on the life of Edith Head. It is, still, a most
impressive study of the films she has designed, with sections
analyzing 27 of the films for which she has been nominated for an
Academy Award; an additional section analyzes 431 costumes from
the above films, ranging from lingerie to beachwear, as to how
frequently they appear in the films and how successfully they were
designed. Some 55 sketches and stills are included, with a list
of credits from 1927 to 1973. The bibliography is extensive but
often consists of incomplete clippings from Head's own files, which
are consequently impossible to locate. Other topics: studios no
longer keep fabrics in stock (the designer shops for them in fabric
stores); the guests in a reception sequence of "Pocketful of Miracles" wore vintage costumes from Head's collection; and copies of
costumes from "Topaz" and "Airport" were marketed for retail
stores, with Head also allowing other film costumes to be marketed as patterns through Advance Pattern Company, circa 1960.
Hirsch notes: " ... we should expect the history of film costume
design and techniques of the outstanding designers to be well documented. Unfortunately, quite the opposite is true."

1403 "Hitch Your Fashions to a Star." New Movie, 6 (6): 52-5,
79, December 1932.
Radio Pictures brought Josette de Lima to Hollywood after she
had achieved success as a theatrical designer working at an (unnamed) Fifth Avenue store, where she had her own salon. She
discusses designing a gown for Myrna Loy in "Thirteen Women";
Loy comments on how the gowns helped her performance. She
discusses at length the actresses she has designed for and how
women can find their own style by studying them. One gown each
is modeled by Constance Bennett from "Rock-a-Bye" and Jill Esmond from "Is My Face Red."

1404 Hoadley, Ray. "Wardrobe and Costumes," in How They Make
a Motion Picture. New York: Crowell, 1939. p. 39-44.
Discussion of how a film is costumed, with mention of the importance of Western Costume Company in supplying costumes for
extras.

1405 Hoffman, Catherine. "From Fashion to Fame." Modern
Movies, 2 (6): 32-3, 58, December 1938.
Discussion of the career of Vyvyan Donner, director of the weekly
fashion newsreel of Twentieth Century-Fox, begun in 1929.

1406 Hoffman, Hugh. "New York Fashion Show in Pictures." Moving Picture World, 18 (1): 32, October 4, 1913.
In order to film the biannual New York Fashion Show, and with only a few days in which to do so, newspaperman Wilbur W. Nugent formed the Ny-Fax Company and hired camerman Herman Obrock, Jr., who soon assumed full responsibility. The film, and the proposed series, will be shown in theaters and department stores. A number of suggestions are included, especially that professional actresses be hired instead of fashion models.

1407 "Hoffman, Pat." American Film Institue Catalog, 1961-70, p.295.
Pat Hoffman is credited with the wardrobe of "Women of Desire."

1408 "Hoffman, Walt." American Film Institute Catalog, 1961-70, p.295.
Walt Hoffman is credited with the wardrobe of "Lassie's Great Adventure" and the men's wardrobe of "Wild, Wild Winter."

1409 Holden, Lansing C. "Color! The New Language of the Screen." Cinema Arts, 1 (2): 64, July 1937.
Holden discusses his role as a film color designer; he coordinated costumes and set decorations for "The Garden of Allah" and "A Star Is Born." He discusses the colors, and symbolism, of costumes worn by Janet Gaynor in "A Star Is Born" in relation to the lawn, pond, and pool colors.

1410 _____. "Designing for Color," in We Make the Movies, edited by Nancy Naumburg. New York: Norton, 1937. p.239-52.
Discussion by color designer Lansing C. Holden of the importance of the lighting and colors in a film, including of the costumes, in relation to the background, emotional values and impact upon the audience. The people he must work with include the costume designer; the two coordinate the different colors worn by each person in a scene, and with the sets.

1411 Holdon, Courtland. "Hollywood's Fashion Parade." Christian Science Monitor Magazine, January 22, 1936, p.8-9, 15.
Discussion of whether Hollywood or Paris is really influenced by the other, and debates whether Hollywood is becoming the fashion capital of the world. Includes comments by Adrian, Bernard Newman, Milo Anderson, and Travis Banton, who notes that many film costumes should not be copied, citing a popular dress worn in "Luxury Liner." One still of Greta Garbo in a gown by Adrian from "Anna Karenina."

1412 "Holger, Helmut." American Film Institute Catalog, 1961-70, p.296.
Helmut Holger is credited with the costumes of "The Corpse of Beverly Hills" and "How to Seduce a Playboy."

1413 Holland, Jack. "Glamour Does a Pratt Fall." Motion Pic-

ture, 61 (5): 24-5, 80-1, 86, June 1941.
Discussion of the numerous actresses who have forsaken their
glamour-girl images, including Ann Sothern, Marlene Dietrich,
Greta Garbo, Lana Turner, Carole Lombard, Ann Sheridan, Jean
Arthur, Irene Dunne, Ginger Rogers, and Joan Crawford; with
brief filmographies to illustrate the changes. Brief costume comments, including that Hedy Lamarr's "Comrade X" wardrobe consisted mainly of a motorman's uniform and a trenchcoat.

1414 Hollander, Anne. "Costume and Convention." American
        Scholar, 42: 671-5, 1972-3.
Discussion of the many films made of the life of Queen Elizabeth,
as well as theatrical and television versions. The audience has
been conditioned to accept inauthentic period costumes by seeing
the wrong costumes until they look right; clues have become sufficient to tell the audience what period they are witnessing, as
with ruffs to signify the Elizabethan era. Neither of the two
versions starring Bette Davis was authentically costumed, nor
was "Mary Queen of Scots," with Vanessa Redgrave and Glenda
Jackson. The costumes of such current period films are often
made inauthentic through the use of nylon ruffs and bodices of
elastic and aluminum springs, rather than the stiffened ruffs and
bodices worn in the era. Period costumes nearly always reflect
the body proportions of the era in which they are made, as with
the native girls in "Bridge over the River Kwai," who wore up-
lift bras under their tunics, and Edwige Feuillere in "L'Aigle à
Deux Têtes" (1947), who wore authentic costumes of the 1870s,
but with large shoulder pads. The author notes some film exceptions: some British films, films by Luchino Visconti, and
Franco Zeffirelli's Shakespeare films. Period films require that
the actors, if wearing military uniforms, wear sharply contrasting colors, and that women be dressed to appear sexy by current
standards.

1415 _____. "Movie Clothes: More Real Than Life." New York
        Times Magazine, December 1, 1974, p. 68, 70-1.
The author describes the basic Hollywood uniform for women and
states that Hollywood tends to confirm fashion trends rather than
create them and that film costumes tend to be two years behind
the times. Discussion of costumes in the "Romantic and Glamorous Hollywood Design" exhibit, and their significance to film and
fashion history, their fantasy nature, and the symbolism of fabrics
and accessories, such as furs, feathers, and satin for different
stereotyped women's roles. Discussion also of the "Basic Exotic
Vamp Suit" first worn by Theda Bara in "Cleopatra" in 1917,
which has become generalized for use by heroines in either ancient
or futuristic civilizations. Modern-day film costumes appear to
be more natural and authentic but are still glamorized and as in-
accessible as previous costumes.

1416 _____. "The 'Gatsby Look' and Other Costume Movie
        Blunders." New York, 7 (21): 54-5, 58-9, 62, May 27,
        1974.

Discussion of inauthentic or inappropriately costumed period films, including Anne Baxter in "The Ten Commandments"; Bette Davis in "Jezebel"; "Gone with the Wind"; Greta Garbo in "Camille"; Raquel Welch in "The Three Musketeers" (1973); Elizabeth Taylor in "Taming of the Shrew" (by Irene Sharaff). Also discussed are other genres: Mae West in "My Little Chickadee," a western, and science fiction films, including "Things to Come" and "Planet of the Apes." Among the illustrations is an inauthentic hat worn by Lois Chiles in "The Great Gatsby." Examples of authentic costumes include those worn in "Pride and Prejudice," Geraldine Chaplin's costumes in "The Three Musketeers" (1973), and Cecil Beaton's costumes for "Gigi" and "My Fair Lady." Many other films are discussed.

1417   Holliday, Kate.   "Fame on Two Yards of Silk."   Motion Pic-
          ture, 69 (5): 41, 122-30, June 1945.
Discussion of the importance of Dorothy Lamour's sarong to her career, with references to her initial shock at seeing one for "The Jungle Princess"; her donating a sarong to the Los Angeles Museum and to a gun-battery crew during the war; and having her hair cut and a sarong burned by cannibals--a final tribute and publicity stunt when she decided to change her image.

1418   Hollyette.   "Fashionettes by Hollyette."   Hollywood Star, 12
          (25): 18, July 30, 1932.
A white cape and dress similar to those worn by Joan Crawford in "Letty Lynton" are being worn by many women in the Los Angeles area.

1419   "Hollywood."   Harper's Bazaar, 2713: 106-7, 145, 147, Sep-
          tember 1, 1938.
Five film designers have joined Carolyn Modes to design retail fashions. Includes brief biographical information on the five-- Edith Head, Orry-Kelly, Walter Plunkett, Travis Banton, and Howard Greer. The last two were freelance designers; Edith Head succeeded them both when they left Paramount.

1420   "Hollywood Costume Designers."   What's Happening in Holly-
          wood, 13: 6p., December 4, 1939.
Topics discussed include: Hollywood's influence on fashion, as opposed to Paris, with examples of costumes worn in "The Ad- ventures of Robin Hood," and by Bette Davis in "Jezebel" and "The Old Maid," with additional comments by Adrian; how a film is costumed, with mention of Walter Plunkett's costumes for Vi- vien Leigh in "Gone with the Wind"; and the major women de- signers, including Edith Head, Royer (who actually was a man), and Gwen Wakeling, one of whose costumes for Loretta Young in "Suez" was copied in Paris and advertised as an original. With the 5,000 costumes worn in "Gone with the Wind" a major ex- pense was daily laundering, required by state law, even if the costumes had to be specially dirtied the next day. To illustrate the poverty of the times in "GWTW," women wore corn husk or carpet-made hats and shoes with wooden soles.

1421 "Hollywood: Dreams for Sale." Newsweek, 75 (18): 36-7,
    May 4, 1970.
MGM auctioned most of its 46-year collection of props and costumes, including the shoes worn by Judy Garland in "The Wizard
of Oz"; Ramon Novarro's brass helmet from "Ben-Hur"; the uniform worn by Charles Laughton in "Mutiny on the Bounty," made
by the same tailoring firm that dressed the real Captain Bligh;
and the wedding gown worn by Elizabeth Taylor in "Father of the
Bride."

1422 "The Hollywood Fashion Parade." Screen Romances, 1 (7):
    32-3, December 1929.
One fur coat each is modeled by Joan Crawford from "Our Modern
Maidens" and Josephine Dunne from "Sierra."

1423 _____. Screen Romances, 2 (10): 24-5, March 1930.
One fur coat each is modeled by Billie Dove from "The Other
Tomorrow" and Helen Kane from "Pointed Heels."

1424 _____. Screen Romances, 2 (11): 28-9, April 1930.
Fifi Dorsay models a gown from "Hot for Paris."

1425 "Hollywood Fashions." Movie Mirror, 5 (2): 58-61, 63,
    January 1934.
Constance Bennett models three costumes by Gwen Wakeling from
"Moulin Rouge," with the designer's sketches for these and three
additional costumes. Discussion of these costumes and costumes
worn by Katharine Alexander in "Vinegar Tree," Myrna Loy in
"The Prizefighter and the Lady," and Elissa Landi in "By Candlelight."

1426 _____. Screen Romances, 9 (52): 58, September 1933.
Madge Evans models four gowns by Adrian from "Dinner at
Eight."

1427 "Hollywood Fashions Becoming 'Sensible.'" New York Times,
    February 1, 1944, p. 24.
Edith Head feels that L-85, the government's limiting of fabric,
"was the greatest boon" for Hollywood, since it would bring about
more sensible film costumes. Her costumes for Ginger Rogers
in "Lady in the Dark," made before L-85, mark the end of past
luxury. She had gone to New York to study the city's fashions,
where she found as much inspiration as she had previously in
Paris, and to study women workers at the Kaiser shipyards for
a film she was currently working on.

1428 "Hollywood Fashions: Ida Lupino's Summer Frocks." Holly-
    wood, 24 (6): 40-1, June 1935.
Ida Lupino models a costume from "Paris in Spring," which is
sketched along with another costume she wears in the film; patterns were available for both.

1429 "Hollywood Hints ... Spring Suits." Screen Romances, 10 (59):

72-3, April 1934.
Irene Dunne models one hat from "Transient Love," and one dress
each is modeled by Irene Ware from "Orient Express," Suzanne
Kaaren from "Coming Out Party," Mona Barrie from "Sleepers
East," and an unidentified woman from "Fashions of 1934," by
Orry-Kelly.

1430 "Hollywood Men's Store." American Film Institute Catalog,
1961-70, p. 297.
Hollywood Men's Store is credited with the wardrobe of "Motel
Confidential."

1431 "Hollywood Military Hobbies." American Film Institute Cata-
log, 1961-70, p. 297.
Hollywood Military Hobbies is credited with the uniforms of "Love
Camp 7."

1432 " 'Hollywood No Arbiter.' " New York Times, November 26,
1935, p. 31.
Walter Plunkett addressed the (New York) Fashion Group on the
topic of Hollywood's influence on American fashion. Speaking for
the film designers, he stated that they have no time to promote
fashions, and the only movement to have Hollywood usurp the
fashion influence of Paris was that of the New York fashion jour-
nalists.

1433 "Hollywood Paints the Fashion Picture." Picture Play, 52 (3):
16-7, 75, May 1940.
Discussion of the influence of period-film costumes on fashion,
with mention of Alice Faye in "Lillian Russell"; Greta Garbo in
"The Kiss"; Shirley Temple in "Wee Willie Winkie" and "Heidi";
Loretta Young in "Love Under Fire"; and Norma Shearer in "Romeo and Juliet"; "Gone with the Wind"; and "Three Smart Girls."

1434 "Hollywood Rayon Ball." Vogue, 90 (3): 56-7, August 1, 1937.
Two unidentified Vogue models appearing in "Vogues of 1938" each
model one costume from the film.

1435 "Hollywood Sets the Summer Fashions." Photoplay, 35 (6):
58-9, May 1929.
Norma Shearer models six garments, one (or more) of which she
wears in "The Last of Mrs. Cheyney."

1436 "Hollywood Styles for Men." Cinema Arts, 1 (1): 93, September 1936.
A general discussion of the influence of men's film costume on
men's fashions, especially as a result of Hollywood tailor James
Oviatt and his establishment, Oviatt's.

1437 "Hollywood's Creative Custom Made Workrooms Present Their
1961 Costume Entries for the Adam 'N Eve Awards."
Motion Picture Costumers, 1961, n. p.
One costume each is modeled by Rosalind Russell from "Five

Finger Exercise," by Orry-Kelly; Ingrid Thulin and Lee J. Cobb
from "Four Horsemen of the Apocalypse" and Hope Lange from
"How the West Was Won," by Walter Plunkett; Barbara Stanwyck
from "Walk on the Wild Side," by Charles Le Maire; worn but not
modeled by Judith Evelyn from "The Thriller," by Burton Miller;
Shirley Jones and Robert Preston from "The Music Man" and
Marilyn Monroe from "Let's Make Love," by Dorothy Jeakins; Hope
Lange from "Pocketful of Miracles," Shirley MacLaine from "My
Geisha," and Lucille Ball from "Facts of Life," by Edith Head;
Nancy Kwan, Miyoshi Yumeki, and Irene Tsu from "Flower Drum
Song," by Irene Sharaff; and Frank Sinatra, Dean Martin, and
Peter Lawford from "Sergeants 3," by Western Costume Company.

1438   "Hollywood's Star Styles." Hollywood, 26 (7): 37, July 1937.
One costume each is modeled by Anita Louise from "That Certain
Woman" and Bette Davis from "Kid Galahad," by Orry-Kelly.

1439   "Hollywood's Star Styles." Hollywood, 26 (12): 30-4, De-
       cember 1937.
Carole Lombard models one gown from "Nothing Sacred."

1440   "Hollywood's Star Styles." Hollywood, 27 (3): 33-4, March
       1938.
Three costumes each are modeled by Deanna Durbin from "Mad
About Music" and Bette Davis from "Jezebel."

1441   Holmsway, Sten. "Living Ghosts." Screen Guild, 3 (6):
       6-8, August 1936.
Lou Burns founded Western Costume Company and moved it to
Hollywood in 1915. It began as a hobby, supplying cowboy and
Indian costumes for early western film producers. The collections
on the different floors are discussed, including the departments
with costumes, hats, and the library. Basil Rathbone, C. Aub-
rey Smith, and an unnamed actor each model one costume from
"Romeo and Juliet."

1442   _____. "Wardrobe Worries." Screen Guild, 3 (7): 11-2,
       September 1936.
Bert Offord, secretary of the Associated Motion Picture Costumers,
discusses the jobs in, and the duties of, the wardrobe department.
Offord, who costumed "What Price Glory," "Seventh Heaven,"
"Hell's Angels," and others, humorously notes the problems caused
when there is insufficient time for costuming a film, or when costumes are lost.

1443   "Höltz, Nicola." American Film Institute Catalog, 1961-70,
       p. 298.
Nicola Höltz was the costume designer of "Jack of Diamonds."

1444   "Hoops My Dear, but by the Ton!" MGM Studio News, 5 (6):
       n.p., August 15, 1938.
Adrian ordered one ton of metal hoops, with an average diameter
of 16 feet, for 400 gowns to be worn in "Marie Antoinette."

1445 Hopper, Hedda. "The Cosmopolite of the Month: Adrian."
Version 12, p. 12, circa 1938. [A monthly feature of
Cosmopolitan but apparently never published. Housed at
the Academy of Motion Picture Arts and Sciences.]
A biography of Adrian, with discussion of his costume designing
and personal lifestyle. He is paid $75,000 annually by MGM and
sketches in pencil and watercolor from 50 to 75 designs per day.
His favorite costumes were for "The Great Ziegfeld," "Idiot's
Delight," and the over 4,000 costumes for "Marie Antoinette."

1446 Horn, Marilyn J. "Entertainment and the Arts," in The
Second Skin: An Interdisciplinary Study of Clothing.
Boston: Houghton Mifflin, 1975, p. 116-8.
Notes, with brief examples, the fashion influence of Rudolph
Valentino in "The Sheik"; Cecil Beaton's costumes for "My Fair
Lady"; Albert Finney in "Tom Jones"; "Cleopatra" (1961); "Bonnie
and Clyde"; "The Great Gatsby" (1963); Theda Bara; and Pola
Negri.

1447 "Horn, Van." American Film Institute Catalog, 1921-30, p.
1159.
Van Horn was the costume designer of "Scaramouche" (1923).

1448 "Horrors! It Snowed in Hollywood This Week." Screen News,
4 (51): 13, December 26, 1925.
Colleen Moore and 60 models wore fur coats and other winter
clothing for a fashion sequence in "Irene," with simulated snow-
fall.

1449 "Hosiery Heyday." Screenland, 53 (3): 48, January 1949.
June Haver models bejeweled stockings designed for dancer
Marilyn Miller at the peak of her career for $2,500; Haver also
models stockings designed by Willys De Mond that she will wear
in "Look for the Silver Lining," a film based on Miller's life.

1450 "Hot from Hollywood; Publicity." Stage, 16 (6): 61, March
15, 1939.
A dilapidated cloak was needed for Frank Morgan in "The Wizard
of Oz," but the costume department's cloak photographed too well,
so that agents were sent to secondhand shops. One coat brought
back was approved, cleaned, and fitted for Morgan, who found a
label in the pocket that revealed it had been originally owned by
L. Frank Baum, author of The Wizard of Oz. It was verified,
but most people thought that it was made up by the publicity department. (It was true, and only once was the story published,
according to author Aljean Harmetz.)

1451 Hotchner, A. E. "Clothes," in Doris Day: Her Own Story. New
York: Morrow, 1976, p. 304-5.
Doris Day learned how not to dress through the "ludicrous"
costumes she wore in her Warner Brothers films--which caused
her to cry after seeing herself in them.

1452 Hover, Helen. "Popping Questions at Joan Fontaine." <u>Motion
         Picture,</u> 69 (5): 46-7, 73-6, June 1945.
      Joan Fontaine models two gowns from "The Affairs of Susan" and
      notes that it was her favorite film because the part was exciting
      and she wore the most numerous and varied costumes of her
      career.

1453 "How a Good Tailor Lifted Adolphe Menjou from Poverty to
         Riches." <u>Screen News,</u> 4 (22): 8, May 30, 1925.
      Adolphe Menjou received considerable help in his film career
      when he was given four costly suits from an established tailor;
      he convinced the tailor (Eddie Schmidt) that his career would be
      more secure if he were well dressed.

1454 "How Does a Girl Become a Woman?" <u>Photoplay,</u> 60 (5): 68-
         9, November 1961.
      Alongside three stills of Audrey Hepburn from "Breakfast at
      Tiffany's," Deborah Walley models similar clothing and jewelry
      to give her and the readers a chic appearance without the Given-
      chy price.

1455 "How Is Your Clothes Line?" <u>Photoplay,</u> 33 (4): 85, Sep-
         tember 1948.
      Brief mention by Travis Banton of a dress he designed for Rosa-
      lind Russell in "The Velvet Touch."

1456 "How It Was Made." <u>MGM Studio News,</u> 5 (6): n.p., August
         15, 1938.
      20,000 pairs of stockings were required for the male cast of
      "Marie Antoinette." Adrian researched the film's costumes in
      Vienna and Paris. Norma Shearer wears 34 costumes weighing
      a total of 1,768 pounds. Two poodles were also costumed for
      the film.

1457 "How Many Yards of Goods Does It Take to Dress a Costume
         Film?" <u>Screen News,</u> 2 (23): 12, June 9, 1923, col. 3.
      Walter Israel, designer for "Ashes of Vengeance," had his staff
      of 35 dressmakers sewing around the clock for several months
      on approximately 3,000 costumes, which averaged about seven
      yards of fabric per costume. Norma Talmadge wears 15 gowns,
      averaging ten yards of fabric each.

1458 "How $1,600,000 Was Spent on 'Robin Hood.'" <u>Screen Guide,</u>
         2 (11): 40-3, March 1938.
      The suits of armor for "The Adventures of Robin Hood" were
      made in studio shops, with wool painted to resemble metal for the
      mail on the helmets.

1459 "How Talmadge Sisters Express Personality in Art of Dress."
         <u>Screen News,</u> 3 (10): 22, March 8, 1924.
      Charles Le Maire discusses designing for Constance and Norma Tal-
      madge. He finds designing for the screen much more difficult than
      for the stage because of the way color, fabrics, and lines photograph.

1460 "How They Save Crawford's Time." Photoplay, 42 (1): 76,
      June 1932.
Photographs illustrate the steps in constructing a silver lamé
dress for Joan Crawford in "Letty Lynton," designed by Adrian.
In the conventional draping method muslin is fitted to a dress
form according to the original sketch; the muslin is then used as
a pattern, and the dress in the fashion fabric is fitted to Crawford.

1461 "How to Adapt Screen Costumes to Suit Your Wardrobe."
      Motion Picture Studio Insider, 1 (3): 46-7, 61, June 1935.
Adrian discusses general ways in which the average woman can
dress attractively by learning to adapt screen costumes, with
restraint.

1462 "How to Costume a Production or (Things You Never Learn in
      School.)" Motion Picture Costumers, 1957, n.p.
A film is costumed by breaking down a script to determine how
many costumes and duplicates will be needed; how much research
is required, which fabrics and colors are most appropriate and
which costumes must be dyed, aged, or altered; and then by cop-
ing with any problems that might arise during film production.

1463 "How to Spoil the Effect of Beautiful Clothes." Photoplay,
      29 (2): 64-5, January 1926.
Travis Banton, born in Texas, was brought over from Paris to
design Leatrice Joy's costumes in "The Dressmaker from Paris."

1464 "How to Stop Perspiration from Ruining Clothes." National
      Enquirer, 53 (1): 40, August 15, 1978.
Perspiration stains in film costumes, a problem that afflicts
actresses under hot lights, is avoided by dress shields, sewn
all around the shield to make them lie flat--according to designer
Edith Head.

      Howard, Kathleen see "Photoplay Fashions"

1465 Howard, Lillian. "Back to Babylon for New Fashions."
      Photoplay, 11 (5): 39-40, April 1917.
The Babylonian costumes worn in "Intolerance" immediately influenced fashion. Four sketches of dresses adapted from the
film are included.

1466 _____. "Beverly Bayne a Living Van Dyke." Photoplay,
      11 (4): 107-8, March 1917.
Beverly Bayne insisted upon historically accurate costumes for
"Romeo and Juliet"; she models one that was adapted from a
Van Dyke portrait. Three months were spent making the cos-
tumes. She discusses the trend to adapt historical costumes for
modern fashion.

1467 _____. "Fashions and the Screen." Photoplay, 8 (6): 27-
      8, November 1915.

Film actresses have influenced the fashions of countless women, often by reinforcing what is dictated in Paris.

1468 _____. " 'Genevieve, Your Stockings!' " Photoplay, 9 (6): 104-6, May 1916.
Discussion of the importance of quality fabrics in film costumes because of the magnification on the screen. Nearly-new costumes, worn only a few weeks during filming, are either kept for personal use or are sold to used-clothing shops. An actress may be given a clothing bonus if the costumes become especially expensive for a certain film. Extras provide all modern clothing, but are provided with character costumes.

1469 _____. " 'How I Teach My Gowns to Act.' " Photoplay, 9 (3): 89-93, February 1916.
Marguerite Courtot discusses how she selects her film costumes to complement her performance, with mention of color, line, and mood--line being the most important.

1470 Howard, Oscar. "What Did She Have On?" Collier's, 98 (13): 22, 53, September 26, 1936.
Includes biographical information on Omar Kiam, descriptions of some of the workrooms at United Artists studios, and discussion of how a film is costumed. Ruth Chatterton models one of her 28 costumes from "Dodsworth."

1471 "Howard Greer, Designer, Dies; Couturier for Hollywood Stars." New York Times, April 21, 1974, p. 53.
Howard Greer, one of the first custom designers and wholesalers on the West Coast, died at age 78 from an undisclosed cause. He began his career sketching for Madame Lucile and Lady Lucy Duff Gordon (actually the same).

1472 "Howard Greer Draws Throng to Gown Show." San Francisco Chronicle, April 23, 1934, p. 26.
Howard Greer said that "movie actresses have the most horrible taste in the world."

1473 Howell, Georgina. In Vogue: Sixty Years of International Celebrities and Fashion from British Vogue. New York: Schocken, 1976.
1920s film costumes were generally regarded as too vulgar to influence fashion, though by the 1930s working women and designers looked to Hollywood for fashion inspiration. It is felt that in 1932-3 Hollywood was at its most influential period, and in 1933 Vogue tried to determine whether Hollywood or Paris was the most influential (see "Does Hollywood Create?"). Examples are given of fashion having been influenced by costumes from "The Private Life of Henry VIII," "Catherine the Great," "Little Women," and "Romeo and Juliet."

1474 "Huarte, Mario." American Film Institute Catalog, 1961-70, p. 302.

Mario Huarte is credited with Stella Stevens's dresses in "Rage."

1475 "Huber, Charles." American Film Institute Catalog, 1921-30,
           p. 1163.
Charles Huber was the master of wardrobe for "Evangeline."

1476 "Hubert, Ali." American Film Institute Catalog, 1921-30,
           p. 1163.
Ali Hubert is credited with the wardrobe of "The Student Prince
in Old Heidelberg" and the costumes of "The Patriot."

1477 Hubert, Ali. Legende und Wirklichkeit. Leipzig: Seemann,
           1930.
Does not include sketches or photographs useful to researchers of
Ali Hubert's film costumes. See the review by Carringer, Robert,
and Barry Sabath. German text.

1478 Hubert, Rene. "Corrective Costuming." Motion Picture
           Studio Insider, 1 (2): 32-3, May 1935.
Rene Hubert, head of the Fox wardrobe department, discusses
camoflauging figure flaws. Dixie Lee models a gown from "Redheads on Parade," by William Lambert, also with Fox.

1479 _____. "Fashion Forecast from Hollywood." Photoplay,
           48 (5): 53, 84, October 1935.
Anita Louise models a costume from "Here's to Romance," by
Rene Hubert, who discusses fashion trends.

1480 "Hubert, Rene." American Film Institute Catalog, 1921-30,
           p. 1164.
Rene Hubert is credited with the wardrobe of "Adam and Evil,"
"After Midnight," "Body and Soul" (1927), "The Callahans and
the Murphys," "Foreign Devils," "Frisco Sally Levy," "On ze
Boulevard," "Quality Street" (1927), "Twelve Miles Out," "Min
and Bill," "Those Three French Girls," and "War Nurse."

1481 "Hubert, Rene." American Film Institute Catalog, 1961-70,
           p. 302.
Rene Hubert was the costume designer of "The Four Horsemen of
the Apocalypse" (1962), and the wardrobe designer for Ingrid
Bergman in "The Visit."

1482 Hudson, Richard. "The Incredible Costumes," in Sixty Years
           of Vamps and Camps: Visual Nostalgia of the Silver
           Screen. New York: Drake, 1973, n. p.
58 stills are presented of actresses and actors in vamp/camp
costumes, many of which were either publicity stills only, or are
without film titles. Included are Theda Bara in "Salome" (1918);
Mae West in "I'm No Angel" and "Belle of the Nineties"; the same
gown worn by Norma Shearer in "Marie Antoinette" and Jeanette
MacDonald in "New Moon"; elaborate oriental costumes worn by
Greta Garbo in "Mata Hari," Hedy Lamarr in "Lady of the Tropics," and Doris Day in "The Glass Bottom Boat"; and man-

tailored suits worn by Marlene Dietrich in "Seven Sinners,"
Raquel Welch in "Myra Breckenridge," and Annabella in "Wings
of the Morning." Numerous men appear in women's costumes,
including Tony Curtis and Jack Lemmon in "Some Like It Hot."

1483 Huff, Theodore. "The Career of Rudolph Valentino." Films
        in Review, 3 (4): 145-63, April 1952.
Includes references to Rudolph Valentino's second wife, Natacha
Rambova, notorious for her control over his Paramount films.

1484 _____. Charlie Chaplin. New York: Schuman, 1951.
In a 1923 article (not identified) Charlie Chaplin discussed the
symbolism of his famous costume, namely that of being an "under-
dog" trying to put on a front for himself and the world. The
derby, cane, and coat symbolized dignity and gallantry, and the
moustache was for vanity.

1485 Hughes, Eileen Lanouette. On the Set of "Fellini Satyricon":
        A Behind-the-Scenes Diary. New York: Morrow, 1971.
Danilo Donati, the designer of "Fellini Satyricon," could not
determine how many costumes were used in the film since many
were made up as the film progressed. He extensively researched
the costumes worn by the ancient Greeks and Romans but used
only the tunic, since the toga was worn only at official occasions,
he found. Piero Tosi, who had previously designed the costumes
for Federico Fellini's "Toby Dammitt," was a costume consultant
for the film. The fabric was often handwoven and specially dyed,
and the costumes were constructed by four dressmakers and
tailors. Clara Baldassarre, the wardrobe mistress, has been a
film seamstress for over 20 years. An American manufacturer
wanted to market adapted versions of the costumes, but was
turned down since Donati does not sketch the costumes.

1486 "'The Hunchback of Notra [sic] Dame' Is Immense." Screen
        News, 2 (14): 26, April 7, 1923.
3,500 different costumes were required for the period film "The
Hunchback of Notre Dame."

1487 "A Hunger for Updated Glamor." Review of Hollywood Cos-
        tume Design, by David Chierichetti. Los Angeles Times,
        December 15, 1976, sec. 4, p.15.
David Chierichetti, author of Hollywood Costume Design, was
compelled to end his book with the 1950s since designers ceased
to receive challenging assignments, many buying clothes at specialty
shops rather than designing. Both women and costume have been
stifled in films since then despite audiences' desire for a return
to glamour Chierichetti's favorite designer is the late Travis
Banton. Until designers are given larger budgets, Chierichetti
recommends that young persons looking for a career in costuming
choose television rather than films.

1488 "Hunt, Grady." American Film Institute Catalog, 1961-70,
        p.304.

Grady Hunt is credited with the costumes of "Munster, Go Home!,"
"The Perils of Pauline" (1967), "Jigsaw," "The Shakiest Gun in
the West," "Angel in My Pocket"; the wardrobe of "The Brass
Bottle"; the men's wardrobe of "The Hook"; and the costume
supervision of "Torn Curtain."

1489 Hunt, Julie. "Hollywood Career Chart." Picture Play, 50
        (1): 31-4, March 1939.
Features charts of film-related occupations, including costume designers, seamstresses, and wardrobe workers, with such information as training one should have, and expected salary and working conditions. One photo each, with brief captions, of designer
Edith Head, seamstress Wilma Christianson, and wardrobe worker
Arfie Mundy.

1490 Hunt, Julie Lang. "They Aren't All Actresses in Hollywood."
        Photoplay, 50 (3): 50-1, 92-4, September 1936.
Designer Edith Head and dressmaker Sally Paige discuss their
careers, including their job qualifications, how they obtained their
jobs, and working conditions.

1491 _____. "Trials and Triumphs of a Hollywood Dress De-
        signer." Photoplay, 49 (4): 23-5, 108-9, April 1936.
Discussion of the career of designer Travis Banton, with mention
of his costumes for Norma Talmadge in "Poppy," his first film,
in New York in 1916; his first Hollywood film, in 1924, for Leatrice Joy in "The Dressmaker from Paris"; and his costumes for
Joy in "Grounds for Divorce," which were altered for Florence
Vidor when she replaced Joy in the film.

1492 _____. "Trials and Triumphs of a Hollywood Dress De-
        signer." Photoplay, 49 (5): 54-5, 86, 88, May 1936.
Reminiscences by Travis Banton of the many actresses he has
designed for, including Nancy Carroll in "Abie's Irish Rose,"
"Follow Thru," and "Burlesque"; Jeanette MacDonald in "The Love
Parade"; and Clara Bow.

1493 _____. "Trials and Triumphs of a Hollywood Dress De-
        signer." Photoplay, 49 (6): 50-1, 84, 86, 88, June 1936.
Includes references to costumes worn by Claudette Colbert in
"Manslaughter" (which she bought in New York) and in "The Man
from Yesterday," "The Bride Comes Home," "Imitation of Life,"
and "The Gilded Lily" (all designed by Travis Banton). Also includes a list of superstitions that Mae West has concerning her
film costumes.

1494 Hunter, Paul. "Hollywood Costume Designer Keynotes Color."
        Christian Science Monitor, June 15, 1970, p. 12.
Renie, once an assistant to Edith Head and a designer for many
period films, "cheats" a little if the costumes of a period film
do not flatter the actress. Many of her costumes for "Cleopatra"
were simply draped on the person and tied.

1495 Hyde, Nina S.   "Cardin: Pioneer Designer's Logo Now on
          Bikes, Chocolate." <u>San Jose Mercury News</u>, October 15,
          1978, sec. L, p. 2.
Pierre Cardin, at age 23, made the costumes and masks for
"Beauty and the Beast," with designer Christian Berard.   He
designed for other (unnamed) films during this period, but the
salaries were meager, so he began working with Parisian couturiers rather than in film.

1496 "Hyde, Sally."   <u>American Film Institute Catalog, 1961-70,</u>
          p. 307.
Sally Hyde is credited with the costumes of "Peer Gynt."

1497　"'I Do' Fashions for June." <u>Photoplay with Movie Mirror,</u> 21
　　　　(1):　55-9, June 1942.
Claudette Colbert models five costumes by Irene from "Palm
Beach Story."

1498　"'I Look My Best In....'" <u>Hollywood Pattern,</u> 7 (2): 26-7,
　　　　Summer 1938.
Alice Faye would wear period costumes all the time if she could;
she mentions Royer's costumes for her in "In Old Chicago."

1499　"I Love My Shoes." <u>Screen News,</u> 1 (12): 27, May 13, 1922.
For the sake of comfort Harold Lloyd has worn patent-leather
shoes in most of his films since he first discovered them--and
occasionally at peril to his life, as when climbing girders in "Never
Weaken," or performing stunts on a train in "Now Or Never."
The two exceptions were the navy regulation shoes he wore in
"A Sailor-Made Man" and the children's shoes in "Grandma's
Boy."

1500　"IATSE & MPMO [International Alliance of Theatrical Stage
　　　　Employees and Moving Pictures and Machine Operators]
　　　　Local." <u>Women and Film,</u> 1 (1): 74, 1972.
Of the 914 persons in the costumers union # 705, 529 are women.

1501　"Ichida, Kiichi." <u>American Film Institute Catalog, 1961-70,</u>
　　　　p. 307.
Kiichi Ichida is credited with the costumes of "Latitude Zero."

1502　"Imagination in Costume Design." <u>Motion Picture Studio In-</u>
　　　　<u>sider,</u> 2 (4): 46-7, August 1936.
Ernst Dryden had considerable freedom in designing the costumes
for "Lost Horizon" since he did not need to adhere to any particular country or era, though some costumes resemble those of
Tibet.　Jane Wyman models a costume from the film.　Includes
one sketch for the dancing girls' costume in "The Garden of
Allah."

1503　"The Importance of the Crepe de Chine Wrap...." <u>Screen</u>
　　　　<u>News,</u> 1 (29): 20, September 9, 1922, col. 3.
Description of a draped overcape worn by Hope Hampton in "The

202

Light in the Dark. "

1504 "Important Spring Fashions ... from Hollywood. " Movies, 5
       (11): 44-5, May 1942.
       One costume each is modeled by Jane Wyman from "My Favorite
       Spy," by Irene; Betty Field from "Mr. and Mrs. Cugat," by
       Edith Head; and Gene Tierney from "Rings on Her Finger," by
       Gwen Wakeling.

1505 "In Royal Robes. " Picture Play, 24 (6): 77, August 1926.
       Mythical royalty remains popular on the screen, as shown in one
       costume each worn by Jetta Goudal in "The Coming of Amos,"
       Constance Wiley in "The Only Thing," Dorothy Dwan in "The
       Wizard of Oz," Norma Talmadge in "Graustark," and Pola Negri
       in "The Crown of Lies" (closeups of Talmadge and Negri).

1506 "In the Air ... the Moroccan Look. " Harper's Bazaar, 3170:
       88-95, January 1976.
       Numerous retail fashions are modeled, many "inspired" by the
       costumes of "The Man Who Would Be King. "

1507 "In the Grand Manner. " Movieland, 6 (8): 28-9, September
       1948.
       Gene Tierney models five costumes by Oleg Cassini from "That
       Wonderful Urge. "

1508 "In the Spring a Young Girl's Fancy...." Silver Screen, 10
       (6): 46-9, April 1940.
       Deanna Durbin models seven costumes by Vera West from "It's
       a Date. "

1509 "In 'The Young Rajah'...." Screen News, 1 (40): 12, No-
       vember 25, 1922, col. 3.
       Rudolph Valentino wears the most varied costumes of any of his
       films in "The Young Rajah," including (as a descendant of the
       Hindu god Krishna) costumes of India in addition to New England
       clothes and riding habits.

1510 "The Indispensable Suit. " Motion Picture, 74 (4): 60-1, No-
       vember 1947.
       One suit each is modeled by Lucille Ball from "Her Husband's
       Affairs," by Jean Louis, and Eve Arden from "The Voice of the
       Turtle. "

1511 "Informally Yours. " Motion Picture, 56 (1): 38-9, August
       1938.
       Rosalind Russell models a beach robe from "Four's a Crowd,"
       adapted from a monk's robe.

1512 "Ingrid's Greatest Role. " Screenland, 53 (2): 45, December
       1948.
       One still shows Ingrid Bergman being fitted into her armor for
       "Joan of Arc. " The white aluminum suit was hand-tailored by

the armorer of the Metropolitan Museum of Art in New York.

1513   "Inside a Studio Wardrobe Department." What's Happening
       in Hollywood, 25: 6p, March 2, 1942.
Lengthy interview with designer Milo Anderson, a specialist in
period costumes; he is designing about 14 contemporary costumes
for Mary Astor in "Across the Pacific." Discussion at length of
the costuming of a film, including various phases of wardrobe
department involvement.

1514   International Motion Picture Almanac. New York: Quigley,
       1929-   .
Consists of biographies of persons in the film industry, addresses
of film periodicals, award winners, and other information. The
title has varied from Motion Picture Almanac to International
Motion Picture and Television Almanac to International Motion
Picture Almanac.

1515   International Who's Who. London: Europa, 1935-   .

1516   "Interpreting Boyish Fashions Girlishly." Screen News, 3
       (22): 28, May 31, 1924.
Discussion of current boyish styles, which Sylvia Breamer has
adopted in part for her costumes in "Woman on the Jury"; she
models one of the costumes, which has also been sketched.

1517   "Intlekofer, John." American Film Institute Catalog, 1961-70,
       p. 310.
John Intlekofer is credited with the wardrobe of "Hand of Death"
and "The Day Mars Invaded Earth."

1518   Irene. "Dress Up to Romance." Photoplay, 33 (1): 101,
       June 1948.
Irene dresses actresses to please men, since the producers have
the final approval of film costumes.

1519   _____. "Gentleman's Choice." Screenland, 53 (4): 46-7,
       68-9, February 1949.
Irene discusses her early life and film-costume designing, and
she notes that her 1860 costumes for Ava Gardner in "The Great
Sinner" will influence the details of clothes in her next retail
collection. Jeanette MacDonald models six costumes from "Sun
in the Morning."

1520   _____, as told to Gladys Hall. "Have You a 'Clothes
       Personality?'" Screenland, 49 (10): 34-5, 88-90,
       August 1945.
Irene discusses many of the actresses she has worked with, including Katharine Hepburn in "Without Love"; Hedy Lamarr in
"Her Highness and the Bellboy"; and Lana Turner in "Weekend at
the Waldorf"; with six sketches of Miss Turner.

1521   "Irene." American Film Institute Catalog, 1961-70, p. 310.

Irene is credited with the gowns for Doris Day in "Lover Come Back" and Mary Peach in "A Gathering of Eagles."

1522 "Irene." Current Biography. 1946, p. 276-7.
Biographical information on Irene Gibbons, who succeeded Adrian as chief designer for MGM in 1942. While the chief designer for Bullock's Wilshire store she designed for many films, 17 credits of which are listed, beginning in 1938. She notes that actresses are not allowed to buy their film costumes after a film's production and refers briefly to Irene Dunne's costumes in "The White Cliffs of Dover." She supervises a staff of designers, each assigned to one film; she designs "a bit here and there where it pleases her."

1523 "Irene." Southern California Prompter, 1 (1): 18-20, July 1960.
Irene's fashion collection for 1960 was inspired in part by her recent costumes for Doris Day in "Midnight Lace."

1524 "Irene (Gibbons)." World of Fashion. 1976, p. 226-7.
Notes erroneously that Irene was married to set designer Cedric Gibbons (she was married to his brother, screenwriter Eliot Gibbons.)

1525 "Irene (Gibbons)." Fairchild's Who's Who in Fashion. 1975, p. 125.

1526 "Irene, Designer for Women, Dies." New York Times, November 16, 1962, p. 21.
Irene leaped to her death, worried by business problems and her husband's poor health. She headed a staff of 200 persons at MGM but decreased her assignments there to form "Irene, Inc.," for retail fashions.

1527 "Irene Designs Gracious-Lady Fashions." Screenland, 47 (5): 54-5, September 1943.
Mary Astor models six costumes by Irene from "Young Ideas."

1528 "'Irene' Is Going to Follow 'Sally' into the Movies." Screen News, 4 (20): 14, May 16, 1925.
"Irene" will feature the largest and most colorful fashion show yet seen on the screen.

1529 "Irene Rich as Vamp." Senator Newsette, 2 (10): 4, March 7, 1926.
Description of a gown worn by Irene Rich in "Lady Windermere's Fan," designed by Sophie Wachner.

1530 "Irene Sharaff...." Photoplay, 32 (4): 107, March 1948.
Brief biographical information on Irene Sharaff.

1531 "'Irene' to Be Partly in Color." Screen News, 4 (45): 3, November 14, 1925.
The fashion sequence of "Irene" will be filmed in Technicolor.

Weeks of wardrobe testing kept Colleen Moore busy; she will wear gowns she helped design with Cora McGeachy.

1532 Iribe, Paul. "The Elimination of Geographical Lines." <u>Screen News,</u> 3 (28): 8, July 12, 1924.
Paul Iribe, art director for De Mille studios, was a fashion designer for seven years with Paul Poiret and Pacquin. He feels that American women should not be slaves to French fashion and believes that motion pictures have done a great deal to establish distinctive American fashions, since film designers must originate new styles rather than depend on current fashions.

1533 "Iribe, Paul." <u>American Film Institute Catalog, 1921-30</u>, p. 1170.
Paul Iribe is credited with the costumes of "Manslaughter" and "The World's Applause."

1534 "Is Fashion an Art?" <u>Metropolitan Museum Bulletin,</u> 26 (3): 134-5, November 1967.
Irene Sharaff notes that the Asian color scheme and Thai silks used in the film version of "The King and I" influenced fashion considerably.

1535 "Israel, Walter J." <u>American Film Institute Catalog, 1921-30</u>, p. 1171.
Walter J. Israel is credited with the costumes of "The Eternal Flame," "Oliver Twist," "The Sea Hawk," and "Abraham Lincoln."

1536 "It Has 'It'; Clara Bow's Bathing Suit Free." <u>Screenland,</u> 17 (3): 40-1, July 1928.
Clara Bow models a bathing suit with matching coat, cap, and shoes from "Red Hair"; to be given as a contest prize.

1537 "'It's a Lie--I Don't Hate Sarongs!'" <u>Screen Guide,</u> 4 (12): 20-1, April 1940.
Despite previous publicity, Dorothy Lamour is grateful for the sarong because it led her to her first film break. Recently, in "The Road to Singapore," she wore a sarong called a "sinjang"; though she likes sarongs, she objects to the roles that give her a limited vocabulary and character.

1538 "It's the 'Dolly' Influence." <u>Screenland,</u> 50 (2): 42-3, December 1945.
Betty Grable and June Haver model many costumes and hats from "The Dolly Sisters," by Orry-Kelly, as well as retail adaptations.

1539 "Jackie Wears Crown Jewels." <u>Screen News,</u> 2 (24): 22,
June 16, 1923.
Jackie Coogan was lent about $100,000 worth of the Russian
Crown jewels, from a private collection, for use in "Long Live
the King."

1540 "Jackie Will Wear 'Kid's' Rags Again." <u>Screen News,</u> 3 (29):
6, July 19, 1924.
Jackie Coogan will again wear rags, in "Dynamite," including a
worn-out derby.

1541 "Jackson, Jackie." <u>American Film Institute Catalog, 1961-70,</u>
p. 313.
Jackie Jackson is credited with the wardrobe of "Why Bother to
Knock" and was the wardrobe mistress of "Hand in Hand" and
"Tamahine."

1542 "Jacobs, Sally." <u>American Film Institute Catalog, 1961-70,</u>
p. 314.
Sally Jacobs is credited with the costumes of "Having a Wild
Weekend" and as the production designer of "The Persecution and
Assassination of Jean-Paul Marat As Performed by the Inmates
of the Asylum of Charenton Under the Direction of the Marquis
de Sade" and the designer of "Tell Me Lies."

1543 "Jacobs, Sally (née Rich)." <u>Who's Who in the Theatre.</u> 16th
ed., 1977, p. 774.
Sally Jacobs's film-costume credits include "Nothing but the Best,"
"Catch Us if You Can," and "The Persecution and Assassination
of Jean-Paul Marat...."

1544 "Jamandreu, Paco." <u>American Film Institute Catalog, 1961-</u>
<u>70,</u> p. 315.
Paco Jamandreu is credited with Isabel Sarli's wardrobe in
"Woman and Temptation."

1545 Jamison, Jack. "Garbo on the Set." <u>Modern Screen,</u> 3 (4):
32-4, 114-5
Brief mention of Greta Garbo refusing to wear one of her costumes for "Mata Hari." She stayed in her dressing room for

seven hours until she was given permission to wear something
other than the approximately $3000 gown; the delay cost at least
as much as the gown, but she thought it was wrong for the scene.

1546 _____. "How Clothes 'Made' Garbo." Hollywood, 20 (6):
          15-6, 61, July 1931.
The author attributes Greta Garbo's success to Adrian, who
changed her fashion image when he came to MGM; she had been
unhappy in her previous costumes, which Adrian himself felt were
too bizarre. She prefers simplicity and clothes with line as the
focal point and yet will wear almost anything the script requires,
if Adrian designs it. Adrian denies that her figure is boyish;
rather it is well developed but appears differently to the camera.

1547 "Jane Novak in ... 'I Want a Divorce.'" Screen News, 3 (3):
          31, January 19, 1924, cols. 1-2.
Jane Novak models a gown with a fur cape from "I Want a
Divorce."

1548 "Janet, Janine." American Film Institute Catalog, 1961-70,
          p. 316.
Janine Janet is credited with the costumes of "Testament of Orpheus."

1549 "Jax." American Film Institute Catalog, 1961-70, p. 317.
Jax is credited with Tuesday Weld's wardrobe in "Lord Love a
Duck."

1550 "Jeakins, Dorothy." American Film Institute Catalog, 1961-70,
          p. 317.
17 credits are listed for designer Dorothy Jeakins.

1551 "Jeakins, Dorothy." Biographical Encyclopaedia and Who's
          Who of the American Theatre. 1966, p. 569.

1552 "Jeakins, Dorothy." Who's Who in America. 38th ed., 1975-
          6, p. 1578.
Dorothy Jeakins's costume design credits include "Joan of Arc,"
"Samson and Delilah," and "The Greatest Show on Earth." She
has been nominated for six Academy Awards and received two
(as of this date, she had been nominated 11 times and received
three Academy Awards).

1553 "Jean Desses, 65, Fashion Designer." New York Times,
          August 4, 1970, p. 31.
Jean Desses, who died after a long illness at age 65, was famous
for his draped designs and classic suits.

1554 "Jean Louis." American Film Institute Catalog, 1961-70, p.
          318.
26 credits are listed for designer Jean-Louis.

1555 "Jean-Louis." Who's Who in America. 38th ed., 1975-6, p.
          1578.

Jean-Louis was Columbia's head designer from 1943 to 1960, and now freelances for Universal. He is also the president of Jean-Louis, Inc.

1556 "Jeanette Calm As Flames Catch Gown in Spectacle Scenes."
      MGM Studio News, 5 (10): n.p., October 8, 1938.
Jeanette MacDonald's voluminous gown caught fire as it touched one of thousands of electric bulbs decorated as wistaria blossoms during the filming of the finale of "Sweethearts." The flames were extinguished by Nelson Eddy, with whom she was singing, and a gloved electrician. The scene was refilmed with MacDonald in a different position to conceal the damaged part.

1557 Jeanne, René. "Max Linder: France's First Star." Unifrance
      Film, 8: 2-3, December 1950.
Max Linder, unlike other film comedians, would not wear sloppy or dirty-appearing costumes, preferring instead a neat appearance with well-pressed trousers, jacket, topper, and yellow gloves.

1558 "Jefferies, Wesley V." American Film Institute Catalog, 1961-
      70, p.318.
Wesley V. Jefferies is credited with the wardrobe of "X-15," "The Manchurian Candidate," and "Sergeants 3."

1559 "Jeffries, Wes." American Film Institute Catalog, 1961-70,
      p.318.
Wes Jeffries is credited with the wardrobe of "Irma La Douce," "Kiss Me Stupid," "Seven Days in May," "The Young Lovers," "The Hallelujah Trail," "The Satan Bug," and "The Russians Are Coming The Russians Are Coming" and the men's wardrobe/costumes of "The Cabinet of Caligari," "Fitzwilly," and "Gaily, Gaily."

1560 Jennings, C. Robert. "Body by MacLaine--in Originals by
      Edith Head." Saturday Evening Post, 236 (42): 24-9,
      November 30, 1963.
Shirley MacLaine models eight of her 73 costumes from "What a Way to Go," which cost approximately $500,000; worn with $3,000,000 worth of jewelry from Harry Winston. Head reminisces about other actresses and films she has designed for, including Barbara Stanwyck in "The Lady Eve."

1561 Jenssen, Elois. "Fall-Winter Wardrobes." Silver Screen,
      17 (11): 50-1, 83-4, September 1947.
Elois Jenssen, age 23 and the designer for Hunt Stromberg's films, discusses designing for Lucille Ball in "Lured"; Ball models six costumes.

1562 "Jeunique Fashions." American Film Institute Catalog, 1961-
      70, p.319.
Jeunique Fashions is credited with Carrie Rochelle's wardrobe in "Africa Erotica."

1563 "Jewels That Shine in 'The Midnight Sun.'" Photoplay, 29
      (1): 88, December 1925.

Four dancers each model one costume by Alice O'Neill from "The Midnight Sun." The dancers are dressed as jewelry or representative of jewels.

1564/5 "Joan Crawford, One of the Newcomers of the Screen
       .... " Screen News, 4 (41): 15, October 17, 1925, cols.
      1-3.
Joan Crawford models a new ensemble costume from "Sally, Irene and Mary" consisting of a dress with two skirts, the outer skirt being trimmed with ostrich feathers and lace, designed so that it can also be raised to her shoulders to form a cape. Three photos show how it can be worn differently.

1566 "Joan Wears Her Newest." Photoplay, 43 (4): 80, March
      1933.
Joan Crawford models three gowns by Adrian from "Today We Live."

1567 "Jobe, Bill." American Film Institute Catalog, 1961-70, p.
      320.
Bill Jobe is credited with the wardrobe of "The Art of Love" and "Where Were You When the Lights Went Out?" and the costume supervision of "Paint Your Wagon."

1568 "Joe Rapf." New York Times, January 31, 1939, p. 21.
Joe Rapf, formerly MGM's wardrobe supervisor for 11 years, died at age 53 from a stroke.

1569 "Johns, Bertram." American Film Institute Catalog, 1921-
      30, p. 1176.
Bertram Johns was the wardrobe technical adviser for "Seven Days Leave."

1570 "Johnson, Judge." American Film Institute Catalog, 1921-30,
      p. 1177.
Judge Johnson is credited with the wardrobe of "The Trespasser."

1571 Johnston, Carol. "The Girl Who Wouldn't Undress." Motion
      Picture Classic, 28 (6): 51, 87, February 1929.
Alice Day lost her job with the Sennett studio when she refused to wear a scanty costume in "The Romance of the Bathing Girl." In her previous two-reel Sennett comedies she had been the only star not to wear a bathing suit.

1572 "Johnstone, Anna Hill." American Film Institute Catalog,
      1961-70, p. 322.
16 credits are listed for designer Anna Hill Johnstone.

1573 "Johnstone, Anna Hill." Biographical Encyclopaedia and Who's
      Who of the American Theatre. 1966, p. 574.
Biographical information on Anna Hill Johnstone, whose film-

costume credits include "Portrait of Jennie," "On the Waterfront,"
"East of Eden," "Baby Doll," "Edge of the City," "A Face in the
Crowd," "Against Tomorrow," "Wild River," "Splendor in the
Grass," "David and Lisa," "America America," "Ladybug," and
"The Pawnbroker."

1574   Jones, Charles Reed. "The Costume Designer," in <u>Your</u>
          <u>Career in Motion Pictures.</u> New York: Sheridan House,
          1949, p. 161-7.
Edith Head, with advice for would-be designers, stresses attending
art school after completing a college education. She discusses
her own education and how she first obtained her job at Paramount
(without mentioning that she borrowed a great number of sketches
from her students).

1575   "Jones, Disley." <u>American Film Institute Catalog, 1961-70,</u>
          p. 323.
Disley Jones is credited with the costumes of "The Mikado."

1576   "Jones, Disley." <u>Who's Who in the Theatre.</u> 16th ed., 1977,
          p. 788.

1577   Jones, Mary W. "The Small, Private World of Audrey Hep-
          burn." <u>Photoplay,</u> 51 (2): 66-7, 94-7, February 1957.
Hubert de Givenchy is erroneously credited with having sketched
all of Audrey Hepburn's costumes in "Funny Face." He did only
her Parisian wardrobe, with the remaining costumes by Edith
Head; Gladys de Segonzac was the wardrobe supervisor for Givenchy's costumes.

1578   Jopp, Fred Gilman. "The Ask Me Another Man." <u>Photoplay,</u>
          33 (3): 34-7, 92, 114-5, February 1928.
Lengthy article on Western Costume Company, with information
from Edward Phillips Lambert, the vice-president, research director, and purchasing director. Includes many photos of the
collection as well as some of the information found in the next
article, as with the collection bought for "The Wedding March."

1579   _____. "If It Can't Be Done--He Does It!" <u>Youth's Com-</u>
          <u>panion,</u> 103 (5): 261, 295, May 1929.
Edward Phillips Lambert founded Associated Costumers so that
anything needed for films, especially costumes and props, could
be researched and added to the collection. Lambert bought the
uniforms of the "lackies, footmen and postillions" from the Venice
Museum for "The Wedding March"; they were once owned by the
late Emperor Franz Josef of Austria. The finest fabrics are
used for film costumes, and white clothing is never used because
of halation. (Associated Costumers later became Western Costume Company.)

1580   "Jordan, Sally." <u>American Film Institute Catalog, 1961-70,</u>
          p. 325.

Sally Jordan is credited with the wardrobe of "The Cycle Savages."

1581 "Joseph, Dina." American Film Institute Catalog, 1961-70,
          p. 325.
Dina Joseph is credited with the wardrobe of "Captain Newman,
M.D.," "For Love or Money," "Murderers' Row," and "How to
Save a Marriage--and Ruin Your Life."

1582 "Joseph Urban Dies; Versatile Artist." New York Times,
          July 11, 1933, p. 17.
Joseph Urban died at age 61 from a heart attack. Includes lengthy
biographical information on Urban and notes that daughter Gretl
Urban is a painter in Paris.

1583 "Judge Can't Afford New Coat So Actor Clings to Old One."
          MGM Studio News, 5 (11): n.p., November 1938.
The wardrobe department submitted a sketch for a new frock-coat
for Lewis Stone to wear in "Out West with the Hardys," but director George B. Seitz insisted that Stone wear the jacket he had
worn in previous Hardy films, since the judge, the character Stone
plays, did not have a large enough budget to allow for a new coat.

1584 "Julie Plays Gertie." Look, 31 (19): 63-8, September 19, 1967.
Donald Brooks has designed 124 costumes for Julie Andrews in
"Star!," seven of which she models. The costumes, which appear
contemporary, will probably influence his retail collection. He
traveled to London to research the original clothing worn by Gertrude Lawrence, upon whose life the film is based, but used flair
and a feel for the period of the 1920s and 1930s rather than copying her clothing.

1585 "June Elvidge's Clothes Club." Moving Picture World, 33 (3):
          459-60, July 21, 1917.
June Elvidge, an actress with World-Brady, has started a club
to help film actresses with their costumes; they will study line,
color, fashion history, and psychology and employ a "style doctor." Elvidge discusses selecting one gown for "The Whip."

1586 "Just a Bit of News and Gossip About Film Folks." Screen
          News, 3 (31): 30, August 2, 1924.
Actor James Morrison has an extensive collection of books on the
history of costume, which he has made available for research of
several motion pictures.

1587 "Just a Bit of News and Gossip About Film Folks." Screen
          News, 3 (32): 30, August 9, 1924.
Alberta Vaughn will wear a necklace of beads made from petrified
eucalyptus buds in "The Go-Getters," given to her by the Boy
Scouts.

1588 "Just a Little Touch of Repressed Daring." Screen News, 4
          (33): 13, August 22, 1925.

Evelyn Brent discusses the difficulty of selecting clothing to appear
as a "girl crook" in films, as in "Three Wise Crooks"; since
fashion is becoming so daring, it is harder to distinguish those
who are disreputable.

1589   "--Just to Be Different Gloria Goes Back to an Old Fashion."
         Photoplay, 30 (3): 86, August 1926.
Gloria Swanson models three costumes from "Fine Manners," in
which she will wear corsets and ankle-length dresses.   Billed as
"Swanson Versus Paris," in the article.

1590 Kahn, Sylvia. "On the Set with 'Pot O' Gold.'" Modern
          Screen, 22 (5): 40-1, April 1941.
Helen Taylor designed dozens of housedresses for Paulette Goddard
and others in "Pot O' Gold."

1591 Kaiser, Joan. "Women's World: Edith Head." Los Angeles
          Herald-Examiner, January 5, 1970, sec A, p.14.
Edith Head discusses the practicality of her costumes in "Airport"
for traveling. Included are three sketches of "Airport" costumes
that will be available in department stores.

1592 Kalloch. "Fashion Forecast for Early Fall." Photoplay, 48
          (3): 53-5, 95, August 1935.
Grace Moore models six costumes from "Love Me Forever," by
Kalloch, who discusses fashion trends.

1593 _____. "Gowns for Summer Backgrounds." Motion Picture
          Studio Insider, 2 (3): 44, 59, July 1937.
Kalloch discusses film-costume designing and his costumes for
Fay Wray in "Once a Hero," two of which Wray models. Includes
also the original sketches.

1594 Kaminsky, Stuart. John Huston: Maker of Magic. Boston:
          Houghton Mifflin, 1978.
Director John Huston developed the "special rig" that allowed José
Ferrer to appear stunted as Toulouse-Lautrec in "Moulin Rouge"
by strapping his calves backwards so that he walked and wore
shoes on his knees. Huston stopped shooting late one night since
he wanted a woman to wear a feather boa; stores were closed so
he convinced a female impersonator in a nightclub to lend him
one. For a sequence in "Freud: The Secret Passion" he had
costumes duplicated from a painting by Brouillet, as the painter
had imagined the scene; rather than trying to recreate the im-
possible--what had actually been worn on the occasion. The red
cardinal vestments worn by Huston in "The Cardinal" were sent
to him at his request after the film's completion since he liked
wearing them; they had been purchased at a New York ecclesiasti-
cal shop. The sets and costumes for the Sodom sequence in
"The Bible" were designed by Mirko (he was not listed in the
American Film Institute Catalog's credits for the film). Edith

Head briefly discusses working with Huston on the costumes of "The Man Who Would Be King," and in general.

1595 "Kara, Edmund." American Film Institute Catalog, 1961-70, p. 330.
Edmund Kara is credited with the costumes of "The Moonshine War."

1596 "Karinska." American Film Institute Catalog, 1961-70, p. 331.
Karinska is credited with the costumes of "A Midsummer Night's Dream" (1967).

1597 "Karinska." Biographical Encyclopaedia and Who's Who of the American Theatre. 1966, p. 579.

1598 "Karinska, Barbara." Current Biography. 1971, p. 210-3.
Extensive biographical information on Karinska, ballet, theatrical, and film costumer and designer. She was the seamstress for the costumes of "Lady in the Dark," "Gaslight," "Frenchman's Creek," "Kismet," and "Kitty" and shared an Academy Award with Dorothy Jeakins for the costume design of "Joan of Arc."

1599 "Karinska, Barbara." Who's Who of American Women. 8th ed., 1974-5, p. 495.

1600 "Karmolińska, Maria." American Film Institute Catalog, 1961-70, p. 331.
Maria Karmolińska is credited with the costumes of "Jovita."

1601 "Karp, Soni." American Film Institute Catalog, 1961-70, p. 331.
Soni Karp is credited with the wardrobe of "The Delta Factor."

1602 "Kasparova, T." American Film Institute Catalog, 1961-70, p. 332.
T. Kasparova is credited with the costumes of "The Sun Shines for All" and "Peace to Him Who Enters."

1603 "Katharine Hepburn as 'Mary of Scotland.'" Vogue, 88 (2): 34-5, July 15, 1936.
Katharine Hepburn models one costume from "Mary of Scotland," in color.

1604 "Katherine MacDonald." Screen News, 1 (28): 3, September 2, 1922.
Two gowns worn by Katherine MacDonald in "White Shoulders" are described.

1605 "Katherine MacDonald in White Shoulders." Screen News, 1 (15): 31, June 3, 1922.
Katherine MacDonald was superstitious about wearing 13 gowns in "White Shoulders"; an extra scene was added so that she could wear 14. She models one of the gowns.

1606   "Katherine MacDonald Makes Traveling of 'Lonely Road' Cheer-
           ful Journey." Screen News, 1 (31): 18, September 23,
           1922.
       Description of one gown worn by Katherine MacDonald in "The
       Lonely Road"; she supervised the making of all of her costumes,
       ranging from velvet gowns to gingham costumes.

1607   "Katherine MacDonald Shows How to Be Well Dressed on $2.20."
           Screen News, 1 (33): 14, October 7, 1922.
       Katherine MacDonald wears a wedding gown in "The Lonely Road"
       that cost $2.20, the amount of which she estimated would be
       authentic for the type of role she plays in the film.   Four yards
       of sateen were used for the straight-lined gown, and turban, at
       a cost of $1.80; and one yard of crepe de chine was also bought
       at the price of $.45 per yard, used for trimming the gown.   (Sic;
       $1.80 + .45 = $2.25.)

1608   "Kathleen Kay Is Here Shown Wearing...." Screen News, 4
           (32): 4, August 15, 1925, col. 2.
       Kathleen Key models a costume from "The Midshipman."

1609   "Katona, Piroska." American Film Institute Catalog, 1961-70,
           p.332.
       Piroska Katona is credited with the costumes of "Dialogue."

1610   "Kaufmann, Hermann J." American Film Institute Catalog,
           1921-30, p.1183.
       Hermann J. Kaufmann is credited with the wardrobe of "Ben-Hur."

1611   "Kay, Andrew." American Film Institute Catalog, 1961-70,
           p.333.
       Andrew Kay is credited with the wardrobe of "Joe."

1612   "Kay, Kathleen." American Film Institute Catalog, 1921-30,
           p.1184.
       18 costume-related credits are listed for Kathleen Kay.   (Except
       for two films, all were codesigned with Maude Marsh.)

1613   "Kay's Newest Costumes." Photoplay, 39 (2): 76, January
           1931.
       Kay Francis models two costumes by Adrian from "Passion
       Flower."

1614   "Keehne, Chuck." American Film Institute Catalog, 1961-70,
           p.335.
       32 costume-related credits are listed for Chuck Keehne, most in
       conjunction with a costume designer.

1615   Keene, Dave.   "Visit to Wardrobe Department Likened to Trip
           into Vanished Age." Motion Picture Studio Insider, 1
           (2): 15, 39, May 1935.
       The author describes many of the costumes he saw during a tour
       of Paramount's wardrobe department.   One of the employees, a

goldsmith, made 100 brass medals for "The Lives of a Bengal Lancer."

1616 "Keep Your Head on Your Feet; Cecil B. De Mille Depicts
          His Characters by Their Footwear." Photoplay, 28 (1):
          46-7, June 1925.
Discussion of the importance of shoes to one's appearance, with brief mention of the contrasting shoes worn by Lillian Rich and Vera Reynolds in "Feet of Clay." Illustrated with stills of Reynolds and of shoes worn in "The Golden Bed."

1617 Kehler, Alice V., ed. Movie Workers. New York: Harper,
          1939.
Brief mention of film costume, noting that the costumes are designed by artists.

1618 Kelly, Katie. The Wonderful World of Women's Wear Daily.
          New York: Saturday Review Press, 1972.
John Fairchild, publisher of Women's Wear Daily waged a personal crusade in the newspaper to have hemlines drop, due to his enthusiasm over the costumes worn in "Dr. Zhivago" (which Marc Bohan of the House of Dior immediately adapted) and as worn by Faye Dunaway in "Bonnie and Clyde" and Ingrid Thulin in "The Damned." Paris followed in dropping hemlines. When young, Norman Norell dropped out of two fashion-design schools and had been laboring in a library drawing sketches when he decided to submit them to a film studio; the costumes were worn later by Gloria Swanson.

          Kelly, Orry see also Orry-Kelly

1619 "Kelly, Orry." Fairchild's Who's Who in Fashion. 1975,
          p. 140.
Orry-Kelly began film-costume designing with Warner Brothers in 1932 and later designed for Twentieth Century-Fox, Universal, and MGM. He designed 30 costumes for Rosalind Russell in "Auntie Mame" and designed for Bette Davis for over 20 years. Notes erroneously that his last film was "Gypsy."

1620 "Kemp, Jan." American Film Institute Catalog, 1961-70,
          p. 337.
Jan Kemp is credited with the wardrobe of "The Canadians" and "Batman" and the costumes of "Nikki, Wild Dog of the North."

1621 "Kerwin, Barbara." American Film Institute Catalog, 1961-
          70, p. 339.
Barbara Kerwin is credited with the wardrobe of "The Hooked Generation."

1622 Kessler, Agnes. "Moving Picture Actresses' Fashions."
          Moving Picture Stories, 5 (127): 29, June 4, 1915.
Discussion of one costume each worn by Mary Fuller in an unnamed film; Billie Rhodes in "When Cupid Crossed the Bay";

Vicky Forde, who designs most of her film costumes, in "They Were Heroes"; Doris Pawn in "Diamonds of Fate"; and Viola Dana in "The House of the Lost Court." Also, brief mention of Dorothy Phillips in "A Fireside Realization." Grace Cunard models a gown from "The Broken Coin."

1623   Kessler, Marjorie. "Tony Duquette: Magic Remembered."
            The Californian, 9 (4): 58-61, 66, May 1950.
Biographical information on Tony Duquette, artist, architect, sculptor, and set and costume designer.

1624   Keyes, Marion Herwood. "For Campus or Career." Silver
            Screen, 17 (10): 50-1, 82-3, August 1947.
Two costumes each are modeled by Joan Lorring from "The Other Love" and Lilli Palmer from "Body and Soul"; both films were designed by Marion Herwood Keyes, who discusses fashion trends.

1625   Kezich, Tullio, ed. Federico Fellini's "Juliet of the Spirits."
            Translated by Howard Greenfeld. New York: Orion, 1965.
Rather than hire actors for their acting ability Federico Fellini searches for sensitive faces and then utilizes costumes to help define the psychology of the character. Designer Piero Gherardi, with suggestions by director Fellini, designed the costumes for the apparitions in "Juliet of the Spirits," based on cartoon characters, which gave an Oriental look. Fellini also discusses his need for understanding with Giulietta Masina, in the title role as Juliet. When she complained Fellini thought she was rejecting her role, but she really just wanted costume changes, they found.

1626   "Khoury, Marc." American Film Institute Catalog, 1961-70,
            p. 340.
Marc Khoury is credited with the wardrobe of "One Shocking Moment."

1627   Kiam, Omar, as told to Sonia Lee. "Rules for the Well-
            Dressed Woman." Hollywood, 24 (6): 34-5, 57, June
            1935.
Omar Kiam discusses working with figure flaws, noting briefly how he works with film costume to make Merle Oberon look taller and uses padding for Ann Sothern's small figure and transparent sleeves to emphasize Loretta Young's hands and arms.

1628   "Kiam, Omar." Current Biography. 1945, p. 321-3.
Omar Kiam has designed some film costumes that have been mass-marketed, including the wedding gown worn by Merle Oberon in "Wuthering Heights" and a fur-lined coat for "Clive of India." Lengthy biographical information.

1629   "Kiam, Omar." Current Biography (Necrology). 1954, p. 377.

1630   "Kiam, Omar." Motion Picture Almanac. 1943-4, p. 317.

1631   "Kiam, Omar (Alexander)." World of Fashion. 1976, p. 324-5.

Omar Kiam was a costume designer with Goldwyn studios from
1935 to 1941 and then returned with much acclaim to fashion designing.

1632   Kiesling, Barrett C.   "Costuming the Picture," in <u>Talking Pic-</u>
            <u>tures</u>. Richmond, Va.: Johnson, 1937, p.112-8.
Includes a discussion of the wardrobe department, with biographical information on "Mother" Lucy Coulter, a character-wardrobe
mistress.   5,000 costumes were required for "Romeo and Juliet,"
with hundreds of paintings in Italian and French galleries used
for research.   Each of 40 costumes worn in "The Great Ziegfeld"
required over 50 yards of lightweight fabric.

1633   "Kinds, Karl."   <u>American Film Institute Catalog, 1961-70</u>,
            p.342.
Karl Kinds is credited with the costumes of "Seven Guns for the
MacGregors."

1634   "King, Joe."   <u>American Film Institute Catalog, 1961-70</u>, p.
            342.
Joe King is credited with the wardrobe of "Advise and Consent"
and "The Cardinal"; the costumes of "Judgment at Nuremberg,"
"Guess Who's Coming to Dinner," and "The Secret of Santa
Vittoria"; and the costume/wardrobe supervision of "It's a Mad,
Mad, Mad, Mad World," "Ship of Fools," and "R.P.M."

1635   "King, Muriel."   <u>Current Biography</u>. 1943, p. 379-80.
Lengthy biography of fashion designer Muriel King, artist for
<u>Vogue</u> and frequent film designer.   Beginning in 1935 King oc-
casionally commuted from New York to Hollywood to design film
costumes, until 1942, when she moved to Hollywood to resume her
film career.   For her first film, "Sylvia Scarlett," she flew twice
to Hollywood to design Katharine Hepburn's costumes, but only a
dress, clown suit, and raincoat were worn in the film.

1636   "King, Muriel (Mrs.)."   <u>American Women; the Standard Bio-</u>
            <u>graphical Dictionary of Notable Women.</u> Vol. III, 1939-
            40. Los Angeles: American Publications, 1939, p.487-8.

1637   "King, Roger Milner."   <u>American Film Institute Catalog, 1961-</u>
            <u>70</u>, p.342.
Roger Milner King designed and created the jewelry for "Deadfall."

1638   Kingsley, Grace.   "'Clothes.'"   <u>Photoplay,</u> 7 (6): 98-104,
            May 1915.
Actresses often help designers by wearing the latest fashions in
their films and consequently spreading them to women who may
have only seen them before in fashion magazines.   Film-costume
selection is discussed briefly by Mary Pickford, Fritzi Scheff,
and Mabel Normand, who had recently researched the costumes of
the 1820s for an (unnamed) film in a library, which she then had
sewn.   Discussion also of authentic period costumes worn by Anita

King in "The Girl of the Golden West," "The Man from Home,"
and, briefly, "Snobs"; and Blanche Sweet in "The Warrens of
Virginia" and "The Captive." One costume each is modeled by
King and Sweet from their first films, as listed.

1639 Kinkead, Jean, and Ann Ward. "Modern Screen's Fashion
          Guide." Modern Screen, 30 (4): 50-1, 141, March 1945.
Davenshire (the retail manufacturer) designed the pants worn by
Merle Oberon in "A Song to Remember."

1640 Kirkland, Sally. "McCardell," in American Fashion, edited
          by Sarah Tomerlin Lee. New York: Quadrangle/New
          York Times, 1975, p. 290-315.
Fashion designer Claire McCardell's look is typified by her fashions
from the 1940s, which the author feels are timeless, as compared
with revivals of film costumes of the same era worn by Greta
Garbo and Betty Grable, which are usually "campy" and quickly
fade away as fads.

1641 "Kiselyova, V." American Film Institute Catalog, 1961-70,
          p. 344.
V. Kiselyova is credited with the costumes of "Sound of Life"
and "Nine Days of One Year."

1642 "Kitty." Motion Picture, 71 (1): 25, February 1946.
The eighteenth-century fashions of "Kitty" were researched by a
London unit, with the assistance of Hilda Grenier, a special consultant. Paulette Goddard, in the title role, models two costumes
from the film.

1643 Klein, Carole. Aline: The First Biography of Aline Bernstein,
          Famed Stage Designer and Mistress of Thomas Wolfe.
          New York: Harper & Row, 1979.
An in-depth biography of distinguished writer and theatrical-costume
and set designer Aline Bernstein, founder in 1938 of the Costume
Museum (absorbed by the Metropolitan Museum of Art in 1944).
She took a brief respite from theatrical-costume designing in 1935
to design the costumes for "She," starring Helen Gahagan Douglas, who comments briefly on Bernstein's costumes for her. (She
designed for one other film, the same year, "The Last Days of
Pompeii.") Circa 1928 Irene Sharaff, another accomplished film
and theatrical designer, became Bernstein's design assistant;
Sharaff quit working with Bernstein in 1932, when the theater
where they had been working was closed.

1644 "Klein, Janine." American Film Institute Catalog, 1961-70,
          p. 345.
Janine Klein is credited with the costumes of "Mister Freedom."

1645 Klemesrud, Judy. " 'Funny Girl' Takes Whirl into Fashion."
          New York Times, June 8, 1968, p. 20.
More than ten designers and manufacturers intend to market clothes
based on the "Funny Girl" costumes; many of the ready-to-wear

fashions only vaguely resemble the film's costumes. Irene Sharaff
authenticated the costumes for Barbra Streisand by studying original photos of Fanny Brice, upon whose life story the film is
based. A 20-minute film was shown before the fashion show in
which Streisand modeled Sharaff's costumes; she designed 20 for
Streisand to wear in the film. In addition to the furs, jewelry,
and purses marketed, a manufacturer will sell a men's-wear line
inspired by the wardrobe of Omar Sharif.

1646 "Klotz, Florence." American Film Institute Catalog, 1961-70,
        p. 345.
Florence Klotz was the costume designer of "Something for Everyone."

1647 "Klotz, Florence." Who's Who in the Theatre. 16th ed.,
        1977, p. 820.
Biographical information on Florence Klotz, who began costume
designing for German films in 1969 and began in the U.S.A. with
"Something for Everyone."

1648 "Klotz, Florence." Who's Who of American Women. 8th ed.,
        1974-5, p. 522.

1649 Klumph, Inez and Helen. "The Influence of Costume," in
        Screen Acting: Its Requirements and Rewards. New
        York: Falk, 1922, p. 148-50.
Includes a discussion of the importance of costume to the performances of Richard Barthelmess, Jean Paige, and Hugo Ballin,
who sketches a character the way he thinks it should look and
then sends the sketches to the casting agencies in order to find
someone who looks the part. A ragged dress for Dorothy Gish
in "Orphans of the Storm" required so much research and experi-
menting that its final cost was close to $150, designed by studio
designer O'Kane Cornwell.

1650 "Kniepert, Erni." American Film Institute Catalog, 1961-70,
        p. 346.
Erni Kniepert is credited with the costumes of "Der Rosenkavalier."

1651 Knight, Arthur. "Arthur Knight Looks at the Influentials."
        Hollywood Reporter 49th Annual [1979], p. 11, 14-5.
Discussion of how movies have influenced American culture, as
with advertising and political ideologies. The most typical example of film's influence on American society was the drop in
underwear sales after Clark Gable was shown undressing to a
bare chest in "It Happened One Night." Fashion history has
been changed by stars wearing designer clothes in their films.

1652 Knox, Donald. The Magic Factory: How MGM Made "An
        American in Paris." New York: Praeger, 1973.
Irene Sharaff discusses researching the costumes for "An American
in Paris," and though she had little time to design the 500 cos-

tumes, she listened to the George Gershwin score over and over
so that she could let her subconscious assist her in her sketches,
as with the gendarme uniforms. She also discusses her color
selections for many costumes, and the different parts of the ballet
sequence. She and the other two costume designers, Orry-Kelly
and Walter Plunkett, won an Academy Award; includes Plunkett's
acceptance speech on the designers' behalf. Mary Ann Nyberg,
the "Freed Unit Dress Designer," designed only Leslie Caron's
gown for the Academy Awards.

1653 Kobal, John. Gotta Sing, Gotta Dance; A Pictorial History of
        Film Musicals. London: Hamlyn, 1970.
Walter Plunkett discusses the effect of sound films on costume
fabrics, with brief mention of the costumes for "Dixiana"; the
difficulty of working with color and costumes for "Rio Rita"; and
his costumes for Bebe Daniels in "Rio Rita," Deanna Durbin in
"Can't Help Singing," Marilyn Maxwell in "Summer Holiday," and
for Mae West in "The Heat's On"--she requested that he design
costumes that female impersonators would enjoy wearing.

1654 _____. Rita Hayworth: The Time, the Place and the Wo-
        man. New York: Norton, 1978.
Though the sets and costumes had been made for her, Rita Hayworth's lead role in "Ramona" was given to Loretta Young when
Darryl Zanuck's Twentieth Century merged with Fox; the film was
felt to be too important for the beginning actress, and her contract was soon terminated. She acted in a number of "B" westerns and spy films; in "The Lone Wolf Spy Hunt," she first had
a studio-designed wardrobe, by Kalloch, rather than wardrobe-
department castoffs. Includes references to both Fred Astaire
and Gene Kelly being worried about Hayworth wearing high-heels
and appearing too tall in their films; with both she wore flat heels.
At Columbia she began her long and famous association with designer Jean Louis; he first designed her costumes for "Tonight
and Every Night." He was inspired by John Singer Sargent's
portrait of Mrs. X in designing Hayworth's famous strapless,
black satin gown for "Gilda." Her comeback film after years off
from Columbia and filmmaking was "Affair in Trinidad"; designer
Jean Louis was one of few people with whom Hayworth worked who
still remained at the studio, though his "fifteen breathtaking gowns"
for her couldn't save the film. A "saving grace" for "Salome"
was his innovative plastic body stocking for Hayworth; she appeared
nude under the multicolored, semitransparent veils without the
need for a bra since the straps would have shown. Her marriage
to Dick Haymes did not endear either of them to Columbia when
Haymes began dictating even the style of her costumes for "Joseph
and His Brethren"; both film and marriage were abandoned.

1655 "Kobald, Jerry." American Film Institute Catalog, 1961-70,
        p. 347.
Jerry Kobald is credited with the wardrobe of "Cover Me Babe."

1656 "Koch, Norma." American Film Institute Catalog, 1961-70,
        p. 347.

Norma Koch was the costume designer of "Cry for Happy, " "Taras
Bulba, " "What Ever Happened to Baby Jane?, " "4 for Texas, "
"Hush ... Hush, Sweet Charlotte, " and "The Flight of the Phoenix";
the wardrobe designer of "Mackenna's Gold"; and is credited with
the costumes of "The Last Sunset, " "Kings of the Sun, " and "The
Way West. "

1657 "Kohlschein, Margot. " American Film Institute Catalog, 1961-
          70, p.348.
Margot Kohlschein is credited with the costumes of "False Shame. "

1658 Korda, Michael. "The Influentials; American Authors Assess
          Hollywood. " Hollywood Reporter 49th Annual [1979], p.
          68-9.
Reminiscences of Hollywood by writer/publisher Michael Korda,
son and nephew of filmmakers Vincent Korda and Alexander Korda,
respectively. He notes that Alexander Korda insisted that Paulette
Goddard wear real jewelry in "An Ideal Husband" since she would
feel better.

1659 "Kosloff, Theodore. " American Film Institute Catalog, 1921-
          30, p.1196.
Theodore Kosloff is credited with the wardrobe of "Forbidden
Fruit. "

1660 Krier, Beth Ann. "Movie Memories. " Los Angeles Times
          West Magazine, November 7, 1971, p.16-7.
Following auctions of film props and costumes many designers'
sketches are being auctioned by Sotheby Parke Bernet, with pro-
ceeds going to the Costume Designers' Guild. Included are cos-
tume sketches of Lana Turner in "The Merry Widow" (1952), by
Helen Rose; John Wayne in "The Cowboys, " by Anthea Sylbert;
Faye Dunaway in "Bonnie and Clyde, " by Thea Van Runkle; Joan
Blondell in "Waterhole #3, " by Jack Baer; Bette Davis in "What
Ever Happened to Baby Jane?, " by Norma Koch; and Jane Russell
in "The Revolt of Mamie Stover, " by Jean Louis.

1661 _____. "Thea in the Big Budget World of 'Mame.'" Los
          Angeles Times, January 12, 1973, sec. 4, p.1, 9.
Thea Van Runkle designed over 700 costumes for "Mame, " with
a budget of $150,000, and was allowed to design the shoes, hats,
and other accessories. She researched copies of Vogue and Harper's Bazaar, and emphasized the Art Deco of the 1920s. She
discusses designing for Lucille Ball in the title role; she feels
the shoes were the best part of the costumes for Ball. She used
few colors for the costumes and notes that Preston Foster was
the easiest person to costume for the film. She regretted not
having enough time to design the costumes for "The Great Gatsby. "
Includes several sketches of Ball.

1662 "Kristos, Dimitri. " American Film Institute Catalog, 1961-
          70, p.353.
Dimitri Kristos is credited with Melina Mercouri's wardrobe
in "A Man Could Get Killed. "

1663   "Kruchinina, O." American Film Institute Catalog, 1961-70,
          p.353.
       O. Kruchinina is credited with the costumes of "The Magic Voyage
       of Sinbad" and "The Ballad of a Hussar."

1664   "Krumbachová, Ester." American Film Institute Catalog, 1961-
          70, p.353.
       Ester Krumbachová is credited with the costumes of "Diamonds of
       the Night."

1665   "Kufel, Stanley." American Film Institute Catalog, 1961-70,
          p.354.
       Stanley Kufel is credited with the wardrobe of "Lonely Are the
       Brave."

1666   Kugler, Dorothy. "How Carole Lombard Became the Best-
          Dressed Star." Movie Classic, 8 (3): 28-9, 76-7, May
          1935.
       Travis Banton, who designs Carole Lombard's film costumes, con-
       siders her the best-dressed actress in films. She discusses her
       personal wardrobe.

1667   "Kuhn, Grace." American Film Institute Catalog, 1961-70,
          p.354.
       Grace Kuhn is credited with the costumes of "The Three Stooges
       Go Around the World in a Daze" and "One Man's Way."

1668   "Kumar, Milena." American Film Institute Catalog, 1961-70,
          p.354.
       Milena Kumar is credited with the costumes of "Carmen, Baby."

1669   "Kunkle, Peggy." American Film Institute Catalog, 1961-70,
          p.354.
       Peggy Kunkle is credited with the costumes of "Darker Than
       Amber" and the wardrobe of "Birds Do It" and "Gentle Giant."

1670   Kutner, Nanette. "Irene of Hollywood." Cosmopolitan, 115
          (4): 8, 12-3, October 1943.
       Biographical information on Irene, who designed seven costumes
       for Irene Dunne in "The White Cliffs of Dover"; she had to de-
       sign a new type of shoes for Dunne because of war scarcities.

1671   Kuwalsky, Freddy. "Our Profession...." Motion Picture
          Costumers, July 11, 1953, n.p.
       The profession of costumers includes those who are responsible
       for costume research, cutting, draping, hand-finishing, tailoring,
       beading, and breaking down the script for a costume plot; they
       also must have a knowledge of how different colors photograph.
       Includes comments by designers Edith Head, Walter Plunkett, and
       Helen Rose as to their value to actresses and designers.

1672 "Ladies: Good, Bad and Indifferent." <u>Motion Picture,</u> 30 (6):
       35, January 1926.
Norma Shearer models a costume from "Free Lips" ("His Secretary").

1673 " 'The Lady from Shanghai.'" <u>Motion Picture,</u> 75 (4): 26-7,
       May 1948.
Rita Hayworth models four costumes from "The Lady from Shanghai," in color, with references to the scenes they are worn in.

1674 "Lady of the Evening." <u>Motion Picture,</u> 56 (6): 46-7, January
       1939.
Joan Crawford models five costumes from "The Shining Hour."

1675 "Laeerfeld, Karl." <u>American Film Institute Catalog, 1961-70,</u>
       p. 357.
Karl Laeerfeld is credited with the costumes of "Succubus."

1676 "Lafon, Madeleine." <u>American Film Institute Catalog, 1961-</u>
       <u>70,</u> p. 357.
Madeleine Lafon is credited with the wardrobe of "La Guerre Est
Finie."

1677 Lahr, John. <u>Notes on a Cowardly Lion: The Biography of</u>
       <u>Bert Lahr.</u> New York: Knopf, 1969.
Jack Haley's Tin Man costume in "The Wizard of Oz" left him
nearly immobile, so that he rested on a leaning board (usually
used by actresses in tight gowns, since they often cannot sit down).
Bert Lahr's Cowardly Lion costume was bolstered with shoulder
pads.   The Tin Man's helmet and the Scarecrow's burlap sack on
his sandbag head were made of rubber.

1678 Laitin, Joseph. "Up in Edie's Room." <u>Collier's,</u> 136 (5):
       26-31, September 2, 1955.
The emphasis is upon Edith Head's personal relationships with the
actresses she designs for.   Includes references to costumes worn
by Grace Kelly in "The Bridges at Toko-Ri" and "Rear Window,"
Jeanmaire in "Anything Goes," Carol Ohmart in "The Scarlet Hour,"
and Nina Foch in "The Ten Commandments."

1679 "Lalique, Suzanne." American Film Institute Catalog, 1961-70,
       p. 358.
Suzanne Lalique is credited with the costumes of "The Marriage
of Figaro."

       Lambert, Eleanor see World of Fashion

1680 Lambert, Gavin. GWTW: The Making of "Gone with the Wind."
       Boston: Little, Brown, 1973.
5, 500 items of clothing were made for "Gone with the Wind"; the
total cost of the wardrobe was $153,818. The cost of laundry
during the filming was $10,000.

1681 _____. "Romeo and Juliet," in On Cukor. New York:
       Putnam's, 1972, p. 102-4.
Some of the costumes of "Romeo and Juliet" (1936), were adapted
from Botticelli, but director George Cukor wishes there had been
more of an Italian, Mediterreanean look. The costumes of Adrian
and Oliver Messel were competing with each other.

1682 Lambert, Will. "Some Suggestions for the Coming Modes."
       Hollywood Life, 2 (5): 57-63, April 1927.
Will Lambert was the Director of Costumes at Hal Roach Studios
at this time (a unique reference); he has sketched many actresses
in apparently nonfilm costumes.

1683 Lambourne, Norah. Review of Hollywood Costume Design, by
       David Chierichetti. Journal of the Costume Society, 11:
       142, 1977.
The author found Hollywood Costume Design fascinating and an
excellent reference source. Mentioned are David Chierichetti's
study of the influence of film costume upon fashion; the major
decades, studios, and designers; and the changes created by the
introduction of the microphone, color films, and Cinemascope of
1953, which magnified everything on a larger screen. Universal
is the only studio today that has a full-time designer under contract, Edith Head; the other designers work free-lance.

1684 Lamour, Dorothy. "Should She ... Or Not?" Screenland,
       53 (8): 38-9, 65-6, June 1949.
Dorothy Lamour has asked the readers to write her concerning
whether or not she should make any more "sarong" films. She
only starred in seven such films, and has not been in one for
five years. She discusses the pros and cons of wearing the sarong costume, and sarong roles.

1685 Lamparski, Richard. Whatever Became of ... ? New York:
       Crown, 1967.
Elizabeth Bergner set fashion trends for shorts when she wore
them in "Escape Me Never" and for bare-midriff costumes when
she wore them in "Dreaming Lips."

1686 _____. Whatever Became of ... ? Second Series. New

York: Crown, 1968.
Binnie Barnes received considerable publicity in 1941, when she
announced plans to sue Columbia because she had been "duped"
into appearing in black lace panties and bra for "This Thing Called
Love" (does not say what became of the lawsuit).   Notes Ina
Claire's popularity for playing well-groomed character parts and
that she influenced fashion with many styles.

1687 _____. Whatever Became of ... ? Third Series.   New
          York: Crown, 1970.
Peggy Fears's New York dress shop went broke, and her plans
for being her own movie producer (and costume designer) fell
through.

1688 _____. Whatever Became of ... ? Fifth Series.   New
          York: Crown, 1974.
Anita Colby acted in and designed some of the costumes for
"Cover Girl. "

1689 "Lana Turner Wears Clothes of Future. " MGM Studio News,
          6 (16): n.p., March 25, 1939.
Lana Turner's wardrobe for "Calling Dr. Kildare" will feature
"futuristic" clothes, including the first clothes made of glass and
metal fabric.   A gown adapted for the Nautch dancers consists of
a full skirt with an unattached bodice.

1690 "Lancaster, Osbert. " American Film Institute Catalog, 1961-
          70, p. 359.
Osbert Lancaster was the costume designer of "Those Magnificent
Men in Their Flying Machines; or How I Flew from London to
Paris in 25 Hours and 11 Minutes. "

1691 "Lancetti (Roma), Pino. " American Film Institute Catalog,
          1961-70, p. 359.
Pino Lancetti (of Roma) is credited with Sylva Koscina's costumes
in "Three Bites of the Apple. "

1692 "Landers, Ann. " American Film Institute Catalog, 1961-70,
          p. 360.
Ann Landers is credited with the women's wardrobe/costumes in
"Blue" and "Inside Daisy Clover, " the wardrobe of "Love with
the Proper Stranger, " and Natalie Wood's costumes in "This
Property Is Condemned" and "Penelope" (with Edith Head).

1693 Lane, Jerry. "The Girl Who Learned How to Dress. " Photo-
          play with Movie Mirror, 18 (3): 48-9, 87-8, February
          1941.
Carole Lombard wears at least two 3/4-length coats in "Mr. and
Mrs. Smith, " which she had Irene design for her because she
grew tired of the usual short jackets.   She models a gown from
the film.   Notes also the trend started by her wearing a beaded
shirtwaist dinner dress (which she wore in many films).

1694   Lane, Lydia. "Edith Head Looks to Future." Los Angeles
              Times, May 21, 1972, sec. E, p. 17.
       Elizabeth Taylor specifically chose Edith Head to design her 12
       costumes in "Hammersmith Is Out."

1695   Lane, Virginia T. "Chart Your Wardrobe Colors for Spring."
              Motion Picture, 51 (2): 44-5, 84-5, March 1936.
       Adrian and Orry-Kelly discuss the personal coloring of many
       actresses they have designed for; with a color chart by Adrian
       for nine of MGM's leading actresses. Bette Davis models a
       costume from "Dangerous," by Orry-Kelly, which is discussed.

1696   _____. "Fashions--Yesterday, Today, and Tomorrow."
              Motion Picture, 51 (1): 44-6, 76, February 1936.
       Adrian discusses film costume's fashion influence; Lucien Lelong
       credits designer Travis Banton with the popularity of clothes with
       feathers; and there are references to Banton's research for Ruby
       Keeler's costumes in "Colleen." It has taken Hollywood 25 years
       to become a fashion capital, as opposed to 300 years it took Paris.
       Miscellaneous film costumes modeled, without film titles, present
       a visual history of film costume. Costumes that have influenced
       fashion include the sleeves worn by Joan Crawford in "Letty Lyn-
       ton," Greta Garbo's pill-box hat, tailored evening gowns by Carole
       Lombard, and Mae West's period costumes.

1697   _____. "Secrets of the Hollywood Stylists." Part II.
              Modern Screen, 1 (5): 60-3, 102, April 1931.
       The author and Travis Banton discuss the influence of film cos-
       tume on fashion, as with the Victorian revival sparked by Adrian's
       costumes for "Bitter Sweet." Banton also discusses the fashion
       image of many of the actresses he has designed for. Includes one
       of his sketches for Ruth Chatterton in "New Morals."

1698   _____. "Secrets of the Hollywood Stylists." Part III.
              Modern Screen, 1 (6): 62-5, 119, May 1931.
       Sophie Wachner discusses actresses she has designed for, includ-
       ing Irene Rich in "Lady Windermere's Fan" and Jeanette MacDonald
       in "Oh, for a Man!"; MacDonald models two of the costumes. Ex-
       amples of trend-setting costume details by the designer include a
       dress worn by Sharon Lynn in "Sunny Side Up," with a bow worn
       on the back (which popularized a bustle effect), and a trick clasp
       worn on a hat worn by Catherine Dale Owens in "Such Men Are
       Dangerous."

1699   _____. "Secrets of the Hollywood Stylists." Part IV.
              Modern Screen, 2 (1): 70-3, 103-4, June 1931.
       Earl Luick discusses film-costume designing, and costumes worn
       by Loretta Young in "Big Business Girl" and "Upper Underworld,"
       by Doris Kenyon in the latter film, and by Dorothy Mackaill in
       "The Reckless Hour." Young models one costume each from the
       two films.

1700   _____. "Style Your Wardrobe the Hollywood Way!" Motion

Picture, 51 (4): 44-5, 88-9, May 1936.
A costume worn by Grace Moore in "The King Steps Out" will be
adapted for retail sale; it is described simply as white chiffon with
ruffles, draped bodice, and worn with a picture hat, being from
the 1850s.   Moore notes the influence of the "Romeo and Juliet"
costumes on fashion.

1701   Lang, Harry.   "Clothes Make the MEN-JOU."   Motion Picture,
        54 (2): 29, 84-5, September 1937.
Adolphe Menjou, the "Best-Dressed Man in the Movies" and the
"Finest Male Clothes-Hoss in Hollywood," owes much of his
success to his wardrobe and to his tailor, Eddie Schmidt, who
lent him $1,000 worth of clothes when he first began his film
career.

1702   _____.   "This Odd Chap Barrymore."   Photoplay, 39 (4):
        31-2, 119-21, March 1931.
John Barrymore submits his own sketches to the wardrobe department as guidelines for his film characters, which the department
follows.

1703   "Langbein, Barbara."   American Film Institute Catalog, 1961-
        70, p.361.
Barbara Langbein is credited with the costumes of "Heidi."

1704   "Lange, Brigitte."   American Film Institute Catalog, 1961-70,
        p.361.
Brigitte Lange is credited with the costumes of "Beyond Control."

1705   "Lannes, Horace."   American Film Institute Catalog, 1961-70,
        p.362.
Horace Lannes was the costume designer of "No Exit."

1706   "Lanvin."   American Film Institute Catalog, 1961-70, p.362.
Lanvin is credited with the wardrobe for Danielle Darrieux and
Anne Vernon in "Friend of the Family" and the costumes of "The
Girl on a Motorcycle."

1707   "Lanvin-Castillo."   American Film Institute Catalog, 1961-70,
        p.362.
Lanvin-Castillo is credited with the Paris originals of "A New
Kind of Love."

1708   "Lanz."   American Film Institute Catalog, 1961-70, p.362.
Lanz is credited with the fashions of "13 Frightened Girls."

1709   La Roche, Bill.   "High Cost of Being a Movie Cowboy."
        Hollywood Star, 12 (17): 14-5, May 14, 1932.
William Powell's modern costumes are not as expensive as those
of the following "cowboy" actors, but his wardrobe consistently is
worth $9,000, since his clothes wear out quickly with frequent
laundering and must be replaced.   He has 20 suits with exactly
20 duplicates, each suit averaging $200; they are worn with scores

of shirts, socks, and shoes, of which he owns 40 pairs. Tom
Mix's 150 riding outfits average $75-$100 apiece, with three
duplicates made of each outfit because of wear and tear. His
100 Stetson broad-brim hats are specially made, costing $50-75
apiece; he gives one to his leading lady after each film. He also
has about 100 hand-tailored shirts. Newcomer Tom Keene has a
dozen economical Stetson hats worth $400, four pairs of boots
worth $100, three sets of spurs worth $90, and wears whatever
shirts or pants he has handy; he has not needed any special riding
suits yet.

1710   "Laroche, Guy."   American Film Institute Catalog, 1961-70,
            p. 363.
Guy Laroche is credited with the wardrobe for Sophia Loren in
"Five Miles to Midnight" and Nancy Kwan in "Tamahine."

1711   Lasky, Jesse L., with Don Weldon.   I Blow My Own Horn.
            Garden City, N.Y.: Doubleday, 1957.
Jesse L. Lasky, founder of Famous Players-Lasky studios, which
later merged with Paramount, admired Natacha Rambova's costumes for Rudolph Valentino in "Monsieur Beaucaire" (Barbier
received credit), but feels she badly mismanaged his career.
Julian Eltinge's three or four films started with him as a man,
later appearing in women's clothes; he was hired because he could
put the leading ladies of the day to shame with his costumes.
Hollywood became a world style center, with women everywhere
copying costumes they had seen in films. Brief mention of Paramount designers Howard Greer, Travis Banton, and Edith Head.

1712   "The Last of the Mohicans."   Cinema Arts [Preview Issue],
            1 (1): 24-5, September 1936.
Edward Lambert researched the customs and costumes for "The
Last of the Mohicans," for the colonial women, the soldiers' uni-
forms of various nationalities, and the different Indian tribes.
Mention also of hundreds of costume sketches drawn by Franc
Smith from his researching of the period for the film.

1713   "Latest Adrian Gowns Displayed by Models During 'Manne-
            quin.'"   MGM Studio News, 4 (16): n.p., October 15,
            1937.
Joan Crawford and professional models will model Adrian's fashions
for the future in the fashion-show sequence of "Mannequin."

1714   "Latest Details Embodied in the Costumes of Anna Q. Nils-
            son."   Screen News, 3 (11): 19, March 15, 1924.
The latest fashion trends are discussed, as shown in a gown worn
by Anna Q. Nilsson in "Flowing Gold."

1715   "Latest Lingerie Confection."   Screen News, 3 (24): 13, June
            21, 1924.
Clare West, designer for various Schenck organizations, has designed lingerie for Kathryn McGuire in "The Navigator," including
a "step-in" of flesh-colored net with bird-of-paradise fringe trim,

worn with fringed, matching satin mules.

1716 "Laurence, Ken." American Film Institute Catalog, 1961-70,
        p. 365.
      Ken Laurence is credited with the wardrobe of "Brainstorm."

1717 "Laver, James." American Film Institute Catalog, 1961-70,
        p. 366.
      James Laver is credited as a period adviser (probably for the
      costumes) of "The Amorous Adventures of Moll Flanders."

1718 Laver, James. "Cleavage and Other Devices," in Film Today.
        London: Saturn, 1948, p. 33-6.
      James Laver, British fashion historian, discusses the "Shifting
      Erogenous Zone" upon which fashion is based, and the trend toward
      censorship of costume in British and American films, particularly
      on the part of American censors in not allowing British films to
      be seen in which cleavage is shown in décolleté gowns.   Refer-
      ences and/or stills include costumes worn by Marlene Dietrich,
      in black stockings and exposed thigh, in "The Blue Angel"; Mar-
      garet Lockwood in "The Wicked Lady"; Rita Hayworth in "Tonight
      and Every Night"; Sid Field and Kay Kendell in "London Town";
      Jane Russell in "The Outlaw"; and chorus girls in "A Midsummer
      Night's Dream" (1935).

1719 _____. "Dates and Dresses." Sight and Sound, 8 (30): 50-
        1, Summer 1939.
      James Laver discusses historical inaccuracies in costume design,
      which film has inherited from the theater. A subtle change to
      make a garment more fashionable also dates the whole film.   In-
      cludes one still each of Sarah Bernhardt in "Queen Elizabeth,"
      Wendy Barrie in "The Private Life of Henry VIII," Katharine
      Hepburn in "Mary of Scotland," and Flora Robson in "Fire over
      England"; all examples of attempts at Elizabethan films.

1720 "La Vine, W. Robert." American Film Institute Catalog, 1961-
        70, p. 366.
      W. Robert La Vine was the costume designer of "Boys in the
      Band." [see entry 1835a.]

1721 "Lavish Costumes for 'Monsieur Beaucaire.'" New York
        Times, February 17, 1924, sec. 7, p. 5.
      George Barbier, a Parisian illustrator, designed and supervised
      the construction of 40 of the costumes in "Monsieur Beaucaire,"
      the remainder of which were adapted from imported costumes.
      The only costume described extensively is one worn by Rudolph
      Valentino, including his stockings, hat, and shoes.

1722 "The Lavish Use of Furs." Screen News, 4 (7): 12, February
        14, 1925.
      Discussion of current trends in furs, with a description of a coat
      modeled by Constance Talmadge and worn in "Her Night of "Ro-
      mance."

1723   Lavoisier, Madame Therese.   "The Latest Fashions in Moving
           Pictures. "   Motion Picture, 9 (6): 117-20, July 1915.
       Discussion of the growing importance of film costume and film
       costume designers.   Jane Lewis, chief designer of Vitagraph, has
       labored to amass 3,000 gowns for the wardrobe department.   An
       actress usually requires from eight to ten gowns per picture, but
       Anita Stewart recently wore 31 in an (unnamed) picture.

1724   "Lawton, Ken. "   American Film Institute Catalog, 1961-70,
           p. 367.
       Ken Lawton is credited with the wardrobe of "One More Time. "

1725   "Laykin et Cie. "   American Film Institute Catalog, 1961-70,
           p. 367.
       Laykin et Cie is credited with Doris Day's jewelry in "Lover Come
       Back. "

1726   "Lear, Frances. "   American Film Institute Catalog, 1961-70,
           p. 368.
       Frances Lear was the assistant costume designer of "Divorce
       American Style. "

1727   "Leatrice Joy. "   Motion Picture, 29 (3): 15, April 1925.
       Leatrice Joy's costumes for "The Dressmaker of Paris" should
       create fashion trends through 1925 and 1926.

1728   "Leave Her to Heaven. "   Motion Picture, 71 (1): 52, Feb-
           ruary 1946.
       Gene Tierney wears 28 costumes in "Leave Her to Heaven, " in-
       cluding a one-piece bathing suit.

1729   "Le Barbenchon, Odette. "   American Film Institute Catalog,
           1961-70, p. 368.
       Odette Le Barbenchon is credited with the costumes of "Mouchette. "

1730   "Leder, Walter. "   American Film Institute Catalog, 1961-70,
           p. 369.
       Walter Leder is credited with the wardrobe of "Heldinnen. "

1731   Lederer, Josie P.   "Clothes Make the Film. "   Picturegoer,
           12 (68): 32-3, August 1926.
       Cora McGeachy has the distinction of designing the costumes for
       the first film with a color fashion-show sequence, "Irene. "   Col-
       leen Moore, Dolores Costello, and several unnamed persons ap-
       pear in one costume each from the film, with additional costume
       descriptions; the costumes were sent from Paris.   Mme. Frances
       and Corinne Griffith evolved Griffith's costumes for "Mlle. Mo-
       diste, " one of which she models; her hats were designed by Peggy
       Hoyt.   Gloria Swanson spends about $125,000 per year on her
       film costumes, wears about 25 pairs of shoes per film, and rents
       her film jewelry for 10 percent of the cost.   Jetta Goudal started
       the trend away from fitted costumes with her bouffant film cos-
       tumes.   Dorothy Mackaill models one costume from "The Dancer

of Paris"; her costumes for "Chickie" and "Joanna" were widely
copied by women.

1732 Lee, Carol. "Individuality in Dress." Motion Picture Classic,
      4 (5): 27-8, June 1917.
Ann Murdock intends to design her future film costumes. She
models six costumes from "Where Love Is."

1733 _____. "War-Time Economy in Dress." Motion Picture
      Classic, 5 (2): 25-7, October 1917.
Due to the war actress Marguerite Clayton has cut down considerably on her expenses for new clothes, but a clause in her
prewar contract forbids her from cutting down on her film wardrobe expenses.

1734 Leese, Elizabeth. Costume Design in the Movies. Bembridge,
      Isle of Wight: BCW, 1976.
This excellent reference book is essentially a "who's who of film
costume," consisting mainly of biographies and extensive credits
of over 150 British and American designers, both film and fashion.
Many original photos and sketches are included, with eight in color.
A most helpful index lists thousands of film titles with designer
credits and the year of production. The main problem is not an
abundance of errors but the omission of many films. Also included is a list of all costume-design and film nominees of the
Academy Awards from 1948 to 1975 and of the British Academy
of Film and Television Arts from 1964 to 1975. Besides the above
credits, biographies, and award nominees, film-costume history
is discussed specifically only in the introductory chapter, "Couture on the Screen." In both this chapter and in the illustrations
there is a wealth of material from the earliest film decades, particularly from the 1910s on. The biographies suffer from being
too brief and often lack such information as whether the designer
is now living.

1735 "Lehmann, Olga." American Film Institute Catalog, 1961-70,
      p. 371.
Olga Lehmann was the wardrobe designer of "The Guns of Navarone"
and "The Victors" and the costume designer of "Captain Nemo and
the Underwater City."

1736 "Leighton, Maxine." American Film Institute Catalog, 1961-
      70, p. 371.
Maxine Leighton was the wardrobe designer for Jacqueline Pearce
in "Don't Raise the Bridge, Lower the River."

1737 Leisen, Mitchell. "You Women Won't Like This!" Silver
      Screen, 16 (7): 40-1, 80-3, May 1946.
Director, producer, and art and costume designer Mitchell Leisen
gives the readers an idea of the inconveniences actresses must
endure; for example, Paulette Goddard had to wear many costumes
weighing 50 to 60 pounds over a corset that pinched her waist to
17 inches, in "Kitty."

1738 "Leisen, Mitchell." American Film Institute Catalog, 1921-30,
       p. 1211.
      Mitchell Leisen was the costume designer of "The Thief of Bag-
      dad" and is credited with the costumes of "Robin Hood."

1739 "LeKang, Per." American Film Institute Catalog, 1961-70,
       p. 372.
      Per LeKang is credited with the costumes of "Bamse."

1740 "Le Maire, Charles." American Film Institute Catalog, 1961-
       70, p. 372.
      Charles Le Maire is credited with the costumes of "Walk on the
      Wild Side."

1741 Le Maire, Charles. "How the Screen Influences Fashion."
       Screen News, 3 (28): 19, July 12, 1924.
      Charles Le Maire believes that the screen is the greatest in-
      fluencer of fashion since many women can examine the latest
      fashions on actresses and then have their dressmakers copy them.
      Simple lines make the most attractive film costumes.

1742 _____. "The Star's Selection of Line and Color Serves as
       a Guide to Average Woman." Screen News, 3 (13): 18,
       April 5, 1924.
      Charles Le Maire discusses how he designs for a film, and the
      fashion images of Constance and Norma Talmadge. He mentions
      that Norma Talmadge will wear costumes with low shoulder lines
      and bouffant skirts in "Secrets," and Constance will wear essen-
      tially simple gowns in "The Goldfish."

1743 _____. "The Tie-Up." Theatre Arts, 9 (8): 533-5, August
       1925.
      Charles Le Maire discusses costume designing for the theater,
      noting that the main difference in designing for the screen is the
      restriction placed on a designer because of the black-and-white
      film, so he emphasizes line and pattern rather than color.

1744 "Le Maire, Charles." International Motion Picture Almanac.
       1975, p. 131.
      Charles Le Maire became the executive director of the Twentieth
      Century-Fox wardrobe department in 1943 and has since won
      Academy Awards for "All About Eve" (with Edith Head), "The
      Robe" (with Emile Santiago), and "Love Is a Many Splendored
      Thing."

1745 "Lentini Creations." American Film Institute Catalog, 1961-
       70, p. 373.
      Lentini Creations is credited with Ben Gazzara's wardrobe in
      "Husbands."

1746 "Leon, Idel." American Film Institute Catalog, 1961-70, p.
       373.
      Idel Leon is credited with the wardrobe of "Shameless Desire."

1747 "Leong, Terry." <u>American Film Institute Catalog, 1961-70,</u>
       p. 374.
Terry Leong was the costume designer of "Puzzle of a Downfall
Child."

1748 Lerman, Leo. "The Gatsby File." <u>Vogue,</u> 162 (6): 158-65,
       December 1973.
A photographic collage of costumes worn in "The Great Gatsby,"
designed by Theoni V. Aldredge. Included are stills, though
seldom full-length or in color, of Robert Redford, Mia Farrow,
Lois Chiles, Karen Black, and Bruce Dern. Also includes a
small photograph of the $1 million worth of jewelry from Cartier.

1749 _____. "The Million Dollar Costume Bash: Hollywood's
          Sumptuous Glad Rags on Show." <u>Vogue,</u> 164 (6): 168-9,
          December 1974.
15 color photos are presented of costumes that were exhibited at
the "Romantic and Glamorous Hollywood Design" exhibit in 1974.
On page 70 the present owners of the costumes are listed (see
"Movie Costumes"). All costumes are modeled with a mask of
the original actress, and are in color. The costumes modeled
include those originally worn by Pola Negri in "Fedora," Mary
Pickford in "Sparrows," Greta Garbo in "Romance," Carole Lom-
bard in "No Man of Her Own," Mae West in "She Done Him
Wrong," Claudette Colbert in "Cleopatra," Marlene Dietrich in
"Angel," Joan Crawford in "The Bride Wore Red," Jean Harlow
in "Personal Property," Vivien Leigh in "Gone with the Wind,"
Ginger Rogers in "Lady in the Dark," Katharine Hepburn in
"Without Love," Rita Hayworth in "Pal Joey," Marilyn Monroe in
"Let's Make Love," and Barbra Streisand in "Hello, Dolly!"

1750 Le Roy, Mervyn. "Your Career as a Dress Designer," in
          <u>It Takes More Than Talent.</u> New York: Knopf, 1953,
          p. 156-67. 292-3, passim.
Mervyn Le Roy discusses the careers of Helen Rose, Walter Plunkett, Howard Greer, Bill Thomas, and Adrian, with reference
to Adrian's costumes for "Lovely to Look At" and Plunkett's costumes for "Singin' in the Rain" and "Million Dollar Mermaid."
Also, brief mention of the effectiveness of the costumes to the
plots of "Pandora and the Flying Dutchman" and "A Place in the
Sun." The emphasis is on preparing for and obtaining a career
in the film-costume industry, with recommended education, job
qualifications, and salaries. The above information concerning
designers is usually brief and career-oriented, as with the mention of Bill Thomas, who was once Plunkett's assistant.

1751 "Les Tentations de Pascale." <u>Unifrance Film,</u> 48: 18-9,
          October-December 1958.
Pascale Petit models a dress designed by Jacques Estrel from
"Faibles Femmes." English text provided.

1752 "Leslie (cost)." <u>American Film Institute Catalog,</u> 1961-70, p.
       375.

Leslie was the costume designer of "Terrified!"

1753   " 'Lest We Forget!' " Screen News, 1 (12): 25, May 13, 1922.
Walter Israel, the designer of "Oliver Twist," has 20 women
creating the costumes for the cast and principals.

1754   "Let the Other Girls Go Mannish--Kay Francis Will Stay Femi-
ine! (And Here's How!)." Movie Classic, 4 (21): 40-1,
April 1933.
Kay Francis models six costumes by Orry-Kelly from "The Keyhole."

1755   "Let's Get Acquainted with 20th Century Fox Research."
Jones' Magazine, 1 (3): 36-7, October 1937.
Frances Richardson, the head of the research department of Twentieth Century-Fox studios, gives the final approval on requests for
costume information.   Books for research are either bought or
borrowed from public libraries.

1756   "Let's Get Acquainted with Warner Brothers Craftsmen."
Jones' Magazine, 1 (4): 44-5, November 1937.
The property department is responsible for making suits of armor.

1757   Let's Study Ours.   Let's Study Theirs." Hollywood Pattern,
7 (1): 22-3, Spring 1938.
General discussion of film-costume design, with brief mention of
costumes worn by Loretta Young, designed by Gwen Wakeling;
Ethel Merman in costumes designed by Royer; Greta Garbo, by
Adrian; Carole Lombard, by Travis Banton; and Bette Davis in
"Jezebel," by Orry-Kelly.   One costume is modeled by each
actress, with only Davis's film identified.

1758   "Leva, Carlo."   American Film Institute Catalog, 1961-70,
p. 375.
Carlo Leva is credited with the costumes of "Spirits of the Dead."

1759   "Levasseur, André."   American Film Institute Catalog, 1961-
70, p. 375.
André Levasseur is credited with the costumes of "A Flea in Her
Ear."

1760   Levin, Phyllis.   "Costumer's Art Raises Dressmaking to the
Highest Level."   New York Times, April 13, 1960, p. 42.
Words of praise for the talented designer/costume maker Barbara
Karinska; George Balanchine said, "There is Shakespeare for liter-
ature and Mme. Karinska for costumes."   Her daughter makes
costumes under the name of Karinska in Paris.

1761   "Levine, Alan."   American Film Institute Catalog, 1961-70,
p. 376.
Alan Levine is credited with the wardrobe of "In Harm's Way,"
"Hurry Sundown," "In the Heat of the Night," "The Thomas Crown
Affair," and "Monte Walsh"; the costumes of "Bullitt"; and the

men's costumes of "The Reivers."

1762 Levitt, Rosalind.   "Happy or Not Those Days Are Here Again."
       Show, 1 (9): 12-7, July 23, 1970.
      A lengthy discussion of the nostalgia craze for the 1930s, with
      comments by Thea Van Runkle concerning her costumes for
      "Bonnie and Clyde," with a still of Faye Dunaway, and by Sidney
      Pollack concerning his costumes for "They Shoot Horses, Don't
      They?," with a still of Susannah York and Bonnie Bedelia.   The
      emphasis of the article is on how the film costumes are period
      and yet fit well into contemporary fashion, and are influencing
      fashion, as with the beret worn by Faye Dunaway and the longer
      hemlines worn in "The Damned" and by Maggie Smith in "The
      Prime of Miss Jean Brodie"--all being promoted heavily by Wo-
      men's Wear Daily.   Even department-store mannequins are dressed
      like Jane Fonda and others in "They Shoot Horses, Don't They?"

1763 Levy, Sam G.   "The World's New Fashion-Plate."   Photoplay,
       15 (1): 62-4, December 1918.
      Levy, a Los Angeles tailor, discusses the influence of film actors'
      clothing on fashion and how he learned how to costume men by
      studying photography, photogenic colors and fabrics, and scripts.
      He is responsible for the wardrobes of Herbert Rawlinson, Elliot
      Dexter. Wallace Reid, William Desmond, and Franklyn Farnum.
      He feels the screen's best-dressed actor is Harold Lockwood, who
      owns a character wardrobe in addition to a modern wardrobe of
      27 suits and accessories, valued at $3,500.

1764 "Lewin, Maggie."   American Film Institute Catalog, 1961-70,
       p. 377.
      Maggie Lewin is credited with the wardrobe of "Nearly a Nasty
      Accident" and "Billion Dollar Brain," the women's wardrobe of
      "Carry on Constable" and "The Singer Not the Song," and was the
      wardrobe mistress of "Anne of the Thousand Days."

1765 "Lewington, Ken."   American Film Institute Catalog, 1961-70,
       p. 377.
      Ken Lewington is credited with the wardrobe of "If It's Tuesday,
      This Must Be Belgium" and was the wardrobe master of "Lock
      Up Your Daughters."

1766 Lewis, Ernest D.   "A Guide to the Discussion of ... 'Con-
       quest'; Costumes."   Photoplay Studies, 3 (10): 20, Series
       of 1937.
      Adrian designed 2,000 costumes for "Conquest," which were then
      made by his staff, and used authenticity and flare for the costumes
      of Greta Garbo and Charles Boyer, whose costumes will be limited
      to uniforms.   Garbo will wear a sash, as well as many pieces of
      jewelry given to Maria Louisa Walewska, whom she portrays, by
      Napoleon, including a tiara and clasp.

1767 "Lewis, Frank."   American Film Institute Catalog, 1961-70,
       p. 377
      Frank Lewis is credited with the costumes of "Orgy Girls '69."

1768   Lewis, Lilian. "In Style with the Stars." Screenland, 51 (4):
          48-9, 93, February 1947.
       Discussion of how film costumes can be adapted to one's wardrobe,
       with examples of costumes worn by Shirley Temple in "Honey-
       moon," by Edward Stevenson; and Laraine Day in "The Locket."
       Miss Temple models five, and Day two costumes from their films.

1769   _____. "In Style with the Stars." Screenland, 51 (5): 40,
          98, March 1947.
       Discussion of how six costumes worn by Gene Tierney in "The
       Razor's Edge" can be adapted to one's wardrobe, with small stills
       of the costumes shown in scenes from the film, set in the 1920s.

1770   Lewis, M.D.A. "Jewellery and the Period Film." Sight
          and Sound, 16 (63): 99-101, Autumn 1947.
       Discussion of the major historical periods of jewelry. The func-
       tions of jewelry in film are to lend further historical background
       to costumes and sets, adorn the body, and lend symbolic interest.
       The author, a gemologist, offers suggestions concerning either
       acquiring or reproducing antique jewelry for period films.

1771   "Lewis Stone Traces Origin of Dignity." Screen News, 2 (24):
          7, June 16, 1923.
       Lewis Stone wears ten costumes, each weighing between 20 and
       30 pounds, in "Scaramouche."

1772   "Lidaková, Anna." American Film Institute Catalog, 1961-70,
          p. 379.
       Anna Lidaková is credited with the costumes of "The Deserter
       and the Nomads."

1773   Lieber, Evaline. "Hollywood's New Champion Best Dresser."
          Photoplay, 43 (1): 40, 120-1, December 1932.
       George Raft's salary did not keep up with his fame, so he had
       a tailor lend him $800 worth of clothes for "Night After Night"
       rather than wear the wardrobe the studio provided.

1774   "Like Red Tape." Screen News, 1 (7): 13, April 8, 1922.
       175 pounds of gold braid, gimp, and bullion fringe were used to
       decorate the uniforms worn by Kalla Pasha, Theodore Kosloff,
       Alan Hale, and Wallace Reid in "The Dictator."

1775   "Lili Dramatizes Her Gowns." Photoplay, 42 (6): 54, No-
          vember 1932.
       Lili Damita models three gowns and one cape from "The Match
       King."

1776   "Lillian Gish Prefers American Clothes." Screen News, 2
          (44): 15, November 3, 1923.
       Lillian Gish had her most important costumes for "The White
       Sister" and "Romola" made on Fifth Avenue because she felt that
       American designers were more skilled than Parisians. Both
       movies were filmed in Italy; the costumes required for minor

roles were made in Europe.

1777 "Linda (cost). " American Film Institute Catalog, 1961-70,
          p. 380.
Linda is credited with the costumes of "Love Mates. "

1778 "Lindgren, Katerina. " American Film Institute Catalog, 1961-
          70, p. 380.
Katerina Lindgren is credited with the costumes of "Duet for
Cannibals. "

1779 Lindsay, Cynthia. Dear Boris: The Life of William Henry
          Pratt a. k. a. Boris Karloff. New York: Knopf, 1975.
In "The Criminal Code" Boris Karloff wore special tights with
large pads to conceal his bowed legs, apparently a common practice even with "Barrymore" (John?). Also includes a description
of the costume worn by Karloff in "Frankenstein. "

1780 "Line Appeal. " Photoplay, 36 (2): 83, July 1949.
Leah Rhodes discusses briefly the costumes of "The Girl from
Jones Beach, " for which she made three costumes each for 14
women, including Virginia Mayo.

1781 "Lipsey, A. I. " American Film Institute Catalog, 1961-70,
          p. 382.
A. I. Lipsey is credited with the furs of "Doctor, You've Got to
Be Kidding. "

1782 "Listen, Women--and Envy Walter Israel. " Screen News, 2
          (14): 29, April 7, 1923, col. 3.
Walter Israel, wardrobe department chief for Schenck Studios, recently spent three days and $50,000 in New York shopping for
fabrics and accessories for "Ashes of Vengeance, " some brocades
costing $3,000 per yard.

1783 "Liu Hsian Hui. " American Film Institute Catalog, 1961-70,
          p. 383.
Liu Hsian Hui is credited with the costumes of "The Arch. "

1784 Livingstone, Beulah. Remember Valentino: Reminiscences of
          the World's Greatest Lover. [No publisher], © 1938.
Rudolph Valentino influenced men's and women's fashions through
Spanish sailor hats and bolero jackets worn in "The Four Horse-
men of the Apocalypse, " Russian headgear and capes from "The
Eagle, " and turbans from "The Sheik" and "Son of the Sheik. "
With his large collection of valuable costume books he researched
customs and costumes for all of his films. In "The Big Little
Person" he refused to wear the studio armor and found a suitable
one at a costume company, which the studio would not pay to rent;
he paid $15 from his meager salary. He consulted with Natacha
Rambova about his costumes for "Camille" (1921); they later married, and she insisted on advising him further concerning his
costumes. They spent over $50,000 for costumes and props to be

used in "The Hooded Falcon," which was shelved. He purchased
many Arabian costumes while abroad for "Son of the Sheik," his
last film.

1785 Liza. "Janet Does an Off to Yuma!" Silver Screen, 10 (1):
         16-7, 66, November 1939.
Discussion of the careers of Adrian and Janet Gaynor, their recent marriage, and how they first met in 1933, when Fox arranged
for Adrian to design her costumes for "Paddy the Next Best Thing."

1786 "Lloyd, Dora." American Film Institute Catalog, 1961-70,
         p. 383.
Dora Lloyd is credited with the wardrobe of "Cry of the Banshee"
and was the wardrobe supervisor of "I Thank a Fool" and the
wardrobe mistress of "Scream of Fear."

1787 "Locke, Eric." American Film Institute Catalog, 1921-30,
         p. 1219.
Eric Locke is credited with the wardrobe of "The Student Prince
in Old Heidelberg."

1788 Locker, Linda. "Film Stylist Reveals Backstage Lore."
         Making Films in New York, 8 (16): 24-5, December 1974.
Film stylists usually work independently, never receiving credit,
as either a consultant, or in buying or making costumes for films
or television; they are a cross between a designer and a wardrobe
mistress or master.

1789 Logan, Joshua. Movie Stars, Real People, and Me. New
         York: Delacorte, 1978.
Jean Louis designed Kim Novak's picnic-sequence dress in "Picnic" to look homemade; she wore it with four-inch high-heels.
One costume worn by Marilyn Monroe led her to tell the designer
that it was great, but she then altered it considerably with director
Joshua Logan, e.g., tearing holes in the stockings; they chose the
remainder of her costumes for "Bus Stop" in the wardrobe department. Don Murray wore a sweatshirt under his oversized
shirt in the film to camouflage his thinness. Brief mention of a
costume selected by Logan for Miiko Taka in "Sayonara" and of
Dorothy Jeakins's costumes for "South Pacific." John Truscott's
sets and costumes "contributed more to the final film of 'Camelot'
than anything else." The designer avoided a specific era for the
film, and also the color red, since most medieval-type films have
an abundance of this color. Brief mention of Vanessa Redgrave
and the armor worn by Franco Nero. However, having Truscott
design the sets and costumes of "Paint Your Wagon" "was probably
a major mistake, as John never cares about saving money" (probably said in reference to the designer's insistence upon location
shooting).

1790 "Logan Costumes." American Film Institute Catalog, 1961-70,
         p. 385.
Logan Costumes is credited with the costumes of "The Secret Sex Live

of Romeo and Juliet," "All the Lovin' Kinfolk," "The Joys of
Jezebel," and "The Notorious Cleopatra."

1791 London, Mel. "Costume, Styling, and Wardrobe," in Getting
        into Film. New York: Ballantine, 1977, p. 89-91, passim.
Discussion of career opportunities in the film-costume field, particularly with wardrobe attendants. The costumer usually works
with modern wardrobes and does much of the shopping required
(especially when time is limited or when it may cost less to buy
rather than make a wardrobe). Notes that on the East Coast a
costume designer is also the costumer. The term "stylist" refers
to a wardrobe person in television, commercials, or commercial
films. One of few sources dealing with career opportunities in
the current job market, this book has information on how to join
the unions, with brief mention of Motion Picture Costumers
and the Costume Designers Guild.

1792 "Long Skirts Win; Small Girls Lose; Russia to the Fore."
        Screen News, 1 (34): 8, October 14, 1922.
Sophie Wachner, Goldwyn costume director, has just returned from
New York, where she studied the latest fashion trends, including
the changing hemlines.

1793 "The Long Waist Is Such an Accepted Fact...." Screen News,
        2 (2): 14, January 13, 1923, col. 1.
Includes a description of a costume worn by Colleen Moore in
"Slippy McGee."

1794 Loos, Anita. The Talmadge Girls: A Memoir. New York:
        Viking, 1978.
Norma Talmadge wore gowns by Madame Frances, "New York's
most expensive couturier," in "By Right of Purchase," "Ghosts of
Yesterday," and apparently in most of her films during the late
1910s. Factors in Joseph Schenck moving his studio and actors
and actresses from New York to Hollywood included the conveniences
of using Central Casting and Western Costume Company. Loos
quit writing for the Talmadge sisters in 1925, leaving an unfortunate gap concerning their films, which one hopes will be filled in
by later biographers.

1795 Loper, Don. "Design for Being Chic." Silver Screen, 18 (4):
        50-1, 84-5, February 1948.
Don Loper, who has his own fashion salon, discusses his cos-
tumes for Lucille Bremer, Martha Vickers, and Diana Lynn in
"Prelude to Night"; each models two costumes.

1796 _____. "Why Not Look Like a Star?" Screenland, 53 (10):
        46-8, 74, August 1949.
"Stars used to set the style but now the designers are doing it";
the studios prefer to publicize actresses' abilities in cooking, rather
than as fashion trend-setters, as in the past. The partnership of
Adrian and Joan Crawford has not been replaced in contemporary
fashion. Jane Greer models two costumes by Don Loper from "The
Big Steal."

1797 "Loper, Don." American Film Institute Catalog, 1961-70, p.
         387.
Don Loper was the costume designer of "Looking for Love."

1798 "Los Angeles Dealers Recently Reported a Shortage in ...
         Bandanas." Screen News, 1 (24): 20, August 5, 1922,
         col. 3.
Over 500 bandanas in various colors, stripes, and checks were
bought for the pirates in "To Have and to Hold."

1799 "A Los Angeles Dress Firm Will Market...." Screen News,
         2 (30): 21, July 28, 1923, col. 1.
A gingham frock worn by Colleen Moore in "April Showers" will
be marketed as the "Colleen Moore gown."

1800 "Lo Scalzo, Vincent." American Film Institute Catalog, 1961-
         70, p. 388.
Vincent Lo Scalzo is credited with the costumes of "The Square
Root of Zero" and "Warm Nights & Hot Pleasures."

1801 "Lossman, Ed." American Film Institute Catalog, 1961-70,
         p. 388.
Ed Lossman is credited with the costumes of "Shoot Out at Big
Sag."

1802 "Lost Horizon." Cinema Arts [Preview Issue], 1 (1): 44-6,
         September 1936.
Harrison Forman, an American explorer who had spent much
time in Tibet, was the technical adviser for "Lost Horizon." His
photographs, costumes, and other items gathered during the trip
enabled designer Ernst Dryden to authenticate his Lima costumes
and hats. Extensive searches through the costume companies did
not help the designer in finding costumes resembling those of the
Tibetans, so Forman helped with these also.

1803 "Loud Styles for Men Evoke Togs Tip from Douglas." MGM
         Studio News, 5 (5): n.p., May 31, 1938.
Melvyn Douglas discusses briefly how he avoids self-consciousness
in wearing period costumes, as in "The Toy Wife."

1804 "Louis XV Costumes Require Miles of Cloth in 'Monsieur
         Beaucaire.' " Screen News, 3 (22): 25, May 31, 1924.
Paramount's Long Island costume department made 500 costumes
for "Monsieur Beaucaire," the average woman's dress consisting
of 15 yards of fabric with 12 yards of trimming. The average
man's costume required nine yards of fabric and ten yards of
trimming, for the 100 actors. The 500 costumes required about
7,000 yards of fabric.

         Louis, Jean see also "Jean-Louis"

1805 Louis, Jean. "As a Matter of Chic...." Screenland, 54 (2):
         48-9, 71-2, December 1949.

Jean Louis discusses how his wardrobe for Rosalind Russell in
"Tell It to the Judge" can be adapted to the average-budget wardrobe. Russell models eight of her 18 costumes from the film.

1806 _____. "Whispers from a Hollywood Fitting Room."
        Motion Picture, 78 (2): 38-9, 63-4, March 1949.
Jean Louis discusses designing for Ginger Rogers in "It Had to
Be You," Dorothy Lamour in "Lulu Belle," Joan Fontaine in
"You Gotta Stay Happy," Evelyn Keyes in "Mr. Soft Touch," and,
in general, Rita Hayworth, Claudette Colbert, and Ann Miller (all
of whose film costumes must be approved by her mother).

1807 _____, as told to Bee Bangs. "Alluring Evening Elegance."
        Silver Screen, 17 (4): 56-7, 90-1, February 1947.
One costume each is modeled by Leslie Brooks from "Cigarette
Girl"; Marguerite Chapman from "Mr. District Attorney"; and
Rosalind Russell, with closeups of two others, from "The Guilt
of Janet Ames"; all by Jean Louis.

1808 _____, as told to Bee Bangs. "Let's Be Glamourous!"
        Movie Show, 5 (4): 62-3, 92-4, December 1946.
Jean Louis feels that French actresses are often "badly dressed"
because they choose their own film costumes. He will continue to
keep film costume hemlines $16\frac{1}{2}$ inches from the floor (despite the
New Look). He notes that he hoped a gown with a plunging neck-
line (to the waist), worn by Lizabeth Scott in "Dead Reckoning,"
would pass uncensored by the Hays Office. One costume each is
modeled by Evelyn Keyes from "The Thrill of Brazil," Marguerite
Chapman from "Mr. District Attorney," and Rita Hayworth from
"Gilda." Includes also a sketch of Hayworth in a gown from
"Down to Earth."

1809 "Louis, Jean." Fairchild's Who's Who in Fashion.   1975,
        p. 163.
Jean Louis, born in Paris, was employed by Hattie Carnegie when
he came to New York and in 1943 became a designer at Columbia
Studios. In 1961 he started his own ready-to-wear business and
occasionally designs for films.

1810 "Louis, Jean." International Motion Picture Almanac.   1975,
        p. 138.

1811 "Louis, Jean (Berthault)." World of Fashion.   1976, p. 237-8.
When Jean Louis became the costume designer for Columbia
Studios his former employer, Hattie Carnegie, took Columbia
head Harry Cohn to court for "stealing" Jean Louis away. Of
his 22 Academy Award nominations, he has received one award,
for "The Solid Gold Cadillac."

1812 Love, Bessie. From Hollywood with Love. London: Elm
        Tree Press, 1977.
After a bleak and impoverished childhood Bessie Love and her
mother conspired to get her job as a film actress. Tom Mix had

offered to get her a job, but wardrobe lady Mrs. Christian told
her making cowboy pictures was grueling and she should try D.
W. Griffith's studio. The costume she wore in her first film,
"The Flying Torpedo," as described, is now in the National Film
Archive. Includes references to her costumes in "Sundown,"
"The Lost World," "The Broadway Melody," and "Acquitted" and
"Intolerance," in both of which she wore some of her own clothes.
Curt Rehfeld was in charge of "Stock Wardrobe for Crowd Artistes"
at the Griffith studio, where the collection included costumes origi-
nally worn by Madame Modjewsak and by Clara Butt in theatrical
productions. Costumes originally worn by Douglas Fairbanks and
the cast of "Robin Hood" were reworn by Love and others in "The
Adventures of Prince Courageous," a serial. During World War II
in England she worked as a technician in the prop room for "San
Demetrio, London"; part of her duties was to keep a record of con-
secutive scenes, as to what was being worn, whether or not it was
buttoned, and how many buttons there were.

1813 "A Lovely Beaded Chiffon Evening Gown...." Screen News,
         2 (51): 29, December 22, 1923, cols. 1-2.
Betty Francisco models a gown from "Flaming Youth."

1814 "Lovely Greeters of the Evening." Picture Play, 43 (6): 26-9,
         February 1936.
One gown each is modeled by Geneva Hall and Dena Myles from
"Anything Goes," and Jane Hamilton, Jeannette Warner, and Alice
Daley from "I Dream Too Much."

1815 "Lovely to Look At." Movie Play, 3 (2): 26-7, July 1948.
Barbara Stanwyck models three costumes by Irene from "B.F.'s
Daughter."

1816 Loynd, Ray. "How to Judge on Costume Design in Oscar
         Voting." Hollywood Reporter, 199 (44): 9, February 28,
         1968.
1968 was the first year since the Academy Awards for costume
design began in 1948 that Edith Head was not nominated. Head
and Irene Sharaff have received one-third of the awards. According to Head, the most important criterion in determining the best-
costumed film is whether or not the costumes reinforce the story
by transforming the actress into the character, regardless of the
budget, historical setting, or beauty of the costumes.

1817 "Lucile (Lady Duff-Gordon)." World of Fashion. 1976, p.
         327-8.
Biographical information on Lady Duff Gordon, known professionally
as Lucile, who died virtually forgotten in 1935 (or 1937).

1818 "Lucilla." American Film Institute Catalog, 1961-70, p. 390.
Lucilla is credited with the costumes of "End of Desire."

1819 "Lucille [sic] (Lady Duff Gordon)." Fairchild's Who's Who in
         Fashion. 1975, p. 165.

Biographical information on Lady Duff Gordon, whose fashions
were sold under the name of Lucile.

1820 "Lucille [sic] Ltd." American Film Institute Catalog, 1921-30,
          p. 1225.
Lucille Ltd. is credited with the costumes of "Heedless Moths."

1821 "Lucretia Had Her Troubles." Screen News, 4 (47): 5,
          November 28, 1925.
Estelle Taylor has discovered why many women held their waists
in old paintings; she must do the same in "Don Juan," in order
to hold up her silver embroidered girdle.

1822 "Luick, Earl." American Film Institute Catalog, 1921-30,
          p. 1225.
Earl (or Earle) Luick is credited with the costumes of "The King
of Kings" (1927), "Conquest" (1928), "On Trial," "The Desert
Song" (1929), "Gold Diggers of Broadway," and "Old English."

1823 Luick, Earle, as told to Mary Brush Williams. "Costuming
          the Movies." Saturday Evening Post, 206 (11): 18-9, 32,
          36, 38, September 9, 1933.
Earle Luick discusses researching and designing the costumes for
Diana Wynyard, Irene Brown, and extras in "Cavalcade"; color
photography; a gown worn by Claudette Colbert in "Sign of the
Cross," by Travis Banton, who had greatly influenced fashion,
with Adrian; and many other topics. He prefers to tell actresses
what to wear rather than spend great amounts of time in con-
sultations. One gown each is modeled by Mary Pickford from
"Secrets" and Edwina Booth from "Trader Horn."

1824 "Luick, Earle." Motion Picture Almanac. 1930, p. 123.
Earle Luick has been a film-costume designer for four years,
working for Cecil B. De Mille, then freelance, and for Warner
Brothers. His credits include "Alimony Annie."

1825 "Luise Rainer Dictates Fashions." MGM Studio News, 4 (9):
          n. p., June 5, 1937.
Adrian has designed 15 gowns for Luise Rainer in "The Emperor's
Candlesticks," some of which were adapted from Russian Imperial
styles. Her previous three films, "Escapade," "The Good Earth,"
and "The Great Ziegfeld," did not allow her to wear modern
clothes.

1826 "Luise Rainer Pluming...." Harper's Bazaar, 2681: 96,
          March 1936.
One still of Luise Rainer surrounded by many hats from "The
Great Ziegfeld," by Adrian.

1827 Luther, Marylou. "Edith Head: From Elephants to Oscars."
          Los Angeles Times, May 19, 1974, sec. 4, p. 1, 18-9.
Edith Head discusses her career, favorite director and actress,
and the most difficult person she has designed for (Nancy Car-

roll). She arranges film-fashion shows two to three times per
year for charity.

1828 _____. "No-Nonsense 'Wantables' by Jean Louis." Los
         Angeles Times, February 21, 1974, sec. 4, p.1-2.
The trademark of Jean Louis is clothes that move with the body;
the older actresses knew how to walk and move right.

1829 _____. "The Paramount Look for Fall: 20th Century Foxy."
         Los Angeles Times, August 26, 1973, Home, p.16-9.
Many of the fashions modeled show a continued influence of modern and older film costumes upon retail fashion, as with a copy
of a slip worn by Elizabeth Taylor in "Butterfield 8."

1830 _____. "She Works with Hollywood Ghosts of Fashion's
         Past." Los Angeles Times, July 28, 1974, sec. 10,
         p.1, 14.
Diana Vreeland borrowed many film costumes for the "Romantic
and Glamorous Years of [sic] Hollywood Design" but found that
many Adrian gowns, and gowns worn by Ginger Rogers, no longer
exist. MGM, before its auction, donated some of its costumes
to the Fashion Institute of Technology in New York. Skills employed in film-costume construction were superior to French couture methods.

1831 _____. "Timeless Pull of Glamor." Los Angeles Times,
         September 20, 1974, sec. 4, p.1-2.
A three-hour fashion show of film costumes by more than 20 designers was held to benefit the Motion Picture and Television
Fund; over 850 persons attended. In addition to the many costumes and film titles listed, there are stills of one costume each
worn by Debbie Reynolds in "Hit the Deck," Julie Andrews in
"Darling Lili," and Lee Grant in "Shampoo," Elizabeth Taylor
in "A Place in the Sun," and Kim Novak in "Jeanne Eagels."

1832 Lydia. "'Thanks, Paris!' Says Mae West." Screen Book,
         11 (4): 14-5, 73, November 1933.
Screen Book cabled three couturiers--Schiaparelli, Jean Patou,
and Mainbocher--when they heard that Paris was being influenced
by the 1890s costumes worn by Mae West in her recent films; the
designers denied being influenced. The author mentions the influence on Paris of film costumes worn by Greta Garbo and Marlene Dietrich; and West discusses at length her fashions and their
influence.

1833 Lyle, Joe. "The Other Man in Liz' Life." Photoplay, 61
         (5): 39-41, 76-7, May 1962.
A $100,000 wardrobe for Elizabeth Taylor in "Cleopatra" was
discarded because the costumes did not fit right, and apparently
did not look as regal as one 22-carat gold costume she was wearing during the interview.

1834 "Lyon, Agnes." American Film Institute Catalog, 1961-70,

p. 394.

Agnes Lyon is credited with the wardrobe of "The Dunwich Horror."

1835   Lytle, Frederick E.   "Style Invading the Mennonites: Are the
          'Movies' Responsible?"   Photoplay, 21 (2): 84, January
          1922.
An unusual example of how film costume may have influenced
fashion, though not well supported, concerning the changing Men-
nonite women's clothing.   (Would such women ever attend the
movies?)

1835a [LATE ENTRY] La Vine, W. Robert.   In a Glamorous Fashion:
          The Fabulous Years of Hollywood Costume Design.   New
          York: Scribner's 1980.
The publication of yet another excellent book on film-costume
history also marked the passing of two accomplished film- and
theatrical-costume designers, W. Robert La Vine, the author,
and the great Cecil Beaton, who wrote the foreword.   (La Vine
died August 6, 1979, following heart surgery, at the age of 59.
Sir Cecil Beaton died in his sleep on January 19, 1980, at the
age of 76.)   The sole reference to La Vine's own film work is
made by Beaton, associated with La Vine on numerous unnamed
films.   The book consists of two sections: a history of the
studio system's better-known designers during the decades of the
1920s to 1960s (with brief mention of the 1910s and 1970s), and
biographical sections on designers Adrian, Travis Banton, Cecil
Beaton, Howard Greer, Edith Head, Irene, Walter Plunkett, Helen
Rose, and Irene Sharaff.   Appendixes, also, of designers who
received Academy Awards from 1948 to 1979; a bibliography of
books related to film, fashion, and fashion designers; and an
excellent index.   Several hundred black-and-white illustrations
complement the text; for example, Howard Greer at work among
dozens of seamstresses in the Paramount workroom, and a page
of the "Conquest" wardrobe plot.   The designers are written
about in-depth, their methods of designing and their personal
lives--alcoholism suffered by Travis Banton and Irene, and the
latter's bouts of depression, particularly after an alleged, unsuccessful affair with Gary Cooper.   The names of designers
Clare West, Madame Frances, and Gile Steele are misspelled.
Comparison with Chierichetti's Hollywood Costume Design seems
inevitable--both are excellent and, happily, do not particularly
overlap in either text or illustrations.

1836   "Mabel Normand, Designer." Screen News, 2 (40): 15, October 6, 1923.
Mabel Normand designs all of her hats and film costumes, including the original and humorous hats she wore in "The Extra Girl." She also supervises the construction of the costumes and helps other cast members with their costumes.

1837   "Mabry, Moss." American Film Institute Catalog, 1961-70, p. 395.
32 credits are listed for designer Moss Mabry.

1838   "Mabs of Hollywood," in Fashion is Our Business, by Beryl Williams [Epstein]. Philadelphia: Lippincott, 1945, p. 184-205.
Mabs Elizabeth Ryden was a film dancer when she decided to redesign the tights the studio provided. Her innovative design, which is standard today (but not described), was worked out with MGM's wardrobe mistress, Inez Schrodt. She eventually marketed the tights and became a famous bathing-suit designer known as Mabs of Hollywood.

1839   McAndrew, Maureen. "Polly Platt Sets the Style." Cinema (Beverly Hills), 35: 39-40, 1976.
On every film she is associated with, Polly Platt is both the costume and production designer. The production designer is responsible for the visual theme of a film, which the set designer carriers out through blueprints.

1840   _____. "Shirley Russell; Filmmaking: A Family Affair." Cinema (Beverly Hills), 35: 36-8, 1976.
Shirley Russell discusses working on Ken Russell's films, which she usually designs and costumes. Includes references to and/or stills of costumes worn in "Women in Love" and worn by Twiggy in "The Boyfriend," a low-budget film that had Twiggy wearing old shoes that were falling apart; Fiona Lewis, Roger Daltry, and Sara Kestelman in "Lisztomania"; and brief mention of the color selection of costumes worn in "The Devils" and by Richard Chamberlain, Glenda Jackson, and Madame von Meck in "The Music Lovers."

1841   "MacBeth, Ian." American Film Institute Catalog, 1961-70, p. 395.

Ian MacBeth is credited with the costumes of "Devil in Velvet."

1842 McC., C.E. "The Breeze." Screen News, 1 (30): 23, Sep-
          tember 16, 1922.
      60 dressmakers spent over one month constructing the costumes
      for the female cast of "To Have and to Hold."

1843 McCabe, John. Charlie Chaplin. Garden City, N.Y.: Double-
          day, 1978.
      Brief mention of Charlie Chaplin's costume in "Making a Living,"
      his first film. His tramp costume was first seen in "Kid Auto
      Races at Venice," his second film, lasting only five minutes--
      though Chaplin and others reported that it had first been worn in
      "Mabel's Strange Predicament," his third film. The costume con-
      sisted of Fatty Arbuckle's pants, Charlie Avery's coat, Ford Ster-
      ling's shoes (size 14 and put on the wrong feet), and Minta Dur-
      fee's father's small derby. According to Charlie Chaplin, Jr.,
      his father had told him that the tramp costume had really been
      born long before his Sennett comedies. Two actors particularly
      copied Chaplin's costume, Billy Ritchie and Charlie Aplin (who
      had changed his name from Charles Amador). Chaplin sued Ap-
      lin, and despite Aplin's defense concerning the historical origin
      of the costume from previous stage actors, Chaplin won the case
      since the judge ruled that elements of the costume were not as
      important as the ensemble. The author notes that the tramp cos-
      tume, which Chaplin wore in only 13 films, may have been partly
      inspired by that of Max Linder; Chaplin had stated his indebtedness
      to the French comedian. Brief mention of the influence Chap-
      lin's uniform in "The Dictator" had over him, and the role of his
      derby and cane in his comedies.

1844 "McCandless, Kathleen." American Film Institute Catalog,
          1961-70, p.396.
      Kathleen McCandless is credited with the costumes of "Synanon";
      the women's wardrobe of "The Cabinet of Caligari"; and the ward-
      robe of "What Ever Happened to Baby Jane?" "Lady in a Cage,"
      "Alvarez Kelly," and "Madame X" (1966).

1845 "McCann, Gerald." American Film Institute Catalog, 1961-70,
          p.396.
      Gerald McCann is credited with the costumes of "Hot Girls for
      Men Only."

1846 MacCann, Richard Dyer. "Costumes for Bob Hope's New
          Film--Wardrobe Adviser Trained by Queen Mary of Eng-
          land." Christian Science Monitor, October 21, 1953, p.
          7.
      Hilda Grenier, once the royal dresser to Queen Mary of England,
      has worked as a film adviser on etiquette and wardrobes. Her
      credits include "Bride of Vengeance" (her first film), "Botany
      Bay," "Prisoner of Zenda" (1952), "My Cousin Rachel," and
      "Young Bess." She said that the costumes worn by Bob Hope and
      the cast of "Casanova's Big Night" were absolutely correct, de-
      signed by studio designers.

1847 "McCarter, Jerry." American Film Institute Catalog, 1961-70,
        p. 396.
Jerry McCarter is credited with the wardrobe of "101 Acts of
Love."

1848 "MacCharty, Mary." American Film Institute Catalog, 1961-
        70, p. 397.
Mary MacCharty is credited with the costumes of "The Ghost."

1849 McClelland, Doug. "Production," in Down the Yellow Brick
        Road: The Making of "The Wizard of Oz." New York:
        Pyramid, 1976, p. 93-117, passim.
Adrian designed a special corset to flatten Judy Garland's bosom
in "The Wizard of Oz" so that she would appear younger. He
also designed over 100 special Munchkin costumes; oversized
vests, jackets, and jewelry were worn by the men to emphasize
their smallness. Over 4,000 costumes were designed for the
approximately 1,000 cast members. Gale Sondergaard was once
considered for the role of the Wicked Witch, and a glamorous,
sequined costume with a sequined, high-pointed hat was made; the
studio chose to stick with the book's original conception of the
Wicked Witch and her costume. Cinematographer Harold Rosson
mentions problems with lighting and the costumes of Margaret
Hamilton, Jack Haley, Judy Garland, and Billie Burke. Notes
also that Bert Lahr's tail as the Cowardly Lion was usually man-
euvered by a person walking on a catwalk with a fishing pole.
Includes many illustrations, all in black-and-white.

1850 McConathy, Dale. "Mainbocher," in American Fashion. New
        York: Quadrangle/New York Times, 1975, p. 109-208.
The author contrasts the styles of designers Mainbocher and Coco
Chanel, whose costumes for "Last Year at Marienbad" played a
large part in the story because, like the heroine, Chanel was
caught between the past and present.

1851 _____, with Diana Vreeland. Hollywood Costume--Glamour!
        Glitter! Romance! New York: Abrams, 1976.
As suggested by the title, this is a lavish treatment of film costume, with an abundance of original stills and many photos of the
surviving costumes, originally shown in the "Romantic and Glamorous Hollywood Design" exhibit several years earlier. Much of
the book, as with the biographical essays of major actresses and
the bibliography, deals more with general film history than
with costume history. Only major actresses, designers, and
films are discussed, but (despite some negative comments) it is a
valuable contribution to film-costume history. One can only wish
that the sources of the text had been identified. Also, it is odd
that Carol Burnett's television show should receive more coverage
than any other actress or film. Includes also a section of biographical notes of 21 costume designers and two set designers.

1852 "McCorry, John." American Film Institute Catalog, 1961-70,
        p. 397.

John McCorry is credited with the wardrobe of "Guns at Batasi,"
"The Third Secret," and "Khartoum" and the wardrobe/costume
supervision of "Tom Jones," "A High Wind in Jamaica," and "Sword
of Sherwood Forest."

1853 MacCullers, Maris, and Kay Hardy. " 'Hello, Frisco, Hello';
        Production." <u>Modern Screen</u> 26 (4): 40-1, 106, March
        1943.
Alice Faye lost seven pounds before the production of "Hello,
Frisco, Hello," causing much extra work for over 70 persons, as
her dress form had to be discarded and a new one made, and her
costume designs changed. Other production departments were
similarly affected.

1854 _____. " 'Hers to Hold'; Production." <u>Modern Screen</u>, 26
        (4): 40-1, 96, September 1943.
Deanna Durbin wears overalls designed by Adrian in "Hers to
Hold."

1855 _____. " 'Lady in the Dark'; Production." <u>Modern Screen</u>,
        28 (5): 52-3, 89-90, April 1944.
Ray Milland was embarrassed by his loud circus costume for
"Lady in the Dark," consisting of white pants, red suede boots,
and a coat and top hat of red, blue, and purple sequins in a sunflower pattern. Ginger Rogers could not enjoy her mink and sequin costume, by Edith Head, because she kept getting electrical
charges from the floor.

1856 _____. " 'Lucky Jordan'; Production." <u>Modern Screen</u>, 26
        (5): 32-3, 79, April 1943.
Indicative of a change in roles, Alan Ladd wore tattered clothes
in "This Gun for Hire" but wore a tailored raincoat of good fabric
in "Lucky Jordan."

1857 MacCullers, Maris, and Charis Zeigler. " 'Spellbound'; Pro-
        duction." <u>Modern Screen</u>, 30 (5): 38-9, 121-2, April
        1945.
Ingrid Bergman was required to stand still for hours while wearing
a wet robe as a plaster statue of her was made for a dream sequence of "Spellbound"; featuring a Grecian gown with a train.

1858 "McDonald, Donald J." <u>American Film Institute Catalog, 1961-</u>
        <u>70</u>, p. 398.
Donald J. McDonald is credited with the wardrobe of "The Graduate" and the costumes of "Hail, Hero!"

1859 MacDonald, Margaret I. "Alice Brady Talks About Dress and
        Make-Up." <u>Moving Picture World</u>, 33 (3): 426, July 21,
        1917.
Alice Brady discusses the importance of line and fabric design in
clothing selections for her films; she is careful to select clothes that
emphasize her role. She acts in about one film a month but, unlike
other actresses, does not wear the clothes again for another film.

1860 "MacDonald Sings 'Mme. Butterfly' in 1939 Setting." MGM
        Studio News, 5 (13): n.p., January 14, 1939.
The chorus girls of the Mme. Butterfly sequence in "Broadway
Serenade" have departed from the traditional costume by wearing
pastel kimonos.

1861 McDonough, Jane. "Gloria ... Dictatrix Extraordinary."
        Hollywood, 19 (3): 13, March 1930.
Gloria Swanson has influenced fashion more than any Parisian designer because she creates or adapts styles rather than follows
them.

1862 McEvoy, J. P. "I Remember Gloria." Motion Picture, 80
        (6): 10-11, 64, January 1951.
One of many false publicity stories about Gloria Swanson, she
notes, was that her jewel-encrusted wedding gown in "Her Love
Story" cost $100,000.

1863 "McFarland, Hugh." American Film Institute Catalog, 1961-
        70, p. 399.
Hugh McFarland is credited with the wardrobe of "Clambake."

1864 McGaffey, Bessie. "Meet Your Research Department."
        Screen Guilds' Magazine, 4 (9): 30-2, November 1937.
Bessie McGaffey, founder of the first studio research department,
notes that Edward Stevenson researched the period costumes for
"The Toast of New York" with copies of Godey's Lady's Book,
Woman's Repository, and Peterson's Magazine. The research
department sent hundreds of photographs to the men's-wardrobe
department to design costumes for Cary Grant, Edward Arnold,
Donald Meek, and others not mentioned.

1865 McGaffey, Kenneth. "Clothes Do Not Make the Woman."
        Photoplay, 13 (2): 84-7, 135, January 1918.
Julian Eltinge is the stage name of the "ambi-sextrous" Bill Dalton, female impersonator, who has completed three films. Although he came equipped with 20 trunks of gowns, he had to return to New York for more. He designs some of his costumes.
Photos of the actor in men's and women's costumes.

1866 "McGee, Lois." American Film Institute Catalog, 1961-70,
        p. 399.
Lois McGee is credited with the wardrobe of "Johnny Tiger."

1867 "McHorter, Evelyn." American Film Institute Catalog, 1921-
        30, p. 1236.
Evelyn McHorter is credited with the costumes of "Potash and
Perlmutter."

1868 "McIntosh, Heather." American Film Institute Catalog, 1961-
        70, p. 401.
Heather McIntosh is credited with the costumes of "Dr. Frankenstein on Campus."

1869   Mack, Grace.   "Garbo's Fashion Splurge--and Other Style
          Notes."   Screen Book, 14 (6): 58-9, 81, July 1935.
Includes brief descriptions of costumes worn by Joan Crawford
in "No More Ladies," Greta Garbo in "Anna Karenina," and Dixie
Lee in "Redheads on Parade."

1870   _____.   "Hollywood Shop Talk."   Screen Book, 15 (5): 18,
          65-7, December 1935.
Discussion of costumes worn by Billie Burke and Joan Bennett in
"She Couldn't Take It," by Kalloch; Gail Patrick in "Two Fisted";
Ginger Rogers in "Tamed," by Bernard Newman; Wendy Barrie in
"A Feather in Her Hat"; Gladys Swarthout in "Rose of the Rancho";
and Carole Lombard in "Hands Across the Table," by Travis
Banton.   Brief mention of Marlene Dietrich in "Desire," Mae
West in "Goin' to Town," Katharine Hepburn in "Sylvia Scarlett,"
and Barbara Stanwyck in "Annie Oakley."   One costume each is
modeled, from their respective films, by Patrick, Barrie, and
Swarthout.   Marsha Hunt models three hats from "The Virginia
Judge."

1871   _____.   "Screen Book's Spotlight; Starred Styles."   Screen
          Book, 14 (4): 46-7, 61, 69, May 1935.
Discussion of costumes worn by Verree Teasdale in "The Goose
and the Gander"; Jean Harlow in "Reckless," one of which she
models; and Dolores Del Rio in "In Caliente."   Brief mention of
Marlene Dietrich in "The Devil Is a Woman."

1872   _____.   "That New Hollywood Elegance."   Screen Book, 15
          (4): 50-1, 76-7, November 1935.
Discussion of costumes worn by Ann Sothern in "Grand Exit," by
Murray Mayer, and brief mention of hats and a coat worn by
Marlene Dietrich in "Desire," and of Joan Crawford's jewelry in
an unnamed film.

1873   "Mack, Wanda."   American Film Institute Catalog, 1961-70,
          p. 401.
Wanda Mack is credited with the wardrobe of "Cottonpickin'
Chickenpickers."

1874   "McKay, Rosemarie."   American Film Institute Catalog, 1961-
          70, p. 401.
Rosemarie McKay is credited with the wardrobe of "Spiked Heels
and Black Nylons" and "Scarlet Negligee."

1875   McKegg, William H.   "What a Man Should Not Wear."   Picture
          Play, 26 (2): 85-6, 106, April 1927.
John Bowers insists upon appropriate and never faddish clothing,
as he wears in "Confessions of a Queen" and "The Dice Woman";
with a still from the latter film of Bowers and Priscilla Dean.
He discusses what is good taste in fashion and notes that author
Elinor Glyn and director Erich von Stroheim always insist upon
good taste and accurate costuming in their films.

1876 Mackenzie, Norman A. <u>The Magic of Rudolph Valentino.</u>
London: Research Publishing, 1974.
The author acknowledges immediately that he made "free use" of
biographies of Rudolph Valentino written by Natacha Rambova, S.
George Ullman, and Beulah Livingstone. Those books should be
referred to (see each entry) since the only original thing said
here in regard to costume is that the hat worn by Valentino in
"The Eagle" was awarded to a <u>Picture Show</u> reader as a contest
prize.

1877 McKenzie, Richard. "What They'll Do for Publicity." <u>Motion
Picture,</u> 58 (3): 38-9, 60-1, April 1939.
Two alleged publicity stunts include Norma Shearer wearing tight
and low-cut dresses in "Idiot's Delight," with one still, and Marlene Dietrich wearing pants on and off screen.

1878 Mackie, Bob, with Gerry Bremer. <u>Dressing for Glamour.</u>
New York: A & W, 1979.
Bob Mackie's first "real" costume-designing job was as a sketch
artist at Paramount for Frank Thompson, the wardrobe designer
for "Love Is a Ball"; Mackie was the men's, and eventually women's, sketch artist for the film. He next worked as Jean Louis's
sketch artist for Marilyn Monroe's gowns in the never-completed
"Something's Got to Give"; he learned a lot working with Jean
Louis but returned, as Edith Head's sketch artist, to Paramount
where he found it more exciting because of the numerous films
she was working on. He next worked with Ray Aghayan on many
television and entertainment assignments and on the films "Funny
Lady" and "Lady Sings the Blues," both Academy Award nominees.
Each of Barbra Streisand's costumes in "Funny Lady" was worn
with Art Deco jewelry personally chosen by her from her extensive
collection. Illustrations include a sketch and finished costume
modeled by Diana Ross from "Lady Sings the Blues," a sketch
of Ann-Margret in "The Villain," and two stills of Streisand from
"Funny Lady." Mackie discusses costume designing at length but
one could only wish for more specifics on the above films.

1879 "Mackie, Bob." <u>American Film Institute Catalog, 1961-70,</u>
p. 402.
Bob Mackie was the costume designer of "Divorce American Style."

1880 "Mackie, Bob." <u>Fairchild's Who's Who in Fashion.</u> 1975,
p. 172.
Bob Mackie has worked as a sketch designer for Jean-Louis, and
with Edith Head, and has won the Costume Designers Guild Award
several times, for nonfilm designs.

1881 MacLean, Barbara Barondess. "Billowy and Romantic."
<u>Screenland,</u> 53 (9): 46-7, 72-3, July 1949.
Barbara Barondess MacLean, an actress and designer, designed
five costumes for Stephanie Paull in "Million Dollar Weekend,"
three of which Paull models.

1882 "MacLean, Barbara Barondess." <u>Who's Who of American</u>
         <u>Women.</u> 10th ed., 1977-8, p. 558.

1883 "MacPhee, Duncan." <u>American Film Institute Catalog, 1961-</u>
         <u>70</u>, p. 403.
      Duncan MacPhee is credited with the costumes of "The Bofors
      Gun," the wardrobe of "Hell Boats," and was the wardrobe
      master of "Carry on Constable," "Carry on Regardless," and
      "Africa--Texas Style!"

1884 "Made in Hollywood." <u>Vogue,</u> 87 (11): 102, June 1, 1936.
      Two sketches of retail gowns by former film designers Lettie Lee
      and Howard Greer (one of few sources that mention Lettie Lee as
      a film designer).

1885 "Mae Busch." <u>Screen News,</u> 4 (43): 2, October 31, 1925.
      Mae Busch models an ermine coat from "Time, the Comedian."

1886 "Mae Murray Prefers Simple and Restful Dress for Home."
         <u>Screen News,</u> 2 (12): 28, March 24, 1923.
      Mae Murray wears exotic gowns on screen and simple ones at
      home, both types of which she enjoys designing. She will wear
      many of her own designs in her next film, "The French Doll."

1887 "Mafai, Giulia." <u>American Film Institute Catalog, 1961-70,</u>
         p. 405.
      Giulia Mafai is credited with the costumes of "The Pirate of the
      Black Hawk" and "Love, the Italian Way."

1888 "Magahay, Robert." <u>American Film Institute Catalog, 1961-</u>
         <u>70</u>, p. 405.
      Robert Magahay is credited with the costumes of "Harlow" and
      "Slaves," the wardrobe of "Who's Got the Action?" and "Project
      X," the men's wardrobe of "The Caper of the Golden Bulls" and
      Stephen Boyd's wardrobe in "The Oscar."

1889 "Mager, Kitty." <u>American Film Institute Catalog, 1961-70,</u>
         p. 405.
      Kitty Mager is credited with the women's costumes in "A Thunder
      of Drums" and the wardrobe of "Angel, Angel, Down We Go" and
      "The Traveling Executioner."

1890 "Magic Modes for May." <u>Photoplay with Movie Mirror,</u> 18
         (6): 53-7, May 1941.
      Merle Oberon models five costumes by Irene from "That Uncer-
      tain Feeling."

1891 "Magnificence!" <u>Hollywood,</u> 27 (9): 24-5, September 1938.
      Norma Shearer models seven costumes by Adrian from "Marie
      Antoinette."

1892 <u>Magnificent Costumes.</u> [An auction of uniforms, film and
         theater costumes of Max Berman & Sons, Inc., in June

1971.] Los Angeles: Sotheby Parke Bernet, 1971.
Photos are included, with a description of the costume auctioned,
for the suit of armor worn by Ingrid Bergman in "Joan of Arc";
a coat worn by Orson Welles in "The Third Man"; and four of the
15 auctioned costumes worn in "Gaily, Gaily," designed by Ray
Aghayan. Eight costumes from "Mary of Scotland" were auctioned,
including three worn by Katharine Hepburn and one by Florence
Eldredge; and two costumes each, worn by Ginger Rogers in "The
Story of Vernon and Irene Castle," Irene Dunne in "Cimarron,"
Jane Russell in "The French Line," and Linda Darnell in "Forever Amber." Many other film costumes were auctioned, and
many others were identified only by actor or actress, without
film titles.

1893 "Mago." American Film Institute Catalog, 1961-70, p. 406.
Mago was the costume designer of "Through a Glass Darkly,"
"Winter Light," "All These Women," "The Swedish Mistress,"
"To Love," "Persona," "Hour of the Wolf," "Shame," "The
Passion of Anna," and "The Ritual."

1894 Maillefert, Julia. "Glamour Fashions for You." Picture Play,
        49 (5): 57-9, 78, January 1939.
Many of the actresses Edward Stevenson designs for buy their
wardrobes when their films are completed; the average prices
range from one-half to two-thirds of the original cost to make the
garment, with specific examples of prices. He also designs and
selects hats worn with the film costumes and discusses the many
actresses he has designed for, with emphasis on their figure flaws
and assets. He has designed 65 costumes for seven women in
"The Mad Miss Manton," three of which Barbara Stanwyck models
(the other women are not identified).

1895 "Maison Repetto." American Film Institute Catalog, 1961-70,
        p. 407.
Maison Repetto is credited with the special costumes for Robert
Hirsch in "Impossible on Saturday."

1896 "Makau, Marge." American Film Institute Catalog, 1961-70,
        p. 407.
Marge Makau is credited with the wardrobe of "Don't Worry, We'll
Think of a Title."

1897 "The Making of 'Marie Antoinette' in Pictures." Souvenir
        Program ... of the Metro-Goldwyn-Mayer Production
        "Marie Antoinette." 1938, p. 3, 19-20, passim.
Closeup photos show elaborately embroidered cuffs for John Barrymore in "Marie Antoinette," and women attaching spangles and
beads onto lace for costumes worn by Norma Shearer. Gile
Steele was the supervisor of the men's costumes. Many additional
closeups of costumes being constructed.

1898 "Making Toys Interesting for Little Girls." Screen News, 3
        (7): 9, February 16, 1924.

Includes a detailed description of how to make a doll costume
identical to a costume worn, and modeled, by Constance Talmadge
in "The Dangerous Maid."

1899   "Malabar."   American Film Institute Catalog, 1961-70, p.407.
Malabar is credited with Leela Naidu's costumes in "The Guru."

1900   "Male Legs Attract Feminine Eyes in Royal Court Fetes."
          MGM Studio News, 5 (6): n.p., August 15, 1938.
Each of Norma Shearer's costumes in "Marie Antoinette" were
made of over 30 yards of fabric and weighed about 50 pounds
each; they covered her feet, required for authenticity.

1901   Malmgreen, Henry P.   " 'Honky Tonk'; Production."   Modern
          Screen, 23 (6): 44-5, 99, November 1941.
Adrian designed Lana Turner's period costumes for "Honky Tonk"
so that they would not hide her figure and designed a costume for
Claire Trevor consisting mainly of ostrich feathers in numerous
colors.

1902   "Maltzeff, C."   American Film Institute Catalog, 1961-70,
          p.408.
C. Maltzeff is credited with the costumes of "Les Gauloises
Bleues."

1903   "Mami."   American Film Institute Catalog, 1961-70, p.409.
Mami is credited with the costumes of "The Green Slime."

1904   " 'Man Dresses Women to Please the Eyes of Other Men.' "
          Screen News, 2 (39): 10, September 29, 1923.
The Jackie Coogan film "Long Live the King" will feature as
many as 1,500 women in gowns created by the Coogan wardrobe
department, with the help of six wardrobe mistresses.

1905   " 'The Man of the Seven Trunks.' "   Screen News, 3 (36): 12,
          September 6, 1924, col. 1.
Holmes Herbert is prepared for most any role since he has kept
all of his old film costumes.   He brought seven trunks of costumes to location for "Wilderness."

1906   Manchel, Frank.   Terrors of the Screen.   Englewood Cliffs,
          N.J.: Prentice-Hall, 1970.
Lon Chaney's painful costume for "The Hunchback of Notre Dame"
(1923) consisted of football-player-sized shoulder pads attached to
a breastplate in the front, a 70-pound hump worn on his back,
with a lightweight leather harness worn over these to force him to
hunch over, and a tinted rubber suit covered with animal hair to
cover the harness.

1907   Mandelbaum, Nathan.   "Edith Head: The Way She Lives."
          Ladies' Home Journal, 93 (4): 106-9, April 1976.
Includes many statements by Edith Head about some of the actors
and actresses she has designed for.   In John Wayne's films the

actresses "conform with what he's wearing"; Fred Astaire inad-
vertantly started a fashion trend when Head copied his style of
wearing a tie as a substitute for a belt; and Dorothy Lamour's
first sarong was held with tape, which came undone in the water.

1908 "Manela, Sabine." American Film Institute Catalog, 1961-70,
       p. 409.
Sabine Manela is credited with the costumes of "Gun Street,"
"Secret of Deep Harbor," and "Deadly Duo" and the wardrobe of
"Flight That Disappeared," "The Gambler Wore a Gun," "Gun
Fight," "The Last Time I Saw Archie," "Jack the Giant Killer,"
"Saintly Sinners," and "Big Daddy."

1909 Mann, Ronald. "Walter Plunkett." [Letters]. Films in Re-
       view, 24 (1): 61 , January 1973.
The author's favorite designer is Walter Plunkett; includes a lengthy
list of his design credits, and notes when he collaborated with
another designer on a film.

1910 Manners, Dorothy. "Devastating Daytime Styles." Motion
       Picture, 50 (6): 43-5, 54, January 1936.
Discussion of costumes worn by Ann Sothern in "Grand Exit,"
Billie Burke and Joan Bennett in "She Couldn't Take It," and
Bennett in "The Man Who Broke the Bank at Monte Carlo." Ben-
nett models one costume from each film, and Billie Burke models
one and Ann Sothern three from their films.

1911 _____. "Fall Fashions--and Grace Moore." Motion Pic-
       ture, 50 (2): 43-5, 72, September 1935.
Discussion of costumes worn by Grace Moore in "Love Me Forever" and Ann Sothern in "The Girl Friend"; they each model
four costumes by Kalloch.

1912 _____. "Have You a Theme Gown in Your Wardrobe?"
       Motion Picture, 50 (3): 43-5, 72, October 1935.
Discussion of costumes worn by Lyda Roberti, Gracie Allen, and
Wendy Barrie in "The Big Broadcast of 1936"; Gail Patrick in
"Smart Girl"; and clothing adapted for, and from costumes worn
by, Joan Bennett from "Two for Tonight" and Patrick from "The
Crusades," by Travis Banton. One costume each is modeled,
from the above films, by Roberti, Allen, Barrie, and Patrick.

1913 _____. "The New Styles are Your Styles." Motion Picture,
       49 (5): 43-5, 66, June 1935.
Discussion of costumes worn by Jean Harlow in "Reckless," Virginia Bruce in "Times Square Lady," and Elizabeth Allen in "Mark
of the Vampire," all by Adrian. One costume each is modeled by
Harlow and Allen.

1914 _____. "New Styles Have Rhythm." Motion Picture, 50
       (5): 43-5, 76, December 1935.
Includes references to Eleanor Powell's costumes in "Broadway

Melody of 1936, " three of which she models.

1915 _____. "Round the Mid-Summer Fashion Clock. " Motion
            Picture, 50 (1): 43-5, 68, August 1935.
Discussion of costumes by Helen Myron worn by Pat Paterson in
"Charlie Chan in Egypt"; Claire Trevor in "Dante's Inferno, " by
Royer; Dixie Lee in "Redheads on Parade, " by William Lambert;
and Mae Clarke in "The Daring Young Man" and Ketti Gallian in
"Under the Pampas Moon, " both by Rene Hubert.   Two costumes
each are modeled by Lee and Gallian, and one by Clarke, from
their films.

1916 _____. "Taking Off Their Clothes. " Motion Picture
            Classic, 31 (4): 38-9, 87, June 1930.
Discussion of the trend toward brief costumes, as worn by Corinne
Griffith in "Lilies of the Field, " Kay Johnson in "Madame Satan, "
Edwina Booth in "Trader Horn, " and Sue Carol in "The Golden
Calf"; all briefly mentioned.   M. Sammy Lee, formerly with
Florenz Ziegfeld, discusses his new job with MGM to glorify the
Hollywood girl.   Brief mention of other films, and many photos.

1917 "The Manufacturing Workrooms of Hollywood Present Their
            1960 Costume Entries for an Adam 'N Eve Award. "
            Motion Picture Costumers, 1960, n. p.
One costume each is modeled by Sophia Loren from "Heller in
Pink Tights, " by Edith Head; Diane McBain from "Parrish, " by
Howard Shoup; Capucine from "Song without End, " by Jean-Louis;
Joan Collins from "Seven Thieves, " by Bill Thomas; Debbie Rey-
nolds from "It Started with a Kiss, " by Helen Rose; and Shirley
MacLaine from "Can-Can, " by Irene Sharaff.

1918 "Marcel Vertes, Painter, 66, Dies. " New York Times, No-
            vember 1, 1961, p.39.
Marcel Vertes, who began film-costume designing in 1932, died
of a heart attack at the age of 66.

1919 "March Mode-Makers. " Photoplay with Movie Mirror, 20
            (4): 57-61, March 1942.
Gene Tierney models five costumes from "Shanghai Gesture, "
by Oleg Cassini.

1920 "March Modes. " Picturegoer, 11 (33): 33, March 1926.
Five unidentified women model one costume each from "The Dressmaker from Paris" (probably from the fashion-show sequence).

1921 "Marchand, Anne-Marie. " American Film Institute Catalog,
            1961-70, p.413.
Anne-Marie Marchand is credited with the costumes of "Fanny. "

1922 "Marchesi, Pia. " American Film Institute Catalog, 1961-70,
            p.413.
Pia Marchesi is credited with the costumes of "Il Grido. "

1923 Marcus, Stanley. Minding the Store; A Memoir. Boston:
          Little, Brown, 1974.
The author notes that Gilbert Adrian entered ready-to-wear designing with greater recognition than any other American designer
because of the fame of his previous film-costume designing.
"There will be many who may dispute any attribution of 'greatness'
to him," but his considerable influence on American fashion is
here limited to six years since he was "the only show in town"
while Paris was occupied.

1924 "Mariani, Fiorella." American Film Institute Catalog, 1961-
          70, p. 414.
Fiorella Mariani is credited with the costumes of "Song of Norway."

1925 "Marie-Martine." American Film Institute Catalog, 1961-70,
          p. 414.
Marie-Martine is credited with Brigitte Bardot's dresses in "A
Very Private Affair" and was the clothes designer for Ingrid
Thulin in "La Guerre Est Finie."

1926 Marilyn. "Clothes Gossip from Hollywood." Motion Picture,
          45 (1): 44-7, 86, February 1933.
Discussion and stills of costumes worn by Nancy Carroll in "Child
of Manhattan" and "Undercover Man"; Constance Bennett in
"Rockabye"; Thelma Todd in "Air Hostess," by Kalloch; Carole
Lombard in "No Man of Her Own"; and Clara Bow in "Call Her
Savage," by David Cox. Mae Clarke models two hats from "Ac-
quitted," by Stetson.

1927 _____. "Clothes Gossip from Hollywood." Motion Picture,
          45 (2): 44-7, 84, March 1933.
Discussion and stills of costumes worn by Irene Dunne in "The
Lady"; Boots Mallory in "Handle with Care"; Ann Harding in "The
Animal Kingdom"; Jean Arthur in "The Past of Mary Holmes";
Raquel Torres in "That's Africa"; Sally Eilers in "Second-Hand
Wife"; and Adrienne Ames in an unnamed film, by Travis Banton.

1928 _____. "Clothes Gossip from Hollywood." Motion Picture,
          45 (3): 44-7, 80, April 1933.
Discussion and stills of costumes worn by Joan Crawford in
"Today We Live," by Adrian; Claudette Colbert in "Tonight Is
Ours" and Sari Maritza in "A Lady's Profession," both by Travis
Banton; Kathleen Burke in "Murders in the Zoo"; Constance Ben-
nett in "Our Betters"; and Katharine Hepburn and Helen Chandler
in "A Great Desire."

1929 _____. "Clothes Gossip from Hollywood." Motion Picture,
          45 (4): 44-7, 81, May 1933.
Discussion and stills of costumes worn by Carole Lombard in
"From Hell to Heaven" and Peggy Hopkins Joyce in "International
House," both by Travis Banton; Genevieve Tobin in "Infernal Ma-
chine," by Rita Kaufman; Miriam Jordan in "Dangerously Yours";

and Helen Twelvetrees in "A Bedtime Story."

1930 _____. "Clothes Gossip from Hollywood." <u>Motion Picture,</u>
        45 (5): 44-7, 89, June 1933.
Discussion and stills of costumes worn by Diana Wynyard in "Reunion in Vienna"; Karen Morley in "Gabriel over the White House"
and Madge Evans in "Hell Below," both by Adrian; Genevieve
Tobin in "Pleasure Cruise," by Rita Kaufman; Adrienne Ames in
"A Bedtime Story," Carole Lombard in "Supernatural," and Sari
Maritza in "International House," all three by Travis Banton;
Muriel Kirkland and Mae Clarke in "Fast Workers"; Benita Hume
in "Clear All Wives"; Lilian Bond in "When Strangers Marry";
and Bebe Daniels in her next film (probably "Cocktail Hour"),
by the American Maid Shop.

1931 _____. "Clothes Gossip from Hollywood." <u>Motion Picture,</u>
        45 (6): 44-7, 71, July 1933.
Discussion and stills of costumes worn by Lilian Harvey in "My
Lips Betray"; Marlene Dietrich in "Song of Songs" and Sari Maritza
in "International House," both by Travis Banton; Ginger Rogers
in "Gold Diggers of 1933," by Orry-Kelly; Fay Wray in "Ann Carver's Profession," by Lettie Lee; Patricia Ellis in "The Narrow
Corner"; and Heather Angel in "Pilgrimage."

1932 _____. "Clothes Gossip from Hollywood." <u>Motion Picture,</u>
        46 (1): 44-7, 67, 73, August 1933.
Discussion and stills of costumes worn by Mae West in "I'm No
Angel"; Constance Bennett in "Bed of Roses"; Elissa Landi in
"I Loved You Wednesday," by Rita Kaufman; Adrienne Ames and
Helen Twelvetrees in "Disgraced"; Bebe Daniels in "Cocktail
Hour"; and Loretta Young in "Lady of the Night," Myrna Loy,
Alice Brady, and Ann Harding in "When Ladies Meet," and Marion
Davies in "Peg O'My Heart," the last three by Adrian.

1933 _____. "Clothes Gossip from Hollywood." <u>Motion Picture,</u>
        46 (2): 44-7, 85, September 1933.
Discussion and stills of costumes worn by Lyda Roberti in "Three-
Cornered Moon"; Kay Francis in "Storm at Daybreak," by Adrian;
Miriam Hopkins in "Stranger's Return"; Glenda Farrell in "Lady
for a Day," by Kalloch; Gloria Stuart in "The Secret of the Blue
Room"; Ginger Rogers in "Don't Bet on Love"; and Elizabeth
Young in "The Big Executive." Notes the continual influence of
the sleeves worn by Joan Crawford in "Letty Lynton," and that
she will wear 20 gowns in "The Dancing Lady."

1934 _____. "Clothes Gossip from Hollywood." <u>Motion Picture,</u>
        46 (3): 44-7, 97, October 1933.
Discussion of one costume worn by Lupe Velez in "The Hollywood
Party," by Adrian, which Velez models.

1935 _____. "Clothes Gossip from Hollywood." <u>Motion Picture,</u>
        46 (4): 44-7, November 1933.
Discussion and stills of costumes worn by Joan Crawford in "The

Dancing Lady"; Raquel Torres in "Duck Soup"; Claudette Colbert
in "Torch Singer," by Travis Banton; Judith Allen in "Too Much
Harmony"; and Heather Angel in "Charlie Chan's Greatest Case,"
by Rita Kaufman.

1936 "Maring, Misty." American Film Institute Catalog, 1961-70,
       p. 414.
Misty Maring is credited with the wardrobe of "The Hellcats."

1937/8 "Marinucci, Luciana." American Film Institute Catalog, 1961-
        70, p. 415.
Luciana Marinucci was the costume designer of "The Conjugal
Bed" and is credited with the costumes of "Love and Marriage,"
"Danger: Diabolik," and "We Still Kill the Old Way."

1939 "Mark, Bob." American Film Institute Catalog, 1961-70,
       p. 415.
Bob Mark is credited with the wardrobe of "Police Nurse."

1940 Markel, Helen. "Adrian Talks of Gowns--and of Goats."
       New York Times Magazine, May 27, 1945, p. 14-5, 25.
The emphasis is on Adrian's salon, and mentions his beginning
film-costume design at the request of Natacha Rambova, and that
he later worked for Cecil B. De Mille until he joined MGM, where
he stayed for 16 years.

1941 "Marks, Edward." American Film Institute Catalog, 1961-70,
       p. 415.
Edward Marks is credited with the costumes of "A Man Called
Horse" and the wardrobe of "The Traveling Executioner" and
"Zigzag."

1942 "Marks, Lambert." American Film Institute Catalog, 1961-70,
       p. 416.
11 wardrobe-related credits are listed for Lambert Marks.

1943 "Markwordt, Margarete." American Film Institute Catalog,
       1961-70, p. 416.
Margarete Markwordt is credited with the wardrobe of "Cry
Double Cross."

1944 "Marlene Dietrich." Vogue, 88 (12): 50, December 15, 1936.
Features a color sketch of Marlene Dietrich in a costume from
"Knight Without Armour."

1945 "Marolt, Annie." American Film Institute Catalog, 1961-70,
       p. 416.
Annie Marolt is credited with the wardrobe of "Temptation" (1962)
and was the dresser of "Wise Guys."

1946 "Marrini, Gitt." American Film Institute Catalog, 1961-70,
       p. 417.
Gitt Marrini is credited with the costumes of "Two or Three Things

I Know About Her. "

1947 Marsh, Mae. "Linking Moods and Clothes. " Screen News,
        3 (1): 14, January 5, 1924.
      Mae Marsh discusses the importance of knowing the psychology of
      color in clothing selections and was especially careful in buying
      her costumes for "Daddies. "

1948 "Marsh, Maude. " American Film Institute Catalog, 1921-30,
        p. 1248.
      Designer Maude Marsh is credited with 16 films.   (All co-designed
      with Kathleen Kay.)

1949 "Martell, Jack. " American Film Institute Catalog, 1961-70,
        p. 418.
      Jack Martell was the costume designer of "Castle Keep" and is
      credited with the costumes of "A Man Called Horse, " the ward-
      robe of "The Professionals" and "In Cold Blood, " and the men's
      wardrobe of "The Collector. "

1950 "Martelli, Marissa. " American Film Institute Catalog, 1961-
        70, p. 419.
      Marissa Martelli is credited with the additional costumes for
      Monica Vitti in "Modesty Blaise. "

1951 "Martien, Elva. " American Film Institute Catalog, 1961-70,
        p. 419.
      Elva Martien is credited with the wardrobe of "Jumbo, " "A Tick-
      lish Affair, " "Girl Happy, " "Made in Paris, " "Hang 'Em High, "
      "Stay Away, Joe, " and "Dirty Dingus Magee. "

1952 "Martin, Alice Manougian. " American Film Institute Catalog,
        1961-70, p. 419.
      Alice Manougian Martin was the costume designer of "Love Story. "

1953 Martin, Carolyn. " 'Before the Fact' in Fashions. " Silver
        Screen, 11 (11): 52-5, September 1941.
      Joan Fontaine models seven costumes by Edward Stevenson and
      one hat by John Frederic [sic], from "Before the Fact. "

1954 _____. "Latin-American Treasure Trove. " Silver Screen,
        11 (7): 54-7, May 1941.
      Maureen O'Hara models five costumes and several hats by Edward
      Stevenson from "They Met in Argentina. "

1955 _____. "Please Copy!" Silver Screen, 12 (9): 46-7, June
        1942.
      Joan Bennett models one costume (or more) by Irene from "The
      Wife Takes a Flyer. "

1956 Martin, John. "Dance: Award to Karinska. " New York Times,
        December 31, 1961, sec. 2, p. 10.
      Biographical information on Mme. Karinska, noted for her ability

to translate a sketch into something that can be worn, with frequent departures according to her own judgment.

1957 _____. "Karinska." Center, 2 (1): 21-5, February 1955.
        Karinska has spent her life in theatrical costuming after leaving
        a palace in Petrograd, settling first in France, where she de-
        signed some film costumes (no credits) and worked with Christian
        Bérard.

1958 "Martin of California." American Film Institute Catalog, 1961-
        70, p.420.
        Martin of California is credited with James Coburn's wardrobe in
        "In Like Flint."

1959 Martin, Sally. "Between Seasons with Loretta Young." Motion
        Picture, 53 (2): 47-9, March 1937.
        Loretta Young models a robe by Royer from "Love Is News."

1960 _____. "Fashions." Movie Classic, 11 (4): 42-3, De-
        cember 1936.
        Irene Dunne models two costumes by Bernard Newman from
        "Theodora Goes Wild."

1961 _____. "4 Star Dresses." Movie Classic, 10 (6): 38-9,
        64-5, August 1936.
        Ida Lupino models one costume from "Yours for the Asking."

1962 _____. "History Repeats--in Fashions!" Screen Play,
        20 (139): 40-1, 66, October 1936.
        Walter Plunkett started the wardrobe department at FBO studios,
        which later became RKO. He left in 1930 to work at Western
        Costume Company but returned in 1932; he remained until 1935,
        when he began designing for a wholesale house in New York. He
        returned once again to design Katharine Hepburn's 15 costumes for
        "Mary of Scotland" and designed a total of 420 costumes for the
        film. Hepburn models three of the costumes; with two sketches
        of adapted costumes for modern wear. He discusses the rivalry
        between Hollywood and Paris for title of the fashion center of the
        world.

1963 _____. "If Winter Comes--Will We Be Far Behind?"
        Motion Picture, 52 (4): 44-7, November 1936.
        Carole Lombard models three costumes by Travis Banton, and
        Gail Patrick five by Edith Head, from their "My Man Godfrey"
        wardrobes.

1964 _____. "Melody at Midnight." Screen Play, 20 (141):
        42-3, 72, December 1936.
        Gladys Swarthout models several gowns by Travis Banton from
        "Champagne Waltz."

1965 _____. "Shirley's Personal Wardrobe." Hollywood, 25
        (11): 40, 64, November 1936.

Shirley Temple's film costumes must be smart, ahead of fashion, and yet youthful, since her costumes set trends in children's wear, according to designer Rene Hubert. The fabrics must be easy to clean, and Miss Temple will wear only pastels.

1966 _____. "Suede Clothes--Newest Fad." Hollywood, 25 (5): 38, 55, May 1936.
Discussion of the fad for suede clothes as a result of Voris Linthacum, who had started her shop three years earlier. Her specialty is in designing and sewing a new kind of soft suede, usually in novel colors and color combinations. Bette Davis will wear a chamois evening coat in "Golden Arrow."

1967 "Martinson, A." American Film Institute Catalog, 1961-70, p. 421.
A. Martinson is credited with the costumes of "Violin and Roller" and "Forty-nine Days."

1968 Marx, Arthur. "A Mink's-Eye View of Hollywood." Collier's, 130 (11): 38-41, September 13, 1952.
Al Teitelbaum, whose fur company has been serving actresses and the motion picture industry since 1917, is the "official" furrier for the industry and has started many fur fashion trends, with examples listed. He discusses furs worn in "The Ten Command-ments," and worn by Rita Hayworth in "Gilda," Barbara Stanwyck in "The Mad Miss Manton," Paulette Goddard in "Anna Lucasta," Joan Crawford in "Sudden Fear," and Rosalind Russell and Bette Davis in unnamed films.

1969 Marx, Samuel. Mayer and Thalberg: The Make-Believe Saints. New York: Random House, 1975.
MGM's wardrobe department kept shelves of artificial but com-pletely realistic breasts for their actresses lest they appear un-endowed to their public; custom-made for each actress.

1970 "Mary Astor Displays Beautiful Modes." Hollywood Vagabond, November 17, 1927, p. 18.
Mary Astor models five gowns by Sophie Wachner from "No Place to Go."

1971 "Mary Kay Dodson." Photoplay, 33 (6): 85, November 1948.
Brief mention of Lucille Ball's preference for nonhampering clothes, as designed by Mary Kay Dodson for "Sorrowful Jones." She had her favorite costume from the film made up in several colors for her personal wear.

1972 "Mary Philbin: A Maid of Modes." Screenland, 17 (2): 48, June 1928.
Notes that the premiere audience of "Drums of Love" broke into applause when they saw Mary Philbin in her wedding gown.

1973 "Mary Philbin Shows the Wardrobe of an Extra Girl." Screen-land, 17 (5): 38-9, September 1928.

Mary Philbin models five costumes that would meet the costume
needs for most extras.

1974 "Mary's New Clothes." Photoplay, 22 (1): 76, June 1922.
Mary Pickford models three of the 49 gowns she bought from
Jeanne Lanvin in Paris and which she will wear in forthcoming
films.

1975 "Marzot, Véra." American Film Institute Catalog, 1961-70,
p. 422.
Véra Marzot was the assistant costume designer of "The Leopard,"
the costume designer of "Marriage Italian Style," and is credited
with the costumes of "The Damned."

1976 "Mathie, Marion." American Film Institute Catalog, 1961-70,
p. 424.
Marion Mathie is credited with the wardrobe of "Dracula Has
Risen from the Grave."

1977 "Mathieson, Johanna." American Film Institute Catalog, 1921-
30, p. 1252.
Johanna Mathieson was the costume designer of "Broadway."

1978 Mathieu, Beatrice. "Hollywood Déshabillé." Stage, 15 (2):
108-9, November 1937.
Many film designers design in their leisure hours for ready-to-
wear shops, for example, Omar Kiam, Orry-Kelly, and Edward
Stevenson.

1979 _____. "Hollywood, I Love You!" Stage, 14 (2): 52-7,
September 1937.
Discussion of Hollywood fashion, film and nonfilm. Genuine
jewelry has become important in films, as worn by Claudette
Colbert in "I Met Him in Paris," the models in "Vogues of 1938,"
and Greta Garbo in "Conquest," wearing famous Napoleonic pieces
lent from Mauboussin's collection. Includes photos and/or sketches
of costumes worn by Carole Lombard in "Nothing Sacred," by
Travis Banton; Luise Rainer in "Big City," by Dolly Tree; Olivia
de Havilland in "Gentlemen at Midnight," by Orry-Kelly; Joan
Crawford in "The Bride Wore Red," and Greta Garbo in "Conquest," both by Adrian.

1980 "Matthews, Marilyn." American Film Institute Catalog, 1961-
70, p. 425.
Marilyn Matthews is credited with the wardrobe of "The Traveling
Executioner."

1981 "Maureen Uses Many Costumes." MGM Studio News, 4 (10):
n. p., June 28, 1937.
Maureen O' Sullivan appeared to wear only one white uniform in
"Between Two Women," but was provided with 24 copies so that
each uniform would be without wrinkles during filming.

1982   "Max Ree." New York Times, March 8, 1953, p. 89.
Max Ree died at age 64, of undisclosed causes; noted only as an
art director.

1983   "Maxwell, Barbara." American Film Institute Catalog, 1961-
70, p. 426.
Barbara Maxwell is credited with the wardrobe of "The Clown
and the Kid," "When the Clock Strikes," "You Have to Run Fast,"
and "Incident in an Alley."

1984   Maxwell, Julia. "Night and Day." Screen Romances, 13 (74):
78-9, July 1935.
Helen Vinson models one gown from "The Wedding Night," by
Omar Kiam, which she bought for her personal wardrobe.

1985   "Maxwell, Nora." American Film Institute Catalog, 1961-70,
p. 426.
Nora Maxwell is credited with the wardrobe of "Girl in Gold
Boots."

1986   "May, Cynthia." American Film Institute Catalog, 1961-70,
p. 427.
Cynthia May is credited with the wardrobe of "Downhill Racer."

1987   "Maybe There's an Idea for You in What They're Wearing On
and Off the Screen." Photoplay, 38 (3): 24-5, August
1930.
One costume each is modeled by Gloria Swanson from "What a
Widow" and Ruth Roland from "Reno."

1988   "Mayer." American Film Institute Catalog, 1961-70, p. 427.
Mayer is credited with the costumes of "Investigation of a Citizen
Above Suspicion."

1989   "Mayer, Gabriele." American Film Institute Catalog, 1961-70,
p. 427.
Gabriele Mayer is credited with the costumes of "Planet of the
Vampires."

1990   "Mayo." American Film Institute Catalog, 1961-70, p. 427.
Mayo is credited with the costumes of "The Cheaters."

1991   Mayo, Edna. "Fashions on the Film." Pictures and the Picturegoer, 10 (113): 58, April 15, 1916.
Edna Mayo has been credited as the best-dressed film actress
and has received considerable publicity as a result, which she
discusses.   She wore nine gowns in "The Misleading Lady," by
Lady Duff Gordon; and 24 in "The Strange Case of Mary Page,"
also specially designed, by Lucile (Lady Duff Gordon and Lucile
were the same).

1992   "Meet Jean-Pierre Dorleac: The Designer Who's Dressed--

and Undressed--Everyone from Brooke Shields to Jane
Fonda!" Rona Barrett's Hollywood, 11 (4): 42-4, 72-3,
December 1979.
Biography of French designer Jean-Pierre Dorleac, who first designed for a film, "Barbarella," while working for designer Jacques Fonteray. He attributes much of the start of his career in
America to Edith Head. He discusses at length designing for
Brooke Shields in "Blue Lagoon," the film he considers "his best
to date"; and briefly, designing for Christopher Reeve in "Somewhere in Time." Includes one sketch each of costumes for Shields,
and Reeve and Jane Seymour in "Somewhere in Time."

1993 "Menasco, Milton." American Film Institute Catalog, 1921-
       30, p.1256-7.
Milton Menasco is credited with the costumes of "Lorna Doone"
(1922).

1994 "Mendleson, Anthony." American Film Institute Catalog, 1961-
       70, p.431.
17 credits are listed for designer Anthony Mendleson.

1995 "Menichelli, Rosalba." American Film Institute Catalog, 1961-
       70, p.431.
Rosalba Menichelli is credited with the costumes of "El Che
Guevara."

1996 Menjou, Adolphe, and M.M. Musselman. It Took Nine Tailors.
       New York: Whittlesey House, 1948.
Adolphe Menjou discusses costumes he wore in "The Man Behind
the Door," "The Crucial Test," "Rupert of Hentzau," "The Sorrows of Satan," and "A Woman of Paris," for which he had had
a special suit made for a racetrack scene, and since it was not
needed he had a scene added specially in one of his films a few
years later so that he could wear it. He knew that he would get
better, and more, roles if he had a good wardrobe, so he asked
tailor Eddie Schmidt to give him on credit six suits at $125 each;
he has much praise for the tailor, and together they started many
fashion trends. He once sued, and won, a manufacturer who was
manufacturing an "Adolphe Menjou Tie" and shirt without his permission. His suits often had to be fitted as many as ten times
since the camera magnifies any flaws, and he was, of course, a
perfectionist. After the Depression he found that his "dress suit
character" was no longer needed, but his career was saved with
"The Front Page." He tried to locate a suitably dilapidated blue-
serge suit and hat for "Little Miss Marker" at Western Costume
Company and Paramount's wardrobe department, and finally found
a suit at RKO's wardrobe department, which he had aged at Paramount. That year the Merchant Tailors' Association left him off
their list of the ten best-dressed men. He wore four suits by
Hawes and Curtis in "Cafe Metropole." Includes anecdotes about
a tuxedo George Murphy was supposed to wear in a film, and
Menjou convincing Kay Kyser to buy four suits from Schmidt's
store for his first film, "That's Right, You're Wrong." Menjou

and Johnny Gallup, the cutter for Schmidt's store, supervised
Kyser's final fitting.

1997 "Merangel, Charles." American Film Institute Catalog, 1961-
        70, p.431.
Charles Merangel is credited with the wardrobe of "Cloportes."

1998 Merrill, Kay. "Beltless, Form Fitting Gowns Supplanting the
        Chemise Frocks." Screen News, 4 (11): 6, March 14,
        1925.
Discussion of gowns worn by Paulette Duval in "Cheaper to Marry,"
three of which she models.

1999 "Merrill, Mary." American Film Institute Catalog, 1961-70,
        p.433.
Mary Merrill is credited with the costumes of "A Lovely Way to
Die."

2000 "Mervyn Le Roy: The Costumer's 'Man of the Year' Honorary
        Award." Motion Picture Costumers, 1963, n.p.
Director Mervyn Le Roy began his film career as a wardrobe
assistant.

2001 "A Mesh Evening Gown." Screen News, 4 (25): 8, June 20,
        1925.
Eleanor Boardman models a gown from "Proud Flesh," consisting
of gold beaded net, with hundreds of ermine tails forming the
train and cuffs, and a gold cloth turban.

2002 Messel, Oliver. " 'Romeo and Juliet' Costumes," in "Romeo
        and Juliet"; a Motion Picture Edition, by William Shake-
        speare. New York: Random House, 1936, p.265-8.
Oliver Messel, the costume designer of "Romeo and Juliet" (with
Adrian), discusses the paintings used in designing costumes for
Norma Shearer and other cast members, with mention of the
fabric research.

2003 "Messel, Oliver," in Art and Design in the British Film, by
        Edward Carrick. London: Dobson, 1948. p.85-7.
Oliver Messel was a well-known theatrical costume and set designer when MGM employed him as a costume and set designer
for "Romeo and Juliet" (1936). He was released from the army
to design the costumes of "Caesar and Cleopatra," with Hein
Heckroth assisting him.

2004 "Messel, Oliver." Biographical Encyclopaedia and Who's Who
        of the American Theatre. 1966, p.679.
Lengthy biographical information on Oliver Messel, with film-
costume credits listed, including "The Private Life of Don Juan"
and "The Queen of Spades."

2005 "Messel, Oliver." Who's Who in the Theatre. 16th ed.,
        1977, p.931-2.

2006   Metcalfe, Leigh.   "The Wardrobe Lady: The Bradstreet and
         Dun of the Motion Picture Business."   Photoplay, 17 (1):
         66, December 1919.
       A cartoon, with three drawings, of the problems the wardrobe
       mistress encounters, particularly with temperamental actresses
       and remodeling costumes for different actresses.   Sketched by
       Russell Patterson (probably the designer).

2007   "Metro's 'Wise Cracking' Office Boy Describes Studio Setting."
         Screen News, 2 (5): 27, February 3, 1923.
       Tongue-in-cheek article containing references to the costumes of
       "Desire."

2008   "Meyers, Greta."   American Film Institute Catalog, 1961-70,
         p.436.
       Greta Meyers is credited with the costumes of "Mondo Mod."

2009   "Mialkovszky, Erzsébet."   American Film Institute Catalog,
         1961-70, p.436.
       Erzsébet Mialkovszky is credited with the costumes of "Father."

2010   Michael, Paul, ed.   The American Movies Reference Book:
         Sound Era.   Englewood Cliffs, N.J.: Prentice-Hall, 1969.
         p.10-1.
       One of the most important aspects of the "woman's picture" from
       the 1930s to 1940s was the jewelry and costumes worn by leading
       clotheshorses--many of whom are listed, with examples of their
       films.

2011   "Micheli, Dario."   American Film Institute Catalog, 1961-70,
         p.436.
       Dario Micheli is credited with the wardrobe of "The Bird with the
       Crystal Plumage."

2012   "Micheli, Elio."   American Film Institute Catalog, 1961-70,
         p.436.
       Elio Micheli is credited with the costumes of "The Hills Run Red"
       and was the wardrobe assistant of "The Mystery of Thug Island."

2013   "Micheline."   American Film Institute Catalog, 1961-70, p.437.
       Micheline is credited with the costumes of "How to Succeed in
       Business Without Really Trying."

2014   "Micheline & Jacqueline."   American Film Institute Catalog,
         1961-70, p.437.
       Micheline & Jacqueline were the costume designers of "Good
       Neighbor Sam."

2015   "Michelson, Ed."   American Film Institute Catalog, 1961-70,
         p.437.
       Ed Michelson is credited with the costumes of "Adios Gringo."

2016   "Midnitems."   Midnight/Globe, 25 (3): 9, August 15, 1978.

Victor Mature asked and was allowed to keep his evening clothes and shoes from "Firepower"; he wanted them to wear to funerals.

2017 "Midwinter, Dulcie." American Film Institute Catalog, 1961-
          70, p.437.
Dulcie Midwinter is credited with the wardrobe of "The Snake Woman," "Sandy, the Reluctant Nature Girl," "The Vulture," and "Mumsy, Nanny, Sonny and Girly," with additional wardrobe mistress/supervisor credits.

2018 "Milady Dresses for Fall." Hollywood, 26 (9): 39-40, Sep-
          tember 1937.
Rochelle Hudson models three costumes by Herschel from "Born Reckless."

2019 "Milady's Wardrobe." Silver Screen, 6 (12): 48-9, October
          1936.
Hollywood has taken over Paris's influence on fashion, and film costumes are becoming more simplified, which makes it easier for fans to copy them.

2020 Milinaire, Caterine, and Carol Troy. Cheap Chic. New
          York: Harmony, 1975.
Diana Vreeland notes that Joan Crawford's red buglebead gown in "The Bride Wore Red" was shaded around the hip area by shaded beads to make her look slimmer and more seductive, and that such work was proof that the workmanship of Hollywood film costumes was at least equal to that of Paris couture. Many chapters deal with persons whom the authors feel have good fashion sense, including Carrie White, a Beverly Hills beauty salon manager who rented out some of her clothing from 1968 for "Shampoo." Jean-Paul Goude's tailor, Maurice Breslave, made the suits for "Borsalino"; Goude thinks that Tony Perkins lost his style after he started making European films and tried to look French.

2021 _____, and _____. Cheap Chic Update. New York:
          Harmony, 1978.

2022 "Miller, Burton." American Film Institute Catalog, 1961-70,
          p.439.
Burton Miller is credited with the costumes of "Kitten with a Whip," "Sullivan's Empire," "Valley of Mystery," "Counterpoint," and "Company of Killers."

2023 Miller, Lyn. "Fashions from the New Films." Hollywood,
          24 (7): 37, 41, 50-1, July 1935.
Brief mention of costumes worn by Greta Garbo in "Anna Karenina" and Joan Crawford in "No More Ladies," by Adrian; Katharine Hepburn in "Break of Hearts," by Bernard Newman; Loretta Young in "The Crusades," by Travis Banton; Binnie Barnes in "Diamond Jim," by Vera West; Grace Moore in "Love Me Forever," by Kalloch; Mae Clarke in "The Daring Young Man";

Ginger Rogers in "Star of Midnight"; Ketti Gallian in "Under the Pampas Moon"; Dolores Del Rio in a bathing suit from "In Caliente"; Bette Davis in "Girl from Tenth Avenue"; and Sally Eilers in "Alias Mary Dow," one of which she models.   Brief mention also of a costume worn by Shirley Temple in "Our Little Girl," and of "The Crusades" creating a trend for capes fastened at the shoulder with a large clasp.

2024 _____. "You Wear What They Tell You." Movie Classic, 9 (1): 40-1, 78, September 1935.
"You wear what a handful of men in Hollywood tell you to wear, and it is of no use to argue." Discussion of the fashion influence of costumes worn by Kay Francis in "One-Way Passage" and Dolores Del Rio in an unnamed film, by Orry-Kelly; Joan Crawford in "Letty Lynton" and Greta Garbo in "Mata Hari" and "Anna Karenina," by Adrian; Dixie Lee in "Redheads on Parade" and Janet Gaynor in "Servants' Entrance," by Rene Hubert; Carole Lombard in "No Man of Her Own"; and Katharine Hepburn in "Christopher Strong," by Howard Greer.   Also discussed are costumes worn in "The Crusades," and in "Little Women" and "Cimarron," by Walter Plunkett, and hats worn by Mae West in "She Done Him Wrong," by Travis Banton (Edith Head received credit for this film; Banton had been out of town, though he may have designed the hats).

2025 "Miller, Nolan." American Film Institute Catalog, 1961-70, p.439.
Nolan Miller was the costume designer of "Harlow" (the version starring Carol Lynley in the title role, released May 14, 1965, as distinguished from the version starring Carroll Baker, released June 23, 1965, with Edith Head as costume supervisor) and "How to Commit Marriage."

2026 "Millings & Son, Dougie." American Film Institute Catalog, 1961-70, p.440.
Dougie Millings & Son is credited with the wardrobe for the Beatles in "A Hard Day's Night."

2027 "Millstein, Dan." American Film Institute Catalog, 1961-70, p.441.
Dan Millstein is credited with Shirley Eaton's wardrobe in "The Girl Hunters."

2028 Minnelli, Vincente, with Hector Arce. I Remember It Well. Garden City, N.Y.: Doubleday, 1974.
Vincente Minnelli once worked as a theatrical costume designer for Paramount Theatre because he could not get into the set designers union.   He discusses selecting the costumes for the Halloween sequence in "Meet Me in St. Louis"; Irene Sharaff's costumes for "The Ziegfeld Follies"; Robert Mitchum's clothes in "Undercurrent"; Karinska's costumes for "The Pirate," with Minnelli's own costume designs for Gene Kelly and Judy Garland; his own costume design for Garland in "Summer Stock"; Cecil

Beaton's costumes for "Gigi" and for Barbra Streisand in "On a Clear Day You Can See Forever"; with brief mention of Walter Plunkett's costumes for Jennifer Jones in "Madame Bovary." Although he did not receive credit, Minnelli directed the fashion-show sequence of "Lovely to Look At," which featured over 40 costumes by Adrian at a cost of $100,000; the chorus costumes were designed by Tony Duquette. In "The Cat People" director Val Lewton decided not to use studio "cat" costumes but rather to suggest the cats' presence through imagination. Also included are many photos of Minnelli's daughter, Liza Minnelli, as a child in many film costumes copied for her by Irene and Adrian, with specific film titles listed.

2029 "Mintz, Sid." American Film Institute Catalog, 1961-70, p. 442.
Sid Mintz is credited with the wardrobe of "Seven Days in May."

2030 "Mir, David." American Film Institute Catalog, 1921-30, p.1266.
David Mir is credited with the costumes of "The Only Thing."

2031 "Miss Breamer Uses Costumes Rather Than Cosmetics to Accentuate Her Loveliness." Screen News, 3 (19): 6, May 10, 1924.
Sylvia Breamer models a costume from "The Woman on the Jury."

2032 "Miss Rambova, 69, Film Figure, Dead." New York Times, June 8, 1966, p.47.
Natacha Rambova died at the age of 69 from dietary complications. Natacha Rambova was the stage name used by Winifred Shaunessy, who was later adopted by stepfather Richard Hudnut; her name was changed to Winifred Hudnut. Her varied career centered on her writing newspaper columns after her film career ended. Includes comments by Rambova concerning her quarrel with Jetta Goudal over Goudal's wardrobe for "A Sainted Devil."

2033 "Mitchell, Alexandria." American Film Institute Catalog, 1961-70, p.444.
Alexandria Mitchell is credited with the costumes of "Scare Their Pants Off."

2034 "Mitchell, Don." American Film Institute Catalog, 1961-70, p.444.
Don Mitchell is credited with the wardrobe of "The Shepherd of the Hills."

2035 "Mitchell Leisen, Director, Dies; 'To Each His Own' Among Films." New York Times, November 1, 1972, p.48.
Mitchell Leisen died at the age of 74 of undisclosed causes. He began his film career as a set and costume designer with Cecil B. De Mille. He was a director for most of the remainder of his career.

2036   "Mitzou of Madrid. "   American Film Institute Catalog, 1961-
          70, p.445.
Mitzou of Madrid designed the original costumes and dresses worn
by Martha Hyer in "Pyro. "

2037   Mix, Paul E.   The Life and Legend of Tom Mix.   South
          Brunswick, N. J.: Barnes, 1972.
Tom Mix's fancy clothes, hand-carved boots (of which he had a
room full), and Stetson hats were an important part of his show-
manship, and were not intended to represent typical cowboy attire.
Many cowboy actors dressed like Mix, and one actor, Buck Jones,
imitated cowboy actor William S. Hart's manner of dress.   After
Mix's death in 1940 his western regalia changed hands, until it
was bought by a group that founded the Tom Mix Museum, in
Dewey, Oklahoma, in 1968.

2038   "Modas de Cinelandia. "   Cinelandia, 12 (1): 34-7, January
          1938.
Kay Francis models a gown from "La Primera Dama" (English
title "The First Lady).   Spanish text.

2039   "Modas de Cinelandia. "   Cinelandia, 14 (8): 28-30, August
          1940.
Virginia Bruce models a wedding gown from "Angeles de la Tierra"
("Angels Wash Their Faces").

2040   "Modas de Cinelandia. "   Cinelandia, 14 (12): 34-5, 39, 50,
          December 1940.
Rosalind Russell models four costumes by Irene from "Hired
Wife, " which are discussed at length.   Spanish text.

2041   "Modas de Cinelandia. "   Cinelandia, 15 (3): 33-5, March 1941.
Ginger Rogers models one costume from "Kitty Foyle, " and Kay
Francis models five costumes, three from "Play Girl, " one of
which is credited to Bernard Newman and another to I. Magnin,
though Newman is also referred to as "Bernard Newman de la
casa I. Magnin. "   Spanish text.

2042   "Modas de Cinelandia. "   Cinelandia, 18 (5): 24-5, May 1944.
Four costumes each are modeled by Jane Wyman from "Make
Your Own Bed, " by Milo Anderson, and Ann Sheridan from her
latest film.   Spanish text.

2043   "Modas de Cinelandia, " by Carmen.   Cinelandia, 7 (14):
          18-21, 57, April 1933.
Joan Crawford models a gown from "Dancing Lady, " which is
credited to Schiaparelli (this credit is baffling since Adrian received credit for the film).   A gown worn by Pat Paterson in
"Bottoms Up" is described.   Spanish text.

2044   "Modas de Hollywood. "   Cinelandia, 5 (10): 53-6, October
          1931.
One costume each is modeled by Mae Murray from "Bachelor

Apartments" and Marion Davies from "Five and Ten." Spanish text.

2045 "A Modern Role for Robin Hood." Screen News, 1 (11): 18,
        May 6, 1922.
A fire in the costume department of the Pickford-Fairbanks Studio
probably started from spontaneous combustion of the silk "Robin
Hood" costumes in the hot weather. Of the 2,800 period costumes
for the film, valued at $250,000, there was about $800 worth of
damage.

2046 "The Modes of Lilyan Tashman Are Always Right in Style."
        Motion Picture, 42 (4): 64-5, November 1931.
Lilyan Tashman models 12 garments from her on- and off-screen
wardrobe, without film titles. (Like this nonspecific article, many
articles were written about Tashman, who was usually billed as
the best-dressed woman of Hollywood.)

2047 "Modes of the Movies." Screen News, 3 (4): 14, January 26,
        1924.
Discussion of gowns worn by Anna Q. Nilsson in "Painted People,"
Maude George in "Torment," and Barbara La Marr in "Eternal
City."

2048 "Modesty in Dress Will Return." Screen News, 3 (19): 6,
        May 10, 1924.
Walter J. Israel spent $85,000 on the sixteenth-century costumes
he designed for "The Sea Hawk."

2049 Moews, Daniel. Keaton; The Silent Features Close Up.
        Berkeley: University of California Press, 1977.
Buster Keaton often used clothing and occupational uniforms to
give a professional image to the wearer, and as a contrast to
the wearer's actual intelligence. Includes references to costumes
worn by Keaton and other cast members in "Sherlock Junior,"
"The Navigator," "Battling Butler," "The General," "College,"
and "Steamboat Bill Junior."

2050 Monde, Nance. "A Fitting Finish or, a Day with the Ward-
        robe Mistress." Motion Picture, 16 (7): 58-9, August
        1918.
Jane Lewis, head of Vitagraph's wardrobe department, has a
great volume of costumes so that extras need not spend their
meager salaries on expensive wardrobes--this, in contrast to
other studios which hire extras because of their clothes.

2051 Montanye, Lillian. "Clothes May Not Make the Man, But--."
        Motion Picture, 18 (9): 60-1, 122, October 1919.
Betty Blythe designs all of her film costumes to fit the scene and
the people with whom she appears, which she discusses. She
models a gown from "Undercurrents."

2052 _____. "The Dollar Princess: Emmy Wehlen Dresses the
        Part." Motion Picture, 17 (2): 61-2, 103, March 1919.

Includes descriptions of some of Emmy Wehlen's film costumes,
without film titles. Her clothes must be of the finest fabrics
since they are made over for other clothes or given to charity
after a film's completion.

2053   "Montgomery, Elizabeth." Biographical Encyclopaedia and
          Who's Who of the American Theatre. 1966, p.690.
Montgomery's credits are listed collectively with those found under
Motley; she was a cofounder of the firm.

2054   "Mongtomery, Elizabeth." Who's Who in the Theatre. 16th
          ed., 1977, p.949.

2055   Mook, Samuel Richard. "He Has to Have 40 Suits." Picture
          Play, 47 (6): 38-9, 71, February 1938.
Studios seldom provide clothing for actors, who are expected to
be dressed appropriately for their films by their own tailors.
Ray Milland owns 40 suits and rotates them so that the audience
does not recognize them.

2056   Moore, Colleen. "Flapper Frills Cast Aside by We Modern
          Girls." Screen News, 4 (51): 14, December 26, 1925.
Discussion of current fashions, with comments by Cora McGeachy,
First National designer, who designed the Fashion Review sequence
costumes for Colleen Moore and others in "Irene," and by Alphretta Hoffman, also a First National designer.

2057   _____. Silent Star. Garden City, N.Y.: Doubleday, 1968.
Colleen Moore was given her first film contract because of her
uncle's having helped D.W. Griffith; and, similarly, wardrobe
head Mrs. Harris was rewarded for her costume expertise with
a contract for her daughter Mildred. Silent western films often
had unrealistic plots, but the cowboys and Indians were real, with
the Indians wearing headdresses and costumes handed down from
their ancestors. Cowboy and actor Tom Mix wore the best, and
most expensive, clothes made by Porter's in Prescott, Arizona.
Sophie Wachner designed all the Goldwyn film costumes, including
a $500 beaded gown worn by Moore in "Look Your Best"; she also
wore a bathing suit in the film made with gelatin sequins, which
melted, causing the scene to be cut out. She changed her image
in the first flapper film, "Flaming Youth," the costumes of which
were copied everywhere. Hollywood's flapper clothes were made
by later film designer Irene. Howard Greer was the first film
designer to design nontheatrical-looking costumes. Moore later
signed a contract with First National that allowed her to keep all
of her film costumes. Illustrated with costume stills from many
films.

2058   _____. "The Younger Generation." Screen News, 3 (1):
          31, January 5, 1924.
Colleen Moore discusses her costumes from "Flaming Youth," one
of which she models; with two sketches of additional costumes.

2059   Moore, Deedee. "Inspiration and Information: The Costume
           Institute." <u>Metropolitan Museum of Art Bulletin</u>, 30 (1):
           2-10, August/September 1971.
Edith Head, Patricia Zipprodt, and Donald Brooks, among others,
discuss why the Metropolitan Museum of Art's Costume Institute
is such an important research source. Head states that there is
little research material in Los Angeles, and today's historical-
film costumes must be authentic.

2060   "Moore, Doris Langley." <u>American Film Institute Catalog,</u>
           <u>1961-70</u>, p. 450.
Doris Langley Moore was the costume designer of "Freud."

2061   "Moore, Doris Langley." <u>Contemporary Authors.</u> Detroit:
           Gale, 1967, p. 678-9.
Doris Langley Moore, clothing authority, film- and theatrical-
costume designer, and author, founded the Museum of Costume in
Bath, England.

2062   "Moore, Mrs. D[oris] Langley." <u>Who's Who.</u> 125th ed.,
           1973, p. 2275.
Moore, costume authority and period-film costume designer, has
written many fiction and nonfiction books, 20 of which are listed.

2063   "Moore, John." <u>American Film Institute Catalog, 1961-70</u>,
           p. 450.
John Moore was the costume designer of "El Cid" and "55 Days
at Peking."

2064   "Moreau, Jacqueline." <u>American Film Institute Catalog, 1961-</u>
           <u>70</u>, p. 451.
Jacqueline Moreau is credited with the costumes of "The Umbrellas
of Cherbourg," "Up to His Ears," "The Young Girls of Rochefort," and "The Milky Way" and the wardrobe supervision of
"Diary of a Chambermaid."

2065   Morella, Joe, and Edward Z. Epstein. <u>Gable & Lombard &</u>
           <u>Powell & Harlow.</u> New York: Dell, 1975.
Typical remarks about costars of Clark Gable--Jean Harlow,
Carole Lombard, and Norma Shearer not wearing lingerie on and/
or off screen to charge up film or photographic sessions. Gable
was reportedly worried about the effect his "prissy" period costumes of "Mutiny on the Bounty" would have on his image. He
supervised his wardrobe in all of his films, but was apathetic
over his "Gone with the Wind" costumes, in part because he was
told he could have any tailor, except his usual one, Eddie Schmidt.
Producer David O. Selznick corrected the situation when
he learned of it. Carole Lombard's favorite designer, after
leaving Paramount, was Irene, who considered Lombard the most
exciting woman she had ever designed for.

2066   _____, and _____. <u>The "It" Girl: The Incredible Story</u>

of Clara Bow. New York: Dell, 1976.
In a beauty contest Clara Bow won a guaranteed part in a film;
she spent $40 of her $50 salary on the costumes, but her part
was cut out of "Beyond the Rainbow." One unnamed designer
feels that Bow's frequent wearing of lingerie in her films influenced fashion in the 1920s to the extent that Lana Turner did in
the 1940s with sweaters, and Brigitte Bardot did in the 1950s and
1960s with the bikini. Since her roles were usually not high-
fashion, she was passed on from Travis Banton to Edith Head,
Banton's assistant. Bow refused to dress according to the "flat
look" and wore belts with everything, in the bust-less and waist-
less 1920s.

2067 "Morelli, Mirella." American Film Institute Catalog, 1961-
        70, p.452.
Mirella Morelli is credited with the costumes of "The Railroad
Man."

2068 "Moreno, Catalina." American Film Institute Catalog, 1961-70,
        p.452.
Catalina Moreno is credited with the wardrobe of "Murieta."

2069 "Morgan, Ann." American Film Institute Catalog, 1921-30,
        p.1273.
Ann Morgan is credited with the wardrobe of "The Trespasser."

2070 "Morgan, Terence, II." American Film Institute Catalog,
        1961-70, p.452.
Terence Morgan II was the costume designer of "Sword of Lancelot."

2071 "Morley, Ruth." American Film Institute Catalog, 1961-70,
        p.453.
Ruth Morley was the costume designer of "The Hustler," "Lilith,"
"A Thousand Clowns," "The Brotherhood," and "Diary of a Mad
Housewife" and is credited with the costumes of "The Young
Doctors," "The Connection," and "The Miracle Worker."

2072 Morley, Sheridan. Marlene Dietrich. New York: McGraw-
        Hill, 1976.
Includes comments by Louise Brooks on Marlene Dietrich's
"fantastic" costumes in "I Kiss Your Hand, Madame" and Josef
von Sternberg's comments on Dietrich's male costumes in "Morocco" (see von Sternberg, Josef. Fun in a Chinese Laundry).
After "Shanghai Express" most films would feature her equally
in uniforms and evening gowns.

2073 "Morn to Midnight." Movie Play, 3 (3): 18-9, September
        1948.
Doris Day models three costumes by Milo Anderson from "Romance
on the High Seas" and Esther Williams three costumes by Irene
either from or adapted from "On an Island with You."

2074   "Morning, Noon or Night--the Circular Skirt." Screen News,
          3 (10): 19, March 8, 1924.
Virginia Brown Faire has bought circular skirts for her upcoming
films.

2075   Morrin, Frances. "Designs for Dorothy." Movies, 5 (1): 42-
          3, 65, July 1941.
Discussion of costumes worn by Dorothy Lamour in "Caught in the
Draft," three of which she models, by Edith Head; and worn by
Rosalind Russell in "The Uniform," by Adrian.

2076   Morris, Bernadine. "A Lasting Hollywood Alliance." New
          York Times, October 17, 1967, p. 50.
Irene Dunne discusses her long-held fondness for the film and
nonfilm fashions of Jean Louis, who came from France and started
designing for Hattie Carnegie in 1935.   In 1938 he began his 17-
year career with Columbia, left to start his own business, and in
1967 was designing for about four films per year.   Dunne notes
that he designed her costumes for "The Awful Truth" and "Theodora Goes Wild" (but the designers credited, respectively, were
Kalloch and Bernard Newman, and Jean Louis is credited in other
sources as having begun designing for Columbia in 1944).

2077   _____. " 'Heaven' in the 40's: A Man-Tailored Suit." New
          York Times, March 26, 1971, p. 34.
Rosalind Russell feels that the clothes from the 1940s, which she
helped popularize, were horrible, particularly the padded-shouldered
suits, which she used to buy from Irene for her films "by the
carload."   At the time she felt they were her idea of heaven.
Designer Valentino had recently admitted that his collection was
inspired by films from this era.

2078   _____. "Hollywood Casts Fashion in a Featured Role."
          New York Times, August 26, 1967, p. 16.
Hollywood hopes to increase its box-office receipts by returning
to trend-setting fashions and is encouraging Seventh Avenue designers and manufacturers to copy the costumes for additional
publicity.   Discussion of fashions copied from "Tony Rome," with
one photo of Gena Rowlands; "Far from the Madding Crowd," with
one photo of Julie Christie; and "Valley of the Dolls," with one
photo of Barbara Parkins, designed by Bill Travilla, who designed
130 costumes for the film.   Film designers are departing from an
old tradition by designing costumes that reflect current fashion
trends, as with the especially short skirts worn in "The Bobo" and
"Inspector Clouseau."

2079   _____. "Norell," in American Fashion. New York:
          Quadrangle/New York Times, 1975, p. 317-408.
Norman Norell's first salaried job as a costume designer came
at age 22, when he designed for Gloria Swanson in "Zaza" and
for Rudolph Valentino in "A Sainted Devil"; but the studio soon
shut down.   Notes also that Hollywood was Paris's chief rival in

its control of world fashion in the 1940s, and though not related
to Norell's fashions, it is noted that Ginger Rogers's white-collared
dress in "Kitty Foyle" widely influenced fashion but "was a far
cry from originality. "

2080 _____. "Norman Norell, Designer, Dies; Made 7th Avenue
         the Rival of Paris. " New York Times, October 26, 1972,
         p. 1, 46.
Norman Norell died at the age of 72 following a stroke.

2081 _____. "The Pleasure of Being Among Friends. " New
         York Times, March 15, 1973, p. 48.
22 persons and companies purchased franchising rights for clothing
and other items from "Lost Horizon. " Jean Louis, the film's costume designer, was licensed and adapted 12 of the film's costumes
for his ready-to-wear collection, especially the caftans. Jewelry
inspired from the film was marketed by Pierre Cardin, and lounge-
wear by Periphery.

2082 _____. "Shirley MacLaine, Concerned with Causes and
         Fashion Also. " New York Times, January 15, 1971, p. 17.
Shirley MacLaine wore about 175 costumes in "What a Way to
Go"; in "The Possession of Joel Delaney" she played the part of
a woman with a small budget but who spent all she could on cloth-
ing, which included her wearing some evening gowns by George
Stavropoulos and a mink cape from Frank Somper.

2083 _____. "Stuff of Tinsel Dreams: Silver Screen Costumes. "
         New York Times, November 22, 1974, p. 24.
Discussion of the opening night of the "Romantic and Glamorous
Hollywood Design" exhibit, organized by Diana Vreeland, whose
favorite film designers are Adrian and Travis Banton. Mentions
some of the costumes included in the exhibit.

2084 "Morris, Hope. " American Film Institute Catalog, 1961-70,
         p. 454.
Hope Morris is credited with the formal wear worn by Donna
Kerness in "Unstrap Me. "

2085 "Morris, Jane. " American Film Institute Catalog, 1961-70,
         p. 454.
Jane Morris is credited with the wardrobe of "Red Runs the River. "

2086 "Morroni, Renata. " American Film Institute Catalog, 1961-70,
         p. 455.
Renata Morroni is credited with the costumes of "Chronicle of
Anna Magdalena Bach. "

2087 "Morse, Tiger. " American Film Institute Catalog, 1961-70, p.
         455.
Tiger Morse is credited with the costumes of "The Secret Life of
Hernando Cortez. "

2088 "Moser, Earl. " American Film Institute Catalog, 1921-30,
         p. 1275.

Earl Moser was the master of wardrobe for "The Big Trail."

2089   "Moss, Sandy."   American Film Institute Catalog, 1961-70,
          p. 456.
Sandy Moss is credited with the costumes of "Goodbye Gemini"
and was the fashion coordinator of "Here We Go 'Round the Mulberry Bush," and the costume adviser of "The Touchables."

2090   "Mostoller, Ramse."   American Film Institute Catalog, 1961-
          70, p. 456.
Ramse Mostoller was the wardrobe designer of "House of Dark
Shadows" and the costume director of "Santa Claus Conquers the
Martians."

2091   "The Motion Picture Costumers--1929-50."   The Costumer,
          June 1950, p. 2, 12.
Discussion of the founding of the Motion Picture Costumer union
in 1929, the diverse background of its members, the variety of
craftsmen, and the typical duties of the costumer.   Notes that the
Tin Man costume in "The Wizard of Oz" was troublesome for
studio specialists in the property department, metal experts, and
makers of armor, but the problem was solved by Sam Winters
of the studio's tailor shop, by making the costume of metallic
cloth with buckram to stiffen it.

2092   "The Motion Picture Costumers Present a Special Award to
          George Stevens."   Motion Picture Costumers, 1962, n. p.
Clinton Sandeen, the costume supervisor for "The Greatest Story
Ever Told," is closely cooperating with Western Costume Company, who will be making 2, 000 new costumes for the film, including those needed for the over 150 male principals.   With a
staff of over 35 costumers Sandeen works closely with director
George Stevens in conferences.

2093/4 Motley.   Designing and Making Stage Costumes.   New York:
          Watson-Guptill, 1964, 1974.
Motley, consisting of designers Sophie Devine, Margaret Harris,
and Elizabeth Montgomery, discusses adapting an authentic costume for Katharine Hepburn in "Long Day's Journey into Night."
Hepburn had tried on a period costume at an unnamed New York
museum, and since Motley was pressed for time, they copied
the fabric and style, placing the seams in the same exact places.

2095   "Motley."   American Film Institute Catalog, 1961-70, p. 456.
Motley was the costume designer of "The Innocents" and is cred-
ited with the costumes of "Long Day's Journey into Night," "The
Pumpkin Eater," "The Spy Who Came in from the Cold," and
"A Study in Terror."

2096   "Motley."   Who's Who in the Theatre.   16th ed. , 1977, p.
          959-60.
This costume-design firm was originated by Audrey Sophia Devine, Margaret F. Harris, and Elizabeth Montgomery.   Only
theatrical-design credits are listed.

2097 "Mott, Caroline." <u>American Film Institute Catalog, 1961-70,</u>
        p.456.
Caroline Mott is credited with the costumes of "Just Like a Woman"
and "All Neat in Black Stockings" and the wardrobe of "The Shuttered Room."

2098 Mount, Laura. "Designs on Hollywood." <u>Collier's,</u> 87 (14):
        21, 60-1, April 4, 1931.
Coco Chanel, hired by Sam Goldwyn to visit Hollywood periodically
and send designs from Paris, may go the way of Erté and Gilbert
Clarke, both of whom quit when Lillian Gish and Greta Garbo,
respectively, refused to wear their costumes. Chanel will leave
several of her fitters in Hollywood for permanent employment and
will reorganize the studio dressmaking department. As one of
the more demanding stars Chanel will design for, Gloria Swanson
wore about 15 gowns in "What a Widow," which she bought from
a leading fashion salon in New York; though she changed the simple
costumes drastically to suit herself. Brief mention of Carolyn
Putnam being the designer for Paramount's Long Island studio.
Elsa Maxwell asked Paramount producer Walter Wanger if she
should hire Jean Patou, Parisian couturier, when she heard that
Goldwyn had hired Chanel; Wanger decided against it.

2099 "Movie Costumes Worth Millions." <u>Popular Mechanics,</u> 65
        (1): 82-4, 116A, January 1936.
Discussion of Western Costume Company, which houses thousands
of costumes, all catalogued and ready to be used at any time.
Discussion of how costumes are researched and aged; outfitting
large crowd scenes; and how synthetic chain mail for armor is
made.

2100 "Movie Designer to Do Custom Work in Fall." <u>New York</u>
        <u>Times,</u> May 15, 1947, p.29.
Irene announced that she will begin custom designing in addition
to her duties as the chief costume designer of MGM. She re-
grets that, probably due to the war, she has not been designing
glamorous or exciting costumes.

2101 "Movie Mermaid." <u>Life,</u> 24 (6): 91-2, 94, February 9, 1948.
For Ann Blyth in "Mr. Peabody and the Mermaid" a mermaid
tail was created by Bud Westmore, who discusses how the tail
was made. It cost $18,000 and took 14 weeks to make. Stills
illustrate how the tail was made, and show Blyth wearing the
completed tail.

2102 "Movie Modes." <u>Screen News,</u> 1 (2): 30, March 4, 1922.
Discussion of costumes worn by Katherine MacDonald in "Do-
mestic Relations," May Collins in "Red Hot Romance," and Anita
Stewart in "The Woman He Married."

2103 "Movie Modes." <u>Screen News,</u> 1 (20): 8, 20, July 1, 1922.
Discussion of costumes worn by Ora Carew in "Smudge," Gertrude Astor in "Heroes and Husbands," Dorothy Phillips in

"Hurricane's Gal," and Agatha Bemis in a Katherine MacDonald film, not named (Agatha Bemis was a character played by Mona Kingsley in "Heroes and Husbands." This same error was repeated in the following article).

2104 "Movie Modes." Screen News, 1 (30): 18, September 16, 1922.
Discussion of costumes worn by Ora Carew in "Smudge," Dorothy Phillips in "Hurricane's Gal," and Agatha Bemis in a Katherine MacDonald film (see previous entry).

2105 "Movie Show Window." Movie Show, 4 (2): 56-7, October 1945.
Includes two sketches of costumes worn by Lucille Bremer in "Yolanda and the Thief" and one costume each worn by Esther Williams in "Early to Wed" and Joan Blondell and Greer Garson in "Big Shore Leave"; all by Irene.

2106 "Movie Show Window." Movie Show, 4 (7): 58-9, March 1946.
Dorothy Lamour models five costumes and one hat from "Masquerade in Mexico," by Edith Head.

2107 "Movie Show Window." Movie Show, 4 (10): 64-5, June 1946.
Barbara Stanwyck models six costumes by Edith Head from "The Bride Wore Boots."

2108 "Movie Show Window." Movie Show, 4 (12): 65-4, August 1946.
Sylvia Sidney models two hats by Florell and five costumes by Michael Woulfe from "Mr. Ace and the Queen."

2109 "Movie Show Window." Movie Show, 5 (2): 46-7, October 1946.
Lucille Ball models six costumes by Travis Banton from "Lover Come Back."

2110 "Movie Show Window." Movie Show, 5 (3): 62-3, November 1946.
Three costumes each are modeled by Esther Williams from "Fiesta" and Ilona Massey from "Holiday in Mexico"; both films by Irene.

2111 "Movie Show Window." Movie Show, 5 (5): 52-3, January 1947.
Paulette Goddard models a costume from "Suddenly It's Spring."

2112 "Movie Show Window." Movie Show, 5 (6): 56-7, February 1947.
Ella Raines models six costumes by Yvonne Wood from "White Tie and Tails."

2113 "Movie Show Window." Movie Show, 5 (7): 64-5, March 1947.
Eve Arden models six costumes by Irene from "The Arnelo Affair."

2114 "Movie Show Window." Movie Show, 5 (8): 58-9, April 1947.
Alexis Smith models a costume by Milo Anderson from "Stallion
Road," and Hedy Lamarr models a beret from "Dishonored Lady."

2115 "Movie Test." Modern Screen, 15 (1): 58-9, June 1937.
Two stills show Joan Bennett being fitted in a gown from "Vogues
of 1938."

2116 "Movies as Style Guide." New York Times, July 26, 1935,
       p. 33.
While speaking to the New York Fashion Group's press section
Adrian said that film costumes are not as trend-setting as they
could be because of the time it takes to release a film. He suggested that his costumes for Greta Garbo in "Anna Karenina"
would influence spring fashions.

2117 "Movietown's Fashion Parade." Movie Mirror, 5 (5): 48-50,
       85-6, April 1934.
Discussion of costumes worn by Norma Shearer in "Lady Mary's
Lover" ("Riptide"), by Adrian; a chorus girl's costume in "Scan-
dals"; and costumes Travis Banton adapted for Carole Lombard
from her wardrobe for "Bolero," three of which she models.
Barbara Stanwyck models a costume from "Gambling Lady."

2118 "'Mr. Blackwell.'" American Film Institute Catalog, 1961-70,
       p. 457.
"Mr. Blackwell" was the wardrobe designer for Jayne Mansfield
in "Promises! Promises!"

2119 "Mr. Mike." American Film Institute Catalog, 1961-70, p.
       457.
Mr. Mike is credited with the costumes of "The Curse of Her
Flesh."

2120 "Mugge, Vera." American Film Institute Catalog, 1961-70,
       p. 457.
Vera Mugge is credited with the costumes of "The Terror of Dr.
Mabuse" and "Frozen Alive" and the wardrobe of "Fanny Hill:
Memoirs of a Woman of Pleasure."

2121 "Muir, Jean." American Film Institute Catalog, 1961-70, p.
       457.
Jean Muir was the clothes designer for Eleanor Bron in "Bedazzled."

2122 Mullen, Sarah McLean. "Following the Films; Costume Pic-
       tures." Scholastic, 26 (7): 29, March 16, 1935.
Historical films, according to the author, are often called "costume pictures" so that the costumes can be less authentic, and
adapted so that the audience will not find them ridiculous. Authentic fabrics are often no longer available or are discarded for
more photogenic ones; as with "Cleopatra," though there was no
loss of beauty.

2123 "Muller, N." American Film Institute Catalog, 1961-70, p.
      458.
N. Muller is credited with the costumes of "Dimka."

2124 Mullett, Mary B. "Dressing the Movie Stars." Woman's
      Home Companion, 53 (8): 13-4, August 1926.
Designer H.M.K. Smith discusses average costume costs, including costumes worn in "society pictures." The wardrobe of "Monsieur Beaucaire" came to $60,000, including about 750 costumes
and specially made accessories, including shoes; also, $85,000
worth of antique jewelry was rented. The costumes of "Madame
Sans Gêne" cost about $125,000, and all of the jewelry was copied
from authentic pieces and made in Paris. Famous Players stocks
about $10,000 worth of paste jewelry. Includes a list, with costs,
of costumes worn by Gloria Swanson in "Her Love Story," including the $60,000 wedding ensemble. Discussion of costumes
worn by Bebe Daniels and Maud Turner Gordon in "The Palm
Beach Girl" and transparent celluloid slippers worn by Betty
Bronson in "A Kiss for Cinderella"; with brief mention of costumes for "Too Many Kisses." Billie Burke once withdrew from
a film because the director insisted that she wear costumes in a
color she hated. Gloria Swanson brought Rene Hubert over from
Paris to be her designer. Smith allows only a few actresses to
select their own costumes, for instance Alice Joyce, though he
accompanies her to her couturière, Frances (Madame Frances?);
he usually chooses all of the cast's costumes.

2125 Mulvey, Kate. "Hollywood." Woman's Home Companion, 73
      (5): 10-1, May 1946.
One beaded gown worn by Rita Hayworth in "Gilda" was so tight
that two wardrobe persons had to help her into it after she had
eaten only concentrated food for several days.

2126 "Munden, Jesse." American Film Institute Catalog, 1961-70,
      p. 459.
Jesse Munden is credited with the wardrobe of "The Last Time I
Saw Archie" and "Munster, Go Home!," the men's wardrobe of
"Buckskin," and the costumes of "The Misfits."

2127 "Munson, Byron." American Film Institute Catalog, 1961-70,
      p. 459.
Byron Munson is credited with the wardrobe of "The Gambler
Wore a Gun" and "Look in Any Window."

2128 "Murata, Yoshiaki." American Film Institute Catalog, 1961-
      70, p. 459.
Yoshiaki Murata is credited with the wardrobe of "The Big Wave."

2129 "Murder, He Says." Motion Picture, 69 (5): 56, June 1945.
The cotton dress worn by Jean Heather in "Murder, He Says"
cost $1.95, but $200 was spent on labor and materials for aging
the dress--through bleaching, tearing, mending, aging in brick
dust, washing, and then repeating the processes.

2130 "Muriel Has Real Wardrobe." <u>Screen News,</u> 3 (26): 19, June
        28, 1924.
Discussion of three costumes worn by Muriel Frances Dana in
"The Husbands of Edith."

2131 "Murray, Gene." <u>American Film Institute Catalog, 1961-70,</u>
        p. 460.
Gene Murray is credited with the wardrobe of "For Singles Only"
and "Hang 'Em High."

2132 "Murray, Gordon." <u>American Film Institute Catalog, 1961-70,</u>
        p. 460.
Gordon Murray is credited with the wardrobe of "Twenty Plus
Two," "McHale's Navy," and " ... And Now Miguel."

2133 "My Favorite Dress." <u>Hollywood Pattern,</u> 5 (4): 14-5, De-
        cember 1937/January 1938.
One favorite costume each is modeled by Ann Sothern in "There
Goes My Heart"; Loretta Young in "Wife, Doctor, and Nurse";
Pat Patterson in "52nd Street"; Irene Dunne in "The Awful Truth"
and Grace Moore in "I'll Take Romance" (both by Robert Kalloch);
Alice Faye in "In Old Chicago"; Barbara Stanwyck in "Breakfast
for Two," by Edward Stevenson; and Joan Bennett, from an un-
named film.

2134 "Myers, Mickey." <u>American Film Institute Catalog, 1961-70,</u>
        p. 461.
Mickey Myers is credited with the wardrobe of "The Human Duplicators."

2135 "Myers, Ruth." <u>American Film Institute Catalog, 1961-70,</u> p.
        461.
Ruth Myers is credited with the costumes of "Smashing Time"
and "3 into 2 Won't Go," and the wardrobe of "Isadora" and was
the wardrobe mistress of "The Sailor from Gibraltar."

2136 "Myrtil, Odette." <u>Biographical Encyclopaedia and Who's Who
        of the American Theatre.</u> 1966, p. 703.
Biographical information on actress Odette Myrtil, who was a
fashion designer in Beverly Hills from 1930 to 1936; no mention
of her film-costume designs.

2137 "Nakajima, Hachiro." American Film Institute Catalog, 1961-
70, p. 463.
Hachiro Nakajima was the costume designer of "Buddha."

2138 Nangle, Eleanor. "Movie Fashion Chief Attempts a Triple
Play." Review of The Dress Doctor, by Edith Head.
Chicago Tribune, March 15, 1959, sec. 4, p. 3.
The author finds Edith Head's sketches and general clothes advice
excellent, the movie chit-chat somewhat laborious, and the autobiographical information interesting; The Dress Doctor's force,
however, has been dissipated by its organization of the above
three subjects.

2139 "Nasalli-Rocca, Annalisa." American Film Institute Catalog,
1961-70, p. 464.
Annalisa Nasalli-Rocca was the costume designer of "Jessica"; the
wardrobe coordinator of "Hornets' Nest"; the wardrobe supervisor
of "Francis of Assisi," "Boom!," "Viva Max!," and "A Walk
with Love and Death"; and is credited with the costumes of
"Romanoff and Juliet."

2140 "Nasalli-Rocca, Orietta." American Film Institute Catalog,
1961-70, p. 464.
Orietta Nasalli-Rocca was the costume designer of "The Shoes of
the Fisherman" and is credited with the costumes of "Romanoff
and Juliet" and the additional costumes for "Those Daring Young
Men in Their Jaunty Jalopies."

2141 Nash, Paul. "The Colour Film," in Footnotes to the Film,
edited by Charles Davy. New York: Oxford University
Press, 1937, p. 116-34.
Color director Natalie Kalmus discusses the color and lighting of
"Wings of the Morning," with brief mention of the gypsy costumes
worn in the prologue. Rene Hubert, the film's costume designer,
determines an actress's color scheme from her lips, which he
feels should be the dominant color so that the costume colors do
not steal the scenes.

2142 "Nastat 'Real,' Arlette." American Film Institute Catalog,
1961-70, p. 465.

Arlette Nastat (of Réal) is credited with Julie Christie's costumes in "Petulia."

2143   "Natacha Rambova Launches Her Own Film Productions."
            Screen News, 4 (21): 14, May 23, 1925.
Description of one costume by Adrian worn by Nita Naldi in "What Price Beauty."

2144   Nathan, Archie.   "Films," in Costumes by Nathan.   London:
            Newnes, 1960, p.158-75, passim.
The London firm known as "L. and H. Nathan," "Nathans of London," or "House of Nathan" began as a theatrical-costume company in 1790, but now furnishes mostly British and American films.   Their complete credits are not given, but are still numerous, ranging from silent films of D.W. Griffith to war propaganda films produced by Leslie Howard.   In addition to brief mention of many films, subjects discussed include the armor for "Helen of Troy," "Richard III," and "Saint Joan"; authentic tartan plaid fabric for "Rob Roy" and its remake by Walt Disney ("Rob Roy," 1954); and problems with costumes for Laurence Olivier in "Richard III" and those for "The Seekers," "The Prince and the Showgirl;" "Lust for Life," with Walter Plunkett insisting on authentic coats from 1875 for the actors; and "John Paul Jones," with costumes by Phyllis Dalton and uniforms by Don Hatswell.   Brief mention of designers Julie Harris, Roger and Margaret Furse, Beatrice Dawson, Emma Selby-Walker, Doris Zinkeisen, Tom Heslewood, and Elizabeth Haffenden.   Good, but few, sketches and stills.

2145   "Nathan, L. and H."   American Film Institute Catalog, 1961-
            70, p.465.
The firm of L. and H. Nathan is credited with the costumes of "Dr. Crippen."

2146   "Nathans of London."   American Film Institute Catalog, 1961-
            70, p.465.
Nathans of London is credited with the costumes of "Captain Sinbad."

2147   "Natili, Giovanna."   American Film Institute Catalog, 1961-
            70, p.465.
Giovanna Natili was the costume designer of "The Tartars" and is credited with the costumes of "David and Goliath."

2148   Naumburg, Nancy.   "'Juarez': The Life History of a Movie."
            Photoplay, 52 (5): 22-3, 93-5, May 1939.
Bette Davis wore 14 costumes designed by Orry-Kelly in "Juarez." All but one of the costumes were fairly simple, made with French fabric.   Each gown had a complete set of jewelry brought from either Europe or Mexico City, one set of which is described; the jewelry had already influenced fashion.   Davis didn't mind wearing authentic costumes, the colors of which reflected the character's mental breakdown.   One sketch and a wardrobe-test still are included.

2149 "Naumova, L." American Film Institute Catalog, 1961-70,
        p.465.
      L. Naumova is credited with the costumes of "The Letter That
      Was Never Sent."

2150 Naylor, Hazel Simpson. "A Chat with Madge Kennedy's Frills."
        Motion Picture, 15 (2): 74-5, March 1918.
      Several gowns worn by Madge Kennedy in "My Little Wife" are
      described, with stills. All of her gowns are made by Lucile.

2151 "Nazemi, Shai." American Film Institute Catalog, 1961-70,
        p.466.
      Shai Nazemi was the costume designer of "The Invincible Sex."

2152 Neagle, Anna, as told to Gladys Hall. "What I Know About
        You Fans." Motion Picture, 61 (3): 30-1, 88-90, April
        1941.
      Anna Neagle models her Alice Blue Gown from "Irene," with
      comments concerning how fans reacted to the gown when she was
      on a personal-appearance tour.

2153 "Nearly Every Young Man...." Screen News, 1 (44): 10,
        December 23, 1922, col. 1.
      Jack Holt had to wear a rented tuxedo two sizes too small in
      "The Tiger's Claw," for three days because the presser had
      burnt a hole in his own tuxedo's pants.

2154 "Negri, Sandro." American Film Institute Catalog, 1961-70,
        p.467.
      Sandro Negri is credited with the costumes of "The Magic World
      of Topo Gigio (The Italian Mouse)."

2155 "Negulesco, Dusty." American Film Institute Catalog, 1961-
        70, p.467.
      Dusty Negulesco was the costume designer of "Jessica."

2156 Nelson, Kay. "Gentlemen Prefer Simplicity." Silver Screen,
        18 (5): 46-7, 78-9, March 1948.
      Kay Nelson discusses designing for "Gentleman's Agreement," and
      the look she wanted for Celeste Holm, who models three costumes,
      and for Dorothy McGuire, who models four costumes. Her cos-
      tumes for Gene Tierney in "Leave Her to Heaven" prompted sev-
      eral hundred men to write in hoping to purchase some of the cos-
      tumes for their wives.

2157 _____. "Give a Thought to Color." Screenland, 53 (11):
        46-7, 68-9, September 1949.
      Kay Nelson discusses designing for Linda Darnell and Celeste
      Holm in "Everybody Does It," with mention of their color types
      and the color schemes used. Holm models seven costumes from
      the film.

2158 _____. "Kay Nelson's Fashion Flashes." Screenland, 53

(5): 46-7, 70-1, March 1949.
Kay Nelson discusses designing for Loretta Young in "Mother Was a Freshman," eight costumes from which Young models.

2159 _____. "Keep It Simple!" Silver Screen, 18 (12): 44-5,
        66-7, October 1948.
Kay Nelson, who once worked for Irene, dicusses her costumes for Ida Lupino in "Roadhouse," seven of which Lupino models. References are also made to her first assignment, and Joan Bennett's film debut, in "Bulldog Drummond," and to a suit worn by Gene Tierney in "Leave Her to Heaven."

2160 _____, as told to Bee Bangs. "Put the Accent on Color."
        Silver Screen, 17 (2): 58-9, 82-3, December 1946.
Kay Nelson has designed 30 costumes for Maureen O'Hara in "Home Stretch," four of which O'Hara models; with one original sketch. She also discusses how she selected the colors according to O'Hara's coloring.

2161 "Nelstedt, Björn." American Film Institute Catalog, 1961-70,
        p.468.
Björn Nelstedt is credited with the costumes of "My Sister, My Love."

2162 "Nelstedt, Eva-Lisa." American Film Institute Catalog, 1961-
        70, p.468.
Eva-Lisa Nelstedt is credited with the costumes of "Le Viol."

2163 Nemy, Enid. "Film Titles Starring in a Fashion Role." New
        York Times, February 3, 1966, p.27.
Old films still influence fashion, but current films reflect fashion rather than initiate it. Film tie-ins are big business for retailers, who publicize their clothing as being adapted from such a film as "Made in Paris," by Helen Rose. The films discussed, as to the extent of their fashion influence, are "Dr. Zhivago," "The Agony and the Ecstasy," "Sound of Music," "Viva Maria," and "Darling," with a $40,000 wardrobe for Julie Christie. Fashion designers Cosmo Sirchio, Scassi, Adolpho, and Oscar de la Renta join the discussion. Photos of Ann-Margret in "Made in Paris" and Geraldine Chaplin in "Dr. Zhivago" show how the retail copies, modeled alongside, show little resemblance.

2164 _____. "Mata Hari Lives Again--in 30 Designs by Irene
        Sharaff." New York Times, November 9, 1967, p.60.
Irene Sharaff's costumes for "The King and I" started trends in vibrant color schemes and popularized Thai silks.

2165 "Nesterovskaya, G." American Film Institute Catalog, 1961-
        70, p.468.
G. Nesterovskaya is credited with the costumes of "Mother and Daughter."

2166 "Neumann, Margarete." American Film Institute Catalog,

<u>1961-70</u>, p.469.
Margarete Neumann is credited with the wardrobe of "Escape from East Berlin" and "Heldinnen."

2167   "Never Give Up the Slip, Girls." <u>Screen News,</u> 3 (28): 31, July 21, 1924.
Jacqueline Logan refuses to wear the new tight-waisted dresses, preferring instead the currently popular, loose slip-dress.   In "Dynamite Smith" Logan wore a flannel shirtwaist and woolen skirt, which were pinned together for comfort under an old-fashioned leather belt, for the Alaskan sequences.

2168   "New Arbiter of Women's Movie Styles." <u>Literary Digest,</u> 105 (6): 23, May 10, 1930.
The emergence of sound films has restricted actresses in what they can wear.   Certain dress styles, accessories, and fabrics have been eliminated, including trains on dresses, long dresses, wedding veils, and silk fabrics--all of which actress Lilian Harvey learned the hard way.

2169   "New Career, Coiffure, Clothes for Colbert!" <u>Screenland,</u> 33 (3): 39, July 1936.
Claudette Colbert models one gown from "The New Divorce."

2170   "The New Films Show the Smart New Fashions." <u>New Movie,</u> 7 (6): 38-41, June 1933.
Discussion and/or illustrations of costumes worn by Miriam Hopkins in "The Story of Temple Drake," Carole Lombard in "Supernatural," Shirley Grey in "Terror Aboard," and Peggy Joyce in "International House," all by Travis Banton; Janet Gaynor in "Adorable," by William Lambert; Joan Crawford in "Today We Live," and Myrna Loy in "The Barbarian."

2171   "The New Fur Coats." <u>Screenland,</u> 16 (2): 48-9, December 1927.
June Marlowe models a pony and seal coat from "The Grip"; with a small still and description of Mary Philbin's fur coat from "Surrender."

2172   "New Gowns Worn in Current Photoplays." <u>Photoplay,</u> 17 (1): 76-7, December 1919.
Gowns are modeled by May Allison from "Fair and Warmer" and Bebe Daniels from "Everywoman."

2173   "The 'New Look' for Old Clothes." <u>Life,</u> 23 (11): 109-10, 112, September 15, 1947.
Edith Head discusses how she had about 1,450 studio garments made over into the New Look, with photographs of three dresses, before and after.

2174   "New Movie Fields Weighed by Board." <u>New York Times,</u> November 6, 1940, p.19.
At a meeting of the National Board of Review of Motion Pictures

Ilka Chase stated that the presentation of fashion in films has
been inadequate. Mark Starr of the International Ladies Garment
Workers Union stated that the entire garment industry has felt the
impact of film fashions, through production improvements as
standards change. Vyvyan Donner, who directs fashion shorts
(for Fox Movietone), spoke on the problems of time restrictions
and finding photogenic fashions. Also, Chase said that there is
insufficient authority exercised in the selection of film costumes,
so that the varying qualities confuse the audience.

2175   "New Movie's Hollywood Fashions."   New Movie, 8 (4): 38-
            41, October 1933.
One costume each is modeled by Lilian Bond from "Double Har-
ness," Wynne Gibson from "Her Bodyguard," Kay Francis from
"Storm at Daybreak," and Frances Dee from "Headline Shooters."

2176   "New Movie's Hollywood Fashions."   New Movie, 8 (6): 53-5,
            December 1933.
One costume each is modeled by Claire Trevor from "The Mad
Game" and Sally Eilers from "Walls of Gold."

2177   "New Movie's Hollywood Fashions."   New Movie, 9 (2): 54-7,
            February 1934.
Claire Trevor models three costumes from "Jimmy and Sally"
and Irene Dunne one from "Behold We Live." One hat each is
modeled by Patricia Ellis from "Convention City," Dolores Del
Rio from "Flying Down to Rio," Madge Evans from "Transcontinental Bus," and Miriam Hopkins from "All of Me."

2178   "New Movie's Hollywood Fashion."   New Movie, 10 (6): 35-8,
            December 1934.
Gail Patrick models one costume from "Wagon Wheels."

2179   "The New Screen 'Lady of the Ensemble.'"   Hollywood, 19
            (1): 26, January 1930.
Included are numerous stills of chorus girls in their film costumes, with only one identified, Maxine Cantway from "The Show
of Shows."

2180   "The New Skirts Are Slashed."   Screen News, 3 (17): 22,
            April 26, 1924.
A slashed skirt is modeled by an unnamed actress from "Lilies
of the Field"; with description.

2181   New York (City).   Metropolitan Museum of Art Costume
            Institute.   "Romantic and Glamorous Hollywood Design."
            [Catalogue of an exhibition, prepared by Diana Vreeland
            and others.]   New York: Metropolitan Museum of Art,
            1974.
This booklet might well be considered a synopsis of Hollywood
Costume: Glamour! Glitter! Romance!, since both were written
as a result of the above exhibit, and both were coauthored by
Diana Vreeland. With both, film costume is discussed, along

with much film history and the most widely known designers, with such generalizations as, Adrian was a "great costumer," and Travis Banton was a "superb dressmaker."

2182   "Newell, Catherine." American Film Institute Catalog, 1961-
       70, p. 470.
Catherine Newell is credited with the wardrobe of "Erika's Hot Summer."

2183   Newman, Bernard. "You Always Can Look Even Lovelier."
       Silver Screen, 17 (6): 50-1, 83-6, April 1947.
Bernard Newman, formerly the chief designer at Bergdorf Good-man for 15 years, is now the executive designer at Warner Brothers. He believes that film actresses and designers have more influence over fashion than any other group in the world, including Paris and socialites. He discusses working with Lauren Bacall in "Dark Passage," three costumes from which she models, with one sketch. Bette Davis models one costume from "Decep-tion," with additional sketches.

2184   "Newsmakers." Newsweek, 82 (21): 64, May 23, 1977.
Marlon Brando complained that the iridescent Kryptonian costumes were like "portable saunas" under the lights during production of "Superman--The Movie."

2185   "Next Season's Styles Paraded in 'Sweethearts' Color Scene."
       MGM Studio News, 5 (10): n. p., October 8, 1938.
The fashion show in "Sweethearts" includes Jeanette MacDonald modeling 12 costumes. Many of Adrian's costumes for MacDonald and others are described.

2186   "Nice Legs Having Long Been an Important Item...." Screen
       News, 4 (47): 4, November 28, 1925, col. 2.
Edmund Lowe's success as an actor is attributed, in part, to his attractive legs, especially in short breeches and silk stockings, as worn in "Palaces of Pleasure."

2187   "Nicholls, Tiny." American Film Institute Catalog, 1961-70,
       p. 471.
Tiny Nicholls is credited with the costumes of "The McKenzie Break," and the wardrobe supervision of "The Chairman."

2188   "Nickols, Vicki." American Film Institute Catalog, 1961-70,
       p. 472.
Vicki Nickols is credited with the wardrobe of "Hold On!"

2189   "Nightingale, Laura." American Film Institute Catalog, 1961-
       70, p. 472.
Laura Nightingale is credited with the wardrobe of "A Kind of Loving," with additional credits as a wardrobe mistress and ward-robe/costume supervisor.

2190   "Nikki of Just Men." American Film Institute Catalog, 1961-
       70, p. 473.

Nikki of Just Men is credited with the costumes for Ian McShane
in "Pussycat, Pussycat, I Love You."

2191 Ninon. "Banton, Back in Hollywood, Talks Style." San
            Francisco Chronicle, June 13, 1935, p. 20.
Travis Banton recently returned from Paris, where he helped design some new silk fabrics with the house of Ducharne, for an
(unnamed) Marlene Dietrich film.

2192 _____. "Famous Designer at Hollywood." San Francisco
            Chronicle, May 1, 1934, p. 22.
Ninon visited the Hollywood set of "She Loves Me Not," where
Kitty Carlisle is acting; with one costume description, designed
by Travis Banton. Maud Turner Gordon, in the same film, has
knitted many dresses, which her daughter has been wearing
in films (the writer could find no record of her daughter). Also,
includes one photo of shoes worn by Mae West in "It Ain't No
Sin" ("Belle of the Nineties") and Miriam Hopkins in "She Loves
Me Not," both designed by Banton.

2193 _____. "Fashion's Honored Four; Neiman-Marcus Awards
            Announced." San Francisco Chronicle, August 24, 1948,
            p. 6.
Brief biographical information of Antonio Castillo, who assisted
Jean Cocteau with the costumes of "Beauty and the Beast." Bonnie
Cashin also received a Neiman-Marcus award.

2194 _____. "Hollywood's Stylist Real Genius." San Francisco
            Chronicle, May 6, 1934, p. 57.
Travis Banton discusses briefly his costumes for Claudette Colbert
in "Cleopatra" and for Marlene Dietrich in "The Scarlet Empress."
He notes that interviewers want him to say that Hollywood and its
films are the leaders in world fashion, but that this is impossible
to determine. His research for period films indirectly influences
his modern costumes. Includes a sketch of Colbert in a costume
from "Cleopatra."

2195 _____. "Ninon in Hollywood; Movies Will Not and Cannot
            Accept World Fashion Crown." San Francisco Chronicle,
            August 20, 1940, p. 7.
Travis Banton, Walter Plunkett, Edith Head, Edward Stevenson,
Milo Anderson, Robert Kalloch, and Adrian discuss the extent to
which movies will influence fashion while Paris is occupied. They
all agree that because they do not produce seasonal collections their
influence will continue to be the same as before the war, but as
Adrian noted, "it will be we who provide the caviar for the world
of style. That we have done for years, right along with Paris."

2196 "Nisskaya, V." American Film Institute Catalog, 1961-70,
            p. 473.
V. Nisskaya is credited with the costumes of "The Duel."

2197 "Nita Naldi Had Considerable Trouble...." Screen News, 2

(28): 29, July 14, 1923, col. 3.
Nita Naldi did not know what type of headdress she should wear
as Cleopatra in the prologue of "Lawful Larceny, " and after con-
flicting research she chose a gold crownlike headpiece with an
asp decoration in the front and a lotus flower in the back.

2198 "Nixdorf, Gisela. " American Film Institute Catalog, 1961-70,
         p. 474.
Gisela Nixdorf is credited with the costumes of "The Return of
Dr. Mabuse. "

2199 "No More a Silken Gloria. " Motion Picture, 27 (2): 56, March
         1924.
Gloria Swanson models a man-styled costume from "The Humming
Bird, " which illustrates how she has tried to change her image,
according to the author, from that of a clotheshorse to one of a
more serious actress.

2200 Noerdlinger, Henry S. "Costumes and Adornments, " in Moses
         and Egypt: The Documentation to the Motion Picture "The
         Ten Commandments. " Los Angeles: University of Southern
         California Press, 1956.
This book was written as a result of the massive research done
for "The Ten Commandments. " Discussion of research done and
decisions made concerning costumes, headdresses, crowns and
other royal insignia, shoes, gloves, handkerchiefs, leather and
other animal skins, and jewelry, including the significance of
different gemstones and their use by the Hebrews and Egyptians.
Includes stills of Yul Brynner and others not identified, alongside
the original photographs or sketches from which the costumes
were copied. Certain aspects of authentic clothing were eliminated
if they would detract from the performances. The actors and
actresses discussed are virtually never identified, and no designer
or wardrobe-person credits are given. (The designers were Edith
Head, Dorothy Jeakins, Ralph Jester, John Jensen (or Jenssen),
and Arnold Friberg.)

2201 "Nola Luxford Has Arrived. " Screen News, 2 (31): 8, August
         4, 1923.
Nola Luxford spent months researching the costumes and background
of her role as Melissa in "The Flying Dutchman. "

2202 Norden, Helen Brown. "Passion for the Past. " Vogue, 89
         (5): 84-5, 124, March 1, 1937.
The majority of films in 1937 are historical; the author discusses
those actors and actresses who are not suited to historical garb,
with the hope of starting a "Back-to-the-Present" movement.
Merle Oberon models one costume from "I, Claudius. "

2203 "Norell, Norman. " American Film Institute Catalog, 1961-70,
         p. 475.
Norman Norell is credited with the fashions of "That Touch of
Mink, " the costumes of "Sex and the Single Girl, " and was Lee
Remick's wardrobe designer for "The Wheeler Dealers. "

2204   "Norell, Norman." Current Biography. 1964, p.321-3.
Norman Norell became a costume designer for Paramount in 1922,
but the job ended when the studio closed. He then became a
theatrical designer, and eventually an accomplished fashion designer. Doris Day wore three costumes selected off-the-rack in
Norell's showroom by costar Cary Grant, in "That Touch of Mink."

2205   "Norell, Norman," in Fashion Is Our Business, by Beryl
           Williams [Epstein]. Philadelphia: Lippincott, 1945, p.
           94-115.
In Norman Norell's first fashion-related jobs he worked with many
film and theatrical designers. Gilbert Clark, formerly with Henri
Bendel and then the owner of his own establishment, believed in
Norell's ability, as did Herman K. Smith, a film designer in
Astoria, New York. Norell was soon working with Natacha Rambova and Adrian designing for Rudolph Valentino in "A Sainted
Devil." He then designed Gloria Swanson's costumes for "Zaza,"
also at the Paramount Astoria studio, and for some of Mae Murray's films (unnamed). Like many film designers, he moved on
to the Greenwich Village Follies, and then Brooks Costume Co.,
where he worked with Charles Le Maire.

2206   "Norell, Norman." Who's Who in America. 33rd ed., 1964-5,
           p. 1492.
Norman Norell began designing in 1927 with Hattie Carnegie (his
film career had begun before), and had his first collection in 1941
with Traina-Norell, a partnership with Anthony Traina.

2207   "Norma Shearer." Screen News, 4 (43): 15, October 31,
           1925.
Norma Shearer models a costume with chinchilla wrap from "The
Tower of Lies."

2208   "Norma Shearer Wears Clothes in Keeping with Her Mood."
           Screen News, 3 (36): 14, September 6, 1924.
Norma Shearer wears clothes on and off screen that best suit
her mood. Designer Sophie Wachner has taught her much about
color psychology, which Shearer believes is the most important
factor in her clothing selections.

2209   "Norma Shearer Wears These Gowns in 'A Slave of Fashion.'"
           Screen News, 4 (33): 15, August 22, 1925.
Norma Shearer models three costumes from "A Slave of Fashion."

2210   "Norma Talmadge Has Largest Motion Picture Set Ever
           Screened." Screen News, 1 (23): 6-7, July 29, 1922.
The huge ballroom set in "The Eternal Flame" will feature 800
persons in costumes of the Second Restoration period, made by
45 persons, including designers, costumers, and wardrobe mistresses.

2211   "Norma Talmadge in an Empire Gown of Brocaded Blue Silk."
           Screen News, 2 (38): 17, September 22, 1923.

Norma Talmadge models a gown from "The Eternal Flame"; the
same gown as in the following entry.

2212   "Norma Talmadge in 'The Eternal Flame.'" Screen News, 1
         (17): 4, June 10, 1922.

2213   "Norma Talmadge Introduces Empire Fashions in 'The Eternal
         Flame.'" Screen News, 1 (22): 22, 26, July 22, 1922.
Norma Talmadge will wear about 20 costumes from the Louis
XVIII period in "The Eternal Flame." The jewels and costumes
are authentic reproductions, but many of the fans are originals.
Many costumes are described.

2214   "Norman Norell Borrows 2 Dresses Designed by the Late
         Travis Banton...." Women's Wear Daily, November 29,
         1963, p.1.
Norman Norrell feels that Travis Banton has been underrated and
that his talent surpassed Adrian's, since Banton's costumes were
timeless and established many famous images, as with the Mae
West look. He was making a comeback with his costumes for
"Auntie Mame"; though it is not specified as to whether this was
for his film or theatrical costumes for "Auntie Mame."

2215   North, Jeanne. "Do You Want a Job in the Studios?" Photo-
         play, 39 (6): 68-70, 116-20, May 1931.
"Mother" Coulter has been MGM's wardrobe department head for
12 years, and earns $125 per week. Aged 65, she has been a
theatrical and film costumer for over 40 years. She prefers to
hire seamstresses who have learned at home rather than in dressmaking shops. Seamstresses begin at $22.50 per week, and head
cutters at $60 per week; 40 women are employed at busy times.

2216   " 'Not an Ounce to Her Back.'" Screen News, 4 (36): 15,
         September 12, 1925.
Evelyn Brent has compared the weight of a previously worn period-
film costume with a contemporary costume she wore in "Three
Wise Crooks," with the obvious conclusion that she prefers the
more comfortable, if skimpy, modern one.

2217   "Not 'Moore' Than a Half Day?" Screen News, 1 (8): 28,
         April 15, 1922.
Tom Moore spent half a day with his tailor and his cameraman
studying red fabrics with a test glass to find the color that would
photograph best for his coat as a Royal Mounted policeman in
"Over the Border" and that would contrast with his dark uniform
pants.

2218   "Not So Many Years Ago." Photoplay, 29 (1): 34-5, Decem-
         ber 1925.
Nine stills show actresses in film costumes from as far back as
1914, without film titles, for Gloria Swanson, Alma Rubens,
Dorothy Gish, Colleen Moore, Lila Lee, Anna Q. Nilsson, Lillian
Gish, Doris Kenyon, and Mae Murray (in "Nell Brinkley").

2219 "Not the Only Woman Wearing Them." Screen News, 1 (6): 8,
         April 1, 1922.
Dorothy Dalton's last three films required that she wear trousers,
including overalls for a seaman's role in "Moran of the Lady
Letty," western knickerbockers in "The Crimson Challenge," and
an English riding habit in "The Woman Who Walked Alone."

2220 "Notes on Contributors." Journal of the Costume Society, 8:
         93, 1974.
Joseph S. Simms, a high school history teacher, and an expert on
and avid fan of Adrian, often writes and lectures on the late designer.

2221 "Nothing Like a Tall Collar to Make One Feel Pompous."
         Screen News, 4 (33): 4, August 22, 1925.
Edward Earle wears a $2-\frac{1}{4}$ inch collar specially created for his
role as an official in "The Viennese Medley."

2222 "Nourry, Hélène." American Film Institute Catalog, 1961-70,
         p. 476.
Hélène Nourry is credited with the wardrobe of "Belle de Jour"
and the costumes of "The Sicilian Clan."

2223 "Nourry, Pierre." American Film Institute Catalog, 1961-70,
         p. 476.
Pierre Nourry is credited with the costumes of "Is Paris Burning?"
and was the wardrobe master for "Borsalino."

2224 "Novak, Kim." American Film Institute Catalog, 1961-70,
         p. 476.
Kim Novak designed her own costumes for "Boys' Night Out"
(with Bill Thomas) and "The Notorious Landlady."

2225 "Novarese, Vittorio Nino." American Film Institute Catalog,
         1961-70, p. 476.
Vittorio Nino Novarese was the costume designer of "Francis of
Assisi," "The Agony and the Ecstasy," "The Greatest Story Ever
Told," and "Cromwell" and the costume supervisor of "The War
Lord," and is credited with the costumes of "The King's Pirate"
and "The Savage Innocents" and the men's costumes of "Cleopatra."

2226 "Novello, Roselle." American Film Institute Catalog, 1961-70,
         p. 477.
Roselle Novello is credited with the costumes of "The Young Savages."

2227 Nowland, Lucille. "The Dressing Room." It, 5 (4): 10, No-
         vember 1, 1919.
Katherine MacDonald wears 14 costumes, which she bought at
Robinson's, in "Japonette."

2228 _____. "The Dressing Room." It, 5 (7): 12, December
         15, 1919.

Discussion of gowns worn by Bessie Barriscale in "Beckoning Roads."

2229 _____. "The Dressing Room." It, 5 (8): 12, January 1, 1920.
Discussion of two costumes worn by Edith Johnson in a Vitagraph film with William Duncan. (Johnson appeared in many films at this time with husband, actor/director Duncan.)

2230 _____. "The Dressing Room." It, 2 (4): 12, February 15, 1920.
Discussion of many gowns worn by Fritzi Brunette in "The Green Flame."

2231 _____. "The Dressing Room." It, 2 (6): 12, March 15, 1920.
Discussion of many gowns worn by Gloria Swanson in a film in which she begins as a poor, young girl and marries (probably "Something to Think About").

2232 Nowland-Semnacher, Lucille. "The Dressing Room." It, 2 (7): 10, April 15, 1920.
Discussion of four costumes worn by Kathleen Kirkham in "Parlor, Bedroom and Bath."

2233 _____. "The Dressing Room." It, 2 (9): 16, May 1, 1920.
Discussion of gowns owned by Bebe Daniels, many worn in "Hunting Trouble"; not clearly identified.

2233a "Un Nuevo Servicio de Cinelandia." Cinelandia, 12 (12): 30-1, 34-5, December 1938.
Brief mention of how Norma Shearer's costumes in "Marie Antoinette" have influenced fashion, especially evening clothes. One of her dresses was reproduced with modifications along with her hat and purse, and these are discussed at length and available for purchase. Spanish text.

2234 Nugent, Frank S. "Assignment in Hollywood." Good Housekeeping, 122 (1): 12-3, 128, January 1946.
The author was taken on a tour of MGM's wardrobe department by its head designer, Irene, and Sam Kress, wardrobe department head. Discussion of the major departments and average costume costs, and notes that some costumes are disposed of yearly; employees ranges from 300 to 450 depending on the work load. Irene discusses designing Esther Williams's costumes in "Fiesta"; she wore at least ten matador costumes at $1,000 each.

2235 "Nyby, Thelma." American Film Institute Catalog, 1961-70, p. 477.
Thelma Nyby is credited with the gowns of "Operation CIA."

2236 "Nykjaer, Berit." American Film Institute Catalog, 1961-70, p. 477.
Berit Nykjaer is credited with the costumes of "Without a Stitch."

2237 Oberfirst, Robert. Rudolph Valentino: The Man Behind the Myth. New York: Citadel, 1962.
More of the same material found in other Valentino biographies, except that this features tedious and impossible recreations of everyday conversations, including Natacha Rambova advising Valentino to refuse "The Sheik" because the costumes would make him appear comical. Byron (or Bryan; sources disagree) Foy said that Valentino would rather go hungry than appear poorly or inappropriately dressed in his films. References also to his argument with director Rex Ingram over one costume for "The Four Horsemen of the Apocalypse," his replacing the armor the studio had provided for him in "The Big Little Person" with a suit he rented, and his wearing a monocle on and off screen to identify more with his role in "The Conquering Power."

2238 "O'Brian [sic], Sheila." American Film Institute Catalog, 1961-70, p.478.
Sheila O'Brien was the costume designer of "Never Too Late" and is credited with the wardrobe of "The Deadly Companions."

2239 "O'Dell, Robert." American Film Institute Catalog, 1961-70, p.480.
Robert O'Dell is credited with the costumes of "Varan the Unbelievable."

2240 Odell, Rosemary. "Interesting Assignment," in Hollywood Album. London: Sampson, 1949, p.73-4.
Rosemary Odell discusses researching and designing the costumes for Andrea King and Mona Freeman in "I Was a Shoplifter," with such historical shoplifting aids as booster bloomers, fake sleeves and pockets, and special hooks and garters.

2241 "Odell, Rosemary." American Film Institute Catalog, 1961-70, p.480.
29 films are listed for designer Rosemary Odell.

2242 "Odette Myrtil, Designer of Claire Trevor's Suit in 'The Lucky Stiff.' " Photoplay, 34 (3): 87, February 1949.
Odette Myrtil, costume designer of "The Lucky Stiff" and a former actress, notes that film is the best medium for promoting fashion.

2243 "Of Interest to Women." Grauman's Magazine, 4 (34): 7,
      August 28, 1921.
Motion-picture censors have forbidden wearing of the one-piece
bathing suit, so that film designers have worked hard at finding
an attractive substitute--generally, a suit with a skirt midway to
the knee, as worn in the "Bathing Girl Revue."

2244 "Of Interest to Women." Grauman's Magazine, 5 (46): 8,
      December 3, 1922.
Marion Davies has had six screen marriages, that in "When
Knighthood Was in Flower" being the most elaborate of any film
wedding yet. Her wedding gown is made of silver cloth with
ermine trim, worn with a headdress of filigree and pearls, and
a long, heavily embroidered veil also decorated with pearls.

2245 "Of Interest to Women." Grauman's Magazine, 5 (47): 8,
      December 10, 1922.
Rudolph Valentino's bride, Winifred Hudnut, known professionally
as Natacha Rambova, is a famous film designer known especially
for her bizarre costumes. An example of her "striking and
original" costumes are those worn by Valentino in "The Young
Rajah," with silver and gold brocades, jewels for trimming, and
unique headdresses.

2246 "Of Interest to Women, and Perhaps to Men." Grauman's
      Magazine, 4 (41): 20, October 16, 1921.
Women are expressing more and more their concern over motion
pictures by their silent pressure at the box office, not just over
the gowns, but over concerns of decency, esthetics, and ethics.

2247 Ogden, Helen. "The Wear and Tear in Comedies." Picture
      Play, 20 (2): 88-9, April 1924.
Comedians often have large bills for their costumes because so
many duplicates are needed to anticipate wear and tear. The
costume needs of Harold Lloyd, Buster Keaton, Al St. John,
Larry Semon, and Charlie Chaplin are discussed.

2248 "Oglesbee, Michael." American Film Institute Catalog, 1961-
      70, p.480.
Michael Oglesbee is credited with the wardrobe of "His Wife's
Habit."

2249 "Oh, Girls, Don't You Envy Gloria Joy, Screen Star of 11?
      She Has Her Own Modest [sic] Shop." Screen News,
      1 (29): 19, September 9, 1922.
Director Sherwood MacDonald had a special wardrobe department
built at the R-C studios to costume Gloria Joy and other child
stars who would normally have great difficulty finding period and
modern costumes.

2250 "Oh, What a Gown!" Photoplay, 39 (1): 58, December 1930.
Jeanette Loff models a gown from "The Boudoir Diplomat," by
Andre-Ani.

2251 "Old King Tut-Ankh-Amen of Egypt Sets the Fashion for the
         American Girl's Summer Gowns and Hats." Photoplay,
         23 (6): 41, May 1925.
Bebe Daniels models a hand-painted shawl from "Glimpses of the
Moon."

2252 "Old Romance." Motion Picture, 24 (10): 23, November 1922.
Features three stills of Marion Davies in costumes from "When
Knighthood Was in Flower." A caption reads that "Charles Urban designed both the settings and costumes." (The author undoubtedly meant Joseph Urban, though this is the only source in
the bibliography that refers to Urban as having designed the costumes for any Hearst film; he often collaborated with his daughter,
Gretl, who designed the costumes, and he the sets.)

2253 O'Leary, Dorothy. "Lesson from Lili." Screenland, 54 (4):
         45, 66-8, February 1950.
French fashion designer Lili feels that film costumes worn by
American actresses are not as sexy and individualistic as they
should be, as compared with the costumes of French actresses.
Also, too many American women imitate the over-elaborately
costumed actresses, and lose their distinctiveness.

2254 "Olivas, Robert." American Film Institute Catalog, 1961-70,
         p. 482.
Robert Olivas is credited with the wardrobe of "Battle at Bloody
Beach," the costumes of "Sniper's Ridge," and the men's ward-
robe of "The Two Little Bears."

2255 "Omar Kiam, Noted for Dress Designs." New York Times,
         March 30, 1954, p. 27.
Omar Kiam died at the age of 60 due to a heart ailment. He
was a film designer in Hollywood from 1935 to 1940; he then
worked as a designer for a New York manufacturer. He believed in simple lines with elaborate detail.

2256 "Omar of Omaha." American Film Institute Catalog, 1961-70,
         p. 483.
Omar of Omaha is credited with Phyllis Diller's costumes in
"Did You Hear the One About the Traveling Saleslady?"

2257 "Omar's Screen Clothes." Screen News, 1 (18): 28, June 17,
         1922.
The silk fabrics used in "Omar the Tentmaker" were sent from
the same Persian silk merchant, unidentified, who supplied the
fabrics for the stage version.

2258 "On Stage--and Off." New York Times Magazine, March 30,
         1941, p. 22.
One costume each is modeled by Ginger Rogers from "Kitty Foyle,"
Vivien Leigh from "That Hamilton Woman," and Lily Pons from
"Daughter of the Regiment," alongside models in modified copies
that were selected from ready-to-wear collections. Parisian de-

signer Schiaparelli once designed a collection with a Mae West film as her inspiration.

2259 "On the Date Front." Photoplay with Movie Mirror, 21 (4): 59-61, September 1942.
Anne Shirley models three costumes by Edith Head from "Lady Bodyguard."

2260 "On the First Day of the Shooting of ... 'The Humming Bird.' ... " Screen News, 2 (45): 23, November 10, 1923, col. 3.
Shooting of "The Humming Bird" was stopped until the wardrobe department could find suspenders for the actors, since it was learned that Parisian men prefer them to belts.

2261 "On the Set for Parnell." Harper's Bazaar, 71 (4): 188, April 1937.
Myrna Loy models three costumes by Adrian from "Parnell."

2262 "On the Set with 'All This, and Heaven Too.' " Modern Screen, 21 (1): 32-3, 73, June 1940.
The $35,000 wardrobe for "All This, and Heaven Too" included 35 plain costumes for Bette Davis.

2263 "On the Set with 'Kitty Foyle.'" Modern Screen, 22 (1): 52, December 1940.
Ginger Rogers's costume as a 15-year-old, in the beginning of "Kitty Foyle," consisted of a blue middy worn with black cotton stockings. Besides an evening gown made of imported French gold lamé, which cost $24 per yard and was the last exported from France because of the war, she wore clothes that any secretary might; New York department store Bonwit Teller had wired the studio requesting it, but the studio preferred it for Rogers.

2264 "On the Set with 'Lady Be Good.'" Modern Screen, 23 (1): 42-3, June 1941.
Ann Sothern wears 35 gowns by Adrian in "Lady Be Good."

2265 "On the Set with 'Lillian Russell.' ... " Modern Screen, 20 (6): 34-5, 103, May 1940.
In "Lillian Russell" Alice Faye wore copies of Russell's original stockings, which cost $100 per pair and were made by Willys DeMond, who earned $3,000; the stockings were embroidered with butterflies and had lace inserts. The female extras' 800 costumes came to over $25,000. Faye will wear 27 costumes and a copy of a $3,900 corset made for Russell by Mme. Rosa Binner, who will supervise the reproduction of the corset and act as technical adviser for corsets worn in the film. The original corset featured gold stays, diamond clasps, and $700 worth of Belgian lace trim. Also, the corset was the first one made with a corset garter--to keep the corset down, rather than hold up stockings.

2266   "On the Set with 'The Californian.'"   Modern Screen, 21 (6):
            40-1, November 1940.
        Linda Darnell's costumes in "The Californian" cost $10,000, but
        Tyrone Power's 22 costumes, consisting of tight velvet pants,
        satin shirts, and embroidered waistcoats, cost $15,000.

2267   "On the Set with 'The Little Foxes.'"   Modern Screen, 23
            (5): 8-10, October 1941.
        Bette Davis's Edwardian costumes for "The Little Foxes" required
        tight corsets, made with steel instead of whalebone, which was
        hard to find; she collapsed once due to her corset.   Her ward-
        robe, designed by Orry-Kelly, included a gown of black taffeta
        and lace, and a gown of white lace, identified as heirlooms.   She
        is shown in a closeup of a hat with a bird, and since the use of
        birds on hats has been banned, the studio borrowed the hat from
        the Louisiana Museum.

2268   "On the Set with 'The Mortal Storm.'"   Modern Screen, 21
            (2): 34-5, 88, July 1940.
        The Nazi uniforms for 200 men in "The Mortal Storm" cost $75
        each, worn with swastika-trimmed hats, armbands, and buttons.
        Also, the studio had to make them, since no local manufacturer
        would.

2269   "On the Set with 'Tom, Dick and Harry.'"   Modern Screen,
            23 (2): 40-1, 97, July 1941.
        Ginger Rogers wore 45 costumes in "Tom, Dick and Harry,"
        "which is more than any actress has had since the birth of
        pictures."   A costume stand-in was hired, another first, with
        Rogers's exact measurements, for fittings.   The fantasy roles of
        Rogers required costumes ranging from housedresses matching
        her curtains to a wedding gown made from flour sacks, to a
        pearl-encrusted gown.

2270   "Once Paris,--Now Los Angeles."   Grauman's Magazine,
            5 (36): 3, September 24, 1922.
        Fashion geography has shifted, and Paris no longer dictates
        fashion since the film is the most practical and farthest reaching
        medium for disseminating fashions.   Clare West purchases all
        costume materials needed in the Los Angeles area, as she did
        for Leatrice Joy in "Manslaughter," the furs of which cost over
        $100,000.

2271   "One Frog Paddled."   Time, 40 (9): 23, August 31, 1942.
        Announces the opening of Adrian's salon in Beverly Hills, and
        consequently his leaving film-costume design as a full-time pro-
        fession.

2272   "One Hour and Forty-Five Minutes in One Position."   Screen
            News, 1 (40): 6, November 25, 1922, col. 2.
        Gloria Swanson stood 1-3/4 hours while being sewn into a cos-
        tume resembling a statue for a ball scene in "The Impossible
        Mrs. Bellew."

2273   "One of Constance Talmadge's Most Charming Gowns...."
          <u>Screen News</u>, 2 (33): 6, August 18, 1923, col. 3.
Constance Talmadge wears a gown of soft black fabric, with cut-
work decorating the yoke and spiral panels, in "Dulcy."

2274   "O'Neill, Alice." <u>American Film Institute Catalog, 1921-30</u>,
          p. 1293.
Alice O'Neill was the costume designer of "Just Imagine" and is
credited with the wardrobe of "Married in Hollywood" and "Lummox" and the costumes of "The Ladybird," "Drums of Love,"
"Tempest," "Fox Movietone Follies of 1929," "Lady of the Pavements," "The Bad One," "Be Yourself!," "The Lottery Bride," and
"Puttin' on the Ritz."

2275   "Original Hollywood Designs." <u>Screen Romances</u>, February
          1932, p. 66-7.
Three costumes each are modeled by Greta Garbo from "Mata
Hari," by Adrian, and Pola Negri from "A Woman Commands."
Includes the original sketches from which the costumes were made;
without designer credit for Negri.

2276   Orlando, Joe, Jack C. Harris, and Michael L. Fleisher.
          "Costume Designer Yvonne Blake," in <u>Superman--the</u>
          <u>Movie Magazine</u>, 8 (C-62): 61-2, 1979.
Includes brief biographical information on designer Yvonne Blake,
whose credits include costumes worn by Diana Dors in "Passport
to Shame" and Margaret Rutherford in "I'm All Right." Does not
include references to her costumes for "Superman--The Movie,"
but does include one sketch each of costumes worn by Marlon
Brando, Sara Douglas, and Christopher Reeve, who each model
the finished costume.

2277   Orry Kelly [sic]. "Charmingly Yours." <u>Screenland</u>, 53 (8):
          48-9, 68-9, June 1949.
Orry-Kelly's costumes for Barbara Stanwyck in "The Lady Gambles" were designed with an average woman's budget in mind so
that they could be easily copied; Stanwyck models seven of the
costumes.   He notes that film costumes in the 1930s lacked restraint, and when independent productions increased over 100 designers were trying to succeed.

2278   Orry-Kelly. "Clothes to Help You Win." <u>Picture Play</u>, 48
          (5): 35, 68, July 1938.
Tips on how to look one's best before the camera, by designer
Orry-Kelly.

2279   _____. "Hollywood Fashion Defended!" <u>Screenland</u>, 38 (1):
          27-9, 93, January 1938.
This article was written as a rebuttal to Elizabeth Hawes's article,
"Hollywood Fashion Is Spinach."   Orry-Kelly likes Elizabeth
Hawes's fashion designs but emphasizes the difference in design-
ing for the screen and high fashion.   For example, Chanel was
an excellent designer, but her film costumes were unsuccessful.

Many actresses also find their film costumes suitably in style to
buy and wear in their personal lives.

2280   _____.   "Presenting the September Look."   Silver Screen,
            18 (11): 46-7, 68-9, September 1948.
        Orry-Kelly discusses his costumes for Joan Caulfied in   "Larceny,"
        which he feels would be suitable for any woman with coloring
        similar to Caulfield's.   She models six costumes from the film.

2281   "Orry-Kelly."   American Film Institute Catalog, 1961-70, p.
            485.
        Orry-Kelly was the costume designer of "Two for the Seesaw"
        and for Rosalind Russell and Natalie Wood in "Gypsy"; the ward-
        robe designer of "Sunday in New York" and for Jane Fonda in
        "In the Cool of the Day"; and is credited with the costumes of
        "The Chapman Report," "A Majority of One," "Sweet Bird of
        Youth," and "Irma La Douce"; the gowns for Rosalind Russell in
        "Five Finger Exercise"; and some of Ingrid Thulin's gowns in
        "The Four Horsemen of the Apocalypse" (1962).

2282   "Orry-Kelly."   International Encyclopedia of Film.   New York:
            Crown, 1972, p.385.
        Orry-Kelly was less concerned than Adrian with "good taste fash-
        ion."

2283   "Orry-Kelly."   Motion Picture Almanac.   1943-4, p.448.
        80 film credits are listed for designer Orry-Kelly, from 1933 to
        1941.

2284   "Orry-Kelly."   Photoplay, 34 (1): 88, December 1948.
        Brief mention of a suit worn by Deanna Durbin in "For the Love
        of Mary," featuring the currently popular and simple slim skirt,
        and jacket with wrist-length sleeves.

2285   "Orry-Kelly."   Time, (Milestones), 83 (10): 98, March 6,
            1964.
        Orry-Kelly died at age 66 (or 67; he was born in 1897) due to
        cancer of the liver.   Some of the more famous costumes he de-
        signed are Rosalind Russell's black lace pajamas in "Auntie
        Mame," Natalie Wood's few spangles for "Gypsy," and the shimmy
        Marilyn Monroe wore in "Some Like It Hot."

2286   "Orry-Kelly Dies; Movie Designer."   New York Times, Febru-
            ary 27, 1964, p.31.
        Orry-Kelly, dead at age 67 due to cancer of the liver, was the
        chief designer at Warner Brothers from 1931 to 1945.   He then
        moved to Twentieth Century-Fox, where he remained until his
        death; he had been designing for "Kiss Me Stupid" at that time.
        He won Academy Awards for "An American in Paris" and "Les
        Girls."

2287   Osborne, Kay.   "Portfolio of Fashion and Beauty; Ginger
            Rogers."   Motion Picture, 49 (4): 43-5, 62, May 1935.

RKO hired Bernard Newman, a designer at Bergdorf Goodman in New York, to design the costumes for "Roberta." Newman discusses designing the hats and costumes, and the remodeling of Ginger Rogers and Irene Dunne, each of whom discuss the effect of his efforts. Dunne models four costumes, and Rogers, Lucille Ball, and Virginia Reid each model one from the film.

2288   "Osborne, Marie." American Film Institute Catalog, 1961-70, p. 486.
Marie Osborne is credited with the costumes of "Love Is a Funny Thing" and the wardrobe of "The Chase," "The Killing of Sister George," and "The Legend of Lylah Clare."

2289   O'Shea, Beth. "Alma Rubens Collects Smart Wardrobe for Latest Picture." Screen News, 4 (18): 14, May 2, 1925.
Discussion of many gowns worn by Alma Rubens in "She Wolves."

2290   _____. "Film Fashions." Screen News, 3 (10): 18, March 8, 1924.
Discussion of gowns worn by Betty Compson in "You Can't Get Away with It," Shirley Mason in "Love Letters," and Brenda Bond in "The Fool."

2291   _____. "Film Fashions." Screen News, 3 (11): 18, March 15, 1924.
Discussion of one gown each worn by Pauline Starke in "The Arizona Express," Brenda Bond in "The Fool," Violet Mersereau in "The Shepherd King," and Kathleen Key in "North of Hudson Bay."

2292   _____. "Film Fashions." Screen News, 3 (12): 18, March 22, 1924.
Discussion of gowns worn by Peggy Shaw in "The Plunderer" and Rose Blossom in "The Fool."

2293   _____. "Film Fashions." Screen News, 3 (15): 18, April 12, 1924.
Includes a description of one gown worn by Rose Blossom in "The Fool."

2294   _____. "Film Fashions." Screen News, 3 (21): 8, May 24, 1924.
Discussion of gowns worn by Shirley Mason in "The Strange Woman," Frances Beaumont in "Strathmore," and Pauline Starke in "The Man Without a Country."

2295   _____. "Film Fashions." Screen News, 3 (22): 8, May 31, 1924.
Discussion of gowns worn by Frances Beaumont in "Strathmore" and Pauline French in "The Last Man on Earth."

2296   _____. "Film Fashions." Screen News, 3 (23): 24, June 7, 1924.
Discussion of gowns worn by Virginia Faire in "Romance Ranch,"

Evelyn Brent in an untitled film (she was in many films in this period), and Dorothy Mackaill in "The Man Who Came Back."

2297 _____. "Film Fashions." Screen News, 3 (24): 24, June 14, 1924.
Discussion of gowns worn by Grace Cunard in "The Last Man on Earth" and Lucille Ricksen in "The Painted Lady."

2298 _____. "Film Fashions." Screen News, 3 (30): 6, July 26, 1924.
Includes a description of one gown worn by Florence Gilbert in "Sylvia."

2299 _____. "Film Fashions." Screen News, 4 (48): 7, December 5, 1925.
Alma Rubens is finally in a modern picture, "The Gilded Butterfly," which will require a different gown for almost every scene; many were bought and many she designed, with one gown description.

2300 "Ostler, Gene." American Film Institute Catalog, 1961-70, p. 486.
Gene Ostler is credited with the wardrobe of "Kissin' Cousins," "Harum Scarum," "Hold On!," "Angel, Angel, Down We Go," and "Zigzag."

2301 "Ostrich Feathers Latest in Paris." Screen News, 3 (41): 2, October 11, 1924.
Ostrich feathers are the chief trimming of gowns worn by Claire Windsor in "For Sale" and "Born Rich." Windsor also wears a long scarf of ostrich feathers, rather than the usual chiffon.

2302 "Oswald, Tye." American Film Institute Catalog, 1961-70, p. 487.
Tye Oswald is credited with the costumes of "Which Way to the Front?" and the wardrobe of "An American Dream," "The Cool Ones," and "More Dead Than Alive."

2303 "Otto, Theo." American Film Institute Catalog, 1961-70, p. 487.
Theo Otto was the costume designer of "Faust."

2304 "Otto, Vera." American Film Institute Catalog, 1961-70, p. 487.
Vera Otto is credited with the costumes of "Buddenbrooks."

2305 "Ottobre." American Film Institute Catalog, 1961-70, p. 487.
Ottobre is credited with June Wilkinson's clothes in "Twist All Night."

2306 "Over-Dressed 'Sets' and Under-Dressed Actresses Will Cause Social Unrest." Screen News, 1 (35): 24, October 21, 1922.

Novelist Gene Stratton Porter feels that such great amounts of money are spent on unrealistic sets and costumes that people are discontent with their comparably simple lives.   Eight of her novels will soon be produced at Thomas H. Ince studios.

2307   "Owen-Smith, Brian."   <u>American Film Institute Catalog, 1961-</u>
          <u>70</u>, p.488.
Brian Owen-Smith is credited with the wardrobe of "The Last Safari," "Robbery," and "The Magus" and was the wardrobe master of "The Lion," "Lisa," "Of Human Bondage" (1964), and "Oh! What a Lovely War."

2308   "Ozerova, D."   <u>American Film Institute Catalog, 1961-70</u>, p.
          488.
D. Ozerova is credited with the costumes of "Meet Me in Moscow."

2309 "Page, Pat." American Film Institute Catalog, 1961-70, p.
       490.
Pat Page is credited with the wardrobe of "13 West Street" and
the costumes of "The Three Stooges in Orbit."

2310 Paige, Norman. "Gadgets, Garb, and Glamour!" Movie
       Classic, 11 (6): 54-5, 72-4, February 1937.
Western Costume Company is one of Hollywood's finest museums,
with a library housed in one of its eight floors. Includes references to researching and construction of costumes, the different
departments, and costuming "Mary of Scotland."

2311 "The Painted Shawl." Screen News, 5 (2): 4, January 16,
       1926.
Myrtle Stedman models one of two gowns described from "The
Desert Flower."

2312 "Pajama Game Fashions." Photoplay, 52 (4): 85, October 1957.
Doris Day, John Raitt, Eddie Foy, Jr., and Carol Henry model
pajamas from "The Pajama Game"; with prices for retail copies.

2313 "Palace of Versailles Will Be Shown in New Talmadge Pic-
       ture." Screen News, 1 (17): 25, June 10, 1922.
"The Eternal Flame" featured 400 couples in one ballroom sequence, dressed in costumes of the Second Restoration period of
France, made by 40 wardrobe mistresses of the First National
studios.

2314 "Pallack, Andrew." American Film Institute Catalog, 1961-
       70, p. 491.
Andrew Pallack is credited with Joel Holt's wardrobe in "Karate,
the Hand of Death" and Soupy Sales's wardrobe in "Birds Do It."

2315 Palmer, Adele. "When Dollars Are Scarce." Silver Screen,
       19 (5): 46-7, 73-4, March 1949.
Adele Palmer discusses assembling an economical wardrobe, with
examples from her costumes for Lizabeth Scott in "Too Late for
Tears," eight of which Scott models.

2316 "Palmer, Alma." American Film Institute Catalog, 1961-70,

p. 491.
Alma Palmer is credited with the wardrobe of "Invitation to Ruin."

2317 Palmer, Constance. "Shirley, Today!" Screenland, 49 (10):
        32-3, 94-5, August 1945.
Shirley Temple models three costumes from "Kiss and Tell."

2318 "Palmer, Roger." American Film Institute Catalog, 1961-70,
        p. 492.
Roger Palmer is credited with the costumes of "Isabel," "Dr.
Frankenstein on Campus," and "King of the Grizzlies."

2319 "Palmieri, Remo." American Film Institute Catalog, 1961-70,
        p. 492.
Remo Palmieri is credited with the costumes of "Everybody Go
Home!"

2320 "Palmstierna-Weiss, Gunilla." American Film Institute Cata-
        log, 1961-70, p. 492.
Gunilla Palmstierna-Weiss is credited with the costumes of "The
Persecution and Assassination of Jean-Paul Marat as Performed
by the Inmates of the Asylum of Charenton Under the Direction
of the Marquis de Sade."

2321 "Paltscho of Vienna." American Film Institute Catalog, 1961-
        70, p. 492.
Paltscho of Vienna is credited with the jewelry of "The Cardinal."

2322 "Panaro, Maria Luisa." American Film Institute Catalog,
        1961-70, p. 492.
Maria Luisa Panaro is credited with the costumes of "Caesar the
Conqueror" and "This Man Can't Die."

2323 "Pancani, Gianni." American Film Institute Catalog, 1961-70,
        p. 492.
Gianni Pancani is credited with the costumes of "Paranoia."

2324 "Panova, N." American Film Institute Catalog, 1961-70, p.
        493.
N. Panova is credited with the costumes of "Farewell, Doves."

2325 "Papi, Giuliano." American Film Institute Catalog, 1961-70,
        p. 493.
Giuliano Papi is credited with the costumes of "Atlas Against
Cyclops," "The Hours of Love," and "The Little Nuns."

2326 "Par 'Exposes' Fashions; Hostess Brings Screens to Protect
        the Clergy." Variety (weekly), September 25, 1963, p. 3.
Edith Head presented a fashion show of the $200,000 worth of
costumes from "A New Kind of Love" at New York's Franklin
Simon department store.

2327 "Parade of Notables Fills 88 Speaking Roles in Garbo Pro-

duction of 'Camille.'"   MGM Studio News, 3 (17): n.p.,
August 31, 1936.
Greta Garbo wears 18 costumes and Robert Taylor 14 in "Camille."
An additional 250 costumes were made by MGM seamstresses for
female extras and others, over a six-month period.

2328 "Paramount News." Grauman's Magazine, 6 (16): 14, April
          22, 1923.
For "The Ten Commandments" 100 dressmakers have been employed to create the thousands of costumes needed for those in
the Egypt and Palestine scenes. The dressmakers are working
in a new wardrobe department established in the old Lasky labo-
ratory's top floor.

2329 "Paramount News." Grauman's Magazine, 6 (17): 31, April
          29, 1923.
Clare West is supervising over 100 seamstresses working on the
over 3,000 costumes needed for "The Ten Commandments."

2330 "Paramount News." Grauman's Magazine, 6 (20): 10, May
          20, 1923.
Over eight months have been spent in the preparation of costumes,
sets, and properties for "The Ten Commandments." It is the cost-
liest production yet made, and the many delays were a result of
the hundreds of crafts-people required for the great number of
items needed, including thousands of costumes.

2331 "Paramount News." Grauman's Magazine, 6 (21): 12, May
          27, 1923.
"The Ten Commandments" has the largest number of costumes
ever sewn for a film.

2332 "Paris' Long Skirts Decree Catches H'wood Short on the Gam-
          Line." Variety, September 10, 1947, p. 3.
The new, longer skirts present a threat to many films now in
production, some of which are two to three years old.   27 films
by seven studios are listed, all of which are in danger of being
dated if the new fashion catches on.

2333 "Paris Points." Screen Romances, 11 (66): 92, November
          1934.
A listing of the newest Parisian fashion trends, though it is noted
that Adrian's costumes for Joan Crawford are also quite influential.

2334 "Parisian Artist Turns Talent to Film Studio." Screen News,
          4 (21): 15, May 23, 1925.
Erté recently arrived at MGM and has designed Aileen Pringle's
costumes for "The Mystic."

2335 Parker, Gladys, and Mrs. Jimmie Fidler. "Don't Call It
          Spinach!" Screen Guide, 4 (9): 30-1, January 1940.
The authors, who have opened their own fashion salon, note that
film costume has been referred to as "spinach" (by Elizabeth

Hawes) because the average woman finds them too extreme, and manufacturers too costly, to copy. A factor in Hollywood's not becoming the world's style center is that the designers cannot get a bill through Congress to copyright their designs.

2336 Parks, Florence Porter. "Women in the Movies." Camera!
        Year Book, 2 (9): 91-2, June 1, 1919.
An "extra girl" is hired according to her wardrobe since the studio must rent whatever she does not have. She is paid little with which to acquire a fashionable wardrobe, and must constantly replace or remodel her clothes, on $5-$7.50 per day. A price list of wardrobe essentials is included, with a recommended initial investment of $359.

2337 "Parmenter, Adele." American Film Institute Catalog, 1961-
        70, p.496.
Adele Parmenter was the costume designer of "It Happened in Athens" and is credited with the wardrobe of "Advise and Consent."

2338 Parsons, Louella O. "Hollywood and Censorship." Cosmo-
        politan, 136 (4): 8, 10, April 1954.
"The French Line" did not receive the Motion Picture Producer Association's seal of approval because Jane Russell was over-exposed. Includes a photo of Russell in one offending costume.

2339 "Parvin, Ted." American Film Institute Catalog, 1961-70,
        p.497.
Ted Parvin is credited with the costumes of "A Man Called Horse," "Soldier Blue," and "Wild Seed"; the wardrobe of "Hurry Sundown," "Little Fauss and Big Halsy," "Skidoo," and "A Man Called Gannon"; and the men's wardrobe/costumes of "The Lawyer" and "Rio Lobo."

2340 "Paterson, Ronald." American Film Institute Catalog, 1961-
        70, p.498.
Ronald Paterson is credited with the costumes of "The Adventurers."

2341 "Pathe Fashion Film to Have Wide Publicity." Moving Pic-
        ture World, 29 (4): 640, July 22, 1916.
Pathé has made its first fashion film, "A Day with a Society Girl," with the supervision of Florence Rose, fashion editor of several New York newspapers, with new reels to be released every two weeks. Unlike other fashion films, these will feature advance-season fashions, and not just those of Paris and New York's Fifth Avenue.

2342 "Patou, Jean." American Film Institute Catalog, 1961-70,
        p.498.
Jean Patou is credited with the gowns of "The Empty Star" and the wardrobe of "Act of the Heart."

2343 "Patriarca, Walter." American Film Institute Catalog, 1961-
        70, p.498.

Walter Patriarca is credited with the costumes of "Samson and the Slave Queen," "Samson vs. the Giant King," and "Seven Slaves Against the World."

2344   "Patterning After the Stars." Motion Picture, 39 (4): 68-9, May 1930.
Lois Wilson models two dresses by Walter Plunkett from "Lovin' the Ladies." The dresses are also sketched, with a layout of the pattern pieces and directions given for drafting the patterns to one's size.

2345   "Patterning After the Stars." Motion Picture, 39 (5): 68-9, June 1930.
Jean Arthur models a wedding gown from "The Return of Dr. Mabuse," with one sketch and sketches for adaptations, and drafting information.

2346   "Patterning After the Stars." Motion Picture, 39 (6): 68-9, July 1930.
Lila Lee models a gown from "Under Western Skies," with sketches by Edward Stevenson and drafting instructions for the gown and adaptations.

2347   "Pauli, Irms." American Film Institute Catalog, 1961-70, p. 499.
Irms Pauli is credited with the costumes of "Apache Gold," "The Invisible Dr. Mabuse," "Frontier Hellcat," "Last of the Renegades," "Rampage at Apache Wells," "The Desperado Trail," "Flaming Frontier," "The Blood Demon," and "Treasure of Silver Lake," and the wardrobe supervision of "Something for Everyone."

2348   "Pauline Garon Wins Degree of 'F.C.D.'" Screen News, 1 (24): 21, August 5, 1922.
Pauline Garon, actress and "first class dressmaker," believes every woman ought to design her own clothes.

2349   "Pauline Starke." Screen News, 4 (43): 8, October 31, 1925.
Pauline Starke models a coat from "Paris."

2350   "Pauzer(s), U." American Film Institute Catalog, 1961-70, p. 499.
U. Pauzer(s) is credited with the costumes of "Yolanta."

2351   "Pawloff, Irène." American Film Institute Catalog, 1961-70, p. 500.
Irène Pawloff is credited with the costumes of "Night Affair."

2352   Peak, Mayme Ober. "Study the Stars and Dress Your Line." Ladies' Home Journal, 49 (6): 8-9, 105, June 1932.
The emphasis is on figure flaws; Adrian discusses designing for Joan Crawford and Norma Shearer, and Greta Garbo in "A Woman of Affairs" and "Mata Hari"; Travis Banton discusses designing

for Carole Lombard, Miriam Hopkins, Tallulah Bankhead, Lilyan
Tashman and Ruth Chatterton; Max Ree for Irene Dunne; Guy Duty,
who formerly worked with Gloria Swanson, for Sally Eilers; Gwen
Wakeling for Constance Bennett, Dolores Del Rio, and Ann Harding;
and Earl Luick for Loretta Young. Adrian also discusses the influence of his costumes for Greta Garbo on fashion.

2353 "Pearlman, Lilli." American Film Institute Catalog, 1961-70,
      p. 501.
Lilli Pearlman is credited with Jayne Mansfield's wardrobe in
"The Fat Spy."

2354 "Peasant Embroidery." Screen News, 4 (16): 6, April 18,
      1925.
European peasant fashions are currently popular, as shown in a
gown modeled by Doris Kenyon, from "The Half Way Girl."

2355 "The Peasant Influence." Hollywood, 26 (8): 41-2, August
      1937.
One costume each is modeled by Helen Vinson and Ruth Martin
from "Vogues of 1938," and Jeanette MacDonald from "Firefly."
Luise Rainer models a scarf from "The Emperor's Candlesticks."

2356 "Pechanz, W." American Film Institute Catalog, 1961-70,
      p. 501.
W. Pechanz is credited with the costumes of "Snow White."

2357 "Peck, Ann B." American Film Institute Catalog, 1961-70,
      p. 501.
Ann B. Peck was the costume designer of "Cheyenne Autumn"
and is credited with the ladies' costumes of "McLintock!"

2358 "Penezis, I." American Film Institute Catalog, 1961-70, p.
      502.
I. Penezis is credited with the costumes of "They Came to Rob
Las Vegas."

2359 Penn, Virginia. "Behind the Fitting-Room Door." Motion
      Picture Classic, 30 (1): 52-3, 105, August 1925.
Howard Greer discusses designing for Pola Negri in general and
in "The Spanish Dancer," and for Betty Compson, Nita Naldi,
Betty Bronson, and Lois Wilson.

2360 _____. "Behind the Fitting-Room Door." Motion Picture
      Classic, 30 (2): 72-3, 88-9, 119, September 1925.
Howard Greer discusses designing for Jetta Goudal, Trixie Friganza, Lillian Rich, Louise Fazenda, Dorothy Mackaill, Viola
Dana, Anna Q. Nilsson, Agnes Ayres, Constance Bennett, and
others briefly.

2361 "Perelyotov, V." American Film Institute Catalog, 1961-70,
      p. 504.
V. Perelyotov is credited with the costumes of "Clear Skies" and
"Grown-Up Children."

2362 "Pericoli, Ugo." <u>American Film Institute Catalog, 1961-70,</u>
       p. 504.
       Ugo Pericoli is credited with the costumes of "Everybody Go
       Home!," "Let's Talk About Women," "Love on the Riviera,"
       "Il Successo," and "Anzio."

2363 "Peris." <u>American Film Institute Catalog, 1961-70,</u> p. 504.
       Peris is credited with the wardrobe of "Kid Rodelo" and "A Bullet
       for Sandoval."

2364 "Persian Expert for 'Omar the Tentmaker.'" <u>Screen News,</u>
       1 (13): 18, May 10, 1922.
       François Nazare Aga, the costume and set adviser for "Omar the
       Tentmaker," was born in France but mostly grew up in Persia.
       He has since become an authority on Persian customs, as well
       as an accomplished sketch artist; a book of his sketches for news-
       papers and magazines has been published.

2365 "Personal Appearance." <u>Stage,</u> 16 (6): 54, March 15, 1939.
       Merle Oberon's chief costume in "Wuthering Heights," by Omar
       Kiam, was a dress made of imported wool, painstakingly aged,
       which cost about $200 and was given as much attention as a
       glamorous dress. Oberon models the dress.

2366 "Personal Appearance." <u>Stage,</u> 16 (9): 48, May 1, 1939.
       Bette Davis is said to adapt well to her period costumes in
       "Juarez" and to her modern costumes in "Dark Victory." A
       piece of jewelry she wears in "Juarez" is described and is being
       copied by costume jewelers for retail sale.

2367 "Personal Notes on Bonnie Cashin." <u>Screenland,</u> 49 (8): 65-
       6, June 1945.
       This biography of Bonnie Cashin traces her career from growing
       up in Los Angeles and in her mother's dressmaking shop, to her
       being hired by Twentieth Century-Fox in August 1943.

2368 Perutz, Kathrin. "Celebrities," in <u>Beyond the Looking</u>
       <u>Glass: America's Beauty Culture.</u> New York: Morrow,
       1970, p. 216-27.
       "Movie stars are not considered swinging and therefore aren't
       imitated," though such movies as "Bonnie and Clyde," and less
       so "Cleopatra" and "Dr. Zhivago," do influence fashion. "Bonnie
       and Clyde" influenced fashion because the clothes gave a tough
       look, but were dated enough not to threaten one's image of sweet-
       ness. Elvis Presley shot to stardom dressed in clothes similar
       to those worn by Marlon Brando in "The Wild One"--essentially
       tight, black, and of leather.

2369 "Peruzzi." <u>American Film Institute Catalog, 1961-70,</u> p. 506.
       Peruzzi is credited with the costumes of "Guns of the Black
       Witch" and "The Minotaur."

2370 "Peruzzi, Ditta." <u>American Film Institute Catalog, 1961-70,</u>
       p. 506.

Ditta Peruzzi is credited with the costumes of "David and Goliath."

2371   Peta.   "The Fashions Go Round and Around!"   Film Pictorial,
           9 (218): 24-5, April 25, 1936.
       Brief mention of a hat worn by Helen Vinson in "The Tunnel" and
       a dress worn by Norma Shearer in "Romeo and Juliet," the cos-
       tumes of which are influencing fashion.   Dolores Costello models
       a costume and a hat from "Little Lord Fauntleroy," and Nancy
       Burne models a retail copy of the hat.

2372   _____.   "These Films Will Affect Our Fashions."   Film
           Pictorial, 9 (220): 24-5, May 9, 1936.
       One costume each is modeled by Ann Harding from "The Lady
       Consents," Marlene Dietrich from "Desire," Miriam Hopkins from
       "These Three," and Helen Vinson from "Love in Exile" (by Schia-
       parelli).   Brief mention of each.

2373   _____, "Ginger, Grace and Gaiety!"   Film Pictorial, 9
           (223): 24-5, May 30, 1936.
       Discussion of costumes by Bernard Newman worn by Ginger Rogers
       in "Top Hat" and "Follow the Fleet."   She models three costumes
       from the latter.

2374   _____.   "Jessie Matthews--Simplicity and Splendour."   Film
           Pictorial, 9 (227): 24-5, June 27, 1936.
       Discussion of costumes by Joe Strassner worn by Jessie Matthews
       in "It's Love Again," five costumes and two hats from which she
       models.

2375   _____.   " 'Mary of Scotland' Fashions Reveal 1936 Trend."
           Film Pictorial, 9 (230): 16-7, July 18, 1936.
       A collage of costumes, hats, gloves, and a purse worn by Katha-
       rine Hepburn in "Mary of Scotland"; with additional stills and
       closeups of others, including Molly Lamont.   Includes comments
       concerning how they compare with current fashion.   Mme. Hilda
       Grenier was the film's adviser.

2376   _____.   "Peta Reveals Secrets of the Spring."   Film Pic-
           torial, 9 (213): 24-5, March 21, 1936.
       Brief mention of the trend in hemlines, as worn by Claudette
       Colbert in "The Bride Comes Home" and Marlene Dietrich in
       "Desire," both by Travis Banton.   Brief mention also of fashion
       trends created by "Romeo and Juliet," through trimmings and
       embroidery.   Ginger Rogers models a beret from "Follow the
       Fleet."

2377   Petrou, David Michael.   The Making of "Superman--The Movie."
           New York: Warner, 1978.
       Extensive references to the costumes of "Superman--The Movie,"
       including Yvonne Blake's researching the original comics, though
       director Richard Donner did not want them too similar for "Super-
       man"; Ruth Morley, who had previously worked on "Annie Hall,"
       helped with the British and American costumes and researched

the guard costumes at the White House; Betty Adamson, wardrobe
supervisor, applied reflector paper costing hundreds of dollars
per roll to the costumes of Susannah York and Marlon Brando;
Brando wore an "S," one of the departures from the comics, to
signify the bond between father and son; Jack O'Halloran wore
five-inch platform shoes to be almost seven feet tall; $52,000
was lost per day for several days due to Gene Hackman's costume and wig fittings during script revisions; Eddie Albert's
measurements were telexed to Blake due to his last-minute hiring;
Valerie Perrine discusses her gauche wardrobe; and brief mention
of Ned Beatty's costume. Christopher Reeve, in the title role,
required costumes with extra lining and dress shields due to perspiration, and required 25 costume and seven cape duplicates
due to different positions and special effects. Costume duplicates
were also required for a midget in a long shot and stuntmen.
Kirk Alyn discusses changes in the Superman costume since he
played the role (in "Superman," 1948, and "Atom Man vs. Superman," in 1950); mainly, that he had to keep stretching out the
cotton tights and costume. The credits read: costumes designed
by Yvonne Blake, wardrobe supervisor, and additional designs by
Betty Adamson, additional costumes by Ruth Morley, costumes
[made] by Bermans & Nathans Ltd., Clark Kent's wardrobe by
Barneys Inc., jewelry by Cartier, and watches by Timex.

2378   "Phelps, Ray." American Film Institute Catalog, 1961-70,
         p. 508.
Ray Phelps is credited with the costumes of "Barquero" and the
wardrobe of "Thunder Alley" and "Pieces of Dreams."

2379   "Philippe, J. Claude." American Film Institute Catalog, 1961-
         70, p. 509.
J. Claude Philippe is credited with the costumes of "The Night of
the Generals."

2380   Phillips, Dorothy. "Screen Style Gossip." Screen News, 1
         (27): 26, August 26, 1922.
Currently fashionable Chinese and Persian shawls are a result
of the costumes worn in "Omar the Tentmaker."

2381   _____. "Screen Style Gossip." Screen News, 1 (33): 8,
         October 7, 1922.
Includes a description of one gown worn by Madge Bellamy in
"Hottentot."

2382   _____. "Screen Style Gossip." Screen News, 2 (6): 20,
         February 10, 1923.
Includes descriptions of costumes bought by Norma Talmadge in
Paris for "Within the Law" and of skirt lengths as worn by Ruth
Clifford in "The Dangerous Age."

2383   "Phillips, Thalia." American Film Institute Catalog, 1961-70,
         p. 509.
Thalia Phillips is credited with the costumes of "Barquero," the

wardrobe of "Johnny Reno" and "They Shoot Horses, Don't They?," and the women's costumes of "The April Fools."

INTRODUCTION TO "PHOTOPLAY FASHIONS"

The four sections of columns from Photoplay consist of "Seymour--Photoplay's Style Authority," "Photoplay Fashions," "Fashion Letter," and "Photoplay's Pattern of the Month"; all are arranged in chronological sequence.

The page numbers included are somewhat misleading, in that ads and nonfilm costume stills were often mixed within the sections of "Seymour--Photoplay's Style Authority" and "Photoplay Fashions." "Photoplay's Pattern of the Month" was often included within the "Photoplay Fashions" section. Determining even the beginning page of some of the fashion sections was often difficult because there might be no title page or because it would be presented on several pages within the sections.

The authors of the "Photoplay Fashions" articles were Rita Kaufman for March 1935; Courtenay Marvin for July 1935; Katherine Howard for April 1936 to December 1936, March 1937 to September 1937, and December 1939; Gwenn Walters from January 1937 to February 1937, November 1937 to November 1939, and January and October 1940; Adele Whiteley Fletcher for October 1947; Peggy Thorndike for October 1948 to September 1949; and Jacqueline Dempsey for issues from October 1949 to October 1951, though she was listed as the "fashion editor" rather than author, as was Peggy Thorndike; and Adele Whiteley Fletcher was credited as the "Director" for the October 1947 issue. Some of the above have written articles that can be found listed under their surnames.

"Seymour--Photoplay's Style Authority"

This column ran from March 1931 to November 1935, though other articles were written by Seymour before and after these, some of which can be found later in this bibliography under "S." The costumes modeled often included such accessories as hats and jewelry, and many costumes could be bought as copies; in the back of each issue appeared a list of stores throughout the country.

2384 "Seymour--Photoplay's Style Authority." Photoplay, 39 (4):
      61-4, March 1931.
   Includes one still each of Greta Garbo in a skullcap from "Inspiration" and Dorothy Mackaill in a hat from "Their Mad Moment."

2385 _____. Photoplay, 40 (1): 61-4, June 1931.
   One costume each is modeled by Bebe Daniels from "The Maltese Falcon" and Dorothy Mackaill from "Party Husband"; and Lilyan Tashman models four from "Up Pops the Devil."

2386 _____. Photoplay, 40 (2): 43-6, July 1931.

One costume each is modeled by Joan Crawford from "This Modern Age," Rose Hobart from "We Three," Fay Wray from "The Lawyer's Secret," Anita Louise from "Everything's Rosie," Barbara Stanwyck from "Ten Cents a Dance," and Frances Dee from "An American Tragedy"; Mitzi Green models several costumes from "Let's Play King."

2387 _____. Photoplay, 40 (3): 41-4, August 1931.
One costume each is modeled by Bette Davis from "Seed," Virginia Cherrill from "The Brat," Lita Chevret from "Everything's Rosie," and Carole Lombard from "I Take This Woman." Constance Bennett models three costumes, with three of the original sketches, and Hedda Hopper one costume with an original sketch, from "The Common Law."

2388 _____. Photoplay, 40 (4): 41-4, September 1931.
One costume each is modeled by Sylvia Sidney from "An American Tragedy" and Madge Evans from "Guilty Hands," and two each are modeled by Constance Bennett from "Bought," and Barbara Weeks from "Palmy Days," by Chanel.

2389 _____. Photoplay, 40 (5): 56-61, October 1931.
One costume each is modeled by Madge Evans from "Sporting Blood," Dolores Costello from "Expensive Woman," Tallulah Bankhead from "My Sin," Adrienne Ames from "24 Hours," Lilyan Tashman from "Murder by the Clock," Alice McCormack from "Bad Girl," and Sally Blane from "The Star Witness."

2390 _____. Photoplay, 40 (6): 62-5, November 1931.
Frances Dee models one costume from "Rich Man's Folly," and Judith Wood models one and Peggy Shannon two costumes from "Road to Reno."

2391 _____. Photoplay, 41 (1): 42, 62, December 1931.
Mae Clarke models two costumes from "Frankenstein," Kay Francis one and Lilyan Tashman three costumes and one hat from "Girl About Town."

2392 _____. Photoplay, 41 (2): 61-4, January 1932.
One costume each is modeled by Dorothy Lee from "Peach O'Reno," Conchita Montenegro from "Disorderly Conduct," and Joan Crawford from "Possessed." Two costumes each are modeled by Marion Davies from "Polly of the Circus," Dorothy Tree from "Husband's Holiday," and Norma Shearer from "Private Lives."

2393 _____. Photoplay, 41 (3): 61-4, February 1932.
One costume each is modeled by Myrna Loy from "Emma," Judith Wood from "Working Girls," Carole Lombard from "No One Man," and Adrienne Ames from "One Hour with You."

2394 _____. Photoplay, 41 (4): 61-4, March 1932.
Three costumes each are modeled by Carole Lombard from "No One Man" and Miriam Hopkins from "Two Kinds of Woman."

2395 _____. Photoplay, 41 (5): 63-6, April 1932.
One costume each is modeled by Karen Morley from "Arsene
Lupin," Juliette Compton from "Strangers in Love," and Frances
Dee from "Sky Bride." Two costumes each are modeled by
Miriam Hopkins from "Dancers in the Dark," Tallulah Bankhead
from "Thunder Below," and Elissa Landi from "The Devil's
Lottery" (with one sketch).

2396 _____. Photoplay, 41 (6): 61-4, May 1932.
One costume each is modeled by Ruth Chatterton from "The Rich
Are Always with Us," Bette Davis from "The Man Who Played
God," Mae Clarke from "Impatient Maiden," and Mary Doran
from "Beauty and the Boss"; Kay Francis models two from
"Dangerous Brunette," and Dorothy Jordan models four from "The
Wet Parade" (mostly half-shots of Jordan).

2397 _____. Photoplay, 42 (1): 61-4, June 1932.
One costume each is modeled by Anita Louise from "As You De-
sire Me," Kay Francis from "Street of Women," Loretta Young
from "Week-End Marriage," Mary Astor and Edith Knapp from
"A Successful Calamity," Joan Crawford from "Letty Lynton,"
Carole Lombard from "Sinners in the Sun," Adrienne Dore from
"The Rich Are Always with Us," and Madge Evans from "Are You
Listening?"

2398 _____. Photoplay, 42 (2): 58-63, July 1932.
Greta Garbo models a costume from "As You Desire Me," with
one sketch; Florine McKinney models two costumes from "Horse
Feathers," with two sketches; and three costumes each are modeled by Mae Clarke from "Night World," Arletta Duncan from
"Back Street," and Loretta Young from "Week-End Marriage,"
with three sketches of Young's costumes.

2399 _____. Photoplay, 42 (3): 61-4, August 1932.
One costume each is modeled by Marian Brian from "Blessed
Event," Myrna Loy from "Love Me Tonight," and Joan Bennett
from "Week-Ends Only"; and two costumes each are modeled by
Hedda Hopper from "As You Desire Me," Helen Twelvetrees from
"Without Shame," and Ruth Chatterton from "Children of Pleasure";
with sketches of all but for the first two films.

2400 _____. Photoplay, 42 (4): 61-4, September 1932.
One costume each is modeled by Florence Eldredge from "Thirteen Women," Constance Bennett from "Two Against the World,"
and Lila Lee from "War Correspondent"; and two costumes each
are modeled by Susan Fleming from "Million Dollar Legs" and
Karen Morley from "Washington Masquerade." Also includes two
sketches of costumes worn by Irene Dunne in "Thirteen Women";
with sketches for all films except "Washington Masquerade."

2401 _____. Photoplay, 42 (5): 61-4, October 1932.
One costume each is modeled by Katharine Hepburn from "A Bill
of Divorcement," Kay Francis from "One Way Passage," and

Leila Hyams from "The Big Broadcast." Verree Teasdale models
a costume from "Skyscraper Souls," with an additional sketch;
Adrienne Ames models two costumes from "Guilty as Hell," with
an additional sketch; and there is a sketch of a costume worn by
Myrna Loy in "Thirteen Women."

2402 _____. Photoplay, 42 (6): 62-7, November 1932.
One costume each is modeled by Constance Cummings from "Washington Masquerade," Miriam Hopkins from "Trouble in Paradise,"
and Karen Morley from "The Phantom of Crestwood"; and three
costumes, with an additional sketch, are modeled by Dorothy Jordan from "That's My Boy" and Marian Marsh from "Sport Page."

2403 _____. Photoplay, 43 (1): 62-8, December 1932.
One costume each is modeled by Ginger Rogers from "You Said
a Mouthful," by Orry-Kelly; Lillian Miles from "Plainclothes
Man," by Robert Kalloch; Marian Nixon from "Too Busy to Work,"
by Earl Luick; and Lili Damita from "Goldie Gets Along," by
Irene. Also includes one sketch each of costumes worn by Zita
Johann in "The Mummy," by Vera West; and Sari Maritza in
"Evenings for Sale," by Travis Banton, with sketches of her
accessories, including jewelry. Two costumes each are modeled
by Susan Fleming from "He Learned About Women," by Travis
Banton, and Tallulah Bankhead from "Faithless," by Adrian.

2404 _____. Photoplay, 43 (2): 62-7, January 1933.
One costume each is modeled by Helen Vinson from "Lawyer
Man" and by Nancy Carroll from "Undercover Man"; two costumes
each are modeled by Ann Harding and Myrna Loy from "Animal
Kingdom," by Howard Greer, and Sally Eilers and Helen Vinson
from "Second Hand Wife," by David Cox for Eilers and Edith Head
for Vinson; with sketches for the last two films.

2405 _____. Photoplay, 43 (3): 62-7, February 1933.
One costume each is modeled by Ginger Rogers from "Forty-
Second Street," by Orry-Kelly; Nancy Carroll from "Child of
Manhattan"; Joan Blondell from "Blondie Johnson"; Carole Lom-
bard from "No Man of Her Own," by Travis Banton; and Claire
Dodd from "Hard to Handle," by Orry-Kelly; with one sketch of a
costume by Earl Luick worn by Lilian Bond in "Hot Pepper."
Three costumes each are modeled by Jean Arthur from "The Past
of Mary Holmes," by Walter Plunkett, and Constance Cummings
from "Billion Dollar Scandal."

2406 _____. Photoplay, 43 (4): 64-9, March 1933.
One costume each is modeled by Myrna Loy from "Topaze," by
Rose Crowley; Katharine Hepburn from "A Great Desire ("Chris-
topher Strong"), by Howard Greer; Barbara Barondess from
"Fever," by Kalloch; Ginger Rogers from "Broadway Bad"; Sari
Maritza from "A Lady's Profession"; Miriam Jordan from "Dan-
gerously Yours"; Constance Bennett from "Our Betters"; Frances
Dee from "The Crime of the Century," by Travis Banton; and
Sally Eilers from "Central Airport" and Kay Francis from "The

Keyhole, " by Orry-Kelly.

2407 _____. Photoplay, 43 (5): 60-5, April 1933.
One costume each is modeled by Katharine Hepburn from "Christopher Strong, " by Howard Greer; Mae Clarke from "Parole Girl";
and Adrienne Ames from "From Hell to Heaven, " by Travis Banton; Kay Francis models two from "The Keyhole, " by Orry-Kelly;
and three costumes each are modeled by Bette Davis from "Ex-
Lady, " by Orry-Kelly, and Miriam Jordan from "Dangerously
Yours, " by Edward Lambert under the direction of Rita Kaufman.

2408 _____. Photoplay, 43 (6): 62-7, May 1933.
Minna Gombell models one costume and Genevieve Tobin five from
"Pleasure Cruise, " by Edward Lambert; Shirley Grey models one
from "Terror Abroad, " by Travis Banton; and Myrna Loy models
three costumes, with one sketch, from "Man on the Nile. "

2409 _____. Photoplay, 44 (1): 64-9, June 1933.
Ruthelma Stevens models one costume by Kalloch from "The Circus Queen Murder, " and two costumes each are modeled by Fay
Wray from "The Woman I Stole, " by Kalloch; Sari Maritza from
"International House, " by Travis Banton; Nancy Carroll from "I
Love That Man"; and Myrna Loy from "The Barbarian. " Includes
one sketch of one of Wray's costume, and two sketches of costumes worn by Carole Lombard in "Supernatural, " by Travis Banton.

2410 _____. Photoplay, 44 (2): 64-9, July 1933.
One costume each is modeled by Ruth Hall from "I'll Be Hanged
if I Do, " by Nancy of Hollywood, and Lona Andree from "College
Humor, " by Travis Banton; and two costumes each are modeled
by Gloria Stuart from "It's Great to Be Alive"; Marian Nixon from
"Five Cents a Glass, " by Rita Kaufman; and Bebe Daniels from
"Cocktail Hour, " by Kalloch.

2411 _____. Photoplay, 44 (3): 60-5, August 1933.
Adrienne Ames models two costumes and Helen Twelvetrees three
from "Disgraced, " by Travis Banton.

2412 _____. Photoplay, 44 (4): 61-7, September 1933.
Claudette Colbert models one costume from "Three-Cornered
Moon, " and two costumes each are modeled by Helen Vinson from
"Midnight Club" and Carole Lombard from "Brief Moment, " all
three by Travis Banton. Lilian Harvey models two costumes from
"My Lips Betray, " by Joe Strassner, whom she brought from
Europe.

2413 _____. Photoplay, 44 (5): 61-7, October 1933.
One costume each is modeled by Heather Angel from "Charlie
Chan's Greatest Case, " by Royer; Gloria Stuart from "The Se-
cret of the Blue Room, " by Vera West; and Helen Chandler from
"Goodbye Again. " Claire Trevor models two costumes from "The
Last Trail, " by Royer. Includes two sketches of Claudette Col-

bert's costumes from "Torch Singer," by Travis Banton.

2414 _____. Photoplay, 44 (6): 61-7, November 1933.
One costume each is modeled by Irene Bentley from "My Weakness," by Rita Kaufman; Miriam Hopkins from "Design for Living";
Sally Eilers from "Walls of Gold," by Royer; Claire Dodd and
Helen Twelvetrees from "My Women," by Kalloch; Billie Burke
from "Only Yesterday," by Vera West; and Maureen O'Sullivan
from "Stage Mother," by Adrian, with one sketch.

2415 _____. Photoplay, 45 (1): 63-8, December 1933.
One costume each is modeled by Constance Cummings from
"Broadway Thru a Keyhole," by Gwen Wakeling; Claire Trevor
from "The Mad Game" and Sally Eilers from "Walls of Gold,"
both by Royer; Fay Wray from "Master of Men," by Kalloch; and
Claudette Colbert from "Torch Singer" and Miriam Hopkins from
"Design for Living," both by Travis Banton, with one sketch of
Hopkins. Dorothy Tree models two costumes from "East of 5th
Avenue."

2416 _____. Photoplay, 45 (2): 61-6, January 1934.
One costume each is modeled by June Collyer from "Before Midnight," by Kalloch; Marguerite Churchill from "Girl Without a
Room," by Travis Banton; Sally Blane from "Advice to the Lovelorn"; Loretta Young from "Born to Be Bad," by Gwen Wakeling;
and Heather Angel from "7 Lives Were Changed," by Royer.
Two costumes each are modeled by Helen Vinson from "As Husbands Go," by Rita Kaufman, and Fay Wray from "Master of
Men."

2417 _____. Photoplay, 45 (3): 62-7, February 1934.
One costume each is modeled by Marian Marsh from "I Like It
That Way"; Dorothea Wieck from "Miss Fane's Baby Is Stolen";
Claire Trevor from "Woman and the Law," by Royer; Marlene
Dietrich from "Queen Catherine" ("The Scarlet Empress"), Gail
Patrick and Evelyn Venable from "Death Takes a Holiday" and
Miriam Hopkins from "All of Me," all three films by Travis
Banton. Ann Harding models two costumes from "Gallant Lady,"
by Gwen Wakeling, with one sketch.

2418 _____. Photoplay, 45 (4): 61-8, March 1934.
One costume each is modeled by Suzanne Kaaren from "Coming
Out Party," Carole Lombard from "Bolero," and Ida Lupino from
"Search for Beauty," the last two films by Travis Banton. Marian
Nixon models two costumes from "The Line-Up."

2419 _____. Photoplay, 45 (5): 63-9, April 1934.
One costume each is modeled by Carole Lombard from "Bolero,"
and Elissa Landi from "Sisters Under the Skin," by Kalloch; and
two costumes each are modeled by Loretta Young from "The
House of Rothschild," by Gwen Wakeling; Irene Harvey, with a
sketch of a costume for Sally Eilers, from "Three on a Honeymoon," by Royer; and Pat Patterson (Thelma Todd models one)

from "Bottoms Up," by Russell Patterson.   Marlene Dietrich
models a pearl crown from "The Scarlet Empress."

2420 _____. Photoplay, 45 (6): 62-6, May 1934.
One costume each is modeled by Patricia Ellis and Isabel Jewell
from "Let's Be Ritzy," by Vera West; Helen Twelvetrees from
"All Men Are Enemies"; and Irene Harvey from "Three on a
Honeymoon," by Royer.   Two costumes each are modeled by
Adrienne Ames from "You're Telling Me," by Travis Banton, and
Claire Trevor from "Wild Gold"; and three costumes are modeled
by Heather Angel from "Murder in Trinidad," the last two films
also by Royer.

2421 _____. Photoplay, 46 (1): 60-4, June 1934.
Kathryn Williams models a hat from "Where Sinners Meet"; Jean
Arthur models one costume from "Whirlpool"; Sylvia Sidney models
two from "Thirty Day Princess"; and Renee Gadd models one and
Genevieve Tobin two costumes from "Uncertain Lady."

2422 _____. Photoplay, 46 (2): 62-6, July 1934.
Marian Nixon models a costume and a hat from "Embarrassing
Moments," and Mary Carlisle models two costumes from "Merry
Andrew."

2423 _____. Photoplay, 46 (3): 62-7, August 1934.
One costume each is modeled by Billie Burke from "Arabella,"
Claire Trevor from "Baby Take a Bow," Irene Harvey from "Let's
Try Again," and Zita Johann and Madge Evans from "Grand Can-
ary."   Two costumes each are modeled by Dorothy Burgess and
Fay Wray from "Black Moon," by Kalloch.

2424 _____. Photoplay, 46 (4): 60-6, September 1934.
One costume is modeled by Drue Leyton from "Charlie Chan's
Courage," Mae West from "It Ain't No Sin" ("Belle of the Nineties"), Diana Wynyard from "One More River," and Helen Mack
from "Kiss and Make Up" (by Travis Banton).   Julie Haydon and
Kay Johnson each models two from "Afterwards," by Walter Plunkett, and Peggy Wood models three from "Handy Andy," by Royer.

2425 _____. Photoplay, 46 (5): 59-64, October 1934.
Rochelle Hudson models two costumes from "Bachelor Bait," by
Walter Plunkett; Diana Wynyard models one and Jane Wyatt three
from "One More River," by Vera West; and Janet Gaynor models
three from "Servants' Entrance," by Rene Hubert.   Also included
are closeups of Claudette Colbert in a turban and jewelry from
"Cleopatra," Anna Neagle in a necklace from "Nell Gwyn," and of
Patricia Hilliard and Joan Gardner from "The Private Life of Don
Juan," with references to how the above will influence fashion.

2426 _____. Photoplay, 46 (6): 60-6, November 1934.
Claudette Colbert models one costume from "Imitation of Life";
Helen Vinson models two from "Broadway Bill," by Kalloch; and
three costumes each are modeled by Drue Leyton from "Charlie

Chan in London," by Royer, and Fay Wray from "The Richest Girl in the World," by Walter Plunkett.

2427 _____. Photoplay, 47 (1): 62-7, December 1934.
One costume each is modeled by Elissa Landi and Sharon Lynn from "Enter Madame"; Claudette Colbert from "Imitation of Life," by Travis Banton; Gloria Swanson from "Music in the Air"; Claire Trevor from "Elinor Norton," by Rene Hubert; Carole Lombard, with one sketch, from "Part Time Lady"; Karen Morley from "Wednesday's Child," by Walter Plunkett; and Gertrude Michael from "Menace."

2428 _____. Photoplay, 47 (2): 60-5, January 1935.
One costume each is modeled by Helen Vinson from "The Captain Hates the Sea," by Kalloch; Claudette Colbert from "Imitation of Life"; Gertrude Michael from "Menace" and Kitty Carlisle from "Here Is My Heart," by Travis Banton; and Shirley Grey from "Wednesday's Child." Greta Garbo models three costumes from "The Painted Veil."

2429 _____. Photoplay, 48 (4): 54-61, September 1935.
Jean Muir models one costume from "Orchids to You," by Rene Hubert.

2430 _____. Photoplay, 48 (5): 54-61, October 1935.
One costume each is modeled by Rochelle Hudson from "Curly Top" and Jane Hamilton from "The Three Musketeers." Lucille Ball models a hat inspired by "Top Hat."

2431 _____. Photoplay, 48 (6): 54-61, November 1935.
Princess Natalie Paley models one costume by Walter Plunkett from "Sylvia Scarlett."

"Photoplay Fashions"

2432 "Photoplay Fashions," by Rita Kaufman. Photoplay, 47 (4): 58-66, March 1935.
Claudette Colbert models two costumes from "The Gilded Lily," by Travis Banton, with closeups of her jewelry and of a fan used by Marlene Dietrich in "Caprice Espagnole" ("The Devil Is a Woman"). Discussion at length of how a somewhat dowdy Merle Oberon was transformed for the lead role in "Folies Bergère de Paris" ("Folies Bergère"), with a $25,000 wardrobe by Omar Kiam; with photos of before and after.

2433 "Photoplay Fashions." Photoplay, 47 (5): 57-67, April 1935.
Virginia Reid models two costumes, and Margaret McChrystal one, from "Roberta," by Bernard Newman. Lilian Harvey models three from "Let's Live Tonight," by Kalloch.

2434 _____. Photoplay, 47 (6): 58-66, May 1935.
Claire Trevor models a wedding gown by Rene Hubert from

"Spring Tonic."

2435 _____, by Courtenay Marvin. <u>Photoplay</u>, 48 (2): 53-61,
        101, July 1935.
Joan Crawford models a gown by Adrian from "No More Ladies";
one of her gowns required 30 yards of silver tissue at $18 per
yard. "Anna Karenina" will influence fashion through trimmings of
feathers, flowers, ribbons, lace and fur. Shirley Temple models
six costumes by Rene Hubert from "Our Little Girl."

2436 _____, by Courtenay Marvin. <u>Photoplay</u>, 48 (3): 56-63,
        August 1935.
Helen Gahagan models two costumes from "She" and Marion
Davies one from "Page Miss Glory."

<u>See</u> "Seymour--Photoplay's Style Authority" for articles from Sep-
tember to November 1935. Any missing months are indicative of
articles that did not specifically mention film titles. The monthly
articles can be confusing because of changing titles, as with the
next article; all are presented in chronological order regardless of
titles.

2437 "Photoplay's Own Fashions." <u>Photoplay</u>, 49 (1): 61-8, Janu-
        ary 1936.
Marlene Dietrich models three costumes from "Desire," with
closeups of her hat, jewelry, and gloves.

2438 "Photoplay Fashions," by Katherine Howard. <u>Photoplay</u>, 49
        (4): 63-71, April 1936.
Jean Arthur models six costumes from "A Gentleman Goes to
Town," with two original sketches, designed by Lange (probably
Samuel Lange).

2439 _____, by Katherine Howard. <u>Photoplay</u>, 49 (5): 61-70,
        May 1936.
Grace Moore models two costumes by Dryden from "The King
Steps Out," with two sketches for copies also designed by Dryden
and sold at Saks Fifth Avenue. Carole Lombard models three
from "Love Before Breakfast," by Travis Banton.

2440 _____, by Katherine Howard. <u>Photoplay</u>, 49 (6): 61-70,
        June 1936.
Included are numerous stills of costumes, hats, and other ac-
cessories worn by Katharine Hepburn in "Mary of Scotland," with
a closeup of Mary Beaton; all designed by Walter Plunkett. Also
included are photos of shoes, hats, gloves, and jewelry worn by
Loretta Young in "The Guarded Hour"; she models two costumes.
Bette Davis models two costumes by Orry-Kelly from "Golden
Arrow."

2441 _____, by Katherine Howard. <u>Photoplay</u>, 50 (1): 64-5,
        July 1936.
The steps of designing and creating a gown for Carole Lombard

in "The Princess Comes Across" are shown with five stills; designed by Travis Banton.

2442 _____, by Katherine Howard. Photoplay, 50 (2): 61-70,
         August 1936.
Jane Wyman models two costumes from "Lost Horizon," by Ernst
Dryden; Kay Francis two from "Give Me Your Heart," by Orry-
Kelly; Carole Lombard one from "My Man Godfrey" and Dolores
Costello two from "Yours for the Asking," both films by Travis
Banton.

2443 _____, by Katherine Howard. Photoplay, 50 (4): 53-62,
         October 1936.
Madge Evans models two costumes from "Piccadilly Jim," with
closeups of how the costumes appear with different accessories,
including a fur cape.

2444 _____, by Katherine Howard. Photoplay, 50 (5): 53-62,
         November 1936.
Ruth Chatterton models three costumes by Omar Kiam from
"Dodsworth"; and two costumes each are modeled by Ginger
Rogers from "Swing Time," by Bernard Newman, and Shirley
Ross from "The Big Broadcast of 1937," by Travis Banton.

2445 _____, by Katherine Howard. Photoplay, 50 (6): 61-8,
         December 1936.
Merle Oberon models two costumes by Omar Kiam from "Love
Under Fire," and one costume each is modeled by Kay Francis
from "Stolen Holiday," by Orry-Kelly, and Rosalind Russell from
"Craig's Wife."

2446 _____, by Gwenn Walters. Photoplay, 51 (1): 61-70,
         January 1937.
Joan Crawford models two costumes by Adrian from "Love on the
Run," and Grace Moore models a costume by Bernard Newman
for her latest film, "Interlude."

2447 _____, by Gwenn Walters. Photoplay, 51 (2): 61-70,
         February 1937.
Grace Moore models two costumes from "Interlude," by Bernard
Newman and a hat by John Frederics; and Loretta Young models
one costume from "Love Is News." Six photos of the many pieces
of jewelry Greta Garbo wears in "Camille," designed by Adrian.

2448 _____, by Katherine Howard. Photoplay, 51 (3): 61-9,
         March 1937.
Lily Pons models one of her four wedding gowns from "That Girl
from Paris"; Marsha Hunt models three and Eleanore Whitney one
costume from "College Holiday," by Edith Head; and Jean Arthur
models four costumes from "History Is Made at Night," by Bernard Newman.

2449 _____, by Katherine Howard. Photoplay, 51 (4): 61-8,

April 1937.
Gladys Swarthout models one costume by Travis Banton from
"Champagne Waltz," and two costumes each are modeled by Janet
Gaynor from "A Star Is Born," by Omar Kiam, and Maureen
O'Sullivan from "A Day at the Races," by Dolly Tree.

2450 _____, by Katherine Howard. Photoplay, 51 (5): 61-70,
          May 1937.
One costume each is modeled by Loretta Young from "Cafe
Metropole"; Ida Lupino from "Let's Get Married," by Kalloch;
and Anita Louise from "Call It a Day," by Orry-Kelly. Shirley
Ross models three from "Waikiki Wedding," by Edith Head.

2451 _____, by Katherine Howard. Photoplay, 51 (6): 61-70,
          June 1937.
Marlene Dietrich models one costume from "Angel," by Travis
Banton (confusingly worded; may not be a film costume).

2452 _____, by Katherine Howard. Photoplay, 51 (7): 69-78,
          July 1937.
Claudette Colbert models one gown by Travis Banton from "I Met
Him in Paris."

2453 _____, by Katherine Howard. Photoplay, 51 (8): 70-8,
          August 1937.
Marlene Dietrich models three costumes by Travis Banton from
"Angel."

2454 _____, by Katherine Howard. Photoplay, 51 (9): 68-78,
          September 1937.
Joan Bennett models three costumes by Irene, and Helen Vinson,
Peggy Calvin, and Martha Heveran each model one suit, by Omar
Kiam, all from "Vogues of 1938."

2455 _____. Photoplay, 51 (10): 56-63, October 1937.
One costume each is modeled by Madeleine Carroll from "It's
All Yours," by Kalloch; Barbara Stanwyck from "A Love Like
That," by Edward Stevenson; Ida Lupino from "Artists and Models";
and Florence Rice from "Double Wedding," by Adrian. Ginger
Rogers models four from "Stage Door," by Muriel King; and Kay
Francis two from "First Lady," by Orry-Kelly.

2456 _____, by Gwenn Walters. Photoplay, 51 (11): 52-63,
          November 1937.
One costume each is modeled by Sandra Storme from "Sophie
Lang Goes West," by Edith Head, and Loretta Young from "Wife,
Doctor, and Nurse"; and two costumes each are modeled by Anita
Louise from "First Lady," by Orry-Kelly; Joan Blondell from
"Stand-In," by Helen Taylor; and Carole Lombard from "Nothing
Sacred," by Travis Banton.

2457 _____, Gwenn Walters. Photoplay, 51 (1): 48-58, January
          1938.

One costume each is modeled by Miriam Hopkins from "Women
Have a Way"; Simone Simon from "Love and Hisses," by Royer;
and Andrea Leeds from "The Goldwyn Follies," by Omar Kiam.

2458 _____, Gwenn Walters. Photoplay, 52 (2): 56-66, February
1938.
One costume each is modeled by Ann Sothern from "She's Got
Everything" and Ginger Rogers from "Having a Wonderful Time,"
by Edward Stevenson; Claire Trevor from "Big Town Girl," by
Herschel; and Simone Simon from "Love and Hisses," by Royer.

2459 _____, Gwenn Walters. Photoplay, 52 (3): 56-66, March
1938.
One costume each is modeled by Katharine Hepburn from "Bringing Up Baby," by Howard Greer, and Joan Crawford from "Mannequin," by Adrian. Four hats are modeled by actresses, showing
the influence of "Snow White and the Seven Dwarfs."

2460 _____, Gwenn Walters. Photoplay, 52 (4): 56-65, April
1938.
Claudette Colbert models three costumes from "Bluebeard's Eighth
Wife," by Travis Banton, and a swimsuit also worn in the film,
by Mabs Barnes of Hollywood.

2461 _____, Gwenn Walters. Photoplay, 52 (5): 52-61, May
1938.
One costume each is modeled by Loretta Young from "Four Men
and a Prayer"; Simone Simon from "Josette," by Royer; and
Joan Fontaine from "Maid's Night Out," by Edward Stevenson.

2462 _____, Gwenn Walters. Photoplay, 52 (6): 56-64, June
1938.
Dorothy Lamour models one costume by Edith Head and an adaptation, from "Tropic Holiday."

2463 _____, Gwenn Walters. Photoplay, 52 (7): 53-62, July
1938.
Kay Francis models one costume by Orry-Kelly from "Secrets of
an Actress."

2464 _____, Gwenn Walters. Photoplay, 52 (8): 48-58, August
1938.
One costume each is modeled by Barbara Stanwyck from "Always
Goodbye," by Royer, and Gail Patrick from "Wives Under Suspicion."

2465 _____, Gwenn Walters. Photoplay, 52 (9): 58-63, Sep-
tember 1938.
One costume each is modeled by Rosalind Russell from "Four's
a Crowd," by Orry-Kelly; Virginia Bruce from "Woman Against
Woman," by Dolly Tree; Danielle Darrieux from "The Rage of
Paris," by Vera West; and Sonja Henie from "My Lucky Star" and
Barbara Stanwyck from "Always Goodbye," both by Royer.

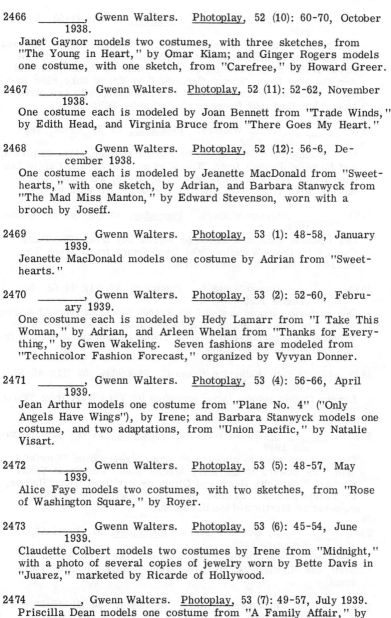

2466 _____, Gwenn Walters. Photoplay, 52 (10): 60-70, October
        1938.
Janet Gaynor models two costumes, with three sketches, from
"The Young in Heart," by Omar Kiam; and Ginger Rogers models
one costume, with one sketch, from "Carefree," by Howard Greer.

2467 _____, Gwenn Walters. Photoplay, 52 (11): 52-62, November
        1938.
One costume each is modeled by Joan Bennett from "Trade Winds,"
by Edith Head, and Virginia Bruce from "There Goes My Heart."

2468 _____, Gwenn Walters. Photoplay, 52 (12): 56-6, De-
        cember 1938.
One costume each is modeled by Jeanette MacDonald from "Sweethearts," with one sketch, by Adrian, and Barbara Stanwyck from
"The Mad Miss Manton," by Edward Stevenson, worn with a
brooch by Joseff.

2469 _____, Gwenn Walters. Photoplay, 53 (1): 48-58, January
        1939.
Jeanette MacDonald models one costume by Adrian from "Sweethearts."

2470 _____, Gwenn Walters. Photoplay, 53 (2): 52-60, Febru-
        ary 1939.
One costume each is modeled by Hedy Lamarr from "I Take This
Woman," by Adrian, and Arleen Whelan from "Thanks for Every-
thing," by Gwen Wakeling.   Seven fashions are modeled from
"Technicolor Fashion Forecast," organized by Vyvyan Donner.

2471 _____, Gwenn Walters. Photoplay, 53 (4): 56-66, April
        1939.
Jean Arthur models one costume from "Plane No. 4" ("Only
Angels Have Wings"), by Irene; and Barbara Stanwyck models one
costume, and two adaptations, from "Union Pacific," by Natalie
Visart.

2472 _____, Gwenn Walters. Photoplay, 53 (5): 48-57, May
        1939.
Alice Faye models two costumes, with two sketches, from "Rose
of Washington Square," by Royer.

2473 _____, Gwenn Walters. Photoplay, 53 (6): 45-54, June
        1939.
Claudette Colbert models two costumes by Irene from "Midnight,"
with a photo of several copies of jewelry worn by Bette Davis in
"Juarez," marketed by Ricarde of Hollywood.

2474 _____, Gwenn Walters. Photoplay, 53 (7): 49-57, July 1939.
Priscilla Dean models one costume from "A Family Affair," by
Howard Shoup; and Billie Burke models several costumes from
"Bridal Suite," which are shown with extra blouses, hats, and
jackets, by Dolly Tree.

2475 _____, Gwenn Walters. Photoplay, 53 (8): 41-50, August
        1939.
One costume each is modeled by Paulette Goddard from "Cat and
the Canary," with a sketch of an additional costume, and Jane
Bryan from "Each Dawn I Die," both films by Edith Head; and
Ann Sheridan from "Winter Carnival," by Erl of Saks Fifth Avenue. Madeleine Carroll models two costumes, with two sketches,
from "Are Husbands Necessary?," also by Edith Head.

2476 _____, Gwenn Walters. Photoplay, 53 (9): 49-58, Sep-
        tember, 1939.
One costume each is modeled by Norma Shearer, Joan Crawford,
and Rosalind Russell from "The Women," by Adrian; Carole Lombard from "The Kind Men Marry," by Irene; and Anita Louise
models three coats from "Hero for a Day," by Vera West.

2477 _____, Gwenn Walters. Photoplay, 53 (10): 49-58, October
        1939.
One costume each is modeled by Myrna Loy from "The Rains
Came," by Gwen Wakeling, and Irene Dunne from "When To-
morrow Comes," by Howard Greer.

2478 _____, Gwenn Walters. Photoplay, 53 (11): 49-58, No-
        vember 1939.
One costume each is modeled by Brenda Marshall from "Espionage
Agent," by Howard Shoup, and Hedy Lamarr from "Lady of the
Tropics," by Adrian; and Loretta Young models two costumes from
"Eternally Yours," by Irene.

2479 _____, by Katherine Howard. Photoplay, 53 (12): 49-58,
        December 1939.
Deanna Durbin models three costumes by Vera West from "First
Love."

2480 _____, by Gwenn Walters. Photoplay, 54 (1): 41-7, Janu-
        ary 1940.
One costume each is modeled by Ann Sheridan from "City of Lost
Men," by Howard Shoup; Mary Martin from "The Great Victor
Herbert," by Edith Head; and Olivia de Havilland from "Raffles,"
by Travis Banton. Includes one sketch each of the costumes
modeled by Martin and de Havilland.

2481 _____, by Gwenn Walters. Photoplay, 54 (2): 49-58,
        February 1940.
Mary Martin models one costume from "The Great Victor Her-
bert" and Madeleine Carroll two from "Safari," both by Edith
Head.

2482 _____, by Gwenn Walters. Photoplay, 54 (3): 49-58,
        March 1940.
One costume each is modeled by Ann Sheridan from "It All Came
True," by Howard Shoup, and Mae West from "My Little Chicka-
dee," by Vera West; and Jane Bryan models two costumes by

Milo Anderson from "Brother Rat and a Baby."

2483 _____, by Gwenn Walters. <u>Photoplay,</u> 54 (4): 53-63, April
        1940.
One costume each is modeled by Zorina from "I Was an Adventuress," by Royer, and Gail Patrick from "My Favorite Wife,"
by Howard Greer.

2484 _____, by Gwenn Walters. <u>Photoplay,</u> 54 (5): 57-68, May
        1940.
Jean Arthur models one costume, with one sketch, from "Too
Many Husbands," by Irene.

2485 _____, by Gwenn Walters. <u>Photoplay,</u> 54 (8): 45-56,
        August 1940.
One costume each is modeled by Paulette Goddard from "The
Ghost Breakers," by Edith Head, and Ann Sothern from "Brother
Orchid," by Howard Shoup.

2486 _____. <u>Photoplay,</u> 54 (9): 35-48, September 1940.
Myrna Loy models one costume by Dolly Tree from "I Love You
Again."

2487 "Photoplay Fashions; Renie, Fashion Designer," by Gwenn
        Walters. <u>Photoplay,</u> 54 (10): 39, October 1940.
Career highlights and biographical information on Renie, whose
credits include "A Bill of Divorcement" (Josette de Lima received credit) and "Stunt Man."

2488 "Photoplay Fashions," by Adele Whitely Fletcher. <u>Photoplay,</u>
        31 (5): 82-6, October 1947.
Joan Caulfield models two suits, and copies, from "Dear Ruth"
and "Welcome Stranger," and Lizabeth Scott models one suit and
a copy from "Desert Fury," all by Edith Head.

2489 _____, by Peggy Thorndike. <u>Photoplay,</u> 33 (5): 80-6,
        October 1948.
Gail Russell models four costumes by Edith Head from "The Night Has
a Thousand Eyes," with retail copies.

2490 _____, by Peggy Thorndike. <u>Photoplay,</u> 36 (1): 80-1, June
        1949.
Jane Wyman models one costume, and two copies, from "A Kiss
in the Dark," by Milo Anderson.

2491 _____, by Peggy Thorndike. <u>Photoplay,</u> 36 (2): 78-9, July
        1949.
Virginia Mayo models one costume, and a copy, from "The Girl
from Jones Beach," by Leah Rhodes.

2492 _____, by Peggy Thorndike. <u>Photoplay,</u> 36 (3): 82-3,
        August 1949.
Marilyn Maxwell models one costume, and a copy, from "Champion,"
by Helen Stepner.

2493 _____, by Peggy Thorndike. <u>Photoplay,</u> 36 (4): 74-5,
        September 1949.
Patricia Neal models one costume, and a copy, from "The Fountainhead," by Milo Anderson.

2494 _____, by Jacqueline Dempsey. <u>Photoplay,</u> 36 (5): 86-7,
        October 1949.
Marta Toren models one costume, and a copy, from "Illegal
Entry," by Yvonne Wood.

2495 _____, by Jacqueline Dempsey. <u>Photoplay,</u> 36 (6): 84-7,
        November 1949.
Joan Caulfield models one costume, and a copy, from "Dear
Wife," by Mary Kay Dodson.

2496 _____, by Jacqueline Dempsey. <u>Photoplay,</u> 36 (7): 80-1,
        December 1949.
Joan Leslie models one costume, and a copy, from "Bed of
Roses," by Michael Woulfe.

2497 _____, by Jacqueline Dempsey. <u>Photoplay,</u> 37 (1): 72-3,
        January 1950.
Laraine Day models one costume, and a copy, from "I Married
a Communist," by Michael Woulfe.

2498 _____, by Jaqueline Dempsey. <u>Photoplay,</u> 37 (2): 80-1,
        February 1950.
Rhonda Fleming models one costume, and a copy, from "The
Great Lover," by Edith Head.

2499 _____, by Jacqueline Dempsey. <u>Photoplay,</u> 37 (3): 80-1,
        March 1950.
Cyd Charisse models one costume, and a copy, from "East Side,
West Side," by Helen Rose.

2500 _____, by Jacqueline Dempsey. <u>Photoplay,</u> 37 (4): 82-3,
        April 1950.
Joanne Dru models one costume, and a copy, from "711 Ocean
Drive," by Odette Myrtil.

2501 _____, by Jacqueline Dempsey. <u>Photoplay,</u> 37 (5): 84-5,
        May 1950.
Mona Freeman models one costume, and a copy, from "I Was a
Shoplifter," by Orry-Kelly.

2502 _____, by Jacqueline Dempsey. <u>Photoplay,</u> 37 (6): 78-9,
        June 1950.
Elizabeth Taylor models a swimsuit and beach dress, and copies,
from "A Place in the Sun," by Edith Head.

2503 _____, by Jacqueline Dempsey. <u>Photoplay,</u> 38 (1): 84-5,
        July 1950.
Jane Powell models one costume, and a copy, from "Nancy Goes to

Rio, " by Helen Rose.

2504 _____, by Jacqueline Dempsey.   Photoplay, 38 (2): 60-1,
            64, August 1950.
Ruth Roman models one costume, and a copy, from "Colt .45, "
by Orry-Kelly; and Vera-Ellen models one costume from "Three
Little Words, " by Helen Rose.

2505 _____, by Jacqueline Dempsey.   Photoplay, 38 (3): 66-7,
            September 1950.
Lizabeth Scott model one costume, and a copy, from "The Wall
Outside, " by Michael Woulfe.

2506 _____, by Jacqueline Dempsey.   Photoplay, 38 (4): 66-7,
            October 1950.
June Allyson models one costume, and a copy, from "Right
Cross, " by Helen Rose.

2507 _____, by Jacqueline Dempsey.   Photoplay, 38 (5): 68-9,
            November 1950.
Viveca Lindfors models one costume, and a copy, from "Dark
City, " by Edith Head.

2508 _____, by Jacqueline Dempsey.   Photoplay, 38 (6): 64-5,
            December 1950.
Nancy Olson models one costume, and a copy, from "Mr. Music, "
by Edith Head.

2509 _____, by Jacqueline Dempsey.   Photoplay, 39 (1): 58-9,
            January 1951.
Patrice Wymore models one costume, and a copy, from "Rocky
Mountain, " by Marjorie Best.

2510 _____, by Jacqueline Dempsey.   Photoplay, 39 (2): 68-9,
            February 1951.
Diana Lynn models one costume, and a copy, from "Bedtime for
Bonzo, " by Rosemary Odell.

2511 _____, by Jacqueline Dempsey.   Photoplay, 39 (3): 64-5,
            March 1951.
Lizabeth Scott models one costume, and a copy, from "The Company She Keeps, " by Michael Woulfe.

2512 _____, by Jacqueline Dempsey.   Photoplay, 39 (4): 64-5,
            April 1951.
Included are stills of two retail garments influenced by the costumes of "Bird of Paradise. "

2513 _____, by Jacqueline Dempsey.   Photoplay, 40 (2): 64-5,
            August 1951.
Sally Forrest models one costume, and a copy, from "The Strip, "
by Helen Rose.

2514 _____, by Jacqueline Dempsey. Photoplay, 40 (4): 66-7,
          October 1951.
Jean Hagen models one costume, and a copy, from "No Questions
Asked, " by Helen Rose.

2515 _____. Photoplay, 40 (5): 64-5, November 1951.
Jeanne Crain models one costume, and a copy, from "People
Will Talk, " by Charles Le Maire.

2516 _____. Photoplay, 41 (2): 64-5, February 1952.
Marie Wilson models one costume, and a copy, from "A Girl in
Every Port, " by Michael Woulfe.

2517 "Photoplay's Star Fashions. " Photoplay, 46 (2): 63, August
          1954.
Cyd Charisse models a costume from "Brigadoon, " which has
been copied for a pattern that can be ordered.

2518 _____. Photoplay, 46 (4): 75-87, October 1954.
Janet Leigh, starring in "The Black Shield of Falworth, " and
others model many "adapted" costumes from the film.   Leigh
also models one costume from the film, with an original sketch.

2519 _____. Photoplay, 48 (3): 71-9, September 1955.
Numerous dresses are modeled, adapted for retail sale from costumes worn in "Lucy Gallant, " by Edith Head.

2520 _____. Photoplay, 49 (4): 66 (63-70), April 1956.
Gregory Peck models a suit from "The Man in the Gray Flannel
Suit, " by Eagle Clothes, costing about $75.

"Photoplay Fashions" has continued, sometime infrequently, to the
present, but without film costumes.

"Fashion Letter"

Photoplay's "Fashion Letter" ran from September 1936 to November
1939.   It was usually a monthly discussion of the fashions featured
in "Photoplay Fashions. "

2521 "Fashion Letter, " by Kathleen Howard.   Photoplay, 50 (3):
          79, September 1936.
Discussion of costumes worn by Jane Wyatt in "Lost Horizon";
Ruth Chatterton in "Dodsworth, " by Omar Kiam; Claudette Colbert
in "Maid of Salem, " by Travis Banton; Billie Burke in "My
American Wife"; and Gail Patrick in "Murder with Pictures, " by
Edith Head; with mention of the fabrics and the potential influence
of the costumes upon fashion.

2522 _____, by Kathleen Howard.   Photoplay, 50 (4): 78, Oc-
          tober 1936.
Discussion of costumes worn by Madge Evans in "Piccadilly Jim, "

Claudette Colbert in "Maid of Salem," Mae West in "Personal
Appearance" ("Go West, Young Man"), and Arline Judge in "Val-
iant Is the Word for Carrie," all of the films designed by Travis
Banton.   Discussion also of fabric Banton designed for Carole
Lombard in "My Man Godfrey," as modeled in "Photoplay Fashions,"
August 1936; made by Ducharne of Paris.

2523 _____, by Kathleen Howard. Photoplay, 50 (5): 90-1,
          November 1936.
Discussion of hats, jewelry, and costumes worn by Greta Garbo
in "Camille" and a costume worn by Joan Crawford in "Love on
the Run," all by Adrian; Kay Francis in "Stolen Holiday," by
Orry-Kelly; and Mae West in "Go West, Young Man," in a fur
cape designed by Irene (Travis Banton was credited with the film);
with brief mention of the influence of the costumes upon fashion
and Adrian's influence through costumes for "Romeo and Juliet"
and "Anna Karenina."

2524 _____, by Kathleen Howard. Photoplay, 50 (6): 78, 99,
          December 1936.
Howard was the commentator at a New York fashion show, for
which she arranged to show period costumes that she felt might
influence fashion; with brief descriptions of costumes worn by
Jean Arthur in "The Plainsman," Olivia de Havilland in "The
Charge of the Light Brigade," Katharine Hepburn in "Portrait of
a Rebel," Claudette Colbert in "Maid of Salem," Loretta Young in
"Ramona," and Joan Crawford in "Gorgeous Hussy."

2525 _____, by Kathleen Howard. Photoplay, 51 (1): 77, 113,
          January 1937.
Some of Omar Kiam's costumes for Merle Oberon in "Beloved
Enemy" are described, two of which she models.   After a year's
absence from Columbia Kalloch noted that he can design film costumes similar to his retail fashions since actresses no longer require exaggerated styles.

2526 _____, by Kathleen Howard. Photoplay, 51 (2): 75, 113,
          February 1937.
Some of Grace Moore's costumes in "Interlude" are discussed,
by Bernard Newman; and costumes worn by Marsha Hunt, Eleanore Whitney, and Olympe Bradna in "College Holiday," by Edith
Head.   Several of Travis Banton's hats for Carole Lombard in
"Swing High Swing Low," made by Lilly Daché, are also discussed.

2527 _____, by Kathleen Howard. Photoplay, 51 (3): 79, 117,
          March 1937.
Discussion of costumes worn by Joan Crawford, Aileen Pringle,
and Phyllis Claire and hats worn by Benita Hume, all in "The
Last of Mrs. Cheyney," by Adrian; with brief mention of Omar
Kiam's costumes for Janet Gaynor in "A Star Is Born." Madeleine Carroll models a suit by Gwen Wakeling from "On the Avenue."

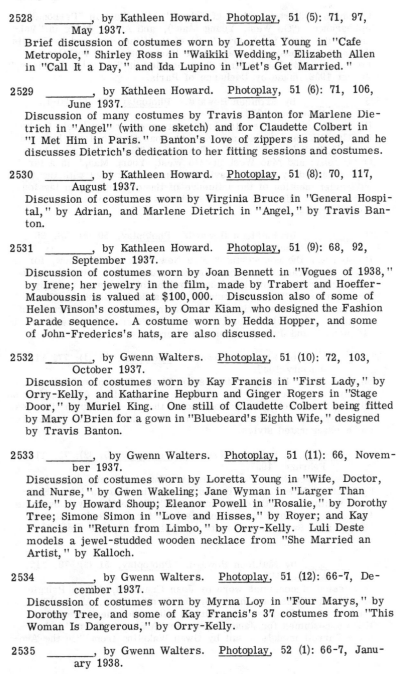

2528 _____, by Kathleen Howard. Photoplay, 51 (5): 71, 97,
        May 1937.
Brief discussion of costumes worn by Loretta Young in "Cafe
Metropole," Shirley Ross in "Waikiki Wedding," Elizabeth Allen
in "Call It a Day," and Ida Lupino in "Let's Get Married."

2529 _____, by Kathleen Howard. Photoplay, 51 (6): 71, 106,
        June 1937.
Discussion of many costumes by Travis Banton for Marlene Dietrich in "Angel" (with one sketch) and for Claudette Colbert in
"I Met Him in Paris." Banton's love of zippers is noted, and he
discusses Dietrich's dedication to her fitting sessions and costumes.

2530 _____, by Kathleen Howard. Photoplay, 51 (8): 70, 117,
        August 1937.
Discussion of costumes worn by Virginia Bruce in "General Hospital," by Adrian, and Marlene Dietrich in "Angel," by Travis Banton.

2531 _____, by Kathleen Howard. Photoplay, 51 (9): 68, 92,
        September 1937.
Discussion of costumes worn by Joan Bennett in "Vogues of 1938,"
by Irene; her jewelry in the film, made by Trabert and Hoeffer-
Mauboussin is valued at $100,000. Discussion also of some of
Helen Vinson's costumes, by Omar Kiam, who designed the Fashion
Parade sequence. A costume worn by Hedda Hopper, and some
of John-Frederics's hats, are also discussed.

2532 _____, by Gwenn Walters. Photoplay, 51 (10): 72, 103,
        October 1937.
Discussion of costumes worn by Kay Francis in "First Lady," by
Orry-Kelly, and Katharine Hepburn and Ginger Rogers in "Stage
Door," by Muriel King. One still of Claudette Colbert being fitted
by Mary O'Brien for a gown in "Bluebeard's Eighth Wife," designed
by Travis Banton.

2533 _____, by Gwenn Walters. Photoplay, 51 (11): 66, Novem-
        ber 1937.
Discussion of costumes worn by Loretta Young in "Wife, Doctor,
and Nurse," by Gwen Wakeling; Jane Wyman in "Larger Than
Life," by Howard Shoup; Eleanor Powell in "Rosalie," by Dorothy
Tree; Simone Simon in "Love and Hisses," by Royer; and Kay
Francis in "Return from Limbo," by Orry-Kelly. Luli Deste
models a jewel-studded wooden necklace from "She Married an
Artist," by Kalloch.

2534 _____, by Gwenn Walters. Photoplay, 51 (12): 66-7, De-
        cember 1937.
Discussion of costumes worn by Myrna Loy in "Four Marys," by
Dorothy Tree, and some of Kay Francis's 37 costumes from "This
Woman Is Dangerous," by Orry-Kelly.

2535 _____, by Gwenn Walters. Photoplay, 52 (1): 66-7, Janu-
        ary 1938.

Discussion of costumes worn by Claudette Colbert in "Bluebeard's Eighth Wife" and a costume worn by Constance Bennett in "Merrily We Live." Shirley Ross models a costume from "The Big Broadcast of 1938," designed by the film's director, Mitchell Leisen.

2536 _____, by Gwenn Walters. Photoplay, 52 (2): 67, February 1938.
Discussion of two costumes worn by Annabella in "The Baroness and the Butler," by Gwen Wakeling; and one costume each worn by Dolores Del Rio and June Lang in "Shanghai Deadline," by Herschel, with jewelry designed by Josephy of Hollywood.

2537 _____, by Gwenn Walters. Photoplay, 52 (3): 76, March 1938.
Discussion of one costume each worn by Irene Dunne in "The Joy of Living," by Edward Stevenson, and Joan Blondell in "There's Always a Woman," by Kalloch. Alice Faye models a wedding gown from "Sally, Irene and Mary," by Gwen Wakeling.

2538 _____, by Gwenn Walters. Photoplay, 52 (4): 76, April 1938.
Discussion of one costume each worn by Simone Simon in "Josette," by Royer, and by Ginger Rogers in "Vivacious Lady," by Irene of Bullocks-Wilshire; and of one hat each worn by Irene Dunne in "The Joy of Living" and Joan Fontaine in "Certified," by Edward Stevenson.

2539 _____, by Gwenn Walters. Photoplay, 52 (5): 66, 85, May 1938.
Gwen Wakeling notes that her costumes for "Alexander's Ragtime Band" will probably influence fashion through the accessories, including lapel watches, shoes with shoelaces tied around the ankle, and purses with beaded-tapestry designs.

2540 _____, by Gwenn Walters. Photoplay, 52 (7): 70, July 1938.
Discussion of many costumes worn by Katharine Hepburn in "Holiday," by Kalloch, with mention of her accessories and several pieces of jewelry by Flato.

2541 _____, by Gwenn Walters. Photoplay, 52 (8): 76, August 1938.
Discussion of costumes worn by Ginger Rogers in "Carefree," by Howard Greer; Margaret Lindsay in "Garden of the Moon," by Howard Shoup; and Danielle Darrieux in "The Rage of Paris," by Vera West. Arleen Whelan models a suit from "Ellis Island," by Gwen Wakeling.

2542 _____, by Gwenn Walters. Photoplay, 52 (9): 74, September 1938.
Discussion of costumes worn by Kay Francis in "Unlawful," by Orry-Kelly, and by Joan Bennett in "Artists and Models Abroad," by Edith Head. The Paris Exposition fashion sequence in the latter film will feature gowns by eight Parisian couturiers, brought by Lillian Fisher from Paris for the film.

2543 _____, by Gwenn Walters. Photoplay, 52 (10): 78, Oc-
          tober 1938.
Discussion of costumes worn by Jeanette MacDonald in "Sweet-
hearts," Norma Shearer in "Idiot's Delight," Joan Crawford in
"The Shining Hour," and Janet Gaynor in "Three Loves Has Nancy"
--all by Adrian, who feels that his costumes for "The Wizard of
Oz" will influence fashion and may start an era of fantasy fashion.

2544 _____, by Gwenn Walters. Photoplay, 52 (11): 72, No-
          vember 1938.
While in Paris Edith Head cabled the author to tell her that her
costumes for Claudette Colbert in "Zaza," Joan Bennett in "Artists and Models Abroad," and Gail Patrick in "Disbarred" had
influenced Parisian fashion.

2545 [In lieu of the "Fashion Letter"] "Close Ups of Hollywood
          Designers," by Gwenn Walters. Photoplay, 52 (10): 74,
          December 1938.
In lieu of her monthly letter Walters introduces her readers to
three retail designers, including suede designer Voris.

2546 ["Fashion Letter"] "Close Ups of Hollywood Designers," by
          Gwenn Walters. Photoplay, 53 (1): 72, January 1939.
Discussion of the careers of Irene of Bullocks-Wilshire, who
occasionally designs for films, including for Virginia Bruce in
"There Goes My Heart"; Willys, who has provided hosiery for
many films, including "Beauty for the Asking," with costumes by
Edward Stevenson; and Joseff of Hollywood, who has rented out
thousands of pieces of costume jewelry to be worn in films.

2547 _____, by Gwenn Walters. Photoplay, 53 (2): 66, Febru-
          ary 1939.
Discussion of costumes worn by Rita Johnson in "The Girl Down-
stairs," by Dolly Tree; with brief mention of Tree's costumes for
"The Ice Follies of 1939."

2548 _____, by Gwenn Walters. Photoplay, 53 (3): 74, March
          1939.
Travis Banton quit Paramount in the fall of 1938 to team up with
his former boss, Howard Greer, at Greer's establishment. Though
the two will design mostly for personal wardrobes, Greer occasionally designs for films, including for Katharine Hepburn in
"Bringing Up Baby" and Ginger Rogers in "Carefree."

2549 _____, by Gwenn Walters. Photoplay, 53 (4): 76, April
          1939.
Robert Kalloch is seen with Ida Lupino holding the wedding veil
of old lace she will wear in "The Lady and the Mob." He is also
designing costumes for Jean Arthur in "Only Angels Have Wings."

2550 _____, by Gwenn Walters. Photoplay, 53 (5): 70, 93, May
          1939.
Discussion of Orry-Kelly's costumes for Bette Davis in "Jezebel,"

"The Sisters," "The Old Maid," "Dark Victory," and "Juarez" (including her jewelry). Includes one photo of Davis in a costume from "The Old Maid" and mention of how some of the above will influence fashion.

2551 _____, by Gwenn Walters. Photoplay, 53 (7): 76, 79, July 1939.
Vera West has designed all of Deanna Durbin's costumes in her six films made since Durbin was age 13, which include "Three Smart Girls Grow Up" and "After School Days."

2552 _____, by Gwenn Walters. Photoplay, 53 (9): 70, 79, September 1939.
Discussion of costumes worn by Norma Shearer, Joan Crawford, and Rosalind Russell in "The Women" and many costumes worn in the film's fashion show, by Adrian. Includes one sketch each of costumes worn by the three actresses.

2553 _____, by Gwenn Walters. Photoplay, 53 (10): 59, 93, October 1939.
Discussion of many costumes worn by Madeleine Carroll in "My Love for Yours," by Edith Head; one of which Carroll models.

2554 _____, by Gwenn Walters. Photoplay, 53 (11): 59, 87, November 1939.
Orry-Kelly spent one year researching the costumes for "The Private Lives of Elizabeth and Essex" before designing the costumes. Discussion of some of the costumes worn by Bette Davis, one of which she models; with sketches of how they can be adapted for modern clothing. Davis found the hoop worn in the film more comfortable than the nineteenth-century type she had worn in "Jezebel," "Juarez," and "The Old Maid." Orry-Kelly adapted some of the above costumes for Zorina and Gloria Dickson in "On Your Toes"; with costume descriptions and brief mention of of their hats and jewelry.

Photoplay's Pattern Of The Month

"Photoplay's Pattern of the Month" was often mixed in with the "Photoplay Fashions" articles, but all are presented separately here, with the exception of August 1954. The actress usually appeared in several stills of the featured dress, often in color, and sketches either by the designer or of the pattern were also frequently included. The pattern purchase information was included on another page (not cited here). Months in which the feature was not included, or when non-film costumes were modeled, have been omitted.

2555 "Photoplay's Pattern of the Month." Photoplay, 31 (4): 103, September 1947.
Shirley Temple models a suit by Edward Stevenson from "Honeymoon."

2556 _____. Photoplay, 31 (5): 87, October 1947.
Lizabeth Scott models a suit by Edith Head from "Desert Fury."

2557 _____. Photoplay, 31 (6): 80, November 1947.
Jane Greer models a dress and turban by Edward Stevenson from "Out of the Past."

2558 _____. Photoplay, 32 (1): 74, December 1947.
Joan Bennett models a dress by Travis Banton from "Secret Beyond the Door."

2559 _____. Photoplay, 32 (2): 74, January 1948.
Ella Raines models a coat by Grace Houston from "The Senator Was Indiscreet."

2560 _____. Photoplay, 32 (3): 78, February 1948.
Betty Hutton models a dress by Edith Head from "Dream Girl."

2561 _____. Photoplay, 32 (4): 74, March 1948.
Loretta Young models a suit and blouse by Irene Sharaff from "The Bishop's Wife."

2562 _____. Photoplay, 32 (5): 88, April 1948.
Claudette Colbert models a dress by Sophie of Saks Fifth Avenue from "Sleep, My Love."

2563 _____. Photoplay, 32 (6): 98, May 1948.
Olivia de Havilland models a suit by Bonnie Cashin from "The Snake Pit."

2564 _____. Photoplay, 33 (1): 92, June 1948.
Janis Paige models a suit by Leah Rhodes from "Wallflower."

2565 _____. Photoplay, 33 (2): 98, July 1948.
Jacqueline White models a dress and jacket by Renie from "Mystery in Mexico."

2566 _____. Photoplay, 33 (3): 88, August 1948.
Diana Lynn models a dress by Mary Grant from "Texas, Brooklyn and Heaven."

2567 _____. Photoplay, 33 (4): 84, September 1948.
Rosalind Russell models a dress by Travis Banton from "The Velvet Touch."

2568 _____. Photoplay, 33 (5): 84, October 1948.
Wanda Hendrix models a suit by Edith Head from "The Tatlock Millions."

2569 _____. Photoplay, 33 (6): 82, November 1948.
Lucille Ball models a dress and stole by Mary Kay Dodson from "Sorrowful Jones."

2570 _____. Photoplay, 34 (1): 86, December 1948.
Deanna Durbin models a suit by Orry-Kelly from "For the Love
of Mary."

2571 _____. Photoplay, 34 (2): 76, January 1949.
Doris Day models a robe by Milo Anderson from "My Dream Is
Yours."

2572 _____. Photoplay, 34 (3): 86, February 1949.
Claire Trevor models a suit by Odette Myrtil from "The Lucky
Stiff."

2573 _____. Photoplay, 34 (4): 86, March 1949.
Lizabeth Scott models a dress by Adele Palmer from "Too Late
for Tears."

2574 _____. Photoplay, 34 (5): 84, April 1949.
Susan Hayward models a dress designed by Herschel from "Tulsa."

2575 _____. Photoplay, 36 (1): 84, June 1949.
Diana Lynn models a dress by Edith Head from "Bitter Victory."

2576 _____. Photoplay, 36 (2): 82, July 1949.
Virginia Mayo models a dress by Leah Rhodes from "The Girl
from Jones Beach."

2577 _____. Photoplay, 36 (3): 86, August 1949.
Marilyn Maxwell models a dress by Helen Stepner from "Champion."

2578 _____. Photoplay, 36 (4): 78, September 1949.
Diana Lynn models a dress by Edith Head from "Bitter Victory."

2579 _____. Photoplay, 36 (5): 90, October 1949.
Lucille Ball models a suit by Edward Stevenson from "Interference."

2580 _____. Photoplay, 36 (6): 88, November 1949.
Marta Toren models a dress by Yvonne Wood from "Illegal Entry."

2581 _____. Photoplay, 36 (7): 84, December 1949.
Kathryn Grayson models a dress by Helen Rose from "That Midnight Kiss."

2582 _____. Photoplay, 37 (1): 76, January 1950.
Shirley Temple models a dress by Leah Rhodes from "The Story
of Seabiscuit."

2583 _____. Photoplay, 37 (2): 84, February 1950.
Jane Powell models a suit by Helen Rose from "Nancy Goes to
Rio."

2584 _____. Photoplay, 37 (3): 84, March 1950.
Teresa Wright models an ensemble by Mary Wills from "The Capture."

2585 _____. Photoplay, 37 (4): 86, April 1950.
Barbara Stanwyck models a dress by Edith Head from "Thelma
Jordan."

2586 _____. Photoplay, 37 (5): 92, May 1950.
Janet Leigh models a playsuit by Michael Woulfe from "Jet Pilot."

2587 _____. Photoplay, 37 (6): 82, June 1950.
Ann Blyth models a bathing suit by Mary Wills from "Our Very
Own."

2588 _____. Photoplay, 38 (1): 88, July 1950.
Jan Sterling models a dress by Mary Kay Dodson from "United
States Mail."

2589 _____. Photoplay, 38 (3): 70, September 1950.
Joan Caulfield models an ensemble by Jean Louis from "The
Petty Girl."

2590 _____. Photoplay, 38 (4): 66-7, October 1950.
June Allyson models a suit by Helen Rose from "Right Cross."

2591 _____. Photoplay, 38 (5): 72, November 1950.
Doris Day models a dress by Leah Rhodes from "Tea for Two."

2592 _____. Photoplay, 38 (6): 68, December 1950.
Ann Blyth models a gown by Rosemary Odell from "Katie."

2593 _____. Photoplay, 39 (1): 62, January 1951.
Alexis Smith models a dress by Bill Thomas from "Undercover
Girl."

2594 _____. Photoplay, 39 (2): 72, February 1951.
Joan Bennett models a dress by Charles Le Maire from "For
Heaven's Sake."

2595 _____. Photoplay, 39 (3): 68, March 1951.
Kathryn Grayson models a dress by Helen Rose from "Grounds
for Marriage."

2596 _____. Photoplay, 39 (4): 66, April 1951.
Debra Paget models one outfit designed by William Travilla,
adopted from a costume worn in "Bird of Paradise."

2597 _____. Photoplay, 39 (5): 70, May 1951.
Mona Freeman models a dress with stole by Edith Head from
"Dear Brat."

2598 _____. Photoplay, 39 (6): 66, June 1951.
Janet Leigh models a playsuit by Michael Woulfe from "Two
Tickets to Broadway."

2599 _____. Photoplay, 40 (1): 68, July 1951.

Ella Raines models a dress by Adele Palmer from "Fighting Coast Guard."

2600 _____. Photoplay, 40 (2): 68-9, August 1951.
Elizabeth Taylor models a dress by Helen Rose from "Love Is Better Than Ever."

2601 _____. Photoplay, 40 (3): 68, September 1951.
Polly Bergen models a suit by Edith Head from "That's My Boy."

2602 _____. Photoplay, 40 (4): 72, October 1951.
Diana Lynn models a dress by Helen Rose from "The People Against O'Hara."

2603 _____. Photoplay, 40 (5): 68, November 1951.
Rhonda Fleming models a jumper with two blouses by Edith Head from "Hong Kong."

2604 _____. Photoplay, 40 (6): 70-1, December 1951.
Polly Bergen models a dress by Edith Head from "The Stooge."

2605 _____. Photoplay, 41 (1): 60, January 1952.
Donna Reed models a dress by Jean Louis from "Scandal Sheet."

2606 _____. Photoplay, 41 (2): 66, February 1952.
Joyce Holden models a dress by Bill Thomas from "Bronco Buster."

2607 _____. Photoplay, 41 (3): 70, March 1952.
Shelley Winters models an ensemble by Bill Thomas from "Meet Danny Wilson."

2608 _____. Photoplay, 41 (5): 68, May 1952.
Loretta Young models a dress by Jean Louis from "Paula."

2609 _____. Photoplay, 41 (6): 69, June 1952.
Mona Freeman models a beach ensemble by Bill Thomas from "Flesh and Fury."

2610 _____. Photoplay, 42 (1): 66-7, July 1952.
Piper Laurie models a dress by Bill Thomas from "No Room for the Groom."

2611 _____. Photoplay, 42 (2): 71, August 1952.
Virginia Mayo models an ensemble by Travilla from "She's Working Her Way Through College."

2612 "Photoplay's Star Pattern: Sew Easy." Photoplay, 42 (5): 65, November 1952.
Anne Baxter models a suit from "My Wife's Best Friend," by Charles Le Maire.

2613 _____. Photoplay, 42 (6): 62, December 1952.

June Haver models a dress from "The Girl Next Door."

2614 _____. Photoplay, 43 (2): 65, February 1953.
Doris Day models a suit by Leah Rhodes from "April in Paris."

2615 "Photoplay's Advance Star Pattern." Photoplay, 44 (2): 58,
      August 1953.
Janet Leigh models a dress by Jay Morely, Jr., from "Walking
My Baby Back Home."

2616 _____. Photoplay, 45 (1): 53, January 1954.
Jane Powell models a skirt and top by Moss Mabry from "Three
Sailors and a Girl."

[End of Photoplay's Pattern of the Month]

2617 "Photoplay Sneak Previews 'The Heiress.'" Photoplay, 36
      (5): 46-9, October 1949.
Edith Head researched Olivia de Havilland's costumes for "The
Heiress" from century-old photographs and museum clothes.

2618 "Photoplay's Designer of the Month." Photoplay, 32 (2): 88,
      January 1948.
Biographical information on Grace Houston, who briefly discusses
film- and theatrical-costume design.

2619 "Photoplay's Fashion History: 1913-1937." Photoplay, 52
      (1): 28-31, January 1938.
39 actresses model film and nonfilm fashions, not specifically
identified, but including Joan Crawford in the "Letty Lynton"
gown and Norma Shearer in "Riptide."

2620 "Photoplay's Fall Style Forecast." Photoplay, 36 (5): 75-86,
      October 1929.
Hollywood has usurped Paris's position as fashion dictator because
the Hollywood fashions have resisted the masculine influence of
Paris, which is now returning to feminine fashions.

2621 "Photoplay's Fashion Review," by Grace Corson. Photoplay,
      26 (6): 38-40, November 1924.
Grace Corson has sketched costumes, copies of which can be
ordered, as worn by Pola Negri in "Lily of the Dust," Colleen
Moore in "Flirting with Love," Constance Bennett in "Into the
Net," Aileen Pringle in "His Hour," Betty Blythe in "Breath of
Scandal," Mae Murray in "Circe the Enchantress," Eleanor
Boardman in "Sinners in Silk," and Dagmar Godowsky and Hope
Hampton in "Price of a Party."

2622 "Photoplay's Fashion Review of the Month," by Grace Corson.
      Photoplay, 27 (1): 61-3, December 1924.
Grace Corson has sketched costumes, copies of which can be
ordered, as worn by Doris Kenyon in "Lend Me Your Husband,"

Betty Compson and an unidentified actress in "Garden of Weeds,"
Marie Prevost in "Lover of Camille," Bebe Daniels and Dolores
Cassinelli in "Dangerous Money," Jetta Goudal in "Open All Night,"
Virginia Valli in "In Every Woman's Life," Norma Talmadge in
"The Only Woman," and Doris Kenyon in "Restless Wives."

2623 "Photoplay's Spring Style Forecast," by Katherine Albert.
        Photoplay, 35 (4): 73-84, March 1929.
Women throughout the world inadvertently wear film-costume
adaptations originated and established by Hollywood designers,
and not by Paris since the actresses prefer, and the camera requires, costumes designed for their original and photogenic qualities.

2624 "Phunkie Attire." American Film Institute Catalog, 1961-70,
        p. 510.
Phunkie Attire is credited with the wardrobe of "Love Thy
Neighbor and His Wife."

2625 Phyllis, Dorothy. "Screen Style Gossip." Screen News, 1
        (28): 23, 30, September 2, 1922.
Katherine MacDonald will wear approximately 13 gowns and 13
negligees in "White Shoulders." (This article may have been
written by Dorothy Phillips; it is difficult to determine if this is
an error.)

2626 Pickford, Mary. Sunshine and Shadow. Garden City, N.Y.:
        Doubleday, 1955.
Although she was already an experienced stage actress at age
13, Mary Pickford was going to study fashion design in case her
acting career failed. Pickford was allowed to wear her first silk
stockings and high-heeled shoes for the hateful task of visiting
Biograph Studios. For the filming of "Her First Biscuits," she
was provided with a costly costume of shoes and socks, hat, and
a lace and linen dress, costing a total $10.50. The Biograph
wardrobe department then consisted of a "tiny cellar alcove set
aside." Her small stature required that a velvet gown's long
train, worn in "To Save Her Soul," be pinned up, which she hid
from the camera. She refused the lead role in "Man's Genesis"
because the "primitive grass costume" required that she bare her
legs and feet. She interpreted a character she played in "Stella
Maris" to have one shoulder low and a high hip; a subsequent remake featured an actress in a lumpy rubber suit. She had six-
inch platform shoes designed for her in "Little Lord Fauntleroy"
(1921); a three-second scene took 15 hours to film. One 35-
pound costume had to be changed to a lighter, 20-pound costume
for a scene in "Dorothy Vernon of Haddon Hall" because she
could not lift herself onto a horse.

2627 "Pick-ups for Your House Program." It, 3 (35): 25, Janu-
        ary 15, 1921.
Viola Dana is wearing cotton stockings in "Home Stuff," as she
did when she grew up on the farm; according to the press agent,

they may be the same pairs.

2628 "A Pictorial Close-up of the 1964 Costume Entries." Motion
Picture Costumers, 1964, n. p.
One costume each is modeled by George Hamilton from "Your
Cheatin' Heart," by Nudie's; Alan Napier and Baroness de Roths-
child from "My Fair Lady," by Cecil Beaton; Vera Miles from
"The Hanged Man," by Burton Miller; Lana Turner from "Love
Has Many Faces," by Edith Head; Robert Wright, Elizabeth Allen,
and Roy Ritzell from "Kiss Me Kate," by Gwen Wakeling; Paul
Newman and Claire Bloom from "The Outrage," by Don Feld;
Laura Lane from "The Adventures of Ali Baba," by Helen Colvig;
and Julie Andrews from "The Sound of Music," by Dorothy Jea-
kins. Includes one sketch of a costume worn by Natalie Wood in
"The Great Race," by Edith Head.

2629 "A Pictorial View of the 1963 Workroom Entries." Motion
Picture Costumers, 1963, n. p.
One costume each is modeled by Sandra Dee from "Take Her,
She's Mine," by Travilla; Stephen Boyd from "Jumbo," by Morton
Haack; Joanne Woodward from "A New Kind of Love," by Edith
Head; Troy Donahue and Suzanne Pleshette from "A Distant Trum-
pet," by Howard Shoup; Alan Ladd from "The Carpetbaggers," by
Nudie's; and Elizabeth Taylor from "Cleopatra," by Irene Sharaff.

2630 "Picture Play's Fall Fashions." Picture Play, 47 (2): 72-7,
October 1937.
Gail Patrick models five costumes from "Artists and Models."

2631 Pieck, Kaaren. "Mad Hatter." Modern Screen, 24 (2): 46-7,
80, January 1942.
Tips on hat selection by Lilly Daché, whose hats for Loretta
Young in "The Men in Her Life" cost $21,000. Fashion fore-
casts include trends in berets with flowing veils, as worn by
Marlene Dietrich in "The Lady Is Willing," by Daché, and hats
with up-turned brims, as worn by Young in "The Men in Her
Life."

2632 "Pievetti, Alice." American Film Institute Catalog, 1961-70,
p. 511.
Alice Pievetti is credited with the wardrobe of "Girl in Room
13."

2633 "Pilla, Paola." American Film Institute Catalog, 1961-70,
p. 511.
Paola Pilla is credited with the costumes of "Marry Me! Marry
Me!"

2634 "Pinnow, Helga." American Film Institute Catalog, 1961-70,
p. 512.
Helga Pinnow is credited with the costumes of "The Merry Wives
of Windsor."

2635 "Pistek, Theodor." <u>American Film Institute Catalog, 1961-</u>
<u>70</u>, p. 513.
Theodor Pistek is credited with the costumes of "The Death of
Tarzan."

2636 "Pizzi, Pier Luigi." <u>American Film Institute Catalog, 1961-</u>
<u>70</u>, p. 513.
Pier Luigi Pizzi was the wardrobe designer of "The Condemned
of Altona" and is credited with the costumes of "Duel of the Titans," "White Voices," "Made in Italy," "A Maiden for a Prince,"
"The Girl Who Couldn't Say No," and "The Witch."

2637 Platt, Polly. "Dressing Up; On Costume Design." Review of
<u>Hollywood Costume, Hollywood Costume Design,</u> and <u>Cos-</u>
<u>tume Design in the Movies.</u> <u>American Film</u>, 2 (4): 75-7,
February 1977.
Polly Platt, costume and set designer, advises readers not to
buy <u>Hollywood Costume</u>, by Dale McConathy with Diana Vreeland.
Of the remaining two, she is more impressed with <u>Hollywood Cos-</u>
<u>tume Design,</u> by David Chierichetti; she feels it is excellent, for
example, because of the stills and captions, the careful study of
the designers' development, and the relationship of costume to
developments in film technology. <u>Costume Design in the Movies,</u>
by Elizabeth Leese, is impressive for its scholarly undertaking
of supplying credits for 6,000 films, but suffers from the in-
clusion of many designers who have designed for only a handful
of films or without distinction, and from many errors, for example, in the credits for Orry-Kelly, and for herself; briefly,
she designed the costumes for "The Last Picture Show," "Paper
Moon," and "What's Up Doc?" (The problem with her credits is
that she is usually the production designer, but the Costume Designers Guild, of which she is a member, does not allow a production designer to receive credit for both set and costume design.)

2638 "Playing Londoner, Richard Dix Has Clothes Made in London."
<u>Screen News,</u> 3 (3): 17, January 19, 1924.
Richard Dix ordered a "small but complete" wardrobe from London for "The Stranger," but prefers the more fitted American
clothes.

2639 "Ploberger, Herbert." <u>American Film Institute Catalog, 1961-</u>
<u>70</u>, p. 514.
Herbert Ploberger is credited with the costumes of "King in
Shadow," "Arms and the Man," "Buddenbrooks," and "Uncle Tom's
Cabin."

2640 Plunkett, Walter. "Dressing Up the Movies." <u>California</u>
<u>Monthly,</u> 33 (4): 13-5, 43-4, December 1934.
Walter Plunkett seems to have omitted nothing concerning film-
costume design. He discusses the researching, with mention of
specific fashion magazines, of the period costumes for "Cimar-

ron," "Little Women," and "The Age of Innocence" and for Katharine Hepburn in "The Little Minister"; period, yet contemporary,
costumes for Irene Dunne in "Stingaree"; color preferences of
Dunne and Hepburn, Ann Harding, Genevieve Tobin, and Ginger
Rogers; figure flaws, as with concealing Karen Moreley's thinness
in "Wednesday's Child"; the influence of film costume on fashion,
as with Mae West's authentic period costumes (by Travis Banton)
and "Little Women," especially on Paris couture; the aging of
fabric for some of the above films, and for Fay Wray in "King
Kong"; and performances enhanced through costumes for Billie
Burke, Zasu Pitts, and for Bette Davis in "Of Human Bondage,"
with many stills illustrating Davis's character's degeneration.
Erté and Chanel did not succeed as film designers because they
could not adjust to the above problems in costume designing.

2641   "Plunkett, Walter." American Film Institute Catalog, 1961-
         70, p. 514.
Walter Plunkett was the costume designer of "The Four Horsemen
of the Apocalypse" (1962) and "Seven Women," the women's costume designer of "Marriage on the Rocks," and is credited with
the costumes of "How the West Was Won," the men's costumes
of "Pocketful of Miracles," and the wardrobe of "Two Weeks in
Another Town." (See also Walter Pulunkett.)

2642   "Plunkett, Walter." Fairchild's Who's Who in Fashion. 1975,
         p. 203.
During the mid-1920s, Walter Plunkett was hired by FBO as a
designer, and he became the chief designer when the studio became RKO. He left in 1934 to design a retail collection, but
returned at Katharine Hepburn's request for "Mary of Scotland."
He later freelanced until joining MGM, where he remained until
his retirement in 1966.

2643   "Plunkett, Walter." International Motion Picture Almanac.
         1975, p. 179.

2644   "Plunkett, Walter." Motion Picture Almanac.   1946-7, p.
         306.

2645   "Poggioni, Vera." American Film Institute Catalog, 1961-70,
         p. 514.
Vera Poggioni is credited with the costumes of "Chronicle of
Anna Magdalena Bach."

2646   "Pola Negri Starts Work on 'Bella Donna.'" Screen News,
         1 (36): 22, October 28, 1922.
Pola Negri has spent one week trying on dozens of costumes for
"Bella Donna," her first American film. Costumes for the Egyp-
tian sequence were designed from authentic plates.

2647   "Pompei." American Film Institute Catalog, 1960-70, p. 516.
Pompei is credited with the footwear of "The Slave" and "The
Hawks and the Sparrows."

2648   "Pontén, Gunilla." _American Film Institute Catalog, 1961-70,_
          p. 516.
Gunilla Pontén is credited with the costumes of "Dear John" and
the wardrobe of "Fanny Hill."

2649   "Ponting, Roy." _American Film Institute Catalog, 1961-70,_
          p. 517.
Roy Ponting is credited with the costumes of "King and Country"
and was the wardrobe master/supervisor of "The Italian Job" and
"The Last Grenade."

2650   "Poor Feathers Make Poor Birds." _Screen News,_ 3 (28): 20,
          July 12, 1924.
Bessie Love has been feeling melancholy due to her costume from
"Dynamite Smith," consisting of a "pancake" straw hat, a silk
blouse with a choker collar and leg-o'-mutton sleeves, feather
boa, and a long, gored skirt, tight at the waist and flared at the
flounced hem. Of her costume, she said "I understand now why
poor people are apt to stay poor."

2651   Pope, Virginia. "Clothes for Six Motion Pictures Are Shown
          Here by Edith Head." _New York Times,_ January 16,
          1947, p. 33.
A fashion show was held by Edith Head at the Waldorf-Astoria
Hotel; it featured costumes from six movies, worn by Loretta
Young in "The Perfect Marriage," Joan Caulfield in "Dear Ruth"
and "Welcome Stranger," Dorothy Lamour in "My Favorite Brunette," Betty Hutton in "Perils of Pauline," and Joan Fontaine in
"The Emperor Waltz"; with many costumes described. Head
sold the rights to the nightgowns to Macy's, and their copies were
modeled with the originals.

2652   _____. "Movies' Influence on Styles Assayed." _New York
          Times,_ May 2, 1945, p. 20.
In an interview Irene said that Paris has lost some influence due
to the war and would not completely dominate U. S. fashion after
the war; film costumes should never be extreme or overcome the
actress since films are "hardly the means for advancing styles";
costumes cannot be projected too much into the future, despite
the foreseeable trends; and film costumes have improved considerably during the war because of simpler stories and, consequently, costumes.

2653   _____. "Pattern of the Times: American Designer Series."
          New York Times, April 7, 1952, p. 22.
Includes pattern offers of dresses by Adrian, and biographical
information of the designer; his trademarks include geometric
designs, as in tailored suits, and floating panels for a sense of
motion.

2654   _____. "Pattern of the Times: American Designer Series."
          New York Times, July 5, 1954, p. 8.
Includes a biography of Howard Greer, from his career with Lady

Duff Gordon, to Lasky studios, to his starting his own establishment.

2655 "Porteous, Emma." American Film Institute Catalog, 1961-70,
          p. 517.
Emma Porteous is credited with the costumes of "Entertaining Mr.
Sloane."

2656 Porter, Mary E. "A Dressing Room on Wheels." Picture
          Play, 4 (2): 132-3, April 1916.
Betty Eyton had many problems changing costumes on location,
so, with six months of thought, she came up with the idea of a
dressing room set up inside a car.

2657 "Posner, Sylvia." American Film Institute Catalog, 1961-70,
          p. 518.
Sylvia Posner is credited with the wardrobe of "Twilight of
Honor," "Kissin' Cousins," and "The Outrage" and the women's
wardrobe of "Advance to the Rear."

2658 "Postal, Ron." American Film Institute Catalog, 1961-70,
          p. 518.
Ron Postal is credited with Steve McQueen's wardrobe in "The
Thomas Crown Affair."

2659 "The Postman Always Rings Twice." Motion Picture, 71 (4):
          52, May 1946.
Lana Turner's wardrobe in "The Postman Always Rings Twice"
will consist of all-white clothes, with the exception of a black
dress for a funeral sequence--the most simple wardrobe of her
films. (A recent viewing of the film indicated that the one black
dress was worn by Turner in her second-to-last sequence; there
was no funeral.)

2660 "Poulet, Sylvie." American Film Institute Catalog, 1961-70,
          p. 518.
Sylvie Poulet is credited with the costumes of "The Wanderer"
(1969).

2661 "Practical Styles in Crawford Pix." MGM Studio News, 11
          (2): n. p., August 8, 1935.
The trend in film costume is toward simplicity. Joan Crawford
wears the type of clothing that she herself would wear under
similar circumstances in "Glitter" ("I Live My Life").

2662 "Praigg, Peggy." American Film Institute Catalog, 1961-70,
          p. 519.
Peggy Praigg is credited with the costumes of "Jack and the
Beanstalk."

2663 "Praise Heaped on Sennett Suits." Screen News, 3 (35): 18,
          August 30, 1924.
The Sennett studio constantly receives letters regarding the bath-

ing suits worn in their comedies: manufacturers often request
rights to reproduce the suits, and fans ask what colors and
fabrics the suits are made of, who designs them, and where they
can be bought. The bathing suits are designed by Gladys Rousseau, who has designed a special wardrobe for each of the Sennett Bathing Girls, at the rate of one design per week.

2664   Pratt, William. "The Costumes," in Scarlett Fever: The
         Ultimate Pictorial Treasury of "Gone with the Wind."
         New York: Macmillan, 1977, p. 113-42, passim.
Remarkable text and photographic record of the costumes of
"Gone with the Wind." Margaret Mitchell, the author of the
book, had become involved in a controversy when she said how
well Katharine Hepburn looked in her "Little Women" costumes;
the designer, Walter Plunkett, also designed "Gone with the Wind"
and researched fabrics in Atlanta with the help of the author.
Before the film's production, Women's Wear Daily, fashion designer Hattie Carnegie, and Bonwit-Teller, the store, were pro-
fiting from tie-ins with the film's costumes. Clark Gable complained that he had more costume changes than any other actor
in history. If Vivien Leigh had been dressed faithfully to the
book, she would have appeared almost always in green. MGM
arranged a "Traveling Tour of Costumes" for the film's opening
throughout the country. The merchandising tie-ins with the film
included jewelry, brassieres and corsets, Rhett's bow, hats and
other headdresses, and dress patterns--some of which are shown.
The "American Freedom Train," part of the U.S.A. Bicentennial
celebration begun in 1975, included displays of Fred Astaire's
top hat, the chief dress worn by Judy Garland in "The Wizard
of Oz," a suit worn by Robert Redford in "The Sting," and a
brooch worn by Leigh in "GWTW." The vast number of original
wardrobe tests document the major costumes worn by principals
and many extras, including 36 costumes worn by Leigh; with references to how the costumes fit into the plot and how they were
occasionally changed during production, causing confusion when
publicity stills did not match the actual costumes seen in the
film. No other film's costumes have been photographically as
well documented. Includes reviews of Hollywood Costume--
Glamour! Glitter! Romance! and Hollywood Costume Design,
with mention of the passages concerning the costumes of "GWTW."
The film's costume credits read: "Costumes Designed by Walter
Plunkett, Scarlett's Hats by John Frederics, and Edward P. Lambert in Charge of Wardrobe." Notes also that the ape suit used
in "King Kong" (1933) became infested with fleas due to the horse-
tail hair covering.

2665   Pretzfelder, Max. "The Film Costumier's Problems."
         Close Up, 9 (4): 275-80, December, 1932.
Max Pretzfelder, the designer for all Pabst films, discusses his
determination to design authentic and realistic film costumes, unlike the designers of "Romance," "Sign of the Cross," and "The
Congress Dances." He considers the role of the character and
would not hesitate to put a star in grubby rags if the story re-

quired it.   Included are six of his sketches for "Don Quixote."

2666   "Preuss, Helmut."   American Film Institute Catalog, 1961-
          70, p. 521.
Helmut Preuss is credited with the wardrobe of "Escape from
East Berlin" and "Rampage at Apache Wells."

2667   "Preview's Fashion Session: Fantastica!"   Preview, London:
          Spring, 1962, p. 26-7.
Anna Maria Alberghetti models a costume from "Cinderfella," by
Edith Head, which illustrates that the fichu is coming back into
fashion.

2668   "The Principal Error About the Hawaiian Hula Hula Dance...."
          Grauman's Magazine, 6 (8): 20, February 25, 1923,
          cols. 1-2.
While in Hawaii for "The White Flower" Betty Compson was
visited by the Queen Emma Society of Honolulu, which tries to
preserve old Hawaiian customs and which tried to discourage
Compson from wearing the conventional grass skirt in the film.
The grass skirt originated in Samoa, and Hawaiians dance the hula
hula in simple, loose clothes.   Compson met several more times
with the committee, and director Julia Crawford Ivers, but decided to wear the grass skirt.

2669   "Probably No Motion Picture Has Ever Introduced as Many
          Distinct Novelties...."   Grauman's Magazine, 6 (6): 8,
          February 11, 1923, cols. 1-2.
"Adam's Rib" is a contemporary movie with a prehistoric sequence.   Designer Clare West researched what cave people wore;
without stitching 25 costumes were made using either skins or fur,
with the hemlines corresponding to the uneven hemlines of 1923.
Julia Faye's costume of feathers and leopard skins has a long
and short alternating hem, with jewelry made of claws, bones,
and feathers.

2670   Proctor, Kay.   "The Dress Suit All Hollywood Wanted to
          Wear."   Hollywood, 31 (8): 32-3, August 1942.
In "Tales of Manhattan" one suit is worn by nine different men
descending the social ladder.   The suit and the nine actors are
shown; with a plot synopsis.

2671   _____.   "Mitchell Leisen--Perfectionist."   Motion Picture,
          71 (3): 52, 123-5, April 1946.
A lengthy biography of Mitchell Leisen, for 12 years the set and
costume designer for De Mille studios.   He achieves near technical perfection by being active in most production aspects of his
films.

2672   Pryor, Nancy.   "No More 'Nighties' for Jeanette."   Motion
          Picture, 45 (1): 27, 97, February 1933.
Jeanette MacDonald, afraid of being "typed in underwear," hopes
to wear more clothes on the screen in the future.   She has ap-

peared in lingerie in "The Love Parade," "One Hour with You,"
"Love Me Tonight," and "Don't Bet on Women" and models a
boa-trimmed negligee from "Let's Go Native."

2673 Pryor, Thomas M. " 'Fishwife to Her Dressmaker.' " Re-
         view of Designing Male, by Howard Greer. New York
         Times Book Review, September 30, 1951, sec. 7, p. 21.
Designing Male sparkles for its presentation of silent-screen
actresses; Howard Greer's section on Greta Garbo was "the most
affectionate and revealing portrait of the real Garbo that this reviewer has ever read."

2674 Pryor, William Clayton, and Helen Sloman Pryor. "Costumes
         and Make-up," in Let's Go to the Movies. New York:
         Harcourt, Brace, 1939, p. 96-113.
The wardrobe department is discussed at greater length than the
costume-design department since the authors find it more interesting. A general treatment of film costume.

2675 "Pucci, Emilio." American Film Institute Catalog, 1961-70,
         p. 524.
Emilio Pucci was the special wardrobe designer for Maureen
O'Hara in "The Battle of the Villa Fiorita."

       Pulunkett, Walter see also Plunkett, Walter

2676 "Pulunkett, Walter." American Film Institute Catalog, 1921-
         30, p. 1318.
Walter Pulunkett is credited with the costumes of "Hard-Boiled
Haggerty," "Sinners in Love," and "Love in the Desert."

2677 "Pulunkett, Walter." Motion Picture Almanac. 1930, p. 123.
Walter Pulunkett has been RKO's costume designer for two and a
half years, and in addition to the above AFIC credits, he designed "The Red Sword."

2678 "Puppets Invade 'Mickey Mouse's' Domain." Literary Digest,
         119 (17): 20, April 27, 1935.
Russell Patterson, film set and costume designer, has tired of
glamorizing women and is now designing miniature sets and puppets.

2679 Quant, Mary. Quant by Quant. New York: Putnam's 1966.
      For her retail fashions Mary Quant's sources of inspiration have
      included Greta Garbo's films and "Goldfinger." The only other
      film reference is to an 8mm movie that advertised the fashions
      of the retail line Youthquake, featuring models in clothes by
      Quant, Marion Foale, and Sally Tuffin.

2680 "Quant, Mary." American Film Institute Catalog, 1961-70,
          p. 525.
      Mary Quant is credited with the model costumes in "Sing and
      Swing" and the clothes for Claire Bloom in "The Haunting,"
      Charlotte Rampling in "Georgy Girl," and Audrey Hepburn in
      "Two for the Road."

2681 "Quant, Mary." Current Biography. 1968, p. 322-5.

2682 "Quant, Mary." International Who's Who. 38th ed., 1974-5,
          p. 1409.

2683 "Quant, Mary." Who's Who in the World. 2nd ed., 1974-5,
          p. 808.

2684 "Quant, Mary (Mrs. A. Plunket Greene)." Who's Who. 125th
          ed., 1973-4, p. 2639.

2685 "Queen Christina 1934." Modern Screen, 7 (5): 70-1, April
          1934.
      Macy's Cinema Shop has some ready-to-wear garments patterned
      after Greta Garbo's costumes in "Queen Christina." Three stills
      of Garbo in "Queen Christina" are included along with four of the
      copies.

2686 Quinn, Marian H. "Fashion Quiz: Answer to a Gentleman's
          Prayer." Photoplay with Movie Mirror, 18 (3): 46, 84,
          February 1941.
      A sketch of a gown worn by Judy Garland in "Little Nellie Kelly"
      is included along with drafting and sewing instructions.

2687 Quirk, James R. "Presto Chango Valentino!" Photoplay, 27
          (6): 36-7, 117, May 1925.

Natacha Rambova's management of Rudolph Valentino's films, especially "Monsieur Beaucaire" and "A Sainted Devil," has resulted in less successful films, court actions, and delayed production of "The Hooded Falcon." Since Joseph Schenck and others feel that her involvement in his career is not good publicity for his "sheik" image, her services are being decreased (actually, they were eliminated).

2688 "Rabadi, Mani." <u>American Film Institute Catalog, 1961-70,</u>
    p. 526.
Mani Rabadi is credited with the costumes of "Kama Sutra."

2689 "Rabanne, Paco." <u>American Film Institute Catalog, 1961-70,</u>
    p. 526.
Paco Rabanne is credited with Audrey Hepburn's clothes in "Two
for the Road," Jane Fonda's costumes for the last sequence of
"Barbarella," and the costumes of "The Last Adventure."

2690 "Rabanne, Paco." <u>Who's Who in the World.</u> 3rd ed., 1976-
    7, p. 571.

2691 "Raffiné." <u>American Film Institute Catalog, 1961-70</u>, p. 527.
Raffiné is credited with the costumes of "Torture Dungeon."

2692 "Rags Never Hid from Us the Aristocrat That Carol Dempster
    Really Is." <u>Motion Picture,</u> 30 (1): 69, August 1925.
Carol Dempster has progressed from wearing rags in "Isn't Life
Wonderful" (from which she models one costume) to elegant cos-
tumes in "Sally of the Sawdust" (two of which she models).

2693 "Rahvis." <u>American Film Institute Catalog, 1961-70</u>, p. 528.
Rahvis is credited with Ursula Andress's costumes in "Perfect
Friday."

2694 "Rainer a Red-Head in 'Candlesticks.'" <u>MGM Studio News,</u>
    4 (5): n.p., March 27, 1937.
Luise Rainer wears 15 modernized costumes copied by Adrian
from Russian Imperial styles in "The Emperor's Candlesticks."

2695 Rall, Pearl. "Where They Are and What They're Doing."
    <u>Screen News,</u> 4 (13): 10, March 28, 1925.
Vast amounts are now spent on costuming and costume designers
for films; wardrobe mistresses are no longer chiefly responsible
for a film's costumes. Notes, for example, that MGM recently
hired THE foremost designer, Erté.

2696 Rambova, Natacha. <u>Rudolph Valentino, Recollections, Intimate</u>
    <u>and Interesting Reminiscences of the Life of the Late</u>

World-Famous Star by Natacha Rambova, His Wife. New
        York: Jacobsen-Hodgkinson, 1927.
This was the American edition of the following book.

2697 _____ . Rudy: An Intimate Portrait of Rudolph Valentino
        by His Wife. London: Hutchinson, 1926.
Rudolph Valentino insisted upon correct costumes and enjoyed
dressed-up roles in his films, including "Blood and Sand," in
which he wore authentic and complete torero costumes sent over
from Spain, and was dressed by a retired matador. During the
filming of "The Conquering Power" he had a quarrel with director
Rex Ingram over one of his costumes. In a section written by
Rambova's mother it is noted that Rambova designed the costumes
for "The Hooded Falcon," though Rambova later credits Adrian.
She had little interest in Valentino's "Cobra," and just supervised
the costumes. She feels free of charges that she ruined Valentino's career.

2698 "Rambova, Natacha." American Film Institute Catalog, 1921-
        30, p. 1321.
Natacha Rambova is credited with the costumes of "Salome"
(1922).

2699 "Ramoin, Clo." American Film Institute Catalog, 1961-70,
        p. 529.
Clo Ramoin is credited with the wardrobe of "Temptation" (1962).

2700 Ramsaye, Terry. A Million and One Nights: A History of the
        Motion Picture. Vol. 1. New York: Simon and Schuster, 1926.
In 1906 Florence Turner was hired by Vitagraph to work as both
an actress and the wardrobe mistress: the studio's practice in
order to keep the actors/actresses busy with a steady paycheck.

2701 "Rand, June." American Film Institute Catalog, 1921-30,
        p. 1321.
June Rand is credited with the costumes of "Men of Steel."

2702 "Rangel, Germinal." American Film Institute Catalog, 1961-
        70, p. 530.
Germinal Rangel was the costume designer for Maggie Smith in
"Hot Millions."

2703 Rankin, Ruth. "There's Gold in Those Frills." Photoplay,
        47 (5): 56, 62-3, 105, April 1935.
Discussion of Bernard Newman's $250,000 costumes for "Roberta."
He also designed the fabrics--some costing $25 per yard, as
worn by Irene Dunne and Ginger Rogers--and the accessories;
he spared no cost, as with a $19,000 fur coat. Special stockings
were also made for each costume. One costume each is modeled
by Diane Cook, Jane Hamilton, and Margaret McChrystal and two
by Virginia Reid. (See also "Photoplay Fashions," April 1935.)

2704 _____ . "Undraping Hollywood." Photoplay, 45 (3): 28-9,

113-4, February 1934.
Travis Banton, Adrian, Orry-Kelly, and Kalloch discuss the
near-nudity of current film costumes and how it will affect fashion
and future film costumes--namely, by popularizing the covered-
up look. Brief mention of Marlene Dietrich in "The Scarlet Empress," Joan Crawford in "Dancing Lady," and Ginger Rogers in
"Sitting Pretty."

2705 "Ranzato, Jo." American Film Institute Catalog, 1961-70,
        p. 530.
Jo Ranzato is credited with the costumes of "OSS 117--Mission for
a Killer."

2706 "Rapf, Joe." American Film Institute Catalog, 1921-30, p.
        1322.
Joe Rapf is credited with the costumes of "The Hollywood Revue
of 1929."

2707 "Rappoport, E." American Film Institute Catalog, 1961-70,
        p. 530.
E. Rappoport is credited with the costumes of "The Gordeyev
Family."

2708 Ratoff, Gregory. "On the Set with 'The Men in Her Life.'"
        Modern Screen, 23 (4): 48-9, September 1941.
Loretta Young's 30 costumes, and hats by Lilly Daché, for "The
Men in Her Life," cost $21,000. The costumes were designed
by Charles Le Maire.

2709 "Ravnholt, Lotte." American Film Institute Catalog, 1961-70,
        p. 531.
Lotte Ravnholt is credited with the costumes of "People Meet and
Sweet Music Fills the Heart."

2710 Ray, Charles. "I Spent a Million to Dress Up." Photoplay,
        32 (4): 47, 131-2, September 1927.
When Charles Ray dressed poorly on the screen for character
parts, he was popular, but most of his fans dropped him when
he began to dress elegantly in his own film productions. He
lost $1 million on "A Tailor Made Man," and discusses his
career before and since then.

2711 Ray, Marie Beynon. "Curves Ahead." Collier's, 92 (14):
        24, 40, October 7, 1933.
Includes a discussion of the influence of Mae West's costumes in
"She Done Him Wrong" on American and Parisian fashion and on
Marlene Dietrich's costumes in "Song of Songs."

2712 _____. "How Do I Look?" Collier's, 94 (6): 18. 51,
        August 11, 1934.
Adrian discusses designing for Greta Garbo, Norma Shearer,
and Joan Crawford. If one copies these actresses, Adrian advises considerable restraint since he designs for their mind and

personality, and with imagination.

2713   Raymond, Louis. "Original Glamour Girl Returns." Motion
            Picture, 63 (3): 40-1, 80-1, October 1941.
Gloria Swanson, whose former clotheshorse films of the 1920s
enriched herself and Cecil B. De Mille, now thinks the clothes
hysterical and finds it hard to believe that she wore them.

2714   "Raymonde." American Film Institute Catalog, 1961-70, p. 532.
Raymonde was the costume designer of "Peek-a-boo."

2715   "Reachi, Renita." American Film Institute Catalog, 1961-70,
            p. 533.
Renita Reachi is credited with the costumes of "Yours, Mine, and
Ours."

2716   "Réal." American Film Institute Catalog, 1961-70, p. 533.
Réal is credited with the wardrobe for Catherine Deneuve in "The
Umbrellas of Cherbourg" and for Sylvia Vartan in "Friend of the
Family."

2717   "Real Thirties by Travis Banton." New York Herald Tribune,
            May 29, 1964, p. 10.
Unlike that of other designers, Travis Banton's work has not been
preserved.

2718   Ree, Max. "Costume Designing," in Breaking into the Movies,
            edited by Charles Reed Jones. New York: Unicorn, 1927,
            p. 172-7.
Max Ree, costume director of First National, feels that the two
most important factors in designing costumes for black-and-white
films are line and psychology. His previous jobs as an architect and
stage designer have helped his designing, though he cannot cut out or
sew a dress. He discusses the basics of design, with references to
Billie Dove in "The Tender Hour."

2719   "Ree, Max." American Film Institute Catalog, 1921-30, p.
            1325-6.
   21 costume-related credits are listed for Max Ree.

2720   "Ree, Max." Motion Picture Almanac. 1930, p. 123.
   15 credits are listed for designer Max Ree.

2721   "Ree, Max." Motion Picture News Blue Book. New York:
            Motion Picture News, 1929, p. 182.

2722   Reed, Dena. "If You Would Be as Chic as Norma." Modern
            Screen, 8 (2): 58-9, 86-7, July 1934.
Discussion of costumes worn by Norma Shearer in "Riptide";
Shearer models two hats from the film. Adrian discusses how
he designs for a film, and designing for Shearer.

2723   Reed, Rex. "Wiz 'Fabulous' Because of the Wonderful Things

It Does." San Francisco Sunday Examiner and Chronicle,
Datebook, October 29, 1978, p. 28-9.
Diana Ross, starring as Dorothy in "The Wiz," wore Capezio
rhinestone slippers, but was limited to simple costumes for her
role as a schoolteacher. She at first envied the others in designer clothes, but found it better to be identified with the role
in correct costumes. 2,000 costumes were worn in the film.
The designers included Halston, Bill Blass, and Oscar de la
Renta.

2724   "Reed, Rose Marie." American Film Institute Catalog, 1961-
          70, p. 534.
Rose Marie Reed is credited with the swimsuits of "Look in Any
Window," and the girls' beachwear in "Beach Ball."

2725   Reed, Ruth Brown.   "These Designing Young Americans."
          Independent Woman [absorbed by National Business Wo-
          man], 14 (9): 298-300, September 1935.
Katharine Hepburn once visited Muriel King's New York studio
and was later to have her fly to Hollywood to design her 15
costumes in "Sylvia Scarlett." Adrian discusses the competition
between New York, Paris, and Hollywood; each will continue to
have distinctive fashions regardless of prejudice between the cities.

2726   "Regal Mode: Coronation, Lower Tariffs and Costume Movies
          Aid Revival of Lace." Literary Digest, 122 (13): 34-5,
          September 26, 1936.
The renewed interest in lace is due in part to the popularity of
period films and their costumes. Walter Plunkett notes that the
popularity for feminine clothing is just part of the cycle that
swings from tailored clothes to feminine ones. Studios can pay
from four cents to $65 a yard for lace.

2727   Rehrauer, George. Review of Fair Lady (or Cecil Beaton's
          Fair Lady), by Cecil Beaton, in Cinema Booklist.
          Metuchen, N. J.: Scarecrow, 1972, p. 111.
Includes a summary of Fair Lady, which the author found impressive.

2728   _____. Review of The Dress Doctor, by Edith Head
          and Jane Kesner Ardmore, in Cinema Booklist. Metu-
          chen, N. J.: Scarecrow, 1972, p. 94.
The author finds this book disappointing due to its lack of autobiographical information and its general treatment of costume design.

2729   Reid, James. "How Hepburn Is 'Queening' It." Motion Pic-
          ture, 51 (6): 33, 66-7, 79, July 1936.
Katharine Hepburn has worn "fashion-plate" gowns only in "Christopher Strong," and now in "Mary of Scotland." Her costumes
from "Little Women" influenced fashion, as will the "Mary of
Scotland" costumes, which designer Walter Plunkett has already
adapted for retail sale.

2730 _____. "Sex Is Here to Pay." Motion Picture, 58 (4): 26-
        7, 58-9, May 1939.
Includes mention of the importance of sex appeal and tight, sexy
costumes to the success of Jeanette MacDonald, Sonja Henie, and
Bette Davis, and to Norma Shearer in "Idiot's Delight" and Lana
Turner in "They Won't Forget"; with brief mention of others.

2731 Reid, James E. "Color--and You." Movie Classic, 8 (6):
        6, August 1935.
Predicts that film costumes will become more practical with color
films, and that women will be better able to plan their color
schemes through what the actresses will wear. Includes two
sketches of costumes worn by Miriam Hopkins in "Becky Sharp,"
with notes and photos of fabric samples; designed by Robert Edmond Jones, who worked as a color consultant for the film.

2732 Reid, Janet. "Are They Heroines to Their Costume Designer?"
        Motion Picture, 33 (1): 46-7, 110-1, February 1927.
André-Ani discusses designing for Greta Garbo, Claire Windsor,
Marion Davies, Mae Murray, Carmel Myers, and Aileen Pringle,
with regard to their fashion preferences, and temperament. In-
cludes also one sketch each of costumes worn by Marion Davies
in "The Red Mill," Greta Garbo in "Flesh and the Devil," Mae
Murray in "Altars of Desire," and Claire Windsor in "Dance
Madness."

2733 Reid, Margaret. "Do the Stars Dress Badly?" Picture Play,
        30 (2): 16-8, 92, April 1929.
The author feels that Hollywood women are the worst dressed in
America, particularly off screen; their on-screen clothes do not
come up to the usual standards of fashion due to the need for dramatic value, and are consequently not suitable for wear by the
public. "Simplicity is a lost art in Hollywood."

2734 "Reimann, Walter." American Film Institute Catalog, 1921-30,
        p. 1327.
Walter Reimann is credited with the costumes of "Eternal Love."

2735 "Reiss & Fabrizio." American Film Institute Catalog, 1961-
        70, p. 537.
Reiss & Fabrizio is credited with the furs of "Funny Girl."

2736 "'Rendezvous' Proves 1917 Fashions Same as Modes of Today."
        MGM Studio News, 3 (1): n.p., October 12, 1935.
While studying for their costumes in "Rendezvous" Rosalind Russell and others were amazed that the fashions of 1917 were so
similar to current styles. This is attributed to fashion moving
back in time to 1917, rather than a result of film costumes of the
period influencing 1935 fashions.

2737 "Rendlesham, Clare." American Film Institute Catalog, 1961-
        70, p. 538.
Clare Rendlesham was the wardrobe supervisor for "Staircase"

and for Audrey Hepburn in "Two for the Road" and the fashion consultant of "Bedazzled."

2738 Renie. "Be Your Age, Girls!" Silver Screen, 17 (8): 58-9, 90-1, June 1947.
Renie, who has been with RKO for ten years, discusses costumes worn by Barbara Hale in "A Likely Story," five of which she models. Brief mention of her costumes for Joan Davis in "If You Knew Susie."

2739 "Renie." American Film Institute Catalog, 1961-70, p. 538.
Renie was the costume designer of "Snow White and the Three Stooges," "The Pleasure Seekers," "The Sand Pebbles," and "The Legend of Lylah Clare" and is credited with the women's costumes of "Cleopatra" and the costumes of "Circus World," "The Killing of Sister George," and "What Ever Happened to Aunt Alice?"

2740 "Renie." Photoplay, 33 (2): 97, July 1948.

2741 "Ressl, Eldean." American Film Institute Catalog, 1961-70, p. 538.
Eldean Ressl is credited with the Indian wardrobe of "Deadwood '76."

2742 "Reversible Jacket." Movies, 5 (4): 42, October 1941.
Barbara Stanwyck models one suit by Edith Head from "You Belong to Me." (The table of contents indicated that many suits were modeled, but they could not be found.)

2743 Review of Designing Male, by Howard Greer. Booklist, 48 (9): 158, January 1, 1952.
A summary and recommendation of Designing Male.

2744 Review of Hollywood Costume Design and Hollywood Costume --Glamour! Glitter! Romance! Newsweek, 88 (24): 107, December 13, 1976.
Hollywood Costume Design, less ostentatious than Hollywood Costume--Glamour! Glitter! Romance!, includes shoptalk with problems many designers have encountered with their films; the latter includes fashion essays on many "eclipsed divas."

2745 Review of Hollywood Costume Design and Hollywood Costume --Glamour! Glitter! Romance! Village Voice, 21 (50): 70, December 13, 1976.
In brief, sentence-length reviews, the reviewer finds it somehow appropriate that the rival books, one plush and one not, should have forewords, respectively, by Diana Vreeland and Edith Head.

2746 Review of Hollywood Costume--Glamour! Glitter! Romance!, by Dale McConathy and Diana Vreeland. Booklist, 73 (5): 442, November 1, 1976.
Brief but positive summary.

2747   Review of <u>The Dress Doctor,</u> by Edith Head and Jane Kesner
            Ardmore.   <u>Booklist,</u> 55 (21): 591, July 1, 1959.
       Too brief to be of value.

2748   Review of <u>The Dress Doctor.</u>   <u>Bookmark,</u> 11 (3): 146, March
            1959.
       The reviewer finds <u>The Dress Doctor</u> engaging, with sensible ad-
       vice for the average woman.

2749   Review of <u>The Dress Doctor.</u>   <u>Kirkus Bulletin,</u> 27: 76, Janu-
            ary 15, 1959.
       A brief summary of the "pleasantly informal" <u>The Dress Doctor.</u>

2750   "Revillard, Suzanne."   <u>American Film Institute Catalog, 1961-</u>
            <u>70,</u> p. 539.
       Suzanne Revillard is credited with the costumes of "Hotbed of
       Sin."

2751   "Revuelta, Manuel."   <u>American Film Institute Catalog, 1961-</u>
            <u>70,</u> p. 539.
       Manuel Revuelta is credited with the wardrobe of "The Savage
       Guns."

2752   "Rex Ingram Designed and Painted ... the Color Plates...."
            <u>Screen News,</u> 2 (25): 22, June 23, 1923, col. 2.
       Rex Ingram, an artist and the director of "Scaramouche," de-
       signed each of the color plates from which the costumes were
       made.   (Conflicts with the film's credits.)

2753   Rhea, Marian.   "Are Modern Women Copy-Cats?"   <u>Movie</u>
            <u>Classic,</u> 9 (4): 44-5, 70, December 1935.
       Bernard Newman is disappointed to see so many women wearing
       clothes patterned after historical or foreign costumes, since the
       early twentieth century is unique and its fashions should also be.
       Includes one sketch by the designer of a costume worn by Lily
       Pons in "Love Song."

2754   _____.   "Fashions for the Freshman Co-ed."   <u>Hollywood,</u>
            25 (2): 36, 38, 40, February 1936.
       The discussion includes several costumes worn by Patricia Ellis
       in "Freshman Love," one of which she models.

2755   _____.   "Glamour--and the Clothes You Wear."   <u>Motion</u>
            <u>Picture,</u> 63 (2): 38-9, 92-3, March 1942.
       Discussion of costumes worn by Ruth Hussey in "Married Bachelor"
       and Eleanor Powell in "Ship Ahoy," by Kalloch; Betty Grable in
       "I Wake Up Screaming," by Gwen Wakeling; and Ginny Simms in
       "Playmates," by Edward Stevenson.   Orry-Kelly is working on
       his autobiography, to be titled <u>Women I've Undressed.</u>   (It is noted
       in <u>Hollywood Costume--Glamour! Glitter! Romance!</u> that he was
       working on this at the time of his death, several decades later.)

2756   _____.   "Let's Go Collegiate!"   <u>Hollywood,</u> 24 (8): 40-5,
            August 1935.

Arline Judge discusses her fashion preferences and some of the
costumes she wears in "College Scandal." Includes photos and
sketches of some of the costumes, with pattern offers.

2757 Rhode, Eric. A History of the Cinema. London: Butler and
Tanner, 1976.
Brief mention of Paramount designers Howard Greer, Travis
Banton, "and especially Edith Head." Notes that Adrian excelled
with silhouette costumes of black-and-white.

2758 "Rhodes, Leah." American Film Institute Catalog, 1961-70,
p. 540.
Leah Rhodes was the costume designer of "Tickle Me" and is
credited with the costumes of "Village of the Giants," "Picture
Mommy Dead," "Good Times," and "5 Card Stud."

2759 "Ribas, Marian." American Film Institute Catalog, 1961-70,
p. 540.
Marian Ribas is credited with the costumes of "Savage Pampas"
and "Dr. Coppelius."

2760 "Riber, Bente." American Film Institute Catalog, 1961-70,
p. 540.
Bente Riber is credited with the costumes of "Crazy Paradise."

2761 "Ricci, Nina." American Film Institute Catalog, 1961-70,
p. 540.
Nina Ricci is credited with the gowns of "L'Immortelle," Claudia
Cardinale's gowns in "The Magnificent Cuckold," and the execution
of Ingrid Bergman's gowns in "The Visit."

2762 Rice, Janet. "Hollywood Fashion Letter." New Movie, 7
(4): 52-5, April 1933.
Discussion and stills and/or sketches of costumes worn by Joan
Crawford in "Today We Live"; Joan Blondell in "Broadway Bad"
and Lupe Velez in "Hot Pepper," both by Earl Luick; Katharine
Hepburn in "Christopher Strong"; Adrienne Ames in "From Hell
to Heaven"; and Nancy Carroll in "The Woman Accused."

2763 _____. "Last Minute Fashions from the New Films."
New Movie, 8 (2): 52-5, August 1933.
Discussion of costumes worn by Gloria Stuart in "It's Great to
Be Alive"; Jean Harlow in "Black Orange Blossoms" (she was in
no film with this title), by Adrian; Loretta Young in "Lady of
the Night"; Elissa Landi in "I Loved You Wednesday," by Orry-
Kelly; Lilian Harvey in "My Lips Betray," by Joe Strassner;
Helen Twelvetrees in "Disgraced"; Constance Bennett in "Bed of
Roses"; Joan Crawford in "Today We Live"; Miriam Hopkins in
"Stranger's Return"; and Joan Bennett in "Arizona to Broadway."
Sketches and/or stills are included of costumes worn by Young
and Landi in the above films, Benita Hume in "Gambling Ship,"
Colleen Moore in "The Power and the Glory," and Fay Wray and
Claire Dodd in "Ann Carver's Profession" (designed by Lettie Lee

and sketched by Kalloch; Lettie Lee received film credit).

2764   _____. "The Newest Fashions in the Latest Films." New
              Movie, 7 (5): 48-51, May 1933.
       One gown each is modeled by Barbara Stanwyck from "Baby Face,"
       Constance Bennett from "Our Betters," Gloria Swanson from "Per-
       fect Understanding," and Genevieve Tobin from "Pleasure Cruise";
       Bette Davis models two gowns from "Ex-Lady."

2765   Rich, Irene. "Do Men Like Daring Clothes on Women?"
              Screen News, 2 (51): 14, December 22, 1923.
       Irene Rich discusses dressing attractively, with brief mention of
       her role in "Lucretia Lombard."

2766   Rich, Lillian. "Fashions from Filmdom." Screen News, 2
              (37): 31, September 15, 1923.
       Irene Rich, having completed "The Love Master," is designing
       the costumes for her next films.

2767   "Richards, Robert." American Film Institute Catalog, 1961-
              70, p. 541.
       Robert Richards is credited with the wardrobe of "Wall of Noise,"
       "The Incredible Mr. Limpet," and "The Baby Maker" and the
       men's wardrobe of "The Good Guys and the Bad Guys."

2768   Richmond, Jack. Hollywood. The City of a Thousand Dreams;
              the Graveyard of a Thousand Hopes. Facts and Fancies
              of Filmdom. Los Angeles, no publisher, [1928].
       The author advises that those who hope for a film career bring
       sufficient money with them for clothing since they may have to
       rent or buy these, as the studios usually do not supply any.

2769   "Richter, Ilse." American Film Institute Catalog, 1961-70,
              p. 542.
       Ilse Richter is credited with the costumes of "Explosion."

2770   "Richter-Visser, Anna." American Film Institute Catalog,
              1961-70, p. 542.
       Anna Richter-Visser was the costume designer of "Dingaka" and
       is credited with the costumes of "Kimberley Jim."

2771   "Rickards, Jocelyn." American Film Institute Catalog, 1961-
              70, p. 542.
       Jocelyn Rickards was the dress designer of "Blow-Up"; the cos-
       tume designer of "From Russia with Love," "The Sailor from
       Gibraltar," "The Bliss of Mrs. Blossom," "Interlude," "Alfred
       the Great," and "Ryan's Daughter"; and is credited with the cos-
       tumes of "The Knack ... and How to Get It" and "Mademoiselle."

2772   "Rickart, Evelyn." American Film Institute Catalog, 1961-70,
              p. 542.
       Evelyn Rickart is credited with the wardrobe of "Your Cheatin'
       Heart."

2773 "Ricketts, Charles." American Film Institute Catalog, 1961-
70, p. 542.
Charles Ricketts is credited with the costumes of "The Mikado."

2774 "Ridard, Henriette." American Film Institute Catalog, 1961-
70, p. 542.
Henriette Ridard is credited with the costumes of "Vice Dolls."

2775 Riddle, Melvin M. From Pen to Silversheet. Los Angeles:
Harvey White, 1922.
The following three articles by Riddle were adapted from chapters
in this book; no specific designers or films are discussed, though
the following articles all refer to Famous Players-Lasky studio
departments.

2776 Riddle, Malvin [sic] M. "From Pen to Silversheet: Architec-
ture, Decoration, Research." Photo-Dramatist, 3 (8):
35-7, January 1922.
The researching of Paramount films begins in the research de-
partment/library established by Elizabeth McGaffey when it was
the Lasky studio. The department has vast holdings of periodicals,
books, and files on costuming, fashion, and other subjects.

2777 Riddle, Melvin M. "From Pen to Silversheet: Costuming the
Players." Photo-Dramatist, 3 (9): 29-30, February 1922.
A discussion of the Lasky character wardrobe department, which
houses about 50,000 costumes and is supervised by Roy Diem.
Some of the duties of the wardrobe department are discussed, with
mention of the costuming of 200 extras for a cafe scene in "At
the End of the World."

2778 _____. "From Pen to Silversheet: Filmland's Fashion
Shop." Photo-Dramatist, 3 (10): 31-2, March 1922.
The fashion department of Lasky studio is extensively discussed,
as to the number and type of employees, and the various branches.
Ethel Chaffin, the chief designer, has designed the costumes for
Gloria Swanson in "The Great Moment" and "The Husband's Trade-
mark" and for Betty Compson in "At the End of the World," some
of which are discussed.

2779 "Riggs, Rita." American Film Institute Catalog, 1961-70,
p. 543.
Rita Riggs was the costume designer of "Number One" and is
credited with the costumes of "The Happy Ending" and "The Model
Shop," the wardrobe of "The Art of Love" and "Petulia," the
women's costumes/wardrobe of "Marnie" and "The Lawyer," and
the wardrobe supervision of "The Birds."

2780 "The Right Dress Triumphs." New Movie, 5 (6): 35-7, 98-9,
June 1932.
Norma Shearer prefers a simple gown of black or white for dra-
matic film scenes. She models two costumes from "Strangers
May Kiss."

2781   "Right for the Occasion." <u>Motion Picture,</u> 82 (4): 46, No-
           vember 1951.
Diana Lynn models a blouse and dress that have been adapted for
retail sale and the originals from "The People Against O'Hara,"
designed by Helen Rose.

2782   "Riley, Laurie." <u>American Film Institute Catalog, 1961-70,</u>
           p. 543.
Laurie Riley is credited with the wardrobe of "Wild in the Streets."

2783   Riley, Robert.   "Adrian," in <u>American Fashion.</u>   New York:
           Quadrangle/New York Times, 1975, p. 3-105.
Adrian's talent as an artist was obvious even as a child.   He
eventually changed his name from Adrian Adolph Greenburg to
Gilbert Adrian, the Gilbert from his father's name; his father
was upset but decades later changed his own name to Mr. Adrian.
Norman Norell designed the costumes for "A Sainted Devil," but
Natacha Rambova did not like his "crabbed little sketches" and
asked Adrian to come to Hollywood to design for "The Hooded
Falcon."   "Costumes by Adrian" first appeared in the credits of
"Cobra."   He then began designing for Cecil B. De Mille's films
and moved with him to MGM, where David Cox was the designer.
Limited mostly to Adrian's costumes in the 1930s, references include his hats for Greta Garbo, the fashion influence of her costumes in "A Woman of Affairs," and her ornate petticoats in
"Camille"; notes also that a single embroidered panel on her
coronation robe in "Queen Christina" cost $1,800 (the dress had
many such panels), and his depression over Garbo appearing like
a "supermarket housewife" in "Two-Faced Woman."   In 1935 he
organized a fashion show with Omar Kiam, Travis Banton, and
other designers (not named) for visiting designer Schiaparelli.
His staff at MGM included embroiderer Mrs. Cluett; Hannah
Lindfors, who cut and supervised modern costumes, and left
MGM with Adrian when he opened his salon; and Inez Schrodt,
who was in charge of films with period and unusual costumes,
including "The Wizard of Oz."   In 1930 Janet Gaynor requested
and was allowed to have Adrian design her costumes for "Daddy
Long Legs" (see Deaner, Frances.   "The New Janet Gaynor--
Designed by Adrian").   After leaving MGM Adrian designed the
costumes for a Carole Landis film, "The Powers Girl," to fi-
nance the building of his salon and designed the costumes for a
12-minute fashion show in "Lovely to Look At."   Fashion magazines <u>Vogue</u> and <u>Harper's Bazaar</u> virtually ignored him--"The
popular success of his clothes was certainly a concrete challenge
to their editorial authority."   To date, this is the most extensive
biography of Adrian and gives one a touching portrait of the designer, as with his marvelous sense of humor.

2784   "Road to Utopia." <u>Motion Picture,</u> 71 (2): 25, March 1946.
Edith Head's costumes for Dorothy Lamour in "Road to Utopia"
include a fur-lined sarong.

2785   Roberts, Catherine.   "Vacation Story: Primp-Up for Playing."

> Motion Picture, 71 (1): 38-9, February 1946.
> Anita Louise models a retail "interpretation" of one of her cos-
> tumes from "The Bandit of Sherwood Forest."

2786 "Roberts, Frank." American Film Institute Catalog, 1961-70,
       p. 546.
Frank Roberts is credited with the wardrobe of "36 Hours," "Wel-
come to Hard Times," "The Legend of Lylah Clare," and "The
Extraordinary Seaman."

2787 "Roberts, Ricky." American Film Institute Catalog, 1961-70,
       p. 547.
Ricky Roberts is credited with the costumes of "The Strawberry
Statement."

2788 Robin, Toni. "Irene of Hollywood." Holiday, 4 (2): 132-7,
       August 1947.
Biographical information on Irene, who discusses film-costume
designing. The average film costume is completed in one to one
and a half weeks, with two fittings; the majority of furs are rented,
and the jewelry is usually rented from Joseff of California. Ann
Miller models one costume from "Easter Parade," with costly
embroidered stockings that frequently had to be replaced because
of her vigorous dancing.

2789 "Robins of Dallas." American Film Institute Catalog, 1961-
       70, p. 548.
Robins of Dallas is credited with the wardrobe of "She Mob."

2790 "Robinson Co., J.W." American Film Institute Catalog, 1961-
       70, p. 548.
J.W. Robinson Co. is credited with the costumes of "Young
Americans."

2791 Robinson, David. "Showbiz Glamour." Times (London),
       November 30, 1974, p. 9.
Discussion of film-costume design and history, with examples of
costumes displayed in the "Romantic and Glamorous Hollywood
Design" exhibit. Notes that a costume worn by Lillian Gish in
"Romola" was made by the costumier of the Milan opera in Flo-
rence and that Travis Banton once worked with Madame Francine
(Frances).

2792 Robinson, Julian. "The Hollywood Image--1933 to 1936," in
       Fashion in the '30s. London: Oresko, 1978, p. 19-84.
The book, and the decade of the 1930s, is divided into three chapters. The title is misleading; film costume is limited to several
very general paragraphs. Designer Schiaparelli was the first to
acknowledge film costumes' fashion influence; she said that "the
film fashions of today are your fashions of tomorrow." Illustrations include Ginger Rogers in five costumes and a hat from "In
Person," by Bernard Newman; and one costume each worn by
Mary Brian from "Two's Company," Antoinette Cellier from "The

Tenth Man," and Helen Vinson from "The Tunnel" (by Schiaparelli). Some of the illustrations were reproduced from film or fashion magazines.

2793 Robinson, Selma. "Look at Yourself." Collier's, 100 (17): 20, 36, October 23, 1937.
Muriel King briefly discusses selecting flattering costumes for Katharine Hepburn, Gail Patrick, and Ginger Rogers in "Stage Door"; their respective roles required well-bred, seductive, and cute costumes.

2794 Robyns, Grace. Princess Grace. New York: McKay, 1976.
Edith Head discusses how she and Grace Kelly would collaborate on fabric selections and other aspects of Kelly's costumes before Head would begin the actual sketching. Kelly was so certain that she would receive the lead role in "To Catch a Thief" that she convinced Head to design the costumes beforehand. Notes that it was unusual that Kelly consented to wear a bathing suit in "The Bridges at Toko-Ri." She wore the diamond engagement ring given her by Prince Rainier in "High Society," which was shown in a closeup.

2795 "Rockne, Rose." American Film Institute Catalog, 1961-70, p. 549.
Rose Rockne is credited with the wardrobe of "Operation Eichmann" and "Welcome to Hard Times" and was the wardrobe woman of "The Young Lovers."

2796 "Rodgers, Dorothy." American Film Institute Catalog, 1961-70, p. 550.
Dorothy Rodgers is credited with the costumes of "Hail, Hero!"

2797 "Rodrigues, Pedro." American Film Institute Catalog, 1961-70, p. 550.
Pedro Rodrigues is credited with Rita Hayworth's wardrobe in "The Happy Thieves."

2798 "Rodriguez, Domingo." American Film Institute Catalog, 1961-70, p. 550.
Domingo Rodriguez was the costume designer of "Mickey One," and is credited with the costumes of "Rachel, Rachel," "The Angel Levine," "The Landlord," and "The Sidelong Glances of a Pigeon Kicker."

2799 "Rodriguez, Oscar." American Film Institute Catalog, 1961-70, p. 550.
Oscar Rodriguez is credited with the costumes of "Wild Harvest," "The War Wagon," and "Flap"; the wardrobe of "The Magic Sword," "The Private Navy of Sgt. O'Farrell," "The Wicked Dreams of Paula Schultz," "100 Rifles," and "Angel Unchained"; and the men's wardrobe of "The Phantom Planet."

2800 "Roger Furse Dies; Stage Designer." New York Times,

August 22, 1972, p. 46.
Roger Kemble Furse died at age 68 from undisclosed causes. Notes
his famous association with Laurence Olivier.

2801   "Rogers, Joyce." American Film Institute Catalog, 1961-70,
           p. 551.
Joyce Rogers is credited with the costumes of "4 for Texas," the
women's costumes of "Palm Springs Weekend," and the wardrobe
of "More Dead Than Alive."

2802   Roland, Ruth. "Personality in Dress." Photoplay, 8 (1):
           134-5, June 1915.
Ruth Roland discusses the importance of the psychology of clothing
in the selection of her film costumes.

2803   " 'Rollerball's' Futuristic Fashions Bedazzle." Times-Picayune
           (New Orleans), July 20, 1975, sec. 4, p. 6.
Julie Harris designed her first futuristic costumes for "Rollerball," for which she designed over 1,000 costumes with a goal of
comfort, classic simplicity, and fluidity. The specific costumes
for James Caan, and for the men in general, are discussed, with
reference to color and fabric selections, jewelry creation, and
problems with the modern fabrics. She won an Academy Award
for Julie Christie's costumes in "Darling"; in most of her films
she works with wardrobe supervisor John Hilling and wardrobe
mistress Dorothy Edwards.

2804   "Romanini, Gaia." American Film Institute Catalog, 1961-70,
           p. 552.
Gaia Romanini was the costume designer of "Hercules, Samson
& Ulysses," "The Libertine," and for Sophia Loren in "Judith"
and is credited with the costumes of "The Warrior Empress,"
"Family Diary," "The Wastrel," "Operation Kid Brother," "A
Rose for Everyone," and "Seven Golden Men" and the wardrobe
of "The Sweet Body of Deborah."

2805   "Root, Sandy." American Film Institute Catalog, 1961-70,
           p. 554.
Sandy Root is credited with the wardrobe of "Diamond Stud" and
"The Joys of Jezebel," as wardrobe girl for "The Secret Sex
Lives of Romeo and Juliet," and for costume coordination of "The
Notorious Cleopatra."

2806   Rose, Helen. "How I Dress the Stars." Motion Picture,
           80 (2): 48, September 1950.
Helen Rose discusses designing one dress each, with one photo
of each, for Elizabeth Taylor in "Father of the Bride," June
Allyson in "Right Cross," Jane Powell in "Nancy Goes to Rio,"
Vera-Ellen in "Three Little Words," and Lana Turner in "A Life
of Her Own."

2807   _____. "How to Be a 'Designing Woman.' " Photoplay,
           51 (4): 77, 81, April 1957.

Helen Rose discusses how she designs for a film; how one can
become a film designer; and designing for Lauren Bacall and
Dolores Gray in "Designing Woman," with references to specific
costumes, the stars' preferences, and their selections. Gray
models one costume. Rose was also a story consultant (the film
was based in part upon her life).

2808 _____. "Just Make Them Beautiful": The Many Worlds of
       a Designing Woman. Santa Monica, Calif.,: Dennis-
       Landman, 1976.
Helen Rose was a successful theatrical costume designer when
she moved to Hollywood, and for a short while worked in a costume company started by Walter and Ethel Israel. There she researched and sketched costumes for "Abraham Lincoln," and
others (unnamed). She later worked with Rita Kaufman, supervising designer for Twentieth Century-Fox, in 1936, but Kaufman
received costume-design credit without designing. They were both
fired several months later when the heads of the studio changed.
Later, at the same studio, Fanchon was hired as a musical coordinator (and costume supervisor) and asked Rose to assist her.
When Fanchon didn't like the present designers' sketches, the two
designers (Earl Luick, and probably Herschel) quit, and Rose
finished and received credit for "Coney Island," "Hello, Frisco,
Hello," and "Stormy Weather." She again quit film design and
was later hired by MGM and paid $750 per week just so that she
could not design for her previous studio, MGM's competitor in
musicals. At least half of the book deals with her film costumes,
with references to the three-year influence on fashion of the corset
worn by Lana Turner in "The Merry Widow" (1952); the only film
she refused credit for--Jane Fonda in "A Period of Adjustment,"
since Fonda redesigned everything; piracy (the stealing of a costume idea) of a costume worn by Cyd Charisse in "Deep in My
Heart"; and the successful sales in her retail collections of one
costume worn by Elizabeth Taylor in "Cat on a Hot Tin Roof"
and "Butterfield 8." Includes 34 sketches of film costumes in
color and over 70 black-and white stills. The actresses most
often shown are Esther Williams (whose bathing suits cost thousands of dollars), Lana Turner, Grace Kelly, and Lauren Bacall.

2809 "Rose, Helen." American Film Institute Catalog, 1961-70,
       p. 554.
Helen Rose was the costume designer of "Ada," "Bachelor in
Paradise," "Go Naked in the World," "The Honeymoon Machine,"
"Goodbye Charlie," and "How Sweet It Is!" and is credited with
the costumes of "The Courtship of Eddie's Father," the gowns for
"Made in Paris," and for Jean Simmons's gowns in "Mister Budd-
wing."

2810 "Rose, Helen." Fairchild's Who's Who in Fashion. 1975,
       p. 225.
Helen Rose was a costume designer at Twentieth Century-Fox
until 1942, when she switched to MGM. In the 1950s she began
designing her own ready-to-wear line and has received two Aca-

demy Awards, for "The Bad and the Beautiful" and "I'll Cry
Tomorrow."

2811 "Rose, Helen." World of Fashion. 1976, p. 247.
Helen Rose was a costume designer for Twentieth Century-Fox
from 1939 to 1942 and for MGM from 1942 to 1963.

2812 "Rosemary Theby Finds Compensations in Being a Vamp...."
        Screen News, 3 (32): 17, August 9, 1924, cols. 2-3.
As a vamp, Rosemary Theby may lose the hero, but she has
beautiful gowns in "The Best in Life," all but one of which are
American-made. (Contradicts following article.)

2813 "Rosemary Theby Is Wearing Some of Her Beautiful French
        Gowns...." Screen News, 3 (34): 9, August 23, 1924,
        col. 3.
While in Paris for another film, Rosemary Theby had some
gowns made for "The Best in Life."

2814 Rosen, Marjorie. "Movie Costumes." Film Comment, 11
        (2): 34-5, March/April 1975.
The author was enthusiastic about the "Romantic and Glamorous
Hollywood Design" exhibit at the Metropolitan Museum of Art,
referring to the gowns as "artifacts of the Hollywood myth" and
" ... of the American Dream"; with a discussion of the fantasy
nature of film costume, and nine stills of costumes from the
exhibit.

2815 "Rosenbach, Gina." American Film Institute Catalog, 1961-
        70, p. 555.
Gina Rosenbach is credited with the costumes of "Sallah" and
"Impossible on Saturday" and the wardrobe of "Trunk to Cairo."

2816 "Rosenquest, Barbara." American Film Institute Catalog,
        1961-70, p. 556.
Barbara Rosenquest is credited with the costumes of "Macho
Callahan."

2817 "Rosier, Michele." American Film Institute Catalog, 1961-
        70, p. 556.
Michele Rosier is credited with the parachute jump-suits worn by
Raquel Welch in "Fathom" and Audrey Hepburn's clothes in "Two
for the Road."

2818 Ross, Clark. Stars and Strikes: [The] Unionization of Holly-
        wood. New York: Columbia University Press, 1941.
Before the days of Central Casting (pre-1926) extras often traveled from studio to studio with complete wardrobes to meet any
role offer. Dress extras are the highest paid extras because of
the expense of keeping an extensive wardrobe and purchasing the
latest fashions and indoor and outdoor clothing with added upkeep
of laundering and repairs. In 1939 the daily rate for extras was
$15 for the "Class A," modern-dress extra; $10 for those with

modern but less formal, or character wardrobes; $7.50 if the studio provided the wardrobe, and $5 if no specific wardrobe was required.

2819 "Ross, Clark." American Film Institute Catalog, 1961-70,
         p. 556.
Ross Clark is credited with the wardrobe of "The Little Shepherd of Kingdom Come."

2820 Ross, Lillian. Picture. New York: Discus, 1969.
The budget for "The Red Badge of Courage" included 20 pairs of carbine boots at $150 each in the Rent and Purchase Props category. The $43,000 spent on Wardrobe included 25 Union soldier uniforms at $50 each, and 25 Union officer's and ten Confederate officer's uniforms costing $75 each--in addition to what the wardrobe department already had supplied. The uniforms cost more than those originally worn by both sides in the Civil War. Extras changed uniforms and sides throughout the film during production.

2821 "Rosse, Herman." American Film Institute Catalog, 1921-30,
         p. 1341.
Herman Rosse is credited with the costumes of "The King of Jazz."

2822 "Rossi, Vittorio." American Film Institute Catalog, 1961-70,
         p. 557.
Vittorio Rossi is credited with the costumes of "The Colossus of Rhodes," "The Revolt of the Slaves," "Goliath Against the Giants," "Hercules and the Captive Women," "My Son, the Hero," "Goliath and the Vampires," and "Journey Beneath the Desert."

2823 "Roth, Ann." American Film Institute Catalog, 1961-70, p.
         558.
Ann Roth was the costume designer of "A Fine Madness," "Up the Down Staircase," "Pretty Poison," "Sweet November," and "Midnight Cowboy" and the wardrobe designer of "Jenny" and is credited with the costumes of "The World of Henry Orient," "The Owl and the Pussycat," and "The People Next Door."

2824 "Roth, Eve." American Film Institute Catalog, 1921-30, p.
         1342.
Eve Roth was the costume designer of "Scaramouche" (1923) and is credited with the wardrobe of "The Silent Watcher."

2825 Rotha, Paul. "Technique of the Art-Director," in Rotha on
         the Film: A Selection of Writings About the Cinema.
         Fair Lawn, N.J.: Essential, 1958, p.40-3.
The author was fired from his job as an art director for an unnamed studio when this article was published in 1928. He felt that film costume had been virtually unexplored and poorly treated, as with expensive but bad period costumes in "The Man Who Laughs," though supervisor Paul Leni was excellent with the cos-

tumes of "Manon Lescaut." The men's costumes of "Casanova" failed because they were poorly proportioned; Walter Röhrig's designs for "Tartuffe" were successful; Claude Autant-Lara's designs for "Nana" were charming; Rudolph Bamberger's for "A Glass of Water" were adequate; and "Federicus Rex" featured the most historically accurate costumes yet seen.

2826 "Roughly Speaking." Motion Picture, 69 (3): 58, April 1945.
Rosalind Russell wore over 50 costumes that spanned half of a century, from the early 1900s on, in "Roughly Speaking."

2827 "Rous, Bucky." American Film Institute Catalog, 1961-70, p. 558.
Bucky Rous is credited with the wardrobe of "Jack the Giant Killer," "Kitten with a Whip," "The Night Walker," "Bus Riley's Back in Town," and "Five Easy Pieces" and the men's wardrobe of "Ensign Pulver."

2828 Roux-Parassac, E. "The Cinema and Fashion; Costume on the Screen." International Review of Educational Cinematography, 9: 1096-8, September 1930.
The author's ideas about film costume are very similar to Paul Rotha's; specifically, that film costume has been neglected, unlike scenery, despite famous designers and big budgets; film costume has not surpassed theatrical costumes of the past; and too often a dress is made for originality, and distorted when it must be changed to meet screen requirements. Large studios neglect the extras in order to clothe the chief actors, who are usually also neglected and poorly fitted, so that films are soon dated. The author recommends that expert costumers, aware of the functions and influence of dress, be given more freedom to design authentic period costumes, and more realistic contemporary clothes, considering the influence of film costume on fashion.

2829 "Rouzot, Renée." American Film Institute Catalog, 1961-70, p. 559.
Renée Rouzot is credited with the costumes of "Vice Dolls" and was wardrobe mistress for "Nights of Shame" and "The Soft Skin." She is also known as Renée Rouzeau (but there are no references to this other name).

2830 "Rovatti, Cesare." American Film Institute Catalog, 1961-70, p. 559.
Cesare Rovatti is credited with the costumes of "Matchless."

2831 "Roy, Hazel." American Film Institute Catalog, 1961-70, p. 559.
Hazel Roy was the costume designer of "Andy" and is credited with the wardrobe of "Charly."

2832 "Royal Robe Uses 2500 Ermine Pelts." MGM Studio News, 5 (6): n.p., August 15, 1938.
For the wedding sequence of "Marie Antoinette" Robert Morley

wore a copy of the robe the French king Louis XVI wore, lined
with 2,500 ermine pelts and with the upper portion made of blue
velvet, heavily embroidered with gold thread.

2833 "The Royal Robes That Pola Negri Wears in Her Latest Pic-
         ture." Motion Picture, 28 (12): 46, January 1925.
Pola Negri models five costumes from "Forbidden Paradise," with
detailed descriptions of each.

2834 Royer. "Fashion Forecast for Summer." Photoplay, 49 (5):
         53-5, 120-1, June 1935.
Mona Barrie models two costumes from "Ladies Love Danger,"
by Royer, who discusses fashion trends.

2835 _____. "The Magic of Coiffures." Movie Classic, 8 (6):
         64-5, August 1935.
When Royer sketches film costumes he usually also sketches the
hair styles to give the hair stylist an idea of what the completed
look should be. He discusses how a gown worn by Mona Barrie
in "Ladies Love Danger" was complemented through her hairstyle.

2836 "Royer (Louis Royer Hastings)." World of Fashion. 1976,
         p. 202.
Rare biographical information on Royer, who left Hollywood in
1939 to design film costumes and retail fashions in Mexico.

2837 Rubin, Joan Alleman. "Costumes by Karinska." Dance, 41
         (6): 49-51, 84, June 1967.
Contains biographical information on Mme. Karinska, costumer-
perfectionist, who stayed briefly in Hollywood in 1938, when she
first came to the United States from France. (Does not elaborate
on what she did in Hollywood.)

2838 Rubinstein, Helena. "Defense of Glamour." Cinema Arts, 1
         (2): 66, 90, July 1937.
Greta Garbo's hat in "Romance," christened the "Empress Eugenie,"
was worn by women everywhere; includes a still of Garbo in the
hat. Mae West's 1890 figure and costumes in "She Done Him
Wrong" induced Parisian couturiers to follow, away from the slim
look.

2839 "Ruckman, Nan." American Film Institute Catalog, 1961-70,
         p. 560.
Nan Ruckman is credited with the wardrobe of "No Man's Land."

2840 "Rudolph, Rod." American Film Institute Catalog, 1961-70,
         p. 561.
Rod Rudolph is credited with the wardrobe of "Wife Swappers."

2841 "Ruffing, Nancy." American Film Institute Catalog, 1961-70,
         p. 561.
Nancy Ruffing is credited with the costumes of "Nothing But a
Man."

2842   Russell, Frederick.   "How John Barrymore Helped Carole. "
         Film Pictorial, 9 (229): 28-9, July 11, 1936.
       Carole Lombard was happy to learn of the simple uniforms re-
       quired for "Hands Across the Table" since she had wanted more
       lifelike roles.   She often helps designer Travis Banton as he
       sketches her costumes, and accompanies him on shopping trips
       for her fabrics.

2843   Russell, Rosalind, and Chris Chase.   Life Is a Banquet.   New
         York: Random House, 1977.
       Norma Shearer selected a period costume made for "Marie An-
       toinette, " but which had not been worn, for the fitting-room se-
       quence in "The Women" rather than wear the dress that had been
       designed for her.   Rosalind Russell's usual wardrobe for her
       many career-woman films included a variety of suits, with a
       negligee for the obligatory bedroom scene.   She tells of an inci-
       dent with Harry Cohn, president of Columbia Studios, who charged
       her $600 apiece for her old film costumes, but she charged him
       $100 per day rental for a fur worn in an unnamed film, and came
       out receiving money from him; the fur was rented from furrier
       Mr. Hoffman.   Russell wanted Jean Louis to design her costumes
       for "Never Wave at a Wac, " but he recommended unknown James
       Galanos for her costume designer; Galanos designed 13 costumes
       for the film, Jean Louis designed one costume, and Hattie Carne-
       gie designed her military uniform.   Years later, Mainbocher copied
       one of Galanos's costumes for his own collection.   Travis Banton
       died before he could design her costumes for "Auntie Mame, "
       having designed them for her Broadway production; Orry-Kelly
       did them.   Coco Chanel gave a 10-percent discount to those who
       wore her fashions in their films.

2844   "Russell, Shirley. "   American Film Institute Catalog, 1961-
         70, p. 562.
       Shirley Russell was the costume designer of "Women in Love. "

2845   "Ruth Clifford ... in ... 'The Dangerous Age'.... "   Screen
         News, 1 (42): 6, December 9, 1922, col. 1.
       Ruth Clifford models one costume (different from the following
       two entries and costumes modeled) from "The Dangerous Age, "
       by Paul Poiret.   (Following dresses not credited to Poiret.)

2846   "Ruth Clifford ... in ... 'The Dangerous Age'.... "   Screen
         News, 1 (42): 27, December 9, 1922, col. 3.

2847   "Ruth Clifford ... in ... 'The Dangerous Age'.... "   Screen
         News, 1 (43): 22, December 16, 1922, col. 1.

2848   "Ruth Clifford Wears Poiret Gown [in] 'The Dangerous Age.' "
         Screen News, 1 (27): 23, August 26, 1922.
       Description of a gown worn by Ruth Clifford in "The Dangerous
       Age, " designed by Paul Poiret, worn with a cape and hat.

2849   "Ruth Roland Wears Unique Esquimaux Furs in 'The Timber

Queen.'" Screen News, 1 (27): 23, August 26, 1922.
In "The Timber Queen" Ruth Roland wears a parka made of reindeer, fox, and ermine furs, with checkerboard trimming made
from ermine and darker reindeer.

2850 "Ryan, Florence." American Film Institute Catalog, 1961-70,
          p. 563.
Florence Ryan is credited with the costumes of "Sin in the Suburbs."

2851 Ryan, Rita. "The 'Best Dressed Woman' Jinx." Shadoplay,
          3 (1): 42-3, 64-6, March 1934.
Lilyan Tashman has long been considered the "best dressed"
actress on and off the screen. A number of actresses, including
Tashman, Kay Francis, and Hedda Hopper, discuss the importance
of being well dressed, as opposed to being noticed for one's costumes while acting.

2852 "Ryndina, V." American Film Institute Catalog, 1961-70, p.
          564.
V. Ryndina is credited with the costumes for a ballet sequence in
"Bolshoi Ballet 67."

2853 "Sabatelli, Luca." American Film Institute Catalog, 1961-70, p. 564.
Luca Sabatelli was the costume designer of "I Married You for Fun."

2854 "Sabbatini, Enrico." American Film Institute Catalog, 1961-70, p. 565.
Enrico Sabbatini was the costume designer of "Candy," "Ghosts --Italian Style," and "A Place for Lovers" and the assistant costume designer of "More Than a Miracle" and is credited with the costumes of "Camille 2000," "A Fine Pair," "The Laughing Woman," "The Lickerish Quartet," "Machine Gun McCain," and "Sunflower."

2855 Sabol, Blair. "Flick Fashions Headed for Disaster?" Los Angeles Times, January 5, 1975, sec. 4, p. 1, 14.
Brief mention of the influence on fashion of "Bonnie and Clyde," "Elvira Madigan," "Superfly," "Shaft," "Borsalino," "The Great Gatsby," "The Damned," "Cabaret," and "Pink Flamingos." Also a somewhat tongue-in-cheek discussion of how the audiences of "Earthquake," "Towering Inferno," and "Airport '75" have learned to prepare for disasters by wearing durable clothing; with occasional comments on how well the clothing of the actors/actresses withstood the disaster conditions.

2856 "Safas, Sartoria." American Film Institute Catalog, 1961-70, p. 565.
Sartoria Safas is credited with the costumes of "The Leopard" and Sophia Loren's costumes in "More Than a Miracle"; she made Elizabeth Taylor's costumes for "The Taming of the Shrew."

2857 "Sagoni, Luciano." American Film Institute Catalog, 1961-70, p. 566.
Luciano Sagoni is credited with the costumes of "The Five Man Army."

2858 "Sailor in Need of a Tailor." Photoplay, 53 (4): 42-3, April 1958.
Mitzi Gaynor's oversized sailor uniform in "South Pacific" required three copies made of seven yards each of regulation fab-

ric, at a cost of $350 each. Despite the jumbo size, six fittings were required to ensure her being able to dance; designed by Dorothy Jeakins.

2859 "St. Hill, Loudon." American Film Institute Catalog, 1961-
       70, p. 566.
    Loudon St. Hill was the costume designer of "Can Heironymus Merkin Ever Forget Mercy Humppe and Find True Happiness?"

2860 St. Johns, Adela Rogers.   "'From the Skin Out.'" Photoplay,
       15 (6): 32-5, 97-101, May 1919.
    Discussion of the growing importance of realism, authenticity, appropriateness, and harmony in film costume, through research; consequently, actresses usually have their costumes supplied by the studio. Discussion also of the wardrobe departments of Lasky, Sennett, Universal, Goldwyn, and Triangle studios; and the jobs of Mrs. A.B. Hoffman, Lasky's designer and modiste; Violet Schroeder, Sennett studio designer; and Mrs. Duncan, wardrobe mistress for the De Mille studio, with references to her costumes for Sylvia Ashton in "Old Wives for New," extras and Carmel Myers in "The Little White Savage," and Mabel Normand in "Sis Hopkins," with illustrations from the three films. The Goldwyn wardrobe department houses the costumes left in it by the Triangle studio, though many of designer Peggy Hamilton's costumes have already been remade for other films; costumes were also left from films made by D.W. Griffith and Thomas Ince. Pauline Frederick spends about $75,000 per year for film costumes, usually bought on Fifth Avenue. References also to the research and costuming of "The Woman God Forgot," with Geraldine Farrar in this and "The Hell Cat," the costumes of which were widely criticized for inauthenticity.

2861 _____. "Gloria! An Impression." Photoplay, 24 (4): 28-9,
       104-5, September 1923.
    The author states that "I always hope that Gloria Swanson has not forgotten Peggy Hamilton." Hamilton, costume designer for Triangle studios, had the "genius," "instinct," and "Parisian training" to know that a less than chic and immaculate Gloria Swanson could be groomed and costumed into the image she has become associated with, having costumed her in her first Triangle film (her first Triangle film was "Society for Sale").

2862 _____. "Judy--the Girl Who Became the 'World's Best-
       Dressed Woman.'" Photoplay with Movie Mirror, 27
       (6): 30-1, 121-3, November 1945.
    Irene discusses designing Judy Garland's costumes for "Presenting Lily Mars" and, briefly, "The Ziegfeld Follies" and "The Clock."

2863 "Saint-Laurent, Yves." American Film Institute Catalog,
       1961-70, p. 566.
    Yves Saint-Laurent is credited with the costumes of "Black Tights"; the wardrobe of "Live for Life" and "Hello--Goodbye"

and for Claudia Cardinale and Capucine in "The Pink Panther," Leslie Caron in "A Very Special Favor," and Jean Seberg in "Moment to Moment"; and Catherine Deneuve's costumes/wardrobe in "Belle de Jour" and "La Chamade."

2864 "Saint-Laurent, Yves." International Who's Who. 38th ed., 1974-5, p.1513.

2865 "Saint-Laurent, Yves." Who's Who in France. 6th ed., 1963-4, p.2149.

2866 "Saint-Laurent, Yves (-Mathieu)." Current Biography. 1964, p.385-7.
Yves St.-Laurent has been fond of theatrical costumes since childhood; lengthy biographical information on the designer.

2867 "St. Moritz, Ruth." American Film Institute Catalog, 1961-70, p.566.
Ruth St. Moritz was the costume designer of "Dingaka."

2868 "Salamero, Flora." American Film Institute Catalog, 1961-70, p.567.
Flora Salamero is credited with the wardrobe of "Gunfighters of Casa Grande" and "Son of a Gunfighter."

2869 "Salcedo, Felisa." American Film Institute Catalog, 1961-70, p.567.
Felisa Salcedo is credited with the costumes of "Cry of Battle."

2870 "Salcedo, Paquito." American Film Institute Catalog, 1961-70, p.567.
Paquito Salcedo is credited with the wardrobe of "The Ravagers" and "Beast of Blood."

2871 "Saldutti, Peter." American Film Institute Catalog, 1961-70, p.567.
Peter Saldutti is credited with the costumes of "Strange Bedfellows"; the wardrobe of "Lonely Are the Brave," "For Love or Money," "Blindfold," and "The Reluctant Astronaut"; the men's wardrobe of "Forty Pounds of Trouble," "Man's Favorite Sport?," and "I Love My Wife"; the men's costume supervision of "Topaz"; and the costume supervision of "The Plainsman" (1966).

2872 "Saling, Norman." American Film Institute Catalog, 1961-70, p.568.
Norman Saling is credited with the costumes of "The Gay Deceivers."

2873 "Sally Tuffin, Ltd." World of Fashion. 1976, p.99.
Sally Tuffin and Marion Foale have dissolved their firm, Foale and Tuffin, Ltd.; the firm continues as Sally Tuffin, Ltd.

2874 "Salome's Seven Veils Just Six Too Many." Screen News, 4

(33): 15, August 22, 1925.
Seven women in "The Wedding Song" will wear costumes made
from one scarf each, designed by Adrian.

2875 "Samazeuilh, Alyette." American Film Institute Catalog, 1961-
         70, p. 569.
Alyette Samazeuilh is credited with the costumes of "Cleo from
5 to 7."

2876 "Sammaciccia, Angela." American Film Institute Catalog,
         1961-70, p. 569.
Angela Sammaciccia is credited with the wardrobe of "The Climax"
and the costumes of "Seduced and Abandoned," "The Birds, the
Bees, and the Italians," "Investigation of a Citizen Above Suspicion," and "Serafino."

2877 Sammis, Constance Sharp. "Miss Rose Dresses Stars."
         Christian Science Monitor, October 2, 1956, p. 14.
Helen Rose discusses costume design and recent assignments in
general; she advises that aspiring costume designers obtain all
the clothing experience and education they can before coming to
Hollywood.

2878 "Sandeen, Jack." American Film Institute Catalog, 1961-70,
         p. 570.
Jack Sandeen is credited with the wardrobe of "Brewster McCloud."

2879 "Sanjust, Filippo." American Film Institute Catalog, 1961-70,
         p. 571.
Filippo Sanjust was the costume designer of "Morgan the Pirate"
and "Seven Seas to Calais" and is credited with the costumes of
"The White Warrior" and "The Young Lord."

2880 "Sånnell, Bertha." American Film Institute Catalog, 1961-70,
         p. 571.
Bertha Sånnell is credited with the costumes of "Bamse."

2881 "Santiago, Emile." Who's Who in America. 39th ed., 1976-
         7, p. 2745.
Emile Santiago has been a costume designer for Hal Roach Studios,
MGM, Paramount, RKO, Warner Brothers, and Universal studios,
and won an Academy Award for "The Robe."

2882 "Save Profits." It, 2 (12): 16, June 15, 1920.
Over ten studios, as listed, hope to save the $20 million they
spend annually on "everything needed in the production of pictures"
by financing and building their own warehouse, to be called Cinema
Mercantile Company.

2883 "Say Europe's Designers Using Our Film Ideals." Screen
         News, 2 (10): 14, March 10, 1923.
Clare West, costume designer for De Mille Studios, has just returned from a trip to Europe, gathering ideas, jewelry, and ma-

terials for "The Ten Commandments." West believes motion-
picture costumes are ahead of European fashion and have a greater
fashion influence throughout the world than Paris.

2884 Scagnetti, Jack. The Intimate Life of Rudolph Valentino.
          Middle Village, N.Y.: Jonathan David, 1975.
      Rudolph Valentino influenced fashion with the bolero fad from
      "The Four Horsemen of the Apocalypse" and with Spanish shirts,
      shawls, and bandanas from "Blood and Sand" and the turban from
      "The Young Rajah," and men's clothes became generally more
      colorful. S. George Ullman withdrew Valentino's clothes from
      the auction of his estate so that he could buy them himself for
      sentimental reasons (they apparently were auctioned). A rare
      collector's item for Valentino fans is a costume replica of Valen-
      tino's "Sheik" costume made by Chessler Company in 1930, a
      masquerade costume called the "Desert Chief." Includes refer-
      ences found in the other Valentino biographies, including his re-
      lationship to wife and costume designer Natacha Rambova.

2885 "Scales, John." American Film Institute Catalog, 1961-70,
          p. 575.
      John Scales was the costume designer of "Voyage to the End of
      the Universe."

2886 Scallon, Virginia. "The Adrian Story." The Californian,
          9 (4): 20-1, 62, May 1950.
      A biography of Adrian, with emphasis on his career since leaving
      the film industry.

2887 "Scandariato, Itala." American Film Institute Catalog, 1961-
          70, p. 576.
      Itala Scandariato was the costume designer of "The Biggest Bundle
      of Them All" and the wardrobe designer of "Story of a Woman"
      and is credited with the wardrobe of "Up the MacGregors" and
      "House of Cards" and the costumes of "Madame" and "A Place
      Called Glory."

2888 "Scarano, Gildo." American Film Institute Catalog, 1961-70,
          p. 576.
      Gildo Scarano is credited with the costumes of "The Carpetbaggers,"
      the wardrobe of "In Harm's Way," and the men's wardrobe of
      "The Molly Maguires."

2889 "Scarano, Tony." American Film Institute Catalog, 1961-70,
          p. 576.
      Tony Scarano is credited with the wardrobe of "Apache Uprising"
      and the costumes of "An Eye for an Eye."

2890 "Scarfiotti, Ferdinando." American Film Institute Catalog,
          1961-70, p. 576.
      Ferdinando Scarfiotti is credited with the costumes of "Listen,
      Let's Make Love."

2891 "Scassi, Arnold." <u>American Film Institute Catalog, 1961-70</u>,
        p. 576.
      Arnold Scassi was the designer of Barbra Streisand's contempo-
      rary clothes in "On a Clear Day You Can See Forever."

2892 "Scatena, Luce." <u>American Film Institute Catalog, 1961-70</u>,
        p. 576.
      Luce Scatena is credited with the costumes of "Hotbed of Sin"
      and "Sellers of Girls."

2893 "Scenes in Natural Colors Feature of 'Stage Struck.'" <u>Senator
        Newsette</u>, 2 (49): 1, 3, December 6, 1925.
      Three costumes worn by Gloria Swanson in a color, dream se-
      quence in "Stage Struck" are described, along with the headdresses.

2894 "Schaffer, Judit." <u>American Film Institute Catalog, 1961-70</u>,
        p. 576.
      Judit Schaffer was the costume designer of "The Boys of Paul
      Street."

2895 Schar, Robert. "Piero Tosi." <u>Cinema Papers</u>, 12: 322-3,
        378, April 1977.
      Italian designer Piero Tosi discusses film-costume design, with
      many stills and examples from his films with Federico Fellini,
      and from his 27 years with Luchino Visconti. Includes a partial
      list of his credits, and photos from "Fellini Satyricon," "Death
      in Venice," and "The Damned."

2896 Schiaparelli, Elsa. <u>Shocking Life.</u> New York: Dutton, 1954.
      Elsa Schiaparelli notes that she designed the costumes for "The
      Ghost Goes West"; discusses how she started the fad for padded
      shoulders, which she claims Adrian and Joan Crawford copied to
      excessive proportions; and describes some of Mae West's cos-
      tumes (For "Every Day's a Holiday"). She notes that she once
      dressed a woman to look like Gloria Swanson in "Sunset Boule-
      vard" to advertise the film in Paris.

2897 "A Schizophrenic Wardrobe!" <u>Los Angeles Herald-Examiner</u>,
        January 10, 1967, sec. C, p. 6.
      Edith Head discusses her quarter-million-dollar wardrobe for
      Natalie Wood in "Penelope," consisting of a high-fashion ward-
      robe and a separate "way out" one for the split personality charac-
      ter played by Wood.

2898 "Schmidt, Günther." <u>American Film Institute Catalog, 1961-
        70</u>, p. 578.
      Günther Schmidt is credited with the costumes of "Naked Among
      the Wolves."

2899 Schmitz, Virginia. "How Garbo Puts Glamour into Clothes."
        <u>New Movie</u>, 7 (3): 46-7, 84, March 1933.
      The look of Greta Garbo has been a steady influence on fashion

for years; the look attempts to capture her mood rather than copy the costumes completely. Retail fashion was influenced by the high-neck, low-back gown she wore in "As You Desire Me." Includes reprints of Garbo-inspired fashion ads by Saks Fifth Avenue and Gimbel Brothers department store.

2900   Schnurnberger, Lynn Edelman. "Star Trek--the Motion Picture" Make-Your-Own Costume Book. New York: Pocket Books, 1979.
A one-of-a-kind book, it is astonishing that, even before its release, a film's costumes should be the subject of a "how to" book. Robert Fletcher, the costume and jewelry designer of "Star Trek--the Motion Picture," has written the preface, in which he discusses designing the film's costumes, including how they differ from the television show. Draping instructions are given for three basic costumes, and patterns are supplied for many of the accessories; supplies needed are also noted. Most of the book consists of sections of costumes for characters from the film, with rare information as to the symbolism of colors, trims, and accessories; it is these paragraph-length analyses that really reveal the characters, crew members, or aliens, in a way that one could not discover from the film itself or through other sources. The majority of illustrations include nonfilm persons in costumes made from the book's instructions. Nine stills are included, in color or black-and-white, of characters, whose real names are not identified, from the film; with four closeups of jewelry from the film.

2901   Schoen, Juliet P. Silents to Sound: A History of the Movies. New York: Four Winds, 1976.
George Melies designed the costumes for his film "Cinderella." The expressionistic style of "The Cabinet of Dr. Caligari" included stylized, unrealistic costumes. Buster Keaton's comedy film "The General" included authentically copied costumes.

2902   "Schofield, Violet." American Film Institute Catalog, 1921-30, p. 1352.
Violet Schofield is credited with the costumes of "Molly O'."

2903   "Scholz, Brigitte." American Film Institute Catalog, 1961-70, p. 579.
Brigitte Scholz is credited with the costumes of "The Trapp Family."

2904   Schrader, Marie B. "The Gown Quest: The Problem of a Screen Star." Motion Picture Classic, 8 (4): 38, 68, 74, June 1919.
Actress Bessie Barriscale discusses traveling to New York for gowns for her pictures. She no longer feels the need for Parisian gowns and prefers not to wear her film costumes in her personal life.

2905   "Schreckling, Walter." American Film Institute Catalog, 1961-

<u>70</u>, p. 580.
Walter Schreckling is credited with the wardrobe of "Cry Double
Cross. "

2906 "Schröder, Eva Maria. " <u>American Film Institute Catalog,</u>
      <u>1961-70</u>, p. 580.
Eva Maria Schröder is credited with the costumes of "Freddy
Unter Fremden Sternen. "

2907 Schumach, Murray. "Boudoirs and Blood; Sex, " in <u>The Face</u>
      <u>on the Cutting Room Floor: The Story of Movie and Tele-</u>
      <u>vision Censorship.</u> New York: Morrow, 1964. p. 160-70,
      passim.
Marilyn Monroe's penchant for tight clothes, low necklines, and
no underclothes frustrated her designers and the censors.   Current fashions often determine whether costumes will be approved;
the bikini, previously rejected for other films, was allowed to
be worn in "Town Without Pity. " Brief mention of Elizabeth Taylor in "Cleopatra, " and of Lana Turner in suggestive and tight
knit sweaters, which caused the censors to issue a general warning about such knitwear.   The Production Code is included, which
for costumes forbade nudity and indecent exposure, unless applied
to foreign cultures, for example, in a documentary.   Includes
references also to Jane Russell in "The Outlaw" and how her
bustline and low-cut clothes caused "mammary madness" and,
eventually, a considerable relaxation in censorship.

2908 "Scott, Jay Hutchinson. " <u>American Film Institute Catalog,</u>
      <u>1961-70</u>, p. 582.
Jay Hutchinson Scott is credited with the costumes of "Berserk. "

2909 "Scott, Jay Hutchinson. " <u>Who's Who in the Theatre.</u>   16th
      ed. , 1977, p. 1105.

2910 "Scott, Ken, cost. " <u>American Film Institute Catalog, 1961-</u>
      <u>70</u>, p. 582.
Ken Scott is credited with Audrey Hepburn's clothes in "Two for
the Road. "

2911 "Scott, Ron. " <u>American Film Institute Catalog, 1961-70</u>, p.
      582.
Ron Scott is credited with the wardrobe of "A Bullet for Pretty
Boy. "

2912 "[Scrap Book]; Designer Karinska. " <u>Harper's Bazaar</u>, 2682:
      92-3, April 1936.
Much praise for Varia Karinska's ability as a seamstress.

2913 "Screen Fashion Designer Quits. " <u>Los Angeles Times</u>, No-
      vember 3, 1925, sec. 2, p. 1-2.
Erté looked forward to returning to Paris, having spent seven
frustrated months with MGM stars, including Lillian Gish, who
had unrealistic demands.   He found the actresses no more in-

spiring than his usual couture clientele.

2914 "Screen Glamour to Sell Fashions to Fans." Design for
         Industry, 19 (109): 19, July 1935.
      Marianne Horn, wardrobe supervisor of Gaumont British Studios,
      has arranged with Scott, Son & Co. to have film costumes mar-
      keted as "Marianne models" at the time of a film's release. Four
      stills show copies of costumes from "The Clairvoyant," designed
      by Joe Strassner. Costumes will also be marketed from "The Thirty-
      nine Steps."

2915 "Screen Guide Fashions." Screen Guide, 1 (6): 48, October
         1936.
      Katharine Hepburn models one costume (or two) and her stand-in
      three adaptations of Hepburn's costumes from "Mary of Scotland";
      the original and adapted costumes designed by Walter Plunkett.

2916 "Screen Play Style Scenes." Screen Play, 21 (150): 41-7,
         September 1937.
      Joan Bennett models three costumes by Irene, and Ruth Martin
      one by Omar Kiam, from "Vogues of 1938." Dorothy Day, Peggy
      Calvin, and Betty Wyman each model one hat from the film, de-
      signed by John Frederics.

2917 "Screen Play's Style Scenes." Screen Play, 21 (149): 43-8,
         August 1937.
      Mary Carlisle models one hat from "Double or Nothing"; Gail
      Patrick one costume from "Artists and Models," by Edith Head;
      and Claudette Colbert two costumes from "I Met Him in Paris,"
      by Travis Banton.

2918 "Screen Styles." Screen News, 1 (24): 31, August 5, 1922.
      Discussion of gowns worn by Virginia Brown Faire in "Omar the
      Tentmaker" and Kathryn McGuire in "The Silent Call."

2919 "Screen Styles." Screen News, 2 (23): 27, June 9, 1923.
      Includes a description of one gown worn by Pauline Garon in
      "Children of Dust."

2920 "Screen Styles Suggest Spring." Photoplay, 29 (5): 52-3,
         April 1926.
      One sketch each is presented of costumes worn by Blanche Sweet
      in "The Far Cry" and Clara Bow in "Dancing Mothers"; readers
      can order copies of the costumes.

2921 "Screen-Test for Fashion." Vogue, 90 (3): 54-5, August 1,
         1937.
      For "Vogues of 1938" Jaeckel designed the furs, John Frederics
      and Sally Victor the hats and Trabert and Hoeffer Mauboussin the
      jewels. Mary Oakes, Betty Douglas, Betty Wyman, and Katherine
      Aldridge each model one costume; all four are models who have
      worked for Vogue before. Joan Bennett models a dress by Irene
      and Hedda Hopper a coat by Omar Kiam from the film. Macy's

will copy one of the model's dresses, designed by Omar Kiam.

2922 "Screenland Glamor School." Screenland, 29 (2): 30-1, June
      1934.
      Norma Shearer models two costumes by Adrian from "Riptide";
      with closeups of additional costumes.

2923 "Screenland Glamor School." Screenland, 30 (1): 20-1, No-
      vember 1934.
      Joan Crawford models four costumes by Adrian from "Chained."

2924 "Screenland Glamor School." Screenland, 33 (1): 56-9, May
      1936.
      Bette Davis models six costumes by Orry-Kelly from "Golden
      Arrow," and Carole Lombard models one costume by Travis Ban-
      ton from "Love Before Breakfast."

2925 "Screenland Glamor School." Screenland, 34 (1): 56-9, No-
      vember 1936.
      Ruth Chatterton models two costumes from "Dodsworth."

2926 "Screenland Glamor School." Screenland, 35 (5): 56-9, Sep-
      tember 1937.
      Helen Vinson models seven costumes from "Vogues of 1938," and
      Martha Raye one from "Double or Nothing."

2927 "Screenland Glamor School." Screenland, 36 (3): 52-5, Janu-
      ary 1938.
      Frances Drake models two costumes from "She Married an Artist."

2928 "Screenland Glamor School." Screenland, 26 (6): 56-7, April
      1938.
      Kay Francis models six costumes by Orry-Kelly from "Women
      Are Like That."

2929 "Screenland Glamor School." Screenland, 37 (1): 60-2, May
      1938.
      Loretta Young models six costumes by Royer from "Four Men and
      a Prayer," and Claudette Colbert models three by Travis Banton
      from "Bluebeard's Eighth Wife."

2930 "Screenland Glamor School." Screenland, 37 (6): 58-9, Oc-
      tober 1938.
      Sonja Henie models six costumes from "My Lucky Star."

2931 "Screenland's Glamor School." Screenland, 27 (4): 56-7,
      August 1933.
      Helen Vinson models one gown from "Disgraced."

2932 "Screenland's Glamor School." Screenland, 27 (5): 54-5, Sep-
      tember 1933.
      One costume each is modeled by Jean Harlow from "Dinner at
      Eight" and Constance Cummings from "Heads We Go."

2933 "Screenland's Glamor School." Screenland, 32 (3): 24-7, January 1936.
Ginger Rogers models two costumes by Bernard Newman from "Tamed."

2934 "Screenland's Special Glamor Guide." Screenland, 30 (1): 62-3, November 1934.
Travis Banton has adapted some of his costumes for Claudette Colbert in "Cleopatra," for her personal wardrobe; she models two of the adaptations.

2935 "Search for the Spectacular." Screen Guide, 2 (5): 44-5, September 1937.
Royer designs the costumes for about one musical per month. Included are numerous sketches and stills of the completed costumes for chorus girls in "You Can't Have Everything."

2936 "Seasons to Be Represented by Beautiful Girls." Screen News, 4 (46): 7, November 21, 1925.
The four seasons will be shown through costumed models in the fashion sequence of "Irene."

2937 "Secretarial Success Fashions." Screenland, 49 (12): 50-1, October 1945.
Frances Gifford models six suits by Irene, one (or more) from "Our Vines Have Tender Grapes."

2938 "Seelig, Eric." American Film Institute Catalog, 1961-70, p. 584.
Eric Seelig is credited with the costumes of "A Dream of Kings"; the wardrobe of "What Ever Happened to Baby Jane?" "In Harm's Way," "Hawaii," "Return of the Seven," "Guns of the Magnificent Seven," and "Cannon for Cordoba"; and the costume supervision of "King of Kings" (1961) and "Villa Rides."

2939 "Seid, Tauhma." American Film Institute Catalog, 1961-70, p. 585.
Tauhma Seid is credited with the wardrobe of "Gone Are the Days!"

2940 "Selby-Walker, Emma." American Film Institute Catalog, 1961-70, p. 585.
Emma Selby-Walker is credited with the costumes of "Follow That Camel."

2941 "Sellers, Bridget." American Film Institute Catalog, 1961-70, p. 585.
14 wardrobe-related credits are listed for Bridget Sellers.

2942 "Selli, Sergio." American Film Institute Catalog, 1961-70, p. 585.
Sergio Selli is credited with the costumes of "The Tramplers."

2943 "Selling Gowns by the Pound!" Screen News, 3 (29): 22, July
          19, 1924.
      Some merchants are starting to sell clothes by the pound; fortu-
      nately, this was not done with a 40-pound beaded gown worn by
      Anna Q. Nilsson in "Vanity's Price."

2944 "Seltenhammer, Paul." American Film Institute Catalog, 1961-
          70, p. 586.
      Paul Seltenhammer was the costume designer of "The Corrupt
      Ones" and is credited with the costumes of "Die Fledermaus"
      and "And So to Bed."

2945 "Senne, Agnès." American Film Institute Catalog, 1961-70,
          p. 586.
      Agnès Senne is credited with the wardrobe of "Chappaqua."

2946 "Sennett Bathing Girl Gets Lead." Screen News, 3 (38): 10,
          September 20, 1924.
      Thelma Hill, remembered for her mah jongg bathing suit, was
      one of the first girls to reappear when Mack Sennett announced
      that the bathing girls would return to his comedies.

2947 "Sennett Styles Have Changed." Screenland, 20 (3): 70-1,
          January 1930.
      Nine stills of former Sennett bathing girls; those identified are
      Gloria Swanson, Phyllis Haver, Marie Prevost, Kathryn Stanley,
      and Winnie Law, all in vintage bathing suits.

2948 "Sequins ... Sheers ... and Swirling Skirts." Movies, 5 (9):
          46, March 1942.
      Betty Field models a sequined-plaid gown from "Mr. and Mrs.
      Cugat."

2949 "Servants Refuse to 'Wear Out' His Clothes--Are Fired."
          Screen News, 1 (30): 14, September 16, 1922.
      Claude Gillingwater recently paid $125 for a wardrobe, which is
      listed, for "The Strangers' Banquet." The clothes were old-
      fashioned but had to be aged by rubbing sandpaper and rough stones
      over them and hosing them down. His servants eventually quit,
      and the actor is aging them himself.

2950 Service, Faith. "Who Are the Best-Dressed Women on the
          Screen--and Why?" Motion Picture, 32 (3): 22-4, 111-3,
          October 1926.
      Fashion designers Maybelle Manning, Mme. Frances, and Harry
      Collins discuss the screen appearance of Gloria Swanson, Irene
      Castle, Anita Loos, Norma Talmadge, Carol Dempster, Bebe
      Daniels, Corinne Griffith, Diana Kane, Blanche Sweet, and Alice
      Joyce. When designing film costumes Mme. Frances tries to
      keep the director in mind so that the costume will also inspire
      him.

2951 "Session, Ermon." American Film Institute Catalog, 1961-70,

p. 587.
Ermon Session is credited with the wardrobe of "They Call Me
MISTER Tibbs."

2952   Seton, Lindsay, ed.   "Beauty & the Bath."   House Beautiful,
            113 (13): 14, 16-7, March 1971.
The influence of film costume on fashion was shown in the '20s
when Clara Bow popularized the cloche hat and knee-length skirts.
In the '30s Greta Garbo's midis and broad-brimmed hats were
popular, and remain so today.

        Seymour see also "Seymour--Photoplay's Style Authority"
        in the "Photoplay" section.

2953   Seymour.   " 'A Lovely June Bride' Votes Seymour."   Photo-
            play, 40 (1): 108, June 1931.
Marguerite Churchill models a wedding gown from "Quick Millions."

2954   _____.   "Little Tricks Make Hollywood Fashions Individual."
            Photoplay, 42 (4): 104, September 1932.
Brief mention of a gown worn by Joan Crawford in "Letty Lynton,"
by Adrian and a riding habit worn by Billie Dove in "Blondie of
the Follies."   Norma Shearer's costumes in "Smilin' Through" do not
include the daring type that she is associated with.

2955   _____.   "A Royal Wedding Gown for Any Princess."   Photo-
            play, 40 (1): 102, June 1931.
Miriam Hopkins models a wedding gown from "The Smiling Lieutenant."

2956   "Shades of Captain Kidd!"   Photoplay, 13 (1): 68, December
            1917.
Edna Goodrich is making a comeback in style, as shown in two
stills of her wearing two crowns and a "dog collar" covered with
diamonds and other jewels; all worn in "Reputation."

2957   Shaffer, Rosalind.   "Marlene Dietrich Tells Why She Wears
            Men's Clothes."   Motion Picture, 45 (3): 54-5, 70, April
            1933.
Marlene Dietrich created a sensation when she appeared in a
man-tailored suit in "Morocco" and "Blonde Venus."   She likes
wearing men's clothes because they do not change every three
months or so, and she claims to have never felt comfortable in
dresses, including her film costumes.

2958   _____.   "Spring Is Here!"   New Movie, 3 (4): 66-71, 104,
            106, April 1931.
Max Ree and Adrian discuss designing for many actresses concerning their most attractive styles, as does Sophie Wachner,
with reference to Mary Pickford in "The Taming of the Shrew."

2959   "Shakespeare and the Cinema...."   Cinema Arts, [Preview

Issue] 1 (1): 19-21, June 1937.
Oliver Messel and a crew of two cameramen took more than
2,769 photographs in Verona, Italy, of buildings, frescoes, and
engravings for use by Messel and Adrian for the costumes of
"Romeo and Juliet," and for the set designs.

2960 "Shakespeare Was Right!" Picture Play, 28 (6): 54-5, August
      1928.
Ethnic film costumes are modeled by Olga Baclanova from "The
Man Who Laughs," Warner Oland from "Stand and Deliver,"
William Austin from "Drums of Love," Josephine Borio and Renee
Adoree from "The Cossacks," Dolores Del Rio from "The Red
Dancer," Emil Jannings from "The Patriot," Ramon Novarro
from "Forbidden Hours," and Theodore Kosloff from "The King
of Kings."

2961 "Shall We Waltz?" Cinema Arts, 1 (3): 86-91, September
      1937.
Loretta Young models a gown from "Love Under Fire"; one fur
or skin coat each is modeled by Joan Bennett, Frances Joyce,
and a model from "Vogues of 1938," by Jaeckel, and Gail Patrick
from "Artists and Models," by Willard George Ltd.

2962 Shanklin, Gertrude. "He Blueprints His Movies." Movieland,
      4 (8): 46, 76, September 1946.
Includes biographical information on Mitchell Leisen, whose quick
work with costumes for "The King of Kings" (1927) landed him a
12-year job as a set and costume designer for De Mille Studios.
He insists upon authenticity in period films, as with the costumes
of "To Each His Own," which progressed from 1918 to 1944.

2963 "Shannon, Jon." American Film Institute Catalog, 1961-70,
      p. 589.
Jon Shannon was the costume designer of "C.C. and Company"
and the costume coordinator of "Blood of Dracula's Castle."

2964 Sharaff, Irene. Broadway and Hollywood. New York: Van
      Nostrand Reinhold, 1976.
In her autobiography Irene Sharaff discusses designing for Judy
Garland in "Meet Me in St. Louis" and "A Star Is Born"; Leslie
Caron in the ballet sequence of "An American in Paris"; Irene
Dunne and Yul Brynner in "The King and I"; Jean Simmons in
"Guys and Dolls"; Pearl Bailey in "Porgy and Bess"; Elizabeth
Taylor and Rex Harrison in "Cleopatra"; Taylor in "The Sand-
piper," with Sandy Dennis, and in "The Taming of the Shrew";
Barbra Streisand in "Hello, Dolly!"; Anouk Aimee in "Justine";
for Jane Alexander and James Earl Jones in "The Great White
Hope"; and "Can-Can" and "West Side Story." Other persons in
the above films are occasionally and briefly discussed; the writer
was disappointed with the brevity of the discussions for most of
the films. Sharaff also discusses costume research for the above;
censorship; costume colors in color photography; and her memories
of MGM, Samuel Goldwyn, and working with Karinska. Many

stills, in black-and-white, and sketches, some in color, are included from most of the above films. Includes also complete
film and theatrical credits for the designer (both Hollywood Costume Design and Costume Design in the Movies include credits
not listed in this autobiography).

2965 _____. "Color Is an Invitation to be Inventive." House
         and Garden, 102 (3): 106-7, September 1952.
Irene Sharaff discusses how colors become fashionable, symbolic,
and trademarks; with brief mention of the costumes' color schemes
in "The King and I" and "An American in Paris."

2966 _____. "Hollywood Dress Parade." Good Housekeeping,
         183 (3): 78, 80-2, 84, September 1976.
Consists of excerpts from Sharaff's autobiography, Broadway and
Hollywood, with references to her replacing Adrian, at a time
when emphasis was changing from broad shoulders to bosoms;
censorship and realism in film costume; and designing for Judy
Garland in "Meet Me in St. Louis" and "A Star Is Born," Loretta
Young in "The Bishop's Wife," and Elizabeth Taylor and Rex
Harrison in "Cleopatra." Includes stills not found in the book.

2967 _____, as told to Bee Bangs. "Your Clothes Tell Exactly
         What You Are." Silver Screen, 17 (5): 48-9, 92-4,
         March 1947.
Irene Sharaff discusses designing for Teresa Wright, Myrna Loy,
Virginia Mayo, and Cathy O'Donnell in "The Best Years of Our
Lives," with references to their roles and figure types; for Olivia
de Havilland in "The Dark Mirror"; and for Mayo in "The Secret
Life of Walter Mitty"; with stills from all three films.

2968 "Sharaff, Irene." American Film Institute Catalog, 1961-70,
         p. 590.
Irene Sharaff was the costume designer for Elizabeth Taylor in
"Cleopatra" and "The Taming of the Shrew"; Barbra Streisand
in "Funny Girl"; and "West Side Story," "The Sandpiper," "Who's
Afraid of Virginia Woolf?," "Hello, Dolly!," "Justine," and "The
Great White Hope"; and she is credited with the costumes of
"Flower Drum Song."

2969 "Sharaff, Irene." Biographical Encyclopaedia and Who's Who
         of the American Theatre. 1966, p. 819.

2970 "Sharaff, Irene." Fairchild's Who's Who in Fashion. 1975,
         p. 243.

2971 "Sharaff, Irene." Who's Who in America. 38th ed., 1974-5,
         p. 2789.

2972 "Sharaff, Irene." Who's Who in the Theatre. 15th ed., 1972,
         p. 1398.

2973 "Sharaff, Irene." Who's Who in the World. 2nd ed., 1974-5,
         p. 904.

2974   "Sharaff, Irene." <u>World Who's Who of Women.</u> 2nd ed.,
         1974-5, p. 1120.

2975   "Sharon of Hollywood." <u>American Film Institute Catalog, 1961-</u>
         <u>70</u>, p. 590.
Sharon of Hollywood is credited with the wardrobe of "Tropic of
Scorpio."

2976   "Sharpe, Norah." <u>American Film Institute Catalog, 1961-70,</u>
         p. 590.
Norah Sharpe is credited with the wardrobe of "The George Raft
Story," "Twenty Plus Two," "King of the Roaring 20's--The Story
of Arnold Rothstein," "Confessions of an Opium Eater," "Convicts
4," and "Black Zoo."

2977   "She Finishes 'Fashion Row.'" <u>Screen News,</u> 2 (47): 24,
         November 24, 1923.
Mae Murray wears 30 gowns in "Fashion Row" and is followed
rather than led by New York and Paris in her fashion selections.

2978   "She Sets the Styles for the Stars." <u>Photoplay,</u> 25 (2): 82,
         January 1924.
Clare West, formerly the designer for De Mille Studios, is now
designing exclusively for Norma and Constance Talmadge, having
already completed "Ashes of Vengeance," "Dust of Desire," and
"Secrets."

2979   "She Wears Dress of 18,000 Pearls." <u>Senator Newsette,</u> 1
         (10): 2, February 22, 1925.
In "A Thief in Paradise" Aileen Pringle wore a skirt, top, and
headdress of solid pearl ropes, and a cape of silver net, also
strung with pearls.

2980   "She Wears French Gowns and Didn't Go to Paris." <u>Screen</u>
         <u>News,</u> 4 (48): 3, December 5, 1925.
Explanation of how Evelyn Brent obtained Parisian gown copies,
with the help of fashion artist Mlle. Dagenais, for her eight forthcoming pictures.

2981   "She Went to the Head of the Class." <u>San Francisco Chronicle,</u>
         August 30, 1974, p. 20.
Biography of Edith Head and historical summary of her career;
illustrations include one costume each worn by Yvonne de Carlo
in "Hurricane Smith," Grace Kelly in "Rear Window," and Gloria
Swanson in "Sunset Boulevard."

2982   "She's from Paris, So She Knows Clothes." <u>Screen News,</u>
         3 (4): 17, January 26, 1924.
A Parisian gown worn by Vella Lavella in a party scene in "Just
Off Broadway" is described.

2983   "Shearer Fashions." <u>MGM Studio News,</u> 5 (13): n. p., Janu-
         ary 14, 1939.

Norma Shearer will have her first modern wardrobe in almost
five years since "Riptide," for "Idiot's Delight."

2984 "Shearer Gowns Set New Record." MGM Studio News, 4: n.p.,
        December 24, 1937.
Adrian has designed over 500 costumes for "Marie Antoinette,"
including 34 for Norma Shearer. Shearer spent three weeks with
Adrian in fitting sessions of four to five hours a day, three to
four days per week. Adrian spent seven months designing the
costumes after returning from a research trip to Paris and Vienna.

2985 "Shearer Starts New Fad." MGM Studio News, 6 (13): n.p.,
        January 14, 1939.
Norma Shearer started a fad for square bracelets after wearing
them in "Idiot's Delight"; once popularly worn by Russian nobility.

2986 "Shearer's 34 Changes." MGM Studio News, 5 (6): n.p.,
        August 15, 1938.
Norma Shearer wears 34 costumes in "Marie Antoinette." (This
small bit of information was repeated endlessly in this MGM
publicity paper, and in other articles included in the bibliography.)

2987 Sheldon, Donna. "Ginger Rogers--Past, Present and Future."
        Movie Classic, 9 (1): 38-9, 66, 71, September 1935.
Ginger Rogers models four costumes from "In Person," by Bernard Newman, who said that she would soon be the most trend-
setting film actress.

2988 Sheldon, Isabel. "Fashion Flashes from Hollywood." Pic-
        ture Play, 51 (3): 56-9, November 1939.
Rosemary Lane models one costume and a copy from "Return of
Dr. X," illustrating the return of the bustle, as influenced by
period-film costumes. Six film designers discuss fashion trends.
Walter Plunkett notes that his costumes for Scarlett O'Hara in
"Gone with the Wind" illustrate what is becoming fashionable;
particularly the sloped shoulders and tiny waists, and emphasis
on bustlines.

2989 _____. "Glamour Fashions for Evening." Picture Play,
        50 (1): 56-60, March 1939.
One gown each is modeled by Loretta Young from "Wife, Husband, Friend," by Royer; Dorothy Lamour from "St. Louis Blues,"
by Bernard Newman; and Elaine Barrie from "Midnight."

2990 _____. "Glamour Fashions for You." Picture Play, 50
        (2): 57-9, April 1939.
Ann Morris models two costumes from "Four Girls in White,"
and Grace Allen one hat and Eleanor Powell one dress from
"Honolulu." Lilyan Graves and Lucille Ball model costumes
from unnamed films.

2991 _____. "Glamour Fashions for You." Picture Play, 50 (6):
        40-4, August 1939.
Discussion of current fashion trends, including the return of the

bustle and crinoline, due to period-film costumes; and notes that
John Frederics's hats for Vivien Leigh in "Gone with the Wind"
will influence fashion.   One costume each is modeled by Andrea
Leeds from "Music School" and Joan Perry from "Good Girls Go
to Paris."

2992 Shelton, Patricia. "Designs in Floating Chiffons." Christian
          Science Monitor, July 17, 1967, p.6.
Helen Rose spent 22 years as a costume designer with MGM,
where she began working with Irene.   Rose added a simple chiffon
dress to her retail collection that she had designed for Elizabeth
Taylor for "Cat on a Hot Tin Roof" and sold hundreds for $250
each.

2993 _____.   " 'The Star' Is Center Stage." Christian Science
          Monitor, June 17, 1968, p.12.
Donald Brooks included some of his costumes from "Star" in his
fall collection, as did Helen Rose with her costumes for "How
Sweet It Is."   "Maybe movies really are going to be better than
ever this year.   They are if the movie influence on the fall fashion picture is a good yardstick."

2994 Shepard, Rosalind. "Your New Spring Wardrobe Straight from
          Hollywood." Screen Play, 14 (96): 33-4, 60-1, March
          1933.
The author and Orry-Kelly discuss the influence of film costume
on fashion, Kelly noting that Hollywood is the center of world
fashion, with a list of the nine actresses he feels are the most
copied.   Also discussed are costumes worn in "Alexander Hamilton"; by Greta Garbo in "Romance"; Joan Crawford in "Letty
Lynton"; Ruth Chatterton in "The Rich Are Always with Us," by
Howard Greer; Loretta Young in "The Hatchet Man" and "Week-
End Marriage"; and Ruth Chatterton in "The Crash"; Lili Damita
in "The Crash" and "The Match King," and Kay Francis in "The
Keyhole," by Orry-Kelly.

2995 "Sheppard, Dolores." American Film Institute Catalog, 1961-
          70, p.592.
Dolores Sheppard is credited with the wardrobe of "Fluffy" and
"Love and Kisses" and the women's costumes of "Billie."

2996 "Sheriff, Earl." American Film Institute Catalog, 1961-70,
          p.593.
Earl Sheriff is credited with the costumes of "Shannon's Women."

2997 "Sherman, Stanley." American Film Institute Catalog, 1961-
          70, p.593.
Stanley Sherman is credited with Virginia Grey's wardrobe in
"Tammy Tell Me True."

2998 "Sherrard, Mickey." American Film Institute Catalog, 1961-
          70, p.593.
Mickey Sherrard is credited with the costumes of "Terrified!"

and the wardrobe of "Move Over, Darling," "John Goldfarb, Please
Come Home!," "Von Ryan's Express," and "The Great White
Hope."

2999   "Sherrard, Wesley." American Film Institute Catalog, 1961-
          70, p. 593.
       Wesley Sherrard is credited with the wardrobe of "House of the
       Damned," "Lilies of the Field" (1963), "Young Guns of Texas,"
       and "Doctor Dolittle," and the wardrobe supervision of "Francis
       of Assisi."

3000   "Sherrick, Arthur." American Film Institute Catalog, 1961-
          70, p. 593.
       Arthur Sherrick is credited with the costumes of "Girl in Trouble."

3001   "Shieff, Maxwell." American Film Institute Catalog, 1961-70,
          p. 594.
       Maxwell Shieff is credited with the costumes of "Mother Goose
       à Go-Go."

3002   "Shields, Chuck." American Film Institute Catalog, 1961-70,
          p. 594.
       Chuck Shields is credited with the costumes of "Greetings."

3003   "Shildknekht, L." American Film Institute Catalog, 1961-70,
          p. 594.
       L. Shildknekht is credited with the costumes of "Song over Moscow."

3004   Shirley, Lois. "How Studio Designers Use Lines to Remedy De-
          fects." Photoplay, 37 (2): 66-7, January 1930.
       Max Ree, previously the set and costume designer for Max Rein-
       hardt, has become the chief set and costume designer for RKO.
       He discusses camouflaging figure flaws, the only film reference
       being that he helped Greta Garbo disguise her too-long neck.

3005   _____. "Secrets of the Fitting Room." Photoplay, 37 (2):
          32-3, 104, January 1930.
       Brief mention of Howard Greer's costume designs for Mary Pick-
       ford in "Coquette"; with general references to other actresses he
       has designed for.

3006   _____. "Your Clothes Come from Hollywood." Photoplay,
          35 (3): 70-1, 130-2, February 1929.
       Discussion of how film costumes have influenced fashion; how
       colors photograph; figure flaws of some actresses; Max Ree's
       "Freudian" costumes for Zasu Pitts and Maude George in "The
       Wedding March"; Howard Greer's costumes for Greta Garbo in
       "The Torrent," with one still; Peggy Hamilton's costumes for
       Gloria Swanson's first big role, not identified, which Hamilton
       made over from her own clothes since she had a low budget, then
       being a teenager and the manager of Triangle studio's costume
       department; Adrian's costumes for Leatrice Joy (probably in "Fig-
       leaves"); Sophie Wachner's costumes for Aileen Pringle in "Three

Weeks" and "The Wife of the Centaur"; Travis Banton's for Florence Vidor in "The Grand Duchess and the Waiter"; Howard Greer's for Jetta Goudal, whose fussiness had previously caused a year-long silence with Adrian, and for Pola Negri. Harry Collins, of the House (?) of Collins, came from New York to Hollywood to design film costumes, but after he said that there were almost no smartly dressed women there, the stars went elsewhere rather than wear his film costumes.

3007 "Shoe Trouble!" Screen News, 1 (8): 20, April 15, 1922.
Because of the demanding comedy roles Marie Mosquini appears in, she wears out about one pair of shoes per week. She wears black satin pump shoes in most films, and silver shoes for dressy roles; she pays from $17 to $24 per pair. Her frequent costar, Harry "Snub" Pollard, wears out one silk hat per week, and in "Some Baby" wore out five. He has popularized the hats, made by a New York firm.

3008 "Short Hair, Military Dress Will Make a Man of Her." Screen News, 4 (48): 9, December 5, 1925.
Marion Davies had her hair cropped and wore a military uniform through much of "Beverly of Graustark," for her role as Prince Oscar.

3009 "The Short Skirt Is Doomed." Screen News, 4 (19): 2, May 9, 1925.
Mlle. Henriette Dallot, Parisian designer, will make her film-designing debut with Leatrice Joy's costumes in "Hell's Highroad." She discusses fashion trends, including longer hemlines, that Joy will wear.

3010 "Short Skirts Have Come to Stay, Says Corinne Griffith." Screen News, 4 (29): 3, July 25, 1925.
Corinne Griffith returned from New York with trunks of clothes for forthcoming films, including "Classified." Actresses have been wearing short skirts in films and have contributed considerably in spreading the fashion.

3011 "Shortly After the First of the Year Ethel Chaffin ... Will Return...." Grauman's Magazine, 6 (1): 8, January 7, 1923.
Ethel Chaffin, wardrobe-department head of Lasky Studios, has gone to New York to hire a designer she can supervise for Paramount's (Lasky was absorbed by Paramount) leading actresses.

3012 "Shoup, Howard." American Film Institute Catalog, 1961-70, p. 596.
17 credits are listed for designer Howard Shoup.

3013 "Shubette of London." American Film Institute Catalog, 1961-70, p. 596.
Shubette of London is credited with Cherry Roland's costumes in "Just for Fun."

3014 Shulman, Irving. <u>Valentino.</u> New York: Trident, 1967.
      Notes that "Rudolph Valentino continued to waste his time in ...
      research into Spanish dress and costumes" for "Blood and Sand."
      Valentino's staff at Paramount for "Monsieur Beaucaire" included
      a costume director and four wardrobe women, and designer/wife
      Natacha Rambova supervised George Barbier, who designed 60
      costumes. Two French period experts spent one month research-
      ing the costumes for authenticity before they were made. Men-
      tions also his shopping for "The Hooded Falcon" and his wardrobe
      and jewelry for "The Son of the Sheik" (see the article by John
      Abbot). Concerning the feud between Rambova and Jetta Goudal,
      it is noted that Goudal announced in a newspaper interview that
      she was disappointed with Rambova as a designer; at the first
      fitting she screamed insults--she would not even look at such
      costumes, and Rambova was best suited to designing for men
      who were not men. Paramount announced almost immediately
      that Goudal had withdrawn; her replacement, Dagmar Godowsky,
      was ecstatic about the costumes in subsequent interviews (see
      Godowsky, Dagmar). The money netted from the auctioning of
      Valentino's possessions was especially disappointing, including
      Adrian's $20,000 worth of costumes for "The Hooded Falcon";
      Adrian came and purchased one (see Scagnetti, Jack). Rudolph
      Florentino, born Dominic Giordano, an avid imitator of Valentino,
      received considerable press coverage around 1953 because of his
      idolizing him, and his collection of memorabilia. He acquired
      and authenticated many items from Valentino's wardrobe, includ-
      ing a gaucho hat from "The Four Horsemen of the Apocalypse";
      the museum he opened of his collection folded.

3015 Shute, Nerina. "Dress Personality." <u>Picturegoer,</u> 17 (97):
           15-6, January 1929.
      Actresses ensure their box-office appeal by having unique style
      and personality in their roles, reinforced through their costume
      selections. One costume each is modeled by Joan Crawford in
      "Spring Fever" and Dorothy Sebastian in "On ze Boulevard "

3016 "Side View of Edward Stevenson, Miracle Man." <u>Photoplay,</u>
           31 (4): 106, September 1947.
      Before graduation from high school Edward Stevenson designed
      film costumes during summers off, and began his first full-time
      job as assistant designer for Fox studios, later leaving to become
      head designer for First National and RKO.

3017 "Sievewright, Alan." <u>American Film Institute Catalog, 1961-</u>
           <u>70</u>, p. 597.
      Alan Sievewright was the costume designer of "Wonderful to Be
      Young!"

3018 "Sigal, Joann." <u>American Film Institute Catalog, 1961-70,</u>
           p. 597.
      Joann Sigal is credited with the wardrobe of "Bigfoot."

3019 "Silich, L." <u>American Film Institute Catalog, 1961-70</u>, p. 598.
L. Silich is credited with the costumes of "Springtime on the
Volga."

3020 Silke, James R. "The Costumes for George Stevens' 'The
Greatest Story Ever Told.'" <u>Cinema</u> (Beverly Hills), 1
(6): 17-9, November/December 1963.
Designer Nino Novarese's first Hollywood assignments were for
"Spartacus" and the men's costumes of "Cleopatra." He discusses
his 14 months with "The Greatest Story Ever Told," including the
research methods and the significance of some color selections;
with some costume descriptions. Nine of his sketches are included with photos of John Wayne, Donald Pleasence, Charlton
Heston, Roddy McDowall, Joanna Dunham, David McCallum, Ed
Wynn, and Telly Savalas.

3021 "The Silken Gowns Worn by a Siren." <u>Motion Picture,</u> 29 (5):
46-7, June 1925.
Barbara La Marr models four of her 18 costumes from "The
Heart of a Siren"; with four of Charles Le Maire's sketches.

3022 "Silverstein, Jason." <u>American Film Institute Catalog, 1961-
70</u>, p. 598.
Jason Silverstein is credited with the special wardrobe for Faye
Dunaway in "The Happening."

3023 "Simi, Carlo." <u>American Film Institute Catalog, 1961-70</u>, p.
599.
Carlo Simi is credited with the costumes of "For a Few Dollars
More," "The Good, the Bad, and the Ugly," "The Big Gundown,"
"Day of Anger," "Once Upon a Time in the West," and "Sabata."

3024 "Simmons, Elinor." <u>American Film Institute Catalog, 1961-
70</u>, p. 599.
Elinor Simmons was the women's fashion designer of "Tony Rome."

3025 Simmons, Patricia. "Betty Boop, a.k.a. Aunt Bluebell, Wears
Her Age Well." <u>San Jose Mercury News,</u> October 15,
1978, sec. L, p. 3.
Betty Boop, star of the animated cartoons of the 1930s, was required to quit wearing her single black garter because the Hays
office found it suggestive. Paramount complied but was deluged
with complaint letters from fans; the Hays office allowed the cartoon character to resume wearing the garter.

3026 Simms, Joseph. "Adrian--American Artist and Designer."
<u>Journal of the Costume Society</u>, 8: 13-7, 1974.
A biography of Adrian, whom the author considers the "Father of
the American Silhouette"; the fashion press, however, virtually
ignored him. Few of Adrian's sketches remain because he always
tore them up after completion of a film. References to his costumes for "Madam Satan," his replacing Mitchell Leisen as the

costume designer for the De Mille Studios so that Leisen could
concentrate on the set designs, and his being influenced by Erté.
Illustrations include a sketch and completed costume worn by Anita
Louise in "Marie Antoinette" and a still of Greta Garbo in a hat,
which revolutionized the millinery industry, from "A Woman of
Affairs."

3027 "Simon, Margarete." American Film Institute Catalog, 1961-
        70, p. 599.
Margarete Simon is credited with the wardrobe of "Red-Dragon."

3028 "Simpkins, Mildred." American Film Institute Catalog, 1961-
        70, p. 600.
Mildred Simpkins is credited with the wardrobe of "Birds Do It."

3029 "Sinclair, Anthony." American Film Institute Catalog, 1961-
        70, p. 600.
Anthony Sinclair is credited with Warren Beatty's wardrobe in
"Kaleidoscope."

3030 Sinclair, Upton. "Success and the Movies." Screenland, 9
        (2): 38, 103, May 1924.
Upton Sinclair suggests that movies may seek to entertain, but
more often they incite social discontent with lavish costumes and
jewelry, among other things, that the masses can not possibly
afford.

3031 " 'The Single Track' a Spectacular Photoplay." Screen News,
        1 (7): 24, April 8, 1922.
Corinne Griffith wears her standard beautiful gowns in the beginning of "The Single Track" and then changes to calico and
khaki clothes worn with sun bonnets and sombreros.

3032 "$60,000 Wardrobe." Life, 20 (5): 33-4, 36, February 4,
        1946.
Rita Hayworth models three of her 15 costumes from "Gilda"; she
will also wear a $35,000 chinchilla coat and drag around a
$10,000 ermine wrap. Other costumes she wears in the film
are noted, designed by Jean Louis.

3033 "Skalicky, Jan." American Film Institute Catalog, 1961-70,
        p. 602.
Jan Skalicky is credited with the costumes of "Così Fan Tutte."

3034 "Skarżyński, Jerzy." American Film Institute Catalog, 1961-
        70, p. 602.
Jerzy Skarżyński is credited with the costumes of "The Saragossa
Manuscript."

3035 "Skarżyński, Lidia." American Film Institute Catalog, 1961-
        70, p. 602.
Lidia Skarżyński is credited with the costumes of "The Saragossa
Manuscript."

3036 "Skolmen, Ada." American Film Institute Catalog, 1961-
         70, p. 602.
Ada Skolmen is credited with the costumes of "Hunger."

3037 Skolsky, Sidney. "Tintypes." Hollywood Citizen-News,
         October 1, 1940, p. 9.
Biographical information on Adrian; his methods of film-costume
design are discussed, with brief mention of his working with
Greta Garbo, Joan Crawford, and Norma Shearer.

3038 "Skorepová." American Film Institute Catalog, 1961-70, p.
         602.
Skorepová is credited with the costumes of "Do You Keep a Lion
at Home?"

3039 "Slender Lines for Spring." Screen News, 3 (7): 18, Febru-
         ary 16, 1924.
Corinne Griffith models one gown from "Lilies of the Field."

3040 Slide, Anthony. The Big V: A History of the Vitagraph Com-
         pany. Metuchen, N. J.: Scarecrow, 1976.
As was the custom of employment for many stage mothers, Mrs.
Turner, the mother of Vitagraph star Florence Turner, worked
as a wardrobe mistress for Vitagraph. Vitagraph later formed a
Western studio with Bill Duncan in charge of wardrobe, as a
member of the Western Vitagraph Stock Company. J. Stuart
Blackton, a cofounder of Vitagraph, was producer and supervisor
of "The Battle Cry of Peace," for which he designed the uniforms
and helmets so that they would resemble those of no other country.
He also produced and directed several of his own films in England, with his whole family contributing; Paula Blackton acted as
costume adviser.

3041 Sloan, Robin Adams. "Was 'The Warriors' Done for Pub-
         licity?" San Francisco Sunday Examiner & Chronicle,
         Datebook-TV Week, May 13, 1979, p. 6-7.
One fan wrote in to say "Jane Fonda always seems so well-
dressed. Where does she get her clothes?" Fonda dislikes
shopping and wears her film costumes in her private life, as
with those from "Julia" and "The China Syndrome."

3042 "Slovtsova, Ye." American Film Institute Catalog, 1961-70,
         p. 603.
Ye. Slovtsova is credited with the costumes of "Queen of Spades."

3043 "Smart Simplicity." Movie Classic, 10 (1): 50, March 1936.
Lettie Lee is currently designing for Republic Pictures and owns
her own dress-manufacturing business.

3044 "Smarten Up Your Gowns with Smarty Jewelry." Photoplay,
         39 (4): 70-1, March 1931.
Claire Luce models a necklace, earrings, and bracelet of dia-
monds and emeralds, designed for her to wear in "The Painted
Woman."

3045   Smith, Darr. "Upon Receipt, Men, of the Horrible Rumor
               . ..." Los Angeles Daily News, March 5, 1949, p. 19.
       Edith Head discusses the styles of 1900, as worn in "The Emper-
       or Waltz"; censorship; and the two basic types of costume de-
       signing, period and character.

3046   Smith, Ella. Starring Miss Barbara Stanwyck. New York:
               Crown, 1974.
       In "Stella Dallas" Barbara Stanwyck wore lumpy padding around
       her body, legs, and occasionally in her cheeks, with gauche and
       trashy costumes to appear unkempt; designed by Omar Kiam.
       References to Edith Head's costumes, often from The Dress Doctor,
       include costumes worn by Stanwyck in "The Lady Eve, " "The
       Great Man's Lady, " "California, " and "Roustabout. " Stanwyck
       was not so pleased to work with Sterling Hayden in "Crime of
       Passion" because of his ill-fitting and sloppy clothes, as discussed.

3047   "Smith, Esther. " American Film Institute Catalog, 1961-70,
               p. 604.
       Esther Smith was the costume designer of "Voyage to the End of
       the Universe. "

3048   Smith, H. M. K. "Be Careful of Your Colors. " Photoplay,
               39 (2): 74-5, 116-7, January 1931.
       H. M. K. Smith discusses the psychology of color, how he works
       with it to establish a certain mood or image of a character, and
       working with many actresses' fashion preferences.   One photo of
       Pola Negri from "Bella Donna, " wearing a symbolic black gown
       for her role as a vamp.

3049   "Smith, H. M. K. " American Film Institute Catalog, 1921-30,
               p. 1369.
       H. M. K. Smith is credited with the wardrobe of "Jealousy. "

3050   Smith, Jack. "Sex and the Old Movie. " San Francisco
               Chronicle, August 11, 1978, p. 52.
       Movies have always influenced style, as when Clark Gable was
       shown in "It Happened One Night" without an undershirt, nearly
       bankrupting some of the industry of undershirt makers.

3051   "Smith, James, cost. " American Film Institute Catalog, 1961-
               70, p. 605.
       James Smith is credited with the costumes of "Sands of the Kala-
       hari" and the wardrobe of "Where's Jack?"

3052   "Smith, William, cost. " American Film Institute Catalog,
               1961-70, p. 606.
       William Smith is credited with the wardrobe of "Harper" and
       "Chubasco. "

3053   "Snajderová, Zdena. " American Film Institute Catalog, 1961-
               70, p. 607.
       Zdena Snajderová is credited with the costumes of "The Firemen's
       Ball. "

3054 Snow, Marguerite. "Clothes and the Camera." Pictures and
         the Picturegoer, 10 (132): 412, August 26, 1916.
Marguerite Snow discusses her favorite colors and explains how
she must carefully choose her costume colors because of the way
they photograph.

3055 "Soares, Paulo Gil." American Film Institute Catalog, 1961-
         70, p. 607.
Paulo Gil Soares is credited with the costumes of "Earth Entranced."

3056 "Söderlund, Ulla Britt." American Film Institute Catalog,
         1961-70, p. 607.
Ulla Britt Söderlund is credited with the costumes of "Hagbard
and Signe" and "People Meet and Sweet Music Fills the Heart"
and the wardrobe of "Doctor Glas."

3057 "Soft Suits." Movies, 7 (10): 42-3, May 1944.
Ella Raines models two costumes from "Phantom Lady," and
Louise Allbritton models one from "Her Primitive Man," both
by Vera West.

3058 "Soldati, Sebastiano." American Film Institute Catalog, 1961-
         70, p. 608.
Sebastiano Soldati is credited with the costumes of "The Violent
Four."

3059 "Somber All Day but a Riot of Colors at Night; Edith Head:
         Famed Designer for Movie Stars." Christian Science
         Monitor, June 7, 1974, sec. B, p. 5.
Edith Head's eighth Academy Award, for "The Sting," was the
first time the award was given her primarily for men's costumes.
Head always gives the star several sketches of the same costume.
She gave Robert Redford three sketches for each costume in "The
Great Waldo Pepper," each dominantly sensitive, aggressive, or
romantic; he always picks the most masculine.

3060 "Some Interesting Facts Concerning 'The Wanderer.'" Senator
         Newsette, 2 (2): 3-4, January 10, 1926.
For the biblical film "The Wanderer" 100 seamstresses worked
up to one month creating thousands of costumes. 3,000 rings,
bracelets, and arm bands were also made.

3061 "Something New in the Way of Clothes...." Screen News, 2
         (33): 11, August 18, 1923, col. 1.
Nearly every screen comedienne has worn striped stockings in
imitation of Dorothea Wolbert. One day Wolbert could not find
her stockings and was rushing to the set when she grabbed some
striped canvas from a trash can and wrapped it around her legs.

3062 "Somner, Pearl." American Film Institute Catalog, 1961-70,
         p. 609.
Pearl Somner was the costume designer of "Love Story" and is
credited with the costumes of "The Cross and the Switchblade."

3063 "Somohano, Georgette." <u>American Film Institute Catalog,</u>
         <u>1961-70</u>, p. 609.
      Georgette Somohano is credited with the wardrobe of "Nazarin"
      and the costumes of "The Exterminating Angel."

3064 "Somper, Frank." <u>American Film Institute Catalog, 1961-70</u>,
         p. 609.
      Frank Somper is credited with the furs of "If a Man Answers."

3065 " 'Song of the Open Road' Fashions." <u>Modern Screen</u>, 28 (6):
         70, May 1944.
      The designers of Freshy Playclothes, manufactured by Goldman
      Co., created exclusive playclothes for the starlets of "Song of the
      Open Road."

3066 "Sophie (Gimbel)." <u>World of Fashion</u>. 1976, p. 254.
      Biographical information on Sophie Haas, whose married name was
      Sophie Gimbel. For her costume designs at Saks Fifth Avenue
      she was known as Sophie of Saks Fifth Avenue.

3067 "Sophie ... Who Believes in the Feminine." <u>Photoplay</u>, 32 (5):
         92, April 1948.
      Brief biographical information on Sophie of Saks Fifth Avenue,
      who designed Claudette Colbert's costumes for "Sleep, My Love."

3068 "Sørenson, Edith." <u>American Film Institute Catalog, 1961-70</u>,
         p. 610.
      Edith Sørenson is credited with the costumes of "Crazy Paradise."

3069 "Southgate, Michael." <u>American Film Institute Catalog, 1961-</u>
         <u>70</u>, p. 610.
      Michael Southgate is credited with the costumes of "The Crimson
      Cult."

3070 "Spadoni, Luciano." <u>American Film Institute Catalog, 1961-</u>
         <u>70</u>, p. 611.
      Luciano Spadoni is credited with the costumes of "The Witch's
      Curse."

3071 Spanier, Ginette. <u>It Isn't All Mink.</u> New York: Random
         House, 1960.
      When Ginette Spanier was the director for Pierre Balmain's
      salon she helped Marlene Dietrich in her selection of their most
      expensive mink stole and cape; though she did not seem impressed,
      she wore them in "No Highway in the Sky."

3072 "Spanish Mantillas, High Tortoise Shell Combs and Gay Fiesta
         Costumes...." <u>Screen News</u>, 2 (31): 20, January 20,
         1923, cols. 1-2.
      Several old Spanish families lent priceless costumes to May Mc-
      Avoy and Eric Mayne to wear in a New Orleans fiesta sequence
      in "Her Reputation."

3073   "Sparrow, Bernice." <u>American Film Institute Catalog, 1961-</u>
           <u>70</u>, p. 611.
   Bernice Sparrow is credited with the costumes of "The Wild, Wild
   Planet."

3074   "Speaking of Pictures ... Cecil Beaton Photographs the Cos-
           tumes He Designed." <u>Life</u>, 23 (6): 14-6, August 11, 1947.
   Strelsa Brown, Mary Midwinter, Mary Nash, Roma Goy, Rosalie
   Hillan, Joy Adams, and Glynis Johns each model one costume,
   and Diana Wynyard two, from "An Ideal Husband"; by Cecil Beaton.

3075   "Spencer, Bob." <u>American Film Institute Catalog, 1961-70</u>,
           p. 612.
   Bob Spencer is credited with the wardrobe of "Don't Worry, We'll
   Think of a Title."

3076   Spencer, Charles. "Films," in <u>Cecil Beaton; Stage and Film</u>
           <u>Designs</u>. New York: St. Martin's, 1975, p. 81-93.
   Discussion, often briefly, of Cecil Beaton's film costumes, in-
   cluding the research methods used, and the reactions of the press.
   Discussion and/or illustrations of costumes worn by Diana Wynyard
   and Phyllis Calvert in "Kipps," Sally Gray in "Dangerous Moonlight," Agnes Lauchlan in "The Young Mr. Pitt," Beatrice Lillie
   in "On Approval," Lilli Palmer in "Beware of Pity," Paulette
   Goddard in "An Ideal Husband," Vivien Leigh in "Anna Karenina,"
   Leslie Caron in "Gigi" and "The Doctor's Dilemma," Barbra
   Streisand in "On a Clear Day You Can See Forever," and unnamed
   actresses in "Major Barbara" and "The Truth About Women."

3077   _____. "Hollywood--A Frustrating Episode," in <u>Erte</u>.
           New York: Potter, 1970, p. 88-138, passim.
   Commendable biography of Erté, with extensive theater, ballet,
   and film credits, sketches and photos, and a bibliography. Erté,
   already famous for his <u>Harper's Bazaar</u> covers, was commissioned
   by the magazine's owner, William Randolph Hearst, to design
   Marion Davies's costumes for a sequence of "Restless Sex" (1919).
   He later designed for, as discussed, Carmel Myers in an extra
   scene for "Ben-Hur"; Aileen Pringle in "The Mystic" and "Dance
   Madness"; Lillian Gish and Renee Adoree in "La Bohème"; and in
   "Time the Comedian" and "A Little Bit of Broadway," with illustrations for all except the latter film.

3078   Spensley, Dorothy. "The Most-Copied Girl in the World."
           <u>Motion Picture</u>, 53 (4): 30-1, 69, 93, May 1937.
   Joan Crawford, in costumes by Adrian, has influenced fashion
   with starched jabots, hats, and the wide-lapel polo coat. Adrian
   usually shows Crawford two varied sketches of each costume,
   and then she helps with suggestions for the details. When she
   did improvise with a gown, with huge lapels for "No More Ladies,"
   the audience found it comical, since it made her shoulders appear even larger than Adrian usually has them. Two of her most
   copied costumes were worn in "Letty Lynton" and "Today We Live."
   The proof that the "Letty Lynton" gown influenced fashion is that

the fashion cycle had swung away from puffed sleeves, and consequently returned to them.

3079   "Spiller, Joey." American Film Institute Catalog, 1961-70,
          p. 612.
Joey Spiller is credited with Reinet Maasdorp's wardrobe in
"After You, Comrade."

3080   "The Spirit of Chivalry Has Descended on the Fairbanks'
          Lot...." Screen News, 1 (4): 25, March 18, 1922,
          col. 1.
For "The Spirit of Chivalry" ("Robin Hood") Douglas Fairbanks
has not yet decided whether his tights should be made of wool or
silk, since silk may result in excess halation.

3081   "The Spirit of 'Paris.' " Screenland, 20 (1): 76, November
          1929.
Irene Bordoni models a gown from "Paris," with sequins and
ostrich trim, and matching headdress.

3082   "Sport Coats Replace Sweaters--Carmelita Geraghty Wears One
          of Latest Models." Screen News, 3 (3): 7, January 19,
          1924.
The end of the war and changing lifestyles have influenced sweater
styles. Carmelita Geraghty models their replacement, a flannel
sports coat, from "Jealous Husbands."

3083   "Spring Fling." Screenland, 51 (6): 54-5, April 1947.
Maureen O'Hara models four costumes by Kay Nelson from "The
Home Stretch."

3084   "Spring Is Coming--But Fay Wray Is Here--with New Frocks!"
          Hollywood, 24 (3): 42, March 1935.
Fay Wray models one gown by Kalloch from "White Lies." Two
dresses from the film are sketched, with pattern offers.

3085   "Spring Softness." Motion Picture, 67 (3): 115, April 1944.
Janet Blair models two coats and a dress by Travis Banton from
"Curly."

3086   "Spring Swing." Motion Picture, 55 (3): 38-41, April 1938.
Kay Francis models eight costumes by Orry-Kelly from "Women
Are Like That."

3087   " 'Spring Will Come Again.' " Silver Screen, 10 (5): 50-3,
          March 1940.
Joan Bennett models eight costumes from "House Across the
Bay."

3088   "Springtime for Judy!" Screenland, 47 (1): 50-1, May 1943.
Judy Garland models five costumes from "Presenting Lily Mars."

3089   Squire, Marian. "Guile and Grandeur." Modern Screen, 18

(1): 48-9, 93, December 1938.
Includes descriptions of costumes worn by Barbara Stanwyck,
Frances Mercer, Vicki Lester, Eleanor Hansen, and Whitney
Boume in "The Mad Miss Manton." Stanwyck models three cos-
tumes, and Mercer one from the film; by Edward Stevenson.

3090 _____. "It's Fashionable to Be Feminine." Modern Screen,
         17 (3): 48-9, 79, August 1938.
The discussion includes costumes worn by Virginia Bruce and
Binnie Barnes in "The First Hundred Years," by Dolly Tree;
Loretta Young in "Four Men and a Prayer"; and Irene Dunne in
"Joy of Living." Young and Dunne each model two costumes from
the films.

3091 _____. "Social Security." Modern Screen, 17 (5): 44-5,
         79, October 1938.
Discussion of costumes worn by Danielle Darrieux in "The Rage
of Paris," Katharine Hepburn and Doris Nolan in "Holiday,"
Binnie Barnes and Loretta Young in "Three Blind Mice," Barbara
Stanwyck and Lynn Bari in "Always Goodbye," Ginger Rogers in
"Having a Wonderful Time," Hedy Lamarr in "Algiers," and Harriet
Hilliard in "Cocoanut Grove"; brief mention of Dorothy Lamour in
"Tropic Holiday." One costume each is modeled by Darrieux,
Nolan, and Bari.

3092 _____. "Suiting the Season." Modern Screen, 17 (6): 48-
         9, 80, January 1938.
Discussion of costumes worn by Rosalind Russell and Olivia de
Havilland in "Four's a Crowd" (by Orry-Kelly), Maureen O'Sulli-
van and Jane Wyman in "The Crowd Roars," Martha Raye and
Betty Grable in "Give Me a Sailor," Arleen Whelan in "Gateway,"
and Anne Shirley and Ruby Keeler in "Mother Carey's Chickens."
One costume each is modeled by de Havilland and O'Sullivan, and
two by Russell.

3093 _____. "Wardrobe Weapons." Modern Screen, 17 (4): 48-
         9, 85, September 1938.
Discussion of costumes worn by Rosemary Lane and Gloria Dickson in "Gold Diggers in Paris"; Simone Simon and Joan Davis in
"Josette," by Royer; Ginger Rogers and Frances Mercer in "Vivacious Lady"; and Margaret Sullavan in "Three Comrades." One
costume each is modeled by Simon and Sullavan and two by Rogers.

3094 Squire, Nancy Winslow. "Duchess on Wheels." Modern
         Screen, 29 (3): 42-3, 117, August 1944.
Greer Garson spent weeks in costume tests of her 36 costumes
for "Mrs. Parkington."

3095 "Staffel, Laurel." American Film Institute Catalog, 1961-70,
         p. 614.
14 wardrobe-related credits are listed for Laurel Staffel.

3096 Stanley, John. "Darth Vader Goes Through Inter-Galactic

Identity Crisis." <u>San Francisco Sunday Examiner and
Chronicle</u>, Datebook, August 6, 1978, p.15.
David Prowse was disappointed when he found out that his costume for the role of Darth Vader in "Star Wars" would completely
cover him.   The fiberglass mask, worn under a helmet, was
padded with rubber so that it would move when he did.   In addition to gauntlets and plastic shinguards worn with calf-length
boots, the costume consisted of leather pants, and a fiberglass
shoulder-breastplate worn under a bolero jacket, leather jacket,
and cape.

3097 _____. " 'Day the Earth Stood Still' Withstood the Test of
Time." <u>San Francisco Sunday Examiner and Chronicle</u>,
Datebook, March 4, 1979, p.18-9.
The robot Gort in "The Day the Earth Stood Still" was actually
7'7" Lock Martin in an eight-foot foam rubber costume painted
silver to resemble metal--though metal was used to make the
hands, feet, and detachable headpiece.

3098 _____. "30 Years Later, Kirk Alyn Is Still Flying 'Super'
High." <u>San Francisco Sunday Examiner and Chronicle</u>,
Datebook, February 11, 1979, p.20-1.
Kirk Alyn, perhaps best remembered as Superman in several
Columbia serials, once made a serial called "Blackhawk" and
bought the television rights since he thought it would be popular.
No one would show the serial because the black flying uniforms
were too reminiscent of the Nazi uniform.

3099 Stanley, May. "Jazzing Up the Fashions." <u>Photoplay,</u> 17 (5):
57-8, 131, April 1920.
Discussion of the extent to which film costume has "revolutionized"
fashion throughout the United States, with references to Gloria
Swanson in "Male and Female" and Alice Brady in "Field of the
Cloth of Gold."

3100 Stanwyck, Barbara.   "My Favorite Designer Is Edith Head."
<u>Movieland,</u> 6 (1): 16-7, 108, February 1948.
Barbara Stanwyck discusses her fondness for Edith Head and her
film costumes, including those she wore in "The Lady Eve,"
"The Other Love," and "Internes Can't Take Money," their first
film together.   They did not always work together after their first
film, but Stanwyck decided they would after she saw herself in
"Stella Dallas" and was disappointed by the costumes, designed by
Omar Kiam.

3101 Stanyan, Mary. "Helga Howie Always Goes First Class."
<u>San Francisco Sunday Examiner & Chronicle</u>, Scene, July
30, 1978, p.2.
Helga Howie's shop in San Francisco has become a fashion land-
mark established in part by her selling her own hand-crocheted
dresses.   Brenda Vaccaro wore one when she met Jon Voight in
"Midnight Cowboy," and Paula Prentiss wore one in "Catch 22."

3102 _____. "Mr. John Is Old Hat These Days." <u>San Fran-</u>
        <u>cisco Sunday Examiner and Chronicle</u>, Scene, May 27,
        1979, p. 4.
Biographical information on John P. John, whose hats were worn
by Greta Garbo in "The Painted Veil" (attributed elsewhere to
Adrian), Irene Dunne in "The Awful Truth," Carole Lombard in
"Love Before Breakfast," and Joan Crawford in "The Women."
He owns still, apparently the original, above hats, though others
are in the Metropolitan Museum of Art. He also owns a hat worn
by Vivien Leigh in "Gone with the Wind"; the hats for the film
cost "$20,000 apiece." (His credits were under the name of
John Frederics; it is unfortunate that the origin of the name is
not explained, since this is the only biographical reference to the
designer in this bibliography.)

3103 "Star Fashions." <u>Movie Mirror,</u> 14 (1): 44-8, December 1938.
Olivia de Havilland models one suit by Orry-Kelly from "Wings
of the Navy," worn with a piece of jewelry by Joseff of Hollywood.

3104 "Star Fashions." <u>Movie Mirror,</u> 14 (2): 40-4, January 1939.
Jeanette MacDonald models five costumes by Adrian from "Sweethearts."

3105 "Star Gets London Clothes for Role." <u>MGM Studio News,</u> 2
        (12): n.p., August 30, 1935.
Robert Montgomery visited many tailors in London, where he purchased a trunk full of clothes for "Piccadilly Jim."

3106 "Star Loses Gloves--New Style Is Born!" <u>MGM Studio News,</u>
        5 (10): n.p., October 8, 1938.
Adrian designed a new style of gloves for Jeanette MacDonald in
"Sweethearts" since she often loses them. The "glove sleeves"
attach to the cuff of a dress with a hook so that they can be removed or folded back as cuffs with petals; contrasting or matching
fabrics and colors can be used.

3107 "Star Makers." <u>It</u>, 4 (23): 13, August 15, 1919.
Sophie Wachner is the new costume designer for Goldwyn films.

3108 " 'Star Pilots.' " <u>San Francisco Sunday Examiner and Chroni-</u>
        <u>cle</u>, Datebook, November 27, 1977, p. 4.
Allan Shackleton, European film producer, came across the original "Flash Gordon" (serial) costumes at a studio sale and had an
original screenplay written around them for "Star Pilots."

3109 "Star, Slacks Devotee, Now Clothes-Conscious." <u>MGM Studio</u>
        <u>News,</u> 5 (5): n.p., May 31, 1938.
Luise Rainer wears 24 costumes in "The Toy Wife."

3110 "Star Styles." <u>Hollywood</u>, 27 (1): 36-7, January 1938.
Ann Dvorak and Tamara Geva each model one gown from "Manhattan Merry-Go-Round."

3111   "Star Styles." Hollywood, 27 (4): 30, April 1938.
       Constance Bennett models three gowns from "Merrily We Live."

3112   "A Star Test for 'Jezebel.'" Screenland, 36 (4): 44, February
       1938.
       Included are several wardrobe tests of Bette Davis in costumes
       from "Jezebel," designed by Orry-Kelly. The tests are required
       before a film is started so that the different members of the pro-
       duction team can judge the suitability of the costumes.

3113   The "Star Wars" Album. New York: Ballantine, 1977.
       Jack Haley's costume as the Tin Man in "The Wizard of Oz" was
       as "primitive and uncomfortable" as that worn by Anthony Daniels
       as C3PO in "Star Wars." Daniels had to be propped up (on a
       leaning board) between takes since he could not sit down, and he
       "sweated off close to 4 pounds per day," especially with location
       filming in Tunisia. Extras in the stormtrooper costumes also
       became very hot. Ralph McQuarrie designed the two robots, R2D2
       and C3PO, and the look of the Sandpeople, who were designed to
       resemble Arabs and other desert people with their faces covered
       to protect themselves from the sand. Carrie Fisher wore a rubber
       suit in the garbage-room sequence that no longer fit after two
       hours in the "garbage."

3114   "Starly, Inoa." American Film Institute Catalog, 1961-70, p.
       616.
       Inoa Starly is credited with the costumes of "The Horrible Dr.
       Hichcock."

3115   Starr, Helen. "Dressing for the Movies." Photoplay, 13 (2):
       133-4, January 1918.
       A general discussion of film costume, with references to how
       colors and fabrics photograph, with comments by Theda Bara
       concerning checks and plaids; the costume needs of an extra,
       mainly that the costumes be clean and not necessarily costly;
       and notes that costume jewelry often photographs as well as the
       real thing. Louise Glaum avoids stiff costumes, despite prevail-
       ing fashions, and prefers clinging, draped gowns for more impact
       in her movements. Geraldine Farrar spends about $2,000 per
       month on clothing.

3116   _____. "Flirting with Fads." Screenland, 7 (4): 57-8,
       94, 97-9, July 1923.
       Notes that each well-dressed actress must have a fur coat, follow
       the fads, and claim to design her own clothes.

3117   "Starr, Malcolm." American Film Institute Catalog, 1961-70,
       p. 616.
       Malcolm Starr was the women's fashion designer of "Tony Rome."

3118   "Stars' Salaries Small Item in Film Spectacle." Screen News,
       1 (26): 13, 20, August 19, 1922.
       The largest part of the budget of "Manslaughter," about one-sixth,

was for the creation and renting of costumes. Everything worn
was new and made specially for the film, ranging from Leatrice
Joy's velvet gown with pearls, barbarian costumes made of fur
and decorated with claws, armor for the gladiators, and brief
costumes for the dancing girls.

3119 "The Stars Set the Fashions." Photoplay, 58 (6): 44-5, De-
          cember 1960.
Photoplay looks back on its past fashion reporting of Mae Murray,
Greta Garbo, Bette Davis, and Katharine Hepburn; with one photo
of each, not necessarily from their films. Retail garments of
1960 are modeled, reminiscent of the fashions modeled by the
actresses, who, along with Carole Lombard, brought about the
"American Look" through their costumes.

3120 "Staub, Richard." American Film Institute Catalog, 1961-70,
          p. 616.
Richard Staub is credited with the wardrobe of "Tales of Terror."

3121 "Stavropoulou, Anna." American Film Institute Catalog, 1961-
          70, p. 616.
Anna Stavropoulou is credited with the wardrobe of "Zorba the
Greek" and the execution of the costumes of "The Day the Fish
Came Out" and was the wardrobe mistress of "Oedipus the King."

3122 Steen, Mike. "Costume Design: Edith Head," in Hollywood
          Speaks! An Oral History. New York: Putnam's, 1974,
          p. 247-58, 379.
Edith Head discusses her long career; the difference between
being a fashion designer and a costume designer; her Academy
Awards and nominations; and her costumes for Gloria Swanson
in "Sunset Boulevard," Ginger Rogers in "Lady in the Dark,"
Dorothy Lamour in "The Jungle Princess," Barbara Stanwyck in
"The Lady Eve," and Joanne Woodward in "Winning"; with occasional reference to the fashion influence of these and other
films and actresses.

3123 "Stefan, Ivan." American Film Institute Catalog, 1961-70,
          p. 617.
Ivan Stefan is credited with the costumes of "The Seventh Continent."

3124 "Stein, Ina." American Film Institute Catalog, 1961-70, p.
          617.
Ina Stein is credited with the costumes of "The 1000 Eyes of Dr.
Mabuse."

3125 "Stein, Madame." American Film Institute Catalog, 1921-30,
          p. 1377.
Madame Stein is credited with the costumes of "Potash and Perlmutter."

3126 Steinberg, Cobbett. Reel Facts: The Movie Book of Records.

New York: Vintage, 1978.
Includes the Academy Award winners for best costume design, and
the Production Code established by the film industry to regulate
itself and prevent government censorship, with passages concerning costume.   The greatest test of the Code was with Jane Russell's revealing costumes in "The Outlaw," which resulted in the
film being held from release for several years, after it had been
released in 1943 without the approval and seal of the Motion Picture Producers and Distributors of America.

3127 "Stella, Ruth." American Film Institute Catalog, 1961-70, p.
          618.
Ruth Stella is credited with the costumes of "The Carpetbaggers"
and "Harlow"; the wardrobe of "The Children's Hour," "Who's Got
the Action?," and "The Nutty Professor"; and the ladies' wardrobe/
costumes of "Buckskin," "The Molly Maguires," and "Will Penny."

3128 "Stephans, Peggy." American Film Institute Catalog, 1961-70,
          p. 618.
Peggy Stephans is credited with the wardrobe of "Daddy, Darling."
(Stephans also has noncostume credits under the name of Peggy
Steffans.)

3129 "Stephen, John." American Film Institute Catalog, 1961-70,
          p. 619.
John Stephen was the costume designer for the band The Smart
Alecs in "Sing and Swing."

3130 Stephenson, Ralph, and J. R. Debrix.   "Costume," in The
          Cinema as Art.   Baltimore: Penguin, 1965, p. 152-4,
          passim.
Film costume serves primarily as an aesthetic part of a film and
an actor's performance, and should reinforce the role of the
character rather than the image of an actor or actress.   Realism
should be avoided in musical films because of the generally unrealistic nature of such films.   The authors also discuss (on
pages 167-8) the symbolism of color, with examples of a purse
worn by the heroine in "Marnie" and costumes worn in "West
Side Story."

3131 Stephenson, Ron.   "Edith Head: She Dresses Elephants, Too."
          Andy Warhol's Interview, 4 (1): 14-6, January 1974.
Edith Head discusses designing for Hedy Lamarr in "Samson and
Delilah"; traveling with a retail line of garments from "Airport"
to tie-in with the film costumes; and states that there should be
two Academy Awards for costume design, for period and modern
costumes.

3132 "Sterling, Arleen." American Film Institute Catalog, 1961-
          70, p. 619.
Arleen Sterling is credited with the wardrobe of "Riverrun."

3133 "Stern, Henri." American Film Institute Catalog, 1961-70,
          p. 619.

Henri Stern is credited with the furs of "Live for Life."

3134   "Stevens, Douglas." American Film Institute Catalog, 1961-
          70, p. 620.
       Douglas Stevens is credited with the wardrobe of "The Boy Who
       Caught a Crook."

3135   "Stevens, Jane Kip." American Film Institute Catalog, 1961-
          70, p. 620.
       Jane Kip Stevens is credited with the costumes of "A Woman in
       Love.

3136   "Stevens, John." American Film Institute Catalog, 1961-70,
          p. 620.
       John Stevens is credited with Mark Wynter's costumes in "Just
       for Fun."

3137   Stevens, Lorraine, and Kay Hardy. " 'They Died with Their
          Boots On'; Production." Modern Screen, 24 (2): 50-1,
          75, January 1942.
       The cost of Olivia de Havilland's 15 costumes in "They Died with
       Their Boots On" was comparable to the cost of the battle scenes.

3138   Stevenson, Edward. "Hollywood Fashion 'Tricks' for Clever
          Copy Cats." Movie Mirror, 3 (5): 46-7, March 1933.
       Edward Stevenson was a freelance film designer at this time
       (and did not design film costumes for several years). Includes
       one sketch of gloves worn by Carole Lombard in "No More Or-
       chids."

3139   _____. "Let's Be Practical." Screenland, 53 (6): 46-7,
          66-7, April 1949.
       Edward Stevenson discusses designing for Lucille Ball in "Inter-
       ference," seven costumes from which she models; with brief
       mention of a gown worn by Lizabeth Scott in the same film.

3140   _____. "The 'New Look' Is Not." Silver Screen, 18 (6):
          46-7, 75-6, April 1948.
       Edward Stevenson has asked women to pay attention to his cos-
       tumes for "I Remember Mama" because the fashions of 1910 to
       1914 are very similar to the New Look. He discusses several
       costumes worn by Irene Dunne, including one he copied from his
       own family album, and antique jewelry worn by Dunne and Bar-
       bara Bel Geddes. Includes a photo of Dunne in the copied dress
       and a sketch of how it can be adapted for modern wear.

3141   _____. "The Perfect Marriage." Movieland, 4 (5): 17,
          June 1946.
       Loretta Young models a wedding gown from "The Stranger," by
       Edward Stevenson, who discusses wedding-gown selection.

3142   _____, as told to Gladys Hall. "Hitch Your Wardrobe to
          a Rainbow." Screenland, 50 (1): 38-40, 94-6, November
          1945.

Edward Stevenson discusses color selection of Maureen O'Hara in
"The Fallen Sparrow," "Kitten on the Keys," and "The Spanish
Main"; Joan Fontaine in "Suspicion"; and Audrey Long in "The
Most Dangerous Game"; and color preferences of the actresses.

3143 "Stevenson, Edward." American Film Institute Catalog, 1921-
        30, p.1379.
Edward Stevenson was the costume designer of "Song of the Flame"
and is credited with the costumes of "Sally," "Smiling Irish Eyes,"
and "A Notorious Affair."

3144 "Stewart, Elizabeth." American Film Institute Catalog, 1961-
        70, p.621.
Elizabeth Stewart is credited with the swimwear of "The Swimmer."

3145 "Stewart, Larry." American Film Institute Catalog, 1961-70,
        p.621.
Larry Stewart is credited with the wardrobe of "The Password Is
Courage" and "A Study in Terror" and was the wardrobe master
of "The Mummy's Shroud," "Macbeth," and "Frankenstein Created
Woman."

3146 "Sthamer, Frauke." American Film Institute Catalog, 1961-
        70, p.621.
Frauke Sthamer is credited with the costumes of "Call Girls of
Frankfurt."

3147 "The Stockingless Fad Hits Hollywood." Screen News, 4 (18):
        2, May 2, 1925.
Nita Naldi wears the latest fashions in "The Lady Who Lied,"
without hosiery.

3148 "Stockings and Such." It, 3 (35): 8, January 15, 1921.
A previous film reviewer (see "The U.P. Trail") and a reader
have both complained about the inauthentic corset and stockings
worn by Kathlyn Williams, and the modern hat worn by Roy
Stewart, in "The U.P. Trail."

3149 Stoianovich, Diana. "Hollywood's Golden Years." L'Officiel/
        USA, 1 (2): 184-9, Holiday Issue, 1976.
Two years after the "Romantic and Glamorous Hollywood Design"
exhibit another film-costume exhibit was held (apparently the same
costumes, as the exhibit traveled around the United States, also)
in Paris, from which the black-and-white photos were taken; all
the costumes are seen on mannequins, and all can be found in
Hollywood Costume--Glamour! Glitter! Romance!

3150 "Stom, Nancy." American Film Institute Catalog, 1961-70,
        p.622.
Nancy Stom is credited with the wardrobe of "Count Yorga, Vampire."

3151 "Stone Wears Own War Togs in Films." MGM Studio News,

5 (4): n.p., April 23, 1938.
Lewis Stone wore the original uniform he had worn in World War
I in "Yellow Jack" and had previously worn it in "West Point of
the Air."

3152   "Stoney, Yvonne." American Film Institute Catalog, 1961-70,
          p. 623.
Yvonne Stoney is credited with the wardrobe of "Hercules in New
York" and "The Landlord."

3153   " 'Stork Club' Fashions." Screenland, 50 (3): 50-1, January
          1946.
Betty Hutton models six costumes by Edith Head from "The Stork
Club."

3154   "Strahm, Shirlee." American Film Institute Catalog, 1961-70,
          p. 624.
Shirlee Strahm is credited with the wardrobe of "The Misfits,"
"Escape from Zahrain," "Donovan's Reef," "Soldier in the Rain,"
"The Disorderly Orderly," "Tickle Me," and "Project X" and was
the wardrobe woman of "On a Clear Day You Can See Forever"
and "The Owl and the Pussycat."

3155   "Straight Lines for Summer." Screen News, 3 (27): 9, July
          5, 1924.
Claire Windsor bought her costumes for "Born Rich" in New York's
most fashionable shops.

3156   Strickling, Howard. "Adrian." MGM Studios, circa 1935,
          4 p. (Housed at the Academy of Motion Picture Arts and
          Sciences; was probably used as a publicity release for
          newspapers and magazines.)
Those costumes by Adrian that have influenced fashion the most
include costumes worn by Joan Crawford in "Letty Lynton" and
"Chained" and Greta Garbo's Chinese costumes in "The Painted
Veil," her feminine costumes in "Anna Karenina," and the pillbox
hat.

3157   "Strictly Collegiate or What the Well-Dressed Freshman Will
          Wear." Motion Picture, 30 (5): 34, December 1925.
Donald Keith and Gilbert Roland each model one outfit from "The
Plastic Age."

3158   "Stroheim, Erich von." American Film Institute Catalog, 1921-
          30, p. 1382.
Erich von Stroheim is credited with the costumes of "Merry-Go-
Round" and "The Merry Widow" (1925).

3159   "Stuart, Barbara, cost." American Film Institute Catalog,
          1961-70, p. 626.
Barbara Stuart was the wardrobe designer of "Sweet Bird of
Aquarius."

3160 "Stuart, Pat." American Film Institute Catalog, 1961-70, p. 626.
Pat Stuart is credited with the wardrobe of "The Landlord."

3161 "Studio Gossip." Grauman's Magazine, 5 (25): 27, July 9, 1922.
Rudolph Valentino will wear some of the most colorful costumes yet worn by an actor, in "The Young Rajah." Dorothy Dalton left for a summer in New York so that she could restock her wardrobe for future films.

3162 "Studio Makes 207 Corsets for 'Father' Cinema." Los Angeles Times, September 9, 1947, sec. 2, p. 3.
The wardrobe department of Warner Brothers made 207 corsets, circa 1880, for "Life with Father," 18 of which were worn by Irene Dunne and other cast members; the remainder were used for department store sequence displays.

3163 " ... Studio Rambles." Hollywood Star, 12 (17): 15, May 14, 1932.
Costumes worn in films are allowed to rest about one year in the wardrobe department before being worn by extras. Marie Dressler recognized the hat she wore in "Anna Christie" worn by an extra in "Prosperity."

3164 "Studio Wardrobes and Costume Design." What's Happening in Hollywood, 28: 6 p., March 24, 1941.
Discussed at length are the influence of film costume on fashion, and MGM's wardrobe department, where 50 seamstresses, ten tailors, one milliner, and 15 bead workers execute Adrian's designs. Valles designs the men's period costumes and advises them on their modern wardrobes. Costumes for actors provided by the studios included Gary Cooper's jeans and war uniforms in "Sergeant York," homespun costumes for Walter Huston and Thomas Mitchell in "The Devil and Daniel Webster," Tyrone Power's matador suits in "Blood and Sand," and over 30 uniforms for Ray Milland in "I Wanted Wings." Brief mention of many films designed by Adrian, Edith Head, and Travis Banton.

3165 "Stutz, Ursula." American Film Institute Catalog, 1961-70, p. 627.
Ursula Stutz is credited with the costumes of "Cry Double Cross" and the costume supervision of "Brainwashed."

3166 "Style, Comfort, and Durability in Favorite Footwear of the Stars." Photoplay, 26 (3): 42-3, August 1924.
Many photos of shoes worn by actresses, including a pair worn by Mae Busch in "Bread."

3167 "Style Designers Have Some Funny Orders...." Screen News, 2 (10): 20, March 10, 1923, col. 2.
In "Adam's Rib" Anna Q. Nilsson, Pauline Garon, and Julia Faye wore cavewomen costumes made of skins, which were constructed

with skin strips and wood pieces, rather than stitching.

3168   "Style of Footgear New Medium of Individuality." <u>Screen</u>
        <u>News</u>, 4 (43): 15, October 31, 1925.
        June Marlowe discusses shoe styles and selection, including a
        pair she wears in "The Pleasure Buyers."

3169   "Styled by Loper." <u>Movie Show</u>, 3 (7): 28, March 1945.
        Don Loper designed $145,000 worth of costumes for Dinah Shore,
        Gypsy Rose Lee, and others (not identified) in "Belle of the Yu-
        kon." Shore and Lee model costumes from the film, with sketches
        of how they can be adapted for contemporary wear.

3170   "Styles Change for Next Season." <u>Screen News</u>, 2 (33): 18,
        August 18, 1923.
        Madame Antoinette, a Parisian designer, was so impressed with
        Patsy Ruth Miller's 40 costumes in "The Hunchback of Notre
        Dame," while visiting the set, that she plans to incorporate some
        into her next collection.

3171   "Styles for That 'Siren' Mood." <u>Movie Mirror</u>, 3 (4): 38-9,
        February 1933.
        Myrna Loy models four costumes from "The Animal Kingdom" and
        Irene Dunne three from "No Other Woman."

3172   "Such a Vogue for Ruffles, Bows and Pleatings!" <u>Screen News</u>,
        2 (33): 31, August 18, 1923, col. 1.
        A peach satin gown worn by Sylvia Breamer in "Thundergate"
        features a pleated collar that resembles a cape (since it is almost
        waist-length) and a ruffled skirt.

3173   "Suedes by Voris," in <u>Fashion Is Our Business</u>, by Beryl
        Williams [Epstein]. Philadelphia: Lippincott, 1945, p.
        184-205.
        Voris Linthacum Marker is the suede and leather expert whose
        innovations have made the skins a high-fashion staple. (This
        biography does not mention her film costumes, and she seldom
        received screen credit since an actress might buy items from her
        store, Suedes by Voris.) (Included in a chapter titled "Mabs of
        Hollywood and Suedes by Voris"; see also "Mabs of Hollywood.")

3174   " 'Suez.' " <u>Screen Guide</u>, 3 (7): 32-5, November 1938.
        The research department of Twentieth Century-Fox made over
        700 costume sketches for "Suez." A small part of the wardrobe
        budget was the 900 Arab costumes, costing $18,000. Loretta
        Young's elaborate dedication gown, as Empress Eugenie, included
        an embroidered train, and a crown replica that cost $10,500 and
        took five jewelers four months to make.

3175   "Suit Wins Actor Twenty Thousand Dollars or More." <u>Screen</u>
        <u>News</u>, 2 (45): 26, November 10, 1923.
        De Witte Jennings has worn one suit for at least three years on
        stage, and in the films "Within the Law," "The Way Men Love,"

and "Angel Face Molly," all police-inspector roles. For "Angel
Face Molly" the wardrobe lady simulated a bullet hole by darning
a patch in the actor's jacket since he would not allow the suit to
be ripped.

3176 "Suit-Ed for Fall." Motion Picture, 56 (4): 45-7, November
       1938.
Rosalind Russell models two suits by Orry-Kelly from "Four's a
Crowd."

3177 "Sullivan, Eileen." American Film Institute Catalog, 1961-70,
       p. 628.
Eileen Sullivan is credited with the wardrobe of "The Small World
of Sammy Lee" and "You Only Live Twice," the wardrobe supervision of "Prudence and the Pill," and additional wardrobe mistress credits.

3178 "Summers, Ray." American Film Institute Catalog, 1961-70,
       p. 628.
Ray Summers was the costume designer of "Zabriskie Point" and
is credited with the costumes of "Adam at 6 A.M." and the ward-
robe of "The Purple Hills," "Air Patrol," "The Broken Land," "The
Firebrand," "Petulia," and the men's wardrobe of "With Six You Get
Eggroll."

3179 "Sun Fashions of Hawaii Ltd." American Film Institute Cata-
       log, 1961-70, p. 629.
Sun Fashions of Hawaii Ltd. is credited with the Hawaii fashions
in "Ride the Wild Surf."

3180 "Sundby, Emily." American Film Institute Catalog, 1961-70,
       p. 629.
Emily Sundby is credited with the costumes of "The Horse in the
Gray Flannel Suit," "The One and Only, Genuine Original Family
Band," "The Love Bug," "Rascal," "Smith!," "The Boatniks," and
"The Computer Wore Tennis Shoes."

3181 "Suren, Leyla." American Film Institute Catalog, 1961-70,
       p. 629.
Leyla Suren is credited with the Turkish costumes of "You Can't
Win 'Em All."

3182 Surmelian, Leon. "Studio Designer Confesses." Motion Pic-
       ture, 56 (5): 44-5, 67-8, December 1938.
Travis Banton discusses film-costume designing, as with period
versus modern costumes; the costumes worn by Marlene Dietrich
in "Angel" and "The Scarlet Empress" and Claudette Colbert in
"Zaza" (though he designed one costume, or more, Edith Head
received credit); and, briefly, the fashion influence of costumes
worn by Carole Lombard in "Rhumba" and "Nothing Sacred," one
of which she models. He said that Dietrich's costumes in "The
Scarlet Empress" "represented the finest and most beautiful collection of clothes" he had ever designed, and that "the controversy of Paris versus Hollywood is meaningless."

3183 "Susan and God." Time, 36 (1): 34, July 1, 1940.
Amusing comments by Adrian concerning what he considers dowdi-
ness--Tallulah Bankhead, and the average woman who copies film
costumes.   He recommends that the average woman should limit
herself to the costumes worn by the heroines of light comedies
set in moderate-sized towns.   Joan Crawford models one of her
15 costumes from "Susan   and God."

3184 Swanberg, W.A. Citizen Hearst: A Biography of William
           Randolph Hearst. New York: Scribner's, 1961.
William Randolph Hearst enjoyed seeing Marion Davies in authentic
and luxurious period costumes, and her films continually lost
money because of his insistence upon costly perfection.   Davies
wore over 20 costumes in "Janice Meredith"; over 2,000 military
uniforms were required, the film having over 7,500 actors and
actresses.

3185 Swanson, Gloria. "Do Women Dress to Please Men?" Motion
           Picture, 24 (10): 28-9, 90, November 1922.
Gloria Swanson dresses in her films to please the public, always
appearing in the most recent fashions because of the influence of
film in establishing and spreading fashions; she keeps in touch
with Paris on latest fashion trends.

3186 "Swenson, Aida." American Film Institute Catalog, 1961-70,
           p.631.
Aida Swenson is credited with the costumes of "An Eye for an
Eye" and the wardrobe of "The Lost Man."

3187 "Swenson, Sharon E." American Film Institute Catalog, 1961-
           70, p. 631.
Sharon E. Swenson is credited with the wardrobe of "If He Hollers, Let Him Go!"

3188 Swindell, Larry. Screwball: The Life of Carole Lombard.
           New York: Morrow, 1975.
Carole Lombard and designer Travis Banton began their famous
partnership with "Ladies' Man" (which included the first of their
trend-setting costumes, a beaded shirtmaker dress) and continued
with a long series of clotheshorse roles.   Includes comments by
Banton's successor, Edith Head.

3189 "Sylbert, Anthea." American Film Institute Catalog, 1961-70,
           p.632.
Anthea Sylbert was the costume designer of "Rosemary's Baby,"
"The Illustrated Man," and "Move" and is credited with the cos-
tumes of "The Tiger Makes Out," "John and Mary," and "Some
Kind of a Nut" and the wardrobe of "Where It's At."

3190 "Sylvia Sidney's Fashion Forecast." Movie Mirror, 5 (6):
           44-7, May 1934.
Sylvia Sidney models four costumes by Howard Greer from
"Thirty Day Princess."

3191 "Szeski, Jerzy." <u>American Film Institute Catalog, 1961-70</u>,
       p. 633.
    Jerzy Szeski is credited with the costumes of "Kanal."

3192 "Tadej, Vladimir." American Film Institute Catalog, 1961-70, p. 633.
Vladimir Tadej is credited with the costumes of "Kaya, I'll Kill You."

3193 "Takeuchi, Jack." American Film Institute Catalog, 1961-70, p. 634.
Jack Takeuchi is credited with the wardrobe of "Journey to Shiloh."

3194 "The Talk of Hollywood; Camera Doesn't Lie." Motion Picture, 55 (2): 45, March 1938.
Adrian has been filming Norma Shearer's costumes in "Marie Antoinette" with a 16mm movie camera so that he can better study them.

3195 "Talsky, Ronald." American Film Institute Catalog, 1961-70, p. 635.
Ronald Talsky was the wardrobe designer of "Tell Me That You Love Me, Junie Moon" and is credited with the wardrobe of "The Manchurian Candidate."

3196 Tarleau, Ellen D. "Costuming." Motion Picture, 19 (5): 44-5, 102, June 1920.
Discussion of the importance of film costume to a film; the role of costume companies; and the duties of wardrobe mistress Ethel Clayton, with references to her costumes for John Barrymore in "Dr. Jekyll and Mr. Hyde" and making gold crowns for the rats in "The Seven Swans."

3197 "Tauss, Frank." American Film Institute Catalog, 1961-70, p. 637.
Frank Tauss is credited with the wardrobe of "The Great Sioux Massacre" and "Run, Angel, Run!," the costumes of "The Money Jungle" and "Tiger by the Tail," and the men's costumes of "Flareup."

3198 Taviner, Reginald. "Is It Easy Money?" Photoplay, 39 (4): 52-3, 123-5, March 1931.
Discussion of many studio jobs. Average salaries include $150-

$350 per week for the head costume designer and $60-$125 for assistant designers per week. About 50 seamstresses work under each designer, earning about $18-$22.50 per week.

3199 Taylor, Angela. "An Oracle Analyzes the Course of Fashion." New York Times, December 31, 1974, p. 8.
Diana Vreeland, fashion authority, discusses the last century of fashion, mentioning that women in any part of the country in decades past could go to the movies and dream of looking like Joan Crawford. For example, Macy's in New York sold half a million copies of the "Letty Lynton" dress by Adrian that Joan Crawford wore.

3200 "Taylor, Carol, cost." American Film Institute Catalog, 1961-70, p. 637.
Carol Taylor is credited with Georgine Darcy's wardrobe in "His Wife's Habit."

3201 "Taylor, Edna." American Film Institute Catalog, 1961-70, p. 637.
Edna Taylor is credited with the women's costumes/wardrobe for "Don't Knock the Twist" and "Guess Who's Coming to Dinner," and the wardrobe of "Zotz!," "Diamond Head," "Under the Yum Yum Tree," "The Way West," "A Walk in the Spring Rain," and "Watermelon Man."

3202 "Taylor, Jim." American Film Institute Catalog, 1961-70, p. 638.
Jim Taylor is credited with the wardrobe of "It Happened at the World's Fair," "Twilight of Honor," "The Young and the Brave," and "Made in Paris."

3203 "Taylor, Noel." American Film Institute Catalog, 1961-70, p. 638.
Noel Taylor was the costume designer of "Generation."

3204 "Taylor, Noel." Biographical Encyclopaedia and Who's Who of the American Theatre. 1966, p. 865.

3205 "Taylor, Noel." Who's Who in the Theatre. 16th ed., 1977, p. 1176.

3206 "Taylor, Phyllis." American Film Institute Catalog, 1961-70, p. 638.
Phyllis Taylor is credited with the wardrobe of "The Time Travelers."

3207 Taylor, Theodore. "Art Direction, Set Decoration, and Costumes," in People Who Make Movies. Garden City, N.Y.: Doubleday, 1967, p. 55-75.
Discussion of the role of color in film costumes, including those in "The Great Race"; the purpose of the wardrobe test; and the duties of the wardrobe department chief; though many of the cos-

tumes in a film are supplied through Western Costume Company
or are store-bought.   The jobs of Edith Head and Walter Plunkett
are discussed, including their salaries; Head was paid $6,500 for
her 13 sketches of costumes for Lana Turner in "Love Has Many
Faces." Over half a million dollars was spent on Cecil Beaton's
1,086 costumes for "My Fair Lady." Notes also that local designers are often used when a film is made in a foreign country,
as with "El Cid" (by Veniero Colasanti and John Moore), and with
Elizabeth Haffenden for "Ben-Hur," which are discussed.   A new
school of the Motion Picture Producer's Association prepares
aspirant film-costume designers.

3208   "The Technicolor Director: A New Dictator Comes to Holly-
           wood!" Screen Romances, 2 (9): 55, February 1930.
Natalie M. Kalmus, the only color director in films, and wife
of the president of Technicolor, designed the costumes for "Toll
of the Sea," starring Anna May Wong.   Many other films she has
been associated with are listed, including "The Vagabond King,"
for which she worked several days with designer Travis Banton.
Production costs for films in Technicolor increase costume costs
by about 100 percent.

3209   Teitelbaum, Al.   "Let's Be Glamourous!"   Movie Show, 6 (3):
           52-3, 86-8, November 1947.
Al Teitelbaum discusses many aspects of furs, including a floor-
length ermine coat for Laraine Day in "Tycoon," and a $7,500
ermine dress for Rita Hayworth in "Gilda."

3210   _____.   "Your New Fur Coat."   Silver Screen, 19 (2): 46-
           7, 64-6, December 1948.
Al Teitelbaum has designed most of the furs worn in films for
the last 15 years.   Furs worn by Loretta Young in "And Now
Tomorrow" and by Gene Tierney in "The Razor's Edge" have
started a trend for light-colored furs.   The studios usually keep
the furs so that they can be restyled or recut for use as trimming.

3211   " 'Temptation.' "   Grauman's Magazine, 6 (30): 18, July 29,
           1923.
Actress Eva Novak has spent nearly three months' salary for Paul
Poiret gowns in "Temptation." This amount is in addition to what
film producers customarily pay for the bulk of the wardrobe needed,
though actresses usually supplement this when numerous and lavish
costumes are needed.

3212   "Ten Trained Canaries Add Life to Rainer's 'The Toy Wife'
           Gown." MGM Studio News, 5 (2): n.p., March 23, 1938.
A gown worn by Luise Rainer in "The Toy Wife" featured ten
canaries ranging in color from deep yellow to white, sitting on
taffeta bows around her hooped skirt.

3213   "Ter-Arutunian, Rouben."   American Film Institute Catalog,
           1961-70, p.640.
Rouben Ter-Arutunian was the costume designer of "The Loved One."

3214   "Tetrick, Ted." <u>American Film Institute Catalog, 1961-70</u>,
      p. 641.
Ted Tetrick is credited with the costumes of "The Three Stooges
in Orbit" and "The Three Stooges Go Around the World in a
Daze" and the men's costumes/wardrobe of "The April Fools"
and "There Was a Crooked Man...."

3215   "That Changing Hemline." <u>Photoplay</u>, 33 (1): 93, June 1948.
Leah Rhodes discusses the problem of changing hemlines in relation to Janis Paige's costumes in "Wallflower."

3216   "That Octopus Gown." <u>Photoplay</u>, 20 (4): 20, September 1921.
Bebe Daniels models an "octopus" gown by Clare West from "The
Affairs of Anatol."

3217   "That Well-Dressed Man." <u>Movieland</u>, 6 (5): 36-7, June 1948.
Bing Crosby models a sports costume from "The Emperor Waltz."

3218   "Theadora Van Runkle's Sketch Book of the Thirties." <u>Show</u>,
      1 (9): 16-7, July 23, 1970.
Presented are six sketches of costumes for "Bonnie and Clyde,"
by Thea Van Runkle, who is credited with launching the midi hemline and braless-look of the '70s through this film.

3219   "There Are No Such Things as Rehearsals Out of Costume in
      the Making of Motion Pictures." <u>Screen News</u>, 1 (26):
      20, August 19, 1922, col. 1.
Director Sam Wood has found that Gloria Swanson and others in
"Her Gilded Cage" perform much better before the camera when
they have worn their costumes during rehearsal.

3220   "There Is Nothing New Under the Sun!" <u>Screen News</u>, 1 (30):
      18, September 16, 1922.
Virginia Magee tried to find authentic gowns from the 1870s for
her role in "The Bond Boy," but was unable to, so she researched
the period at a library. She was able to buy similar costumes
on Fifth Avenue.

3221   "They Have Dressed Dorothy Dalton Up...." <u>Screen News</u>,
      1 (19): 9, June 24, 1922, col. 1.
Dorothy Dalton again wears overalls and a sweater in a film, for
"On the High Seas."

3222   "They Like 'Em from Yale or England." <u>Screen News</u>, 1 (42):
      6, December 9, 1922.
Many directors prefer Yale students and English men for their
films because they generally know how to dress well as extras.

3223   "They're All Among the 'Fashions of 1934.'" <u>Motion Picture</u>,
      47 (2): 46-7, March 1934.
Many stills are included of costumes worn by Bette Davis, William
Haines, and chorus girls in "Fashions of 1934."

3224 "They're the Topics!" Movie Classic, 8 (6): 12-3, August
        1935.
Notes that the 1870s costumes worn in "The Little Colonel" have
influenced fashion considerably.

3225 "Thibault, Hélène." American Film Institute Catalog, 1961-70,
        p. 642.
Hélène Thibault is credited with the wardrobe of "The Trial."

3226 "This Dramatic World." Motion Picture, 55 (1): 38-9, Febru-
        ary 1938.
Claire Trevor and Loretta Young each model one gown from
"Second Honeymoon."

3227 "This Picture Reviewed for Fashions." Movie Classic, 11 (4):
        73, December 1936.
Discussion of costumes worn by Gladys Swarthout and Yolanda
(of the dance team Veloz and Yolanda) in "The Champagne Waltz,"
by Travis Banton; Yolanda models one gown.

3228 "Thomas, Bill." American Film Institute Catalog, 1961-70,
        p. 642.
39 films are listed for designer Bill Thomas.

3229 "Thomas, Bill." International Motion Picture Almanac. 1972,
        p. 247.
From 1941 to 1946 Bill Thomas was an assistant at Irene, Inc.,
and was an assistant costume designer for MGM from 1947-8.
He was a costume designer for Universal from 1941 to 1959 and
is currently a freelance designer.

3230 Thomas, Bob. "Edith Head Foresees Striking Changes in
        Women's Fashions." Hollywood Citizen-News, July 1,
        1947, p. 16.
Edith Head discusses the New Look and notes that as a result of
it films made in the previous year will look like period costumes.

3231 _____. Joan Crawford: A Biography. New York: Simon
        and Schuster, 1978.
Edith Head has called Adrian's costumes for Joan Crawford in
"Letty Lynton" "the single most important influence on fashion in
film history"; with a photo of Adrian and Crawford holding a
sketched costume from the film. In response to criticism over
her costumes in "I Live My Life," Joseph Mankiewicz, the film's
writer and producer, told Crawford that the real shopgirls wanted
to see her in Adrian gowns rather than housedresses. Franchot
Tone, her husband then, was limited to "white tie and tails" roles
and was reminded that Robert Montgomery was always available
to slip into his dinner jacket. Her career was considered finished
until the release of "Mildred Pierce"; director Michael Curtiz had
yelled at the designer over her clothes, and at her when she wore
a dress from Sears-Roebuck. She had discussed the film's cos-

tumes with producer Jerry Wald when she accepted the role for
"Torch Song" and selected the jewelry from her own collection
with help from director Charles Walters. Her behavior became
increasingly bizarre, as when she littered, late one night, Mercedes McCambridge's costumes for "Johnny Guitar" all over the road.
She saved the studio money for "Berserk" by wearing her own
clothes but had permission for Edith Head to design her leotard.
Sheila O'Brien designed and made her costumes (no credits) keeping in mind her increasing maturity, and tried to change some of
her habits, including wearing high-heeled shoes with plastic ankle
straps which did not photograph, and her insistence on wearing
Adrian's styles for her. Her costumes became simple, worn with
good furs and jewelry, which were either rented or borrowed for
the film. As she lectured on several occasions, she praised the
talents of designers Adrian and Edith Head; noting that Norma Shearer
had Crawford's dress changed "nineteen times" in "The Wom-
en," but she wore the gold dress and turban anyway. She included
her wardrobe woman, unnamed, in her will.

3232   _____. King Cohn: The Life and Times of Harry Cohn.
        New York: Putnam's, 1967.
Robert Young almost quit acting after one day of filming at
Columbia when Harry Cohn, studio cofounder, cursed him for
being so inappropriately dressed for his role in "Guilty Generation";
his previous films had been period, and he did not know that
actors were supposed to supply their modern wardrobes. Includes
the argument Cohn and Rosalind Russell had when she attempted
to, and finally was able to, buy some of Irene's costumes for use
in an unnamed film. Lucille Ball barely fit into Jean Louis's costumes for her in "The Magic Carpet" from fitting to completion
of her costumes due to her pregnancy; and had to subsequently
drop out of "The Greatest Show on Earth," though her lavish costumes had already been made. Loretta Young's costumes for
"Bedtime Story" had been made by Irene, but, lacking a dress for
an important scene, she bought a $155 sale gown at Magnin's,
and after $400 worth of Irene's changes, charged Cohn $700; she
lost her star billing in the film, was not allowed to wear the gown,
and purposely kept suggesting changes until the studio's substitute
gown cost $5,000. Director George Cukor wanted Judy Holliday
to wear a designer gown in "Adam's Rib" rather than one purchased from a department store so that she could have a glamorous scene in the film, as a reward for both appearing slovenly
early in the film and for dieting toward the end. Rita Hayworth
wore flat-heeled shoes in "You'll Never Get Rich" since Fred
Astaire was insecure about his height. Virginia Van Upp discarded $50,000 worth of Hayworth's costumes for "Cover Girl";
Cohn was angry but agreed when he saw them. She refused to
wear a girdle in "Miss Sadie Thompson" so Cohn ordered that
she be photographed (mostly) from the waist up. Her fourth
husband, Dick Haymes, dictated even the style of her costumes,
and she was eventually dropped by the studio. Notes also that
Cohn and Jean Louis had to insist that Kim Novak wear a bras-
siere.

3233 _____. Marlon: Portrait of the Rebel as an Artist. New
        York: Random House, 1973.
Many references to Marlon Brando's image as "the slob," off
screen and on, as in "A Streetcar Named Desire." He once told
James Dean to stop imitating his "slob" look of T-shirt and jeans.
He selected his boots, cap, leather jacket, and jeans for "The
Wild One" and was later disturbed to find that he was identified
with the "leather jacket of a social renegade." Frances Nuyen
was fired from "The World of Suzie Wong," apparently in part
because she had gained weight and could not wear her costumes.

3234 _____. Selznick. Garden City, N.Y.: Doubleday, 1970.
Walter Plunkett's authentic costumes for "Gone with the Wind"
included petticoats of Val lace at the insistence of producer David
O. Selznick for the sake of the actresses' performances, even
though only they would appreciate the petticoats. Selznick's
voluminous memos often contained references to the film costumes,
demonstrating his concern for authenticity and the actresses'
appearance; he hired Anita Colby to analyze the appearance of
many of the studio's actresses. For each of Jennifer Jones's
costumes in "Duel in the Sun" the research department had to
verify their authenticity, and many were often remade until they
met Selznick's approval.

3235 _____. Thalberg: Life and Legend. Garden City, N.Y.:
        Doubleday, 1969.
Norma Shearer was especially careful over her film costumes,
choosing white satin gowns for most of her films, so that Adrian
referred to them as "Norma's nightgowns." She did not always
get to wear what she wanted, however, as when director Sidney
Franklin had the final say, despite her pleas to husband/producer
Irving Thalberg, for one film, since her contract gave him final
approval. MGM's popularity was due, in part, to Adrian's simple
costumes which most women wanted.

3236 "Thompson, Frank." American Film Institute Catalog, 1961-
        70, p. 643.
Frank Thompson was the costume designer of "Love Is a Ball,"
"Trilogy," and "The Magic Garden of Stanley Sweetheart" and is
credited with the costumes of "Something Wild" and "For Love of
Ivy."

3237 "Thomson, Jill." American Film Institute Catalog, 1961-70,
        p. 644.
Jill Thomson is credited with the wardrobe of "Conqueror Worm."

3238 Thorp, Margaret Farrand. "Cinema Fashions," in America
        at the Movies. New Haven, Conn.: Yale University Press,
        1939, p. 106-34.
The author discusses extensively how Hollywood has influenced
fashion since films have more power than any other medium in
this respect. Ben Waldman of Modern Merchandising Bureau has
started many clothing lines patterned after film costumes with the

cooperation of many film designers. The lines include Cinema Fashions and Cinema Modes and were begun in 1930 with copies from "The King of Jazz" and later included copies from "The Buccaneer." Brief references to the influence on fashion of "Snow White and the Seven Dwarfs," Merle Oberon in "Wuthering Heights," and jewelry for men, as worn by Edward Arnold in "Diamond Jim" and William Powell in "Man of the World."

3239 Thorpe [sic], Margaret. "Hollywood Sets the Style."
       Current History and Forum (formerly Current History),
       51 (3): 35-7, 64, November 1939.
This article, taken from the book in the previous entry, includes only the passages relating to fashion; this chapter in the book is confusingly titled, since it is not limited to fashion.

3240 "Those 'Damned' Fashions Are Turning Up Everywhere."
       Show, 1 (5): 52-5, May 1970.
Five photos with the original sketches of costumes worn by Ingrid Thulin in "The Damned" are included, with references to the research methods of designer Piero Tosi.

3241 "Those Were the Days." Motion Picture Costumers, 1957,
       n. p.
In a salute to early costumers, photographs are included of (former?) president Elmer Elsworth of the union Motion Picture Costumers union, agent Bill Edwards, and costumer Levaughn Larson on location for Fox around 1921.

3242 "Three French Chateaux to Be Built in Hollywood." Screen
       News, 2 (20): 24, May 19, 1923.
"Ashes of Vengeance" will require 12 wardrobe persons to assist the extras.

3243 "Thurlow, Gretl Urban." American Film Institute Catalog,
       1921-30, p. 1395.
Gretl Urban Thurlow is credited with the costumes of "When Knighthood Was in Flower" and "Janice Meredith."

3244 "Ti Leaf Skirts of Hula Dancers N. G. for Sound." MGM
       Studio News, 5 (13): n. p., January 14, 1939.
The traditional grass skirt made of Ti leaves worn by Hawaiians was not suitable for Eleanor Powell in "Honolulu" because of noise produced, so that cellophane was substituted.

3245 "Tiel, Vicki." American Film Institute Catalog, 1961-70,
       p. 645.
Vicki Tiel was the costume designer for Richard Burton, Ewa Aulin, Florinda Bolkan, Marilù Tolo, and Nicoletta Machiavelli in "Candy"; the clothes designer for Paula Prentiss in "What's New Pussycat?"; and is credited with the costumes for Elizabeth Taylor in "The Only Game in Town" and Samantha Eggar in "The Walking Stick" (codesigned with Mia Fonssagrives).

3246 "Tiel, Vicky." World of Fashion. 1976, p.69.
Vicky (apparently Vicki) Tiel and Mia Fonssagrives opened a
boutique in Paris after their successful costumes for "What's New,
Pussycat?" Tiel has since started her own business, financed
in part by a star who has worn many Tiel film costumes, Elizabeth Taylor.

3247 Tierney, Gene, with Mickey Herskowitz. Self-Portrait. New
        York: Simon and Schuster, 1979.
Gene Tierney met Oleg Cassini in 1940, when he was a Paramount
costume designer for $200 per week; he had designed Constance
Moore's and Veronica Lake's costumes in "I Wanted Wings." He
was fired by Henry Ginsberg, "one of the powers at Paramount
Studios," because he had frequently seen Cassini in nightclubs,
usually with Tierney, and assumed he didn't take his job seriously;
also, her parents and her studio, Twentieth Century-Fox, tried
to discourage their relationship. Two weeks after their marriage
in 1941 she left for location filming of "Sundown"; producer Walter
Wanger borrowed some scissors while she was trying on one costume and cut the costume in front, back and at the waist to create
a low-slung skirt, navel exposed, and decorative bra. Cassini
designed the costumes for her next film, "The Shanghai Gesture,"
and then off and on, including "Where the Sidewalk Ends," in which
he made his acting debut (as a dress designer). They were di-
vorced in 1952. Her costumes for "Advise and Consent" were
designed by Bill Blass.

3248 "Tigano & Lo Faro." American Film Institute Catalog, 1961-
        70, p.645.
Tigano & Lo Faro is credited with the costumes of "Last of the
Vikings" and "The Bible ... in the Beginning."

3249 Tildesley, Alice. "If You Cant [sic] Be Pretty, Be Interesting!"
        Motion Picture, 31 (4): 40-2, 120-1, 123, May 1926.
Adrian, aged 22 and the chief designer of the De Mille Studios,
was once offered five studio contracts. He discusses several of
his costumes for Elinor Fair in "The Volga Boatman."

3250 _____. "Wedding in the Fall." Photoplay, 54 (11): 46,
        83, November 1940.
Irene Saltern discusses designing a wedding gown and negligee for
Martha Scott in "The Howards of Virginia," with two sketches, a
photo, and a pattern offer. Travis Banton discusses a gown he
designed for Linda Darnell in "The Californian."

3251 Tildesley, Ruth. "Curves! Hollywood Wants Them--and So
        Will You!" Motion Picture, 45 (6): 34-5, 66, July 1933.
Discussion of the trend with actresses away from boyish figures,
as encouraged by Mae West; with comments by Adrian and Travis
Banton.

3252 "Tingey, Cynthia." American Film Institute Catalog, 1961-70,
        p.646.

Cynthia Tingey was the costume designer of "Genghis Khan,"
"Deadlier Than the Male," and "The Deadly Affair" and is credited
with the costumes of "Double Bunk," "Swingers' Paradise," "Finders Keepers," "Salt & Pepper," "Shalako," and "Where's Jack?"

3253 "Tirelli of Rome." American Film Institute Catalog, 1961-70,
        p. 646.
Tirelli of Rome is credited with the wardrobe of "Better a Widow"
and Florinda Bolkan's clothes in "Investigation of a Citizen Above
Suspicion."

3254 "Tirtoff-Erte Quits Movies." New York Times, November 4,
        1925, p. 31.
After seven months with MGM as a costume designer de Tirtoff-
Erté (Erté) is returning to Paris. He found the actresses no more
inspiring or attractive than his usual clients. He was offended by
Lillian Gish because she wanted simple costumes for the role of a
poor girl made of silks and elegant fabrics. Renee Adoree would
not wear a corset for her 1830 costumes (both actresses in "La
Bohème"). He had to design costumes for one film ("Paris")
four times, as it was constantly rewritten. He looked forward to
being treated considerately in his return to Paris.

3255 " 'Tis Unbelievable." Screen News, 1 (13): 24-5, May 20,
        1922.
Anita Stewart likes fashionable clothes, but hardly for her films
because her maid must keep extensive records of everything she
wears in each scene since one scene may be filmed over several
weeks. Also, she must shop at least six months in advance of a
film's release, and must pack very carefully for location filming.
Her location wardrobe for "A Question of Honor" was limited to
about eight costumes sent to her from New York, which are discussed.

3256 "Tiziani of Rome." American Film Institute Catalog, 1961-70,
        p. 647.
Tiziani of Rome is credited with Elizabeth Taylor's gowns/wardrobe
in "The Comedians" and "Boom!" and the wardrobe of "Better a
Widow."

3257 "Tokyo Costumes Co." American Film Institute Catalog, 1961-
        70, p. 648.
Tokyo Costumes Co. is credited with the costumes of "The Concubines."

3258 "Tolmach, Nat." American Film Institute Catalog, 1961-70,
        p. 649.
Nat Tolmach is credited with the costumes of "The Loved One"
and the wardrobe of "The Legend of Lylah Clare" and "WUSA."

3259 "Toms, Carl." American Film Institute Catalog, 1961-70,
        p. 649.
Carl Toms was the costume designer of "One Million Years B.C.,"

"Prehistoric Women," "The Lost Continent," and "The Vengeance of She" and is credited with the costumes of "She" (1965), "Those Fantastic Flying Fools," and "Moon Zero Two."

3260 "Toms, Carl." Who's Who in the Theatre. 16th ed., 1977,
        p. 1190.

3261 Toni. "Hollywood Summer Fashions." Movies, 5 (3): 28-9,
        July 1934.
      One costume each is modeled by Nancy Lyons from "Hit Me
      Again," by Orry-Kelly and Dorothy Lee from "Cockeyed Cavaliers."

3262 "Toppers Off to Ginger's 'Top Hat' Clothes." Modern Screen,
        11 (4): 46-7, September 1935.
      Ginger Rogers models seven costumes from "Top Hat," with four
      of the original sketches by Bernard Newman.

3263 "Torella." American Film Institute Catalog, 1961-70, p. 650.
      Torella is credited with the wardrobe of "Anna, My Darling."

3264 Tornabene, Lyn. Long Live the King: A Biography of Clark
        Gable. New York: Putnam's, 1976.
      Clark Gable once considered opening a haberdashery shop when
      he was discouraged about his acting in a theater. For "It Hap-
      pened One Night" he did not wear an undershirt because it could
      not be removed gracefully in the sequence in which he partially
      undressed. Another "important American fashion" worn by Gable
      in the film consisted of a V-neck sweater, snap-brim hat, Nor-
      folk jacket, and a trenchcoat with the belt tied rather than buckled.
      The trenchcoat he wore in "Comrade X," made by Burberry, was
      worn for good luck in most of the films he made during the next
      20 years. For "Mutiny on the Bounty" he worried that wearing
      knickers would make him appear like a sissy. The costumes of
      "Gone with the Wind" cost over $150,000, and included handmade
      shoes by an Italian bootmaker, but Clark Gable felt that David
      O. Selznick was taking revenge on him through his own neglected
      wardrobe. Includes excerpts of a memo from Selznick, as found
      in Rudy Behlmer's book, to Edward P. Lambert concerning his
      "GWTW" wardrobe. His clothing for "The Misfits" included a
      Stetson hat, silver cowboy belt, red shirt, and jeans cut more
      loosely than those of the other actors, worn over cowboy boots.
      Includes references to Carole Lombard being the favorite mannequin
      of, and being made a clotheshorse by, Travis Banton. Notes
      that Norma Shearer did not wear underclothes in "A Free Soul,"
      and she wore a series of fur coats. Gable's 1935 contract with
      MGM is included; he would pay for his modern wardrobe, and the
      studio would provide character and period costumes, which would
      remain the studio's property (standard for actors).

3265 "Tosi, Piero." American Film Institute Catalog, 1961-70, p.
        651.
      17 wardrobe-related credits are listed for designer Piero Tosi.

3266 "Tough Guys Wear Derbies!" Hollywood Vagabond, 1 (23): 4,
        8, July 28, 1927.
Lengthy account of why tough guys wear derbies, with apparently
fictional examples from films. "Detectives, cops, politicians,
massive villains and others of the cinema's glowering ilk can be
instantly spotted parading under a huge derby...."

3267 "Tournafond, Françoise." American Film Institute Catalog,
        1961-70, p.651.
Françoise Tournafond is credited with the costumes of "Lafayette"
and "The Milky Way."

3268 "The Train Sweeps In." Picture Play, 30 (2): 91, April 1929.
One costume each is modeled by Geraldine Dvorak from "Masks
of the Devil" and Aileen Pringle from "Dream of Love."

3269 "Traina, Teal." American Film Institute Catalog, 1961-70,
        p.652.
Teal Traina is credited with the fashions of "The Minx."

3270 "Travel in Fashion." Photoplay, 51 (5): 79-81, 84, 86-7,
        May 1957.
18 retail fashions are modeled, all "inspired" by the costumes of
"Designing Woman."

3271 Travilla. "Let's Be Casual." Screenland, 53 (2): 48-9, 67-8,
        October 1949.
Travilla discusses his costumes for Betsy Drake in "Dancing in
the Dark," seven of which she models.

3272 _____. "Save That Suit!" Silver Screen, 18 (2): 50-1,
        83-5, December 1947.
Ann Sheridan models one of her 25 costumes from "Silver River,"
Joyce Reynolds one suit from "Always Together," and Eve Arden
a suit from "Whiplash"; all by Travilla, who is especially proud
of his costumes for Sheridan in "Silver River."

3273 "Travilla." American Film Institute Catalog, 1961-70, p.653.
Travilla is credited with the costumes for "Mary Mary" and "Dad-
dy's Gone A-Hunting"; the costume supervision of "The Boston
Strangler"; the gowns/costumes for Joanne Woodward in "Signpost
to Murder" and "WUSA"; and he designed the gowns for "The
Stripper," "Take Her, She's Mine," "Valley of the Dolls," "The
Secret Life of an American Wife," and "The Big Cube."

3274 "Travilla, Bill." Fairchild's Who's Who in Fashion. 1975,
        p.263.
Bill Travilla is well known for his fashions for ready-to-wear,
television, and film. He has designed for Warner Brothers and
Twentieth Century-Fox and received an Academy Award for "The
Adventures of Don Juan."

3275 "Travis Banton Dies." New York Times, February 3, 1958,
        p.23.

Travis Banton died at age 84 from an undisclosed cause. He had been designing with Marusia the costumes for the film version of "Auntie Mame."

3276 Tredegar, Lillian A. "Advance Fashions from the Films."
      Picture Play, 1 (5): 23-5, May 8, 1915.
Kathlyn Williams discusses the importance of keeping up with Paris so that her costumes will not be three months out of date when her films are released.

3277 "Tree, Dorothy." American Film Institute Catalog, 1921-30,
      p. 1400.
Dorothy (Dolly) Tree was the costume designer of "Just Imagine."

3278 "Triangle's Spring Fashion Show." Photoplay, 8 (4): 79, March
      1918.
Included are four photos of unnamed actresses in costumes by Peggy Hamilton, Triangle's costume designer, and two stills of Alma Rubens in a Hickson gown from "Gown of Destiny."

3279 "Tricky Sleeves Are Something New." Screen Book, 9 (2):
      48, September 1932.
Madge Evans models one suit from "Huddle."

3280 "Trigere, Pauline." American Film Institute Catalog, 1961-70,
      p. 654.
Pauline Trigere is credited with Patricia Neal's wardrobe in "Breakfast at Tiffany's."

3281 "Trist, Wesley." American Film Institute Catalog, 1961-70,
      p. 654.
Wesley Trist is credited with the wardrobe of "The Young Swingers," "Shock Treatment," and "Morituri."

3282 Trow, George S. "Haute, Haute Couture." New Yorker, 51
      (14): 81-8, May 26, 1975.
Lengthy discussion of the "Glamorous and Romantic Hollywood Design" exhibit in an interview with its creator, Diana Vreeland. Many of the costumes are discussed, with notes on the people who assisted in the exhibit.

3283 "Truscott, John." American Film Institute Catalog, 1961-70,
      p. 655.
John Truscott was the costume designer of "Camelot" and is credited with the costumes of "Paint Your Wagon."

3284 "Tsuda, Ikue." American Film Institute Catalog, 1961-70, p.
      656.
Ikue Tsuda is credited with the wardrobe of "The Big Wave."

3285 Tuchman, Mitch. "Styling the Stars." PSA Magazine, 15 (1):
      70-3, 152, January 1980.
Biographical information on designer Yvonne Wood, 45 years in the film-costume industry. Her forte, according to Costume Designers'

Guild founder Sheila O'Brien, is designing for actors. Wood discusses designing for John Wayne in "The Conqueror" and Carmen Miranda in "The Gang's All Here," and designing in general and for television shows. She has designed for many western films, including several with Joel McCrea, but the two never met; his costumes were handled by Eddie Armand, later her second husband. Illustrations include one still each of Signe Hasso in "A Double Life," Ella Raines in "The Web," Miranda in "Something for the Boys," Dan Duryea in "Black Bart," Frank Sinatra in "Dirty Dingus Magee," and John Wayne in "The Conqueror" and one sketch each of Shelley Winters in "Winchester '73" and Bob Hope in "Casanova's Big Night." Includes many credits.

3286   "Tuffin, Sally." American Film Institute Catalog, 1961-70,
          p. 656.
Sally Tuffin is credited with Susannah York's costumes in "Kaleidoscope."

3287   " 'Turn of the Century' Style Themes Live on in 'Zaza' Film
          Costumes." Women's Wear Daily, 57 (77): 3, October
          19, 1938.
Discussion of costumes worn by Claudette Colbert and Genevieve Tobin in "Zaza," including how they will influence fashion; and the hats and jewelry. Includes eight of Edith Head's original sketches; though only one is identified, for Tobin.

3288   "Turner, Rutherford Show Co-Ed Styles in New Music Film."
          MGM Studio News, 6 (25): n. p., September 30, 1939.
Lana Turner wears 17 costumes, and Ann Rutherford 11, in "Dancing Co-Ed." Designer Dolly Tree interviewed students at the University of Southern California to discuss fashion trends; the stars will wear mostly skirts and sweaters.

3289   "Twentieth Century Horsewomen." Picture Play, 25 (6): 86-7,
          February 1927.
Includes stills of various actresses in riding habits to illustrate the changes in several decades, including Mae Murray in "Altars of Desire" and Greta Garbo in "Love."

3290   "Twenty-two New Gowns." Screen News, 3 (34): 12, August
          23, 1924.
Corinne Griffith returned from New York with three trunks filled with 22 gowns for her next picture, "Wilderness."

3291   "Two American Girls Show Paris." Life, 58 (5): 94-6,
          February 5, 1965.
Designers Mia Fonssagrives and Vicky (apparently Vicki) Tiel left for Paris as soon as they graduated from a design school, to design together and with couturier Louis Feraud. They sketch their designs independently, edit together, and use the signature of "Fonssagrives-Tiel." Included are sketches of two costumes for Paula Prentiss in "What's New Pussycat?"

3292 "Two Exclusive Sketches of Garbo's Gowns." Movie Classic,
          8 (6): 34-5, August 1935.
      Features two of Adrian's original sketches for Greta Garbo in
      "Anna Karenina."

3293 "$2,000,000 Hollywood Fire Destroys 'Porgy' Set." New
          York Times, July 3, 1958, p.22.
      The sound stage, sets, and costumes of "Porgy and Bess" were
      destroyed by fire.

3294 Tynan, James J., ed. "The U.P. Trail." It, 3 (31): 20,
          December 18, 1920.
      In a review of "The U.P. Trail" the reviewer doubted that the
      corset worn by Kathlyn Williams was authentic since it had garters
      attached to it, supposedly from 1860.

3295 "Tyson, Joanna." American Film Institute Catalog, 1961-70,
          p.660.
      Joanna Tyson is credited with Rita Tushingham's costumes in
      "The Guru."

3296 "U.S. Lists 217 More Salaries." Motion Picture Herald, 126
(6): 61, February 6, 1937.
Gilbert Adrian's salary was $38,666. Joe Rapf, listed as work-
ing in the property department, earned a yearly salary of $17,984.

3297 "Uhry, Ghislain." American Film Institute Catalog, 1961-70,
p. 660.
Ghislain Uhry was the costume designer of "Viva Maria" and "The
Thief of Paris" and is credited with the costumes of "Spirits of
the Dead."

3298 Ullman, B.L. "Archaeology and Moving Pictures." Art and
Archaeology, 15 (4): 176-83, April 1923.
Discussion of how important moving pictures may be in influencing
the study of archaeology. Two archaeologists were employed to
ensure the accuracy of sets and properties in "Julius Caesar,"
with photos and references to the costumes.

3299 Ullman, S. George. The Real Valentino. London: Pearson,
1927.
Consists mainly of lifted paragraphs from the following book.

3300 _____. Valentino as I Knew Him. New York: Macy-
Masius, 1926.
This is the original book written by Ullman that he himself
and most of the other Valentino biographers have borrowed so
much from. The costume references are: Bryan (or Byron)
Foy's comment about Valentino starving if necessary to be well
dressed in his films; the production delays and subsequent firing
of Jetta Goudal from "A Sainted Devil" because of the time-
consuming creation of the costumes she designed; his life with
designer Natacha Rambova, including their spending about $40,000
of the studio's money for Moorish costumes and jewelry for "The
Hooded Falcon"; his rare and extensive collection of costume-
history books; her buying her wardrobe for "When Love Grows
Cold" in Paris while obtaining a divorce there; Valentino's expensive and mostly original costumes bought abroad for "The Son
of the Sheik"; and a unique reference to his friendship with Cora
McGeachy, a theatrical- and film-costume designer for First
National Studios "whose genius in costuming is almost too well

known to need mention. "

3301 "Ulrich, Trude. " <u>American Film Institute Catalog, 1961-70,</u>
         p. 661.
Trude Ulrich is credited with the costumes of "The Mad Execu-
tioners" and was the costume consultant for "The Monster of
London City. "

3302 "Ultimas en Hollywood. " <u>Cinelandia,</u> 19 (11): 36-9, November
         1945.
One costume each is modeled (some in closeups) by Eleanor Parker
from "Esta Nuestro Amor" (title does not translate directly into
any of her films) and Sonja Henie from "Romance y Fantasia"
(probably "It's a Pleasure, " her only film during a five-year
interval), with mention of their purses; by Andrea King, with a
beret, from her latest film; and by Ida Lupino from "Tormentas
de Pasión" ("Devotion").

3303 "An Ultra Chic Negligee of Lace and Velvet. " <u>Screen News,</u>
         4 (26): 12, June 27, 1925.
Helena D'Algy models a negligee from "The Exquisite Sinner. "

3304 "Ultra Long Skirts Taboo. " <u>Screen News,</u> 1 (45): 31, Sep-
         tember 30, 1922.
Norma and Constance Talmadge, both fashion leaders through their
films, will not be wearing the new long skirts in their films since
they prefer their skirts six to seven inches from the ground.

3305 Underhill, Duncan. "Have You a Hollywood Figure?" <u>Motion
         Picture,</u> 64 (5): 36-7, 76, December 1942.
The Hays Office has requested that film designers, in contrast to
their previous policies, conserve fabric and avoid longer skirts
and any other fabric-using style that would encourage American
women to follow. The War Production Board sent a telegram
from Washington endorsing this.

3306 Underhill, Harriette. "The Clothes of a Perfect Day. " <u>Photo-
         play,</u> 13 (2): 40-3, January 1918.
June Elvidge has supplied the costumes for all of her films in
the past two years, except for "Rasputin, the Black Monk. "
Since she cannot wear the costumes in another film or for her
personal wardrobe because they are easily recognized, she has
them taken apart and remade.

3307 _____. "The Stars Start the Fads. " <u>Screenland,</u> 14 (3):
         28, 88-90, January 1927.
Discussion of how films have influenced fashion trends, with
references to costumes worn by Blanche Sweet in "Diplomacy"
and Mary McAllister in "One Minute to Play. "

3308 "Understated Glamor from Jean Louis. " <u>Los Angeles Times,</u>
         August 29, 1973, sec. 4, p. 1, 7.
Though most of the designers are being inspired by old Hollywood

film costumes, Jean Louis keeps his ready-to-wear line separate
from his film costumes.

3309 Underwood, Peter. Karloff: The Life of Boris Karloff. New
        York: Drake, 1972.
Lon Chaney was skilled in constructing horrible appearances, and
for "The Unknown" he achieved an armless appearance by wearing
a straitjacket that was tight enough to burst his blood vessels.
Boris Karloff was considered by many to be Chaney's successor.
For "Frankenstein" Jack Pierce created Karloff's makeup and
costumes, having to research the role considerably since the
original book was lacking in a detailed description of the character.   Karloff's costume included shoes weighing 18 pounds apiece
and shortened sleeves on a heavily padded suit, with his legs
straightened by steel struts worn under two pairs of pants. Notes
also that, according to one of his last requests, Bela Lugosi was
buried in the "Dracula" cloak that he loved--black with a red
lining.

3309a "An Unusual Partnership...." Screen News, 1 (41): 4,
        December 2, 1922.
Madge Bellamy models a wedding gown designed by Zita Grogan
from "Are You a Failure?"

3310 "The Upward Trend in Fashion." Screen Romances, 1 (7):
        64-5, December 1929.
An aviatrix costume is modeled by both Billie Dove from "The
Man and the Moment" and Anita Page from "Speedway."

3311 "Urban, Dhetl." American Film Institute Catalog, 1921-30,
        p. 1408.
Dhetl Urban (actually Gretl Urban) is credited with the costumes
of "Never the Twain Shall Meet."

3312 "Urban, Gretl." American Film Institute Catalog, 1921-30,
        p. 1408.
Gretl Urban is credited with the costumes of "The Enemies of
Women," "Little Old New York," "Under the Red Robe," "Yo-
landa," and "Zander the Great."

3313 "Urbanic, Elisabeth." American Film Institute Catalog, 1961-
        70, p. 664.
Elisabeth Urbanic is credited with the costumes of "The Spessart
Inn."

3314 "Vácha, Fernand." American Film Institute Catalog, 1961-70,
        p. 665.
Fernand Vácha is credited with the costumes of "Lemonade Joe."

3315 "Vachlioti, Denny." American Film Institute Catalog, 1961-
        70, p. 665.
Denny Vachlioti was the costume designer of "Phaedra" and is
credited with the costumes of "Topkapi" and "Oedipus the King."

3316 "Valentino of Rome." American Film Institute Catalog, 1961-
        70, p. 665.
Valentino of Rome is credited with Christine Kaufmann's gowns
in "Wild and Wonderful" and the wardrobe of "Hello--Goodbye."

3317 "Valentino [of Rome]." Current Biography. 1973, p. 423-5.

3318 Valentino, Rudolph. "High Lights in the Life of Rudolph
        Valentino." Edited by James R. Quirk. Photoplay,
        30 (6): 62-5, 140-9, November 1926.
Rudolph Valentino discusses how he met his second wife, Natacha
Rambova, when she was the set and costume designer for Nazi-
mova's "Aphrodite."

3319 "Valentino to Transfer Producing Company from New York to
        Los Angeles." Screen News, 3 (40): 5, October 4, 1924.
Valentino is abroad selecting costumes and materials for his first
Famous Players-Lasky production, the title of which is a secret
("The Hooded Falcon").

3320 "Valentino Wears 105 Pounds of Clothes in 'Blood and Sand.'"
        Screen News, 1 (8): 7, April 15, 1922.
Rudolph Valentino wore three bullfighter costumes weighing 35
pounds each in "Blood and Sand"; they were made of brown,
purple, and blue velvet with much handwork of silver brocade.
A cape worn with these was made of pink silk with red lining,
also with brocade handwork, of gold.

3321 "Valli." American Film Institute Catalog, 1961-70, p. 666.
Valli is credited with the wardrobe of "Substitution."

3322 Vance, Malcolm. <u>Tara Revisited.</u> New York: Charter, 1976.
Walter Plunkett begged David O. Selznick in a letter for the chance
to design the costumes for "Gone with the Wind," and was soon
awarded with a contract though, several years later, Selznick had
a contest half way through shooting to see if other designers'
sketches could improve the wardrobe. He went to Atlanta and
with the help of author Margaret Mitchell and the Ladies of the
Confederacy researched original fabrics from the Civil War
period; one brown plaid fabric was copied identically for a dress
worn by Hattie McDaniel. He also visited a Pennsylvania mill to
see original cotton print fabric swatches from the period; the mill
had agreed to supply the film's fabrics and merchandise them
concurrently with the film's release. He had all the tiny prints
enlarged and designed himself the green sprig fabric worn by
Vivien Leigh in the barbeque sequence, and had the fabric screen
printed. He discusses the actual circumstances concerning which
producer David O. Selznick wrote memos complaining about Clark
Gable's wardrobe and Vivien Leigh's "breastwork." His large
wardrobe crew included sketch artists who refined his rough
sketches; weavers; fabric agers; and a boy who made shoes from
wood and carpet, buttons from peach pits and pumpkin seeds, and
palmetto and corn-husk bonnets. Plunkett's 5,500 costumes for
the film included 44 for Leigh, 36 for Gable, 21 for Olivia de
Havilland, and 11 for Leslie Howard. He had previously worked
for Western Costume Company and had just completed his autobiography at the time of this book's publication.

3323 Van Den Ecker, Louis. "A Veteran's View of Hollywood
            Authenticity." <u>Hollywood Quarterly,</u> 4 (4): 323-31,
            Summer 1950.
The author, a chief technical adviser for a research department,
discusses several incidents in unnamed films concerning incorrect
military costumes. One union, Local 705, set up an independent
Costumers' Research Group with a library so that they can locate
most anything concerning costume research and construction.

3324 "Vandenecker, Beau." <u>American Film Institute Catalog, 1961-</u>
            <u>70,</u> p.666.
Beau Vandenecker is credited with the wardrobe of "Harum
Scarum."

3325 "Vanderleelie, Roy." <u>American Film Institute Catalog, 1961-</u>
            <u>70,</u> p.666.
Roy Vanderleelie is credited with the wardrobe of "Hell's Angels
on Wheels."

3326 "Van Parys, Blanche." <u>American Film Institute Catalog,</u>
            <u>1961-70,</u> p.667.
Blanche Van Parys is credited with the costumes of "Maxime."

3327 "Van Runkle, Theadora." <u>American Film Institute Catalog,</u>
            <u>1961-70,</u> p.668.
Theadora Van Runkle was the costume designer of "Bonnie and

Clyde," "Bullitt," "I Love You, Alice B. Toklas!," "The Arrangement," "The Reivers," and for Faye Dunaway in "The
Thomas Crown Affair" and "A Place for Lovers" and is credited
with the costumes of "Myra Breckenridge."

3328 "Várdai, Guyula." American Film Institute Catalog, 1961-70,
       p. 668.
Guyula Várdai is credited with the costumes of "The Red and the
White."

3329 "Vassilou, Spyros." American Film Institute Catalog, 1961-
       70, p. 669.
Spyros Vassilou is credited with the costumes of "Electra."

3330 "Vavra, V." American Film Institute Catalog, 1961-70, p.
       669.
V. Vavra was the uniform designer of "War and Peace" (1968).

3331 "Velton, Irene." American Film Institute Catalog, 1961-70,
       p. 670.
Irene Velton is credited with the wardrobe of "Sting of Death."

3332 "Velveteen Is Important!" Vogue, 88 (4): 6, August 15, 1936.
An ad for Walter Plunkett's six retail adaptations of costumes from
"Mary of Scotland," marketed by Modern Merchandising Bureau;
two of them are shown.

3333 "Venet, Philippe." American Film Institute Catalog, 1961-70,
       p. 670.
Philippe Venet is credited with Jean Seberg's wardrobe in "In the
French Style."

3334 "Venezuelan Venture." Theatre Arts, 33 (10): 44-7, Novem-
       ber 1949.
Though Irene Sharaff has had many successful assignments on
Broadway, she feels that her best experience and growth has
occurred as a costume designer with films because of large
budgets and a (comparative) abundance of time; she has, however,
now left Hollywood because of the decreasing budgets and less
imaginative assignments.

3335 "Venus in Finery." Motion Picture, 30 (7): 42, February
       1926.
Fay Lanphier, Nelly Savage, Peggy Fish, and Winifred Hunter
each model one costume designed by Gilbert Clark from "The
American Venus."

3336 Verdone, Mario. La Moda e il Costume nel Film. Rome:
       Bianco e Nero, 1952.
A valuable anthology, in Italian, of film-costume articles and
excerpts from books previously published in French, English,
and Italian; the original sources can be found in the book's
bibliography. Well, but not abundantly, illustrated with costumes

from American, British, German, French, and Italian films. Includes articles written by designers Adrian, Vittorio Nino Novarese,
and Claude Autant-Lara, and actor Laurence Olivier on "Henry
V. "

3337 "Vereyskiy, O." American Film Institute Catalog, 1961-70,
        p. 670.
    O. Vereyskiy is credited with the costumes of "Fate of a Man. "

3338 "Verhille, Guy." American Film Institute Catalog, 1961-70,
        p. 670.
    Guy Verhille was the costume designer of "Which Way to the
    Front?" and is credited with the wardrobe of "A Walk in the
    Spring Rain," the costumes of "The Comic," and the men's ward-
    robe of "The Big Mouth," "Cactus Flower," and "Hook, Line and
    Sinker. "

3339 "Verity, Jack." American Film Institute Catalog, 1961-70,
        p. 670.
    Jack Verity is credited with the wardrobe of "Desert Patrol. "

3340 "Versailles Palace Ballroom Reproduced." Screen News, 1
        (6): 23, April 1, 1922.
    Mr. and Mrs. Walter Israel, of United Studios, executed the
    authentic 800 period costumes of the Second Restoration for the
    ballroom sequence of Norma Talmadge's first independent pro-
    duction, "The Eternal Flame. "

3341 Vertès, Marcel, with Bryan Holme. Art and Fashion. New
        York: Studio Publications, 1944.
    Costumes that might once have been considered "miracles of
    chic," including Gloria Swanson's film costumes in the 1920s,
    appear comical to later generations of movie goers; we might
    also find Mona Lisa comical if movies had existed then.

3342 "Vertès, Marcel." Current Biography. 1961, p. 468-70.
    Artist Marcel Vertès designed his first film costumes for "Les
    Aventures du Roi Pausole," in 1933.

3343 "Vertès, Marcel." Current Biography [Necrology]. 1962, p.
        436.

3344 "Vertes, Marcel." Who's Who in America. 1960-1, p. 2980-1.

3345 "Vertes, Marcel." Who's Who in American Art. Edited by
        Dorothy B. Gilbert. New York: Bowker, 1956, p. 483-4.

3346 "Vertès (Marcel)." Who's Who in France. 4th ed., 1959-60,
        p. 2586-7.

3347 "Vicky." American Film Institute Catalog, 1961-70, p. 672.
    Vicky is credited with the wardrobe of "Finger on the Trigger. "

3348   "Vicze, Zsuzsa." American Film Institute Catalog, 1961-70,
         p. 672.
Zsuzsa Vicze is credited with the costumes of "The Round Up"
and "Winter Wind."

3349   "Vinnie." American Film Institute Catalog, 1961-70, p. 674.
Vinnie is credited with the costumes of "Secrets of an Uncover
Model."

3350   "Viola Dana Designs Her Clothes for New Picture." Screen
         News, 1 (29): 18, September 9, 1922.
Viola Dana is using her vacation between pictures to design the
clothes she will wear in "Miss Emmy Lou." Dana had designed
some of the clothes for her previous picture, "June Madness," including a pajama outfit and a wedding gown.

3351   "Viola Dana Exhibits Mystery Bathing Suit in 'Miss Emmy
         Lou.'" Screen News, 1 (34): 11, October 14, 1922.
Discussion of bathing suits worn by Viola Dana in "Miss Emmy
Lou."

3352   "Viola Dana Finds New Wardrobe Useless." Screen News,
         1 (18): 22, June 17, 1922.
Viola Dana bought four trunks of clothes in New York for her
next films, but will have to wait until after "Page Tim O'Brien,"
in which she will wear a few gingham dresses or other clothes
suitable for an orphan.

3353   "Viola Dana Has Costume That Is Different." Screen News,
         2 (3): 2, January 20, 1923.
Viola Dana will wear an oversized man-tailored costume in "Her
Fatal Millions," this being far removed from her usual costumes.
The costume, which is described, was made in an inexpensive,
local tailor shop.

3354   " 'Viola Dana Pajamas' Make Appearance in 'June Madness.'"
         Screen News, 1 (25): 27, August 12, 1922.
Viola Dana decided to design and sew a pair of pajamas for a
boudoir scene in "June Madness," the fabric, style, and accessories of which are described.

3355   "Viola Dana Selects Elaborate Wardrobe for 'June Madness.'"
         Screen News, 1 (24): 6, August 5, 1922.
Many costumes worn by Viola Dana in "June Madness" are described.

3356   "Viola Dana Wants Fashion Designers to Give Attention to
         Small Women." Screen News, 3 (9): 13, March 1, 1924.
Viola Dana, 4' 11", is limited to certain styles, which she describes and adheres to in "Don't Doubt Your Husband."

3357   "Violet, Madame." American Film Institute Catalog, 1921-

<u>30</u>, p. 1413.
Madame Violet is credited with the costumes of "Suzanna."

3358   "Virginie." <u>American Film Institute Catalog, 1961-70</u>, p. 674.
Virginie is credited with the gowns of "The Cheaters."

3359   "Virsaladze, Solomon." <u>American Film Institute Catalog, 1961-70</u>, p. 674.
Solomon Virsaladze is credited with the costumes of "Hamlet" (1966).

3360   Visart, Natalie. "I Stick Pins in People." <u>Collier's</u>, 104 (6): 17, 46, August 5, 1939.
Natalie Visart, men's-clothes designer for Cecil B. De Mille, discusses working with Joel McCrea in "Union Pacific," Charles Bickford and Gary Cooper in "The Plainsman," and Henry Wilcoxon with armor in "The Crusades"; with anecdotes about fitting-room etiquette and making clothing from metal.

3361   "Vitali, Nadia." <u>American Film Institute Catalog, 1961-70</u>, p. 674.
Nadia Vitali is credited with the costumes of "Tiko and the Shark" and "The Sex of Angels" and the wardrobe of "Superargo vs. Diabolicus," and as assistant costume designer for "Candy."

3362   "Vivian [sic] Leigh Portrays Tolstoy's Anna Karenina." <u>Harper's Bazaar</u>, 81 (10): 180-3, October 1947.
Vivian (she changed her name to Vivien in the 1930s) Leigh models one costume from "Anna Karenina," by Cecil Beaton, which has influenced fashion before its release, as seen in a retail coat by Christian Dior. (These stills are mixed in with an article that is not related.)

3363   "Vogues of 1938." <u>Jones' Magazine</u>, 1 (4): 3, November 1937.
Discussion of the film "Vogues of 1938," with reference to the effectiveness of the fashion background to the plot. The fashions, many made by well-known manufacturers, may help the manufacturers through publicity, but the film is not a "commercial picture."

3364   "Vogues of 1938." <u>Motion Picture Studio Insider</u>, 2 (3): 37, 60, July 1937.
The costumes of "Vogues of 1938," copyrighted by producer Walter Wanger, required three weeks of testing with other properties because of the color film. Buyers traveled three times to Paris for the fabrics. 14 photos of the costumes, including some modeled by Joan Bennett and Helen Vinson.

3365   "Vogues of 1938." <u>Time</u>, 30 (9): 23, August 30, 1937.
The fashion show and plot of "Vogues of 1938" are discussed; notes that 76 of the gowns and hats will be marketed by the Modern Merchandising Bureau.

3366 "Vogues of 1938, ..." Vogue, 90 (3): 52-3, August 1, 1937.
      Included are many stills of costumes from "Vogues of 1938,"
      worn by Vogue models who were hired for the ball and fashion-
      show sequences. Vogue is flattered both by the reference to it
      in the film's title and in the use of many of its models. The
      costumes were copyrighted, and any type of reproduction is for-
      bidden.

3367 "Vogues of 1938: Headlines, Streamlines." Motion Picture,
           54 (2): 39-41, September 1937.
      Seven hats are modeled by models appearing in "Vogues of 1938,"
      made by Sally Victor; and two costumes are modeled by Mary
      Oakes from the film, one designed by Helen Taylor.

3368 Vokaer, Michel. Bibliographie de Marcel Vertès. Bruxelles,
           Belgium: Emile Relecom, 1967.
      The only bibliography that deals solely with someone who had de-
      signed for films, though Marcel Vertès was especially famous as
      an artist. French text.

3369 "Volkmer, Waldemar." American Film Institute Catalog, 1961-
           70, p. 675.
      Waldemar Volkmer is credited with the costumes of "Cinderella."

3370 Volland, Virginia. Designing Woman: The Art and Practice
           of Theatrical Costume Design. Garden City, N. Y.:
           Doubleday, 1966.
      There will probably never be a book written for aspiring film-
      costume designers, but this book is especially helpful for such
      information as recommended education, situations to expect, and
      how to get into the unions (it is also easy reading). The author
      once applied for a job at Western Costume Company, which she
      did not get, but there she did see Dorothy Jeakins's "little works
      of art" translated into Quaker bonnets for "Friendly Persuasion."
      She also wanted, but missed the chance, to design film costumes;
      especially because of the good salaries, which compensate for
      irregular work opportunities, and the opportunities to travel for
      location filming. She notes that there is much "ghost-drawing" in
      Hollywood, as with designer Irene, though she was not sure if
      this was the case with Irene (see "Elissa Langston" and the article
      by Robins, Toni). For film or theatrical designers there is little
      work outside of New York or Hollywood, but in Hollywood it is
      especially difficult to start as more than as assistant to an assist-
      ant designer, since studios depend on big-name designers for
      better publicity. There is also the threat of the costume com-
      panies, which can costume a film as easily as the studio; she
      once saw a row of cobblers making the boots for the chorus of
      "Carousel"--a theatrical costumer could never afford such a
      luxury.

3371 "Vollner, Fern." American Film Institute Catalog, 1961-70,
           p. 675.

Fern Vollner is credited with the wardrobe of "3 in the Attic" and the women's wardrobe of "A Distant Trumpet."

3372 "Volters, Margarete." American Film Institute Catalog, 1961-70, p. 676.
Margarete Volters is credited with the costumes of "Adorable Julia."

3373 "Vongher." American Film Institute Catalog, 1961-70, p. 676.
Vongher is credited with the wardrobe of "Better a Widow."

3374 Von Sternberg, Josef. Fun in a Chinese Laundry. New York: Macmillan, 1965.
Director Josef Von Sternberg's "apprenticeship in the arts began in a millinery shop." For "Morocco" he had Marlene Dietrich wear white tie and tails in a cafe sequence for a slight lesbian appeal, and to show that her allure was not dependent upon her shapely legs. The studio heads argued with him for hours, but he refused to change the scene just because it was not fashionable for women to wear pants; fashion changed after the film's release. The other costume references are that he "dominated" the costumes of "Song of Songs"; a dress extra in 1923 earned $7.50 per day; and Charles Laughton preferred costumes as a disguise so that he could feel transformed into his roles.

3375 "Vos-Lundh, Marik." American Film Institute Catalog, 1961-70, p. 676.
Marik Vos-Lundh is credited with the costumes of "The Silence."

3376   "Wachner, Sophie." American Film Institute Catalog, 1921-
         30, p. 1414.
       58 films are listed for designer Sophie Wachner.

3377   Wagner, Walter.   "Edith Head," in You Must Remember This.
         New York: Putnam's, 1975, p. 224-34.
       Edith Head discusses her career and awards; the lack of flair in
       contemporary film costumes; and her costumes for "Samson and
       Delilah," Olivia de Havilland in "The Heiress," and Ginger Rogers
       in "Lady in the Dark." She feels that she should have won an
       Academy Award for her costumes for Joan Fontaine in "The
       Emperor Waltz," instead of Dorothy Jeakins for "Joan of Arc,"
       and for Grace Kelly in "To Catch a Thief," instead of "Love Is
       a Many Splendored Thing," by Charles Le Maire.

3378   "Wakeling, Gwen." American Film Institute Catalog, 1921-30,
         p. 1415.
       15 films are listed for designer Gwen Wakeling.

3379   "Wakeling, Gwen." American Film Institute Catalog, 1961-70,
         p. 678.
       Gwen Wakeling is credited with the wardrobe of "Most Dangerous
       Man Alive" and was the fashion coordinator of "Frankie and
       Johnny."

3380   "Wakelind [sic], Gwen." Motion Picture Almanac.   1930,
         p. 123.

3381   "Wakhévich [sic], Georges." International Encyclopedia of
         Film. New York: Crown, 1972, p. 498.
       Georges Wakhevitch designed the costumes of "La Grande Illusion"
       and other French films, as listed, and "Ali Baba and the Forty
       Thieves."

3382   "Wakhevitch, Georges." American Film Institute Catalog,
         1961-70, p. 678.
       Georges Wakhevitch was the costume designer of "King of Kings"
       (1961) and is credited with the costumes of "Black Tights," "Crime
       Does Not Pay," "Diary of a Chambermaid," "Scheherazade,"
       "Carmen" (1970), and "I Pagliacci."

3383   "Waldo, Charles." American Film Institute Catalog, 1961-70,
          p. 678.
Charles Waldo is credited with the wardrobe of "Lost Flight" and
"My Sweet Charlie."

3384   Walker, Alexander. Rudolph Valentino. New York: Stein and
          Day, 1976.
Costume was very important to Rudolph Valentino on and off
screen, but he felt he was not as romantic in contemporary
clothes.   In his modern films, including "The Young Rajah,"
"Cobra," and "Camille," period sequences were included because
of the influence of the costumes on his performances. Also,
frequent attacks on his masculinity led him to include scenes in
his films in which he was seen changing his clothes, including
"Blood and Sand" and "Monsieur Beaucaire." Notes the feud
between Natacha Rambova, his wife, and Valentino's costar Jetta
Goudal, when, for "A Sainted Devil," Goudal slighted Rambova's
costume designs; mentions that Rambova and Valentino spent
$100,000 on the costumes and props for "The Hooded Falcon."

3385   Walker, Anne. "Dressing the Movies." Woman's Home
          Companion, 48 (5): 24, May 1921.
Discussion of the basics of film-costume design and career
opportunities in the field, with emphasis on the successful careers
of Sophie Wachner and Clare West. West began designing for
films with "Intolerance" and designs for only about three films
per year; she has a small, specialized staff for all De Mille
films. Wachner, as chief designer for all Goldwyn films, designs
about 25 costumes per week and has a staff housed in a two-story
building.

3386   _____. "The Girls Behind the Screen." Woman's Home
          Companion, 48 (1): 14, 50-1, January 1921.
The many film-related occupations discussed include those of the
researcher, and the secretary who must, for example, make sure
that the same costumes are worn for scenes filmed at different
times. Brief mention of the wardrobe department. Costume designers earn $15,000 per year.

3387   "Walker, David." American Film Institute Catalog, 1961-70,
          p. 678.
David Walker is credited with the costumes of "The Charge of
the Light Brigade" (1968) and "Song of Norway."

3388   Walker, Helen Louise. "Dress Up and Live." Silver Screen,
          8 (7): 18-9, 75, May 1938.
Discussion of current trends in film costume, especially the trend
away from revealing costumes, as discussed by Adrian and Ed-
ward Stevenson. Norma Shearer discusses wearing her costumes
in "Marie Antoinette." Also, discussion of costumes worn by
Joan Fontaine in "The Milkman Rings Twice," Kay Francis in
"This Woman Is Dangerous," and Irene Dunne in "The Joy of
Living"; each models one costume.

3389 _____. "The Perils of the Well-Dressed Man." Motion
          Picture, 31 (5): 44-5, 100, June 1926.
Adolphe Menjou discusses how he has achieved his reputation for
being "best-dressed man on the screen." At the beginning of his
career it looked as though his moustache would limit him to villain roles.

3390 "Walker, Natalie." American Film Institute Catalog, 1961-70,
          p. 679.
Natalie Walker was the costume designer of "Hey, Let's Twist!"
and "Two Tickets to Paris."

3391 "The Walking Encyclopedia of Hollywood." Literary Digest,
          101 (7): 66, 68, 70, May 18, 1929.
Costume specialist Edward Phillips Lambert, of the firm Associated
Costumers, is depended upon by filmmakers for his accuracy, his
voluminous reference sources, and his large warehouse. The
finest fabrics are required since the camera does not lie.

3392 "Walkup, Bruce." American Film Institute Catalog, 1961-70,
          p. 679.
Bruce Walkup is credited with the wardrobe of "Cover Me Babe"
and the men's costumes/wardrobe of "Fantastic Voyage" and
"Hombre."

3393 Wallace, Irving. "Gloria the Glamorous." Modern Screen,
          23 (4): 30-1, 80-3, September 1941.
Rene Hubert and a tattoo artist designed a special blouse for
Gloria Swanson in "Father Takes a Wife," featuring unusual nauti-
tical designs, rather than the typical anchors and life preservers.

3394 Wallace, Pat. "Autumn Sports Fashions." Picturegoer, 18
          (107): 50, 52, 54, November 1929.
The costumes of "High Treason" were designed to be futuristic.
Gloria Swanson's costumes in "The Trespasser" were fashionable
when the film was released, which the author found noteworthy
because film costumes are designed at least six months in advance.

3395 _____. "Can the Stars Choose Clothes?" Picturegoer, 19
          (110): 54, 56, February 1930.
Many film stars would be poorly dressed if the costume managers
did not take care of their film costumes. June Collyer models
one gown from "Illusion."

3396 _____. "Dressing to Type." Picturegoer, 18 (108): 72,
          74, December 1929.
Brief discussion of many actresses and their film-costume styles.
"British screen actresses are the worst dressed of any" because
they often must buy their own wardrobes or choose them from the
wardrobe department.

3397 _____. "Early Summer Fashions in Paris." Picturegoer,
          19 (113): 32-3, May 1930.

A discussion of the latest fashion trends, including the longer hemlines in Paris, though Hollywood is still featuring short skirts.

3398 _____. "The Holiday Wardrobe." Picturegoer, 20 (115): 47-8, July 1930.
Hollywood has popularized tennis clothes, brown-and-white shoes, and the beret.

3399 _____. "Moods and Modes." Picturegoer, 19 (111): 44-5, March 1930.
Several costumes worn by Irene Bordoni in "Paris" are described; with general references to the costumes of "Hallelujah," featuring shapeless muslin and gingham cotton dresses, and the simplicity of Ann Harding's costumes in "Condemned."

3400 _____. "These Film Fashions." Picturegoer, 18 (105): 50, 52, 54, September 1929.
The most common problems in film costuming are excessive accessories, and poor-fitting and skin-tight gowns. Good examples may be seen worn by Laura La Plante in "High Society," Ruth Chatterton in "The Doctor's Secret," "The Broadway Melody," Corinne Griffith in "The Divine Lady," Mary Pickford in "Coquette," and Kay Francis in "Gentlemen of the Press," with brief mention of other actresses. Styles popularized by film costumes include jumpers, sweaters, and brown-and-white shoes.

3401 _____. "They Had to See New York." Picturegoer, 19 (109): 48-9, January 1930.
Film actresses frequently visit New York to learn of the latest Paris fashions. Nancy Carroll models one of her many costumes with the new short hemlines, from "Sweetie." One gown worn by Bebe Daniels in "Rio Rita" is described; the film will shift to color toward its end.

3402 _____. "Where the Film Wins." Picturegoer, 18 (106): 50, 52, 54, October 1929.
A discussion of the three basic types of film costumes: the revue or bizarre type, the period costume (one modeled by Corinne Griffith from "The Divine Lady"), and the modern costume, with which Adrian is particularly skilled. Two other well-costumed period pictures were "Monsieur Beaucaire" and "Ben-Hur." Costumes of taffeta and beaded fabrics are taboo in the talkies, though chiffon and satin are fine.

3403 "Walsh, William." American Film Institute Catalog, 1961-70, p. 680.
William Walsh is credited with the wardrobe of "Trouble in the Sky" and "Othello" (1965).

3404 "Walstrom, Bill." American Film Institute Catalog, 1961-70, p. 680.
Bill Walstrom was the costume designer of "Mad Dog Coll."

3405 "Walter Wanger's 'Vogues of 1938.'" Picture Play, 47 (1):
      78-9, September 1937.
Katherine Aldridge and Phyllis Gilman each model one gown, and
Olive Cawley and Mary Oakes each model two from "Vogues of 1938."

      Walters, Gwenn see also "Photoplay Fashions"

3406 Walters, Gwenn. "Fantasy in Fashion." Photoplay, 53 (8):
      22-3, 88, August 1939.
Nine of Adrian's sketches from "The Wizard of Oz" are presented,
with detailed descriptions and forecasts of how they will influence
fashion through accessories, especially with hats and clothing details. The fantasy costumes are from the Land of Oz sequences
played by extras, including the Munchkins.

3407 _____. "Insure Your Wardrobe." Photoplay, 54 (9): 24-5,
      75, September 1940.
Discussion of how properly to store and care for clothing, with
reference to how film costumes are stored by MGM's wardrobe
department. Gloves, shoes, hats, and clothes are cleaned after
each wearing; sent to the character wardrobe department when they
start to wear out so that they can be remade; and are later given
to charity.

3408 _____. "Star Fashions." Movie Mirror, 5 (7): 43-7, June
      1934.
Norma Shearer models three costumes from "Riptide."

3409 _____. "Star Fashions." Movie Mirror, 9 (6): 49-53, Novem-
      ber, 1936.
Arline Judge models seven costumes by Travis Banton from
"Valiant Is the Word for Carrie."

3410 "Walton, Tony." American Film Institute Catalog, 1961-70,
      p. 681.
Tony Walton was the costume designer of "Fahrenheit 451," "A
Funny Thing Happened on the Way to the Forum," "Petulia," and
"The Sea Gull" and the costume and design consultant of "Mary
Poppins."

3411 "Walton, Tony." Biographical Encyclopaedia and Who's Who
      of the American Theatre. 1966, p. 898.

3412 "Walton, Tony (Anthony John)." Who's Who in the Theatre.
      16th ed., 1977, p. 1221-2.
Film-design credits listed for Tony Walton include "The Boy
Friend" (apparently erroneous) and "Murder on the Orient Ex-
press."

3413 "Wanke, Josef." American Film Institute Catalog, 1961-70,
      p. 681.
Josef Wanke is credited with the costumes of "Emil and the
Detectives."

3414   "Wardrobe, " in The Story of the Making of Ben-Hur.   New
           York: Random House, 1959, n. p.
       Elizabeth Haffenden and Joan Bridge, a color expert, sketched
       over 8, 000 costumes for "Ben-Hur. "   A year before filming a
       staff of over 100 persons began gathering materials for the film,
       including armor from Germany, costume jewelry from Switzerland,
       knee-length boots from Italy, and fabrics from South America,
       Thailand, England, and other countries not mentioned.   The cos-
       tume collection was housed in three buildings and was too large
       for one to obtain an accurate count.

3415   "The Wardrobe Department. "   New York Times, October 19,
           1924, sec. 8, p. 5.
       Jesse L. Lasky doubts that movie viewers could think of some-
       thing his character-wardrobe department lacks.   "Feet of Clay"
       featured close to 1, 000 costumes of different nationalities.   In
       "Empty Hands" Norma Shearer was lost in the wilderness with
       Jack Holt, and her costumes included a bathing suit and a skirt
       made from Holt's bathrobe without benefit of needle or thread.

3416   "Wardrobe Re-Loading. "   Motion Picture Costumers, 1959,
           n. p.
       Brief anecdotes of problems costumers have in film production,
       including Muriel Pool's improvised white envelope bag for Ann
       Sheridan in "The Black Legion, " made of white cardboard and
       stuffed with tissue paper.

3417   "Wardrobes for Chickens and Ducks.... "   Screen News, 1
           (4): 7, March 18, 1922, col. 1.
    . Grace Marvin, studio wardrobe head (studio name not given), re-
       cently created costumes for chickens and ducks in a scene for
       children's comedy reels.

3418   Warga, Wayne.   "Super Stitcher to the Well-Costumed Stars. "
           Los Angeles Times, October 11, 1970, Calendar, p. 24.
       Edith Head discusses contemporary actors/actresses she has
       designed for, the anti-fashion of contemporary films, and the
       possible unimportance and impermanence of film costume; she
       notes that she will soon tour the United States and Europe with
       the "Airport" costumes.

3419   Warren, Virginia Lee.   "Doesn't Anyone Want Mickey Rooney's
           Blazer? "   New York Times, July 18, 1970, p. 16.
       When MGM auctioned off its collection of costumes, Jeffrey
       Joerger and Michael Malcé bought enough to open their own store
       in New York.   Their collection includes costumes worn by Merle
       Oberon in "Deep in My Heart, " Lana Turner in "Honky Tonk, "
       Judy Garland in "The Wizard of Oz, " Hedy Lamarr in "Her High-
       ness and the Bellboy, " and Jane Powell in "Seven Brides for
       Seven Brothers. "

3420   _____.   "Out on the Mini-Midi Limb and Listening for
           Sound of Sawing. "   New York Times, June 10, 1970, p. 52.

Film designers Donald Brooks, Albert Wolsky, Moss Mabry,
Irene Sharaff, and Edith Head discuss the problem of changing
hemlines, which can quickly date a film.   Edith Head is thankful
for an abundance of waist-up scenes and pants suits, Albert Wolsky
planned on staying with miniskirts, and Moss Mabry discusses
specifically and briefly what he designed for Jeanne Moreau,
Rachel Roberts, Kristina Holland, Janice Rule, and Cara Williams,
all in "Alex in Wonderland."   Producer Arthur Broidy allowed
only minis in his film, "B.S. I Love You."   Sharaff was not
currently designing a film but would have chosen minis and pants
suits.

3421   "Warshovsky, Ethel."   American Film Institute Catalog, 1961-
          70, p.684.
Ethel Warshovsky is credited with the costumes of "It's Not My
Body."

3422   Waterbury, Ruth.   "The Commandments of Clothes."   Photo-
          play, 33 (1): 68-9, 125-7, June 1927.
May Allison discusses her costume selections and how they suit
her role in "The Telephone Girl."

3423   _____.   "Fashions in Passions."   Photoplay, 52 (7): 64-5,
          76, July 1938.
Claudette Colbert had a suit made for "Bluebeard's Eighth Wife,"
designed by Travis Banton, which cost $675; only the hat showed
when the film was released.   She models another gown from the
film, designed especially for a spanking she receives from Gary
Cooper in the film.

3424   _____.   "Happiness for Janet--Designed by Adrian."   Photo-
          play, 53 (11): 26, 88, November 1939.
Adrian and Janet Gaynor had not met until he designed her costumes in "Three Loves Has Nancy," since the studio had not felt
her important enough to have her costumes for "Small Town Girl"
designed by Adrian (they were designed by Dolly Tree, who rou-
tinely designed films that were not important enough for Adrian).
(Authors Frances Deaner and Robert Riley each wrote that Adrian
and Gaynor first worked together in two other films.)

3425   "Waterman, Gary."   American Film Institute Catalog, 1961-70,
          p.684.
Gary Waterman is credited with the wardrobe of "The First Time."

3426   "Watteville, E."   American Film Institute Catalog, 1961-70,
          p.686.
E. Watteville is credited with the costumes of "Les Gauloises
Bleues."

3427   "A Way All Her Own."   Picture Play, 42 (1): 32-3, March
          1935.
Josephine Hutchinson models ten costumes by Orry-Kelly from
"The Right to Live."

3428 "Way Out West." Los Angeles Times, December 1, 1976,
      sec. 4, p. 5.
Edith Head has designed a "pure camp" wedding gown for Mae
West to wear in "Sextette." In the film, despite West having
wed six times, she will wear a snow-white gown with the longest
train in film-costume history--40 yards long.

3429 "Wear This Stunning Wynne Gibson Frock." Hollywood, 23
      (6): 45, June 1934.
Wynne Gibson models one gown from "I Give My Life," which is
accompanied by two sketches and a pattern offer.

3430 "Wears Famous Chinese Coat in Picture Series." Screen
      News, 3 (11): 2, March 15, 1924.
Alberta Vaughn has worn a 500-year-old Chinese coat in the
"Telephone Girl" series, owned by a costume rental company.
The coat, insured for $10,000, took approximately seven years
to make; more historical information about the coat.

3431 "Webb, David." American Film Institute Catalog, 1961-70,
      p. 687.
David Webb is credited with the jewels of "If a Man Answers"
and "For Love or Money."

3432 Webb, Jean Francis, and Kay Hardy. "'I Married an Angel.'"
      Modern Screen, 24 (6): 32-3, 68-9, 71, May 1942.
Includes information as to how the wings for Jeanette MacDonald
and six other women in "I Married an Angel" were made and notes
that the wardrobe people try to keep MacDonald dressed in pink
because she acts best in that color.

3433 _____. "In This Our Life." Modern Screen, 24 (5): 60-1,
      86-8, April 1942.
Bette Davis chose all of her costumes for "In This Our Life" for
their well-dressed look; some were in poor taste for a "hussy"
look.

3434 _____. "'Tortilla Flat.'" Modern Screen, 25 (1): 50-1,
      98, June 1942.
The six male stars in "Tortilla Flat" helped age their clothes, a
partial list of which is included. Hedy Lamarr's wardrobe consisted mainly of two thin blouses, skirts, and a white wedding
gown.

3435 "Webster, Ty." American Film Institute Catalog, 1961-70,
      p. 688.
Ty Webster is credited with the wardrobe of "Country Girl."

3436 "Weddings Old and New Show Striking Change in Styles."
      Screen News, 1 (1): 3, 12, February 25, 1922.
General discussion of costumes worn by Norma Talmadge in
"Smilin' Through," by Charles Le Maire. She models two cos-
tumes, including one $1,000 wedding gown, and is seen in an

additional closeup.

3437 Weeks, Brigitte. "Things Strange and Wonderful." Review of
        The Making of "The Wizard of Oz, " by Aljean Harmetz.
        American Film, 3 (4): 77-8, February 1978.
Includes references from the above book concerning the great inconveniences endured by the actors in "The Wizard of Oz, " including taking hours to dress, being very hot in the bulky costumes, and not being able to sit down.

3438 Weinberg, Herman G. The Complete "Wedding March" of
        Erich von Stroheim. Boston: Little, Brown, 1974.
Inaccuracies are often passed on by film historians; the actors in
"The Wedding March" were falsely publicized as wearing silk
underwear.

3439 _____. Josef Von Sternberg: A Critical Study. New York:
        Dutton, 1967.
Includes comments by costume designer John Armstrong concerning the vestal-virgin costumes of "I, Claudius, " quoted from the
television documentary, "The Epic That Never Was. " Brief
mention by critic Ado Kyrou of director Josef Von Sternberg's
"clothes madness" for Marlene Dietrich in erotic film costumes,
so that he was often accused of bad taste.

3440 "Weinberg, Roger J. " American Film Institute Catalog, 1961-
        70, p. 688.
Roger J. Weinberg is credited with the wardrobe of "Dondi, " "The
George Raft Story, " "King of the Roaring 20's--The Story of Ar-
nold Rothstein, " "Twenty Plus Two, " "Confessions of an Opium
Eater, " "Convicts 4, " and "The Gun Hawk. "

3441 "Weintz, Margo. " American Film Institute Catalog, 1961-70,
        p. 689.
Margo Weintz is credited with the wardrobe of "Made in Paris, "
"Spinout, " "Point Blank, " and "For Singles Only, " and "Harum
Scarum, " and the costume coordination of "The Loved One. "

3442 "Weiss, Arnie. " American Film Institute Catalog, 1961-70,
        p. 689.
Arnie Weiss is credited with the wardrobe of "The Harem Bunch;
or War and Piece. "

3443 "Weiss, Ruth. " American Film Institute Catalog, 1961-70, p.
        689.
Ruth Weiss is credited with the wardrobe of "The Time Travelers. "

3444 "Welch, Eileen. " American Film Institute Catalog, 1961-70,
        p. 689.
Eileen Welch is credited with the costumes of "The Terrornauts"
and "The £20,000 Kiss" and the wardrobe of "They Came from
Beyond Space" and was the wardrobe mistress of "Malaga, "

"Ricochet, " "The Share Out, " and "Solo for Sparrow. "

3445 "Welcome Erté to America. " Harper's Bazaar, 2548: 63,
         February 1925.
Erté has arrived in "Movieland" for eight months of film-costume
designing.

3446 "The Well Dressed Man in Hollywood. " Photoplay, 30 (1):
         72, June 1926.
Eddie Schmidt, a tailor, makes the clothes worn by the top film
actors and consequently sets the style throughout the country, as
designed by C. F. Bergman.

3447 Weller, Helen. "The Strange Marriage of Gene Tierney. "
         Motion Picture, 80 (2): 46-7, 73, September 1950.
Gene Tierney and husband Oleg Cassini have arranged their
careers so that they can be together as much as possible, as
when he played a dressmaker in her film "Where the Sidewalk
Ends. " He designs all of her film costumes, as in "The Mating
Season," and designs in California for his New York firm.

3448 Wells, Margery. "On Dress Parade. " Modern Screen, 7
         (4): 72, 114-5, March 1934.
Discussion of costumes worn by Ginger Rogers and Dolores Del
Rio in "Flying Down to Rio, " Ann Harding in "The Right to Romance. " Marion Davies in "Going Hollywood, " and Alice Brady
and Mary Carlisle in "Should Ladies Behave? "; with one still each
of Del Rio and Harding from the above films.

3449 _____. "On Dress Parade. " Modern Screen, 7 (5): 72,
         97-9, April 1934.
Discussion of costumes worn by Madge Evans in "The Fugitive
Kind"; Dorothy Wilson in "Eight Girls in a Boat"; Lilian Harvey
in "I Am Suzanne"; Ann Harding and Janet Beecher in "Gallant
Lady"; and Bette Davis, Claire Augerot, Ricky Newell, and
Verree Teasdale in "Fashions of 1934, " with one costume each
modeled by the last four actresses.

3450 _____. "On Dress Parade. " Modern Screen, 7 (6): 69-
         71, 108-10, May 1934.
Discussion of costumes worn by Constance Bennett in "Moulin
Rouge, " some of which were copied by Cinema Shop; Claudette
Colbert in "It Happened One Night"; Carole Lombard in "Bolero";
Joan Blondell; briefly, the fashion sequence in "Hit Me Again, "
Bette Davis in "Fog over San Francisco, " Marlene Dietrich in
"The Scarlet Empress, " and Elissa Landi in "Sisters Under the
Skin, " and hats worn by Myrna Loy in "Men in White. " Colbert
models a costume from the film, and Norma Shearer models a
hat from "Lady Mary's Lover" ("Riptide").

3451 _____. "On Dress Parade. " Modern Screen, 8 (1): 77,
         86, 88, June 1934.
Discussion of costumes worn by Irene Dunne, Vivian Tobin, and

Constance Cummings in "This Man Is Mine"; Frances Dee and
Billie Burke in "Finishing School"; Marion Davies in "Operator
13"; Genevieve Tobin and Colleen Moore in "Success at Any Price";
Carole Lombard in "Twentieth Century"; Karen Morley in "The
Crime Doctor"; Claire Trevor in "Wild Gold"; and Pert Kelton in
"Sing and Like It"; with one still each of Lombard and Morley
from the above films.

3452 _____. "Screen Stars' Dresses and Hats for You, and You,
        and You." Modern Screen, 7 (6): 72-3, 119, May 1934.
Cinema Shop stores sell film-costume copies from $15 to $35.
Two recent examples are costumes worn by Miriam Hopkins in
"All of Me" and Shirley Grey in "One Is Guilty."

3453 _____. "You Can Have Clothes the Stars Wear...."
        Modern Screen, 7 (2): 70-1, 87, January 1934.
Some of the film costumes copied and marketed by Cinema Shop
are shown in stills of Constance Cummings in "Broadway Through
a Keyhole," Miriam Hopkins in "Design for Living," Irene Dunne
in "Behold, We Live," and Mary Howard in "My Weakness."

3454 "Welsh, Tom." American Film Institute Catalog, 1961-70, p.
        691.
Tom Welsh is credited with the wardrobe of "The Raven," the
costumes of "Twice Told Tales," and the costume supervision of
"Beach Party."

3455 Wenden, D.A. "Have They Dress Suits?" Picturegoer, 16
        (94): 36-7, October 1928.
Those stars who owe much of their success to period costumes
include John Barrymore, Douglas Fairbanks, Sr., Charlie Farrell,
Ivan Mosjoukine, Ramon Novarro, Dolores Costello, Dolores Del
Rio, and Lupe Velez. Rod La Rocque, Vilma Banky, and Ronald
Colman wear both period and modern costumes equally well.

3456 Wennersten, Robert. "The Second Mrs. Valentino." Per-
        forming Arts, 12 (2): 16, 18, 20, 22, 42-5, February
        1978.
Natacha Rambova was a successful dancer with Theodore Kosloff's troup when she settled in Los Angeles to become a teacher
at his studio. As Kosloff had done with a previous De Mille film
(possibly "Forbidden Fruit"), he offered to design the sets and
costumes for Alla Nazimova's "Camille," but merely signed his
name to Rambova's sketches; he was discovered and Rambova
was hired. Discussed are her expressionistic costumes for
"Camille," her 60 designs for "Monsieur Beaucaire" (Barbier
received credit), and "Salome." Includes a sketch for a costume
in "Saturday Night."

3457 Werner, M.R. "Yellow Movies." New Yorker, 41 (31): 61-
        8, September 14, 1940.
William Randolph Hearst's Cosmopolitan Studios existed mainly
for Marion Davies's films. During the author's seven months in

the publicity department he had many opportunities to make up
stories, including the difficulty Eddie Kennedy was supposed to
have had in obtaining a tie for "Get-Rich-Quick Wallingford."
Hearst especially liked Davies in beautiful clothes, so that irrele-
vant fairy-tale sequences were often added to her films. Decades
after the studio had been shut down General Motors sold many
old props for junk, including dozens of suits of armor worn in
"When Knighthood Was in Flower."

3458   "Wessel, Hannelore." American Film Institute Catalog, 1961-
          70, p. 691.
Hannelore Wessel is credited with the costumes of "Only a Woman."

3459   "West, Clare." American Film Institute Catalog, 1921-30,
          p. 1427.
Clare West is credited with the costumes of "Flirting with Love"
and "Sherlock, Jr."

3460   "West, Sue." American Film Institute Catalog, 1961-70, p.
          692.
Sue West was the clothes designer of "Joanna."

3461   West, Vera. "A Bridal Trousseau from the Films." Motion
          Picture Studio Insider, 1 (3): 32-3, June 1935.
Vera West, wardrobe head of Universal, feels that too many
women and manufacturers copy actresses' screen wardrobes,
which are often in bad taste, and that it takes a woman to understand how to dress women. Also, a discussion of designing
practical film costumes.

3462   "West, Vera." American Film Institute Catalog, 1921-30,
          p. 1427.
Vera West is credited with the costumes of "The Man Who
Laughs."

3463   Western Costume Company, Hollywood. There's No Business
          Like Show Business and No Show Business Like Western
          Costume Company. Unpublished, no date, 8p.
Western Costume Company was founded around 1912, when L. L.
Burns began costuming William S. Hart's films. It is now the
largest costuming company in the world, with a stock of over one
million costumes, valued at over $20 million. Its credits include
"The Wedding March," nearly all of Samuel Goldwyn's films, and
"The Robe"; with more information about its history.

3464   "Western Costume Company: World's Most Authentic, Largest
          Costumers." Hollywood Chamber of Commerce, 1977
          annual, p. 25.
Western Costume Company was founded in 1912 to serve the film
industry, has over one million costumes, a library with 10,000
books and periodicals in various languages, and such departments
as for making shoes, hats, and leather goods.

3465 "Western Costuming Co." _American Film Institute Catalog,_
        _1921-30,_ p.1428.
Western Costuming Co. is credited with the wardrobe of "Foolish
Wives."

3466 Westmore, Frank, and Murial Davidson. _The Westmores of_
        Hollywood. New York: Berkley, 1977.
The Westmore dynasty was started in Hollywood by George Westmore and carried on by his sons, Mont, Perc, Ern, Wally, Bud,
and Frank, and now by his grandchildren. Discussed are how
Mont came up with the flat-chested look for Clara Bow in "It"
and made Vivien Leigh's eyes appear green for "Gone with the
Wind" by suggesting special colors for her costumes; Perc's
harness and six-pound hump for Charles Laughton in "The Hunchback of Notre Dame," made of foam, unlike the 40-pound one
Lon Chaney wore in the original film; and Bud's mermaid costume for Ann Blyth in "Mr. Peabody and the Mermaid" and Ricou
Browning's "monster suit" in "Creature from the Black Lagoon,"
which created a fad for monster movies and was a boon for the
film-makeup industry.

3467 "Weston, Irene V." _American Film Institute Catalog, 1961-_
        _70,_ p.693.
Irene V. Weston is credited with the costumes of "Warm Nights
& Hot Pleasures."

3468 Wexman, Virginia Wright, and Patricia Erens. "Clothes-Wise:
        Edith Head." _Take One,_ 5 (4): 12-3, October 1976.
Edith Head discusses her 50+ years costume designing, with
reference to her costumes for Kim Novak in "Vertigo." She
can't sew by machine but can by hand.

3469 "What Happens to the Stars' Clothes." _Film Lovers Annual._
        London: Dean & Sons, 1933, p.51-3.
Constance Bennett donates most of her film costumes to charity
but kept a gown from "Born to Love"; Lilyan Tashman and others
once opened a shop but couldn't keep it stocked; Joan Crawford
has some copied for personal use and Clara Bow buys her film
negligees from the studio; also, the studios reuse and remake
many gowns or have sales. Some occasionally end up in museums,
including a Marion Davies gown from "The Gay Nineties," which
was given to the Los Angeles Exposition Park. The chief dress
worn by Gloria Swanson in "Sadie Thompson" is in a private
collection.

3470 "What the June Bride Will Be Wearing." _Motion Picture,_
        29 (6): 62-3, July 1925.
Wedding gowns are modeled by Blanche Sweet from "His Supreme
Moment," Vivian Welch from "The Exquisite Sinner," May Allison
from "I Want My Man," Mary Astor from "Playing with Souls,"
Mae Murray from "The Merry Widow," and Viola Dana from "The
Necessary Evil."

3471   "What the Stars Will Wear." Woman's Home Companion, 67
          (2): 80, December 1940.
Katharine Hepburn models a slack suit designed by Adrian from "The
Philadelphia Story."

3472   "What Their Clothes Cost." Photoplay, 26 (5): 34-5, 112-4,
          October 1924.
Unique references to the specific amounts spent on the following
actresses' costumes: Gloria Swanson, who models a $96,000
wedding gown from "Her Love Story"; Marion Davies in "Janice
Meredith" and "Yolanda"; Norma Talmadge in "Sacrifice," "Ashes
of Vengeance," and "Secrets"; Pola Negri in "Bella Donna," "The
Cheat," "Spanish Dancer," "Shadows of Paris," "Men," and "Lily
of the Dust"; and Corinne Griffith in "Single Wives," with one
still.   Yearly clothing expenditures are included for Antonio
Moreno and for Claire Windsor, who models one costume from
"Born Rich."   Brief mention of the costume costs for "Black
Oxen."

3473   "What They Are Wearing This Month." Photoplay, 38 (4): 22-3,
          September 1930.
Gowns are modeled by Jeanette MacDonald from "Monte Carlo,"
Irene Rich from "On Your Back," Ann Harding from "Holiday,"
and Natalie Moorhead from "Manslaughter."

3474   "What Walsh Found in Goldwyn Studio." Moving Picture World,
          35 (1): 57, January 5, 1918.
The Goldwyn Studio at Fort Lee, New Jersey, houses $50,000
worth of costumes.

3475   Wheeler, Ralph.   "The Girls Behind the Stars." Screenland,
          21 (1): 24-5, 120-1, May 1930.
Henrietta Frazer has been the assistant manager and designer of
MGM's wardrobe department for three years and formerly worked
in New York and Chicago.   The wardrobe manager is Joseph Rapf.

3476   "'When Love Grows Cold.'" Screen News, 4 (50): 9, De-
          cember 19, 1925.
Natacha Rambova bought many gowns from Parisian couturiers for
"When Love Grows Cold."

3477   "When Mother Was a Girl." Picture Play, 27 (1): 99, Sep-
          tember 1927.
The trend for costumes from the 1890s is shown in costumes
modeled by Alma Rubens from "Marriage License," Mary Astor
from "The Rough Riders," Zasu Pitts from "Casey at the Bat,"
Dolores Costello from "A Million Bid," and Patsy Ruth Miller
from "The First Auto."

3478   "When Rags Are Royal Raiment." Motion Picture, 30 (7): 30,
          February 1926.
Mary Pickford models three costumes from "Scraps."

3479   "Where They Are and What They Are Doing."   Screen News,
       3 (31): 7, August 2, 1924.
Mae Murray has gone to New York to shop for the elaborate wardrobe she will need in "Circe" ("Circe the Enchantress").

3480   "Where They Are and What They Are Doing."   Screen News,
       3 (34): 7, August 23, 1924.
Realism was especially important in the filming of "The Mine with
the Iron Door," for which Dorothy Mackaill and the cast lived like
miners on location in the mountains.   Under her corduroy skirt
and boots Mackaill wore heavy cotton stockings (which could not be
seen) despite the over 100° heat.

3481   "Where They Are and What They Are Doing."   Screen News,
       3 (35): 7, August 30, 1924.
Gloria Swanson wears a wedding dress in "Her Love Story" with
a veil of sixteenth-century lace, and a pearl and diamond coronet.
The $98,000 dress is made of metallic fabric with gold and jewel
embroidery, with a $6\frac{1}{2}$-yard train trimmed with ermine.

3482   "Where They Are and What They're Doing."   Screen News, 2
       (31): 10, August 4, 1923.
Ethel Wales, who usually plays character parts limited to kitchen
scenes, will play the role of a wealthy woman in "Spring Magic,"
with $50 shoes, $45 stockings, and a $66 plume.

3483   "Where They Are and What They're Doing."   Screen News, 4
       (23): 10, June 6, 1925.
Notes Noah Beery's pleasure over wearing one gold earring in
"The Coming of Amos"; he hopes he will wear it in more films.

3484   "Where They Are and What They're Doing."   Screen News, 4
       (26): 10, July 4, 1925.
Helen Ferguson prefers western costumes in her pictures, but her
fans wrote especially to praise her costumes in "Never Say Die"
and "His Neighbor's Wife."

3485   "Where They Are and What They're Doing."   Screen News, 4
       (33): 12, August 22, 1925.
A special studio tailor is employed for Charles Puffy due to his
obesity.

3486   "Whew!"   Screen News, 1 (4): 29, March 18, 1922.
Norma Talmadge's studio costuming department bought 200 pounds
of mothballs so that the 1,100 costumes worn in "The Duchess of
Langeais" ("The Eternal Flame") could be stored at United Studios.

3487   Whitcomb, Jon.   "He Makes the Stars Look That Way."
       Cosmopolitan, 137 (1): 42-5, July 1954.
Designer and choreographer Don Loper has worked as a "star
improver" by redesigning the images of Eartha Kitt, June Allyson,
Betty Hutton, Eleanor Parker, and Teresa Wright.   Biographical

information is included on Loper, with sketches of the actresses.

3488 White, Kay. "Fall Forecast of Film Fashions." Movie
            Mirror, 4 (4): 42-7, September 1933.
Discussion of costumes designed, for unnamed films, by Adrian,
Travis Banton, Earle Luick, Walter Plunkett, Rita Kaufman, Milo
Anderson, and Orry-Kelly. Notes that an (unnamed) Mae West
film is influencing Hollywood and Paris--generally, through feather
and boa scarves and décolleté necklines.

3489 "White, Miles." Biographical Encyclopaedia and Who's Who
            of the American Theatre. 1966, p. 913-4.
Lengthy biographical information on designer Miles White. His
film credits include "Up in Arms," "The Kid from Brooklyn,"
"The Greatest Show on Earth," "There's No Business Like Show
Business," and "Around the World in 80 Days"; he was nominated
for an Academy Award for the last three films.

3490 "White, Miles." Who's Who in the Theatre. 16th ed., 1977,
            p. 1246.

3491 _____. " 'Cleopatra' Evokes an Egyptian Trend." Shado-
            play, 4 (2): 26-7, October 1934.
Claudette Colbert models two adaptations of her costumes from
"Cleopatra," by Travis Banton.

3492 Whitney, Diane. "A Design for Fall Fashions from Hollywood's
            Experts." Shadoplay, 3 (6): 12-3, August 1934.
Most of Grace Moore's costumes in "One Night of Love" are in
black and navy blue, by Kalloch.

3493 _____. "Designers Say Shorter Skirts!" Shadoplay, 3 (5):
            16, July 1934.
"Cleopatra" has influenced fashion accessories, as with clips,
collar details, and bandeaus.

3494 _____. "Evening Pageantry." Shadoplay, 14 (35): 56-9,
            March 1935.
Claire Dodd models one ensemble from "Roberta."

3495 _____. "Five Fashions That Are Pets of Chic Stars."
            Shadoplay, 3 (1): 56-7, March 1934.
One costume each is modeled by Virginia Cherrill from "He
Couldn't Take It" and Claudette Colbert from "It Happened One
Night."

3496 _____. "Hollywood's Costume Pictures Start Style Trends."
            Shadoplay, 3 (2): 12-3, April 1934.
The author predicts that Marlene Dietrich's bouffant costumes in
"The Scarlet Empress," Loretta Young's Empire costumes in "The
House of Rothschild," and Carole Lombard's draped skirts and
large, elaborate hats in "Bolero" will influence fashion. One still
each of Dietrich in "The Scarlet Empress" and of Evelyn Venable

in a hat from "David Harum. "

3497 _____. "Off-Screen Simplicity vs. Film Frills. " Shado-
          play, 3 (4): 8-9, June 1934.
Includes descriptions of some of Joan Crawford's costumes in
"Sadie McKee. " Mae West models a costume for "It Ain't No
Sin" ("Belle of the Nineties").

3498 "Who Said Imported Models?" Motion Picture, 22 (7): 48-9,
          August 1921.
Includes three stills of Gloria Swanson and two of Wanda Hawley,
alongside two costume sketches of each by designer Clare West,
from "The Affairs of Anatol, " with brief mention of the processes
of design and construction.

3499 "Who Stole Marie's Stole?" Screen News, 2 (30): 26, July 28,
          1923.
Production was held up on "The Wanters" because a $2,500 sable
stole was stolen from the dressing room of Marie Prevost, who
needed the fur, made of five sable skins, for connecting scenes.

3500 "The Who What and Why of 'Marie Antoinette'; Settings--
          Costumes. " MGM Studio News, 5 (6): n. p. , August 15,
          1938.
Adrian designed 34 costumes for Norma Shearer in "Marie Antoinette" after touring in France and Austria in the summer, researching especially in Paris and Vienna.

3501 Who's Who: An Annual Biographical Dictionary. New York:
          St. Martin's, 1849 to date.

3502 Who's Who in America. Chicago: Marquis Who's Who, 1899/
          1900-1978/9.

3503 Who's Who in France; Dictionnaire Biographique. Paris:
          Jacques Lafitte and the Central European Publishing Co. ,
          1953/4 to date.
Also known as Who's Who in Paris.

3504 Who's Who in the Theatre: A Biographical Record of the Con-
          temporary Stage. London and New York: Pitman, 1925-
          79.

3505 Who's Who in the World. Chicago: Marquis Who's Who, 1971/
          2-1976/7.

3506 Who's Who of American Women. Chicago: Marquis Who's
          Who, 1958/9-1979/80.

3507 "'Why Gregory Peck Chose Eagle Clothes to Wear in 'The
          Man in the Gray Flannel Suit. ' " Photoplay, 49 (4): 71,
          April 1956.
Gregory Peck chose a moderately priced suit, costing $75, well

tailored and of good quality, to fit realistically the role of a rising
executive in "The Man in the Gray Flannel Suit."

3508   "Why Harold Wears Those Nose Things." Screen News, 2 (19):
          28, May 12, 1923.
Harold Lloyd chose to wear glasses in his films as part of his
own style early in his career, and wears them still due to habit
and gratefulness for their part in his success.

3509   "Wide Demand Abroad for American Styles." New York Times,
          August 15, 1937, sec. 3, p.8.
European women's interest in American fashion is increasing
because of motion-picture fashions and the good fit available in
American patterns.

3510   Wilcox, Grace. "Fashions of the Screen." It, 3 (25): 10,
          January 15, 1920.
Descriptions of two negligees worn by May Allison in "Big Game,"
which comprise most of her wardrobe in the film. (Volume and
numbers changed in February 1920, when It merged with Photoplay
Art.)

3511   _____. "Fashions of the Screen." It, 2 (16): 12, August
          15, 1920.
Discussion of a gown to be worn by Margaret Loomis in her next
film.

3512   _____. "Fashions of the Screen." It, 2 (18): 14, Septem-
          ber 11, 1920.
Discussion of a gown worn by Ann Forrest in "The Faith Healer."

3513   _____. "Fashions of the Screen." It, 2 (19): 29, Septem-
          ber 18, 1920.
Discussion of gowns worn by Wanda Hawley in "Food for Scandal,"
one of which she models.

3514   _____. "Fashions of the Screen." It, 2 (20): 12, 28,
          October 2, 1920.
Discussion of gowns worn by Kathlyn Williams in a De Mille film,
"Forbidden Fruit."

3515   _____. "Fashions of the Screen." It, 2 (22): 13, October
          16, 1920.
Discussion of gowns worn by Carmel Myers in "The Orchid,"
one of which she models.

3516   _____. "Fashions of the Screen." It, 3 (25): 12, Novem-
          ber 6, 1920.
Discussion of gowns worn by Margaret Landis in "Harriet and the
Piper," one of which she models.

3517   _____. "Fashions of the Screen." It, 3 (26): 10, Novem-
          ber 13, 1920.

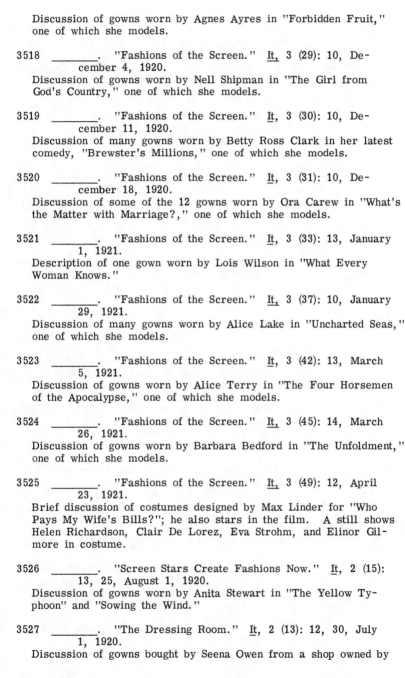

Discussion of gowns worn by Agnes Ayres in "Forbidden Fruit,"
one of which she models.

3518 _____. "Fashions of the Screen." It, 3 (29): 10, De-
        cember 4, 1920.
Discussion of gowns worn by Nell Shipman in "The Girl from
God's Country," one of which she models.

3519 _____. "Fashions of the Screen." It, 3 (30): 10, De-
        cember 11, 1920.
Discussion of many gowns worn by Betty Ross Clark in her latest
comedy, "Brewster's Millions," one of which she models.

3520 _____. "Fashions of the Screen." It, 3 (31): 10, De-
        cember 18, 1920.
Discussion of some of the 12 gowns worn by Ora Carew in "What's
the Matter with Marriage?," one of which she models.

3521 _____. "Fashions of the Screen." It, 3 (33): 13, January
        1, 1921.
Description of one gown worn by Lois Wilson in "What Every
Woman Knows."

3522 _____. "Fashions of the Screen." It, 3 (37): 10, January
        29, 1921.
Discussion of many gowns worn by Alice Lake in "Uncharted Seas,"
one of which she models.

3523 _____. "Fashions of the Screen." It, 3 (42): 13, March
        5, 1921.
Discussion of gowns worn by Alice Terry in "The Four Horsemen
of the Apocalypse," one of which she models.

3524 _____. "Fashions of the Screen." It, 3 (45): 14, March
        26, 1921.
Discussion of gowns worn by Barbara Bedford in "The Unfoldment,"
one of which she models.

3525 _____. "Fashions of the Screen." It, 3 (49): 12, April
        23, 1921.
Brief discussion of costumes designed by Max Linder for "Who
Pays My Wife's Bills?"; he also stars in the film. A still shows
Helen Richardson, Clair De Lorez, Eva Strohm, and Elinor Gil-
more in costume.

3526 _____. "Screen Stars Create Fashions Now." It, 2 (15):
        13, 25, August 1, 1920.
Discussion of gowns worn by Anita Stewart in "The Yellow Typhoon" and "Sowing the Wind."

3527 _____. "The Dressing Room." It, 2 (13): 12, 30, July
        1, 1920.
Discussion of gowns bought by Seena Owen from a shop owned by

Madame Hoffman, who once worked for Lasky studios.

3528 _____. "The Dressing Room." It, 2 (14): 12, 28, July
          15, 1920.
Discussion of gowns worn by Louise Glaum in "Leopard Woman,"
noting that she designs many of her film costumes.

3529 Wilcox, R. [Ruth] Turner. The Mode in Hats and Headdress.
          New York: Scribner's, 1946.
Notes the popularity of the Juliet cap from "Romeo and Juliet"
for evening wear and includes a sketch of the popular Eugenie
hat from "Romance"; both in the 1930s.

3530 "Wilfert, Ingeborg." American Film Institute Catalog, 1961-
          70, p. 698.
Ingeborg Wilfert is credited with the costumes of "The Defector."

3531 "Wilkens, Emily," in Fashion Is Our Business, by Beryl
          Williams [Epstein]. Philadelphia: Lippincott, 1945, p.
          35-52.
Emily Wilkens, children's-fashion designer, was helped considerably in her career when she designed the costumes for a film
starring child actress Ann Todd, though the film was never released.

3532 "Will Screen Portrayal of Girl of 1890 Exert Influence on
          Fashions of Today?" Screen News, 3 (36): 2, September
          6, 1924.
A Hollywood fashion authority, unnamed, believes that Colleen
Moore's 1890s costumes in "So Big" may influence fashion in
small details but not as complete copies.

3533 Willgus, Elizabeth. "For the Modern Miss." Modern Screen,
          26 (4): 71, September 1943.
Virginia Weidler models a costume by Irene from "Best Foot
Forward."

3534 Williams, Louise. "Are You a Velvet or a Calico Girl?"
          Picture Play, 12 (5): 60-1, 80-1, July 1920.
Louise Glaum designed her costumes for "Sex" and many of her
films. She discusses her fashion type, how she selects fabrics
and colors, and other aspects of dress.

3535 _____. "Bebe's Way." Picture Play, 15 (5): 60-1, 103,
          January 1922.
Ethel Chaffin, who supervises 125 women for the Realart and
Players-Lasky costume needs, discusses the appropriateness of
Paris gowns for screen wear, and designing Bebe Daniels's film
costumes, without film titles.

3536 _____. "Flappers--Beware!" Picture Play, 12 (6): 34-5,
          86, August 1920.
May Allison discusses her fashion preferences. She had two

days to buy her seven costumes for "Held in Trust."

3537 _____. "How Clothes Make the Star." Picture Play, 16
          (4): 68-9, 95, June 1922.
Gowns by Madame Frances have helped many actresses in their
rise to stardom, including Corinne Griffith and Norma Talmadge.
Madame Frances has a mansion in New York in which she designs for many film and theatrical performers, and does about
$1 million of business per year. Corinne Griffith models one
gown from "Island Wives."

3538 _____. "Why Bother About Beauty?" Picture Play, 8 (3):
          52-3, 83, November 1920.
Alice Brady models one costume each from "The Dark Lantern"
and "The New York Idea," with a general discussion of her fashion
style and preferences.

3539 Williams, Marion. "What Becomes of Their Clothes?" Photo-
          play, 13 (6): 39-42, May 1918.
Billie Burke, Emmy Whelen, and Alice Brady all give their film
costumes away. Mrs. Sidney Drew and Grace Darmond usually
have their costumes remade or wear as-is in other films. Olga
Petrova, who spends about $40,000 per year on her costumes,
sells them and puts them down as a loss on her income tax; Doris
Kenyon, who wore 90 costumes in a recent serial, remakes them
or gives them away; Pauline Frederick keeps some and gives the
rest away; and Marguerite Clark and Gladys Leslie mostly wear
children's costumes, so they give them to children. Leslie models
an adult gown by Lucile from "The Wooing of Princess Pat," and
Brady models a $900 gown from Bendel, without film title.

3540 "Williams, Peter." American Film Institute Catalog, 1961-70,
          p. 700.
The costumes for "Cinderella" were made from sketches by Peter
Williams.

3541 Williams, Whitney. "Hollywood Newsreel." Hollywood, 27
          (3): 6, March 1938.
In "Marie Antoinette" Norma Shearer wears 34 costumes and had
to endure as much as 12 to 20 hours a week for fittings during
the previous four months.

3542 _____. "If Garbo Wears a Hat." New Movie, 11 (6): 18,
          53-4, June 1935.
Lilly Daché plans to copy some of Travis Banton's hats for
Marlene Dietrich in "The Devil Is a Woman." Exact copies of
period gowns worn in "Little Women" have made their way to the
retail market. Fashion was influences by Kay Francis's backless
gowns in "Jewel Robbery"; Greta Garbo's pillbox hats in "As You
Desire Me"; Marlene Dietrich's boas and feathers in "The Scarlet
Empress"; and Claudette Colbert's turbans, sandals and flowing
gowns in "Cleopatra."

3543 _____. "The New Queen of Fashion in Hollywood." New
Movie, 11 (4): 27, 70, April 1935.
Adolphe Menjou once called Verree Teasdale the "screen's best
dressed woman" and has shared the title himself for actors.
Teasdale was well known in the theater for costumes she herself
designed; she has since married Adolphe Menjou.

3544 _____. "No Glamour for Ginger." Movies, 3 (10): 26-7,
76, April 1940.
Ginger Rogers was "deglamourized" for "The Primrose Path,"
for which her wardrobe cost less than $20.

3545 Wills, Ann. "Accent on Spring." Modern Screen, 16 (6):
98-9, May 1938.
Discussion of costumes worn by Gertrude Niesen and Joan Perry
in "Start Cheering," one of which Perry models; with brief mention of Gail Patrick in "Dangerous to Know."

3546 _____. "College Course in Clothes." Modern Screen, 15
(5): 48-9, 96-7, October 1937.
Discussion of costumes designed by Edith Head and worn by Mary
Carlisle in "Double or Nothing," three of which she models.

3547 _____. "Dressing Your Part." Modern Screen, 18 (4):
48-9, 97-8, March 1939.
Discussion of one costume each worn by Madeleine Carroll in
"Cafe Society" and Rosella Towne in "Adventures of Jane Arden,"
which they model.

3548 _____. "Fall Fashions Forecast." Modern Screen, 15 (4):
40-1, 80-2, September 1937.
Helen Vinson models three of Omar Kiam's costumes for her in
"Vogues of 1938"; she bought the wardrobe for her personal use.
Kiam had been a successful fashion designer in New York when
he left for Hollywood. Rochelle Hudson models one costume
from "She Had to Eat."

3549 _____. "Help Yourself to Style." Modern Screen, 15 (2):
40-1, 82-3, 89-91, July 1937.
Brief mention of one costume each worn by Sally Eilers in "We
Have Our Moments," Ginger Rogers in "Shall We Dance?," and
Doris Nolan in "As Good as Married," and hats worn by Miriam
Hopkins in "The Woman I Love."

3550 _____. "Sentimental Styles." Modern Screen, 18 (6): 48-9,
105-7, May 1939.
The author suggests that the readers follow films rather than
Paris for fashions since film producers prefer to not have their
films dated by extremes of high fashion. The jewelry of "Juarez"
and the costumes of Loretta Young in "Alexander Graham Bell"
are influencing fashion.

3551 _____. "Spring Smartness." Modern Screen, 16 (4): 74,

90, March 1938.
Many costumes worn by Andrea Leeds in "The Goldwyn Follies"
are described, two of which she models. The costumes for her
role as a typical girl can easily be worn and afforded by those
who would like to copy them.

3552   _____. "Summer Starters." Modern Screen, 17 (1): 72,
            79, June 1938.
Includes a discussion of costumes worn by Glenda Farrell in
"Seventh Heaven," two of which she models.

3553   _____. "Swank at Oxford." Modern Screen, 16 (4): 10,
            84-5, March 1938.
Maureen O'Sullivan models two of her 14 costumes from "A Yank
at Oxford," designed by Rene Hubert. Discussion of the above
costumes, and costumes worn by Mary Carlisle in "Hold 'Em
Navy" and Rosalind Russell in "Man-Proof," and hats worn by
Joan Blondell in "The Perfect Specimen." "Snow White and the
Seven Dwarfs" will influence fashion through hats, fabric designs,
and trimmings.

3554   "Wills, Mary." American Film Institute Catalog, 1961-70,
            p. 701.
Mary Wills is credited with the costumes of "Cape Fear" and
"The Wonderful World of the Brothers Grimm."

3555   Willys of Hollywood, as told to Bee Bangs. "Let's Be
            Glamourous!" Movie Show, 5 (7): 58-9, 97-8, March 1947.
Willys discusses, with references to construction and costs, his
hosiery for Alice Faye in "In Old Chicago," Linda Darnell in
"Forever Amber," Gypsy Rose Lee in "Belle of the Yukon,"
Milada Mladova in "Escape Me Never," the chorus girls in "The
Dolly Sisters," Janis Paige in "Cheyenne," Rita Hayworth in
"Down to Earth," Rosalind Russell in "Sister Kenny," Carole
Landis in "One Million B.C.," Marlene Dietrich (with one photo)
in "The Flame of New Orleans," and Barbara Stanwyck in "The
Lady of Burlesque"; also for "The Hunchback of Notre Dame,"
"Stage Door," and "Three Wise Fools"; with photos of Virginia
Welles in "Ladies Man," Jane Wyman in "Magic Town," Karin
Booth in "Unfinished Dance," Lina Romay in "Love Laughs at
Andy Hardy," and Martha Vickers in "Time, Place & Girl."

3556   "Wilmot, Masada." American Film Institute Catalog, 1961-
            70, p. 701.
Masada Wilmot is credited with the women's wardrobe of "Murder
at the Gallop" and the wardrobe of "You Can't Win 'Em All."

3557   Wilson, Elizabeth. "Hollywood Beauties in Corset War!"
            Screenland, 40 (2): 24-7, 70-1, December 1939.
Film actresses are used to enduring torture through historical
costumes with such a fashion accessory as a corset, but most
everyone interviewed, actresses and designers, seemed to hope
that it would not become popular, as a result of "Gone with the Wind."

3558 Wilson, Harry D. "Hollywood's Newest Fad." Motion Picture,
            42 (1): 44-5, 87, August 1931.
      A discussion of the fad for pajamas or pants, which Adrian
      attributes to the influence of films.

3559 "Win a Trip to Hollywood." Photoplay, 51 (5): 72-3, May
            1957.
      A contest to name four costumes from "Designing Woman," de-
      signed by Helen Rose; with prizes, including a visit with Rose
      in her film studio. Two costumes each are modeled by Lauren
      Bacall and Dolores Gray.

3560 "Win This Lovely Frock." Screen Romances, 11 (66): 35,
            October 1934.
      Joan Crawford models a gown from "Chained," to be awarded as
      a contest prize.

3561 Winakor, Bess. "Edith Head Hits Wearing Clothes That Spot-
            light Body's 'Danger Zones.'" Times-Picayune (New
            Orleans), September 29, 1974, sec. 4, p. 10.
      Edith Head notes that 25 years ago stars wore 15- to 20-piece
      wardrobes, but glamour has been replaced by reality. A famous
      star can still create trends and bring back fashions, as with Paul
      Newman and vests worn in "The Sting."

3562 "WINning WARdrobe." Photoplay with Movie Mirror, 24 (1):
            61-3, December 1943.
      Olivia de Havilland models three costumes by Edward Stevenson
      from "Government Girl."

3563 Winship, Mary. "Gloria's Successor." Photoplay, 22 (3):
            31, 111, August 1922.
      Leatrice Joy's being groomed for stardom by Cecil B. De Mille
      included her wearing many pieces of jewelry from his private
      collection, for "Manslaughter." Her costumes for the film cost
      "more than the salary of the president of the United States" and
      included a $32,000 chinchilla coat and an ermine and silver-cloth
      gown.

3564 "Winter, Ingrid." American Film Institute Catalog, 1961-70,
            p. 703.
      Ingrid Winter was the ballet-costume designer of "Captain Sinbad."

3565 "With a Yard of Ribbon and a Little Lace." Hollywood, 18
            (13): 16, December 1929.
      Currently popular brief costumes are modeled, one each, by
      Adrienne Dore from "The Wild Party" and Marguerite Churchill
      from "Seven Faces."

3566 "Witzemann, Wolf." American Film Institute Catalog, 1961-
            70, p. 705.
      Wolf Witzemann is credited with the costumes of "The Elusive
      Corporal."

3567 " 'Wizard' Number Major Problem for Jack Haley." MGM
            Studio News, 6 (22): n.p., August 14, 1939.
Jack Haley's Tin Woodman costume in "The Wizard of Oz" weighed
over 50 pounds, but was specially constructed so that he was able
to dance even though his whole body was enclosed.

3568 Wohlfert, Lee. "What Do Woody, Bob and Diane Have in
            Common? Money, Yes, But Designer Ralph Lauren Too."
            People Weekly, 9 (5): 82-4, February 6, 1978.
Woody Allen and Diane Keaton wore clothes designed by Ralph
Lauren in "Annie Hall," though Keaton also put together her look
with "scraps of antique clothes." One still of Robert Redford in
a Ralph Lauren suit from "The Great Gatsby."

3569 "Wolfe, Bob." American Film Institute Catalog, 1961-70, p.
            705.
Bob Wolfe is credited with the costumes of "Johnny Cool."

3570 "Wolsky, Albert." American Film Institute Catalog, 1961-70,
            p. 706.
Albert Wolsky was the costume designer of "The Heart Is a Lonely
Hunter" and "Where's Poppa?" and is credited with the costumes
of "Popi" and "Loving" and the wardrobe of "Lovers and Other
Strangers."

3571 "Women Need Armor in Marx Pictures." MGM Studio News,
            4 (5): n.p., March 27, 1937.
Esther Muir wore out 14 evening gowns in one week and 12 later
for "A Day at the Races"; they were ruined by paste, water
soaking, and other causes.

3572 "Women Patrons of the Silent Drama...." Screen News, 3
            (19): 4, May 10, 1924, col. 3.
H. M. K. Smith is visiting Paris, where he is studying the latest
fashions.

3573 "Women's Fashions." Hollywood, 26 (7): 38, July 1937.
One costume each is modeled by Anita Louise from "That Certain
Woman" and Bette Davis from "Kid Galahad," both by Orry-Kelly.

3574 Wood, Holly. "Designs on You." Motion Picture, 62 (6):
            40-1, January 1942.
Margaret Sullavan models one coat by Muriel King from "Appointment for Love" and other costumes that may or may not be
from the film.

3575 _____. "Fall Favorites." Motion Picture, 64 (3): 40-1,
            October 1942.
Betty Field models one dress from "Are Husbands Necessary?"

3576 _____. "The Feminine Touch." Motion Picture, 65 (3):
            36-7, April 1943.
Anne Baxter models a playsuit from "Crash Dive."

3577 _____. "Good for the Duration." Motion Picture, 64 (5):
         40-1, December 1942.
    Ann Sheridan models one suit from "George Washington Slept
    Here."

3578 _____. "Junior Miss Glamour." Motion Picture, 63 (2):
         54-5, March 1942.
    Joan Leslie models one dress by Howard Shoup from "The Male
    Animal."

3579 _____. "Spring into Summer." Motion Picture, 65 (2):
         52-3, March 1943.
    Anne Shirley models seven costumes by Adrian from "The Powers
    Girl."

3580 Wood, Yvonne. "Are You the Tailored Type?" Silver Screen,
         18 (1): 50-1, 82-4, November 1947.
    Yvonne Wood discusses designing Ella Raines's costumes in "The
    Senator Was Indiscreet," six of which Raines models; with brief
    mention of her costumes for Gene Tierney in "The Web."

3581 "Wood, Yvonne." American Film Institute Catalog, 1961-70,
         p. 707.
    Yvonne Wood was the costume designer of "Firecreek" and "The
    Good Guys and the Bad Guys" and is credited with the costumes of
    "One-Eyed Jacks," "Duel at Diablo," "Guns for San Sebastian,"
    "The Cheyenne Social Club," and "Dirty Dingus Magee" and the
    wardrobe of "An American Dream" and "The Cool Ones."

3582 Woodmansee, H.A. "Talking Through Their Hats." Motion
         Picture Classic, 27 (1): 63, 81, March 1928.
    Discussion of the more significant styles of men's hats in films,
    and their symbolism, including how the hat is removed or at what
    angle it is worn; with references to Charlie Chaplin, Harold Lloyd,
    Harry Langdon, and Buster Keaton.

3583 "Woollard, Joan." American Film Institute Catalog, 1961-70,
         p. 707.
    Joan Woollard is credited with the costumes of "Leo the Last."

3584 "A Word to the Fashion Wise." Photoplay, 49 (2): 105, Febru-
         ary 1936.
    Adrian has designed a heart-shaped muff of coque feathers with
    matching hat to be worn by an unidentified person or persons in
    "The Great Ziegfeld." In "The Bride Comes Home" Claudette
    Colbert wears a wide pearl-encrusted belt over white satin pajamas,
    designed by Travis Banton.

3585 "Working Girl." Time, 54 (20): 101-2, November 14, 1949.
    Judy Garland was removed from "Annie Get Your Gun," and while
    suspended took a rest and gained needed weight. Her costumes

for her next film, "Summer Stock," were made from her dressform and were then too small; she had not lost the 15 pounds by
the time of rehearsals, prompting a public "spanking" by gossip
columnist Louella O. Parsons.

3586   World of Fashion: People, Places, Resources, by Eleanor
           Lambert.   New York and London: Bowker, 1976.
This resource book and biographical dictionary of fashion notables
has been referred to in this bibliography simply as "World of
Fashion, 1976." Because very many designers are included in
this book, not all of those who have designed for films have been
included, particularly with those who are primarily fashion and
not film designers.

3587   World Who's Who of Women.   Cambridge, England: Melrose,
           1973-8.

3588   "Worner, Dorothy." American Film Institute Catalog, 1961-70,
           p. 708.
Dorothy Worner is credited with the wardrobe of "Catalina Caper."

3589   "Wougher, Roberto." American Film Institute Catalog, 1961-70,
           p. 708.
Roberto Wougher is credited with Glauco Mauri's clothes in "China
Is Near."

3590   "Would You Like to Own Colleen Moore's Bag?" Screenland,
           13 (6): 43, October 1926.
Colleen Moore models a costume from "It Must Be Love"; with a
closeup of her bag, to be given as a costume prize.

3591   Woulfe, Michael.   "Costuming a Film." Films in Review, 6
           (7): 325-7, August/September 1955.
Michael Woulfe discusses designing for modern and period films,
working with a star's personal coloring, the need for research
and authenticity in costuming, and designing for Susan Hayward in
"The Conqueror" (with one still) and for Claudette Colbert in
"Texas Lady."

3592   "Wright, Glen." American Film Institute Catalog, 1961-70,
           p. 709.
Glen Wright is credited with the wardrobe of "The Wild Angels"
and "Hang 'Em High."

3593   "Wright, Joanna." American Film Institute Catalog, 1961-70,
           p. 709.
Joanna Wright is credited with the wardrobe of "Bang! Bang!
You're Dead!" and "Where the Bullets Fly" and the costumes of
"The Bushbaby."

3594   "Wronged by Her Sarong." Screen Guide, 3 (10): 34, Febru-
           ary 1939.
Dorothy Lamour played a semi-autobiographical role in "St. Louis

Blues," in which she tried to get away from "sarong" roles.
Stills include a sarong and period costume worn in the film.

3595 Wyeth, Sandy Brown, and Marc Wanamaker. "Women Behind
the Scenes." Cinema (Beverly Hills), 35: 26-9, 1976.
Brief mention of Edith Head, erroneously credited as the designer
for 202 films (it is almost ten times that), and of Natalie M. Kalmus, Technicolor expert.

3596 "Wyke, Richard." American Film Institute Catalog, 1961-70,
p. 709.
Richard Wyke is credited with the wardrobe of "The Brick Dollhouse."

3597 "Wynigear, Ed." American Film Institute Catalog, 1961-70,
p. 710.
Ed Wynigear is credited with the wardrobe of "Our Man Flint,"
"The Sand Pebbles," "Star!," "Hello, Dolly!," "The Great White
Hope," and "Tora! Tora! Tora!"

3598 Yablonsky, Lewis. <u>George Raft.</u> New York: McGraw-Hill,
1974.
George Raft's extensive wardrobe resulted in his being a trendsetter for many men. The suit he got the most wear out of was
a prison uniform he had made by an exclusive tailor for his many
criminal-role films.

3599 Yaeger, Deborah Sue. "Edith Head Outlasts the Designers'
Era, Still Pleases the Stars." <u>Wall Street Journal,</u>
January 27, 1977, p. 1, 26.
Reminiscences by and biography of Edith Head. Includes com-
ments by designers Dorothy Jeakins, Raoul Pène du Bois, and
Bob Mackie concerning her political acumen and ability as a
costume designer.

3600 "The 'Yankee Doodle Dandy' Girl Poses in Her New 'Young,'
Smart Fall Clothes." <u>Screenland,</u> 46 (1): 56-7, November
1942.
Joan Leslie models one (or more) costume by Orry-Kelly from
"The Hard Way."

3601 "Yelland, Sue." <u>American Film Institute Catalog, 1961-70,</u>
p. 712.
Sue Yelland was the costume designer of "The Walking Stick"
and the dress designer of "The Strange Affair" and is credited
with the costumes of "Secret Ceremony" and the wardrobe of
"Our Mother's House."

3602 Yolanda. "They Can't Be Themselves!" <u>Screen Guide,</u> 6 (5):
36-7, September 1941.
Barbara Stanwyck models five costumes from "You Belong to
Me," and Veronica Lake three from "Sullivan's Travels," both
by Edith Head.

3603 _____. "Women of Hollywood." <u>Screen Guide,</u> 5 (9):
33-5, January 1941.
Discussion of a suit by Irene worn by Carole Lombard in "Mr.
and Mrs. Smith," which she models.

3604 York, Cal. "Cal York's Monthly Broadcast from Hollywood."

Photoplay, 45 (1): 87, December 1933.
Marlene Dietrich's costumes in "The Scarlet Pageant" ("The Scarlet Empress") were all authentically reproduced from portraits and photographs of the period's costumes and were made in duplicate, including the sables.

3605 _____. "Cal York's Monthly Broadcast from Hollywood."
        Photoplay, 45 (3): 126, February 1934.
Travis Banton, having already created a trend for feather-trimmed gowns, intends to include at least one feather-trimmed costume in each of Marlene Dietrich's films, including a gown with curled ostrich plumes for "Catherine the Great" ("The Scarlet Empress"), and in "Shanghai Express."

3606 _____. "Gossip of All the Studios." Photoplay, 35 (5): 48-9, April 1929.
Paul Poiret will soon be spending four months in Hollywood and eight months in Paris each year, as he plans to have an establishment that would sell gowns and other items.

3607 "Yoshida, Yuki." American Film Institute Catalog, 1961-70, p. 713.
Yuki Yoshida is credited with the costumes of "Drylanders."

3608 "You'll Enjoy--'I Love a Soldier.'" Motion Picture, 68 (3): 37, October 1944.
Paulette Goddard wore working-girl clothes for "I Love a Soldier," bought on location in San Francisco where the shipyard workers buy their clothes; with two stills.

3609 "Your Chance to Win a Hollywood-Designed Dress." Photoplay, 40 (4): 56-7, October 1951.
Jane Wyman models a wedding gown from "Here Comes the Groom," with the original sketch by Edith Head.

3610 "Zacha, William T." <u>American Film Institute Catalog, 1961-</u>
       <u>70</u>, p. 715.
William T. Zacha is credited with the wardrobe of "Looking for
Love" and the costumes of "Sam Whiskey."

3611 "Zalabery, Hanny." <u>American Film Institute Catalog, 1961-70,</u>
       p. 715.
Hanny Zalabery is credited with the wardrobe of "Journey to the
Seventh Planet."

3612 "Zamora, José." <u>American Film Institute Catalog, 1961-70,</u>
       p. 715.
José Zamora is credited with the costumes of "The Castilian."

3613 "Zanetti, A. Danilo." <u>American Film Institute Catalog, 1961-</u>
       <u>70</u>, p. 715.
A. Danilo Zanetti is credited with the costumes of "The Christmas
That Almost Wasn't."

3614 "Zarate, Laure de." <u>American Film Institute Catalog, 1961-</u>
       <u>-70</u>, p. 716.
Laure de Zarate was the costume designer of "Battle of the Bulge"
and "Custer of the West," and is credited with the costumes of
"Crack in the World" and "Krakatoa, East of Java."

3615 "Zastupnevich, Paul." <u>American Film Institute Catalog, 1961-</u>
       <u>70</u>, p. 716.
Paul Zastupnevich was the costume designer of "Voyage to the
Bottom of the Sea" and "Five Weeks in a Balloon."

3616 "Zay, Jean." <u>American Film Institute Catalog, 1961-70,</u> p.
       716.
Jean Zay is credited with the costumes of "Is Paris Burning?"
and "Weekend at Dunkirk" and the wardrobe of "The Train" and
"The Lady in the Car with Glasses and a Gun."

3617 "Zay, Léon." <u>American Film Institute Catalog, 1961-70,</u> p.
       716.
Léon Zay is credited with the costumes of "Lafayette" and "Weekend
at Dunkirk."

3618 Zeitlin, Ida. "Catching Up with Norma Shearer." Motion
    Picture, 56 (2): 24-5, 54, September 1938.
Norma Shearer discusses some problems in the filming of "Marie
Antoinette," including running down a flight of stairs in her heavi-
est dress. The problem of being able to hold onto the skirt,
petticoats, and hoops was solved by passing ribbon loops through
each layer.

3619 _____. "Screen Specialists ... Woman Makes the Clothes."
    Modern Screen, 23 (5): 50-1, October 1941.
Discussion of Edith Head's early life and how she designs for
films with a staff of up to 300 persons. She designs all the
fabrics and designs for everyone except the extras.

3620 _____. "Venus in Blue-Jeans." Modern Screen, 38 (4):
    44-5, 88-91, March 1949.
Ava Gardner loved Irene's period costumes for her in "The Great
Sinner," which required a corset that cinched her waist to 21
inches, but she prefers skirts and sweaters.

3621 Zetter, Gwen, as told to Eric L. Ergenbright. "Hollywood's
    Most Successful Extra." New Movie, 11 (5): 18, 52-3,
    May 1935.
Gwen Zetter discusses her successful lifestyle as a dress extra,
for which she must have an extensive modern wardrobe. She
was told that she had to spend about $2,000 for her wardrobe,
which she has amassed for less by designing and sewing. Each
gown costs her about $20 or less, and she spends about $25 per
month for her wardrobe needs.

3622 "Ziegfeld Follies." Motion Picture, 70 (1): 54, August 1945.
75 additional seamstresses made the 400 costumes for principals
and extras in "Ziegfeld Follies."

3623 Zierold, Norman. Sex Goddesses of the Silent Screen.
    Chicago: Regnery, 1973.
Gloria Swanson was not included in this book because she was a
"clotheshorse"; the sex goddesses included wore as few clothes
as possible. For "The Merry Widow" Mae Murray visited Vienna,
where she studied "each detail of dress." Repeats the same inaccuracy as Murray's biographer, Jane Ardmore, in crediting
Adrian as a "young Syrian" designer Murray selected in New
York to design her costumes for "The Merry Widow." Clara
Bow once said that a prime consideration in the films chosen for
her was how quickly she could be undressed. Bow's bust grew
to reflect the changing mode, as in "Hoopla" and "Call Her Savage." Pola Negri wore her own costly jewels in her films and
had designed her own costumes for her German films. Her reputation for being temperamental was not diminished when she
attacked director Ernst Lubitsch because he complained of her
wearing pants instead of a skirt for a sequence as Carmen (in
"Carmen," a German film, 1918). Her wardrobe mistress at
Paramount was Agnes Grunstrom. Theda Bara's trademark cos-

tume included bronze spangles, low necklines, veils and shawls, and satin or sheer fabrics. Her roles were researched for authenticity in libraries and with authorities. For "Cleopatra" (1917) she spent weeks in the Egyptian wing of the Metropolitan Museum of Art and designed many of her costumes. Her contract required that her features be entirely covered when she went to the costumer. Later the torn clothes she wore in "Kathleen Mavourneen," copied after Mary Pickford's, could not help her faltering career. Brief mention of false publicity stories concerning the jewelry she wore in "Sin."

3624 "Zinn, Pat." American Film Institute Catalog, 1961-70, p. 718.
Pat Zinn is credited with the wardrobe of "Wild in the Streets."

3625 "Zippers Speed Period." MGM Studio News, 5 (6): n.p., August 15, 1938.
Marie Antoinette often required five hours to dress, but Norma Shearer, in the title role of "Marie Antoinette," was able to dress in "five minutes" with the aid of hooks, snaps, and zippers.

3626 "Zipprodt, Patricia." American Film Institute Catalog, 1961-70, p. 718.
Patricia Zipprodt is credited with the costumes of "The Graduate" and "The Last of the Mobile Hotshots."

3627 "Zipprodt, Patricia." Who's Who in America. 38th ed., 1974-5, p. 3414.

Abar-Baranovskaya, Mayya, 1
Abbey, Elinor, 749
"Abie's Irish Rose," 1492
"About Face," 400
"Abraham," 185, 186, 1278
"Abraham Lincoln," 1535, 2808
Academy Awards, 251, 277, 279,
    383, 545, 671, 673, 1227, 1353,
    1402, 1552, 1598, 1652, 1734,
    1811, 1816, 2286, 1835a, 2803,
    2810, 2881, 3059, 3122, 3126,
    3131, 3274, 3377, 3489
"Accident," 758
"Accused, The," 1330
"Ace High," 1071
Acker Valentino, Jean, 322
"Acquitted," 1812, 1926
"Across the Bridge," 1289
"Across the Pacific," 296, 1513
"Act of the Heart," 2342
"Act One," 602
"Ada," 2809
Adair, Maudine, 8
"Adam and Evil," 1480
"Adam at 6 A.M.," 3178
Adams, Claire, 570
Adams, Dell, 9
Adams, Joy, 3074
"Adam's Rib," 640, 2669, 3167, 3232
Adamson, Betty, 12, 2377
"Adding Machine, The," 958
"Adios Gringo," 2015
Adolpho, 2163
"Adorable," 2170
"Adorable Julia," 3372
Adoree, Renée, 417, 926, 1174,
    1175, 2960, 3077, 3254
Adrian (Adrian Adolph Greenburg),
    3, 14, 15, 16, 17, 18, 19, 20,
    21, 22, 23, 24, 25, 26, 27, 28,

29, 30, 31, 32, 33, 34, 35, 36,
37, 38, 39, 40, 41, 42, 43, 44,
45, 46, 47, 48, 49, 50, 84, 100,
158, 163, 211, 232, 310, 316,
344, 366, 388, 421, 423, 429, 440,
478, 479, 545, 549, 550, 554, 556,
562, 643, 679, 696, 697, 698, 699,
700, 701, 735, 737, 748, 773, 816,
822, 824, 882, 947, 954, 965, 969,
971, 979, 992, 1003, 1010, 1022,
1025, 1030, 1044, 1046, 1067,
1074, 1087, 1088, 1198, 1206,
1211, 1239, 1268, 1280, 1286,
1295, 1296, 1317, 1318, 1381, 1385,
1389, 1411, 1420, 1426, 1444, 1445,
1456, 1460, 1461, 1522, 1546, 1566,
1613, 1681, 1695, 1696, 1697, 1713,
1750, 1757, 1766, 1785, 1796, 1823,
1825, 1826, 1830, 1835a, 1849, 1854,
1891, 1901, 1913, 1923, 1928, 1930,
1932, 1933, 1934, 1940, 1979, 2002,
2023, 2024, 2028, 2043, 2075, 2083,
2116, 2117, 2143, 2181, 2185, 2195,
2143, 2181, 2185, 2195, 2205, 2214,
2220, 2261, 2264, 2271, 2275, 2282,
2333, 2352, 2403, 2414, 2435, 2446,
2447, 2455, 2459, 2468, 2469, 2470,
2476, 2478, 2523, 2527, 2530, 2543,
2552, 2653, 2694, 2697, 2704, 2712,
2722, 2725, 2757, 2763, 2763, 2783,
2874, 2886, 2896, 2922, 2923, 2954,
2958, 2959, 2966, 2984, 3006, 3014,
3026, 3037, 3078, 3102, 3104, 3106,
3156, 3164, 3183, 3194, 3199, 3231,
3235, 3249, 3251, 3292, 3296, 3336,
3388, 3402, 3406, 3424, 3488, 3500,
3558, 3579, 3584, 3623
Advance Pattern Company, 1402
"Advance to the Rear," 224, 2657
"Adventures, The," 2340

"Adventures of Ali Baba, The," 2628

"Adventures of Don Juan, The," 679, 3274

"Adventures of Prince Courageous, The," 1812

"Adventures of Robin Hood, The," 692, 751, 1420, 1458

"Advice to the Lovelorn," 2416

"Advise and Consent," 404, 1304, 1634, 2337, 3247

"Affair in Trinidad," 1654

"Affairs of Anatol, The," 3216, 3498

"Affairs of Aphrodite, The," 1068

"Affairs of Susan, The," 52, 1326, 1452

"Africa Erotica," 1562

"Africa--Texas Style!," 1883

"After Midnight," 1480

"After School Days," 2551

"After You, Comrade," 3079

"Afterwards," 2424

Aga, Francois Nazare, 1083, 2364

"Against Tomorrow," 1573

"Age of Innocence, The," 2640

"Age of Youth," 533

Aghayan, Ray, 56, 57, 58, 1878, 1892

Agnes, 314

"Agony and the Ecstasy, The," 481, 1391, 2163, 2225

"Aigle à Deux Têtes, L'," 1414

Aimee, Anouk, 2964

"Air Hostess," 1926

"Air Patrol," 3178

"Airport," 1402, 1591, 3131, 3418

"Airport '75," 1335, 2855

"Airport 1977," 829

"Airport 79: The Concorde," 548

Alan, Geoffrey, 62

"Alaskan, The," 1108

Alberghetti, Anna Maria, 2667

Albert, Eddie, 2377

Albray, Maurice, 67

Aldredge, Theoni V., 69, 70, 71, 72, 162, 1748

Aldrich, Georganne, 73

Aldridge, Katherine, 2921, 3405

Aleksandrova, Ye., 75

"Alex in Wonderland," 3420

Alexander, Angela, 76

Alexander, Jane, 2964

Alexander, Katharine, 1425

"Alexander Graham Bell," 3550

"Alexander Hamilton," 2994

"Alexander's Ragtime Band," 2539

"Alfie," 273

Alford, Vi, 77

"Alfred the Great," 2771

"Algiers," 3091

"Ali Baba and the Forty Thieves," 3381

"Alias Mary Dow," 2023

"Alice's Restaurant," 615

"Alien," 552

"Alimony," 1208

"Alimony Annie," 1824

"All About Eve," 526, 679, 713, 1744

"All at Sea," 1091

"All Men Are Enemies," 2420

"All Neat in Black Stockings," 2097

"All of Me," 2177, 2417, 3452

"All the Lovin' Kinfolk," 1790

"All These Women," 1893

"All This, and Heaven Too," 2262

Allan, Geoff, 229

Allbritton, Louise, 3057

Allen, Elizabeth, 7, 1913, 2528, 2628

Allen, Gracie, 1912, 2990

Allen, Judith, 1935

Allen, Woody, 3568

Allison, May, 660, 1309, 2172, 3422, 3470, 3510, 3536

Allyson, June, 1221, 1337, 2506, 2590, 2806, 3487

Almine, 80

"Almost an Angel," 1079

"Almost Angels," 264

Alpert, Jerry, 81

"Alphabet Murders, The," 88

"Altars of Desire," 2732, 3289

Altieri, Ezio, 82

Altman, I., 83

"Alvarez Kelly," 1844

"Always Goodbye," 2464, 2465, 3091

"Always Together," 3273

Alyn, Kirk, 2377, 3098

Amador, Charles 1843

"Amants de Vérone, Les," 996

"Amazing Howard Hughes, The," 797

"Ambition," 854

"Ambushers, The," 492

"America America," 1573

"American Dream, An," 2302, 3581

American Freedom Train, 2664

"American in Paris, An," 390, 1652, 2286, 2964, 2965

American Maid Shop, 1930

"American Tragedy, An,", 2386,

2388
"American Venus, The," 3335
Ames, Adrienne, 727, 1927, 1930, 1932, 2389, 2393, 2401, 2407, 2411, 2420, 2762
"Amiche, Le," 1061
Amies, Hardy, 54, 86, 87, 88, 89, 1135
"Amorous Adventures of Moll Flanders, The," 374, 1259, 1717
"Anatomy of a Murder," 1241
"Anchors Aweigh," 673
" ... And Now Miguel," 2132
"And Now Tomorrow," 91, 3210
"And So to Bed," 2944
Andersen, Elga, 1016
Anderson, John A., 92
Anderson, Judith, 1022
Anderson, Milo, 94, 289, 670, 692, 977, 1008, 1044, 1411, 1513, 2042, 2073, 2114, 2195, 2482, 2490, 2493, 2571, 3488
Anderson, Sara, 96
Andre, 97
André-Ani, 98, 99, 178, 547, 946, 2250, 2732
Andree, Lona, 2410
Andress, Ursula, 283, 1061, 1107, 2693
Andrews, Julie, 379, 383, 642, 775, 875, 1349, 1400, 1584, 1831, 2628
Andrzejewski, Jean Marie, 101
"Andy," 2831
Anemoyannis, George, 102
Angel, Heather, 1931, 1935, 2413, 2416, 2420
Angel, Jack, 105
"Angel," 1211, 1749, 2451, 2453, 2529, 2530, 3182
"Angel, Angel, Down We Go," 634, 1889, 2300
"Angel Face Molly," 3175
"Angel in My Pocket," 1488
"Angel Levine, The," 2798
"Angel Unchained," 2799
"Angel with the Trumpet, The," 1114
"Angeles de la Tierra" (see "Angels Wash Their Faces")
"Angels Wash Their Faces," 2039
"Animal Kingdom, The," 1234, 1927, 2404, 3171
animal skins (leather and others), 161, 295, 640, 903, 1966, 2200, 2545, 2669, 2961, 3167, 3173, 3464
"Ann Carver's Profession," 1931, 2763

Ann-Margret, 1213, 1878, 2163
"Anna and the King of Siam," 675
"Anna Christie," 3163
"Anna Karenina" (1935), 19, 37, 47, 228, 1411, 1869, 2023, 2024, 2116, 2435, 2523, 3156, 3292
"Anna Karenina" (1947), 228, 898, 1266, 3076, 3362
"Anna Lucasta," 1968
"Anna, My Darling," 3263
Annabella, 1482, 2536
"Annabelle Takes a Tour," 1182
Annamode, 107
"Anne Boleyn" (see "Deception" [1920])
"Anne of the Thousand Days," 169, 1764
"Années Follies, Les," 356
Annenkov, Georges, 108
"Annie Get Your Gun," 3585
"Annie Hall," 68, 553, 2377, 3568
"Annie Oakley," 1870
"Anniversary, The," 1158
"Another Dawn," 1067
Ansell, Gail, 110
"Anthony Adverse," 112, 113, 1267
"Antigone," 102
Antoinette, Madame, 3170
Antonelli, A., 115
Antonelli, Franco, 116
"Antony and Cleopatra," 1391
"Anything Goes," 1312, 1678, 1814
"Anzio," 1006, 2362
"Apache Gold," 2347
"Apache Rifles," 736
"Apache Uprising," 475, 2889
"Apartment in Moscow," 425
"Aphrodite," 405, 3318
Aplin, Charlie (see Amador, Charles)
Appel, Wendy, 117
"Applause," 1342
"Appointment, The," 1151
"Appointment for Love," 3574
"April Fools, The," 820, 2383, 3214
"April in Paris," 2614
"April Showers," 1799
"Arabella," 2423
"Arabesque," 805
Arbuckle, Fatty, 106, 916, 1843
Arbuthnot, Molly, 119
"Arch, The," 1783
"Arch of Triumph, The," 1326
Arden, Eve, 1241, 1510, 2113, 3273
"Are Husbands Necessary?," 2475, 3575
"Are Wives to Blame," 1309
"Are You a Failure?," 3309a

"Are You Listening?," 2397
Argüello, Luis, 122
"Arizona Express, The," 2291
"Arizona Raiders," 803
"Arizona to Broadway," 2763
Armand, Edward, 124, 3285
Armand, Jean-Marie, 125
armor (including chain mail), 227,
    266, 388, 502, 692, 762, 1106,
    1113, 1136, 1391, 1458, 1512,
    1756, 1784, 1789, 1892, 2091,
    2099, 2144, 3118, 3360, 3414,
    3457
"Arms and the Man," 2639
Armstrong, John, 3439
Armstrong, Tony, 126
Armstrong Boutique, Tony, 127
"Arnelo Affair, The," 2113
Arnold, Edward, 1864, 3238
Arnold, Harry, 266
"Around the World in 80 Days,"
    605
"Arrangement, The," 526, 3327
Arrico, Charles, 130
"Arrivederci, Baby!," 374, 1259
"Arsene Lupin," 2395
"Art of Love, The," 56, 1567,
    2779
Arthur, Jean, 1268, 1413, 1927,
    2345, 2421, 2438, 2448, 2471,
    2484, 2524, 2549
"Artists and Models," 320, 2455,
    2630, 2917, 2961
"Artists and Models Abroad," 275,
    550, 991, 2542, 2544
"As Good as Married," 3549
"As Husbands Go," 2416
"As You Desire Me," 33, 616,
    1273, 1385, 2397, 2398, 2399,
    2899, 3542
"As Young as You Feel," 398
"Ashes and Diamonds," 558
"Ashes of Vengeance," 1457, 1782,
    2978, 3242, 3472
Ashley, Elizabeth, 379
Ashman, Gene, 139
Ashton, Sylvia, 2860
"Assassination Bureau, The," 743
"Assault on a Queen," 62
"Assignment K," 326, 1322
Associated Costumers (see also
    Western Costume Company), 1579,
    3391
Associated Motion Picture Costumers
    (AFL Local 18067) (see also unions),
    912
Astaire, Fred, 140, 500, 551, 603,
    1654, 1907, 2664, 3232

Astor, Gertrude, 2103
Astor, Mary, 1513, 1527, 1970, 2397,
    3470, 3477
"At First Sight," 121
"At Sword's Point," 679
"At the End of the World," 2777,
    2778
Athena, 146
"Atlas," 626
"Atlas Against Cyclops," 2325
"Atom Man vs. Superman," 2377
"Attack on the Iron Coast," 375
Attenborough, Richard, 711
auctions of film costumes, 597, 691,
    719, 826, 944, 1286, 1421, 1660,
    1830, 1892, 2884, 3014, 3419, 3469
Audran, Stephane, 337, 805
Augerot, Claire, 3449
Aulin, Ewa, 1060, 3245
"Auntie Mame," 188, 1619, 2214,
    2285, 2843, 3275
Auriol, Jean George, 132
Austin, William, 2960
Autant-Lara, Claude, 132, 150,
    2825, 3336
Autre, Tanine, 151
Autry, Gene, 1013
"Avalanche," 994
"Avenger, The," 918
"Aventures du Roi Pausole, Les,"
    3342
Avery, Charlie, 1843
"Awful Truth, The," 551, 2076,
    2133, 3102
Ayres, Agnes, 460, 564, 2360,
    3517
Azevedo, Tereza, 154

"B.F.'s Daughter," 1815
"B.S. I Love You," 3420
Baburina, N., 159
"Baby Doll," 896, 1573
"Baby Face," 2764
"Baby Love," 1321
"Baby Maker, The," 2767
"Baby Take a Bow," 2423
Bacall, Lauren, 860, 1342, 2183,
    2807, 2808, 3559
"Bacchanale," 276
"Bachelor and the Bobby-Soxer,
    The," 291
"Bachelor Apartments," 2044
"Bachelor Bait," 2425
"Bachelor in Paradise," 2809
"Back Street," (1932), 2398

"Backbone," 429
Baclanova, Olga, 2960
"Bad and the Beautiful, The," 2810
"Bad Girl," 2389
"Bad One, The," 2274
Baer, Jack, 1660
Baer, Virginia, 160
Bailey, Pearl, 2964
Baiza, Libertad de, 165
Bake, Hartmut, 166
Baker, Carroll, 172, 515, 896, 2025
Baker, Hylan, 168
Baker, Ivy, 169
Baker, Josephine, 478
Balanchine, George, 1760
Balchus, Frank, 179
Baldassarre, Clara, 1485
Balenciaga, 171
Balestra, 172
Balfour, Betty, 209
Balkan, Adele, 173
Ball, Lucille, 95, 152, 192, 526,
  547, 555, 1011, 1097, 1182, 1437,
  1510, 1510, 1561, 1661, 1971,
  2109, 2287, 2430, 2569, 2579,
  2990, 3139, 3232
"Ball of Fire," 883
"Ballad of a Hussar, The," 1663
"Ballad of Cable Hogue, The,"
  1048
Ballard, Lucinda, 174, 175, 176,
  177, 799, 898
Ballerino, Louella, 178
Ballin, Hugo, 428, 1649
Ballin, Mabel, 428
Balmain, Pierre, 179, 180, 181,
  182, 183, 184, 898, 3071
Balzac, Jeanne, 514
Bamberger, Rudolph, 2825
"Bamse," 1739, 2880
"Bandit of Sherwood Forest,
  The," 2785
"Bandits of Orgosolo," 477
"Bang! Bang! You're Dead!,"
  3593
Bankhead, Tallulah, 2352, 2389,
  2395, 2403, 3183
Banks, Edgar James, Ph.d.,
  185, 186, 1278
Banks, Seth, 187
Banky, Vilma, 3455
Banton, Travis, 16, 188, 189,
  190, 191, 192, 193, 194, 195,
  196, 197, 198, 211, 308, 311,
  312, 351, 365, 366, 423, 465,
  537, 545, 549, 550, 556, 561,
  608, 674, 675, 698, 714, 732,
  766, 817, 822, 857, 917, 984,

997, 1007, 1035, 1046, 1067, 1118,
  1198, 1211, 1231, 1267, 1268, 1273,
  1294, 1297, 1305, 1353, 1394, 1397,
  1411, 1419, 1455, 1463, 1487, 1491,
  1492, 1493, 1666, 1696, 1697, 1711,
  1757, 1823, 1835a, 1870, 1912,
  1927, 1928, 1929, 1930, 1931, 1935,
  1963, 1964, 1979, 2023, 2024, 2066,
  2083, 2109, 2117, 2170, 2181, 2191,
  2192, 2194, 2195, 2214, 2352, 2376,
  2403, 2403, 2405, 2406, 2407, 2408,
  2409, 2410, 2411, 2412, 2413, 2414,
  2415, 2416, 2417, 2418, 2420, 2424,
  2427, 2428, 2432, 2439, 2441, 2442,
  2444, 2449, 2451, 2452, 2453, 2456,
  2460, 2480, 2521, 2522, 2523, 2526,
  2529, 2530, 2532, 2548, 2558, 2567,
  2640, 2704, 2717, 2757, 2783, 2791,
  2842, 2843, 2917, 2924, 2929, 2934,
  3006, 3085, 3164, 3182, 3188, 3208,
  3227, 3250, 3251, 3264, 3275, 3409,
  3423, 3488, 3491, 3542, 3584, 3605
Banucha, Jan, 199
Bara, Theda, 351, 406, 755, 1415,
  1446, 1482, 3115, 3623
"Barabbas," 761
"Barbarella," 1062, 1992, 2689
"Barbarian, The," 2170, 2409
"Barbary Coast," 883
Barbier, George, 203, 777, 1711,
  1721, 3014, 3456
Bardon, Henry, 204, 205
Bardot, Brigitte, 1925, 2066
Bari, Lynn, 370, 1043, 3091
Barnes, Binnie, 1686, 2023, 3090,
  3091
Barnes, Gloria, 207
Barnes, Leah, 229
Barneys Inc., 2377
Barondess, Barbara (see also Mac-
  Lean, Barbara Barondess),
  2406
"Baroness and the Butler, The,"
  2536
"Barquero," 919, 2378, 2383
Barrett, Alan, 208
"Barretts of Wimpole Street, The"
  (1934), 562
Barrie, Elaine, 2989
Barrie, Mona, 584, 1429, 2834,
  2835
Barrie, Scott, 210
Barrie, Wendy, 584, 1719, 1870,
  1912
Barriscale, Bessie, 2228, 2904
Barrymore, Ethel, 158, 439
Barrymore, John, 248, 672, 1702,
  1779, 1897, 3196, 3455

Barthelmess, Richard, 1649
Barthes, Roland, 213
Barthet, Jean, 214
Barto, Pat, 215, 678
Bartolini Salimbeni, Giancarlo, 216
"Bathing Girl Revue," 2243
bathing suits, 103, 137, 262, 263,
     388, 438, 500, 501, 570, 762,
     813, 875, 904, 1338, 1402, 1536,
     1571, 1728, 1838, 2023, 2057,
     2066, 2243, 2263, 2460, 2502,
     2587, 2724, 2794, 2907, 2946,
     2947, 3144, 3351, 3415
Bathsheba, 219
"Batman," 215, 1620
"Battle at Bloody Beach," 2254
"Battle Beyond the Sun," 1187
"Battle Cry of Peace, The," 3040
"Battle of the Bulge," 3614
"Battle of the Villa Fiorita, The,"
     302, 2675
"Battling Butler," 2049
Baudot, Colette, 221
Baum, L. Frank, 1286, 1450
Baxter, Anne, 550, 679, 1416,
     2612, 3576
Baxter, Jane, 312
Baxter, Warner, 981
Bayance, Rita, 222
Baykova, L., 223
Bayless, Luster, 224
Bayne, Beverly, 855, 1466
"Be Yourself!," 2274
"Beach Ball," 630, 2724
"Beach Party," 3454
"Beach Red," 431
Bear, Jack, 226
"Beast of Blood," 2870
Beatles, The, 2026
Beaton, Cecil, 149, 167, 228, 229,
     230, 231, 232, 233, 234, 235,
     237, 238, 239, 240, 241, 242,
     243, 244, 245, 246, 247, 898,
     1088, 1266, 1314, 1323, 1416,
     1446, 1835a, 2028, 2628, 2727,
     3074, 3076, 3207, 3362
Beaton, Mary, 2440
Beatty, Ned, 2377
Beatty, Warren, 3029
"Beau Brummell" (1924), 248,
     672
"Beau Geste" (1926), 296, 385
Beaumont, Frances, 2294, 2295
"Beauty and the Beast" (c.1916),
     905a
"Beauty and the Beast, The" (1947)
     ("Belle et la Bête, La"), 273,
     453, 601, 1314, 1495, 2193
"Beauty and the Boss," 2396

"Beauty for the Asking," 2546
"Beauty Prize, The," 137
"Bebo's Girl," 1001
Beck, Ray, 162
Beck, Ron, 252
"Becket," 723
"Beckoning Roads," 2228
"Becky Sharp," 261, 2731
"Bed of Roses," 1932, 2496, 2763
"Bedazzled," 2121, 2737
Bedelia, Bonnie, 1762
"Bedevilled," 550
Bedford, Barbara, 3524
"Bedtime for Bonzo," 2510
"Bedtime Story" (1941), 993, 3232
"Bedtime Story, A," 1929, 1930
Beecher, Janet, 3449
Beer, Vivian, 254
Beery, Noah, 3483
Beery, Wallace, 138, 255
Beetson, Frank, Jr., 256
Beetson, Frank, Sr., 257
"Before Midnight," 2416
"Before the Fact," 1953
"Before Winter Comes," 354
"Behold a Pale Horse," 374, 1259
"Behold We Live," 2177, 3453
Bei, Leo, 264
Bel Geddes, Barbara, 3140
Belew, Bill, 265
"Bell Jar, The," 548
"Bella Donna," 131, 1238, 2646,
     3048, 3472
Bellamy, Madge, 2381, 3309a
Bellamy, Ralph, 551
"Belle de Jour," 2222, 2863
"Belle et la Bête, La" (see "Beauty
     and the Beast, The," [1947])
"Belle of the Nineties," 1482, 2192,
     2424, 3497
"Belle of the Yukon," 269, 3169,
     3555
Belloni, Nanda, 270
"Bells of St. Mary's, The," 675
Belmont, Mrs. Morgan, 1175
"Beloved Enemy," 2525
belts, 14, 502, 681, 737, 786,
     1907, 2066, 2167, 2260, 3264,
     3584
"Ben-Hur" (1925), 926, 1082, 1421,
     1610, 3077, 3402
"Ben-Hur" (1959), 1391, 3207, 3414
Bendel, Henri, 1174, 1175, 2205
Bendel's, 3539
"Beneath the Planet of the Apes,"
     1254
"Benjamin," 222
Bennett, Belle, 268
Bennett, Constance, 13, 46, 398,

659, 662, 816, 1007, 1042, 1056,
1182, 1231, 1403, 1425, 1926,
1928, 1932, 2352, 2360, 2387,
2388, 2400, 2406, 2535, 2621,
2763, 2764, 3111, 3450, 3469
Bennett, Enid, 528, 915
Bennett, Joan, 321, 526, 981, 991,
1380, 1383, 1870, 1910, 1912,
1955, 2115, 2133, 2159, 2399,
2454, 2467, 2531, 2542, 2544,
2558, 2594, 2763, 2916, 2921,
2961, 3087, 3364
Benny, Jack, 754, 857
Benson, John Brock, 276
Bentley, Irene, 2414
Berankova, Anna, 278
Bérard, Christian, 273, 453, 601,
996, 1314, 1495, 1957
Bergdorf Goodman, 547, 2183,
2287
Bergen, Polly, 2601, 2604
"Bergkatze, Die" (see "Mountain
Cat, The")
Bergman, C. F., 3446
Bergman, Ingrid, 499, 675, 805,
820, 1021, 1326, 1481, 1512,
1857, 1892, 2761
Bergner, Elizabeth, 1685
Berman, David, 280
Berman, Wally, 281
Berman's, 282, 711
Bermans & Nathans Ltd., 2377
Berman's & Sons, 260
Berman's of London, 260, 283
Berne, Israel, 285
Bernhardt, Sarah, 1719
Bernstein, Aline, 78, 766,
1643
Berselli, Adriana, 287
"Berserk," 2908, 3231
Berst, J.A., 815
Best, Marjorie, 292, 671, 2509
"Best Foot Forward," 3533
"Best House in London, The,"
326
"Best in Life, The," 2812, 2813
"Best of Enemies, The," 508,
1098
"Best Years of Our Lives, The,"
883, 2967
Betrue, Gloria, 293
"Better a Widow," 287, 510,
3253, 3256, 3373
"Between Two Women," 1981
Beuf, Colonel, 1224
"Beverly of Graustark," 1247,
3008
"Beware of Children," 910

"Beware of Pity," 3076
"Beyond Control," 1704
"Beyond the Rainbow," 2066
"Beyond the Rocks," 1191
"Beyond the Valley of the Dolls,"
1319
Bibas, 297
"Bible ... In the Beginning, The,"
761, 1061, 1594, 3248
"Bible, The" (see "Bible ... In the
Beginning, The")
"Biches, Les," 67
Bickford, Charles, 3360
"Big Bounce, The," 216
"Big Broadcast, The," 2401
"Big Broadcast of 1936, The," 5,
1912
"Big Broadcast of 1937, The,"
2444
"Big Broadcast of 1938, The," 778,
2535
"Big Business Girl," 1699
"Big City," 1979
"Big Country, The," 896
"Big Cube, The," 3273
"Big Daddy," 1908
"Big Executive, The," 1933
"Big Fix, The," 788
"Big Game," 3510
"Big Gundown, The," 3023
"Big Little Person, The," 1784,
2237
"Big Mouth, The," 3338
"Big Parade, The," 417, 512
"Big Shore Leave," 2105
"Big Sleep, The," 860
"Big Steal, The," 1796
"Big Town Girl," 942, 2458
"Big Trail, The," 2088
"Big Wave, The," 2128, 3284
"Bigfoot," 3018
"Biggest Bundle of Them All, The,"
2887
Biki of Milano, 302
Bilabel, Barbara, 303
"Bill of Divorcement, A," 2401,
2487
"Billie," 81, 2995
Billings, Florence, 658
"Billion Dollar Brain," 357, 1213,
1764
"Billion Dollar Scandal," 2405
"Billy Rose's Diamond Horseshoe,"
485, 1184
Binner, Madame Rosa, 55, 2265
Bird, Adelia, 807
"Bird of Paradise," 2512, 2596
"Bird with the Crystal Plumage, The,"
2011

"Birds, The," 2779
"Birds Do It," 1669, 2314, 3028
"Birds, the Bees, and the Italians, The," 2876
"Birth of a Nation, The," 296, 645, 1175
"Bishop Murder Case, The," 1091
"Bishop's Wife, The," 2561, 2966
Bisset, Jacqueline, 820, 875
"Bitter Sweet," 542, 1088, 1697
"Bitter Victory," 1330, 2575, 2578
Black, Karen, 162, 713, 1335, 1748
"Black Bart," 3285
"Black Hole, The," 552
"Black Klansman, The," 474
"Black Legion, The," 3416
"Black Moon," 2423
"Black Narcissus," 1362
"Black Orange Blossoms," 2763
"Black Oxen," 647, 3472
"Black Sabbath," 1222
"Black Shield of Falworth, The," 2518
"Black Sunday," 1222
"Black Tights," 587, 2863, 3382
"Black Vanities," 245
"Black Zoo," 2976
"Blackhawk," 3098
Blackton, J. Stuart, 3034
Blackton, Paula, 3040
Blaine, Madame, 325
Blaine, Vivian, 1214
Blair, Janet, 250, 3085
Blake, Yvonne, 326, 1202, 2377
Blane, Sally, 2389, 2416
Blass, Bill, 100, 351, 2723, 3247
"Blessed Event," 2399
"Blind Bargain, A," 407
"Blindfold," 668, 1288, 2871
Bliss, Bert, 331
"Bliss of Mrs. Blossom, The," 2771
"Blonde Bombshell, The," 16
"Blonde Venus," 439, 1394, 2957
Blondell, Joan, 485, 754, 1022, 1660, 2105, 2405, 2456, 2537, 2762, 3450, 3553
"Blondie Johnson," 2405
"Blondie of the Follies," 1247, 2954
"Blood," 210
"Blood and Roses," 932
"Blood and Sand" (1922), 332, 502, 528, 682, 1283, 2697, 2884, 3014, 3320, 3384

"Blood and Sand" (1941), 3164
"Blood Demon, The," 2347
"Blood of Dracula's Castle," 2963
"Bloody Mama," 668
Bloom, Claire, 1112, 2628, 2680
Blossom, Rose, 2292, 2293
"Blow-Up," 273, 364, 2771
"Blue," 1692
"Blue Angel, The" (1930), 1718
"Blue Dahlia, The," 1324, 1326, 1348
"Blue Lagoon," 1992
"Blue Max, The," 1015, 1107
"Blue Skies," 1324
"Bluebeard's Eighth Wife," 608, 1190, 2460, 2532, 2535, 2929, 3423
"Bluebird, The," 334, 1332, 1336
"Bluff," 460
Blyth, Ann, 335, 1251, 2101, 2587, 2592, 3466
Blythe, Betty, 388, 826, 870, 2051, 2621
Boardman, Eleanor, 544, 907, 2001, 2621
"Boatniks, The," 3180
"Bobo, The," 287, 2078
"Body and Soul" (1927), 1480
"Body and Soul" (1947), 1624
Boehm, Werner, 336
"Bofors Gun, The," 1883
Bohan, Marc, 337, 338, 339, 340, 805, 1618
"Bohème, La" (1925), 417, 926, 1174, 1175, 3077, 3254
"Bohème, La" (1965), 932
"Bolero," 2117, 2418, 2419, 3450, 3496
Bolger, Ray, 1286
Bolkan, Florinda, 1060, 3245, 3253
Bolongaro, Massimo, 341
"Bolshoi Ballet 67," 725, 2852
Bon Ton of New York, 850
Bond, Brenda, 2290, 2291
Bond, Janice, 342
Bond, Lilian, 1930, 2175, 2405
"Bond Boy, The," 973, 978, 3220
Bonnay, Yvette, 343
"Bonne Soupe, La," 67
"Bonnie and Clyde," 478, 526, 819, 1011, 1051, 1097, 1446, 1618, 1660, 1762, 2368, 2855, 3218, 3327
Bono, Cher (see Cher)
Bono, Sonny, 464
Bonwit Teller, 2263, 2664
"Boom!," 1322, 2139, 3256

Boone, Pat, 785
Boop, Betty, 3025
Booth, Edwina, 1823, 1916
Booth, May, 345
"Bora Bora," 563
Borden, Olive, 1035
"Borderland," 147
Bordoni, Irene, 3081, 3399
Borio, Josephine, 2960
"Born Reckless," 2018
"Born Rich," 657, 2301, 3155, 3472
"Born to Be Bad," 2416
"Born to Love," 3469
Borque, Ralph, 346
"Borsalino," 1062, 2020, 2223, 2855
Bos, Jerry, 347
Boss, Reeder, 348
"Boston Strangler, The," 875, 3273
"Botany Bay," 1846
Botti, Sartoria Sorelle, 349
Bottoms, Joseph, 552
"Bottoms Up," 2043, 2419
"Boudoir Diplomat, The," 2250
"Bought," 2388
Boume, Whitney, 3089
Bourman, Einar, 350
Bow, Clara, 220, 1234, 1275, 1399, 1492, 1536, 1926, 2066, 2920, 2952, 3466, 3469, 3623
Bowers, John, 1875
Box, Brian, 352
Boxer, John, 353
"Boy ... A Girl, A," 771
"Boy, Did I Get a Wrong Number!," 350, 387
"Boy Friend, The," 1213, 3412
"Boy Who Caught a Crook, The," 3134
Boyce, Eddie, 354
Boyd, Betty, 1065
Boyd, Stephen, 1322, 1888, 2629
Boyd, William, 1013
Boyer, Charles, 631, 1766
"Boyfriend, The," 1840
"Boys in the Band," 1720
"Boys' Night Out," 2224
"Boys of Paul Street, The," 2894
Bradley, Grace, 778
Bradna, Olympe, 817, 2526
Brady, Alice, 1859, 1932, 3099, 3448, 3538, 3539
Brady, John, 357

"Brain, The," 151
"Brainstorm," 358, 1716
"Brainwashed," 3165
Brandi, Rose, 358
Brandley, Majo, 359
Brando, Marlon, 1338, 2184, 2276, 2368, 2377, 3233
Brandt, John, 360
"Brass Bottle, The," 1488
brassieres, 696, 797, 870, 947, 1093, 1142, 1198, 1263, 1394, 1414, 1654, 1686, 1849, 2664, 3218, 3232, 3247
"Brat, The," 2387
Brawd, Rose, 361
Brdecka, Jirí, 362
"Bread," 3166
"Break of Hearts," 313, 329, 2023
"Breakfast at Tiffany's," 1178, 1454, 3280
"Breakfast for Two," 2133
Breamer, Sylvia, 618, 1516, 2031, 3172
"Breath of Scandal" (1924), 2621
Breed, Jackie, 364
Breen, Joseph, 588
Bremer, Lucille, 673, 1795, 2105
Brennan, Walter, 883
Brenner, Albert, 367
Brenon, Herbert, 613
Brent, Evelyn, 1065, 1588, 2216, 2296, 2980
Breslave, Maurice, 2020
"Brewster McCloud," 101, 922, 2878
"Brewster's Millions" (1920), 3519
Brian, Marian, 2399
Brian, Mary, 385, 691, 2792
Brice, Fanny, 1645
Brichetto, Bice, 372
"Brick Dollhouse, The," 3596
"Bridal Suite," 2474
"Bride Comes Home, The," 1493, 2376, 3584
"Bride of Vengeance," 550, 1846
"Bride Wore Boots, The," 2107
"Bride Wore Red, The," 1749, 1979, 2020
"Brides of Fu Manchu, The," 1321
Bridge, Joan, 228, 374, 3414
"Bridge at Remagen, The," 170
"Bridge of San Luis Rey, The," 370
"Bridge over the River Kwai," 1414
"Bridges at Toko-Ri, The," 1678, 2794
"Brief Moment," 2412
"Brigadoon," 2517

"Bright Shawl, The," 832, 1174
Brighton, Billy, 377
"Bringing Up Baby," 2459, 2548
"Broadway," 1065, 1977
"Broadway After Dark," 654
Broadway and Hollywood (Sharaff), 2964, 2966
"Broadway Bad," 2406, 2762
"Broadway Bill," 2426
"Broadway Melody, The," 1812, 3400
"Broadway Melody of 1936," 1914
"Broadway Serenade," 1860
"Broadway Thru a Keyhole," 2415
"Broken Barriers," 657
"Broken Blossoms," 1176
"Broken Coin, The," 1622
"Broken Land, The," 1166, 3178
Bron, Eleanor, 2121
"Bronco Buster," 2606
Bronson, Betty, 613, 691, 823, 2124, 2359
Brooks, Donald, 379, 380, 381, 382, 383, 548, 642, 1584, 2059, 2993, 3420
Brooks, Jane, 384
Brooks, Leslie, 1807
Brooks, Louise, 2072
Brooks Costume Co., 2205
"Brother Orchid," 2485
"Brother Rat and a Baby," 2482
"Brotherhood, The," 2071
"Brotherly Love," 12, 326, 1091
Brown, Betty, 405
Brown, Clarence, 388
Brown, Irene, 1823
Brown, Joe E., 843
Brown, Morris, 387
Brown, Pamela, 1112
Brown, Strelsa, 3074
Browning, Ricou, 3466
Bruce, Virginia, 315, 1067, 1913, 2039, 2465, 2467, 2530, 2546, 3090
Brunette, Fritzi, 989, 2230
Bruno, Richard, 403
"Brushfire!," 695
"Brute and the Beast, The," 1177
"Brute Force," 1251
Bryan, Jane, 2475, 2482
Bryce, Hope, 404, 1241
Brymer, 1267
Brynner, Yul, 679, 2200, 2964
Bryson, Winifred, 514
"Buccaneer, The," 976, 1391, 3238
Bucknall, Nathalie, 953

"Buckskin," 2126, 3127
"Buddenbrooks," 2304, 2639
"Buddha," 2137
Budz, Frank R., 409
Bulgarelli, Enzo, 410
"Bulldog Drummond," 2159
"Bullet for a Badman," 124
"Bullet for Pretty Boy, A," 2911
"Bullet for Sandoval, A," 2363
"Bullet for the General, A," 477
"Bullitt," 1761, 3327
Bullock's Wilshire (see also Irene [of Bullock's Wilshire]), 909, 1522
"Bunny Lake Is Missing," 404
"Buona Sera, Mrs. Campbell," 1254
Burberry, 3264
Bürger, Hildegard, 412
Burgess, Dorothy, 2423
Burk, 966
Burke, Billie, 1117, 1218, 1286, 1849, 1870, 1910, 2124, 2414, 2423, 2474, 2521, 2640, 3451, 3539
Burke, Kathleen, 1928
"Burlesque," 1492
Burlison, Heather, 415
"Burn!," 477, 1151
"Burn, Witch, Burn," 784
Burne, Nancy, 2371
Burnett, Carol, 1851
"Burning Sands," 528
Burns, L. L., 3463
Burns, Lou, 1441
Burns, Paul, 416
Burrows, Rosemary, 418
Burton, Richard, 1060, 3245
Burza, Norman, 419
"Bus Riley's Back in Town," 2827
"Bus Stop," 1789
Busch, Mae, 104, 1885, 3166
"Bushbaby, The," 3593
Bushman, Francis X., 1082
bustles (see petticoats)
"Butch Cassidy and the Sundance Kid," 890, 1336
Butler, Forrest T., 422
Butt, Clara, 1812
"Butterfield 8," 1829, 2808
buttons, 54, 953, 1812, 2268
Buzina, N., 424
"By Candlelight," 1425
"By Right of Purchase," 1794
"Bye Bye Birdie," 215, 678
Bykhovskaya, M., 425
Bylek, Rudolph, 528
Byrne, Kiki, 426, 427

"C. C. and Company," 2963
Caan, James, 2803
"Cabaret," 2855
"Cabinet of Caligari, The," 1559,
    1844
"Cabinet of Dr. Caligari, The,"
    2901
Cabrera, Vicente, 431
Cacoyannis, Michael, 432
"Cactus Flower," 3338
"Caesar and Cleopatra," 466, 749,
    898, 1362, 2003
"Caesar the Conqueror," 2322
"Caesar's Wife," 669
"Cafe Metropole," 1996, 2450,
    2528
"Cafe Society," 3547
Caffin, Yvonne, 433
Cagney, James, 843
"Cain and Mabel," 1294
Caine, Irene, 435
Caine, Michael, 273
Calder, Bob, 436
Calder, Magg, 437
"California," 3046
California Museum of Science and
    Industry, 480, 1312
"Californian, The," 2266, 3250
"Call Girls of Frankfurt," 3146
"Call Her Savage," 1234, 1926,
    3623
"Call It a Day," 2450, 2528
"Call Me Madam," 1283
"Callahans and the Murphys, The,"
    1480
"Calling Dr. Kildare," 1689
Calvert, Phyllis, 1088, 3076
Calvet, Corinne, 1221
Calvin, Peggy, 2454, 2916
"Camelot," 1051, 1211, 1789, 3283
"Camille" (1921), 405, 1784,
    3384, 3456
"Camille" (1936), 17, 535, 536,
    789, 944, 1215, 1416, 2327,
    2447, 2523, 2783
"Camille 2000," 2854
Campbell, Alex, 1241
Campbell, Louise, 1354
"Campus Flirt, The," 691
"Can Heironymus Merkin Ever
    Forget Mercy Humppe and
    Find True Happiness?," 2859
"Canadians, The," 1620
"Can-Can," 779, 1917, 2964
"Candy," 1060, 2854, 3245,
    3361
"Cannon for Cordoba," 2938
"Can't Help Singing," 134, 1653

"Cantena de Hollywood, La" (see
    "Hollywood Canteen")
Cantrell, Rebecca, 447
Cantway, Maxine, 2179
"Cape Fear," 3554
Capel, Fred, 447
"Caper of the Golden Bulls, The,"
    1888
capes, 129, 295, 315, 681, 1302,
    1418, 1503, 1547, 1564/5, 1775,
    1784, 2023, 2082, 2377, 2443,
    2523, 2848, 2979, 3071, 3096,
    3172, 3320
Capezio, 2723
"Caprice," 56
"Capricious Summer," 802
"Captain Hates the Sea, The," 2428
"Captain Macklin," 1174
"Captain Nemo and the Underwater
    City," 1735
"Captain Newman, M.D.," 1581
"Captain Sazarac," 296
"Captain Sinbad," 1321, 2146, 3564
"Captive, The," 1638
"Capture, The," 2584
Capucci, Roberto, 448
Capucine, 1917, 2863
Cardi, Gloria, 450
Cardin, Pierre, 273, 451, 452,
    453, 454, 455, 456, 457, 1314,
    1495, 2081
"Cardinal, The," 379, 383, 404,
    615, 1594, 1634, 2321
Cardinale, Claudia, 2761, 2863
Cardinale, Frank, 458
career, film costume as a, 471,
    472, 504, 752, 766, 975, 1228,
    1342, 1489, 1490, 1574, 1750,
    1791, 2215, 2807, 2877, 3198,
    3207, 3385, 3386
"Carefree," 2466, 2541, 2548
"Caretakers, The," 1371
Carew, Ora, 2103, 2104, 3520
Carlisle, Kitty, 2192, 2428
Carlisle, Mary, 2422, 2917, 3448,
    3546, 3553
"Carmen" (1918), 131, 469, 3623
"Carmen" (1970), 3382
"Carmen, Baby," 1668
Carnegie, Hattie, 317, 423, 461,
    462, 698, 816, 917, 1809, 1811,
    2076, 2206, 2664, 2843
Carol, Cindy, 1061
Carol, Martine, 565, 996
Carol, Sue, 823, 1916
Carolyn Modes, 1419
Caron, Leslie, 233, 390, 678,
    1652, 2863, 2964, 3076

"Carousel," 3370
"Carpetbaggers, The," 2629, 2888, 3127
Carpio, Roberto, 463
Carroll, Gordon, 552
Carroll, Madeleine, 312, 314, 2455, 2475, 2481, 2527, 2553, 3547
Carroll, Nancy, 1492, 1827, 1926, 2404, 2405, 2409, 2762, 3401
Carroll, Vana, 474
Carroll, Veda, 475
Carroll and Co., 473
"Carry on Cabby," 910
"Carry on Constable," 1764, 1883
"Carry on Regardless," 910, 1883
Carteney, Marilu, 477
"Carthage in Flames," 607
Cartier's, 162, 875, 1748, 2377
Carver, Kathryn, 1101
"Casanova," 2825
"Casanova '70," 107, 624
"Casanova's Big Night," 1846, 3285
"Case Against Mrs. Ames, The," 314
Casey, Gertrude, 482
"Casey at the Bat," 3477
Cashin, Bonnie, 483, 484, 485, 486. 487, 488, 489, 490, 491, 675, 766, 975, 1170, 1184, 2183, 2367, 2563
"Casino Royale," 273, 283
Cassinelli, Dolores, 2622
Cassini, Oleg, 272, 492, 493, 494, 495, 496, 497, 498, 1507, 1919, 3247, 3447
"Castilian, The," 3612
Castillo (Antonio), 499, 1707, 2193
Castle, Irene, 129, 236, 500, 703, 2950
Castle, Vernon, 500
"Castle, The," 303
"Castle Keep," 1062, 1949
"Cat, The," 899
"Cat and the Canary," 2475
"Cat on a Hot Tin Roof," 2808, 2992
"Cat People, The," 2028
Catalina, 501
"Catalina," 813
"Catalina Caper," 3588
"Catch 22," 3101
"Catch Us if You Can," 1543
Catesby, Sir William, 1112
Catherine, 503
"Catherine the Great," 329, 1473
"Cat's Pajamas, The," 691

Caudrelier, Lily, 505
"Caught in the Draft," 2075
"Caught Short," 1091
Caulfield, Joan, 394, 397, 675, 895, 2280, 2488, 2495, 2589, 2651
"Cavalcade," 439, 1823
Cavalieri, Lina, 206
"Cavalleria Rusticana," 724
Cavanagh, John, 506
Cawley, Olive, 3405
Cecchi, Dario, 508
Cecil Beaton's Fair Lady (Beaton), 229, 234, 2727
Cellier, Antoinette, 2792
censorship of costumes, 220, 438, 556, 588, 737, 1142, 1338, 1718, 1808, 2243, 2338, 2907, 2964, 2966, 3025, 3045, 3126
"Central Airport," 2406
"Centurion, The," 1169
Ceraceni, 510
"Certified," 2538
Chadwick, Helene, 137, 1365, 1366, 1367
Chaffin, Ethel, 405, 460, 511, 512, 528, 824, 935, 1092, 1310, 2778, 3011, 3535
"Chained," 211, 701, 882, 2923, 3156, 3560
"Chairman, The," 880, 2187
Chalif, S. L., 513
"Chamade, La," 2863
Chamberlain, Richard, 1213, 1840
"Champagne Murders, The," 67
"Champagne Waltz," 817, 1964, 2449, 3227
"Champion," 2492, 2577
Chandler, Helen, 1928, 2413
Chanel (Gabrielle), 220, 232, 330, 414, 423, 516, 517, 518, 698, 871, 947, 1029, 1121, 1258, 1380, 1383, 1850, 2098, 2279, 2388, 2640, 2843
Chaney, Lon (Senior), 1906, 3309, 3466
"Change of Habit," 345
"Change of Mind," 110
Chaplin, Charlie, 388, 519, 916, 1258, 1302, 1484, 1843, 2247, 3582
Chaplin, Charlie, Jr., 1843
Chaplin, Geraldine, 1416, 2163
Chapman, Ceil, 520, 521
Chapman, Marguerite, 442, 1807, 1808
"Chapman Report, The," 678, 2281
"Chappaqua," 2945

"Chapter II," 100
"Charade," 1178
"Charge of the Light Brigade, The" (1936), 2524
"Charge of the Light Brigade, The" (1968), 3387
Charisse, Cyd, 349, 2499, 2517, 2808
"Charley's Aunt," 754, 857
"Charlie Bubbles," 326
"Charlie Chan in Eqypt," 1915
"Charlie Chan in London," 2426
"Charlie Chan's Courage," 2424
"Charlie Chan's Greatest Case," 1935, 2413
"Charly," 2831
Chase, Edna Woolman, 527
Chase, Ilka, 988, 1327, 2174
"Chase, The," 820, 2288
"Chastity," 1320
Chatterton, Ruth, 306, 1470, 1697, 2352, 2396, 2399, 2444, 2521, 2925, 2994, 3400
"Che Guevara, El," 1995
"Cheaper to Marry," 51, 824, 1998
"Cheat, The," 3472
"Cheaters, The," 805, 1364, 1990, 3358
"Checkerboard," 1156
"Cheech and Chong Go Hollyweed," 552
"Chelkash," 725
Cheltenham High School, 27, 36, 344
Chepurko, A., 533
Cher, 464
Cherrill, Virginia, 2387, 3495
Cheruit, 983
Chevalier, Maurice, 233
Chevret, Lita, 2387
"Cheyenne," 3555
"Cheyenne Autumn," 257, 2357
"Cheyenne Social Club, The," 3581
Chiari, Maurizio, 534
"Chickie," 662, 1731
Chikovani, Mikhail, 557
"Child of Manhattan," 1926, 2405
"Children of Dust," 2919
"Children of Pleasure," 2399
"Children's Hour, The," 435, 3127
Chiles, Lois, 162, 1416, 1748
"China," 1021
"China Is Near," 3589
"China Syndrome, The," 3041
"Chinatown," 713

"Chink and the Child, The," 1175
"Chisum," 224, 1304
"Chitty Chitty Bang Bang," 374, 1259
Chodorowicz, Katarzyna, 558
Chojkowska, Wieslawa, 559
Chombert, 1213
Christian, Mrs., 1812
Christianson, Wilma, 1489
Christie, Al, 769
Christie, Julie, 2078, 2142, 2163, 2803
Christine, 560
"Christine of the Hungry Heart," 672
"Christmas in Connecticut," 289
"Christmas That Almost Wasn't, The," 3613
"Christopher Strong," 2024, 2406, 2407, 2729, 2762
"Chronicle of Anna Magdalena Bach," 481, 2086, 2645
"Chubasco," 3052
"Churchill, Marguerite, 2416, 2953, 3565
Cicoletti, Piero, 563
"Cid, El," 607, 1391, 2063, 3207
"Cigarette Girl," 1807
"Cimarron," 562, 1892, 2024, 2640
"Cincinnati Kid, The," 820
"Cinderella" (1900), 2901
"Cinderella" (1961), 3540
"Cinderella" (1966), 3369
"Cinderfella," 2667
Cinema Fashions, 3238
Cinema Mercantile Company (or Corporation), 266, 2882
Cinema Modes, 3238
Cinema Shop, 807, 2685, 3450, 3452, 3453
"Circe the Enchantress," 2621, 3479
"Circle, The," 512
"Circle of Deception," 910
"Circle of Love," 814
"Circus Queen Murder, The," 2409
"Circus World," 2739
"Citizen Kane," 547
"City Lights," 1258
"City of Flowers," 675
"City of Lost Men," 2480
Clair, Ethlyn, 1065
Claire, Ina, 1380, 1383, 1686
Claire, Phyllis, 2527
Clairval, Laurence, 574
"Clairvoyant, The," 312, 2914
"Clambake," 1863

Clare and Deborah, 1382
Clark, Betty Ross, 3519
Clark, Buddy, 576
Clark, Edith, 577
Clark, Gilbert (or Clarke), 385,
  578, 750, 1072, 1194, 1231,
  2098, 2205, 3335
Clark, Louise, 1212
Clark, Marguerite, 3539
Clark, Ossie, 579
Clarke, Mae, 1915, 1926, 1930,
  2023, 2391, 2396, 2398, 2407
Clarke, Vanessa, 580
"Classified," 3010
"Classmates," 660
"Claudia," 636
Clave, Antoni, 587
Clayburgh, Jill, 145, 1333
Clayton, Ethel, 936, 3196
Clayton, Marguerite, 1733
"Clear All Wives," 1930
"Clear Skies," 2361
"Cleo from 5 to 7," 940, 2875
"Cleopatra" (1917), 1415, 3623
"Cleopatra" (1934), 472, 550,
  1749, 2122, 2194, 2425, 2934,
  3491, 3493, 3542
"Cleopatra" (1963), 1446, 1494,
  1833, 2225, 2368, 2629, 2739,
  2907, 2964, 2966, 2968, 3020
"Cleopatra's Daughter," 216
Clifford, Ruth, 973, 978, 2382,
  2845, 2846, 2847, 2848
"Climax, The," 2876
"Clive of India," 1007, 1628
Clive of London, 589
"Clock, The," 2862
"Cloportes," 1997
"Closely Watched Trains," 802
"Clown and the Kid, The," 899,
  1983
"Clue of the Twisted Candle,"
  1157
Cluett, Mrs., 2783
"Cluny Brown," 675
"Coal Miner's Daughter," 548
"Coast of Skeletons," 1016
Cobb, Lee J., 1437
"Cobra," 32, 2697, 2783, 3384
Coburn, James, 1958
"Cockeyed Cavaliers," 3261
"Cocktail Hour," 1930, 1932,
  2410
"Cocoanut Grove," 3091
Cocteau, Jean, 601, 1314,
  2193
Cody, Lew, 209
Coffin, Gene, 602

Cohen, Shura, 604
Cohn, Harry, 1811, 2843, 3232
Colasanti, Veniero, 607, 3207
Colbert, Claudette, 211, 275, 344, 550,
  585, 586, 596, 608, 674, 754, 846,
  1067, 1206, 1297, 1318, 1354, 1493,
  1497, 1749, 1806, 1823, 1928, 1935,
  1979, 2169, 2194, 2376, 2412, 2413,
  2415, 2425, 2426, 2427, 2428, 2432,
  2452, 2460, 2473, 2521, 2522, 2524,
  2529, 2532, 2535, 2544, 2562, 2917,
  2929, 2934, 3067, 3182, 3287, 3423,
  3450, 3491, 3495, 3542, 3584, 3591
Colby, Anita, 609, 1688, 3234
"Cold Deck, The," 1303
Cole, Elizabeth, 610
Cole, Grover, 611
"Collector, The," 77, 1949,
"Colleen," 1696
"College," 2049
"College Holiday," 2448, 2526
"College Humor," 2410
"College Scandal," 2756
Collins, Chris, 614
Collins, Harry, 2950, 3006
Collins, Joan, 1917
Collins, May, 2102
Collyer June, 2416, 3395
Colman, Ronald, 3455
"Color Me Dead," 415
"Colossus of Rhodes, The," 2822
Colt, Alvin, 621, 622, 623
"Colt .45," 2504
Coltellacci, Giulio, 624
Colvig, Helen, 625, 2628
"Comancheros, The," 292
"Come One, Come All!," 726
"Come September," 1254
"Come Spy with Me," 73
Comeau, Barbara, 626
"Comedians, The," 3256
"Comedy of Terrors, The," 81
"Comic, The," 3338
"Coming Apart," 740
"Coming of Amos, The," 1505, 3483
"Coming Out Party," 1429, 2418
Comingore, Dorothy, 547
"Common Law, The," 2387
"Company of Killers," 2022
"Company She Keeps, The," 2511
Compson, Betty, 295, 531, 660, 824,
  2290, 2359, 2622, 2668, 2778
Compton, Juliette, 2395
Compton, Sharon, 630
"Computer Wore Tennis Shoes, The,"
  3180
"Comrade X," 944, 1413, 3264
"Concubines, The," 3257

"Condemned," 3399

"Condemned of Altona, The," 2636

"Coney Island," 389, 1214, 2808

"Confessions of a Queen," 512, 1875

"Confessions of an Opium Eater," 2976, 3441

"Confidential Agent," 631

"Congress Dances, The," 2665

"Conjugal Bed, The," 1937

"Connection, The," 2071

Connelly, Glenn, 633

Connely, Renee, 634

Connery, Sean, 1202

Connolly, Sybil, 635

"Conquering Power, The," 2237, 2697

"Conqueror, The," 3285, 3591

"Conqueror Worm," 3237

"Conquerors, The," 439

"Conquest" (1928), 1822

"Conquest" (1937), 944, 950, 953, 1766, 1835a, 1979

"Constant Nymph, The," 366

"Constantine and the Cross," 216

"Convention City," 2177

"Convict Stage," 707

"Convicts 4," 1308, 2976, 3440

Coogan, Jackie, 1539, 1540, 1904

Cook, Diane, 2703

"Cool Ones, The," 2302, 3581

Cooper, Gary, 66, 538, 817, 875, 1835a, 3164, 3360, 3423

Cooper, Gladys, 229

Cooper, Miriam, 645

copyright of costumes, 1311, 3366

"Coquette," 1233, 3005, 3400

Corklin, Peggy, 942

"Corn Is Green, The," 649

Cornejo, Humberto, 650

Cornelius, Marjory, 651

Cornwell, O'Kane, 652, 1649

"Corporate Queen, The," 276

"Corpse of Beverly Hills, The," 1412

"Corrupt Ones, The," 2944

corsets (see also girdles), 55, 120, 261, 269, 389, 839, 857, 870, 1024, 1033, 1044, 1263, 1589, 1737, 1849, 2265, 2267, 2664, 2808, 3148, 3162, 3254, 3294, 3557, 3620

Corso, Marjorie, 653

Cort, Bud, 922

Corteny, Marilu, 663

Cortés, Antonio, 664

"Cosí Fan Tutte," 3033

"Cossacks, The," 2960

Costanzi, Elio, 665

Coste, Christiane, 667

Costello, Dolores, 1731, 2371, 2389, 2442, 3455, 3477

Costich, Thomas, 668

Costume Design in the Movies (Leese), 549, 564, 824, 979, 1734, 2637, 2964

Costume Designers Guild (see also unions), 554, 1660, 1791, 2637

Costume Designers Guild Award, 1880

Costume Institute (see Metropolitan Museum of Art, Costume Institute)

Costume Museum (see also Metropolitan Museum of Art, Costume Institute), 1643

Costumers' Research Group, 3323

"Cottonpickin' Chickenpickers," 1873

Coulter, Lucia, 684, 1174, 1175, 1225, 1632, 2215

"Count Yorga, Vampire," 3150

"Counterpoint," 2022

"Country Girl," 3435

"Country Wife, The," 1345

Courcelles, Christiane, 685

Courtenay, Tom, 1137

Courtot, Marguerite, 1469

"Courtship of Eddie's Father, The," 2809

"Cover Girl," 556, 1688, 3232

"Cover Me Babe," 1655, 3392

Coward, Noel, 1322

"Cowboy and the Lady, The," 1182

"Cowboys, The," 1660

Cox, Brian, 688

Cox, David, 689, 1926, 2404, 2783

"Crack in the World," 3614

Craig, Marla, 694

"Craig's Wife," 2445

Crain, Jeanne, 398, 485, 2515

Cramer, Claire, 695

"Crash, The," 2994

"Crash Dive," 3576

Crawford, Joan, 14, 16, 23, 40, 44, 50, 90, 100, 158, 211, 232, 310, 313, 421, 465, 478, 554, 556, 616, 643, 696, 697, 699, 700, 701, 735, 882, 947, 971, 1067, 1198, 1206, 1211, 1268, 1273, 1295, 1296, 1318, 1381, 1385, 1398, 1413, 1418, 1422, 1460, 1564/5, 1566, 1674, 1696, 1713, 1749, 1796, 1869, 1872, 1928. 1933, 1935, 1968, 1979, 2020, 2023, 2024, 2043, 2170,

2333, 2352, 2386, 2392, 2397,
2435, 2446, 2459, 2476, 2523,
2524, 2527, 2543, 2552, 2619,
2661, 2704, 2712, 2762, 2763,
2896, 2923, 2954, 2994, 3015,
3037, 3078, 3102, 3156, 3183,
3199, 3231, 3469, 3497, 3560
"Crazy Paradise," 2760, 3068
"Crazy Quilt," 1282
"Creature from the Black Lagoon,"
   3466
Creed, Charles, 947
"Crime Doctor, The," 3451
"Crime Does Not Pay," 3382
"Crime of Passion," 3046
"Crime of the Century, The,"
   2406
"Criminal Code, The," 1779
"Crimson Challenge," 2219
"Crimson Cult, The," 3069
"Cromwell," 2225
Crosby, Bing, 1338, 3217
"Cross and the Switchblade, The,"
   3062
"Crowd Roars, The," 3092
Crowley, Rose, 2406
"Crown of Lies, The," 1505
"Crucial Test, The," 1996
"Crusades, The," 312, 786, 1912,
   2023, 2023, 2024, 3360
"Cry Double Cross," 1943, 2905,
   3165
"Cry for Happy," 1656
"Cry of Battle," 2869
"Cry of the Banshee," 1786
"Cry Wolf!," 1326
"Cucaracha, La," 261
Cukor, George, 693, 789, 1681,
   3232
Cummings, Constance,, 2402, 2405,
   2415, 2932, 3451, 3453
Cummings, Dorothy, 824
Cummings, Patrick, 707
Cummins, Jackie, 708
Cunard, Grace, 1622, 2297
Cunningham, Cecil, 817
"Curly," 3085
"Curly Top," 709, 801, 2430
"Curse of Her Flesh, The," 2119
"Curse of the Mummy's Tomb,
   The," 12, 375
Curtis, Mary Ann, 712
Curtis, Tony, 273, 875, 1482
Curtiz, Michael, 696, 697, 3231
"Custer of the West," 3614
"Cycle Savages, The," 1580
"Cytherea," 659, 1056

Dabney, Virginia, 795
Daché, Lilly, 714, 715, 716, 717,
   718, 2526, 2631, 2708, 3542
"Daddies," 1947
"Daddy, Darling," 3128
"Daddy Long Legs" (1931), 2783
"Daddy's Gone A-Hunting" (1969),
   3273
Dagenais, Mlle., 2980
Dahl, Arlene, 393
Dahlke, Edith, 720
Dahlman, Rynol, 721
"Daisies," 278
Daley, Alice, 1814
D'Algy, Helena, 3303
Dallot, Mlle. Henriette, 3009
Dalton, Bill (see Eltinge, Julian)
Dalton, Dorothy, 2219, 3161, 3221
Dalton, Phyllis, 723, 2144
Daltry, Roger, 1213, 1840
Damiani, Luciano, 724
Damita, Lili, 329, 719, 1775,
   2403, 2994
"Damn Yankees," 886, 887
"Damned, The," 118, 819, 1618,
   1762, 1975, 2855, 2895, 3240
"Damon and Pythias," 287
Dana, Muriel Frances, 2130
Dana, Viola, 137, 599, 1622, 2360,
   2627, 3350, 3351, 3352, 3353,
   3354, 3355, 3356
"Dance Madness," 926, 2732, 3077
"Dancer of Paris, The," 1731
"Dancers in the Dark," 2395
"Dancing Co-Ed," 3288
"Dancing Lady," 1933, 1935, 2043,
   2704
"Dancing Mothers," 2920
Danduryan, A., 725
"Dandy in Aspic, A," 12, 451
"Danger: Diabolik," 1151, 1937
"Dangerous," 1695
"Dangerous Age, The," 135, 892,
   893, 894, 973, 978, 1369, 2382,
   2845, 2846, 2847, 2848
"Dangerous Brunette," 2396
"Dangerous Maid, The," 1898
"Dangerous Money," 2622
"Dangerous Moonlight," 3076
"Dangerous to Know," 3545
"Dangerously Yours," 1929, 2406,
   2407
Daniel, Viora, 1092
Danielle, 726
Daniels, Anthony, 3113
Daniels, Bebe, 658, 691, 777,
   1134, 1653, 1930, 1932, 2124,

2172, 2233, 2251, 2385, 2410,
2622, 2950, 3216, 3401, 3535
Daniels, Hugh,   998
"Danish Blue,"   923
"Dante's Inferno,"   1915
Darby, Kim,   1339
Darcy, Georgine,   3200
Darieux, Robert,   731
"Daring Young Man, The,"   1915,
2023
"Dark Angel,"   312
"Dark City,"   2507
"Dark Corner, The,"   733
"Dark Intruder,"   753
"Dark Lantern, The,"   3538
"Dark Mirror, The,"   2967
"Dark Passage,"   2183
"Dark Purpose,"   172
"Dark Victory,"   2366, 2550
"Darker Than Amber,"   1669
"Darling,"   273, 2163, 2803
"Darling Lili,"   226, 379, 383,
1400, 1831
Darmond, Grace,   3539
Darnell, Linda,   547, 675, 1892,
2157, 2266, 3250, 3555
Darrieux, Danielle,   996, 1706,
2465, 2541, 3091
D'Arvil, Yola,   1035
"Daughter of Neptune,"   823
"Daughter of the Regiment,"   2258
Davenshire,   1639
"David and Bathsheba,"   547, 1248
"David and Goliath,"   2147, 2370
"David and Lisa,"   1573
"David Copperfield" (1970),   711
"David Harum,"   3496
Davidoff, Alexis,   736
Davies, Marion,   16, 327, 430,
479, 547, 719, 738, 926, 1247,
1294, 1932, 2044, 2244, 2252,
2392, 2436, 2732, 3008, 3077,
3184, 3448, 3451, 3457, 3469,
3472
Davis, Bette,   53, 294, 366, 526,
538, 539, 554, 649, 670, 679,
713, 739, 864, 1022, 1318,
1342, 1414, 1416, 1420, 1438,
1440, 1619, 1660, 1698, 1757,
1966, 1968, 2023, 2148, 2183,
2262, 2267, 2366, 2387, 2396,
2407, 2440, 2473, 2550, 2554,
2640, 2730, 2764, 2924, 3112,
3119, 3223, 3433, 3449, 3450,
3573
Davis, Francesca,   740
Davis, Joan,   2738, 3093
Davis, Peggy,   1134

Davis, Sammy, Jr.,   1186, 1340
Dawson, Beatrice (also Bumble),
742, 743, 744, 749, 898, 2144
Dawson, Gordon,   745
Dawson, Tom,   746
Day, Alice,   823, 1571
Day, Doris,   56, 556, 633, 1084,
1451, 1482, 1521, 1523, 1725,
2073, 2204, 2312, 2571, 2591,
2614
Day, Dorothy,   2916
Day, Laraine,   1768, 2497, 3209
Day, Lynda,   982
Day, Richard,   747, 824
"Day at the Races, A,"   2449,
3571
"Day Mars Invaded Earth, The,"
1518
"Day of Anger,"   3023
"Day of the Locust, The,"   713
"Day the Earth Stood Still, The,"
3097
"Day the Fish Came Out, The,"
432, 3121
"Day the War Ended, The,"   75
"Day with a Society Girl, A,"   2341
"Days of Wine and Roses,"   422
"Dead End,"   982
"Dead Reckoning,"   1808
"Dead Ringer,"   62, 1277
"Deadfall,"   1637
"Deadlier Than the Male,"   3252
"Deadly Affair, The,"   3252
"Deadly Companions, The,"   257,
2238
"Deadly Duo,"   350, 1908
"Deadwood '76,"   2741
Dean, James,   3233
Dean, Priscilla,   591, 851, 1875,
2474
Deane, Shirley,   307
"Dear Brat,"   2597
"Dear John,"   2648
"Dear Ruth,"   895, 2488, 2561
"Dear Wife,"   394, 397, 2495
"Death in Venice,"   118, 2895
"Death of Tarzan, The,"   2635
"Death Rides a Horse,"   410
"Death Takes a Holiday,"   2417
de Carlo, Yvonne,   2981
"Deception" (1920),   469
"Deception" (1946),   2183
"Declassé,"   750, 824
"Decline and Fall ... of a Bird
Watcher,"   880
Dee, Frances,   817, 2175, 2386,
2390, 2395, 2406, 3451
Dee, Sandra,   2629

Dee, Vincent, 752, 753
"Deep in My Heart," 2808, 3419
"Defector, The," 3530
De Haven, Gloria, 395
de Havilland, Olivia, 112, 113, 275, 526, 550, 670, 805, 1324, 1342, 1979, 2480, 2524, 2563, 2617, 2967, 3092, 3103, 3137, 3322, 3377, 3562
Deighton, Gordon, 756
Delamare, Rosine, 757, 996
de la Motte, Marguerite, 6
de la Renta, Oscar, 100, 2163, 2723
de Lima, Josette, 1403, 2487
De Lorez, Clair, 3525
Del Rio, Dolores, 310, 942, 1871, 2023, 2024, 2177, 2352, 2536, 2960, 3448, 3455
"Delta Factor, The," 1601
De Luca of Rome, 758
De Marchis, Marcella, 759
Demarez, Andree, 760
De Matteis, Maria, 761
De Mille, Cecil B., 50, 161, 220, 405, 472, 509, 657, 762, 763, 926, 935, 1824, 1940, 2035, 2713, 2783, 3360, 3563
De Mond, Willys (see Willys)
Demore, Don, 764
Dempster, Carol, 2692, 2950
Deneuve, Catherine, 2716, 2863
Dennis, Frances, 767
Dennis, Kathleen, 768
Dennis, Sandy, 2964
De Pinna, 770
Derek, John, 771
Dern, Bruce, 162, 1748
de Rothschild, Baroness Bina, 229, 2628
"De Sade," 1301
de Sant'Angelo, Giorgio, 351
de Segonzac, Gladys, 1577
"Desert Flower, The," 2311
"Desert Fury," 895, 1346, 2488, 2556
"Desert Nights," 1091
"Desert Patrol," 3339
"Desert Song, The," (1929), 1822
"Deserter and the Nomads, The," 1772
Desideri, Giorgio, 772
"Design for Living," 2414, 2415, 3453
Designer, Daisy, 774
Designing Male (Greer), 267, 328, 1231, 2673, 2743
Designing Woman (Volland), 3370

"Designing Woman," 2807, 3270, 3559
"Desirable," 1095
"Desire" (1923), 2007
"Desire" (1936), 189, 318, 584, 627, 714, 715, 792, 982, 1870, 1872, 2372, 2376, 2436
"Desire Under the Elms," 120
Desmarets, Sophie, 996
Desmond, William, 1763
"Desperado Trail, The," 2347
Dessès, Jean, 550, 779, 780, 781, 782, 1553
Deste, Luli, 2533
Devaud, Ginette, 783
"Devil and Daniel Webster, The," 3164
"Devil by the Tail, The," 1062
"Devil in Love, The," 534
"Devil in Velvet," 1841
"Devil Is a Woman, The," 190, 211, 311, 1297, 1305, 1871, 2432, 3542
"Devil Is Driving, The," 1067
"Devils, The," 1213, 1840
"Devil's Bedroom, The," 1248
"Devil's Lottery, The," 2395
"Devils of Darkness," 793
"Devil's Own, The," 1321
Devine, Sophie, 783, 2093/4, 2096
Devore, Sy, 785
"Devotion," 670, 3302
Dexter, Elliot, 1763
"Dialogue," 1609
"Diamond Head," 215, 285, 678, 1391, 3201
"Diamond Jim," 1268, 2023, 3238
"Diamond Stud," 2805
"Diamonds of Fate," 1622
"Diamonds of the Night," 1664
"Diane of the Follies," 1174
"Diary of a Chambermaid," 2064, 3382
"Diary of a Mad Housewife," 2071
Di Bari, Dina, 791
"Dice Woman, The," 1875
Dickson, Gloria, 2554, 3093
Dickson, Muriel 793
"Dictator, The," 1774, 1843
"Did You Hear the One About the Traveling Saleslady?," 2256
"Die! Die! My Darling!," 1158
Diem, Roy, 528, 2777
Dietrich, Marlene, 106, 189, 190, 211, 311, 314, 318, 388, 439, 465, 584, 627, 643, 704, 714, 715, 754, 792, 796, 798, 816, 1089, 1118, 1211, 1273, 1297,

1305, 1345, 1394, 1413, 1482,
1718, 1749, 1832, 1870, 1872,
1877, 1931, 1944, 2072, 2191,
2194, 2372, 2376, 2417, 2419,
2432, 2437, 2451, 2453, 2529,
2530, 2631, 2704, 2711, 2957,
3071, 3182, 3374, 3439, 3450,
3496, 3542, 3555, 3604, 3605
Dietz, Howard, 799
Diliberto, Carolyn, 800
Diller, Phyllis, 2256
Dillon, Carmen, 1111
Dillon, John Francis, 4
Dimitrovová, Olga, 802
"Dimka," 2123
Dimmitt, Joseph, 803
"Dingaka," 2770, 2867
"Dinner at Eight," 1426, 2932
Dior, Christian (and House of Dior),
337, 339, 804, 805, 806, 996,
1618, 1394, 3362
"Diplomacy," 3307
"Dirty Dingus Magee," 1951, 3285,
3581
"Disbarred," 2544
"Disgraced," 1932, 2411, 2763,
2931
"Dishonored Lady," 2114
"Disorder," 372
"Disorderly Conduct," 2392
"Disorderly Orderly, The," 576,
3154
"Disputed Passage," 732, 970
"Distant Trumpet, A," 736, 2629,
3371
"Divine Lady, The," 3400, 3402
"Divorce American Style," 1726,
1879
"Divorce--Italian Style," 791
"Divorce Las Vegas Style," 331
"Divorcee, The," 1025
Dix, Richard, 2638
"Dixiana," 1653
"Dixie," 866
"Do Not Disturb," 56
"Do You Keep a Lion at Home?,"
3038
Dobrovolskaya, Ya., 811
"Dr. Coppelius," 463, 2759
"Dr. Crippen," 2145
"Doctor Dolittle," 56, 875, 2999
"Doctor Faustus," 116, 1270
"Dr. Frankstein on Campus," 1868,
2318
"Doctor Glas," 3056
"Doctor, I'm Coming!," 830
"Dr. Jekyll and Mr. Hyde" (1920),
3196

"Dr. No," 357
"Doctor, You've Got to Be Kidding,"
1781
"Doctor Zhivago," 273, 478, 507,
723, 1051, 1618, 2163, 2368
"Doctor's Dilemma, The," 3076
"Doctor's Secret, The," 3400
Dodd, Claire, 2405, 2414, 2763,
3494
Dodson, Mary Kay, 812, 813, 1971,
2495, 2569, 2588
"Dodsworth," 306, 1470, 2444,
2521, 2925
Doelnitz, Marc, 814
"Dolce Vita, La," 1152
"Doll, The," 469
"Doll's House, A," 1331
"Dolly Sisters, The," 1538, 3555
"Domestic Relations," 2102
"Don Juan," 1821
"Don Q, Son of Zorro," 416
"Don Quixote" (1933), 2665
"Don Quixote" (1961), 83
Donahue, Troy, 2629
Donati, Danilo, 818, 1485
"Dondi," 130, 3440
Donen, Stanley, 1213
Donfeld (see also Feld, Don), 819,
820
Donner, Richard, 2377
Donner, Vyvyan, 606, 1405, 2174,
2470
Donovan, Maria, 827
"Donovan's Reef," 257, 1288, 3154
"Don't Bet on Love," 1933
"Don't Bet on Women," 2672
"Don't Doubt Your Husband," 3356
"Don't Drink the Water," 602
"Don't Knock the Twist," 3201
"Don't Make Waves," 273, 820
"Don't Raise the Bridge, Lower the
River," 958, 1246, 1736
"Don't Tell the Wife," 430
"Don't Tempt the Devil," 1372
"Don't Worry, We'll Think of a
Title," 1896, 3075
"Doomsday," 194
"Dorado, El," 422
Doran, Mary, 2396
Dore, Adrienne, 2397, 3565
Doria, Madame, 200
Doris of Mariposa, 830
Dorleac, Jean-Pierre, 552, 1992
"Dorothy Vernon of Haddon Hall,"
550, 2626
Dors, Diana, 2276
Dorsay, Fifi, 1424
"Double-Barrelled Dectective Story,
The," 219

"Double Bunk," 1321, 3252
"Double Harness," 2175
"Double Life, A," 3285
"Double Man, The," 805, 911
"Double or Nothing," 2917, 2926, 3546
"Double Wedding," 2455
"Doughboys," 160
Douglas, Betty, 840, 2921
Douglas, Craig, 1019
Douglas, Melvyn, 1803
Douglas, Sara, 2276
Dove, Billie, 249, 511, 838, 1101, 1423, 2718, 2954, 3310
"Down to Earth," 1808, 3555
"Downhill Racer," 1986
Downs, Cathy, 1170
"Dracula," 3309
"Dracula Has Risen from the Grave," 1976
"Dragonwyck," 839
Drake, Betsy, 399, 3271
Drake, Frances, 2927
"Dramatic School," 969
"Dream Girl," 609, 868, 891, 1242, 1341, 2560
"Dream of Kings, A," 2938
"Dream of Love," 24, 3268
"Dreaming Lips," 1685
Drecol, 844
Dress Doctor, The (Head), 275, 368, 443, 859, 1070, 1279, 1344, 1345, 1402, 2138, 2728, 2747, 2748, 2749, 3046
Dressing for Glamour (Mackie), 1878
Dressler, Marie, 3163
"Dressmaker from Paris, The," 662, 1035, 1463, 1491, 1920
"Dressmaker of Paris, The," 1727
Drew, Mrs. Sidney, 3539
Dru, Joanne, 2500
"Drums of Love," 1972, 2274, 2960
Drury, Joe, 863
Dryden, Ernst, 864, 909, 1220, 1268, 1502, 1802, 2439, 2442
"Drylanders," 3607
Dubois, Ilse, 865
du Bois, Raoul Pène, 550, 766, 866, 985, 3599
Ducharne, House of, 2191, 2522
"Duck Soup," 1935
"Duel, The," 2196
"Duel at Diablo," 3581
"Duel in the Sun," 134, 1228, 3234
"Duel of Champions," 1169
"Duel of the Titans," 2636
"Duet for Cannibals," 1778

Duff Gordon, Lady Lucile (see also Lucile), 479, 500, 698, 870, 1117, 1194, 1231, 1471, 1817, 1819, 1991, 2654
"Duffy," 12, 326
Duflos, Huguette, 790
"Dulcy," 2273
Dunaway, Faye, 526, 1618, 1660, 1762, 3022, 3327
Dunayeva, I., 872
Duncan, Arletta, 2398
Duncan, Bill, 3040
Duncan, Irene, 850
Duncan, Mrs., 2860
Duncan, William, 2229
Dunham, Joanna, 3020
Dunne, Irene, 307, 317, 439, 670, 675, 874, 985, 1022, 1188, 1234, 1298, 1413, 1429, 1522, 1892, 1927, 1960, 2076, 2133, 2177, 2287, 2352, 2400, 2477, 2537, 2538, 2640, 2703, 2964, 3090, 3102, 3140, 3162, 3171, 3388, 3451, 3453
Dunne, Josephine, 1422
"Dunwich Horror, The," 1834
Dupont, Jacques, 876
Duquette, Tony, 877, 1623, 2028
Durbin, Deanna, 134, 136, 754, 976, 1079, 1440, 1508, 1653, 1854, 2284, 2479, 2551, 2570
Durfee, Minta, 1843
Duryea, Dan, 3285
Duse, Anna, 880
Dushina, L., 881
"Dust Flower, The," 1217
"Dust of Desire," 2978
"Dutchman," 1126
Duty, Guy, 2352
Duval, Paulette, 51, 824, 1998
Dvorak, Ann, 1002, 3110
Dvorak, Geraldine, 3268
Dwan, Dorothy, 1505
"Dynamite," 1540
"Dynamite Smith," 2167, 2650

"Each Dawn I Die," 2475
"Eagle, The," 388, 1784, 1876
Eagle Clothes, 2520
Eames, Erica, 162
Earle, Edward, 2221
"Early to Wed," 2105
"Earth Entranced," 3055
"Earthquake," 683, 1077, 2855
"East Is West," 637, 638, 639

"East Lynne," 268, 878
"East of Eden," 1573
"East of 5th Avenue," 2415
"East Side, West Side," 2499
"Easter Parade," 2788
Eaton, Shirley, 2027
Eckart, Jean, 885, 886
Eckart, William J., 887, 888
Eddy, Helen Jerome, 1368
Eddy, Nelson, 1556
"Edge of the City," 1573
Edwards, Bill, 899, 3241
Edwards, Dorothy, 2803
Edwards, J. Gordon, 755
Edwards, Sally, 900
"Egg and I, The," 674
Eggar, Samantha, 337, 805, 1060, 3245
Egidi, Carlo, 901
Ehren, France, 902
"8½," 1151
"Eight Girls in a Boat," 3449
Eilers, Sally, 1927, 2023, 2176, 2352, 2404, 2406, 2414, 2415, 2419, 3549
Eisner, Lotte H., 132
Ekberg, Anita, 1223
Eldredge, Florence, 1892, 2400
"Electra," 3329
"Elegance," 421
Elfstrom, Katherine, 908
"Elinor Norton," 2427
Ellacott, Joan, 910
Elliot, Courtney, 911
Ellis, Mary, 312
Ellis, Patricia, 1931, 2177, 2420, 2754
"Ellis Island," 2541
Ellsworth, Robert, 1212
Elmquist, Marion, 913
Elsworth, Elmer, 912, 3241
Eltinge, Julian (Bill Dalton), 1711, 1865
"Elusive Corporal, The," 3566
Elvidge, June, 1585, 3306
"Elvira Madigan," 2855
"Elvis--That's the Way It Is," 265
"Embarrassing Moments," 2422
"Emil and the Detectives," 264, 3413
"Emma," 2393
"Emperor Waltz, The," 2651, 3045, 3217, 3377
"Emperor's Candlesticks, The," 1825, 2694
"Empty Hands," 3415
"Empty Star, The," 171, 2342
"Enchantment," 883

"End of Desire," 221, 1818
"Enemies of Women, The," 3312
"Ensign Pulver," 2827
"Enter Madame," 575, 2427
"Entertaining Mr. Sloane," 2655
"Epic That Never Was, The," 3439
Equini, Arrigo, 918
Erbele, Carl, 919
Erdmann, Ernst, 920
Ericksen, Leon, 922
"Erik the Conqueror," 1222
"Erika's Hot Summer," 2182
Erl of Saks Fifth Avenue, 2475
"Ermine and Rhinestones," 1393
Ernst, Lone, 923
Erté (Romain de Tirtoff), 36, 212, 213, 417, 479, 553, 710, 871, 901a, 924, 925, 926, 927, 928, 929, 930, 931, 1174, 1175, 1198, 1231, 2098, 2334, 2640, 2695, 2913, 3026, 3077, 3254, 3445
"Escapade," 1825
"Escape from East Berlin," 2166, 2666
"Escape from Zahrain," 576, 3154
"Escape Me Never," 1685, 3555
Escoffier, Marcel, 601, 932
Esmond, Jill, 1403
"Espionage Agent," 2478
"Esta Nuestro Amor," 3302
Estévez, 934
Estrel, Jacques, 1751
Etches, Matilda, 749
"Eternal City, The," 790, 1238, 2047
"Eternal Flame, The," 1032, 1535 2210, 2211, 2212, 2213, 2313, 3340, 3486
"Eternal Love," 2734
"Eternally Yours," 2478
"Eva," 451
"Evangeline," 1475
Evans, Clive, 938
Evans, Edith, 711
Evans, Felix, 939
Evans, Madge, 660, 787, 1380, 1426, 1930, 2177, 2388, 2389, 2397, 2423, 2443, 2522, 3279, 3449
Evein, Bernard, 940
Evelyn, Judith, 1437
"Evenings for Sale," 2403
"Every Day's a Holiday," 947, 1007,
"Everybody Does It," 2157
"Everybody Go Home!," 2319, 2362 2896
"Everything's Rosie," 2386, 2387
"Everywoman," 1134, 2172

"Executioner, The," 354
"Exile," 388
"Ex-Lady," 2407, 2764
"Expensive Woman," 2389
"Experiment Perilous," 948
"Explosion," 2769
"Explosive Generation, The," 736
"Exquisite Sinner, The," 3303, 3470
"Exterminating Angel, The," 3063
"Extra Girl, The," 1836
"Extraordinary Seaman, The," 2786
extras, costume needs of, 258, 274, 322, 914, 1470, 1973, 2336, 2818, 3115, 3621
"Eye for an Eye, An," 2889, 3186
"Eye of the Devil," 1107
Eyton, Betty, 2656

Fabiani, 952
"Face in the Crowd, A," 1573
"Faces in the Dark," 793
"Facts of Life," 1437
Fageol, Christiane, 955
"Fahrenheit 451," 326, 3410
"Faibles Femmes," 1751
Fair, Elinor, 322, 3249
"Fair and Warmer," 2172
Fairbanks, Douglas (Sr.), 209, 266, 327, 528, 532, 550, 1812, 3080, 3455
Fairchild, John, 1618
Faire, Virginia Brown, 2074, 2296, 2918
Fairlie, Jean, 957
"Faith Healer, The," 3512
"Faithless," 2403
Falk, Gabriella, 958
"Fallen Sparrow, The," 3142
"False Colors," 591
"False Shame," 1657
"Family Affair, A," 2474
"Family Diary," 2804
"Famous Mrs. Fair, The," 1063
Fanchon, 2808
"Fanny," 1921
"Fanny Hill," 2648
"Fanny Hill: Memoirs of a Woman of Pleasure," 1376, 2120
"Fantastic Voyage," 3392
"Far Cry, The," 2920
"Far from the Madding Crowd," 208, 2078
"Farewell, Doves," 2324

"Farmer's Daughter, The," 674
Farnum, Franklyn, 1763
Farrar, Geraldine, 388, 762, 962, 1106, 2860, 3115
Farrell, Charlie, 3455
Farrell, Glenda, 1933, 3552
Farrer, Ernest, 93, 963
Farrington, Mrs., 964
Farrow, Mia, 162, 451, 1748
"Fashion Features," 821
Fashion Group, 807, 1432, 2116
Fashion Institute of Technology, 1830
"Fashion Row," 121, 259, 2977
"Fashions of 1934," 438, 795, 1429, 3223, 3449
"Fast Workers," 1930
"Fastnachtsbeichte, Die," 1262
"Fat City," 279
"Fat Spy, The," 2353
"Fate of a Man," 3337
"Father," 2009
"Father Goose," 56
"Father of the Bride," 1421, 2806
"Father Takes a Wife," 3393
"Fathom," 204, 426, 2817
"Faust," 1376, 2303
Fava, Otello, 1001
Fax, Peg, 1004
Fay, Addalyn, 1005
Faye, Alice, 754, 976, 1007, 1079, 1214, 1433, 1498, 1853, 2133, 2265, 2472, 2537, 3555
Faye, Julia, 564, 657, 762, 2669, 3167
Fazenda, Louise, 826, 2360
Fea, Anna Maria, 1006
"Fearless Vampire Killers; or, Pardon Me but Your Teeth Are in My Neck, The," 784
Fears, Peggy, 728, 1687
"Feather in Her Hat, A," 1870
Feathers, Julia, 129
"Federicus Rex," 2825
"Fedora," 351, 1749
"Feet of Clay," 657, 1616, 3415
Feld, Don (see also Donfeld), 1009, 2628
Fellini, Federico, 1152, 1485, 1625, 2895
"Fellini Satyricon," 118, 818, 1485, 2895
"Female, The," 295, 824
"Femme Infidele, La," 67
"Femme Libre, Une," 719
"Femmes des Folies Bergère, Les," 478
Fennell, Elsa, 1015

Fenwick, Trevor, 1031
Féraud, Louis, 1016, 3291
Ferguson, Elsie, 994, 1017, 1018
Ferguson, Helen, 1063, 3484
Ferrer, José, 1594
Ferris, Gamp, 1019
Feuillere, Edwige, 1414
"Fever," 2406
"Few Bullets More, A," 650
Ffolkes, David, 1020
Field, Betty, 867, 1504, 2948, 3575
Field, Sid, 1718
"Field of the Cloth of Gold," 3099
"Fiesta," 848, 2110, 2234
"5th Avenue Girl," 1026
"Fifty-Fifty Girl, The," 194
"55 Days at Peking," 607, 1391, 2063
"52nd Street," 840, 1103, 2133
"Fighting Coast Guard," 2599
"Fighting Parson, The," 74
"Figleaves," 388, 3006
Fill, Dennis, 1028
"Finders Keepers," 3252
"Fine Madness, A," 2823
"Fine Manners," 465, 1589
"Fine Pair, A," 2854
"Finger on the Trigger," 3347
Fini, Leonor, 1037
"Finishing School," 3451
Finney, Albert, 88, 1446
"Fire over England," 1719
"Firebrand, The," 3178
"Firecreek," 3581
"Firefly," 2355
"Fireman, Save My Child," 138
"Firemen's Ball, The," 3053
"Firepower," 2016
"Fireside Realization, A," 1622
"First a Girl," 680
"First Auto, The," 3477
"First Baby, The," 307
"First Hundred Years, The," 1041, 3090
"First Lady, The," 319, 2038, 2455, 2456, 2532
"First Love," 2479
"First Time, The," 3425
Fischer, Lee, 1039
Fischer, Margarita, 853
Fish, Peggy, 3335
Fisher, Carrie, 3113
Fisher, Lillian, 2542
Fitzer, Gwen, 1040
Fitzgerald, F. Scott, 697
Fitzgerald, Geraldine, 94, 192, 1204

Fitzroy, Emily, 809
"Fitzwilly," 76, 1559
"Five and Ten," 2044
"5 Card Stud," 2758
"Five Cents a Glass," 2410
"Five Easy Pieces," 2827
"Five Finger Exercise," 1437, 2281
"Five Golden Hours," 349
"Five Man Army, The," 410, 2857
"Five Miles to Midnight," 1710
"Five Weeks in a Balloon," 3615
"Flame of New Orleans, The," 754, 1089, 3555
"Flaming Frontier," 2347
"Flaming Youth," 1100, 1813, 2057, 2058
"Flap," 1371, 2799
"Flareup," 1040, 3197
"Flash Gordon" (serial), 3108
Flato, 2540
"Flea in Her Ear, A," 1759
"Fledermaus, Die," 1396, 2944
Fleming, Rhonda, 1214, 2498, 2603
Fleming, Susan, 2400, 2403
Fleming, Victor, 898
Flemming, Charlotte, 1045
"Flesh and Fury," 2609
"Flesh and the Devil," 2732
Fletcher, Robert, 552, 1048, 1049, 1050, 2900
"Flight for Freedom," 30, 1021
"Flight of the Phoenix, The," 1656
"Flight That Disappeared," 347, 1908
"Flirtation Walk," 309
"Flirting with Love," 2621, 3459
Florell, 2108
Florence, Gay, 1055
Florentino, Rudolph (Dominic Giordano), 3014
"Flower Drum Song," 1437, 2968
"Flowing Gold," 968, 1714
"Fluffy," 2995
"Flying Down to Rio," 438, 551, 2177, 3448
"Flying Dutchman, The," 2201
"Flying Torpedo, The," 1812
Flynn, Errol, 679
Foale and Tuffin, Ltd., 1057, 2873
Foale, Marion, 1058, 2679, 2873
Foch, Nina, 1678
"Fog over San Francisco," 3450
"Folies Bergère," 211, 1397, 2432
"Follow That Camel," 2940
"Follow the Fleet," 140, 2373, 2376

"Follow Thru," 1492
Fonda, Henry, 555
Fonda, Jane, 678, 819, 1331, 1762, 2281, 2689, 2808, 3041
Fonssagrives, Mia, 1060, 3245, 3246, 3291
Fonssagrives-Tiel, 3291
Fontaine, Joan, 52, 134, 670, 858, 985, 1073, 1250, 1326, 1452, 1806, 1953, 2461, 2538, 2651, 3142, 3377, 3388
Fontana, Graziella, 1382
Fontana (of Roma), Sorelle, 1061
Fonteray, Jacques, 1062, 1992
"Food for Scandal," 3513
"Fool, The," 2290, 2291, 2292, 2293
"Foolish Wives," 3465
"Fool's Paradise," 509
"For a Few Dollars More, 3023
"For Heaven's Sake," 2594
"For Love of Ivy," 3236
"For Love or Money," 1581, 2871, 3431
"For Sale," 824, 2301
"For Singles Only," 1028, 1138, 2131, 3441
"For the Love of Mary," 2284, 2570
"For Whom the Bell Tolls," 1021, 1052
Forbes, Ralph, 985
"Forbidden Fruit," 564, 1659, 3456, 3514, 3517
"Forbidden Hours," 2960
"Forbidden Paradise," 2833
"Foreign Devils," 1480
"Forever Amber," 1892, 3555
"Forever Female," 546
"Forever My Love," 264, 1143
Forman, Harrison, 1802
Forman, Ron, 1068
Forquet, 1069
Forrest, Ann, 3512
Forrest, Sally, 2513
Forrest, Steve, 550
"Forsaking All Others," 882, 1296, 1381, 1398
Forster, Robert, 552
"Fort Courageous," 707
Fortini, Luciana, 1071
"Fortune Cookie, The," 130, 1166
"Forty Carats," 713
"40 Guns to Apache Pass," 803
"Forty-nine Days," 1967
"Forty Pounds of Trouble," 2871

"Forty-second Street," 2405
Foster, Ben, 93
Foster, Preston, 1661
"Fountain of Love, The," 1143
"Fountainhead, The," 2493
Fouquet, Marie-Claude, 1075
"4 for Texas," 1656, 2801
"Four Girls in White," 2990
"Four Horsemen of the Apocalypse, The" (1921), 502, 1784, 2237, 2884, 3014, 3253
"Four Horsemen of the Apocalypse, The" (1962), 877, 1437, 1481, 2281, 2641
"Four Marys," 2534
"Four Men and a Prayer," 2461, 2929, 3090
"Four's a Crowd," 1511, 2465, 3092, 3176
Fox, Ree, 1078
Fox, William, 106
"Fox Movietone Follies of 1929," 2274
"Foxhole in Cairo," 1157
Foy, Bryan/Byron, 2237, 3300
Foy, Eddie, Jr., 2312
Frances, 2124
Frances, Madame, 197, 750, 979, 1080, 1081, 1174, 1731, 1794, 1835a, 2124, 2791, 2950, 3537
Francis, Alec B., 74
Francis, Kay, 16, 64, 319, 816, 1067, 1300, 1613, 1754, 1933, 2024, 2038, 2041, 2175, 2391, 2396, 2397, 2401, 2406, 2407, 2442, 2445, 2455, 2463, 2523, 2532, 2533, 2534, 2542, 2851, 2928, 2994, 3086, 3388, 3400, 3542
"Francis of Assisi," 2139, 2225, 2999
Francisco, Betty, 79, 1813
"Frankenstein," 1779, 2391, 3309
"Frankenstein Created Woman," 3145
Franklin, Pamela, 711
Franklin, Sidney, 3235
Franklin Simon, 2326
Fratini, Gina, 1090
"Fraulein Doktor," 410, 761
Frazer, Henrietta, 1091, 3475
"Freddy Unter Fremden Sternen," 2906
Frederick, Pauline, 660, 1238, 2860, 3539
Frederics, John (see John Frederics)
Fredericks of Hollywood, 1093
"Free Soul, A," 3264

Freeborn, Stuart, 842
Freeman, Mona, 2241, 2501, 2597, 2609
French, Pauline, 2295
"French Doll, The," 121, 1886
"French Line, The," 947, 1892, 2338
"Frenchman's Creek," 985, 1598
"Freshman Love," 2754
Freshy Playclothes, 1096, 3065
"Freud," 2060
"Freud: The Secret Passion" (see "Freud")
Friberg, Arnold, 2200
"Friend of the Family," 1706, 2716
"Friendly Island," 395
"Friendly Persuasion," 3370
Friganza, Trixie, 2360
Frigerio, Ezio, 1098
"Frisco Sally Levy," 1480
Frocks, Brock, 1102
"From Hell to Heaven," 1929, 2407, 2762
"From Russia with Love," 2771
"From the Terrace," 875
Froman, Jane, 317
"Front Page, The" (1931), 1996
"Frontier Hellcat," 2347
"Frozen Alive," 2120
"Frozen Dead, The," 1158
"Fuga, La," 1151
"Fugitive Kind, The," 3449
Fuller, Mary, 1622
Fulton, Meredith, 821
"Funny Face," 100, 1577
"Funny Girl," 1645, 2735, 2968
"Funny Lady," 57, 129, 1211, 1878
"Funny Thing Happened on the Way to the Forum, A," 3410
Furness, John, 1107
furs (as garments or trim), 51, 158, 315, 402, 464, 546, 550, 699, 700, 700, 837, 898, 936, 1003, 1063, 1108, 1195, 1213, 1333, 1383, 1393, 1422, 1423, 1448, 1547, 1628, 1645, 1722, 1781, 1855, 1885, 1968, 2001, 2082, 2171, 2207, 2244, 2270, 2435, 2443, 2523, 2669, 2703, 2735, 2784, 2788, 2832, 2843, 2849, 2921, 2961, 3032, 3064, 3071, 3116, 3118, 3133, 3209, 3210, 3231, 3264, 3481, 3499, 3563, 3604
Furse, Margaret, 749, 1109, 1136, 2144

Furse, Roger, 466, 1110, 1111, 1112, 1113, 1114, 1136, 2144, 2800
"Fury," 225
"Fury at Smuggler's Bay," 723, 1126
"Fusillé à l'Aube," 996

Gaal, Franciska, 976
Gable, Clark, 217, 261, 944, 1224, 1294, 1651, 2065, 2664, 3050, 3264, 3322
"Gable and Lombard," 145, 408, 561, 1312, 1333
"Gabriel over the White House," 1930
Gadd, Renee, 2421
Gahagan Douglas, Helen, 1643, 2436
"Gaily, Gaily," 56, 76, 1559, 1892
Gainsford, Anne, 1119
Galanos, James, 1120, 2843
"Gallant Lady," 2417, 3449
Gallian, Ketti, 1915, 2023
"Galloping Fish, The," 1401
Gallup, Johnny, 1996
"Gambler Wore a Gun, The," 1908, 2127
"Gambling Lady," 2117
"Gambling Ship," 2763
Gaminerie, La, 1122
Ganevskaya, G., 1123
"Gang's All Here, The," 3285
Garbo, Greta, 5, 14, 16, 18, 19, 23, 27, 33, 34, 35, 37, 47, 50, 53, 158, 163, 228, 230, 267, 440, 465, 536, 562, 616, 643, 789, 816, 822, 868, 944, 947, 950, 1121, 1215, 1232, 1239, 1273, 1280, 1295, 1296, 1317, 1383, 1385, 1411, 1413, 1416, 1433, 1482, 1545, 1546, 1640, 1696, 1749, 1757, 1766, 1832, 1869, 1979, 2023, 2024, 2098, 2116, 2275, 2327, 2352, 2352, 2384, 2398, 2428, 2447, 2523, 2673, 2679, 2685, 2712, 2732, 2783, 2838, 2899, 2952, 2994, 3004, 3006, 3026, 3037, 3102, 3119, 3156, 3289, 3292, 3542
García, Rosa, 1124
"Garden of Allah, The," 261, 314, 909, 1409, 1502
"Garden of Eden, The," 823
"Garden of the Moon," 2541

"Garden of Weeds," 2622
Gardner, Ava, 334, 683, 1061,
    1077, 1125, 1331, 1519, 3620
Gardner, Brenda, 1126
Gardner, Eve, 63
Gardner, Joan, 2425
Garland, Judy, 679, 903, 1127,
    1286, 1343, 1421, 1849, 1849,
    2028, 2664, 2686, 2862, 2964,
    2966, 3088, 3419, 3585
Garner, Peggy Ann, 485
Garon, Pauline, 2348, 2919, 3167
Garr, Phyllis, 1129
Garson, Greer, 670, 673, 944,
    1087, 2105, 3094
garters, 2265, 3025, 3294
Gaskin, Bill, 1130
"Gaslight," 1342, 1598
Gasnier, Louis, 1198
Gasparinetti, Alessandro (Major),
    1131
Gastoni, Lisa, 402
"Gateway," 3092
"Gathering of Eagles, A," 1521
"Gaucho, The," 416
"Gauloises Bleues, Les," 1902,
    3426
"Gay Deceivers, The," 2872
"Gay Divorcee, The," 551
"Gay Nineties, The," 3469
Gaynor, Janet, 209, 748, 1409,
    1785, 2024, 2170, 2425, 2449,
    2466, 2527, 2543, 2783
Gaynor, Mitzi, 2858
Gazzara, Ben, 1745
Gee of London, Cecil, 1137
Gellert, Trudy, 1138
"General, The," 2049, 2901
"General Hospital," 2530
"Generation," 3203
"Genghis Khan," 3252
Gentili, Carlo, 1139
"Gentle Giant," 1669
"Gentleman Goes to Town, A,"
    2438
"Gentleman's Agreement," 2156
"Gentlemen at Midnight," 1979
"Gentlemen of the Press," 3400
"Gentlemen Prefer Blondes" (1928),
    1128
George, Gladys, 27, 1211
George, Maude, 2047, 3006
"George Raft Story, The," 2976,
    3440
"George Washington Slept Here,"
    3577
"George White's 1935 Scandals,"
    822

Georgette, 983
Georgiadis, Nicholas, 1140
"Georgy Girl," 2680
Geradino, Zoraida, 1141
Geraghty, Carmelita, 3082
Gerard, Rolfe, 679
Gerdago, 1143
Germès-Vergne, Jeannine, 1144
Gernreich, Rudi, 1145, 1146, 1147,
    1148, 1149
Gerrard, Charles, 966
Gershwin, George, 1652
"Get-Rich-Quick Wallingford," 3457
"Get Yourself a College Girl," 419,
    1256
"Getting Straight," 139
Gettinger, Muriel, 1150
Geva, Tamara, 3110
Gherardi, Piero, 1151, 1152, 1625
Ghidini, Giuliana, 1153
"Ghost, The," 1848
"Ghost Breakers, The," 2485
"Ghost Goes West, The," 2896
"Ghosts--Italian Style," 2854
"Ghosts of Yesterday," 1794
Gibbons, Cedric, 1524
Gibbons, Eliot, 1524
Gibbs, Evelyn, 1155
"Gibier de Potence," 565
Giboyau, Catherine, 1156
Gibson, Freda, 1157
Gibson, George, 821
Gibson, Mary, 1158
Gibson, Virginia, 400
Gibson, Wynne, 2175, 3429
"Gidget Goes to Rome," 215, 1061
Gielgud, Sir John, 1112
Gifford, Frances, 2937
"Gigi," 233, 235, 1416, 2028, 3076
"Gigollette," 727
Gilbert, Bates, 1159
Gilbert, Florence, 2298
Gilbert, Hylda, 1160
Gilbert, John, 121
"Gilda," 351, 478, 556, 1161, 1654,
    1808, 1968, 2125, 3032, 3209
"Gilded Butterfly, The," 2299
"Gilded Cage, The," 1034
"Gilded Lily, The," 121, 211, 1297,
    1493, 2432
Gill, Betina, 1162
Gillett, Barbara, 1163
Gillingwater, Claude, 2949
Gilman, Phyllis, 3405
Gilmore, Elinor, 3525
Gimbel, Sophie (Sophie Gimbel Haas)
    see also (Sophie of Saks Fifth
    Avenue), 1164, 1165, 3066

Gimbel Brothers, 2899
Gimbel family, 883
Ginsberg, Henry, 3247
Giokaris, Paula, 1166
Giokaris, Vou Lee, 1167
Giorgi, Marinella, 1168
girdles (see also corsets), 696,
    1821, 3232
"Girl About Town," 2391
"Girl and the General, The," 761
"Girl and the Legend, The," 1045
"Girl Downstairs, The," 2547
"Girl Friend, The," 1911
"Girl from God's Country, The,"
    3518
"Girl from Hong Kong," 166
"Girl from Jones Beach, The,"
    1780, 2491, 2576
"Girl from Tenth Avenue," 2023
"Girl Happy," 1951
"Girl in Every Port, A," 2516
"Girl in Gold Boots," 1985
"Girl in Room 13," 2632
"Girl in Trouble," 3000
"Girl Hunters, The," 2027
"Girl Next Door, The," 2613
"Girl of the Golden West, The"
    (c.1915), 1638
"Girl of the Golden West, The"
    (1938), 944
"Girl of the Night," 70
"Girl on a Motorcycle, The,"
    1706
"Girl Who Couldn't Say No, The,"
    2636
"Girl Without a Room," 2416
"Girls! Girls! Girls!," 1288
Girosi, Mario, 1169
Gish, Dorothy, 225, 388, 832,
    1116, 1174, 1649, 2218
Gish, Lillian, 53, 417, 553, 926,
    1174, 1175, 1176, 1198, 1211,
    1776, 2098, 2218, 2791, 2913,
    3077, 3254
"Gismonda," 206
Giusti, Silvano, 1177
"Give Me a Sailor," 3092
"Give Me Your Heart," 2442
Givenchy, Hubert de, 100, 1178,
    1179, 1180, 1454, 1577
"Gladiator of Rome," 772
"Gladiators, The," 614
"Gladiators Seven," 1169
"Glass of Water, A," 336, 2825
"Glass Bottom Boat, The," 56,
    1482
Glaum, Louise, 856, 3115, 3528,
    3534

Glazman, Linda, 1185
Glenn, Charles, 1186
"Glimpses of the Moon, The," 943,
    2251
Glinkova, G., 1187
"Gloria's Romance," 1218
"Glory Guys, The," 256
gloves, 286, 502, 535, 1557, 2200,
    2375, 2437, 2440, 3106, 3138,
    3407
Glunt, Ruth, 1197
Glyn, Elinor, 1875
"Go-Getters, The," 1587
"Go Naked in the World," 2809
"Go West, Young Man," 2522, 2523
"God Forgives--I Don't," 663
Goddard, Paulette, 228, 550, 715,
    813, 969, 1201, 1266, 1347, 1590,
    1642, 1658, 1737, 1968, 2111,
    2475, 2485, 3076, 3608
Godey's Lady's Book, 1864
"Godfather II," 1097
"Godless Girl, The," 550
Godowsky, Dagmar, 128, 1199,
    2621, 3014
"Goin' to Town," 1397, 1870
"Going Hollywood," 16, 3448
"Gold Diggers, The," 1276
"Gold Diggers in Paris," 1200,
    3093
"Gold Diggers of Broadway," 1822
"Gold Diggers of 1933," 1931
"Gold for the Caesars," 1169
"Gold Rush, The," 388
"Golden Arrow, The" (1936), 739,
    1966, 2440, 2924
"Golden Arrow, The" (1964), 772
"Golden Bed, The," 175, 1342,
    1616
"Golden Calf, The," 1916
"Golden Cocoon, The," 1366
"Golden Journey, The," 296
"Goldfinger," 2679
"Goldfish, The," 1742
"Goldie Gets Along," 2403
Goldman Company, 1096, 3065
Goldwyn, Frances, 883
Goldwyn, Samuel, 220, 232, 414,
    871, 883, 1029, 1203, 2098,
    2964. 3463
"Goldwyn Follies, The," 261, 2457,
    3551
"Goliath Against the Giants," 2822
"Goliath and the Vampires," 2822
Gombell, Minna, 2408
"Gone Are the Days," 2939
"Gone with the Wind," 138, 261,
    562, 898, 1051, 1066, 1283,

1311, 1416, 1420, 1433, 1680,
1749, 2065, 2664, 2988, 2991,
3102, 3234, 3264, 3322, 3466,
3557
"Good and Naughty," 691
"Good Earth, The," 1825
"Good Girls Go to Paris," 754,
2991
"Good Guys and the Bad Guys,
The," 2767, 3581
"Good Neighbor Sam," 2014
"Good Soldier Schweik, The," 264
"Good, the Bad, and the Ugly,
The," 3023
"Good Times," 422, 464, 2758
"Goodbye Again," 805, 2413
"Goodbye Charlie," 2809
"Goodbye, Columbus," 602
"Goodbye Gemini," 12, 2089
Goodrich, Edna, 2956
"Goose and the Gander, The,"
1871
"Goose Girl, The," 1210
"Gordeyev Family, The," 2707
Gordon, Bob, 1377
Gordon, Kitty, 529
Gordon, Maud Turner, 2124
2192
Gordon & Marx of California, 464
"Gorgeous Hussy, The," 1211,
2524
Görlich, Grete, 1210
"Gospel According to St. Matthew,
The," 818
Goudal, Jetta, 128, 660, 1199,
1505, 1731, 2032, 2360, 2622,
3006, 3014, 3300, 3384
Goude, Jean-Paul, 2020
"Government Girl," 3562
"Gown of Destiny," 3278
Goy, Roma, 3074
Grable, Betty, 389, 1538, 1640,
2755, 3092
Grace, Dick, 388
"Gracias a Tu Buena Estrella"
(see "Thank Your Lucky Stars")
"Graduate, The," 1129, 1858,
3626
"Grand Canary," 2423
"Grand Duchess and the Waiter,
The," 3006
"Grand Exit," 1872, 1910
"Grand Hotel," 556, 696, 816
"Grande Illusion, La," 3381
"Grandma's Boy," 1499
Granger, Stewart, 749
Grani, Tina, 1222
Grant, Cary, 1084, 1334,

1338, 1864, 2204
Grant, Kathryn, 1241
Grant, Lee, 829, 1831
Grant, Mary, 776, 2566
"Grasshopper, The," 820
"Graustark," 1505
Graves, Lilyan, 2990
Gray, Dolores, 2807, 3559
Gray, Sally, 3076
Grayson, Kathryn, 673, 2581, 2595
"Grease," 68
"Great Catherine," 169
"Great Desire, A," 1928
"Great Gatsby, The" (1974), 162,
1416, 1446, 1661, 1748, 2855,
3568
"Great Lover, The," 2498
"Great Man's Lady, The," 3046
"Great Moment, The," 2778
"Great Race, The," 2628, 3207
"Great Sinner, The," 1519, 3620
"Great Sioux Massacre, The," 3197
"Great Victor Herbert, The," 1183,
2480, 2481
"Great Waldo Pepper, The," 729,
3059
"Great White Hope, The," 2964,
2968, 2998, 3597
"Great Ziegfeld, The," 982, 1268,
1445, 1632, 1825, 1826, 3584
"Greatest Show on Earth, The,"
1552, 3232
"Greatest Story Ever Told, The,"
292, 2092, 2225, 3020
"Greco, El," 818
"Greeks Had a Word for Them,
The," 1380, 1383
Green, Mitzi, 2386
"Green Berets, The," 81
"Green Flame The," 2230
"Green Helmet, The," 169
"Green Mare, The," 757
"Green Slime, The," 1903
Greenwich Village Follies, 479,
2205
Greenwood, Jane, 1229, 1230
Greer, Howard, 65, 267, 328,
423, 479, 549, 735, 816, 824,
997, 1044, 1198, 1232, 1233,
1234, 1235, 1236, 1265, 1321,
1419, 1471, 1472, 1711, 1750,
1835a, 1884, 2024, 2057, 2359,
2360, 2404, 2406, 2407, 2459,
2466, 2477, 2483, 2541, 2548,
2654, 2673, 2743, 2757, 2994,
3005, 3006, 3190
Greer, Jane, 1796, 2557
Greer, Minnie, 267

Greet, Dinah,   1237
"Greetings,"   3002
Grenier, Madame Hilda,   985,
    1642, 1846, 2375
Grey, Shirley,   2170, 2408, 2428,
    3452
Grey, Virginia,   2997
"Greyfriars Bobby,"   375
"Grido, Il,"   1922
Griffe, Jacques,   565
Griffith, Corinne,   65, 647, 648,
    669, 823, 824, 828, 979, 1240,
    1731, 1916, 2950, 3010, 3031,
    3039, 3290, 3400, 3402, 3472,
    3537
Griffith, D.W.,   645, 1012, 1174,
    1175, 1198, 2057, 2144, 2860
Griffith, Mrs. D.W.,   1198
"Grip, The,"   2171
Grogan, Zita,   3309a
Gross, Laurence,   1243
Grossbeck, Dan,   566
"Grounds for Divorce,"   1491
"Grounds for Marriage,"   2595
"Grown-Up Children,"   2361
Gründel, Dorit,   1244
Grunstrom, Agnes,   3623
Gryś, Lidia,   1245
"Guarded Hour, The,"   2440
Gucci's,   1223
Guerin, Charles,   1246
"Guerre Est Finie, La,"   1676,
    1925
"Guess What Happened to Count
    Dracula,"   282
"Guess Who's Coming to Dinner,"
    1634, 3201
"Guilt of Janet Ames, The,"   1807
"Guilty as Hell,"   2401
"Guilty Generation,"   3232
"Guilty Hands,"   2388
Guinness, Alec,   93
"Gun Fight,"   350, 1908
"Gun Hawk, The,"   3440
"Gun Street,"   350, 1908
"Gunfight at Comanche Creek,"
    124
"Gunfighters of Casa Grande,"
    2868
"Gunn,"   826
"Guns at Batasi,"   1852
"Guns for San Sebastian,"   3581
"Guns of Navarone, The,"   1735
"Guns of the Black Witch,"   2369
"Guns of the Magnificent Seven,"
    2938
Gunter, Daisy,   1248
"Guru, The,"   756, 1899, 3295

"Guy Named Joe, A,"   670, 985
Guyot, Jacqueline,   1249
"Guys and Dolls,"   2964
"Gypsy,"   678, 1130, 1619, 2281,
    2285

Haack, Morton,   1254, 2629
Hackett, Florence,   1256
Hackman, Gene,   2377
Haddock, Lillias,   1257
Haffenden, Elizabeth,   1259, 2144,
    3207, 3414
"Hagbard and Signe,"   3056
Hagen, Jean,   2514
Hagen, Lilo,   1260
Hahn, Birgitta,   1261
Hahn, Manon,   1262
"Hail, Hero!,"   1858, 2796
Haines, William,   3223
Hale, Alan,   1774
Hale, Barbara,   2738
Hale, Georgina,   1213
Haley, Jack,   1286, 1677, 1849,
    3113, 3567
"Half a Sixpence,"   374, 1259
"Half Angel,"   392
"Half Way Girl, The,"   2354
Hall, Dorothy,   1171
Hall, Geneva,   1814
Hall, Leslie,   1269
Hall, Peter,   1270
Hall, Ruth,   2410
"Hallelujah,"   1091
"Hallelujah the Hills,"   219
"Hallelujah Trail, The,"   1559
Halston,   1271, 1272, 2723
Hamilton, George,   2628
Hamilton, Jane,   1814, 2430, 2433,
    2703
Hamilton, Lloyd,   1302
Hamilton, Margaret,   903
Hamilton, Murray,   1241
Hamilton, Peggy,   629, 1207, 2860,
    2861, 3006, 3278
Hamilton-Kearse, Virginia,   1274
"Hamlet" (1948),   1110, 1111, 1112
"Hamlet" (1964),   1229
"Hamlet" (1966),   3359
"Hammerhead,"   688
"Hammersmith Is Out,"   1694
Hammerstein, Elaine,   296
Hampshire, Susan,   711
Hampton, Hope,   1276, 1503, 2621
Hancock, Ruth,   1277
"Hand, The" (1961),   1126

"Hand in Hand," 1541
"Hand of Death," 1517
"Handle with Care," 1927
"Hands Across the Table," 550, 1870, 2842
"Hands of Orlac, The," 364
"Handy Andy," 2424
"Hang 'Em High," 1951, 2131, 3592
"Hanged Man, The," 2628
"Hanging at Jefferson City, The," 1013
"Hannie Caulder," 57
Hanoszek, Anna, 1281
Hansen, Eleanor, 3089
Hansen, Juanita, 686
"Happening, The," 602, 3022
"Happy Ending, The," 2779
"Happy Landing," 976
"Happy Thieves, The," 2797
Harbeck, Celine, 1282
"Hard Day's Night, A," 2026
"Hard to Handle," 2405
"Hard Way, The," 3600
"Hard-Boiled Haggerty," 2676
Harding, Ann, 439, 1021, 1234, 1927, 1932, 2352, 2372, 2404, 2417, 2640, 3399, 3448, 3449, 3473
Harding, Lynn, 327
Hardwicke, Sir Cecil, 1111
"Harem Bunch; or War and Piece, The," 3442
Harkrider, John, 1067, 1268, 1285
Harlow, Jean, 16, 556, 737, 1231, 1294, 1296, 1399, 1749, 1871, 1913, 2065, 2763, 2932
"Harlow" (5/14/65), 2025
"Harlow" (6/23/65), 515, 1349, 1888, 3127
"Harper," 900, 3052
Harper's Bazaar, 356, 370, 926, 929, 1661, 2783, 3077
Harris, Grace, 1288
Harris, Julie (designer), 967, 972, 1107, 1289, 1290, 1291, 2144, 2803
Harris, Margaret F., 1292, 1293, 2093/4, 2096
Harris, Mildred, 2057
Harris, Mrs., 645, 1303, 2057
Harrison, Rex, 229, 875, 2964, 2966
Harrison, Vangie, 1301
Hart, William S., 304, 1013, 1303, 2037, 3463
Harte, Michael, 1304

Hartnell, Norman, 1307
Harton, Wally, 1308
"Harum Scarum," 2300, 3324, 3441
Harvey, Irene, 2419, 2420, 2423
Harvey, Laurence, 451
Harvey, Lilian, 1931, 2168, 2412, 2433, 2763, 3449
"Harvey Girls, The," 673
Hassler, Emil, 469
Hasso, Signe, 3285
"Hatari!," 256
"Hatchet Man, The," 2994
hats, headdresses, 23, 37, 54, 121, 129, 134, 143, 149, 158, 162, 214, 217, 229, 234, 261, 310, 314, 332, 389, 393, 465, 485, 502, 519, 525, 562, 572, 573, 584, 585, 599, 616, 631, 643, 646, 681, 714, 715, 739, 749, 751, 769, 868, 875, 875, 884, 916, 936, 966, 969, 987, 1007, 1011, 1024, 1044, 1054, 1087, 1106, 1111, 1182, 1198, 1223, 1224, 1273, 1273, 1275, 1283, 1294, 1305, 1311, 1315, 1317, 1349, 1383, 1385, 1416, 1420, 1421, 1429, 1441, 1458, 1484, 1536, 1540, 1557, 1607, 1661, 1677, 1696, 1698, 1700, 1709, 1721, 1731, 1762, 1784, 1798, 1802, 1826, 1836, 1843, 1849, 1855, 1870, 1872, 1876, 1894, 1926, 1954, 2001, 2024, 2037, 2057, 2106, 2108, 2114, 2177, 2197, 2200, 2200, 2233a, 2244, 2245, 2267, 2268, 2371, 2374, 2375, 2376, 2384, 2391, 2419, 2421, 2422, 2425, 2430, 2437, 2440, 2440, 2447, 2459, 2474, 2523, 2526, 2527, 2531, 2554, 2557, 2626, 2631, 2650, 2664, 2708, 2722, 2792, 2838, 2848, 2884, 2893, 2916, 2917, 2921, 2952, 2979, 2990, 3007, 3014, 3026, 3031, 3040, 3078, 3081, 3102, 3148, 3156, 3163, 3164, 3174, 3196, 3231, 3233, 3264, 3266, 3287, 3322, 3365, 3370, 3374, 3398, 3406, 3407, 3450, 3464, 3481, 3482, 3493, 3496, 3529, 3542, 3549, 3553, 3582, 3584
Hatswell, Don, 2144
Hatton, Raymond, 138
"Haunting, The," 2680
Haver, June, 483, 1449, 1538, 2613
Haver, Phyllis, 2947

"Having a Wild Weekend," 1542
"Having a Wonderful Time," 942,
    2458, 3091
Havoc, June, 883
"Hawaii," 1349, 2938
"Hawaiians, The," 1391
Hawes, Elizabeth, 423, 807,
    1318, 2279, 2335
Hawes and Curtis, 1996
"Hawks and the Sparrows, The,"
    563, 818, 2647
Hawley, Vanda, 1134
Hawley, Wanda, 3498, 3513
Hawn, Goldie, 579
Hayden, Sterling, 3046
Haydon, Julie, 2424
Hayes, David, 1319
Hayes, Sadie, 1320
Haymes, Dick, 1654, 3232
Haynes, Harry, 1321
Hays Office, 438, 556, 737,
    1808, 3025, 3305
Hayward, Douglas, 273, 1322
Hayward, Susan, 91, 192, 547,
    952, 984, 1387, 2574, 3591
Hayworth, Rita, 140, 250, 288,
    351, 478, 556, 754, 1161,
    1181, 1345, 1654, 1673, 1718,
    1749, 1806, 1808, 1968, 2125,
    2797, 3032, 3209, 3232, 3555
"He Couldn't Take It," 3495
"He Learned About Women," 2403
Head, Edith, 3, 91, 145, 148,
    275, 289, 290, 320, 334, 368,
    369, 408, 413, 443, 480, 515,
    524, 526, 546, 548, 549, 550,
    554, 556, 561, 609, 617, 666,
    670, 674, 675, 678, 679, 683,
    713, 729, 732, 734, 775, 778,
    788, 829, 859, 867, 868, 883,
    889, 890, 891, 895, 970, 975,
    977, 991, 1022, 1070, 1077,
    1079, 1127, 1183, 1198, 1227,
    1231, 1242, 1252, 1255, 1263,
    1312, 1324, 1325, 1326, 1327,
    1328, 1329, 1330, 1331, 1332,
    1333, 1334, 1335, 1336, 1337,
    1338, 1339, 1340, 1341, 1342,
    1343, 1344, 1346, 1347, 1348,
    1349, 1350, 1351, 1352, 1353,
    1354, 1355, 1356, 1357, 1358,
    1392, 1399, 1402, 1419, 1420,
    1427, 1437, 1464, 1489, 1490,
    1494, 1504, 1574, 1577, 1591,
    1594, 1671, 1678, 1683, 1692,
    1694, 1711, 1744, 1816, 1827,
    1835a, 1855, 1878, 1880, 1907,
    1917, 1963, 1992, 2024, 2025,
    2059, 2066, 2075, 2106, 2107,
    2138, 2173, 2195, 2200, 2259,
    2326, 2404, 2448, 2450, 2456,
    2462, 2467, 2475, 2480, 2481,
    2485, 2488, 2498, 2502, 2507,
    2508, 2519, 2521, 2526, 2542,
    2544, 2553, 2556, 2560, 2568,
    2575, 2578, 2585, 2597, 2601,
    2603, 2604, 2617, 2628, 2628,
    2629, 2651, 2667, 2728, 2742,
    2745, 2747, 2748, 2749, 2757,
    2784, 2794, 2897, 2917, 2981,
    3045, 3046, 3059, 3100, 3122,
    3131, 3153, 3164, 3182, 3188,
    3207, 3230, 3231, 3231, 3287,
    3377, 3418, 3420, 3420, 3428,
    3468, 3546, 3561, 3595, 3599,
    3602, 3609, 3619
"Head," 139
"Head of the Family, The," 932
headdress (see hats/headdresses)
"Headline Shooters," 2175
"Heads We Go," 2932
Hearst, William Randolph, 479,
    926, 1247, 3077, 3184, 3457
"Heart Is a Lonely Hunter, The,"
    3570
"Heart of a Siren, The," 3021
"Hearts of the World," 1175
Heather, Jean, 2129
"Heat's On, The," 1653
"Heavens Above!," 1020
Heckart, Eileen, 69
Heckroth, Hein, 466, 1154, 1361,
    1362, 2003
"Heedless Moths," 1820
Hegarty, Hazel, 1363
"Heidi," 1433, 1703
Heim, 1364
"Heiress, The," 275, 526, 671,
    1342, 2617, 3377
Helbling, Jeanne, 719
"Held in Trust," 3536
"Held to Answer," 411
"Heldinnen," 1045, 1730, 2166
"Helen of Troy," 1114, 2144
Helfgott, Ann, 1371
"Hell Below," 1930
"Hell Boats," 1883
"Hell Cat, The," 2860
"Hell Is for Heroes," 1308
"Hellcats, The," 1936
"Heller in Pink Tights, 1345, 1917
"Hello, Dolly!," 875, 1749, 2964,
    2968, 3597
"Hello, Frisco, Hello," 1214, 1853,
    2808
"Hello--Goodbye," 757, 2863, 3316

"Hell's Angels," 737, 1142, 1231, 1399, 1442
"Hell's Angels on Wheels," 3325
"Hell's Highroad," 3009
Helm, Jacques, 1372
"Help!," 1237
hemlines, 65, 220, 298, 527, 838, 882, 1618, 1762, 1792, 1808, 2078, 2332, 2376, 2382, 2669, 2952, 3009, 3010, 3215, 3218, 3304, 3305, 3397, 3401, 3420
Hemming, Violet, 1134
Henaberry, Joseph, 388
Hendrix, Wanda, 1330, 2568
Henie, Sonja, 702, 976, 2465, 2730, 2930, 3302
Henry, Carol, 2312
"Henry V," 1111, 1112, 1113, 1114, 1136, 3336
Henze, Jurgen, 1375
Hepburn, Audrey, 100, 149, 229, 234, 235, 556, 1057, 1178, 1179, 1202, 1339, 1345, 1454, 1577, 1680, 2689, 2737, 2817, 2910
Hepburn, Katharine, 27, 134, 313, 329, 679, 693, 808, 816, 944, 1268, 1336, 1520, 1603, 1635, 1719, 1749, 1870, 1892, 1928, 1962, 2023, 2024, 2093/4, 2375, 2401, 2406, 2407, 2440, 2459, 2524, 2532, 2540, 2548, 2640, 2642, 2664, 2725, 2729, 2762, 2793, 2915, 3091, 3119, 3471
"Her Better Self," 1238
"Her Bodyguard," 2175
"Her Fatal Millions," 599, 3353
"Her First Biscuits," 2626
"Her Gilded Cage," 3219
"Her Highness and the Bellboy," 673, 1520, 3419
"Her Husband's Affairs," 1510
"Her Love Story," 1862, 2124, 3472, 3481
"Her Man," 1105
"Her Night of Romance," 1722
"Her Own Free Will," 1367
"Her Primitive Man," 3057
"Her Reputation," 3072
"Her Temporary Husband," 966
Herberg, Claudia, 1376
Herbert, Holmes, 826, 1905
Herbert, Jocelyn, 1378, 1379
"Hercules and the Captive Women," 2822
"Hercules in New York," 3152
"Hercules in the Haunted World," 1169

"Hercules, Samson & Ulysses," 2804
"Here Comes Mr. Jordan," 1079
"Here Comes the Groom," 3609
"Here Is My Heart," 2428
"Here We Go 'Round the Mulberry Bush," 85, 2089
"Here's to Romance," 986, 1479
"Hero for a Day," 2476
"Heroes and Husbands," 2103, 2104
"Heroes of Telemark, The," 1015
"Hero's Island," 348
Herrington, George, 1386
"Hers to Hold," 1854
Herschel, 1387, 2018, 2458, 2536, 2574, 2808
Herwood, Marion, 1388
Heslewood, Tom, 2144
Heston, Charlton, 1335, 1391, 3020
Heveran, Martha, 2454
"Hey, Let's Twist!," 3390
Hiatt, Joe, 229
Hickson of Fifth Avenue, 1393, 3278
"High Society" (1929), 3400
"High Society" (1956), 2794
"High Treason," 3394
"High Wind in Jamaica, A," 1852
Higham, Sir Charles, 10
Hilborn, Thelma, 1395
Hildebrandt, Gudrun, 1396
Hill, George Roy, 788
Hill, Thelma, 2946
"Hill, The," 1015
Hillan, Rosalie, 3074
Hilliard, Harriet, 3091
Hilliard, Patricia, 2425
Hilling, John, 2803
"Hills Run Red, The," 2012
Hime, Marvin, 1400
"Hippodrome," 1045
"Hired Wife," 2040
Hirsch, Robert, 1895
"His Hour," 60, 2621
"His Neighbor's Wife," 3484
"His Secretary," 99, 1672
"His Supreme Moment," 3470
"His Tiger Lady," 194
"His Wife's Habit," 2248, 3200
"History Is Made at Night," 2448
"Hit Me Again," 3261, 3450
"Hit Parade of 1943," 30
"Hit the Deck," 1831
Hitchcock, Alfred, 788
"Hitler," 226, 422
Hobart, Rose, 2386
Hoffman, Alphretta, 762, 2056

Hoffman, Madame, 3527
Hoffman, Mr., 2843
Hoffma, Mrs. A.B., 2860
Hoffman, Pat, 1407
Hoffman, Walt, 1408
"Hold Back the Dawn," 550
"Hold 'Em Navy," 3553
"Hold On!," 2188, 2300
Holden, Joyce, 2606
Holden, Lansing C., 1409, 1410
Holger, Helmut, 1412
"Holiday," 990, 2540, 3091, 3473
"Holiday in Mexico," 2110
Holland, Kristina, 3420
Holliday, Judy, 3232
Holloway, Stanley, 229
"Hollywood Canteen," 366
Hollywood Costume Design
    (Chierichetti), 480, 549, 824,
    1487, 1683, 1835a, 2637, 2665,
    2744, 2745, 2964
Hollywood Costume--Glamour!
    Glitter! Romance! (McConathy
    & Vreeland), 11, 355, 824,
    2181, 2637, 2665, 2744, 2745,
    2746, 2755, 3149
Hollywood: Legende und Wirk-
    lichkeit (Hubert, Ali), 470,
    1477
Hollywood Men's Store, 1430
"Hollywood Party, The," 1934
"Hollywood Revue of 1929, The,"
    1091, 2706
Holm, Celeste, 2156, 2157
Holt, Jack, 2153, 3415
Holt, Joel, 2314
Höltz, Nicola, 1443
"Hombre," 820, 3392
Home for Tanya, A," 75
"Home in Indiana," 485
"Home Stretch, The," 2160, 3083
"Home Stuff," 2627
"Homecoming," 944
"Honeymoon," 1091, 1768, 2555
"Honeymoon Machine, The," 2809
"Hong Kong," 2603
"Honky Tonk," 1901, 3419
"Honolulu," 2990, 3244
"Hooded Falcon, The," 128, 502,
    1784, 2687, 2697, 2783, 3014,
    3300, 3319, 3384
"Hoodlum Priest, The," 736
"Hook, The," 1488
"Hook, Line and Sinker," 3338
"Hooked Generation, The," 1621
hoop skirts (see petticoats)
"Hoopla," 3623
Hope, Bob, 1846, 3285

Hopkins, George, 406
Hopkins, Miriam, 670, 1000, 1273,
    1933, 2170, 2177, 2192, 2352,
    2372, 2394, 2395, 2402, 2414,
    2415, 2417, 2457, 2731, 2763,
    2955, 3452, 3453, 3549
Hopper, Hedda, 2387, 2399, 2531,
    2851, 2921
"Hopper," 111
Horn, Marianne, 2914
Horn, Van, 1447
"Hornets' Nest," 2139
"Horrible Dr. Hichcock, The," 3114
"Horror Hotel," 1157
"Horse Feathers," 2398
"Horse in the Gray Flannel Suit,
    The," 3180
hosiery (including socks), 106, 121,
    162, 220, 388, 389, 502, 754,
    883, 1200, 1201, 1449, 1456,
    1709, 1718, 1721, 1779, 1789,
    1838, 2186, 2263, 2265, 2377,
    2546, 2626, 2627, 2703, 2788,
    3061, 3080, 3147, 3148, 3480,
    3482, 3555
"Hostage, The," 913
"Hot for Paris," 1424
"Hot Girls for Men Only," 1845
"Hot Millions," 2701
"Hot Pepper," 2405, 2762
"Hotbed of Sin," 2750, 2892
"Hotel Imperial," 613, 1394
"Hotel Paradiso," 876
"Hottentot," 2381
"Houdini," 1221
"Hour of the Gun," 745
"Hour of the Wolf," 1893
"Hours of Love, The," 2325
"House Across the Bay, The," 3087
"House of Cards," 2887
"House of Dark Shadows," 2090
"House of Rothschild, The," 2419,
    3496
"House of Secrets," 1289
"House of the Damned," 2999
"House of the Lost Court, The,"
    1622
"House of Women," 736, 1256
"House with an Attic," 872
"Houseboat," 1345
"Householder, The," 1162
Houston, Grace, 2559, 2618
"How I Won the War," 1237
"How Sweet It Is!," 2809, 2993
"How the West Was Won," 1437,
    2641
"How to Commit Marriage," 2025
"How to Make It," 800

"How to Save a Marriage--and Ruin Your Life," 387, 1581
"How to Seduce a Playboy," 1412
"How to Steal a Million," 1178
"How to Succeed in Business Without Really Trying," 2013
Howard, Leslie, 2144, 3322
Howard, Mary, 3453
"Howards of Virginia, The" (1940), 3250
Howie, Helga, 3101
Hoyt, Peggy, 1731
Huarte, Mario, 1474
Huber, Charles, 1475
Hubert, Ali, 469, 470, 1476, 1477
Hubert, Rene, 582, 628, 675, 676, 709, 728, 801, 858, 960, 1022, 1052, 1089, 1173, 1214, 1299, 1478, 1479, 1480, 1481, 1915, 1965, 2024, 2124, 2141, 2425, 2427, 2429, 2434, 2435, 3393, 3553
"Hud," 526
"Huddle," 3279
Hudnut, Mrs., 2697
Hudnut, Richard, 2032
Hudnut, Winifred Shaunessy (see Rambova, Natacha)
Hudson, Earl, 1024
Hudson, Rochelle, 313, 2018, 2425, 2430, 3548
Hughes, Howard, 797, 1142
Hulse, Dorothea, 1284
"Human Duplicators, The," 2134
Hume, Benita, 1930, 2527, 2763
"Humming Bird, The," 613, 1189, 2199, 2260
"Humoresque," 100, 554
"Hunchback of Notre Dame, The" (1923), 1486, 1906, 3170, 3466
"Hunchback of Notre Dame, The" (1939), 1085, 3466, 3555
"Hunchback of Rome, The," 1151
"Hunger," 3036
"Huns, The," 1169
Hunt, Grady, 1488
Hunt, Marsha, 1870, 2448, 2526
Hunter, Winifred, 3335
"Hunting Trouble," 2233
"Hurricane, The," 732
"Hurricane Smith," 2981
"Hurricane's Gal," 973, 2103, 2104
"Hurry Sundown," 404, 934, 1129, 1761, 2339
"Husbands," 604, 1745
"Husband's Holiday," 2392
"Husbands of Edith, The," 2130

"Husband's Trademark, The," 2778
"Hush ... Hush, Sweet Charlotte," 1656
Hussey, Ruth, 2755
"Hustler, The," 2071
Huston, John, 1594
Huston, Walter, 3164
Hutchinson, Josephine, 315, 3427
Hutton, Betty, 609, 859, 868, 891, 1242, 1341, 1347, 2560, 2651, 3153, 3487
Hyams, Leila, 2401
Hyde, Sally, 1496
Hyde-White, Wilfred, 229
Hyer, Martha, 2036

IATSE & MPMO (see also unions), 1500
"I Am Suzanne," 3449
"I, Claudius," 2202, 3439
"I Could Go On Singing," 1127, 1343
"I Dream Too Much," 1814
"I Escape from Hong Kong," 1214
I. Frank & Sons, 567
"I Give My Life," 3429
"I Kiss Your Hand, Madame," 388, 2072
ILGWU (see International Ladies Garment Workers Union)
"I Like It That Way," 2417
"I Live for Love," 310
"I Live My Life," 310, 882, 2661, 3231
"I Love a Soldier," 3608
"I Love Lucy," 547, 552
"I Love My Wife," 2871
"I Love That Man," 2409
"I Love You Again," 2486
"I Love You, Alice B. Toklas!," 3327
"I Loved You Wednesday," 1932, 2673
"I Married a Communist," 2497
"I Married an Angel," 3432
"I Married You for Fun," 2853
"I Met Him in Paris," 608, 1067, 1979, 2452, 2529, 2917
"I Never Sang for My Father," 69
"I Pagliacci," 3382
"I Remember Mama," 3140
"I Take This Woman," 33, 363, 562, 2387, 2470
"I Thank a Fool," 1259, 1786
"I Wake Up Screaming," 2755

"I Walk Alone," 1341
"I Want a Divorce," 1547
"I Want My Man," 662, 3470
"I Wanted Wings," 543, 3164, 3247
"I Was a Shoplifter," 2241, 2501
"I Was an Adventuress," 847, 2483
"I Wonder Who's Kissing Her Now," 1170
"Ice Follies of 1939, The," 700, 2547
Ichida, Kiichi, 1501
"Ideal Husband, An," 228, 1266, 1658, 3074, 3076
"Idiot's Delight," 217, 1445, 1877, 2543, 2730, 2983, 2985
"Idol, The," 326
"If ....," 604
"If a Man Answers," 3064, 3431
"If He Hollers, Let Him Go!," 422, 3187
"If I Marry Again," 884
"If I Were Queen," 300
"If It's Tuesday, This Must Be Belgium," 1765
"If You Knew Susie," 2738
"I'll Be Hanged If I Do," 2410
"I'll Cry Tomorrow," 2810
"I'll Never Forget What's 'Is Name," 297
"I'll Take Romance," 2133
"Illegal Entry," 959, 2494, 2580
"Illusion," 3395
"Illustrated Man, The," 1304, 3189
"I'm All Right," 2276
"I'm No Angel," 1482, 1932
"Imitation of Life" (1934), 313, 1493, 2426, 2427, 2428
"Immoral Charge," 1246
"Immortal Story, The," 451
"Immortelle, L'," 2761
"Impact," 827
"Impatient Maiden," 2396
"Importance of Being Earnest, The," 743
"Impossible Mrs. Bellew, The," 1192, 2272
"Impossible on Saturday," 1895, 2815
In a Glamorous Fashion (La Vine), 1835a
"In Caliente," 1871, 2023
"In Cold Blood," 1949
"In Every Woman's Life," 2622
"In Harm's Way," 404, 745, 1288, 1761, 2888, 2938
"In Like Flint," 56, 1958

"In Old Chicago," 976, 1498, 2133, 3555
"In Person," 310, 2792, 2987
"In Search of Gregory," 958
"In Search of the Castaways," 375
"In the Cool of the Day," 169, 2281
"In the Doghouse," 910
"In the French Style," 3333
"In the Heat of the Night," 1761
"In This Our Life," 3433
"Inadmissible Evidence," 1119
Ince, Thomas, 2860
"Incident, The," 1150
"Incident in an Alley," 350, 1983
"Incredible Mr. Limpet, The," 361, 2767
"Infernal Machine," 1929
Ingram, Rex, 2237, 2697, 2752
"Innocents, The," 784, 1126, 2095
"Inserts," 1213
"Inside Daisy Clover," 226, 358, 1692
"Inspector Clouseau," 169, 1237, 2078
"Inspiration," 440, 562, 2384
"Intent to Kill," 402
"Interference," 152, 2579, 3139
"Interlude," 2446, 2447, 2526, 2771
"International," 754
"International House," 1079, 1929, 1930, 1931, 2170, 2409
International Ladies Garment Workers Union (ILGWU), 2174
"International Settlement," 942
"Internes Can't Take Money," 3100
"Interpreter's House, The," 660
Intlekofer, John, 1517
"Into the Net," 2621
"Intolerance," 388, 645, 824, 1174, 1175, 1465, 1812, 3385
"Invasion of the Star Creatures," 9
"Invasion Quartet," 169
"Invasion 1700," 216
"Investigation of a Citizen Above Suspicion," 1988, 2876, 3253
"Invincible Sex, The," 2151
"Invisible Dr. Mabuse, The," 2347
"Invisible Fear, The," 852
"Invitation to Ruin," 2316
"Ipcress File, The," 793
"Iphigenia," 100
Irene (Irene Lentz Gibbons), 36, 371, 550, 554, 586, 596, 673, 698, 735, 792, 841, 909, 993, 1022, 1042, 1125, 1182, 1294, 1388, 1497, 1504, 1518, 1519, 1520, 1521, 1522, 1523, 1524,

1525, 1526, 1527, 1670, 1693,
1815, 1835a, 1890, 1955, 1978,
2028, 2040, 2057, 2065, 2073,
2077, 2100, 2105, 2110, 2113,
2159, 2234, 2403, 2454, 2456,
2471, 2473, 2476, 2478, 2523,
2531, 2546, 2652, 2788, 2862,
2916, 2921, 2937, 2992, 3229,
3232, 3370, 3533, 3603, 3620
"Irene" (1926), 612, 1226, 1448,
1528, 1531, 1731, 2056, 2936
"Irene" (1940), 541, 2152
Irene of Bullocks-Wilshire (see
Irene)
Iribe, Paul, 861, 1198, 1532,
1533
"Irish Luck," 676
"Irma La Douce," 1559, 2281
"Iron Horse, The," 1013
"Iron Mask, The" (1929), 416,
513
"Is My Face Red," 1403
"Is Paris Burning?," 2223, 3616
"Isabel," 2318
"Isadora," 364, 375, 2135
"Island Wives," 3537
"Isn't Life Wonderful," 2692
Israel, Ethel, 2808, 3340
Israel, Walter J., 143, 1457,
1535, 1753, 1782, 2048, 2808,
3340
"It," 1399, 3466
"It!," 1158
"It All Came True," 2482
"It Had to Be You," 1806
"It Happened at the World's Fair,"
3202
"It Happened in Athens," 2337
"It Happened One Night," 754, 1651,
3050, 3264, 3450, 3495
"It Started with a Kiss," 1917
"Italian Job, The," 1237, 2649
"It's a Date," 1508
"It's a Mad, Mad, Mad, Mad
World," 1634
"It's a Pleasure," 3302
"It's All Yours," 2455
"It's Great to Be Alive," 2410,
2763
"It's Love Again," 2374
"It's Not My Body," 3421
"Ivanhoe," 396, 1114
Ivers, Julia Crawford, 2668
Iverson, Stuart, 275
"Ivy," 1250

"Jack and the Beanstalk," 2662
"Jack of Diamonds," 1443
"Jack the Giant Killer," 280, 1908,
2827
Jackson, Glenda, 1213, 1414, 1840
Jackson, Jackie, 1541
Jacobs, Sally, 1542, 1543
Jaeckel, 2921, 2961
Jamandreu, Paco, 1544
"Jane Eyre" (1944), 670, 858,
1073
Janet, Janine, 1548
"Janice Meredith," 3184, 3243,
3472
Jannings, Emil, 2960
"Japonette," 2227
"Jaws," 904, 1212
Jax, 1549
"Jazz Singer, The" (1953), 444
Jeakins, Dorothy, 120, 279, 713,
1437, 1550, 1551, 1552, 1598,
1789, 2200, 2628, 2858, 3370,
3377, 3599
"Jealous Husbands," 3082
"Jealousy," 3049
Jean Louis (Jean Louis Berthault),
58, 351, 478, 556, 713, 874,
1181, 1198, 1510, 1554, 1555,
1654, 1660, 1789, 1805, 1806,
1807, 1808, 1809, 1810, 1811,
1828, 1878, 1917, 2076, 2081,
2589, 2605, 2608, 2843, 3032,
3232, 3308
Jeanmaire, Zizi, 1312, 1678
"Jeanne Eagels," 1831
Jeans, Ursula, 960
Jefferies, Wesley V. (see also
Jeffries, Wes), 1558
Jeffries, Wes (see also Jefferies,
Wesley V.), 1559
Jennings, De Witte, 3175
Jenny, 983
"Jenny," 2823
Jenssen, Elois, 555, 1561
Jenssen, John, 2200
"Jessica," 2139, 2155
Jester, Ralph, 550, 2200
"Jet Pilot," 2586
Jeunique Fashions, 1562
Jewel, Betty, 323
"Jewel Robbery," 3542
Jewell, Isabel, 2420
jewelry, jewels for trim, 2, 7,
95, 141, 162, 201, 211, 286,
536, 546, 601, 605, 676, 687,
696, 714, 715, 749, 763, 790,
794, 875, 936, 949, 950, 1195,
1209, 1215, 1333, 1349, 1454,

1539, 1539, 1560, 1563, 1587,
1637, 1645, 1658, 1698, 1725,
1731, 1748, 1766, 1770, 1849,
1862, 1872, 1878, 1979, 2010,
2081, 2124, 2148, 2200, 2213,
2244, 2245, 2265, 2269, 2321,
2366, 2377, 2403, 2425, 2432,
2437, 2440, 2447, 2468, 2473,
2523, 2531, 2533, 2536, 2539,
2540, 2546, 2550, 2554, 2664,
2669, 2788, 2794, 2803, 2883,
2900, 2921, 2956, 2979, 2985,
3014, 3030, 3044, 3060, 3103,
3115, 3118, 3140, 3174, 3196,
3231, 3238, 3287, 3300, 3414,
3431, 3481, 3483, 3493, 3550,
3563, 3584, 3623
"Jezebel," 1416, 1420, 1440,
1757, 2550, 2554, 3112
"Jigsaw," 1488
"Jimmy and Sally," 2177
"Joan of Arc," 279, 1283, 1512,
1552, 1598, 1892, 3377
"Joan the Woman," 388, 762
"Joanna," 604, 834, 1274, 1731,
3460
Jobe, Bill, 1567
"Joe," 1611
Joerger, Jeffrey, 3419
Johann, Zita, 2403, 2423
"John and Mary," 3189
John Frederics, 562, 1953, 2447,
2531, 2665, 2916, 2921, 2991,
3102
"John Goldfarb, Please Come
Home!," 173, 2998
"John Paul Jones," 2144
"Johnny Cool," 3569
"Johnny Guitar," 3231
"Johnny Reno," 2383
"Johnny Tiger," 447, 1866
Johns, Bertram, 1569
Johns, Glynis, 678, 3074
Johnson, Edith, 2229
Johnson, Judge, 1570
Johnson, Kay, 1916, 2424
Johnson, Rita, 942, 2547
Johnston, Edward, 217
Johnstone, Anna Hill, 886, 1572,
1573
"Jokers, The," 126
Jones, Buck, 1013, 2037
Jones, Disley, 1575, 1576
Jones, James Earl, 2964
Jones, Jennifer, 134, 675,
858, 1228, 2028, 3234

Jones, Mrs., 1175
Jones, Robert Edmond, 2731
Jones, Shirley, 1437
Jordan, Dorothy, 2396, 2402
Jordan, Miriam, 1929, 2406, 2407
Jordan, Sally, 1580
Joseff, 2468
Joseff of California, 2788
Joseff of Hollywood, 2546, 3103
Joseph, Dina, 1581
"Joseph and His Brethren," 1654
Josephy of Hollywood, 2536
"Josette," 2461, 2538, 3093
Jourdan, Louis, 233
"Journey Beneath the Desert," 2822
"Journey to Shiloh," 124, 1269,
3193
"Journey to the Far Side of the Sun,"
1015
"Journey to the Seventh Planet,"
3611
"Jovita," 1600
Joy, Gloria, 2249
Joy, Leatrice, 299, 388, 530, 654,
763, 823, 1105, 1463, 1491, 1727,
2270, 3006, 3009, 3118, 3563
"Joy of Living, The," 2537, 2538,
3090, 3388
Joyce, Alice, 1116, 2124, 2950
Joyce, Frances, 2961
Joyce, Peggy Hopkins, 1929, 2170
"Joys of Jezebel, The," 1790, 2805
"Juarez," 2148, 2366, 2473, 2550,
2554, 3550
"Judex," 685
Judge, Arline, 2522, 2756, 3409
"Judge and the Sinner, The," 1262
"Judge Hardy's Children," 114
"Judgment at Nuremberg," 1634
"Judith," 326, 2804
"Jules et Jim" ("Jules and Jim"),
273, 447, 478
"Julia," 3041
"Juliet of the Spirits," 1151, 1625
"Julius Caesar" (1922), 3298
"Julius Caesar" (1970), 1391
"Jumbo," 1254, 2629
"June Madness," 3350, 3354, 3355
"Jungle Princess, The," 556, 732,
1337, 1417, 3122
"Just for Fun," 3013, 3136
"Just for You," 1221
"Just Imagine," 2274, 3277
"Just Like a Woman," 2097
"Just Off Broadway," 2982
"Justine," 2964, 2968

Kaaren, Suzanne, 1429, 2418
Kagan, Jeremy Paul, 788
Kai-shek, Mme. Chiang, 365
"Kaleidoscope," 1058, 3029, 3286
Kalloch (Robert Kalloch), 313, 990,
  1067, 1231, 1264, 1593, 1654,
  1870, 1911, 1926, 1933, 2023,
  2076, 2133, 2195, 2403, 2406,
  2409, 2410, 2414, 2415, 2416,
  2419, 2423, 2426, 2428, 2433,
  2450, 2455, 2525, 2533, 2537,
  2540, 2549, 2704, 2755, 2763,
  3084, 3492
Kalmus, Herbert, 1286
Kalmus, Natalie, 228, 1044, 1286,
  2141, 3208, 3595
"Kama Sutra," 2688
Kamali, Norma, 100
"Kanal," 3191
Kane, Diana, 658, 2950
Kane, Helen, 1423
Kara, Edmund, 1595
"Karate, the Hand of Death," 2314
Karinska (Barbara), 235, 550, 592,
  1596, 1597, 1598, 1599, 1760, 1956,
  1957, 2028, 2837, 2912, 2964
Karloff, Boris, 1779, 3309
Karmolińska, Maria, 1600
Karp, Soni, 1601
Kasparova, T., 1602
Katash, Ruth, 807
"Katie," 2592
Katona, Piroska, 1609
Kaufman, Rita, 1929, 1930, 1932,
  1935, 2407, 2410, 2414, 2416,
  2808, 3488
Kaufmann, Christine, 3316
Kaufmann, Hermann J., 1610
Kay, Andrew, 1611
Kay, Kathleen, 1612, 1948
"Kaya, I'll Kill You," 3192
Keaton, Buster, 143, 388, 2049,
  2247, 2901, 3582
Keaton, Diane, 3568
Keehne, Chuck, 1614
Keeler, Ruby, 309, 730, 1696,
  3092
Keene, Tom, 1709
"Keeping Company," 373
Keith, Donald, 3157
Keith, Ian, 672
Kellerman, Annette, 103
Kelly, Dorothy, 686
Kelly, Gene, 1654, 2028
Kelly, Grace, 526, 546, 1263,
  1345, 1678, 2794, 2808, 2981,
  3377
"Kelly's Heroes," 1006

Kelton, Pert, 3451
Kemp, Jan, 1620
Kendell, Kay, 1718
Kennedy, Eddie, 3467
Kennedy, Madge, 2150
Kennedy, Merna, 1065
"Kenner," 342
Kenyon, Doris, 662, 777, 1699,
  2218, 2354, 2622, 3539
Kerness, Donna, 2084
Kerr, Deborah, 679
Kerridge, Mary, 1112
Kerwin, Barbara, 1621
Kestelman, Sara, 1840
Key, Kathleen, 1608, 2291
Keyes, Evelyn, 1806, 1808
Keyes, Marion Herwood, 1624
"Keyhole, The," 1754, 2406, 2407,
  2994
Khambatta, Persis, 552
"Khartoum," 1852
Khoury, Marc, 1626
Kiam, Omar, 211, 306, 366, 698,
  732, 883, 1397, 1470, 1627,
  1628, 1629, 1630, 1631, 1978,
  1984, 2255, 2365, 2432, 2444,
  2445, 2449, 2454, 2457, 2466,
  2521, 2525, 2527, 2531, 2783,
  2916, 2921, 3046, 3100, 3548
"Kid Auto Races at Venice," 1843
"Kid Galahad" (1937), 3573
"Kid Galahad" (1962), 435, 1438
"Kid Rodelo," 2363
"Kiev Comedy, A," 223
"Kill or Be Killed," 772
"Kill or Cure," 1259
"Killing of Sister George, The,"
  2288, 2739
"Kimberley Jim," 2770
"Kind Hearts and Coronets," 93
"Kind Men Marry, The," 2476
"Kind of Loving, A," 2189
"Kindred of the Dust," 645
Kinds, Karl, 1633
King, Andrea, 94, 2241, 3302
King, Anita, 1638
King, Joe, 1634
King, Muriel, 693, 1043, 1635,
  1636, 2455, 2532, 2725, 2793,
  3574
King, Roger Milner, 1637
"King and Country," 2649
"King and I, The," 679, 1534,
  2164, 2964, 2965
"King in Shadow," 2639
"King Kong" (1933), 2640, 2664
"King Kong" (1976), 161, 904
"King of Alcatraz," 991

"King of Burlesque," 584
"King of Hearts," 1062
"King of Jazz, The," 567, 2821,
    3238
"King of Kings" (1961), 2938, 3382
"King of Kings, The" (1927), 762,
    1822, 2960, 2962
"King of the Damned," 584
"King of the Grizzlies," 2318
"King of the Roaring 20's--The
    Story of Arnold Rothstein," 2976,
    3440
"King Steps Out, The," 1220, 1267,
    1268, 1700, 2439
"Kings of the Sun," 1656
"King's Pirate, The," 2225
Kingsley, Mona, 2103, 2104
Kingston, Winifred, 741
"Kipps," 1088, 3076
Kirkham, Kathleen, 2232
Kirkland, Muriel, 1930
Kiselyova, V., 1641
"Kismet" (1930), 547
"Kismet" (1944), 1042, 1598
"Kismet" (1955), 877
"Kiss, The," 1433
"Kiss and Make Up," 2424
"Kiss and Tell," 2317
"Kiss for Cinderella, A," 2124
"Kiss in the Dark, A," 662, 2490
"Kiss Me Kate," 2628
"Kiss Me, Stupid," 435, 1559,
    2286
"Kiss the Girls and Make Them
    Die," 761
"Kisses for My President," 226
"Kissin' Cousins," 2300, 2657
Kitt, Eartha, 3487
"Kitten on the Keys," 3142
"Kitten with a Whip," 2022, 2827
"Kitty," 715, 1598, 1642, 1737
"Kitty Foyle," 548, 556, 2041,
    2079, 2258, 2263
Kiviette, 1305
Klein, Janine, 1644
Klotz, Florence, 1646, 1647,
    1648
"Knack ... and How to Get It, The,"
    273, 2771
Knapp, Edith, 2397
Kniepert, Erni, 1650
Knight, Lillian, 657
"Knight Without Armour," 1944
"Knights of the Round Table," 1114
Kobald, Jerry, 1655
Koch, Norma, 1656, 1660
Kohlschein, Margot, 1657
"Konigsmark," 790

Korda, Alexander, 1658
Korda, Michael, 1658
Korda, Vincent, 1658
Koscina, Sylva, 775, 1691
Kosloff, Theodore, 926, 1106, 1659,
    1774, 2960, 3456
"Krakatoa, East of Java," 3614
"Kremlin Letter, The," 1107
Kress, Sam, 2234
Kristos, Dimitri, 1662
Kruchinina, O., 1663
Kruger, Alma, 43, 981
Krumbachová, Ester, 1664
Kubrick, Stanley, 54
Kufel, Stanley, 1665
Kuhn, Grace, 1667
Kumar, Milena, 1668
Kunkle, Peggy, 1669
Kwan, Nancy, 1437, 1710
Kyrou, Ado, 3439
Kyser, Kay, 1996

"Lad: A Dog," 62, 1277
Ladd, Alan, 1856, 2629
"Ladies in Washington," 862
"Ladies Love Danger," 2834, 2835
"Ladies' Man," 813, 3188, 3555
Ladies of the Confederacy, 3322
"Ladies Who Do," 1321
"Lady, The," 1927
"Lady and the Cowboy, The," 538
"Lady and the Mob, The," 2549
"Lady Be Good," 1003, 1079, 2264
"Lady Bodyguard," 2259
"Lady Consents, The," 2372
"Lady Eve, The," 275, 556, 1312,
    1560, 3046, 3100, 3122
"Lady for a Day," 1933
"Lady from Shanghai, The," 1181,
    1673
"Lady Gambles, The," 2277
"Lady in a Cage," 1844
"Lady in the Car with Glasses
    and a Gun, The," 337, 805,
    3616
"Lady in the Dark," 275, 546, 550,
    551, 670, 679, 866, 985, 1047,
    1427, 1598, 1749, 1855, 3122,
    3377
"Lady Is Willing, The," 2631
"Lady L," 932, 1249
"Lady of Burlesque, The," 3555
"Lady of Monza, The," 818
"Lady of the Night," 1932, 2763
"Lady of the Pavements," 2274

"Lady of the Tropics," 1482, 2478
"Lady Sings the Blues," 57, 713, 1878
"Lady Who Lied, The," 3147
"Lady Windermere's Fan" (1925), 1219, 1529, 1698
"Ladybird, The," 2274
"Ladybug," 1573
"Lady's Profession, A," 1928, 2406
Laeerfeld, Karl, 1675
"Lafayette," 1249, 3267, 3617
Lafon, Madeleine, 1676
Lahr, Bert, 903, 1286, 1677, 1849
Lake, Alice, 322, 3522
Lake, Veronica, 1324, 1326, 1347, 1348, 3247, 3602
Lalique, Suzanne, 1679
La Marr, Barbara, 200, 201, 202, 790, 2047, 3021
Lamarr, Hedy, 33, 363, 562, 673, 948, 975, 1413, 1482, 1520, 2114, 2470, 2478, 3091, 3131, 3419, 3434
Lambert, Edward Phillips, 261, 296, 1578, 1579, 1712, 2407, 2408, 2664, 3264, 3391
Lambert, William, 324, 1043, 1268, 1478, 1682, 1915, 2170
Lamont, Molly, 2375
Lamour, Dorothy, 556, 732, 778, 833, 970, 1242, 1312, 1326, 1337, 1338, 1347, 1354, 1417, 1537, 1684, 1806, 1907, 2075, 2106, 2462, 2651, 2784, 2989, 3091, 3122, 3594
Lancaster, Osbert, 1690
Lancetti (of Roma), Pino, 1691
Landers, Ann, 1692
Landi, Elissa, 312, 1425, 1932, 2395, 2419, 2427, 2763, 3450
Landis, Carole, 754, 965, 2783, 3555
Landis, Jessie Royce, 1061
Landis, Margaret, 3516
"Landlord, The," 2798, 3152, 3160
"Landru," 67
Lane, Adele, 853
Lane, Laura, 2628
Lane, Lola, 540
Lane, Rosemary, 2988, 3093
Lang, June, 2536
Langbein, Barbara, 1703
Langdon, Harry, 388, 600, 1302, 3582
Lange, 2438
Lange, Brigitte, 1704
Lange, Hope, 678, 1437

Lange, Jessica, 161
Lange, Samuel, 2438
Langston, Elissa, 909, 3370
Lannes, Horace, 1705
Lanphier, Fay, 3335
Lanvin-Castillo, 1707
Lanvin, Jeanne, 329, 698, 1706, 1707, 1974
Lanz, 1708
La Plante, Laura, 3400
"Larceny," 2280
"Larger Than Life," 2533
Laroche, Guy, 1710
La Rocque, Rod, 333, 3455
Larson, Levaughn, 3241
Lasky, Jesse L., 1711, 3415
"Lassie's Great Adventure," 1408
"Last Adventure, The," 2689
"Last Days of Pompeii, The," 1643
"Last Grenade, The," 2649
"Last Man on Earth, The," 2295, 2297
"Last of Mrs. Cheyney, The" (1929), 1435
"Last of Mrs. Cheyney, The" (1937), 1067, 2527
"Last of the Mobile Hotshots, The," 3626
"Last of the Mohicans, The," 1712
"Last of the Renegades," 2347
"Last of the Vikings," 3248
"Last Picture Show, The," 2637
"Last Safari, The," 2307
"Last Shot You Hear, The," 207
"Last Summer," 69
"Last Sunset, The," 1656
"Last Time I Saw Archie, The," 1908, 2126
"Last Time I Saw Paris, The," 1263
"Last Trail, The," 2413
"Last Year at Marienbad," 273, 516, 940, 1850
"Latitude Zero," 1185, 1501
Lauchlan, Agnes, 3076
"Laughing Woman, The," 2854
"Laughter in the Dark," 354
Laughton, Charles, 275, 1085, 1421, 3374, 3466
Laune, Anne, 229
"Laura," 100, 485
Lauren, Ralph, 162, 3568
Laurence, Ken, 1716
Laurie, Piper, 2610
Lavella, Vella, 2982
Laver, James, 1717, 1718, 1719
La Vine, W. Robert, 1720, 1835a
Law, Winnie, 2947

"Law of the Land," 388
Lawford, Peter, 1322, 1437
"Lawful Larceny," 790, 2197
Lawrence, Gertrude, 1584
"Lawrence of Arabia," 723
Lawton, Ken, 1724
"Lawyer, The," 2339, 2779
"Lawyer Man," 2404
"Lawyer's Secret, The," 2386
Laykin et Cie, 1725
"Lazarillo," 650
"League of Gentlemen, The,"
  910
Lear, Frances, 1726
"Leave Her to Heaven," 1728,
  2156, 2159
Le Barbenchon, Odette, 1729
Le Croix, Mme. Yvonne, 837
"Leda," 1144
Leder, Walter, 1730
Lederer, Otto, 1027
Lee, Belinda, 967
Lee, Dixie, 582, 1478, 1869,
  1915, 2024
Lee, Dorothy, 2392, 3261
Lee, Gypsy Rose, 269, 3169,
  3555
Lee, Jocelyn, 1035
Lee, Julian, 947
Lee, Lettie, 1884, 1931, 2763,
  3043
Lee, Lila, 2218, 2346, 2400
Lee, Peggy, 444
Lee, Sammy, 1916
Leeds, Andrea, 2457, 2991,
  3551
"Legend of Lylah Clare, The,"
  1256, 2288, 2739, 2786, 3258
Legion of Decency, 220
Lehmann, Olga, 1735
Leigh, Janet, 215, 401, 678,
  1221, 2518, 2586, 2598, 2615
Leigh, Vivien, 134, 228, 261,
  562, 898, 1044, 1089, 1266,
  1311, 1420, 1749, 2258, 2664,
  2991, 3076, 3102, 3322, 3362,
  3466
Leighton, Maxine, 1736
Leisen, Mitchell, 388, 528, 550,
  564, 762, 1737, 1738, 2035,
  2535, 2671, 2962, 3026
LeKang, Per, 1739
Lelong, Lucien, 329, 423, 1267,
  1305, 1696
Le Maire, Charles, 36, 141, 398,
  479, 637, 638, 639, 678, 679,
  822, 1263, 1284, 1437, 1459,
  1740, 1741, 1742, 1743, 1744,

  2205, 2515, 2594, 2612, 2708,
    3021, 3377, 3436
Lemmon, Jack, 1482
"Lemonade Joe," 362, 3314
"Lend Me Your Husband," 2622
Leni, Paul, 2825
Lentini Creations, 1745
"Leo the Last," 3583
Leon, Idel, 1746
Leong, Terry, 1747
"Leopard, The," 372, 1131, 1975,
  2856
"Leopard Woman," 3528
Lepape, Georges, 1198
Le Roy, Mervyn, 1750
  2000
"Les Girls," 2286
Leslie, 1752
Leslie, Gladys, 3539
Leslie, Joan, 485, 1184, 2496,
  3578, 3600
Lester, Vicki, 3089
"Let's Be Ritzy," 2420
"Let's Get Married," 2449, 2528
"Let's Go Native," 2672
"Let's Live Tonight," 2433
"Let's Make Love," 1437, 1749
"Let's Play King," 2386
"Let's Talk About Women," 2362
"Let's Try Again," 2423
"Letter That Was Never Sent, The,"
  2149
"Letty Lynton," 16, 23, 330, 478,
  556, 616, 643, 735, 1052, 1198,
  1268, 1295, 1296, 1385, 1418,
  1460, 1696, 1933, 2024, 2397,
  2619, 2954, 2994, 3078, 3156,
  3199, 3231
Leva, Carlo, 1758
Levasseur, André, 1759
Levine, Alan, 1761
Levy, Sam G., 1763
Lewin, Maggie, 1764
Lewington, Ken, 1765
Lewis, Fiona, 1213, 1840
Lewis, Frank, 1767
Lewis, Mrs. Jane, 686, 1723,
  2050
Lewton, Val, 2028
Leyton, Drue, 2424, 2426
"Liberation of L. B. Jones, The,"
  77, 139
"Libertine, The," 2804
"Lickerish Quartet, The," 2854
Licudi, Gabriella, 126
Lidaková, Anna, 1772
"Life and Times of Judge Roy Bean,
  The," 1331

"Life of Her Own, A," 2806
"Life with Father," 3162
"Light Fantastic," 770
"Light in the Dark, The," 1503
"Light in the Piazza," 805
"Likely Story, A," 2738
"Li'l Abner," 622
Lili, 2253
"Lilies of the Field" (1924), 65, 262, 263, 1065, 1159, 1916, 2180, 3039
"Lilies of the Field" (1963), 2999
"Lilith," 2071
"Lillian Russell," 1433, 2265
Lillie, Beatrice, 3076
"Lily of the Dust," 2621, 3472
Linda, 1777
Linder, Max, 1557, 1843, 3525
Lindfors, Hannah, 2783
Lindfors, Viveca, 2507
Lindgren, Katerina, 1778
Lindsay, Margaret, 583, 2541
"Line-Up, The," 2418
lingerie (see also specific categories), 90, 134, 438, 565, 870, 1239, 1294, 1349, 1402, 1715, 1829, 2065, 2066, 2672, 2907, 3264, 3303, 3469, 3510
"Lion, The," 2307
"Lion of St. Mark, The," 216
Lipsey, A.I., 1781
"Liquidator, The," 374, 1259
"Lisa," 169, 2307
"Listen, Let's Make Love," 2890
Lister, Moira, 805
"Lisztomania," 1213, 1840
"Lit à Colonnes," 996
"Little Bit of Broadway, A," 3077
"Little Caesar," 1115
"Little Colonel, The," 1268, 3224
"Little Fauss and Big Halsy," 451, 2339
"Little Foxes, The," 2267
"Little French Girl, The," 691
"Little Lord Fauntleroy" (1921), 2626
"Little Lord Fauntleroy" (1936), 2371
"Little Minister, The," 2640
"Little Miss Marker," 275, 1996
"Little Nellie Kelly," 2686
"Little Nuns, The," 2325
"Little Old New York," 738, 1247, 3312
"Little Prince, The," 1213
"Little Shepherd of Kingdom Come, The," 2819
"Little White Savage, The," 2860

"Little Women" (1933), 329, 562, 808, 1473, 2024, 2640, 2664, 2729, 3542
Liu Hsian Hui, 1783
"Live for Life," 2863, 3133
"Lives of a Bengal Lancer, The," 1615
Lloyd, Dora, 1786
Lloyd, Frank, 522
Lloyd, Harold, 388, 434, 1287, 1302, 1499, 2247, 3508, 3582
Local 705 (see also Motion Picture Costumers), 260, 1500, 3323
"Lock Up Your Daughters," 208, 1765
Locke, Eric, 1787
"Locked Doors," 660, 824
"Locket, The," 1768
Lockwood, Harold, 1763
Lockwood, Margaret, 588, 1718
"Lodger, The," 858
Loff, Jeanette, 2250
Logan Costumes, 1790
Logan, Jacqueline, 2167
Logan, Joshua, 1789
"Logan's Run," 552
"Lolita," 602, 1015
Lollobrigida, Gina, 805
Lombard, Carole, 537, 561, 714, 817, 841, 1267, 1273, 1294, 1312, 1333, 1413, 1439, 1666, 1693, 1696, 1749, 1757, 1870, 1926, 1929, 1930, 1963, 1979, 2024, 2065, 2117, 2170, 2352, 2387, 2393, 2394, 2397, 2405, 2409, 2412, 2418, 2419, 2427, 2439, 2441, 2442, 2456, 2476, 2522, 2526, 2842, 2924, 3102, 3119, 3138, 3182, 3188, 3264, 3450, 3451, 3496, 3603
"London Town," 1718
"Lone Wolf Spy Hunt, The," 1654
"Lonely Are the Brave," 1665, 2871
"Lonely Road, The," 1054, 1606, 1607
Long, Audrey, 3142
"Long Day's Dying, The," 354
"Long Day's Journey into Night," 2093/4, 2095
"Long Duel, The," 364, 1107, 1246
"Long Live the King," 1539, 1904
"Long Ride from Hell, A," 116
"Long Rope, The," 1166
"Long Ships, The," 1020
"Look for the Silver Lining," 1449
"Look in Any Window," 2127, 2724

"Look Your Best," 2057
"Looking for Love," 1256, 1797, 3610
"Looking Glass War, The," 1237
Loomis, Margaret, 3511
Loos, Anita, 914, 1794, 2950
Loper, Don, 269, 766, 1795, 1796, 1797, 3169, 3487
Lord & Taylor, 1074
"Lord Jim," 723
"Lord Love a Duck," 1166, 1549
Loren, Sophia, 120, 805, 1345, 1710, 1917, 2804, 2856
"Lorna Doone" (1922), 1993
"Lorna Doone" (1935), 467, 468
Lorring, Joan, 1624
Los Angeles County Museum of Art, 1030
Los Angeles Exposition Park, 3469
Los Angeles Museum, 1417
Lo Scalzo, Vincent, 1800
"Losers, The," 431
Lossman, Ed, 1800
"Lost Command," 151
"Lost Continent, The," 1158, 3259
"Lost Flight," 3383
"Lost Horizon" (1937), 566, 864, 909, 1502, 1802, 2442, 2521
"Lost Horizon" (1973), 2081
"Lost Lady, The," 209
"Lost Man, The," 3186
"Lost World, The," 1812
"Lotna," 199, 1245
"Lottery Bride, The," 2274
"Lottery Lover," 728
Louis, Jean (see Jean Louis)
Louise, Anita, 112, 113, 317, 1438, 1479, 2386, 2397, 2450, 2456, 2476, 2785, 3026, 3573
Louisiana Museum, 2267
"Louisiana Purchase," 866
Love, Bessie, 1812, 2650
"Love," 29, 3289
"Love and Hisses," 2457, 2458, 2533
"Love and Kisses," 2995
"Love and Marriage," 1937
"Love at Night," 505
"Love Before Breakfast," 2439, 2924, 3102
"Love Boat," 1223
"Love Bug, The," 3180
"Love Camp 7," 1431
"Love Has Many Faces," 1338, 2628, 3207

"Love in Exile," 2372
"Love in the Desert," 2676
"Love Is a Ball," 1878, 3236
"Love Is a Funny Thing," 2288
"Love Is a Many Splendored Thing," 1744, 3377
"Love Is Better Than Ever," 2600
"Love Is News," 1959, 2447
"Love Laughs at Andy Hardy," 3555
"Love Letters" (1924), 2290
"Love Like That, A," 2455
"Love Master, The," 2766
"Love Mates," 1777
"Love Me Forever," 313, 1592, 1911, 2023
"Love Me Tonight," 2399, 2672
"Love on the Riviera," 2362
"Love on the Run," 535, 2446, 2523
"Love Parade, The," 1492, 2672
"Love Song," 310, 2753
"Love Story," 1342, 1952, 3062
"Love, the Italian Way," 665, 1887
"Love Thy Neighbor and His Wife," 2624
"Love Under Fire," 1433, 2445, 2961
"Love with the Proper Stranger," 81, 1349, 1692
"Loved One, The," 3213, 3258, 3441
"Lovely to Look At," 877, 1750, 2028, 2783
"Lovely Way to Die, A," 1999
"Lover Come Back," 192, 1521, 1725, 2109
"Lover of Camille," 660, 2622
"Lovers and Other Strangers," 3570
"Lovers of Teruel, The," 876
"Loves of Pharaoh, The," 469
"Lovin' the Ladies," 2344
"Loving," 3570
"Loving Couples," 1261
Lowe, Edmund, 2186
Loy, Myrna, 1403, 1425, 1932, 2170, 2261, 2393, 2399, 2401, 2404, 2406, 2408, 2409, 2477, 2486, 2534, 2967, 3161, 3450
Lubitsch, Ernst, 470, 3623
Lucas, George, 842
Luce, Claire, 3044
Lucile (see also Duff Gordon, Lady Lucile), 479, 629, 698, 870, 897, 1175, 1321, 1471, 1817, 1819, 1820, 1991, 2150, 3539
Lucilla, 1818
"Lucky Jordan," 1856

"Lucky Mr. Pennypacker, The,"
679
"Lucky Stiff, The," 2242, 2572
"Lucretia Lombard," 2765
"Lucy Gallant," 2519
Lugosi, Bela, 3309
Luick, Earl/Earle 1699, 1822,
1823, 1824, 2352, 2403, 2405,
2762, 2808, 3488
"Lulu Belle," 1806
"Lummox," 2274
"Luna Sobre la Cosecha" (see
"Shine on Harvest Moon")
Lund, John, 550
Lupin, Arny, 161
Lupino, Ida, 94, 1428, 1961,
2159, 2418, 2450, 2455, 2528,
2549, 3302
"Lured," 1561
"Lust for Life," 2144
"Lusting Hours, The," 1102
"Luv," 820
Luxford, Nola, 2201
"Luxury Liner," 1411
Luza, Reynaldo, 370
Lynch, Helen, 1369
Lynch, Ken 1241
Lynley, Carol, 383, 2025
Lynn, Diana, 776, 1795, 2510,
2566, 2575, 2578, 2602, 2781
Lynn, Sharon, 1046, 1698, 2427
Lyon, Agnes, 1834
Lyons, Nancy, 3261
Lytell, Bert, 528, 531

Maasdorp, Reinet, 3079
"Mabel's Strange Predicament,"
388, 1843
Mabry, Moss, 161, 445, 713,
1836, 2616, 3420
Mabs of Hollywood (Mabs Eliza-
beth Ryden), 1838, 2460,
3173
MacAllister, Mary, 3307
"Macao," 797
McAvoy, May, 1219, 3072
McBain, Diane, 1917
"Macbeth" (1963), 1237, 3145
MacBeth, Ian, 1841
McCallum, David, 3020
McCambridge, Mercedes, 3231
McCandless, Kathleen, 1844
McCann, Gerald, 1845
McCardell, Claire, 84, 1640
McCarter, Jerry, 1847

McCarthy, Charlie, 974
MacCharty, Mary, 1848
McChrystal, Margaret, 2433, 2703
McCormack, Alice, 2389
McCorry, John, 1852
McCoy, Tim, 1013
McCrea, Joel, 3285, 3360
McDaniel, Hattie, 3322
McDonald, Donald J., 1858
MacDonald, Jeanette, 191, 542,
679, 944, 1088, 1482, 1492,
1519, 1556, 1698, 2185, 2355,
2468, 2469, 2543, 2672, 2730,
3104, 3106, 3432, 3473
MacDonald, Katherine, 590, 641,
1054, 1604, 1605, 1606, 1607,
2102, 2227, 2625
McDonald, Marie, 520
MacDonald, Sherwood, 2249
McDowall, Roddy, 3020
McFadden, Mary, 100
McFarland, Hugh, 1863
McGaffey, Bessie (Elizabeth), 762,
1864, 2776
McGeachy, Cora, 1226, 1531, 1731,
2056, 3300
McGee, Lois, 1866
McGraw, Ali, 162, 1342
McGuire, Dorothy, 485, 636, 2156
McGuire, Kathryn, 1715, 2918
"McHale's Navy," 2132
Machiavelli, Nicoletta, 1060, 3245
"Machine Gun McCain," 2854
"Machine Infernale, La," 1314
"Macho Callahan," 2816
McHorter, Evelyn, 1867
McIntosh, Heather, 1868
Mack, Helen, 945, 2424
Mack, Wanda, 1873
Mackaill, Dorothy, 662, 834, 835,
1699, 1731, 2296, 2360, 2384,
2385, 3480
McKay, Rosemarie, 1874
"MacKenna's Gold," 1656
"McKenzie Break, The," 2187
Mackie, Bob, 58, 713, 1211, 1878,
1879, 3599
McKinney, Florine, 2398
MacLaine, Shirley, 524, 1312,
1342, 1349, 1437, 1560, 1917,
2082
MacLean, Barbara Barondess (see
also Barondess, Barbara), 1881,
1882
"McLintock!," 256, 2357
McMartin, John, 1340
MacMurray, Fred, 550
McNear, Howard, 1241

MacPhee, Duncan, 1883
McQuarrie, Ralph, 3113
McQueen, Steve, 2658
McShane, Ian, 2190
Macy and Company, R.H., 807
Macy's, 68, 1349, 1370, 2651,
  2685, 2921, 3199
Macy's Cinema Shop, 2685
"Mad About Music," 754, 976,
  1440
"Mad Dog Coll," 3404
"Mad Executioners, The," 3301
"Mad Game, The," 2176, 2415
"Mad Miss Manton, The," 991,
  1894, 1968, 2468, 3089
"Madam Satan," 3026
"Madame," 932, 2887
"Madame Bovary," 2028
"Madame Curie," 670
"Madame Dubarry" (1919), 406,
  469
"Madame Eve," 823
"Madame Sans Gêne," 1193, 2124
"Madame Satan," 1916
"Madame X" (1966), 1844
"Made in Italy," 2636
"Made in Paris," 1374, 1951,
  2163, 2809, 3202, 3441
"Mademoiselle," 2771
"Mademoiselle Modiste," 828,
  979, 1731
"Madison Avenue," 768
"Madwoman of Chaillot, The,"
  757
"Maedchen in Uniform," 1262
Mafai, Giulia, 1886
"Mafia," 477
Magahay, Robert, 1888
Magee, Virginia, 3220
Mager, Kitty, 1889
"Magic Carpet, The," 3232
"Magic Christian, The," 1301
"Magic Garden of Stanley Sweet-
  heart, The," 3236
"Magic Skin, The," 794
"Magic Sword, The," 2799
"Magic Town," 3555
"Magic Voyage of Sinbad, The,"
  1663
"Magic World of Topo Gigio (The
  Italian Mouse), The," 2154
Magna, Madame, 871
"Magnificent Cuckold, The," 534,
  2761
"Magnificent Obsession, The"
  (1935), 317
Magnin, I., 68, 2041
Magnin's, 3232

Mago, 1893
"Magus, The," 2307
"Mahler," 1213
"Maid of Salem," 164, 2521, 2522,
  2524
"Maiden for a Prince, A," 2636
"Maid's Night Out," 2461
Mainbocher, 84, 1832, 1850, 2843
Maison Maurice, 905a
Maison Repetto, 1895
"Major and the Minor, The," 546
"Major Barbara," 3076
"Major Dundee," 746
"Majority of One, A," 2281
Makau, Marge, 1896
"Make Your Own Bed," 2042
"Making a Living," 1843
Malabar, 1899
"Malaga," 3444
Malce, Michael, 3419
"Male and Female," 123, 550, 762,
  1198, 1399, 3099
"Male Animal, The," 3578
Mallory, Boots, 1927
Malone, Dorothy, 836
"Maltese Falcon, The" (1931), 2385
Maltzeff, C., 1902
"Mame," 95, 526, 1011, 1097,
  1661
Mami, 1903
"Man and the Moment, The," 3310
"Man Behind the Door, The," 1966
"Man Called Dagger, A," 474
"Man Called Gannon, A," 2339
"Man Called Horse, A," 1941,
  1949, 2339
"Man Could Get Killed, A," 1662
"Man for All Seasons, A," 1259
"Man from Home, The," 1638
"Man from the Diners' Club, The,"
  215
"Man from Yesterday, The," 1493
"Man I Love, The," 94
"Man in Possession, The" (see
  "Personal Property")
"Man in the Gray Flannel Suit, The,"
  220, 2520, 3507
"Man in the Middle," 169
"Man of the World," 3238
"Man on the Nile," 2408
"Man-Proof," 942, 3553
"Man Who Broke the Bank at Monte
  Carlo, The," 1910
"Man Who Came Back, The," 2296
"Man Who Came to Dinner, The,"
  1079
"Man Who Couldn't Walk, The,"
  1126

"Man Who Had Power over Women, The," 688
"Man Who Knew Too Much, The," 556
"Man Who Laughs, The," 690, 2825, 2960, 3462
"Man Who Played God, The," 2396
"Man Who Understood Women, The," 678
"Man Who Would be King, The," 148, 1332, 1506, 1594
"Man with Connections, The," 760
"Man Without a Country, The," 2294
"Manchurian Candidate, The," 76, 387, 1558, 3195
"Mandalay," 1300
"Mandragola," 818
Manela, Sabine, 1908
Mangano, Silvana, 448
"Manhandled," 598, 657, 1194
"Manhattan Merry-Go-Round," 3110
Mankiewicz, Joseph, 788, 3231
"Mannequin," 44, 699, 971, 1713, 2459
Manning, Maybelle, 2950
Manon, Marcia, 973
"Manon Lescaut," 2825
"Man's Favorite Sport?," 2871
"Man's Genesis," 645, 2626
Mansfield, Jayne, 2118, 2353
Mansfield, Martha, 388
"Manslaughter" (1922), 388, 528, 763, 1493, 1533, 2270, 3118, 3563
"Manslaughter" (1930), 3473
Manuel, Jacques, 132
March, Fredric, 551
Marchal, Arlette, 691
Marchand, Anne-Marie, 1921
Marchesi, Pia, 1922
"Marco Polo," 1169
"Marco the Magnificent," 1062
Marcus, Stanley, 1923
Mariani, Fiorella, 1924
"Marianne," 1247
"Marie Antoinette," 27, 39, 43, 461, 462, 568, 569, 679, 941, 944, 949, 954, 1010, 1211, 1360, 1373, 1444, 1445, 1456, 1482, 1891, 1897, 1900, 2233a, 2832, 2843, 2984, 2986, 3026, 3194, 3388, 3500, 3541, 3618, 3625
Marie-Martine, 1925
Maring, Misty, 1936
Marinucci, Luciana, 1937
Maritza, Sari, 1928, 1930, 1931,

2403, 2406, 2409
Mark, Bob, 1939
"Mark of the Vampire," 1913
Marks, Edward, 1941
Marks, Lambert, 1942
Markwordt, Margarete, 1943
Marlowe, June, 2171, 3168
"Marnie," 753, 2779, 3130
"Maroc 7," 589
Marolt, Annie, 1945
"Marriage Is a Private Affair," 1042
"Marriage Italian Style," 107, 1975
"Marriage of Figaro, The," 1679
"Marriage on the Rocks," 473, 2641
"Married Bachelor," 2755
"Married Flirts," 660
"Married in Hollywood," 2274
"Married People," 428
"Married Too Young," 422
"Married Woman, The," 574
Marrini, Gitt, 1946
"Marry Me! Marry Me!," 2633
Marsh, Mae, 514, 645, 1947
Marsh, Marian, 2402, 2417
Marsh, Maude, 1612, 1948
Marsh, Veronica, 1382
Marshall, Brenda, 2478
Marshall, Trudy, 862
Marshall, Tully, 817
Martell, Jack, 1949
Martelli, Marissa, 1950
Martin, Alice Manougian, 1952
Martin, Dean, 785, 1437
Martin, Lock, 3097
Martin, Mary, 859, 1183, 2480, 2481
Martin, Ruth, 2355, 2916
Martin, Vivian, 854
Martin of California, 1958
Martinelli, Elsa, 492
Martinson, A., 1967
Marusia, 3275
Marvin, Grace, 3417
"Mary Mary," 3273
"Mary of Scotland," 134, 808, 869, 1267, 1268, 1603, 1719, 1892, 1962, 2310, 2375, 2440, 2642, 2729, 2915, 3332
"Mary Poppins," 1349, 3410
"Mary, Queen of Scots," 1414
Marzot, Vera, 1975
Masina, Giulietta, 1625
"Masks of the Devil," 3268
Mason, Marsha, 100
Mason, Sheila, 683
Mason, Shirley, 2290, 2294

"Masquerade in Mexico," 2106
"Masquerader, The," 973, 1032
Massey, Ilona, 1079, 2110
"Master of Men," 2415, 2416
"Mata Hari," 35, 158, 816, 1317,
    1482, 1545, 2024, 2275, 2352
"Mata Hari, Agent H-21," 451
"Match King, The," 1775, 2994
"Matchless," 1069, 2830
Matera, Barbara, 162
Mathie, Marion, 1976
Mathieson, Johanna, 1977
"Mating Season, The," 3447
"Matrimonial Martyr, A," 815
"Matter of Days, A," 1122
Matthews, Jessie, 314, 2374
Matthews, Marilyn, 1980
Mature, Victor, 2016
Mauboussin (see also Trabert and
    Hoeffer-Mauboussin), 1979
Mauri, Glauco, 3589
"Maxime," 757, 3326
Maxwell, Barbara, 1983
Maxwell, Elsa, 2098
Maxwell, Marilyn, 1653, 2492,
    2577
Maxwell, Nora, 1985
May, Cynthia, 1986
May, Doris, 1059
Mayer, 1988
Mayer, Adalyn, 662, 1035
Mayer, Gabriele, 1989
Mayer, Murray, 1872
"Mayerling," 932
Mayne, Eric, 3072
Mayo, 1990
Mayo, Edna, 897, 1991
Mayo, Frank, 593, 884
Mayo, Virginia, 391, 444, 679,
    883, 1780, 2491, 2576, 2611,
    2967
"Maytime," 79, 679
"Meanest Man in the World, The,"
    133
"Meanwhile, Far from the Front,"
    775
Meek, Donald, 1864
"Meet Danny Wilson," 2607
"Meet Me in Moscow," 2308
"Meet Me in St. Louis," 679,
    2028, 2964, 2966
Meighan, Thomas, 676
Melies, George, 2901
"Melody Lingers On, The," 315
Meltzer, Rose, 1286
"Men," 3472
"Men in Her Life, The," 2631,
    2708

"Men in White," 3450
"Men of Steel," 2701
"Men with Wings," 1354
"Menace," 2427, 2428
Menasco, Milton, 1993
Mendleson, Anthony, 93, 711, 1994
Menichelli, Lilli, 901
Menichelli, Rosalba, 1995
Menjou, Adolphe, 209, 459, 1453,
    1701, 1996, 3389, 3543
Menzies, Bill, 1250
Merangel, Charles, 1997
"Mercenary, The," 1375
Mercer, Frances, 991, 3089, 3093
Merchant Tailors' Association, 1996
Mercier, Michele, 1237
Mercouri, Melina, 1662
Merman, Ethel, 1757
Merrick, Doris, 1214
Merrill, Mary, 1999
"Merrily We Live," 2535, 3111
"Merry Andrew," 2422
"Merry Widow, The" (1925), 121,
    747, 825, 3158, 3470, 3623
"Merry Widow, The" (1952), 1660,
    2808
"Merry Wives of Windsor, The,"
    2634
"Merry-Go-Round," 106, 747,
    3158
Mersereau, Violet, 987, 2291
Messel, Oliver, 466, 749, 1389,
    1681, 2002, 2003, 2004, 2005,
    2959
Messrs. Fenwick Ltd., 1031
"Metello," 118
"Metropolitan," 315
Metropolitan Museum of Art, 405,
    1512, 1643, 3102, 3623
Metropolitan Museum of Art, Cos-
    tume Institute, 351, 1643, 2059,
    2814
Metzer, Erno, 469
Meyers, Greta, 2008
Mialkovszky, Erzsébet, 2009
Michael, Gertrude, 2427, 2428
Micheli, Dario, 2011
Micheli, Elio, 2012
Micheline, 2013
Micheline & Jacqueline, 2014
Michelson, Ed, 2015
"Mickey One," 2798
"Midas Run," 116
"Midnight," 550, 2473, 2989
"Midnight Club," 2412
"Midnight Cowboy," 2823, 3101
"Midnight Lace," 1523
"Midnight Sun, The," 1563

"Midshipman, The," 1608
"Midsummer Night's Dream, A"
   (1935), 843, 1718
"Midsummer Night's Dream, A"
   (1967), 1596
Midwinter, Dulcie, 2017
Midwinter, Mary, 3074
"Mikado, The," 1575, 2773
"Mildred Pierce," 696, 3231
Miles, Lillian, 2403
Miles, Vera, 2628
Milgrim's, 1072
"Milkman Rings Twice, The,"
   3388
"Milky Way, The," 1249, 2064,
   3267
Milland, Ray, 550, 551, 1855,
   2055, 3164
Miller, Ann, 1806, 2788
Miller, Burton, 548, 683, 829,
   1077, 1437, 2022, 2628
Miller, Marilyn, 1449
Miller, Nolan, 2025
Miller, Patsy Ruth, 3170, 3477
Miller, Ruby, 1208
Millings & Son, Dougie, 2026
"Million Bid, A," 3477
"Million Dollar Legs," 2400
"Million Dollar Mermaid," 1750
"Million Dollar Weekend," 1881
"Millions in the Air," 584
Mills, Hayley, 635
Millstein, Dan, 2027
Mimieux, Yvette, 552, 678
"Min and Bill," 1480
"Mine with the Iron Door, The,"
   3480
Mineau, Charlotte, 1064
"Mini-Affair, The," 1055
Minnelli, Liza, 2028
Minnelli, Vincente, 2028
"Minotaur, The," 2369
Mintz, Sid, 875, 2029
"Minute to Pray, a Second to
   Die, A," 1071
"Minx, The," 3269
Mir, David, 2030
"Miracle in Soho," 1289
"Miracle of the White Stallions,"
   264
"Miracle Worker, The," 2071
Miranda, Carmen, 714, 715,
   1007, 1043, 1223, 3285
Mirko, 1594
"Misfits, The," 2126, 3154,
   3264
"Misleading Lady, The," 1991
"Miss Bluebeard," 658

"Miss Emmy Lou," 3350, 3351
"Miss Fane's Baby Is Stolen," 16,
   2417
"Miss Sadie Thompson," 3232
"Miss Tatlock's Millions," 1327,
   1328, 1330
"Mission Mars," 611
"Mission to Moscow," 670, 1021
"Mr. Ace and the Queen," 2108
"Mr. and Mrs. Cugat," 734, 867,
   1504, 2948
"Mr. and Mrs. Smith," 841, 1693,
   3603
"Mr. Belvedere Goes to College,"
   484
Mr. Blackwell, 2118
"Mister Buddwing," 1644
"Mr. District Attorney," 1806, 1808
"Mister Freedom," 1644
Mr. John (see also John Frederics),
   3102
Mr. Mike, 2119
"Mr. Music," 2508
"Mr. Peabody and the Mermaid,"
   335, 2101, 3466
"Mr. Sardonicus," 105, 215
"Mr. Skeffington," 366, 1022
"Mr. Soft Touch," 1806
Mitchell, Alexandria, 2033
Mitchell, Cameron, 785
Mitchell, Don, 2034
Mitchell, Margaret, 1044, 1311,
   2664
Mitchell, Thomas, 3164
Mitchum, Robert, 2028
Mitzou of Madrid, 2036
Mix, Tom, 1013, 1709, 1812, 2037,
   2057
Mladova, Milada, 3555
"Model Murder Case, The," 1321
"Model Shop, The," 139, 2779
"Modern Maidens," 21
Modern Merchandising Bureau, 567,
   3238, 3332, 3365
"Modesty Blaise," 273, 744, 1322,
   1950
"Modigliani of Montparnasse," 108
Modjewska, Madame, 1812
Mollo, John, 552
"Molly Maguires, The," 2888,
   3127
"Molly O'," 2902
Molyneux, Captain Edward, 329,
   330, 465, 698
"Moment to Moment," 2863
"Mon Ami Sanfoin," 996
"Mondo Mod," 2008
"Money Jungle, The," 3197

"Money, Money, Money," 641
"Mongols, The," 410
"Monique," 793
Monroe, Marilyn, 235, 1437,
    1749, 1789, 1878, 2285,
    2907
"Monsieur Beaucaire" (1924),
    203, 502, 777, 961, 1173, 1711,
    1721, 1804, 2124, 2687, 3014,
    3384, 3402, 3456
"Monsieur Beaucaire" (1946), 675
"Monsieur Sanfoin," 996
"Monster of London City, The,"
    3301
Montalban, Ricardo, 1340
Montana, Bull, 411
"Monte Carlo," 191, 3473
"Monte Walsh," 367, 1761
Montenegro, Conchita, 2392
Montez, Maria, 192
Montgomery, Elizabeth (designer),
    2053, 2054, 2093/4, 2096
Montgomery, Robert, 3105, 3231
Montt, Christina, 1035
Moody, Ron, 711
"Moon Zero Two," 3259
"Moonshine War, The," 1595
Moore, Colleen, 612, 765, 978,
    1024, 1100, 1216, 1448, 1531,
    1731, 1793, 1799, 2056, 2057,
    2058, 2218, 2621, 2763, 3451,
    3532, 3590
Moore, Constance, 543, 550,
    3247
Moore, Doris Langley, 2060,
    2061, 2062
Moore, Grace, 313, 1220, 1267,
    1268, 1592, 1700, 1911, 2023,
    2133, 2439, 2446, 2447, 2526,
    3492
Moore, John, 2063, 3207
Moore, Matt, 849
Moore, Tom, 2217
Moorhead, Natalie, 3473
Moran, Lois, 388
"Moran of the Lady Letty," 2219
"More Dead Than Alive," 2302,
    2801
"More Than a Miracle," 624,
    2854, 2856
Moreau, Jacqueline, 2064
Moreau, Jeanne, 451, 3420
Morelli, Mirella, 2067
Morely, Jr., Jay, 2615
Moreno, Antonio, 3472
Moreno, Catalina, 2068
Morgan, Ann, 2069
Morgan, Frank, 1286, 1450

Morgan, Terence, II, 2070
"Morgan!," 273
"Morgan the Pirate," 2879
Morison, Patricia, 734
"Morituri," 3281
Morley, Karen, 1930, 2395, 2400,
    2402, 2427, 2640, 3451
Morley, Robert, 679, 2832
Morley, Ruth, 2071, 2377
"Morning Glory," 982
"Morocco," 816, 2072, 2957, 3374
Morris, Clara, 1035
Morris, Hope, 2084
Morris, Jane, 2085
Morris, Mrs. Leslie, 1047
Morrison, James, 1586
Morroni, Renata, 2086
Morse, Tiger, 2087
"Mortal Storm, The," 2268
Morton Gary, 555
Moser, Earl, 2088
Mosjoukine, Ivan, 3455
Mosquini, Marie, 3007
Moss, Sandy, 2089
"Most Dangerous Game, The," 3142
"Most Dangerous Man Alive," 3379
"Most Immoral Lady, A," 299
"Most Wanted Man, The," 757
Mostoller, Ramse, 2090
"Motel Confidential," 1430
"Moth, The," 1023
"Mother and Daughter," 2165
"Mother and the Law, The," 388
"Mother Carey's Chickens," 3092
"Mother Goose à Go-Go," 3001
"Mother Was a Freshman," 2158
Motion Picture and Television Fund,
    1831
Motion Picture Costumers (Local
    705) (see also unions), 260,
    1082, 1205, 1442, 1500, 1671,
    1791, 2091, 3241, 3323
Motion Picture Producers and Dis-
    tributors of America, 3126
Motion Picture Producer's Associa-
    tion, 2338
Motion Picture Producer's Associa-
    tion (school of film-costume de-
    sign), 3207
Motley, 1292, 2053, 2093/4, 2095,
    2096
Mott, Caroline, 2097
"Mouchette," 1729
"Moulin Rouge," 277, 1425, 1594,
    3450
"Mountain Cat, The," 469
"Move," 3189
"Move Over, Darling," 2998

Movietone (fashion newsreels), 606, 1405, 2174
Moya, 1382
"Mrs. Parkington," 944, 3094
"Mrs. Whitney's Fashion Show," 983
Mugge, Vera, 2120
Muir, Esther, 3571
Muir, Jean, 5, 1095, 2121, 2429
Muller, N., 2123
"Mummy, The," 2403
"Mummy's Shroud, The," 3145
"Mumsy, Nanny, Sonny and Girly," 2017
"Mumu," 1123
Munden, Jesse, 2126
"Mundo Depravados," 97
Mundy, Arfie, 1489
Munson, Byron, 2127
"Munster, Go Home!," 1488, 2126
Murata, Yoshiaki, 2128
"Murder at the Gallop," 3556
"Murder at the Vanities," 550
"Murder by the Clock," 2389
"Murder, He Says," 2129
"Murder in Pictures," 1267
"Murder in Trinidad," 2420
"Murder on the Orient Express," 3412
"Murder She Said," 939
"Murder with Pictures," 2521
"Murderers' Row," 387, 1581
"Murders in the Zoo," 1928
Murdock, Ann, 1732
"Murieta," 2068
Murphy, Fidelma, 1307
Murphy, George, 1996
Murray, Don, 1789
Murray, Gene, 2131
Murray, Gordon, 2132
Murray, Mae, 121, 259, 824, 1172, 1886, 2044, 2205, 2218, 2621, 2732, 2977, 3119 3289, 3470, 3479, 3623
Murray, Roseanne, 1214
Museum of Costume, 2061
Music Box Revue, 429
"Music in the Air," 2427
"Music Lovers, The," 1213, 1840
"Music Man, The," 1437
"Music School," 2991
"Mutiny on the Bounty" (1935), 1421, 2065, 3264
"My American Wife," 2521
"My Cousin Rachel," 1846
"My Dream Is Yours," 2571
"My Fair Lady," 149, 229, 234, 235, 237, 247, 1349, 1416, 1446, 2628, 3207
"My Favorite Brunette," 2651
"My Favorite Spy," 1504
"My Favorite Wife," 1326, 2483
"My Geisha," 1437
"My Life to Live," 955
"My Lips Betray," 1931, 2412, 2763
"My Little Chickadee," 1416, 2482
"My Little Wife," 2150
"My Love for Yours," 2553
"My Lover, My Son," 110
"My Lucky Star," 2465, 2930
"My Man Godfrey," 1267, 1963, 2442, 2522
"My Sin," 2389
"My Sister, My Love," 2161
"My Son," 662
"My Son, the Hero," 2822
"My Sweet Charlie," 3383
"My Weakness," 2414, 3453
"My Wife's Best Friend," 2612
"My Women," 2414
Myers, Carmel, 514, 654, 794, 926, 2732, 2860, 3515
Myers, Mickey, 2134
Myers, Ruth, 2135
Myles, Dena, 1814
"Myra Breckenridge," 526, 1339, 1482, 3327
Myrick, Susan, 1044, 1311
Myron, Helen, 1915
Myrtil, Odette, 2136, 2242, 2500, 2572
"Mystery in Mexico," 2565
"Mystery of Thug Island, The," 216, 479, 2012
"Mystic, The," 926, 2334, 3077

NASA, 54
Naidu, Leela, 1899
Nakajima, Hachiro, 2137
"Naked Among the Wolves," 2898
"Naked Kiss, The," 350
"Naked Truth, The," 823
Naldi, Nita, 128, 790, 2143, 2197, 2359, 3147
"Name of the Game is Kill!, The," 96
"Nana" (1928), 2825
"Nancy Goes to Rio," 2503, 2583, 2806
Nancy of Hollywood, 2410
"Nanny, The," 1158

Napier, Alan, 2628
"Narrow Corner, The," 1931
Nasalli-Rocca, Annalisa, 2139
Nasalli-Rocca, Orietta, 2140
Nash, Mary, 3074
"Nashville Rebel," 712
Nastat (of "Réal"), Arlette, 2142
Nathan, L. and H., 2144, 2145
Nathans, 1391
Nathans of London, 2144, 2146
Natili, Giovanna, 2147
National Board of Review of Motion
  Pictures, 2174
National Film Archive, 1812
"National Lampoon's Animal House,"
  1316
National Legion of Decency, 163
National Theatre of Great Britain,
  1378
Naumova, L., 2149
"Navajo Joe," 759
"Navigator, The," 1715, 2049
"Navy Wife," 581
"Nazarin," 3063
Nazemi, Shai, 2151
Nazi regalia, 2268, 3098
Nazimova, 405, 961, 3456
Neagle, Anna, 541, 1076, 2152,
  2425
Neal, Patricia, 2493, 3280
"Neapolitan Carousel," 761
"Nearly a Nasty Accident," 1764
"Necessary Evil, The," 323, 3470
"Ned Kelly," 1378
"Negatives," 938
Negri, Pola, 131, 613, 691, 826,
  1209, 1231, 1446, 1505, 1749,
  2275, 2359, 2621, 2646, 2833,
  3006, 3048, 3472, 3623
Negri, Sandro, 2154
Negulesco, Dusty, 2155
Neil, Hildegard, 1391
Neiman-Marcus, 2193
"Nell Brinkley," 2218
"Nell Gwyn," 2425
"Nellie, the Beautiful Cloak Model,"
  104, 571
Nelson, Frances M., 854
Nelson, Kay, 2156, 2157, 2158,
  2159, 2160, 3083
Nelstedt, Björn, 2161
Nelstedt, Eva-Lisa, 2162
Nero, Franco, 1789
Nesterovskaya, G., 2165
Neumann, Margarete, 2166
"Nevada Smith," 256
"Never Put It in Writing," 1307
"Never Say Die," 3484

"Never the Twain Shall Meet," 3311
"Never Too Late," 2238
"Never Wave at a Wac," 2843
"Never Weaken," 1499
"New Divorce, The," 2169
"New Kind of Love, A," 451, 805,
  1707, 2326, 2629
"New Moon," 1482
"New Morals," 1697
New York Fashion Show, 1406
New-York Historical Society, 120
"New York Idea, The," 3538
Newell, Catherine, 2182
Newell, Ricky, 3449
Newman, Bernard, 284, 310, 313,
  329, 471, 547, 786, 980, 1043,
  1188, 1268, 1298, 1398, 1411,
  1870, 1960, 2023, 2041, 2076,
  2183, 2287, 2373, 2433, 2444,
  2446, 2447, 2448, 2526, 2703,
  2753, 2792, 2933, 2987, 2989,
  3262
Newman, George, 162, 615
Newman, Paul, 526, 1336, 2628,
  3561
"Next Time We Live," 1267
"Nice Girl," 136
Nicholls, Tiny, 2187
Nicholson, Jack, 713
Nickols, Vicki, 2188
Nierenberg, Lou, of New York, 464
Niesen, Gertrude, 3545
"Night Affair," 270, 2351
"Night After Night," 220, 1773
"Night Before Christmas, A," 881
"Night Games," 1261
"Night Has a Thousand Eyes, The,"
  1252, 1325, 1341, 2489
"Night in Paradise, A," 675
"Night of the Generals, The," 757,
  2379
"Night They Raided Minsky's, The,"
  886, 887
"Night Walker, The," 2827
"Night World," 2398
Nightingale, Laura, 2189
"Nightmare Castle," 1169
"Nightmare in the Sun," 707
"Nightmare in Wax," 785
"Nights of Shame," 80, 2829
Nikki of Just Men, 2190
"Nikki, Wild Dog of the North,"
  1620
Nilsson, Anna Q., 661, 968, 1100,
  1714, 2047, 2218, 2360, 2943,
  3167
"Nine Days of One Year," 1641
"Nine Hours to Rama," 12

"Nine Lives Are Not Enough," 1079
"Ninfa Constante, La" (see "Constant Nymph, The")
"Ninotchka," 465, 1280
Nissen, Greta, 1231
Nisskaya, V., 2196
Nixdorf, Gisela, 2198
Nixon, Marian, 2403, 2410, 2418, 2422
"No Blade of Grass," 127
"No Exit," 1705
"No Highway in the Sky," 3071
"No Man of Her Own," 1749, 1926, 2024, 2405
"No Man's Land," 2839
"No Minor Vices," 1388
"No More Ladies," 313, 882, 1869, 2023, 2435, 3078
"No More Orchids," 3138
"No One Man," 2393, 2394
"No Other Woman," 3171
"No Place to Go," 1970
"No Questions Asked," 393, 2514
"No Room for the Groom," 2610
"No Way to Treat a Lady," 69
"Nobody Lives Forever," 94
Nolan, Doris, 990, 3091, 3549
Nolan, Katie, 1022
Noonan, Gerrie, 1214
"Noose Hangs High, The," 902
Norell, Norman, 84, 128, 273, 1084, 1198, 1199, 1618, 2079, 2080, 2203, 2204, 2205, 2206, 2214, 2783
Normand, Mabel, 1638, 1836, 2860
"North of Hudson Bay," 2291
"Norwood," 224
"Nothing But a Man," 2841
"Nothing But the Best," 1543
"Nothing Sacred," 1439, 1979, 2456, 3182
"Notorious Affair, A," 3143
"Notorious Cleopatra, The," 1790, 2805
"Notorious Landlady," 2224
Nourry, Hélène, 2222
Nourry, Pierre, 2223
Novak, Eva, 3211
Novak, Jane, 144, 1547
Novak, Kim, 1345, 1789, 1831, 2224, 3468
Novarese, Vittorio Nino, 2225, 3020, 3336
Novarro, Ramon, 1421, 2960, 3455
Novello, Roselle, 2226
"Now or Never," 1499

"Now Voyager," 294, 988
Nudie's 2628, 2629
Nugent, Wilbur W., 1406
"Number One," 2779
Nureyev, Rudolph, 1213
"Nutty Professor, The," 785, 3127
Nuyen, Frances, 3233
Nyberg, Mary Ann, 1652
Nyby, Thelma, 2235
Nykjaer, Berit, 2236

"OSS 117--Mission for a Killer," 2705
Oakes, Mary, 2921, 3367, 3405
Oakie, Jack, 875
"Oath, The," 645
Oberon, Merle, 312, 476, 538, 675, 858, 883, 960, 1182, 1627, 1628, 1639, 1890, 2202, 2365, 2432, 2445, 2525, 3238, 3419
O'Brian, Hugh, 1338
O'Brien, Eugene, 937
O'Brien, Mary, 2532
O'Brien, Sheila, 554, 2238, 3231, 3285
Obrock, Herman, Jr., 1406
"Occupe-Toi D'Amélie," 996
O'Connell, Arthur, 1241
O'Connor, Kathleen, 528
"Odd Couple, The," 226
"Odd Man Out," 1110
O'Dell, Robert, 2239
Odell, Rosemary, 2240, 2241, 2510, 2592
O'Donnell, Cathy, 2967
"Oedipus the King," 3315
"Of Human Bondage" (1934), 2640
"Of Human Bondage" (1964), 2307
Offord, Bert, 1442
Oglesbee, Michael, 2248
"Oh Dad, Poor Dad, Mama's Hung You in the Closet and I'm Feelin' So Sad," 1120
"Oh, for a Man!," 1698
"Oh Rosalinda," 779
"Oh! What a Lovely War," 2307
O'Halloran, Jack, 2377
O'Hara, Maureen, 302, 675, 679, 1021, 1954, 2160, 2675, 3083, 3142
Ohmart, Carol, 1678
Oland, Warner, 2960
"Old Acquaintance," 670
"Old Chicago," 754
"Old English," 1822

"Old Homestead, The," 528
"Old Maid, The," 1420, 2550, 2554
"Old Wives for New," 2860
Olivas, Robert, 2254
Oliver, Edna May, 439, 1087
Oliver, Fenwick, 142
"Oliver!," 723
"Oliver Twist" (1922), 1535, 1753
Olivier, Sir Laurence, 235, 711,
   1086, 1089, 1110, 1112, 2800,
   3336
Olmstead, Gertrude, 946
Olson, Nancy, 2508
Omar of Omaha, 2256
"Omar the Tentmaker," 1083, 2257,
   2364, 2380, 2918
"On a Clear Day You Can See
   Forever," 237, 2028, 2891,
   3076, 3154
"On an Island with You," 2073
"On Approval," 3076
"On Her Majesty's Secret Ser-
   vice," 357, 651
"On My Way to the Crusades I Met
   a Girl Who ...," 818
"On the Avenue," 2527
"On the High Seas," 3221
"On the Waterfront," 1573
"On Trial," 1822
"On with the Dance," 121
"On Your Back," 3473
"On Your Toes," 2554
"On ze Boulevard," 1480, 3015
"Once a Hero," 1593
"Once Upon a Honeymoon," 1132
"Once Upon a Time in the West,"
   477, 3023
"One and Only, Genuine Original
   Family Band, The," 3180
"One Arabian Night," 131, 469
"One Black Orchid," 1345
"One Clear Call," 572, 573, 831
"One-Eyed Jacks," 1338, 3581
"One Hour with You," 2393,
   2672
"101 Acts of Love," 1847
"100 Rifles," 2799
"One Is Guilty," 3452
"One Man's Way," 105, 1667
"One Million B.C.," 754, 3555
"One Million Years B.C.," 169,
   3259
"One Minute to Play," 3307
"One More River," 2424, 2425
"One More Time," 1724
"One More Tomorrow," 1008
"One Night of Love," 3492
"One Shocking Moment," 1626

"1000 Eyes of Dr. Mabuse, The,"
   3124
"One Way Passage," 64, 2024,
   2401
"One Way Street," 661
"One Way Wahine," 8
O'Neil, Peggy, 1096
O'Neill, Alice, 1563, 2274
"Only a Woman," 3458
"Only Angels Have Wings," 2471,
   2549
"Only Game in Town, The," 1060,
   3245
"Only Thing, The," 1505, 2030
"Only Two Can Play," 793
"Only Woman, The," 1315, 2622
"Only Yesterday," 2414
"Open All Night," 2622
"Operation CIA," 2235
"Operation Eichmann," 1308, 2795
"Operation Kid Brother," 2804
"Operation 13," 1247, 3451
"Orchid, The," 3515
"Orchids to You," 5, 2429
"Orgy Girls '69," 1767
"Orgy of the Dead," 731
"Orient Express," 1429
"Orphans of the Storm," 1174, 1176,
   1649
"Orphée," 1314
Orry-Kelly (John Kelly), 112, 113,
   309, 310, 317, 319, 366, 390,
   547, 583, 671, 678, 679, 730,
   739, 822, 988, 1002, 1067, 1079,
   1086, 1095, 1268, 1300, 1318,
   1419, 1429, 1437, 1438, 1538,
   1619, 1652, 1695, 1754, 1757,
   1931, 1978, 1979, 2024, 2148,
   2267, 2277, 2278, 2279, 2280,
   2281, 2282, 2283, 2285, 2286,
   2403, 2405, 2405, 2406, 2407,
   2407, 2440, 2442, 2445, 2450,
   2455, 2456, 2463, 2465, 2501,
   2504, 2523, 2532, 2533, 2534,
   2542, 2550, 2554, 2637, 2704,
   2755, 2763, 2843, 2924, 2928,
   2994, 2994, 3086, 3092, 3103,
   3112, 3176, 3261, 3427, 3488,
   3573, 3600
Osborne, Marie, 2288
"Oscar, The," 1888
Ostler, Gene, 2300
O'Sullivan, Maureen, 153, 1981,
   2414, 2449, 3092, 3553
Oswald, Tye, 2302
"Othello" (1965), 1378
"Other Love, The," 1624, 3100
"Other Tomorrow, The," 838, 1423

"Otley," 1137
Otto, Henry, 322
Otto, Theo, 2303
Otto, Vera, 2304
Ottobre, 2305
"Our Betters," 1928, 2406, 2764
"Our Blushing Brides," 90
"Our Dancing Daughters," 478, 690
"Our Hospitality," 143
"Our Leading Citizen," 1036
"Our Little Girl," 2023, 2435
"Our Man Flint," 56, 3597
"Our Modern Maidens," 1422
"Our Mother's House," 3601
"Our Very Own," 883, 2587
"Our Vines Have Tender Grapes," 2937
"Out of Luck," 1174
"Out of the Past," 2557
"Out-of-Towners, The," 422, 1288
"Out West with the Hardys," 1583
"Outlaw The," 797, 1013, 1142, 1198, 1718, 2907, 3126
"Outrage, The," 2628, 2657
"Over the Border," 2217
"Over the Moon," 960
Oviatt, James, 1436
Oviatt's, 1436
Owen, Seena, 3527
Owen-Smith, Brian, 2307
Owens, Catherine Dale, 1698
"Owl and the Pussycat, The," 2823, 3154
Ozerova, D., 2308

"PT 109," 736
Pacquin, 453, 601, 983, 1314, 1532
"Paddy-the-Next-Best-Thing" (c.1924), 514
"Paddy the Next Best Thing" (1933), 748, 1785
Page, Anita, 21, 3310
Fage, Pat, 2309
"Page Miss Glory," 2436
"Page Tim O'Brien," 3352
Paget, Debra, 2596
Paige, Janis, 2564, 3215, 3555
Paige, Jean, 1649
Paige, Sally, 1490

"Paint Your Wagon," 1567, 1789, 3283
"Painted Angel, The," 249
"Painted Lady, The," 2297
"Painted People," 2047
"Painted Veil, The," 562, 1296, 2428, 3102, 3156
"Painted Woman, The," 3044
"Pajama Game, The," 885, 887, 2312
"Pal Joey," 1749
"Palaces of Pleasure," 2186
Paley, Princess Natalie, 211, 2431
Pallack, Andrew, 2314
"Palm Beach Girl, The," 2124
"Palm Beach Story, The," 1497
"Palm Springs Weekend," 345, 2801
Palmer, Adele, 2315, 2573, 2599
Palmer, Alma, 2316
Palmer, Lilli, 1624, 3076
Palmer, Roger, 2318
Palmieri, Remo, 2319
Palmstierna-Weiss, Gunilla, 2320
"Palmy Days," 2388
Paltscho of Vienna, 2321
Panaro, Maria Luisa, 2322
Pancani, Gianni, 2323
"Pandora and the Flying Dutchman," 1750
"Pandora La Croix," 884
Panova, N., 2324
Papas, Irene, 100
"Paper Moon," 2637
Papi, Giuliano, 2325
"Paradine Case, The," 674
Paramount School, costume department, 385
"Paranoia," 2323
Paray, Madame, 330
"Paris," 926, 931, 2349, 3081, 3254
"Paris in Spring," 312, 1428
"Paris Love Song," 314
"Paris--Underground," 46
"Paris When It Sizzles," 1179
Parker, Cecil, 749
Parker, Cecilia, 114
Parker, Eleanor, 3302, 3487
Parker, Mary, 550
Parkins, Barbara, 2078
"Parlor, Bedroom and Bath," 2232
Parmenter, Adele, 2337
"Parnell," 1294, 2261
"Parole Girl," 2407
"Parrish," 1917
Parsons, Estelle, 526
Parsons, Louella O., 3585

"Part Time Lady," 2427
"Party, The," 226
"Party Husband," 2385
Parvin, Ted, 2339
Pascal, Gabriel, 749
Pasha, Kalla, 1774
"Passenger, The," 559
"Passion" (1919), 131, 469
"Passion Flower," 1613
"Passion of Anna, The," 1893
"Passport to Shame," 2276
"Password Is Courage, The,"
    3145
"Past of Mary Holmes, The,"
    1927, 2405
Paterson, Pat, 840, 1915, 2043,
    2133, 2419
Paterson, Ronald, 2340
"Pathé's Animated Gazette," 987
Patou, Jean, 329, 330, 366, 1832,
    2098, 2342
"Patria," 129
Patriarca, Walter, 2343
Patrick, Gail, 312, 320, 991,
    1267, 1870, 1912, 1963, 2178,
    2417, 2464, 2483, 2521, 2544,
    2793, 2917, 2961, 3545
"Patriot, The," 470, 1476, 2960
"Patsy, The," 576, 785
Patterson, Russell, 2006, 2419,
    2678
"Paula," 2608
Paulette, Madame, 228
Pauli, Irms, 2347
Paull, Stephanie, 1881
Pauzer(s), U., 2350
Pawloff, Irene, 2351
Pawn, Doris, 831, 1622
"Pawnbroker, The," 1573
"Payment in Blood," 772
Payne, Lily, 93
"Peace to Him Who Enters,"
    1602
Peach, Mary, 1521
"Peach O'Reno," 2392
"Peacock Parade," 121
Pearce, Jacqueline, 1736
Pearlman, Lilli, 2353
Pearson, Jesie, 678
Pechanz, W., 2356
Peck, Ann B., 2357
Peck, Gregory, 220, 2520,
    3507
"Peek-a-boo," 503, 2714
"Peer Gynt," 610, 908, 1496
"Peg o' My Heart," 1932
"Penelope," 1692, 2897
Penezis, I., 2358

"People Against O'Hara, The," 2602,
    2781
"People Meet and Sweet Music Fills
    the Heart," 2709, 3056
"People Next Door, The," 2823
"People Will Talk," 2515
Perelyotov, V., 2361
"Perfect Friday," 426, 2693
"Perfect Marriage, The," 290, 675,
    1326, 1348, 2651
"Perfect Specimen, The," 3553
"Perfect Understanding," 2764
Pericoli, Ugo, 2362
"Perils of Pauline" (1947), 2651
"Perils of Pauline, The" (1967),
    1488
"Period of Adjustment, A," 678,
    2808
Periphery, 2081
Peris, 2363
Perkins, Anthony, 120, 2020
Perrine, Valerie, 2377
Perry, Joan, 1067, 1079, 2991,
    3545
"Persecution and Assassination of
    Jean-Paul Marat as Performed
    by the Inmates of the Asylum of
    Charenton Under the Direction of
    the Marquis de Sade, The," 1542,
    1543, 2320
"Persona," 1893
"Personal Maid's Secret," 583
"Personal Property," 556, 737,
    1749
Peruzzi, 2369
Peruzzi, Ditta, 2370
"Peter Pan," 613
Peterson's Magazine, 1864
Petit, Pascale, 1751
Petrova, Olga, 388, 3539
Pettet, Joanna, 283
petticoats (including bustles and
    hoop skirts), 40, 120, 461, 645,
    809, 857, 882, 883, 1044, 1086,
    1170, 1311, 1373, 1444, 1698,
    2554, 2783, 2988, 2991, 3234,
    3618
"Petty Girl, The," 2589
"Petulia," 2142, 2779, 3178, 3410
"Phaedra," 3315
"Phantasmes," 1198
"Phantom Lady," 3057
"Phantom of Crestwood, The," 2402
"Phantom Planet, The," 694, 2799
"Phantom President, The," 846
"Pharaoh's Woman, The," 216
Phelps, Ray, 2378
"Philadelphia Story, The," 27, 1007,
    3471

Philbin, Mary, 1972, 1973, 2171
Philippe, J. Claude, 2379
Phillips, Dorothy, 973, 1623, 2103, 2104
Phillips, Michelle, 1213
Phillips, Robin, 711
Phillips, Thalia, 2383
Phunkie Attire, 2624
"Phynx, The," 820
"Piccadilly Jim," 2443, 2522, 3105
Pickford, Mary, 209, 439, 550, 645, 719, 870, 1198, 1233, 1638, 1749, 1823, 1974, 2626, 2958, 3005, 3400, 3478, 3623
"Picnic," 1789
"Picture Mommy Dead," 2758
"Pieces of Dreams," 1129, 1271, 2378
Pierce, Jack, 3309
Pievetti, Alice, 2632
"Pigeon That Took Rome, The," 1391
"Pilgrimage," 1931
Pilla, Paola, 2633
"Pink Flamingos," 2855
"Pink Gods," 142
"Pink Panther, The," 2863
"Pink String and Sealing Wax," 588
"Pinocchio," 1244
"Pirate, The," 2028
"Pirate of the Black Hawk, The," 1887
"Pirates of Monterey," 192
Pistek, Theodor, 2635
"Pistol for Ringo, A," 1139
Pitts, Zasu, 2640, 3006, 3477
"Pizza Triangle, The," 82
Pizzi, Pier Luigi, 2636
"Place Called Glory, A," 2887
"Place for Lovers, A," 2854, 3327
"Place in the Sun, A," 556, 1312, 1750, 1831, 2502
"Plainclothes Man," 2403
"Plainsman, The" (1936), 2524, 3360
"Plainsman, The" (1966), 2871
"Planet of the Apes," 1254, 1416
"Planet of the Vampires," 1989
"Plastic Age, The," 3157
Platt, Polly, 526, 1839, 2637
"Play Girl," 2041
"Playgirl and the War Minister, The," 88
"Playhouse, The," 388
"Playing with Souls," 3470

"Playmates," 2755
"Playthings of Destiny," 852
Pleasence, Donald, 3020
"Pleasure and Vices," 505
"Pleasure Buyers, The," 3168
"Pleasure Cruise," 1930, 2408, 2764
"Pleasure Mad," 514
"Pleasure Seekers, The," 2739
Pleshette, Suzanne, 2629
Plitsetskaya, Maya, 334
Ploberger, Herbert, 2639
"Plunder," 1198
"Plunderer, The," 2292
Plunkett, Walter (see also Pulunkett, Walter), 134, 261, 551, 562, 679, 808, 898, 1044, 1067, 1198, 1268, 1311, 1419, 1432, 1437, 1652, 1653, 1671, 1750, 1835a, 1909, 1962, 2024, 2028, 2144, 2195, 2344, 2405, 2424, 2425, 2426, 2427, 2431, 2440, 2640, 2641, 2642, 2643, 2644, 2726, 2729, 2915, 2988, 3207, 3234, 3322, 3332, 3488
"Pocketful of Miracles," 678, 1342, 1402, 1437, 2641
Poggioni, Vera, 2645
"Point Blank," 3441
"Pointed Heels," 1423
Poiret, Paul, 323, 861, 1198, 1231, 1532, 2845, 2848, 3211
"Police Nurse," 1939
Pollack, Sidney, 1762
Pollard, Harry "Snub," 3007
"Polly of the Circus," 2392
Polo, 162
Pompei, 2647
"Ponjola," 1100
Pons, Lily, 310, 1067, 2258, 2448, 2753
Ponten, Gunilla, 2648
Ponting, Roy, 2649
Pool, Muriel, 3416
"Popi," 3570
"Poppy," 1023, 1491
"Popular Skin, The," 655
"Porgy and Bess," 2964, 3293
Porteous, Emma, 2655
Porter, Gene Stratton, 2306
Porter's, 2057
"Portrait of a Rebel," 2524
"Portrait of a Sinner," 1321
"Portrait of Jennie," 174, 1573
"Poseidon Adventure, The," 806a
Posner, Sylvia, 2657
"Possessed," 2392
"Possession of Joel Delaney, The," 2082

Postal, Ron, 2658
"Postman Always Rings Twice,
  The," 2659
"Pot O'Gold," 1590
"Potash and Perlmutter," 325,
  1080, 1081, 1099, 1867, 3125
Poulet, Sylvie, 2660
Poulton, Mabel, 209
"Pound," 117
Powell, David, 1384
Powell, Eleanor, 1003, 1914,
  2533, 2755, 2990, 3244
Powell, Jane, 445, 2503, 2583,
  2616, 2806, 3419
Powell, Robert, 1213
Powell, William, 1709, 3238
Power, Tyrone, 995, 2266, 3164
"Power and the Glory, The,"
  2763
"Powers Girl, The," 965, 2783,
  3579
Praigg, Peggy, 2662
"Prehistoric Women," 364,
  3259
"Prelude to Night," 1795
Preminger, Otto, 1241
Prentiss, Paula, 1060, 3101,
  3245, 3291
"Presenting Lily Mars," 2862,
  3088
"President's Analyst, The,"
  226
Presley, Elvis, 265, 2368
Preston, Robert, 1437
"Pretty Poison," 2823
Pretzfelder, Max, 2665
Preuss, Helmut, 2666
Prevost, Marie, 660, 2622,
  2947, 3499
"Price of a Party," 2621
"Pride and Prejudice," 944,
  1087, 1416
"Prime of Miss Jean Brodie,
  The," 374, 1259, 1762
"Primera Dama, La" (see
  "First Lady, The,")
"Primrose Path, The," 3544
"Prince and the Showgirl,
  The," 235, 743, 2144
"Princess Comes Across, The,"
  2441
Pringle, Aileen, 20, 24, 60,
  61, 659, 926, 2334, 2527,
  2621, 2732, 2979, 3006,
  3077, 3268
Printemps, Yvonne, 996
"Prisoner of the Iron Mask,"
  287

"Prisoner of Zenda" (1952), 1846
"Private Life of Don Juan, The,"
  2004, 2425
"Private Life of Helen of Troy,
  The," 823
"Private Life of Henry VIII, The,"
  227, 329, 1473, 1719
"Private Lives," 2392
"Private Lives of Elizabeth and
  Essex, The," 679, 1086, 2554
"Private Navy of Sgt. O'Farrell,
  The," 2799
"Private Number," 1268
"Privilege," 580
"Prizefighter and the Lady, The,"
  1425
"Prodigal Son, The," 926
"Producers, The," 602
Production Code, 2907, 3126
"Professionals, The," 1949
"Project X," 1888, 3154
"Promise at Dawn," 69
"Promise Her Anything," 375
"Promises! Promises!," 520, 707,
  1167, 2118
"Prosperity," 3163
"Proud Flesh," 544, 2001
Prowse, David, 3096
"Prudence and the Pill," 3177
"Psych-Out," 96
"Psycho," 752
"Psycho-Circus," 1246
"Public Enemy," 982, 1115
Pucci, Emilio, 2675
"Puente de San Luis Rey, El" (see
  "Bridge of San Luis Rey, The")
Puffy Charles, 525, 3485
"Pullman Bride, The," 388
Pulunkett, Walter (see also Plunkett,
  Walter), 2676, 2677
"Pumpkin Eater, The," 2095
"Puppe, Die" (see "Doll, The")
"Purple Hills, The," 1166, 3178
purses, 273, 286, 882, 1250, 1645,
  2233a, 2375, 2539, 3130, 3416,
  3590
"Pursued, The," 1022
"Pussycat Alley," 169
"Pussycat, Pussycat, I Love You,"
  287, 2190
Putnam, Carolyn, 2098
Putnam, Marilyn, 162
"Puttin' on the Ritz," 2274
"Puzzle of a Downfall Child," 1747
"Pyro," 2036

"Quality Street" (1927), 1480
"Quality Street" (1937), 134, 808
Quant, Mary, 2679, 2680, 2681, 2682, 2683, 2684
"Que Juega con Fuego, El" (see "Roughly Speaking")
"Queen Christina," 16, 822, 1295, 2685, 2783
"Queen Elizabeth," 1719
Queen Emma Society, 2668
"Queen of Blood," 630
"Queen of Burlesque," 754
"Queen of Sheba, The," 296, 388
"Queen of Spades" (1950), 2004
"Queen of Spades" (1961), 3042
"Queen of the Nile," 216
"Queen of the Pirates," 216
"Question of Honor, A," 3255
"Quick Millions," 2953
"Quiet Place in the Country, A," 624
"Quincy Adams Sawyer," 202

"R.P.M.," 1634
Rabadi, Mani, 2688
Rabanne, Paco, 2689, 2690
"Rachel, Rachel," 2798
Raffiné, 2691
"Raffles," 2480
Raft, George, 1773, 3598
"Rage," 1474
"Rage of Paris, The," 2465, 2541, 3091
"Rage to Live, A," 1166
"Raging Tide, The," 395
Rahvis, 2693
"Raiders, The," 753
"Raiders from Beneath the Sea," 803
"Railroad Man, The," 2067
Rainer, Luise, 1825, 1826, 1979, 2355, 2694, 3109, 3212
Raines, Ella, 827, 2112, 2559, 2599, 3057, 3285, 3580
Rainier, Prince, 2794
Rains, Claude, 749
"Rains Came, The," 2477
Raitt, John, 2312
Rambova, Natacha (Winifred Shaunessy Hudnut), 36, 128, 271, 405, 564, 879, 961, 1199, 1483, 1711, 1784, 1940, 2032, 2205, 2237, 2245, 2687, 2696, 2697, 2698, 2783, 2884, 3014,

3300, 3318, 3384, 3456
Ramoin, Clo, 2699
"Ramona," 1267, 1654, 2524
"Rampage," 492
"Rampage at Apache Wells," 2347, 2666
Ramsdell, Roger, 1136
"Rancho Notorious," 465
Rand, Ayn, 550
Rand, June, 2701
Rand, Sally, 1035
Randall, Tony, 88
Ranzato, Jo, 2705
Rapf, Joe, 946, 1568, 2706, 3296, 3475
Rappe, Virginia, 106
Rappoport, E., 2707
"Rapture," 1062
"Rascal," 3180
"Rasputin and the Empress," 16, 158, 439
"Rasputin, the Black Monk," 3306
Rathbone, Basil, 1441
"Ravagers, The," 2870
"Raven, The," 3454
Ravnholt, Lotte, 2709
"Raw Deal," 902
Rawlinson, Herbert, 1763
Ray Aghayan/Bob Mackie, 58
Ray, Charles, 209, 2710
Raye, Martha, 778, 2926, 3092
Raymonde, 2714
"Razor's Edge, The," 1769, 3210
Reachi, Renita, 2715
Reagan, Maureen, 1223
Réal, 2716
"Rear Window," 1263, 1345, 1678, 2981
"Reckless," 316, 1871, 1913
"Reckless Hour, The," 1699
"Recoil, The," 844
"Red and the White, The," 1, 3328
"Red Badge of Courage, The," 2820
"Red Dancer, The," 2960
"Red Desert," 758
"Red-Dragon," 3027
"Red Hair," 1536
"Red Hot Romance," 2102
"Red Line 7000," 576
"Red Mill, The," 1247, 2732
"Red Runs the River," 2085
"Red Shoes, The," 1154, 1362
"Red Sky at Morning," 1339
"Red Sword, The," 2677
"Red, White and Black, The," 767
Redford, Robert, 162, 729, 1336,

1748, 2664, 3059, 3568
Redgrave, Corin, 711
Redgrave, Michael, 711, 1088
Redgrave, Vanessa, 1211, 1414, 1789
"Redheads on Parade," 582, 1478, 1869, 1915, 2024
Ree, Marie, 945
Ree, Max, 766, 1982, 2352, 2718, 2719, 2720, 2721, 2958, 3004, 3006
Reed, Donna, 2605
Reed, Oliver, 1213
Reed, Rose Marie, 2724
Reeve, Christopher, 1992, 2276, 2377
"Reflections in a Golden Eye," 1006
"Refuge," 590
Rehfeld, Curt, 1812
Reid, Virginia, 2287, 2433, 2703
Reid, Wallace, 1763, 1774
Reimann, Walter, 2734
Reinhardt, Max, 3004
Reiss & Fabrizio, 2735
"Reivers, The," 526, 1761, 3327
"Relentless," 442
"Reluctant Astronaut, The," 2871
"Reluctant Saint, The," 761
"Remains to Be Seen," 1221
"Remember the Night," 1183
Remick, Lee, 69, 1241, 2203
"Remodeling Her Husband," 1174
"Remote Control," 160
"Rendezvous," 2736
Rendlesham, Clare, 2737
Renie (Irene Brouillet Conley), 547, 548, 556, 1182, 1494, 2487, 2565, 2738, 2739, 2740
"Reno," 1987
"Reputation," 2956
"Requiem for a Heavyweight," 353
Ressl, Eldean, 2741
"Restless Sex," 901a, 926, 3077
"Restless Wives," 2622
"Resurrection," 1123
"Return from Limbo," 2533
"Return of Dr. Mabuse, The," 2198, 2345
"Return of Dr. X," 2988
"Return of Peter Grimm, The,"

945
"Return of the Seven," 2938
"Reunion in Vienna," 1930
Revill, Clive, 204
Revillard, Suzanne, 2750
"Revolt of Mamie Stover, The," 1660
"Revolt of the Slaves, The," 2822
Revuelta, Manuel, 2751
Rex, 393
Reynolds, Burt, 111
Reynolds, Debbie, 1831, 1917
Reynolds, Joyce, 3273
Reynolds, Marjorie, 675
Reynolds, Vera, 657, 1616
"Rhapsody in Blue," 985
Rhodes, Billie, 1622
Rhodes, Leah, 399, 400, 464, 671, 679, 836, 860, 1780, 2491, 2564, 2576, 2582, 2591, 2614, 2758, 3215
"Rhumba," 3182
"Ribald Tales of Robin Hood, The," 1039
Ribas, Marian, 2759
Riber, Bente, 2760
Ricarde of Hollywood, 2473
Ricci, Nina, 2761
Rice, Florence, 2455
"Rich Are Always with Us, The," 2396, 2397, 2994
Rich, Irene, 209, 1219, 1529, 1698, 2765, 3473
Rich, Lillian, 662, 1616, 2360, 2766
"Rich Man's Folly," 2390
"Richard III," 1111, 1112, 2144
Richards, Robert, 2767
Richardson, Frances, 1755
Richardson, Frank, 554
Richardson, Helen, 3525
Richardson, Sir Ralph, 1112
"Richest Girl in the World, The," 2426
Richter, Ilse, 2769
Richter, Kurt, 469
Richter-Visser, Anna, 2770
Rickards, Jocelyn, 2771
Rickart, Evelyn, 2772
Ricketts, Charles, 2773
Ricksen, Lucille, 1401, 2297
"Ricochet," 3444
Ridard, Henriette, 2774
"Ride Beyond Vengeance," 745
"Ride the Wild Surf," 501, 3179
"Rider on a Dead Horse," 803
"Rider on the Rain," 757
Riggs, Rita, 2779

"Right Cross," 2506, 2590, 2806
"Right to Live, The," 3427
Riley, Laurie, 2782
"Ring-a-Ding Rhythm," 1019
"Rings on Her Finger," 1504
"Rio Lobo," 224, 2339
"Rio Rita," 1653, 3401
"Riptide," 16, 1296, 2117, 2619, 2722, 2922, 2983, 3408, 3450
"Rise of Louis XIV, The," 667
Ritchie, Billy, 1843
"Ritual, The," 1893
Ritva, 1382
Ritzell, Roy, 2628
Rivera, Chita, 524
"Riverrun," 3132
"Road to Morocco," 1312
"Road to Reno," 2390
"Road to Singapore, The," 1537
"Road to Utopia," 1354, 2784
"Roadhouse," 2159
"Rob Roy," 2144
"Robbery," 2307
"Robe, The," 1284, 1744, 2881, 3463
"Roberta," 547, 567, 703, 1188, 1268, 1298, 1398, 2287, 2433, 2703, 3494
Roberti, Lyda, 5, 1912, 1933
Roberts, Edith, 429, 892, 893, 894
Roberts, Frank, 2786
Roberts, Lynne, 1214
Roberts, Rachel, 3420
Roberts, Ricky, 2787
Roberts, Theodore, 528
Robertson, John S., 332, 528, 681
Robin, Genevieve, 986
"Robin and Marian," 1202
"Robin Hood," 266, 327, 388, 528, 532, 550, 1738, 1812, 2045, 3080
Robins of Dallas, 2789
Robinson Co., J.W., 2227, 2790
Robson, Flora, 749, 1719
Roc, Patricia, 588
Rochas, Marcel, 329, 1267
Rochelle, Carrie, 1562
"Rockabye," 1403, 1926
"Rocking Moon," 933
Rockne, Rose, 2795
"Rocky Mountain," 2509
Rodgers, Dorothy, 2796
Rodrigues, Pedro, 2797
Rodriguez, Domingo, 2798
Rodriguez, Oscar, 2799
Rogers, Ginger, 140, 275, 310,
500, 556, 550, 556, 670, 679,
703, 754, 786, 947, 980, 985,
1026, 1047, 1132, 1188, 1298,
1347, 1398, 1413, 1427, 1749,
1806, 1830, 1855, 1870, 1892,
1931, 1933, 2023, 2041, 2079,
2258, 2263, 2269, 2287, 2373,
2376, 2403, 2405, 2406, 2444,
2455, 2458, 2466, 2532, 2538,
2541, 2548, 2640, 2703, 2704,
2792, 2793, 2933, 2987, 3091,
3093, 3122, 3262, 3377, 3448,
3544, 3549
Rogers, Joyce, 2801
Rogers, Roy, 1013
Röhrig, Walter, 2825
Roland, Cherry, 3013
Roland, Gilbert, 3157
Roland, Ruth, 815, 1987, 2802, 2849
"Rollerball," 2803
Roman, Ruth, 2504
"Roman Spring of Mrs. Stone, The," 12, 375, 744, 898
"Romance," 23, 465, 616, 643, 868, 1317, 1383, 1385, 1749, 2665, 2838, 2994, 3529
"Romance of the Bathing Girl, The," 1571
"Romance on the High Seas," 2073
"Romance Ranch," 2296
"Romance y Fantasia," 3302
Romanini, Gaia, 2804
"Romanoff and Juliet," 2139, 2140
Romantic and Glamorous Hollywood Design exhibit, 129, 351, 603, 1211, 1415, 1749, 1830, 1851, 2083, 2791, 2814, 3149, 3282
Romay, Lina, 3555
"Romeo and Juliet" (c.1917), 1466
"Romeo and Juliet" (1936), 22, 461, 562, 751, 1389, 1433, 1441, 1473, 1632, 1681, 1700, 2002, 2003, 2371, 2376, 2523, 2959, 3529
"Romeo and Juliet" (1966), 1140
"Romeo and Juliet" (1968), 818
"Romola," 1776, 2791
"Room for One More," 399
"Rooster Cogburn," 1336
Root, Sandy, 2805
"Rosalie," 2533
Rose, Florence, 2341
Rose, Helen, 393, 550, 1038, 1198, 1263, 1374, 1660, 1671, 1835a, 1750, 1917, 2163, 2499, 2503, 2504, 2506, 2513, 2514, 2581, 2583, 2590, 2595, 2600, 2602, 2781, 2806, 2807, 2808, 2809,

2810, 2811, 2877, 2992, 2993, 3559
"Rose for Everyone, A," 2804
"Rose of the Rancho," 1268, 1870
"Rose of Washington Square," 754, 2472
Rosee, Herman, 2821
"Rosemary's Baby," 3189
Rosenbach, Gina, 2815
"Rosenkavalier, Der," 1650
Rosenquest, Barbara, 2816
Rosenstein, Nettie, 1052, 1073
Rosier, Michele, 2817
"Rosita," 550
Ross, Clark, 2819
Ross, Diana, 713, 1878, 2723
Ross, Don, 1241
Ross, Kathryn, 890
Ross, Shirley, 778, 2444, 2450, 2528, 2535
Rossi, Vittorio, 2822
Rosson, Harold, 1849
Roth, Ann, 713, 2823
Roth, Eve, 2824
Rotha, Paul, 2825
Rouff, Maggy, 960, 996
"Rough Riders, The," 3477
"Roughly Speaking," 365, 2826
"Round Up, The," 3348
Rous, Bucky, 2827
Rousseau, Gladys, 2663
"Roustabout," 3046
Rouzot, Renee, 2829
Rovatti, Cesare, 2830
Rowlands, Gena, 2078
Roxy Theatre, 486
Roy, Hazel, 2831
Royer (Louis Royer Hastings), 698, 702, 847, 1043, 1420, 1498, 1757, 1915, 1959, 2413, 2413, 2414, 2415, 2416, 2417, 2419, 2420, 2424, 2426, 2457, 2458, 2461, 2464, 2465, 2472, 2483, 2533, 2538, 2834, 2835, 2836, 2929, 2935, 2989, 3093
Rubens, Alma, 659, 2218, 2289, 2299, 3278, 3477
Ruckman, Nan 2839
Rudolph, Rod, 2840
Ruffing, Nancy, 2841
Rule, Janice, 3420
"Run, Angel, Run!," 3197
"Rupert of Hentzau," 296, 1996
Russell, Gail, 1252, 1325, 1341, 2489

Russell, Jane, 797, 947, 1142, 1198, 1660, 1718, 1892, 2338, 2907, 3126
Russell, Ken, 1213, 1840
Russell, Rosalind, 188, 193, 316, 365, 478, 1021, 1120, 1437, 1455, 1511, 1619, 1805, 1807, 1968, 2040, 2075, 2077, 2281, 2281, 2285, 2445, 2465, 2476, 2552, 2567, 2736, 2826, 2843, 3092, 3176, 3232, 3553, 3555
Russell, Shirley, 1213, 1840, 2844
"Russian Are Coming, The Russians Are Coming, The," 1559
Rutherford, Ann, 373, 1087
Rutherford, Margaret, 2276
Ryan, Florence, 2850
"Ryan's Daughter," 2771
Ryden, Mabs Elizabeth (see Mabs of Hollywood)
Ryndina, V., 2852

"Sabata," 3023
Sabatelli, Luca, 2853
Sabbatini, Enrico, 2854
"Sabrina," 556, 1339, 1345
"Sacrifice," 3472
"Sadie McKee," 697, 3497
"Sadie Thompson," 3469
"Sadist, The," 1005
"Safari," 2481
Safas, Sartoria, 2856
Sagoni, Luciano, 2857
"Sail a Crooked Ship," 105
"Sailor from Gibraltar, The," 2135, 2771
"Sailor-Made Man, A," 1499
Saint, Eva Marie, 1345
Saint Cyr, Renée, 996
St. Hill, Loudon, 2859
"Saint Joan," 2144
St. John, Al, 2247
St. John, Jill, 679
Saint-Laurent, Yves, 339, 2863, 2864, 2865, 2866
"St. Louis Blues," 2989, 3594
St. Moritz, Ruth, 2867
"Sainted Devil, A," 128, 1199, 2032, 2079, 2205, 2687, 2783, 3300, 3384
"Saintly Sinners," 350, 1908
Saks Fifth Avenue, 211, 2439, 2899, 3066
Salamero, Flora, 2868
salaries, 471, 504, 1044, 1489,

1750, 2215, 3198, 3207, 3247,
  3296, 3370, 3386
Salcedo, Felisa, 2869
Salcedo, Paquito, 2870
Saldutti, Peter, 2871
Sales, Soupy, 2314
Saling, Norman, 2872
"Sallah," 2815
"Sally," 3143
"Sally of the Sawdust," 2692
Sally, Tuffin, Ltd., 2873
"Sally, Irene and Mary," 13,
  1564/5, 2537
"Salome" (1918),   755, 1482
"Salome" (1922),   961, 2698,
  3456
"Salome" (1953),   1654
"Salome of the Tenements," 660
"Salt & Pepper," 1186, 1322,
  3252
Saltern, Irene, 1043, 3250
"Salvatore Giuliano," 477
"Sam Whiskey," 3610
Samazeuilh, Alyette, 2875
Sammaciccia, Angela,   901, 2876
"Samson and Delilah," 671, 975,
  1552, 3131, 3377
"Samson and the Seven Miracles
  of the World," 341
"Samson and the Slave Queen,"
  2343
"Samson vs. the Giant King,"
  2343
"San Demetrio, London," 1812
San Juan, Olga, 1324
"Sand Pebbles, The," 2739, 3597
Sandeen, Clinton, 2092
Sandeen, Jack, 2878
"Sandokan the Great," 216
"Sandpiper, The," 2964, 2968
"Sandra," 372
"Sands of the Kalahari," 3051
"Sandy, the Reluctant Nature Girl,"
  2017
Sanjust, Filippo, 2879
Sannell, Bertha, 2880
"Santa Claus Conquers the Mar-
  tians," 2090
Santiago, Emile,   1744, 2881
"Sappho," 1238
"Saragossa Manuscript, The," 3034,
  3035
"Saratoga Trunk," 671
Sarli, Isabel, 1544
Sassard, Jacqueline, 758
"Satan Bug, The," 1559
"Satan's Secret," 570
"Saturday Night," 530, 762, 3456

"Saturday Night Fever," 553, 687
"Saturday Night Out," 1321
Savage, Nelly, 3335
"Savage Guns, The," 2751
"Savage Innocents, The," 2225
"Savage Messiah," 1213
"Savage Pampas," 2759
Savalas, Telly, 3020
"Saxon Charm, The," 812
"Sayonara," 1789
Scales, John, 2885
"Scalphunters, The," 863
"Scandal Sheet," 2605
"Scandals," 2117
Scandariato, Itala, 2887
"Scaramouche" (1923),   652, 1447,
  1771, 2752, 2824
Scarano, Gildo, 2888
Scarano, Tony, 2889
"Scare Their Pants Off," 2033
"Scarface," 1115
"Scarface Mob, The," 347
Scarfiotti, Ferdinando, 2890
"Scarlet Empress, The," 1118,
  1394, 2194, 2417, 2419, 2704,
  3182, 3450, 3496, 3542, 3604,
  3605
"Scarlet Hour, The," 1678
"Scarlet Negligee," 1874
"Scarlet Pimpernel, The," 476
Scassi, Arnold, 2163, 2891
Scatena, Luce, 2892
Schaffer, Judit, 2894
Scheff, Fritzi, 1638
"Scheherazade," 3382
Schenck, Joseph, 1794, 2687
Schiaparelli (Elsa),   330, 366, 423,
  584, 947, 1007, 1832, 2043,
  2258, 2372, 2783, 2792, 2896
Schmidt, Eddie,   261, 1453, 1701,
  1996, 2065, 3446
Schmidt, Gunther, 2898
Schneider, Romy, 383
Schofield, Violet, 2902
Scholz, Brigitte, 2903
"School for Scandal," 1214
Schrader, Abe and Mort,   507
Schreckling, Walter, 2905
Schroder, Eva Maria   2906
Schrodt, Inez, 1838
Schroeder, Violet, 2860
Scott, George C., 602
Scott, Jay Hutchinson,   2908, 2909
Scott, Ken, 2910
Scott, Lizabeth,   895, 1330, 1341,
  1346, 1808, 2315, 2488, 2505,
  2511, 2556, 2573, 3139
Scott, Martha,   3250

Scott, Ron, 2911
Scott, Son & Co., 2914
Scott-Slymon, 749
"Scraps," 1064, 3478
"Scream of Fear," 1786
Screenland, 68
"Scrooge," 169
"Scudda Hoo, Scudda Hay," 483
"Sea Gull, The," 3410
"Sea Hawk, The" (1924), 522, 1535, 2048
"Sea of Grass," 944
"Search for Beauty," 2418
Sears, Heather, 972
Sears-Roebuck, 555, 696, 697, 3231
Seastrom, Dorothy, 1035
Sebastian, Dorothy, 3015
Seberg, Jean, 2863, 3333
"Second Fiddle," 702
"Second Hand Wife," 1927, 2404
"Second Honeymoon," 318, 3226
"Secret Beyond the Door," 2558
"Secret Ceremony," 337, 805, 3601
"Secret Heart, The," 586
"Secret Invasion, The," 630
"Secret Life of an American Wife, The," 3273
"Secret Life of Hernando Cortez, The," 2087
"Secret Life of Walter Mitty, The," 883, 2967
"Secret of Deep Harbor," 350, 1908
"Secret of Madame Blanche, The," 439
"Secret of My Success, The," 506
"Secret of Santa Vittoria, The," 1634
"Secret of the Blue Room, The," 1933, 2413
"Secret of the Storm Country, The," 1023
"Secret of the Submarine, The," 686
"Secret People," 93
"Secret Seven, The," 1169
"Secret Sex Lives of Romeo and Juliet, The," 1790, 2805
"Secret Ways, The," 264
"Secret World," 221
"Secrets" (1924), 620, 809, 1742, 2978, 3472
"Secrets" (1933), 439, 1823
"Secrets of an Actress," 2463
"Secrets of an Uncover Model,"

3349
"Seduced and Abandoned," 901, 2876
"Seed," 2387
"Seekers, The," 2144
Seelig, Eric, 2938
Seid, Tauhma, 2939
Seitz, George E., 1583
Selby-Walker, Emma, 2144, 2940
Sellers, Bridget, 2941
"Sellers of Girls," 2892
Selli, Sergio, 2942
Seltenhammer, Paul, 2944
Selznick, David O., 261, 1044, 1311, 2065, 3234, 3264, 3322
Selznick, Irene Mayer, 1044
Semon, Larry, 2247
"Senator Was Indiscreet, The," 2559, 3580
Senne, Agnes, 2945
Sennett, Mack, 434, 825, 2946
"Senso," 932
"Separate Tables," 1345
"Serafino," 2876
"Sergeant Was a Lady, The," 1395
"Sergeant York," 3164
"Sergeants 3," 76, 1437, 1558
"Servants' Entrance," 2024, 2425
"Service for Ladies," 1101
Session, Ermon, 2951
"Sesso," 450
"Seven Brides for Seven Brothers," 3419
"Seven Consenting Adults," 412
"Seven Daring Girls," 1281
"Seven Days in May," 76, 1559, 2029
"Seven Days Leave," 377, 1569
"711 Ocean Drive," 2500
"Seven Faces," 3565
"Seven Golden Men," 2804
"Seven Guns for the MacGregors," 1633
"7 Lives Were Changed," 2416
"Seven Seas to Calais," 2879
"Seven Sinners," 792, 798, 1482
"Seven Slaves Against the World," 2343
"Seven Swans, The," 3196
"Seven Thieves," 1917
"Seven Women," 1641
"Seven Women from Hell," 707
"Seventh Continent, The," 3123
"7th Dawn, The," 12, 1160, 1246
"Seventh Heaven," 1442, 3552
"Sex," 856, 3534
"Sex and the Single Girl," 2203
"Sex of Angels, The," 3361

"Sextette," 3428
Seymour, Jane, 1992
Seyrig, Delphine, 516
Shackleton, Allan, 3108
"Shadow of a Doubt," 30
"Shadows," 962
"Shadows of Paris," 3472
"Shaft," 2855
"Shakiest Gun in the West, The,"
    1488
"Shalako," 3252
"Shall We Dance?," 909, 3549
"Shame," 1893
"Shameless Desire," 1746
"Shampoo," 1831, 2020
"Shane," 1013
"Shanghai Deadline," 2536
"Shanghai Express," 465, 1273,
    1305, 2072
"Shanghai Gesture, The," 1919,
    3247
Shannon, Jon, 2963
Shannon, Peggy, 2390
"Shannon's Women," 2996
Sharaff, Irene, 679, 875, 883,
    1198, 1416, 1437, 1530, 1534,
    1643, 1645, 1652, 1816, 1835a,
    1917, 2028, 2164, 2561, 2629,
    2964, 2965, 2966, 2967, 2968,
    2969, 2970, 2971, 2972, 2973,
    2974, 3334, 3420
"Share Out, The," 3444
Sharif, Omar, 1645
Sharon of Hollywood, 2975
Sharpe, Norah, 2976
Shaw, George Bernard, 749
Shaw, Peggy, 2292
Shawls/stoles, 121, 535, 832,
    1174, 2251, 2380, 2569, 2597,
    2884, 3032, 3071, 3499, 3623
"She" (1935), 1643, 2436
"She" (1965), 3259
"She Couldn't Take It," 1870,
    1910
"She-Devil, The," 406
"She Done Him Wrong," 55, 275,
    329, 439, 679, 921, 1312, 1399,
    1749, 2024, 2711, 2838
"She Had to Eat," 3548
"She Loves Me Not," 2192
"She Married an Artist," 2533,
    2927
"She Mob," 2789
"She Wolves," 2289
Shea, Eric, 806a
Shearer, Norma, 16, 22, 43, 50,
    461, 462, 478, 562, 643, 657,
    660, 679, 728, 816, 941, 944,

949, 1010, 1025, 1203, 1211,
    1264, 1273, 1296, 1360, 1373,
    1433, 1435, 1456, 1482, 1672,
    1877, 1891, 1897, 1900, 2002,
    2065, 2117, 2207, 2208, 2209,
    2233a, 2352, 2371, 2392, 2476,
    2543, 2552, 2619, 2712, 2722,
    2730, 2780, 2843, 2922, 2954,
    2983, 2984, 2985, 2986, 3037,
    3194, 3231, 3235, 3264, 3388,
    3408, 3415, 3450, 3541, 3618,
    3625
"Sheik, The," 1446, 1784, 2237
"Shenandoah," 746
"Shepherd King, The," 2291
"Shepherd of the Hills, The," 2034
Sheppard, Dolores, 2995
Sheppard, Eugenia, 792
Sheridan, Ann, 366, 1079, 1413,
    2042, 2475, 2480, 2482, 3272,
    3416, 3577
Sheriff, Earl, 2996
"Sherlock, Jr.," 2049, 3459
Sherman, Lowell, 777
Sherman, Stanley, 2997
Sherrard, Mickey, 2998
Sherrard, Wesley, 2999
Sherrick, Arthur, 3000
"She's Back on Broadway," 444
"She's Got Everything," 2458
"She's Working Her Way Through
    College," 391, 2611
Shieff, Maxwell, 3001
Shields, Brooke, 1992
Shields, Chuck, 3002
Shildknekht, L., 3003
"Shining Hour, The," 40, 1674,
    2543
"Ship Ahoy," 2755
"Ship of Fools," 1634
Shipman, Nell, 3518
Shirley, Anne, 2259, 3092, 3579
"Shock Corridor," 350
"Shock Treatment," 3281
shoes, 106, 113, 121, 140, 162,
    249, 255, 266, 286, 388, 467,
    502, 519, 572, 599, 603, 769,
    904, 916, 1007, 1041, 1059,
    1064, 1111, 1196, 1200, 1283,
    1286, 1420, 1421, 1499, 1536,
    1594, 1616, 1654, 1661, 1670,
    1709, 1715, 1721, 1731, 1789,
    1840, 1843, 1855, 2016, 2037,
    2124, 2192, 2200, 2377, 2440,
    2539, 2626, 2647, 2723, 2820,
    3006, 3096, 3166, 3168, 3231,
    3232, 3233, 3264, 3309, 3322,
    3370, 3398, 3400, 3407, 3414,

3464, 3480, 3482, 3542
"Shoes of the Fisherman, The,"
   2140
"Shoot Out at Big Sag," 1801
Shore, Dinah, 269, 3169
"Short Night, The," 788
"Should Ladies Behave?," 3448
Shoup, Howard, 444, 540, 1079,
   1917, 2474, 2478, 2480, 2482,
   2485, 2533, 2541, 2629, 3012,
   3578
"Show of Shows, The," 1065,
   2179
"Show People," 1091
"Showboat" (1936), 307
"Shrike, The," 1337
Shubette of London, 3013
"Shuttered Room, The," 168,
   2097
"Sicilian Clan, The," 2222
"Sidelong Glances of a Pigeon
   Kicker, The," 2798
Sidney, Sylvia, 1007, 2108, 2388,
   2421, 3190
"Sierra," 1422
Sievewright, Alan, 3017
Sigal, Joann, 3018
"Sign of the Cross, The," 275,
   550, 1823, 2665
"Signpost to Murder," 3273
"Silence, The," 3375
"Silent Call, The," 803, 2918
"Silent Watcher, The," 2824
Silich, L., 3019
Sills, Milton, 884
"Silver Chalice, The," 679
"Silver River," 3272
Silverstein, Jason, 3022
Simi, Carlo, 3023
Simmons, Elinor, 3024
Simmons, Jean, 2809, 2964
Simms, Ginny, 2755
Simms, Joseph S., 27, 344,
   1010, 2220, 3026
Simon, Margarete, 3027
Simon, Simone, 2457, 2458,
   2461, 2533, 2538, 3093
Simpkins, Mildred, 3028
"Sin," 3623
"Sin in the Suburbs," 2850
"SINderella and the Golden Bra,"
   331
Sinatra, Frank, 473, 1437,
   3285
Sinclair, Anthony, 3029
Sinclair, Ruth, 1032
Sinclair, Upton, 3030
"Sing and Like It," 3451

"Sing and Swing," 2680, 3129
"Singer Not the Song, The," 1764
"Singin' in the Rain," 1750
"Singing Marine, The," 1000
"Single Man, A," 20, 61
"Single Track, The," 3031
"Single Wives," 648, 3472
"Sinners in Love," 2676
"Sinners in Silk," 2621
"Sinners in the Sun," 2397
Sirchio, Cosmo, 2163
"Sis Hopkins," 2860
"Sister Kenny," 3555
"Sisters, The," 538, 539, 2550
"Sisters Under the Skin," 2419,
   3450
"Sitting Pretty," 2704
"Situation Hopeless--But Not Serious,"
   865
Skalicky, Jan, 3033
Skarzyński, Jerzy, 3034
Skarzyński, Lidia, 3034
"Skidoo," 404, 1129, 1145, 2339
Skillan, Hugh, 749
Skolmen, Ada, 3036
Skorepová, 3038
"Sky Bride," 2395
"Skylark," 596
"Skyscraper Souls," 2401
"Slander the Woman," 837
"Slave, The" (1963), 115, 1169,
   2647
"Slave of Fashion, A," 2209
"Slaves," 1243, 1888
"Slaves of Desire," 514
"Sleep, My Love," 2562, 3067
"Sleepers East," 1429
"Slippy McGee," 968, 1793
Slovtsova, Ye., 3042
"Small Town Girl," 3424
"Small World of Sammy Lee, The,"
   3177
Smart Alecs, The, 3129
"Smart Girl," 312, 1912
"Smash-Up, The Story of a Woman,"
   192, 984
"Smashing Time," 2135
"Smilin' Through" (1922), 3436
"Smilin' Through" (1932), 2954
"Smiling Irish Eyes," 3143
"Smiling Lieutenant, The," 2955
Smith, Alexis, 366, 1008, 2114,
   2593
Smith, C. Aubrey, 1441
Smith, Esther, 3047
Smith, Franc, 1712
Smith, H.M.K., 676, 722, 1194,
   1253, 2124, 2205, 3048, 3049,
   3572

Smith, James, 3051
Smith, Maggie, 1762, 2701
Smith, William, 3052
"Smith!," 3180
Smithsonian Institution, 833
"Smudge," 2103, 2104
Snajderova, Zdena, 3053
"Snake Pit, The," 2563
"Snake Woman, The," 2017
"Sniper's Ridge," 2254
"Snob, The," 660
"Snobs," 1638
Snow, Marguerite, 3054
"Snow White," 2356
"Snow White and the Seven Dwarfs,"
218, 562, 2459, 3238
"Snow White and the Three
Stooges," 2739
"So Big," 765, 1024, 3532
"So This Is College," 1091
"So This Is Marriage," 905
Soares, Paulo Gil, 3055
"Society for Sale," 2861
"Society Scandal, A," 465
Söderlund, Ulla Britt, 3056
"Sodom and Gomorrah," 216
"Soft Cushions," 823
"Soft Skin, The," 2829
Soldati, Sebastiano, 3058
"Soldier Blue," 2339
"Soldier in the Rain," 81, 3154
"Solid Gold Cadillac, The," 1811
"Solo for Sparrow," 3444
"Some Baby," 3007
"Some Kind of a Nut," 3189
"Some Like It Hot," 1482, 2285
"Something for Everyone," 1646,
1647, 2347
"Something for the Boys," 1043,
3285
"Something to Think About," 2231
"Something Wild," 3236
"Something's Got to Give," 1878
"Somewhere in Time," 1992
Somner, Pearl, 3062
Somohano, Georgette, 3063
Somper, Frank, 2082, 3064
"Son of a Gunfighter," 2868
"Son of Samson," 761
"Son of the Red Corsair," 761
"Son of the Sheik, The," 2, 502,
1784, 3014, 3300
Sondergaard, Gale, 1849
"Song of Bernadette," 858
"Song of Love, The," 620
"Song of Norway," 1924, 3387
"Song of Songs," 1931, 1305, 2711,
3374

"Song of the Flame," 3143
"Song of the Forest," 811
"Song of the Open Road," 1096,
3065
"Song over Moscow," 3003
"Song to Remember, A," 1639
"Song Without End," 1917
"Sophie Lang Goes West," 2456
Sophie of Saks Fifth Avenue (see
also Gimbel, Sophie), 2562,
3066, 3067
Sorenson, Edith, 3068
"Sorrowful Jones," 1971, 2569
"Sorrows of Satan, The," 1996
"Sorry, Wrong Number," 1329
Sotheby Parke Bernet, 1660
Sothern, Ann, 1003, 1079, 1397,
1413, 1627, 1872, 1910, 1911,
2133, 2264, 2458, 2485
"Soul Mates," 99
"Souls at Sea," 817
"Souls for Sables," 682
sound, influence of, 16, 141, 692
1118, 1653, 1683, 2168, 3402
"Sound of Life," 1641
"Sound of Music, The," 2163,
2628
"South Pacific," 1789, 2858
Southgate, Michael, 3069
"Sowing the Wind," 3526
"Space Thing," 774
Spadoni, Luciano, 3070
Spanier, Ginette, 3071
"Spanish Dancer, The," 1033,
1231, 2359, 3472
"Spanish Main, The," 3142
Sparrow, Bernice, 3073
"Sparrows," 1749
"Spartacus," 251, 3020
"Speedway," 3310
"Spellbound," 1857
Spencer, Bob, 3075
"Spencer's Mountain," 62, 292
"Spiked Heels and Black Nylons,"
1874
Spiller, Joey, 3079
"Spinout," 3441
"Spirits of the Dead," 1062, 1758,
3297
"Splendor in the Grass," 1573
"Sport Page," 2402
"Sporting Blood," 2389
"Sporting Venus, The," 513
"Spring Fever," 3015
"Spring Magic," 3482
"Spring Tonic," 628, 2434
"Springtime on the Volga," 3019
"Spy Who Came in from the Cold, The,"

2095
"Spy with a Cold Nose, The," 326
"Square Root of Zero, The," 1800
"Squaw Man, The," 1303
Staffel, Laurel, 3095
"Stage Door," 754, 2455, 2532,
    2793, 3555
"Stage Fright," 1394
"Stage Mother," 2414
"Stage Struck," 619, 2893
Stage Women's War Relief, 962
"Stagecoach" (1939), 1013
Stahl, John, 317
"Staircase," 2737
"Stalking Moon, The," 1288
"Stallion Road," 2114
Stamp, Terence, 1322
"Stand and Deliver," 2960
"Stand-In," 2456
"Standing Room Only," 1201
Stanley, Forrest, 564
Stanley, Kathryn, 2947
Stanton, Harry Dean, 552
Stanwyck, Barbara, 275, 289,
    556, 666, 754, 1079, 1183,
    1312, 1326, 1329, 1347, 1392,
    1437, 1560, 1815, 1870, 1894,
    1968, 2107, 2117, 2133, 2277,
    2386, 2455, 2464, 2465, 2468,
    2471, 2585, 2742, 2764, 3046,
    3089, 3091, 3100, 3122, 3555,
    3602
"Star!," 173, 379, 383, 642,
    875, 1584, 2993, 3597
"Star Is Born, A" (1937), 1409,
    2449, 2527
"Star Is Born, A" (1954), 2964,
    2966
"Star of Midnight," 980, 2023
"Star Pilots," 3108
"Star Trek--The Motion Picture,"
    552, 2900
"Star Wars," 552, 842, 904,
    3096, 3113
"Star Witness, The," 2389
Starke, Pauline, 2291, 2294,
    2349
Starly, Inoa, 3114
Starr, Malcolm, 3117
Starr, Mark, 2174
"Stars over Broadway," 317
"Start Cheering," 3545
"Start the Revolution Without
    Me," 208
"State Fair" (1962), 292
Staub, Richard, 3120
Stavropoulos, George, 2082
Stavropoulou, Anna, 3121

"Stay Away, Joe," 1951
"Steamboat Bill Junior," 2049
Stedman, Myrtle, 1063, 1100, 2311
Steele, Gile, 671, 1835a, 1897
Stefan, Ivan, 3123
Stein, Ina, 3124
Stein, Madame, 3125
Stella, Ruth, 3127
"Stella Dallas" (1925), 388
"Stella Dallas" (1937), 3046, 3100
"Stella Maris," 2626
Stephans, Peggy, 3128
Stephen, John, 3129
Stepner, Helen, 2492, 2577
"Steppe, The," 818
Sterling, Arleen, 3132
Sterling, Ford, 916, 1843
Sterling, Jan, 2588
Stern, Ernst, 469
Stern, Henri, 3133
Stetson, 1709, 1926, 2037
Stevens, Douglas, 3134
Stevens, Emily, 406
Stevens, George, 2092
Stevens, Jane Kip, 3135
Stevens, John, 3136
Stevens, Ruthelma, 2409
Stevens, Stella, 1048, 1474
Stevenson, Edward, 152, 547, 555,
    675, 679, 1043, 1067, 1079, 1768,
    1864, 1894, 1953, 1954, 1978,
    2133, 2195, 2346, 2455, 2458,
    2461, 2468, 2537, 2538, 2546,
    2555, 2557, 2579, 2755, 3016,
    3089, 3138, 3139, 3140, 3141,
    3142, 3143, 3388, 3562
Stewart, Anita, 852, 1723, 2102,
    3255, 3526
Stewart, Elizabeth, 3144
Stewart, James, 1007, 1241
Stewart, Larry, 3145
Stewart, Roy, 3148
Sthamer, Frauke, 3146
"Stiletto," 621
"Still Alarm, The," 1365, 1366
"Sting, The," 1336, 2665, 3059,
    3561
"Sting of Death," 3331
"Stingaree," 2640
"Stitch in Time, A," 910
"Stolen Bride, The," 1101
"Stolen Holiday," 2445, 2523
"Stolen Hours," 952
Stom, Nancy, 3150
Stone, Lewis, 135, 1583, 1771,
    3151
Stoney, Yvonne, 3152
"Stooge, The," 2604

"Stop the World--I Want to Get Off," 426, 1090
"Stork Club, The," 859, 3153
"Storm at Daybreak," 1933, 2175
Storme, Sandra, 2456
"Stormy Weather," 2808
"Story of a Woman," 2887
"Story of Esther Costello, The," 972
"Story of Joseph and His Brethren, The," 761
"Story of Seabiscuit, The," 2582
"Story of Temple Drake, The," 2170
"Story of the Count of Monte Cristo, The," 757
"Story of Vernon and Irene Castle, The," 236, 500, 551, 703, 1892
Strahm, Shirlee, 3154
Strand, 966
"Stranded," 691
"Strange Adventures of Sinbad, The," 675
"Strange Affair, The," 3601
"Strange Bedfellows," 2871
"Strange Cargo," 697
"Strange Case of Mary Page, The," 897, 1991
"Strange Interlude," 643
"Strange Love of Martha Ivers, The," 666
"Strange Woman, The," 2294
"Stranger, The" (1924), 2638
"Stranger, The" (1946), 3141
"Strangers' Banquet, The," 907, 2949
"Strangers in Love," 2395
"Strangers May Kiss," 2780
"Strangers of the Night," 849
"Stranger's Return," 1933, 2763
Strassner, Joe, 2374, 2412, 2763, 2914
"Strathmore," 2294, 2295
"Strawberry Statement, The," 419, 2787
"Street of Women," 2397
"Streetcar Named Desire, A," 174, 898, 3233
Streisand, Barbra, 129, 713, 875, 1211, 1645, 1749, 1878, 2028, 2891, 2964, 2968, 3076
Stretton, Tom, 344
Strickling, Howard, 1044
"Strip, The," 2513
"Stripper, The," 3273
Stroheim, Erich von (see von Stroheim, Erich)

Strohm, Eva, 3525
Stromberg, Hunt, 1561
"Strong Man, The," 600
Stuart, Barbara, 3159
Stuart, Gloria, 1933, 2410, 2413, 2763
Stuart, Pat, 3160
"Student Prince in Old Heidelberg, The," 470, 1476, 1787
Studio Styles, Inc., 112, 113, 822
"Study in Terror, A," 2095, 3145
"Stunt Man," 2487
Stutz, Ursula, 3165
"Submarine X-1," 375
"Substitution," 3321
"Subway Sadie," 1072
"Success at Any Price," 3451
"Successful Calamity, A," 2397
"Successo, Il," 2362
"Succubus," 1675
"Such Men Are Dangerous," 1698
"Sudden Fear," 1968
"Suddenly It's Spring," 813, 2111
Suedes by Voris (see also Voris), 3173
"Suez," 1420, 3174
Sullavan, Margaret, 1267, 3093, 3574
Sullivan, Eileen, 3177
"Sullivan's Empire," 2022
"Sullivan's Travels," 3602
"Summer Holiday," 364, 1653
"Summer Stock," 2028, 3585
Summers, Ray, 3178
Sun Fashions of Hawaii Ltd., 3179
"Sun in the Morning," 1519
"Sun Shines for All, The," 1602
"Sunday in New York," 419, 1256, 2281
Sundby, Emily, 3180
"Sundown," 3247
"Sunflower," 2854
"Sunny Side Up," 1046, 1698
"Sunset Boulevard," 2896, 2981, 3122
"Sunya," 656
"Superargo vs. Diabolicus," 3361
"Superfly," 2855
"Superman" (1948), 2377
"Superman--The Movie," 904, 2184, 2276, 2377
"Supernatural," 1930, 2170, 2409
"Support Your Local Sheriff!," 419, 1256
"Suppose They Gave a War and Nobody Came," 81
Suren, Leyla, 3181
"Surf Party," 1386

"Surrender," 2171
"Susan and God," 551, 3183
"Susan Rocks the Boat," 1116
"Suspicion," 3142
Sutherland, Hope, 1081
"Suzanna," 3357
Swanson, Gloria, 106, 123, 388,
    465, 598, 613, 656, 657, 676,
    762, 1034, 1084, 1189, 1190,
    1191, 1192, 1193, 1194, 1195,
    1196, 1203, 1207, 1299, 1380,
    1399, 1589, 1618, 1731, 1861,
    1862, 1987, 2079, 2098, 2124,
    2199, 2205, 2218, 2231, 2272,
    2352, 2427, 2713, 2764, 2778,
    2861, 2896, 2947, 2950, 2981,
    3006, 3099, 3122, 3185, 3219,
    3341, 3393, 3394, 3469, 3472,
    3481, 3498, 3623
Swarthout, Gladys, 1268, 1870,
    1964, 2449, 3227
"Swedish Mistress, The," 1893
Sweet, Blanche, 1638, 2920,
    2950, 3470
"Sweet and Lowdown," 1043
"Sweet Bird of Aquarius," 3159
"Sweet Bird of Youth," 2281
"Sweet Body of Deborah, The,"
    172, 2804
"Sweet Charity," 524, 1312,
    1340
"Sweet Music," 1002
"Sweet November," 2823
"Sweet Ride, The," 875
"Sweet Rosie O'Grady," 1214
"Sweethearts," 992, 1556, 2185,
    2468, 2469, 2543, 3104, 3106
"Sweetie," 3401
Swenson, Aida, 3186
Swenson, Sharon E., 3187
"Swimmer, The," 3144
"Swing High Swing Low," 537,
    817, 1333, 2526
"Swing Time," 2444
"Swingin' Maiden, The," 910
"Sword of Lancelot," 2070
"Sword of Sherwood Forest,"
    1852
"Sword of the Conqueror," 1153
Sylbert, Anthea, 161, 713, 1660,
    3189
"Sylvia," 2298
"Sylvia Scarlett," 693, 1635,
    1870, 2431, 2725
"Synanon," 1844
Szeski, Jerzy, 3191

"T. A. M. I. Show, The," 1308
Tadej, Vladimir, 3192
"Tailor Made Man, A," 2710
Taka, Miiko, 1789
"Take a Letter, Darling," 550
"Take Care of My Little Girl," 398
"Take Her by Surprise," 560
"Take Her, She's Mine," 2629,
    3273
Takeuchi, Jack, 3193
"Tale of Two Cities, A," 7
"Tales of Manhattan," 1094, 2670
"Tales of Terror," 3120
Talmadge, Constance, 637, 638,
    639, 1459, 1722, 1742, 1898,
    2273, 2978, 3304
Talmadge, Norma, 620, 809, 1023,
    1032, 1315, 1457, 1459, 1491,
    1505, 1742, 1794, 2211, 2212,
    2213, 2383, 2622, 2950, 2978,
    3304, 3436, 3472, 3486, 3537
Talsky, Ron, 713, 3195
"Tamahine," 1541, 1710
Tamblyn, Russ, 678
"Tamed," 676, 1870, 2933
"Taming of the Shrew, The" (1929),
    550, 2958
"Taming of the Shrew, The" (1967),
    818, 1416, 2856, 2964, 2968
"Tammy Tell Me True," 2997
Tappe, Herman, 1175
"Taras Bulba," 285, 1656
"Tartars, The," 2147
"Tartuffe," 2825
"Tarzan," 153
"Tarzan and Jane Regained Sort Of,"
    281
"Tarzan and the Jungle Boy," 154
"Tarzan's Three Challenges," 357
Tashman, Lilyan, 430, 816, 1273,
    2046, 2382, 2385, 2389, 2391,
    2851, 3469
"Tatlock Millions, The," 2568
Tauss, Frank, 3197
Taylor, Carol, 3200
Taylor, Edna, 3201
Taylor, Elizabeth, 100, 334, 337,
    556, 805, 1060, 1263, 1312, 1416,
    1421, 1694, 1829, 1831, 1833,
    2502, 2600, 2629, 2806, 2808,
    2856, 2907, 2964, 2966, 2968,
    2992, 3245, 3246, 3256
Taylor, Estelle, 762, 1821
Taylor, Helen, 315, 1103, 1590,
    2456, 3367
Taylor, Jim, 3202

Taylor, Noel, 3203, 3204, 3205
Taylor, Phyllis, 3206
Taylor, Robert, 944, 2327
Taylor, Ruth, 1128
Tcherina, Ludmila, 779
"Tea for Two," 2591
Teasdale, Verree, 795, 843, 1871,
    2401, 3449, 3543
"Technicolor Fashion Forecast,"
    2470
"Teenage Millionaire," 695, 1166
Teitelbaum, Al, 1968, 3209, 3210
"Telephone Girl, The," 3422, 3430
television, costumes of, 547, 551,
    552, 555, 1414, 1734, 1851
"Tell It to the Judge," 1805
"Tell Me Lies," 1542
"Tell Me That You Love Me, Junie
    Moon," 404, 1129, 1271, 3195
"Tempest," 2274
Temple, Shirley, 66, 275, 291,
    324, 484, 709, 801, 1267, 1268,
    1433, 1768, 1965, 2023, 2317,
    2435, 2555, 2582
"Temptation" (1923), 3211
"Temptation" (1962), 359, 1945,
    2699
"Ten Cents a Dance," 2386
"Ten Commandments, The" (1923),
    762, 2328, 2329, 2330, 2331,
    2883
"Ten Commandments, The" (1956),
    161, 1416, 1678, 1968, 2200
"Tender Comrade," 546
"Tender Hour, The," 2718
"Tender Is the Night," 292
Tennant, Barbara, 853
"Tenth Man, The," 2792
"10th Victim, The," 624, 1061
"Teorema," 448, 759
Ter-Arutunian, Rouben, 3213
"Terrified!," 1752, 2998
"Terror Abroad," 2170, 2408
"Terror in the Jungle," 1141
"Terror of Dr. Mabuse, The,"
    2120
"Terrornauts, The," 3444
Terry, Alice, 3523
"Testament of Orpheus," 1548
Tetrick, Ted, 3214
"Texas Across the River," 753
"Texas, Brooklyn and Heaven,"
    776, 2566
"Texas Lady," 3591
"Texican, The," 346
Textile Association of Los
    Angeles, 145
Thalberg, Irving, 3235

"Thank Your Lucky Stars," 366
"Thanks for Everything," 2470
"That Certain Feeling," 1345
"That Certain Woman," 1438, 3573
"That Girl from Paris," 1067, 2448
"That Hamilton Woman," 1089, 2258
"That Midnight Kiss," 2581
"That Night in Rio," 1007
"That Riviera Touch," 880
"That Royale Girl," 1012
"That Touch of Mink," 1084, 2203,
    2204
"That Uncertain Feeling," 1890
"That Wonderful Urge," 1507
"That's Africa," 1927
"That's My Boy," 2402, 2601
"That's Right, You're Wrong," 1996
Theby, Rosemary, 322, 2812, 2813
"Theft of the Crown Jewels, The,"
    1116
"Their Mad Moment," 2384
"Thelma Jordan," 2585
"Theodora Goes Wild," 1960, 2076
"There Goes My Heart," 2133, 2467,
    2546
"There Was a Crooked Man" (1962),
    1246
"There Was a Crooked Man ..."
    (1970), 358, 3214
"There's a Girl in My Soup," 579,
    1301
"There's Always a Woman," 2537
"These Three," 2372
"They Call Me MISTER Tibbs,"
    2951
"They Came from Beyond Space,"
    3444
"They Came to Rob Las Vegas," 2358
"They Died with Their Boots On,"
    3137
"They Got Me Covered," 30
"They Met in Argentina," 1954
"They Shoot Horses, Don't They?,"
    819, 820, 1167, 1762, 2383
"They Were Heroes," 1622
"They Won't Forget," 2730
Thibault, Hélène, 3225
"Thief in Paradise, A," 2979
"Thief of Bagdad, The" (1924), 416,
    550, 1738
"Thief of Paris, The," 3297
Things I Remember (Erté), 213,
    926, 927
"Things to Come," 1416
"Third Day, The," 379
"Third Man, The," 1892
"Third Secret, The," 1852
"13 Frightened Girls," 105, 1708

"13 West Street," 285, 2309
"Thirteen Women," 1403, 2400,
   2401
"Thirty Day Princess," 2421, 3190
"30 Is a Dangerous Age, Cynthia,"
   283
"39 Steps, The," 312, 2914
"36 Hours," 1256, 2786
"This Gun for Hire," 1856
"This Land Is Mine," 1021, 3451
"This Man Can't Die," 2322
"This Modern Age," 2386
"This Property Is Condemned,"
   1692
"This Sporting Life," 784
"This Thing Called Love," 1686
"This Woman Is Dangerous," 2534
Thomas, Bill, 251, 395, 552, 1263,
   1750, 1917, 2593, 2606, 2607,
   2609, 2610, 3228, 3229
"Thomas Crown Affair, The," 526,
   1761, 2658, 3327
Thompson, Frank, 1878, 3236
Thompson, Kay, 1271
Thomson, Jill, 3237
"Thoroughly Modern Millie," 1349
"Those Daring Young Men in Their
   Jaunty Jalopies," 1107, 2140
"Those Fantastic Flying Fools,"
   3259
"Those Magnificent Men in Their
   Flying Machines; or How I Flew
   from London to Paris in 25
   Hours and 11 Minutes," 1237,
   1690
"Those Three French Girls,"
   1480
"Thousand Clowns, A," 2071
"Three Bites of the Apple," 1691
"Three Blind Mice," 3091
"Three Comrades," 3093
"Three Cornered Kingdom," 936
"Three-Cornered Moon," 1933,
   2412
"300 Spartans, The," 783, 1006
"3 in the Attic," 3371
"3 Into 2 Won't Go," 2135
"Three Little Words," 2504,
   2806
"Three Lives of Thomasina," 375
"Three Loves Has Nancy," 2543,
   3424
"Three Musketeers, The" (1921),
   416
"Three Musketeers, The" (1935),
   2430
"Three Musketeers, The" (1973),
   1391, 1416

"Three Nights of Love," 1151
"Three on a Couch," 785
"Three on a Honeymoon," 2419,
   2420
"Three Penny Opera," 1361
"Three Sailors and a Girl," 445,
   2616
"Three Smart Girls," 1433
"Three Smart Girls Grow Up," 2551
"Three Stooges Go Around the World
   in a Daze, The," 1667, 3214
"Three Stooges in Orbit, The,"
   2309, 3214
"Three Weeks," 3006
"Three Wise Crooks," 1588, 2216
"Three Wise Fools," 3555
"Thrill of Brazil, The," 1808
"Thriller, The," 1437
"Through a Glass Darkly," 1893
Thulin, Ingrid, 1437, 1618, 1925,
   2281, 3240
"Thunder Alley," 2378
"Thunder Below," 2395
"Thunder of Drums, A," 1889
"Thundergate," 3172
Thurlow, Gretl Urban (see also Ur-
   ban, Gretl), 3243
Thurman, Mary, 973, 978
"Thy Name Is Woman," 200
"Tickle Me," 2758, 3154
"Ticklish Affair, A," 1951
"Tide of Battle, The," 645
Tiel, Vicki, 1060, 3245, 3246,
   3291
Tierney, Gene, 100, 485, 839,
   1504, 1507, 1728, 1769, 1919,
   2156, 2159, 3210, 3447, 3580
Tigano & Lo Faro, 3248
"Tiger and the Pussycat, The,"
   82
"Tiger by the Tail," 3197
"Tiger Makes Out, The," 3189
"Tiger of the Seven Seas," 216
"Tiger's Claw, The," 2153
"Tiko and the Shark," 3361
"Tillie the Toiler," 430
Timayo, Mineta, 905
"Timber Queen, The," 2849
"Time Bomb," 343, 1144
"Time of Indifference," 932
"Time Out of Mind," 674
"Time, Place & Girl," 3555
"Time, the Comedian," 926, 1885,
   3077
"Time Travelers, The," 3206,
   3443
"Times Square Lady," 1913
Timex, 2377

Tingey, Cynthia, 3252
Tirelli of Rome, 3253
Tiziani of Rome, 3256
"To Bed or Not to Bed," 1168
"To Catch a Thief," 526, 546, 1345, 2794, 3377
"To Each His Own," 1324, 1348, 2962
"To Have and to Hold," 528, 531, 1798, 1842
"To Love," 1893
"To Save Her Soul," 2626
"To the Shores of Hell," 1257
"Toast of New York, The," 1864
Tobin, Genevieve, 1929, 1930, 2408, 2421, 2640, 2764, 3287, 3451
Tobin, Vivian, 3451
"Toby Dammitt," 1485
"Today We Live," 158, 556, 882, 1566, 1928, 2170, 2762, 2763, 3078
Todd, Ann, 674, 3531
Todd, Thelma, 312, 547, 1926, 2419
"Together Again," 874, 1022
Tokyo Costumes Co., 3257
"Toll of the Sea," 3208
Tolmach, Nat, 3258
Tolo, Marilu, 1060, 3245
"Tom, Dick and Harry," 2269
"Tom Jones," 1349, 1446, 1852
Tom Mix Museum, 2037
"Tommy," 1213,
Tompkins, Joe, 548, 552
Toms, Carl, 3259, 3260
Tone, Franchot, 3231
"Tonight and Every Night," 250, 1654, 1718
"Tonight Is Ours," 550, 1928
"Tonight or Never," 1380
"Tony Rome," 2078, 3024, 3117
"Too Busy to Work," 2403
"Too Late for Tears," 2315, 2573
"Too Many Husbands," 2484
"Too Many Kisses," 2124
"Too Many Millions," 873
"Too Much Harmony," 1935
"Top Banana," 622
"Top Hat," 140, 786, 2373, 2430, 3262
"Topaz," 1402, 2871
"Topaze," 2406
"Topkapi," 3315
"Topper," 1042
"Topper Takes a Trip," 1182
"Tora! Tora! Tora!," 3597

"Torch Singer," 1935, 2413, 2415
"Torch Song," 3231
Torchia, Emily, 1044
Torella, 3263
Toren, Marta, 959, 2494, 2580
"Torment," 2047
"Tormentas de Pasion" (see "Devotion")
"Torn Curtain," 775, 1349, 1488
"Torpedo Bay," 772
"Torrent, The," 3006
Torres, Raquel, 1927, 1935
"Tortilla Flat," 3434
"Torture Dungeon," 2691
Tosi, Piero, 118, 1485, 2895, 3240
Totter, Audrey, 812
"Touch of Evil, A," 1391
"Touchables, The," 2089
Tournafond, Francoise, 3267
"Tower of Lies, The," 2207
"Towering Inferno," 2855
"Town Without Pity," 1260, 2907
Towne, Rosella, 3547
"Toy Wife, The," 1803, 3109, 3212
Trabert and Hoeffer, 211
Trabert and Hoeffer-Mauboussin (see also Mauboussin), 2531, 2921
"Trade Winds," 2467
"Trader Horn," 1823, 1916
"Trader Hornee," 1039
"Train, The," 3616
Traina, Anthony, 2206
Traina, Teal, 3269
Traina-Norell, 2206
"Tramplers, The," 2942
"Transatlantic Tunnel," 787
"Transcontinental Bus," 2177
"Transient Love," 1429
Traphagen, Ethel, 471
"Trapp Family, The," 2903
"Traveling Executioner, The," 419, 1889, 1941, 1980
"Traveling Husbands," 719
Travilla, William, 391, 392, 395, 554, 679, 875, 2078, 2596, 2611, 2629, 3271, 3272, 3273, 3274
Travolta, John, 553, 687
"Treasure of San Gennaro," 534
"Treasure of Silver Lake," 2347
"Treasure of the Amazon Women," 1223
Tree, Dolly (Dorothy), 373, 1979, 2449, 2465, 2474, 2486, 2547, 3277, 3288, 3424
Tree, Dorothy (actress), 2392, 2415, 2533, 2534, 3090
Tree, Dorothy (designer; see also

Tree, Dolly), 3277
"Tree Grows in Brooklyn, A," 485, 1022
"Trespasser, The," 1195, 1570, 2069, 3394
Trevor, Claire, 581, 628, 942, 1299, 1901, 1915, 2176, 2177, 2242, 2413, 2415, 2417, 2420, 2423, 2427, 2434, 2458, 2572, 3226, 3451
"Trial, The," 3225
Trigère, Pauline, 84, 917, 3280
"Trilogy," 3236
Trist, Wesley, 3281
"Tristana," 1124
"Triumph," 654, 1092
"Triumph of Venus, The," 823
"Tropic Holiday," 2462, 3091
"Tropic of Scorpio," 2975
"Trouble in Paradise," 64, 2402
"Trouble in the Sky," 3403
"Trouble with Angels, The," 635
"True as Steel," 659
"True Confessions," 561
"Trunk to Cairo," 2815
Trunnelle, Mabel, 1116
Truscott, John, 1211, 1789, 3283
"Truth About Women, The," 3076
Tsu, Irene, 1437
Tsuda, Ikue, 3284
"Tuck Me In," 384
Tuffin, Sally, 2679, 2873, 3286
"Tulsa," 1387, 2574
"Tunnel, The," 2371, 2792
Turner, Florence, 2700, 3040
Turner, Lana, 735, 1042, 1044, 1241, 1413, 1520, 1660, 1689, 1901, 2066, 2628, 2659, 2730, 2806, 2808, 2907, 3207, 3288, 3419
Turner, Mrs., 3040
Tushingham, Rita, 3295
Tutin, Dorothy, 1213
"Twelve Miles Out," 1480
Twelvetrees, Helen, 1929, 1932, 2399, 2411, 2414, 2420, 2763
"Twentieth Century," 3451
"25th Hour, The," 757
"24 Hours," 2389
"20 Mule Team," 255
"Twenty Plus Two," 2132, 2976, 3440
"£ 20,000 Eyes," 803
"£ 20,000 Kiss, The," 3444
"Twice Told Tales," 3454
Twiggy, 1213, 1840
"Twilight of Honor," 2657, 3202
"Twist All Night," 2305

"Two Against the World," 2400
"Two-Faced Woman," 27, 163, 2783
"Two Fisted," 1870
"Two Flags West," 547
"Two for the Road," 88, 1057, 2680, 2689, 2737, 2817, 2910
"Two for the Seesaw," 435, 2281
"Two for Tonight," 312, 1912
"Two Gentlemen Sharing," 958
"Two Guys from Texas," 836
"Two Kinds of Woman," 2394
"Two Little Bears, The," 1166, 2254
"Two or Three Things I Know About Her," 1946
"Two Orphans, The," 1175
"2,000 Weeks," 436, 437
"2000 Years Later," 81, 1145
"2001: A Space Odyssey," 54, 88, 1135
"Two Tickets to Broadway," 401, 2598
"Two Tickets to Paris," 3390
"Two Weeks in Another Town," 2641
"Two Women," 665
"Two's Company," 2792
"Tycoon," 3209
Tyson, Cecily, 334
Tyson, Joanna, 3295

"U-47 Lt. Commander Prien," 720, 920
"U.P. Trail, The," 3148, 3294
Uhry, Ghislain, 3297
Ullman, S. George, 2884, 3299, 3300
Ullmann, Liv, 713
Ulric, Lenore, 17
Ulrich, Trude, 3301
"Umbrellas of Cherbourg, The," 2064, 2716
"Uncertain Lady," 2421
"Uncharted Seas," 3522
"Unchastened Woman, The," 406
"Uncle Harry," 192
"Uncle Tom's Cabin," 2639
"Undefeated, The," 170, 224
"Under Capricorn," 1114
"Under the Pampas Moon," 1915, 2023
"Under the Red Robe," 3312
"Under the Yum Yum Tree," 285, 3201
"Under Western Skies," 2346

"Undercover Girl," 2593
"Undercover Man," 1926, 2404
"Undercurrent," 2028
"Undercurrents," 2051
underpants, 106, 121, 138, 1311, 1686
undershirts, 1651, 3050, 3264
underwear, 3438
"Underworld," 1065
"Unfinished Dance," 3555
"Unfoldment, The," 3524
"Uniform, The," 2075
"Union Pacific," 2471, 3360
unions (wardrobe) (see also Associated Motion Picture Costumers, Costume Designers Guild, ILGWU, and Motion Picture Costumers), 228, 3370
"United States Mail," 2588
"Unknown, The," 3309
"Unlawful," 2542
"Unsinkable Molly Brown, The," 1254
"Unstrap Me," 2084
"Unto Those Who Sin," 989
"Unwilling Agent," 865
"Up in Arms," 883
"Up in the Cellar," 668
"Up Pops the Devil," 2385
"Up the Down Staircase," 2823
"Up the MacGregors," 2887
"Up to His Ears," 2064
"Upper Hand, The," 1062
"Upper Underworld," 1699
"Uptight," 69
Urban, Gretl (see also Thurlow, Gretl Urban), 479, 1247, 1582, 2252, 3311, 3243, 3312
Urban, Joseph, 1247, 1582, 2252
Urbanic, Elisabeth, 3313

"V.I.P.s, The," 100, 451, 1178
Vaccaro, Brenda, 3101
Vácha, Fernand, 3314
Vachlioti, Denny, 3315
"Vagabond King, The" (1930), 194, 3208
Valentina, 423, 550, 1047
Valentino, Rudolph, 2, 121, 271, 322, 332, 388, 502, 528, 606, 681, 777, 826, 879, 1084, 1174, 1446, 1483, 1509, 1711, 1784, 1876, 2079, 2205, 2237,

2245, 2687, 2696, 2697, 2884, 3014, 3161, 3299, 3300, 3318, 3319, 3320, 3384
"Valentino," 1213
Valentino of Rome, 2077, 3316, 3317
"Valiant Is the Word for Carrie," 2522, 3409
Valles, 3164
"Valley of Decision, The," 673
"Valley of Gwangi, The," 1107
"Valley of Mystery," 2022
"Valley of the Dolls," 2078, 3273
Valli (Alida Valli), 674, 3321
Valli, Virginia, 2622
"Valse de Paris," 996
"Vampire Lovers, The," 352
Vandenecker, Beau, 3324
Vanderbilt, Gloria, 553
Vanderleelie, Roy, 3325
Van Horn, Madame, 926
Van Parys, Blanche, 3326
Van Runkle, Theadora, 95, 526, 1011, 1097, 1660, 1661, 1762, 3218, 3327
Van Upp, Virginia, 3232
"Vanity's Price," 2943
"Varan the Unbelievable," 2239
Várdai, Guyula, 3328
Vartan, Sylvia, 2716
Vassilou, Spyros, 3329
Vaughn, Alberta, 1587, 3430
Vavra, V., 3330
Velcoff, Alex, 677
Velez, Lupe, 275, 1934, 2762, 3455
Veloz and Yolanda, 3227
Velton, Irene, 3331
"Velvet Touch, The," 193, 1455, 2567
Venable, Evelyn, 2417, 3496
Venet, Philippe, 3333
"Vengeance of She, The," 3259
Venice Museum, 1579
"Venus of the South Seas," 103
Vera-Ellen, 2504, 2806
Verdone, Mario, 132
Vereyskiy, O., 3337
Verhille, Guy, 3338
Verity, Jack, 3339
Vernon, Ann, 1706
Vertès, Marcel, 277, 449, 1314, 1918, 3341, 3342, 3343, 3344, 3345, 3346, 3368
"Vertigo," 1345, 3468
"Very Private Affair, A," 1925
"Very Special Favor, A," 2863
"Viaccia, La," 118

"Vice and Virtue," 814, 1016
"Vice Dolls," 2774, 2829
Vickers, Martha, 94, 1795
Vicky, 3347
Victor, Sally, 2921, 3367
"Victoria the Great," 1076
"Victors, The," 1015, 1735
Vicze, Zsuzsa, 3348
Vidor, Florence, 655, 691, 1491, 3006
"Viennese Medley, The," 2221
"Viking Queen, The," 1107
"Villa Rides," 2938
"Village of the Giants," 2758
"Villain, The," 1878
"Vinegar Tree," 1425
Vinnie, 3349
Vinson, Helen, 584, 981, 1133, 1370, 1984, 2355, 2371, 2372, 2404, 2404, 2412, 2416, 2426, 2428, 2454, 2531, 2792, 2926, 2931, 3364
"Viol, Le," 2162
"Violated Love," 165
"Violent Four, The," 3058
Violet, Madame, 3357
"Violin and Roller," 1967
"Virgin Soldiers, The," 1246
"Virginia Judge, The," 1870
Virginie, 3358
Virsaladze, Solomon, 3359
Visart, Natalie, 472, 550, 2471, 3360
Visconti, Luchino, 100, 1414, 2895
"Viscount, The," 664
"Visit, The," 1481, 2761
Vitali, Nadia, 3361
Vitti, Monica, 1950
"Viva Maria," 273, 2163, 3297
"Viva Max!," 2139
"Vivacious Lady," 2538, 3093
Vlady, Marina, 1372
Vogue, 527, 1023, 1279, 1434, 1473, 1635, 1661, 2783, 2921, 3366
Vogue Pattern, 546
"Vogues of 1938," 261, 321, 840, 909, 981, 1370, 1434, 1979, 2115, 2355, 2454, 2531, 2916, 2921, 2926, 2961, 3363, 3364, 3365, 3366, 3367, 3405, 3548
"Voice of the Hurricane," 146
"Voice of the Turtle, The," 1510
Voight, Jon, 3101
"Volga Boatman, The," 550, 823, 3249
Volkmer, Waldemar, 3369

Vollner, Fern, 3371
Volters, Margarete, 3372
von Furstenberg, Ira, 1069
Vongher, 3373
von Meck, Madame, 1840
"Von Ryan's Express," 2998
von Sternberg, Josef, 106, 465, 2072, 3374, 3439
von Stroheim, Erich, 106, 824, 1875, 3158
Voris (Voris Linthacum Marker), 1966, 2545, 3173
Vos-Lundh, Marik, 3375
"Voyage to the Bottom of the Sea," 3615
"Voyage to the End of the Universe," 764, 2885, 3047
Vreeland, Diana, 1830, 2020, 2083, 2181, 2745, 2746, 3199, 3282
"Vulture, The," 2017

"WUSA," 3258, 3273
Wachner, Sophie, 388, 405, 905, 1217, 1219, 1529, 1698, 1792, 1970, 2057, 2208, 2958, 3006, 3107, 3376
"Wages of Virtue," 1253
"Wagon Wheels," 2178
"Waikiki Wedding," 2450, 2528
Wakeling, Gwen, 318, 584, 698, 1067, 1079, 1268, 1420, 1425, 1504, 1757, 2352, 2415, 2416, 2417, 2419, 2470, 2477, 2527, 2533, 2536, 2537, 2539, 2541, 2628, 2755, 3378, 3379, 3380
Wakhevitch, Georges, 3381, 3382
Walbrook, Anton, 1076
Wald, Jerry, 3231
Waldman, Ben, 567, 3238
Waldo, Charles, 3383
Wales, Ethel, 3482
"Walk, Don't Run," 1254
"Walk in the Spring Rain, A," 820, 3201, 3338
"Walk on the Wild Side," 1437, 1740
"Walk with Love and Death, A," 1037, 2139
Walker, David, 3387
Walker, Natalie, 3390
"Walking My Baby Back Home," 2615
"Walking Stick, The," 1060, 3245, 3601
Walkup, Bruce, 3392

"Wall of Noise," 1277, 2767
"Wall Outside, The," 2505
Walley, Deborah, 1454
"Wallflower," 2564, 3215
"Walls of Gold," 2176, 2414, 2415
Walsh, William, 3403
Walstrom, Bill, 3404
Walters, Charles, 3231
Walton, Tony, 3410, 3411, 3412
"Waltz of the Toreadors," 12
"Wanda (The Sadistic Hypnotist)," 1078
"Wanderer, The" (1925), 301, 3060
"Wanderer, The" (1969), 2260
"Wanderers of the Wasteland," 511
Wanger, Walter, 1103, 3247, 3364
Wanke, Josef, 3413
"Wanters, The," 3499
war, the influence of, 228, 366, 371, 389, 550, 556, 670, 702, 858, 1017, 1021, 1042, 1117, 1136, 1201, 1214, 1342, 1427, 1670, 1733, 2195, 2263, 2652, 3082, 3305
"War and Peace" (1968), 424, 557, 3330
"War Correspondent," 1214, 2400
"War Game, The," 580
"War Lord, The," 1391, 2225
"War Lover, The," 1015
"War Nurse," 1480
"War of the Zombies, The," 1222
"War Party," 409
War Production Board, 3305
"War Wagon, The," 2799
Ware, Irene, 1429
Warhol, Andy, 553
"Warm Nights & Hot Pleasures," 1800, 3467
Warner, H.B., 762
Warner, Jeannette, 1814
"Warrens of Virginia, The" (c. 1915), 1638
"Warrens of Virginia, The" (1923), 388
"Warrior Empress, The," 2804
Warshovsky, Ethel, 3421
"Washington Masquerade," 2400, 2402
"Wastrel, The," 2804
"Watch Your Stern," 910
"Waterhole #3," 226, 1660
Waterman, Gary, 3425

"Watermelon Man," 139, 3201
Waterston, Sam, 162
Watson, Barbara, 678
Watteville, E., 3426
"Way Down East," 1174, 1175, 1176, 1211
"Way for a Sailor," 254
"Way Men Love, The," 3175
"Way We Were, The," 713
"Way West, The," 745, 1656, 3201
Wayne, John, 1660, 1907, 3020, 3285
"We Have Our Moments," 3549
"We Still Kill the Old Way," 1937
"We Three," 2386
"We Were Dancing," 1264
Weaver, Sigourney, 552
"Web, The," 3285, 3580
Webb, Clifton, 459, 733
Webb, David, 3431
Weber, Fern, 161
Weber, Lois, 823
Webster, Ty, 3435
wedding gowns, 60, 121, 307, 316, 373, 555, 567, 1089, 1294, 1312, 1373, 1421, 1607, 1628, 1862, 1972, 2039, 2124, 2168, 2244, 2269, 2345, 2434, 2448, 2537, 2549, 2953, 2955, 3141, 3309a, 3350, 3436, 3470, 3472, 3481
"Wedding March, The," 296, 1578, 1579, 3006, 3438, 3463
"Wedding Night, The," 1984
"Wedding Song, The," 2874
"Wednesday's Child," 2427, 2428, 2640
"Wee Willie Winkie," 1433
"Weekend at Dunkirk," 3617
"Weekend at the Waldorf," 1520
"Weekend in Havana," 1079
"Week-End Marriage," 2397, 2398, 2994
"Week-Ends Only," 2399
Weeks, Barbara, 2388
Wehlen, Emmy, 2052
"Weib Des Pharao, Das" (see "Loves of Pharaoh, The")
Weidler, Virginia, 817, 3533
Weinberg, Roger J., 3440
Weintz, Margo, 3441
Weiss, Arnie, 3442
Weiss, Ruth, 3443
Welch, Eileen, 3444
Welch, Raquel, 526, 1416, 1482, 2817
Welch, Vivian, 3470
"Welcome Stranger," 895, 2488, 2651

"Welcome to Hard Times," 2786, 2795

Weld, Tuesday, 1549

"Well-Groomed Bride, The," 1324

Welles, Orson, 547, 1073, 1892

Welles, Virginia, 813, 1324, 1348, 3555

"Wells Fargo," 1359

Welsh, Tom, 3454

Wessel, Hannelore, 3458

West, Brooks, 1241

West, Clare, 405, 509, 564, 762, 809, 824, 1715, 1835a, 2270, 2329, 2669, 2883, 2978, 3216, 3385, 3459, 3498

West, Mae, 55, 220, 275, 439, 679, 921, 947, 1007, 1312, 1334, 1339, 1397, 1399, 1416, 1482, 1493, 1653, 1696, 1749, 1832, 1870, 1932, 2024, 2192, 2214, 2258, 2424, 2482, 2522, 2523, 2640, 2711, 2838, 2896, 3251, 3428, 3497

West, Sue, 3460

West, Vera, 1079, 1268, 1508, 2023, 2403, 2413, 2414, 2420, 2425, 2465, 2476, 2479, 2482, 2541, 2551, 3057, 3461, 3462

"West Point of the Air," 3151

"West Side Story," 2964, 2968, 3130

Western Costume Company (see also Associated Costumers), 260, 266, 296, 645, 788, 1175, 1205, 1283, 1404, 1437, 1441, 1578, 1579, 1794, 1962, 1996, 2092, 2099, 2310, 3207, 3322, 3370, 3463, 3464, 3465

Westmore, Bud, 335, 2101, 3466

Westmore, Ern, 3466

Westmore, Frank, 3466

Westmore, George, 3466

Westmore, Mont, 3466

Westmore, Perc, 646, 3466

Westmore, Wally, 3466

Weston, Doris, 1000

Weston, Irene V., 3467

"Wet Parade, The," 2396

"What!," 1004

"What a Way to Go," 1342, 1349, 2082

"What a Widow," 465, 1987, 2098

"What Did You Do in the War, Daddy?," 226

"What Ever Happened to Aunt Alice?," 2739

"What Ever Happened to Baby Jane?," 76, 1167, 1656, 1660, 1844, 2938

"What Every Woman Knows," 3521

"What Price Beauty," 2143

"What Price Glory," 1221, 1442

"What's New Pussycat?," 1060, 3245, 3246, 3291

"What's the Matter with Marriage?," 3520

"What's Up Doc?," 2637

"What's Up Front," 1093

"Wheeler Dealers, The," 2203

Whelan, Arleen, 813, 2470, 2541, 3092

Whelen, Emmy, 3539

"When Cupid Crossed the Bay," 1622

"When Knighthood Was in Flower," 327, 1247, 2244, 2252, 3243, 3457

"When Ladies Fly," 985

"When Ladies Meet," 1932

"When Love Comes," 1368

"When Love Grows Cold," 3300, 3476

"When Love Is Young," 1067

"When Strangers Marry," 1930

"When the Clock Strikes," 350, 1983

"When the Trees Were Tall," 159

"When Tomorrow Comes," 2477

"Where Do We Go from Here?," 485, 1184

"Where It's At," 3189

"Where Love Is," 1732

"Where Sinners Meet," 2421

"Where the Bullets Fly," 3593

"Where the Sidewalk Ends," 3247, 3447

"Where Were You When the Lights Went Out?," 633, 1567

"Where's Jack?," 3051, 3252

"Where's Poppa?," 3570

"Which Way to the Front?," 2302, 3338

"Whip, The," 1585

"Whiplash," 3272

"Whirlpool," 2421

Whistler, Margaret, 388

White, Alice, 298

White, Carol, 297

White, Carrie, 2020

White, Jacqueline, 2565

White, Miles, 605, 3489, 3490

White, Pearl, 1198

"White Christmas," 1338

"White Cliffs of Dover, The," 1522, 1670

"White Flower, The," 2668
"White Lies," 3084
"White Moth, The," 201
"White Shoulders," 1604, 1605,
  2625
"White Sister, The," 1776
"White Sisters, The," 1224
"White Tie and Tails," 2112
"White Tiger," 851
"White Voices," 2636
"White Warrior, The," 2879
"White Woman," 275
Whitehouse, Alice, 673
Whitney, Belle Armstrong, 983
Whitney, Eleanore, 2448, 2526
"Who Pays My Wife's Bills?,"
  3525
"Whoopee!," 1285
"Who's Afraid of Virginia
  Woolf?," 2968
"Who's Got the Action?," 1888,
  3127
"Why Bother to Knock," 1541
"Wicked Dreams of Paula Schultz,
  The," 2799
"Wicked Lady, The," 588, 1718
"Widow from Chicago, The," 298
Wieck, Dorothea, 16, 2417
"Wife, Doctor, and Nurse," 2133,
  2456, 2533
"Wife, Husband, Friend," 2989
"Wife of the Centaur," 3006
"Wife Swappers," 2840
"Wife Takes a Flyer, The,"
  1955
"Wilbur and the Baby Factory,"
  1197
Wilcoxon, Henry, 3360
"Wild and Wonderful," 3316
"Wild Angels, The," 3592
"Wild Bunch, The," 745
"Wild Cat, The," 469
"Wild Gold," 2420, 3451
"Wild Gypsies," 360
"Wild Harvest," 2799
"Wild in the Streets," 2782,
  3624
"Wild on the Beach," 803
"Wild One, The," 2368, 3233
"Wild Party, The," 194, 3565
"Wild River," 1573
"Wild Seed," 2339
"Wild Wheels," 293
"Wild, Wild Planet, The," 3073
"Wild, Wild Winter," 1048,
  1166
"Wilderness," 1905, 3290
Wiley, Constance, 1505

Wilfert, Ingeborg, 3530
Wilkens, Emily, 3531
Wilkinson, June, 2305
"Will Penny," 3127
Willard George Ltd., 2961
Williams, Cara, 3420
Williams, Esther, 848, 2073, 2105,
  2110, 2234, 2808
Williams, Kathlyn, 511, 564, 989,
  3148, 3276, 3294, 3514
Williams, Kathryn, 2421
Williams, Peter, 3540
Wills, Mary, 678, 679, 883, 2584,
  2587, 3554
Willys (of Hollywood) (De Mond,
  Willys), 754, 1449, 2265, 2546,
  3555
Wilmot, Masada, 3556
Wilomez, Babs, 550
Wilson, Dorothy, 3449
Wilson, Lois, 388, 777, 2344,
  2359, 3521
Wilson, Marie, 2516
"Wilson," 858, 1052, 1204
"Winchester '73," 3285
Windsor, Claire, 104, 571, 572,
  573, 657, 682, 824, 2301, 2732,
  3155, 3472
"Wings of the Morning," 1482,
  2141
"Wings of the Navy," 3103
"Winning," 1336, 3122
Winston, Harry, 1560
Winter, Ingrid, 3564
Winter, Laska, 933
Winter, Wanda, 1328
"Winter A-Go-Go," 76, 803
"Winter Carnival," 2475
"Winter Light," 1893
"Winter Meeting," 554
"Winter Wind," 3348
Winters, Sam, 2091
Winters, Shelley, 395, 602, 2607,
  3285
"Wise Guys," 1945
"Wiser Sex, The," 585
"Wishing Ring, The," 854
"Witch, The," 2636
"Witch's Curse, The," 3070
"With Six You Get Eggroll," 633,
  3178
Withers, Googie, 588
"Within the Law," 2382, 3175
"Without a Stitch," 2236
"Without Love," 1520, 1749
"Without Regret," 312
"Without Reservations," 344, 1206
"Without Shame," 2399

"Witness for the Prosecution," 1345
Witzemann, Wolf, 3566
"Wives and Lovers," 576
"Wives Under Suspicion," 2464
"Wiz, The," 2723
"Wizard of Oz, The" (1926), 1505
"Wizard of Oz, The" (1939), 48,
    49, 903, 1085, 1286, 1421, 1450,
    1677, 1849, 2091, 2543, 2664,
    2783, 3113, 3406, 3419, 3437,
    3567
Wolbert, Dorothea, 3061
"Wolf of Debt, The," 987
"Wolf Song, The," 275
Wolfe, Bob, 3569
Wolsky, Albert, 3420, 3570
"Woman Accused, The," 2762
"Woman Against Woman," 2465
"Woman and Temptation," 1544
"Woman and the Law," 2417
"Woman Between, The," 719
"Woman Chases Man," 1000
"Woman Commands, A," 2275
"Woman God Forgot, The," 1106,
    2860
"Woman He Married, The," 2102
"Woman Hunt," 707
"Woman I Love, The," 3549
"Woman I Stole, The," 2409
"Woman in Love, A," 3135
"Woman of Affairs, A," 18, 1239,
    2352, 2783, 3026
"Woman of Paris, A," 1996
"Woman of Sin," 505
"Woman of Straw," 12, 805
"Woman of the World, A," 1209
"Woman on the Jury, The,"
    1516, 2031
"Woman Rebels, A," 679, 808
"Woman There Was, A," 406
"Woman Times Seven," 932
"Woman Who Walked Alone, The,"
    2219
Woman's Repository, 1864
"Women, The," 478, 697, 2476,
    2552, 2843, 3102, 3231
"Women Are Like That," 2928,
    3086
"Women Have a Way," 2457
"Women in Love," 604, 1213,
    1840, 2844
Women I've Undressed (Kelly),
    2755
"Women of Desire," 1407
Women's Wear Daily, 100, 356,
    1618, 1762, 2664
"Wonder Bar," 438
"Wonderful to Be Young!," 364,
3017
"Wonderful World of the Brothers
    Grimm, The," 678, 3554
"Wonders of Aladdin, The," 757,
    772
Wong, Anna May, 3208
Wood, Judith, 2390, 2393
Wood, Natalie, 678, 1349, 1692,
    2281, 2285, 2628, 2897
Wood, Peggy, 2424
Wood, Sam, 3219
Wood, Yvonne, 500, 552, 959, 1043,
    2112, 2494, 2580, 3285, 3580,
    3581
Woodward, Joanne, 2629, 3122,
    3273
"Wooing of Princess Pat, The,"
    3539
Woollard, Joan, 3583
"Working Girls," 2393
"World of Henry Orient, The," 2823
"World of Suzie Wong, The," 3233
"World's Applause, The," 1533
Worner, Dorothy, 3588
Worth, 983
Worth, Jacques, 330
Worth, Jean Charles, 329
Wougher, Roberto, 3589
Woulfe, Michael, 401, 766, 2108,
    2496, 2497, 2505, 2511, 2516,
    2586, 2598, 3591
Wray, Fay, 1593, 1931, 2386,
    2409, 2415, 2416, 2423, 2426,
    2640, 2763, 3084
"Wrecking Crew, The," 785
Wright, Cobina, 1079
Wright, Glen, 3592
Wright, Joanna, 3593
Wright, Robert, 2628
Wright, Teresa, 30, 883, 2584,
    2967, 3487
"Wuthering Heights" (1939), 883,
    1628, 2365, 3238
Wyatt, Jane, 2425, 2521
Wyke, Richard, 3596
Wyler, William, 788, 883
Wyman, Betty, 2916, 2921
Wyman, Jane, 1221, 1388, 1502,
    2042, 2442, 2490, 2533, 3092,
    3092, 3555, 3609
Wymore, Patrice, 2509
Wynigear, Ed, 3597
Wynn, Ed, 3020
Wynter, Mark, 3136
Wynyard, Diana, 16, 228, 439,
    1088, 1823, 1930, 2424, 2425,
    3074, 3076

"X-15," 1558

"Yank at Oxford, A," 3553
"Yank in Viet-Nam, A," 721
Yelland, Sue, 3601
"Yellow Canary, The," 785
"Yellow Jack," 3151
"Yellow Rolls-Royce, The,"
364, 451, 499, 602
"Yellow Typhoon, The," 3526
"Yesterday, Today and Tomorrow,"
805
"Yo Yo," 1249
Yolanda, 3227
"Yolanda," 3312, 3472
"Yolanda and the Thief," 673,
877, 1042, 2105
"Yolanta," 2350
York, Michael, 756
York, Susannah, 326, 819, 1058,
1762, 2377, 3286
Yoshida, Yuki, 3607
"You Belong to Me," 1079, 1392,
2742, 3602
"You Can't Cheat an Honest Man,"
974
"You Can't Get Away with It,"
2290
"You Can't Have Everything,"
2935
"You Can't Win 'Em All," 1237,
3181, 3556
"You Gotta Stay Happy," 1806
"You Have to Run Fast," 350,
1983
"You Must Be Joking!," 126
"You Never Know Women," 691
"You Never Looked Lovelier,"
754
"You Only Live Twice," 3177
"You Only Love Once," 451, 805
"You Said a Mouthful," 2403
"You'll Never Get Rich," 3232
Young, Clara Kimball, 575, 853
Young, Elizabeth, 1933
Young, Loretta, 91, 290, 318, 392,
674, 675, 985, 993, 1007, 1021,
1268, 1318, 1326, 1330, 1347,
1348, 1420, 1433, 1627, 1654,
1699, 1757, 1932, 1959, 2023,
2133, 2158, 2352, 2397, 2398,
2416, 2419, 2440, 2447, 2450,
2456, 2461, 2478, 2524, 2528,
2533, 2561, 2608, 2631, 2651,
2708, 2763, 2929, 2961, 2966,

2989, 2994, 3090, 3091, 3141,
3174, 3210, 3226, 3232, 3496,
3550
Young, Robert, 3232
"Young Americans," 130, 2790
"Young and the Brave, The,"
3202
"Young Bess," 1846
"Young Billy Young," 81
"Young Doctors, The," 2071
"Young Fury," 576, 1363
"Young Girls of Rochefort, The,"
125, 214, 574, 955, 1075,
2064
"Young Guns of Texas," 2999
"Young Ideas," 1527
"Young in Heart, The," 2466
"Young Lord, The," 2879
"Young Lovers, The," 1559, 2795
"Young Mr. Pitt, The," 3076
"Young Rajah, The," 1509, 2245,
2884, 3161, 3384
"Young Rebel, The," 122
"Young Savages, The," 105, 2226
"Young Swingers, The," 3281
"Young, the Evil and the Savage,
The," 107
"Your Cheatin' Heart," 419, 2628,
2772
"Your Friend and Mine," 915, 1027
"You're a Big Boy Now," 69
"You're Telling Me," 2420
"Yours for the Asking," 1961, 2442
"Yours, Mine and Ours," 458, 555,
2715
Youthquake, 2679
Yumeki, Miyoshi, 1437

"Zabriskie Point," 3178
Zacha, William T., 3610
Zalabery, Hanny, 3611
Zamora, José, 3612
"Zander the Great," 3312
Zanetti, A. Danilo, 3613
Zanuck, Darryl F., 875
Zanuck, Richard, 875
Zarate, Laure de, 3614
Zastupnevich, Paul, 806a, 3615
Zay, Jean, 3616
Zay, Léon, 3617
"Zaza" (1915), 1238
"Zaza" (1923), 2079, 2205
"Zaza" (1939), 275, 754, 1354,
2544, 3182, 3287
"Zazie," 814

Zeffirelli, Franco, 1414
Zetter, Gwen, 3621
Ziegfeld, Florenz, 479, 870, 883,
   1916
Ziegfeld Follies, 406, 479, 870,
   883, 1916
"Ziegfeld Follies, The," 2028,
   2862, 3622
"Zigzag," 1256, 1941, 2300

Zinkeisen, Doris, 2144
Zinn, Pat, 3624
zippers, 537, 1333, 2529, 3625
Zipprodt, Patricia, 2059, 3626,
   3627
"Zorba the Greek," 3121
Zorina, 192, 846, 2483, 2554
"Zotz!," 105, 3201
Zukor, Adolph, 861